Systems Analysis & Design

AN OBJECT-ORIENTED APPROACH WITH UML

Sixth Edition

Alan Dennis
Indiana University

Barbara Haley Wixom
Massachusetts Institute of Technology

David Tegarden
Virginia Tech

WILEY

VP AND EDITORIAL DIRECTOR	Mike McDonald
PUBLISHER	Lise Johnson
EDITOR	Jennifer Manias
EDITORIAL ASSISTANT	Kali Ridley
SENIOR MANAGING EDITOR	Judy Howarth
DIRECTOR OF CONTENT OPERATIONS	Martin Tribe
SENIOR MANAGER OF CONTENT OPERATIONS	Mary Corder
PRODUCTION EDITOR	Bharathy Surya Prakash
ASSISTANT MARKETING MANAGER	Rachel Karach
COVER PHOTO CREDIT	© Los Alerces National Park, Patagonia, Argentina © Guaxinim/Shutterstock

This book was set in 10/12 Minion pro by SPi Global.

Founded in 1807, John Wiley & Sons, Inc. has been a valued source of knowledge and understanding for more than 200 years, helping people around the world meet their needs and fulfill their aspirations. Our company is built on a foundation of principles that include responsibility to the communities we serve and where we live and work. In 2008, we launched a Corporate Citizenship Initiative, a global effort to address the environmental, social, economic, and ethical challenges we face in our business. Among the issues we are addressing are carbon impact, paper specifications and procurement, ethical conduct within our business and among our vendors, and community and charitable support. For more information, please visit our website: www.wiley.com/go/citizenship.

Evaluation copies are provided to qualified academics and professionals for review purposes only, for use in their courses during the next academic year. These copies are licensed and may not be sold or transferred to a third party. Upon completion of the review period, please return the evaluation copy to Wiley. Return instructions and a free of charge return shipping label are available at: www.wiley.com/go/returnlabel. If you have chosen to adopt this textbook for use in your course, please accept this book as your complimentary desk copy. Outside of the United States, please contact your local sales representative.

ISBN: 978-1-119-55991-7 (PBK)
ISBN: 978-1-119-71354-8 (EVALC)

Library of Congress Cataloging-in-Publication Data

Names: Dennis, Alan, author. | Wixom, Barbara Haley, 1969- author. | Tegarden, David Paul, author.
Title: Systems analysis & design, an object-oriented approach with UML / Alan Dennis, Indiana University, Barbara Haley Wixom, Massachusetts Institute of Technology, David Tegarden, Virginia.
Other titles: Systems analysis and design, an object-oriented approach with UML
Description: Sixth edition. | Hoboken, NJ : Wiley, [2021] | Original edition published under title: System analysis and design, an object-oriented approach with UML. | Includes bibliographical references and index.
Identifiers: LCCN 2020018700 (print) | LCCN 2020018701 (ebook) | ISBN 9781119559917 (paperback) | ISBN 9781119746102 (adobe pdf) | ISBN 9781119561217 (epub)
Subjects: LCSH: System analysis. | System design. | UML (Computer science)
Classification: LCC QA402 .D395 2021 (print) | LCC QA402 (ebook) | DDC 004.2/1—dc23
LC record available at https://lccn.loc.gov/2020018700
LC ebook record available at https://lccn.loc.gov/2020018701

The inside back cover will contain printing identification and country of origin if omitted from this page. In addition, if the ISBN on the back cover differs from the ISBN on this page, the one on the back cover is correct.

SKY10032377_010622

PREFACE

PURPOSE OF THIS BOOK

Systems Analysis and Design (SAD) is an exciting, active field in which analysts continually learn new techniques and approaches to develop systems more effectively and efficiently. However, there is a core set of skills that all analysts need to know—no matter what approach or methodology is used. All information systems projects require analysts to gather requirements, model the business needs, and create blueprints for how the system should be built; and all projects require an understanding of organizational behavior concepts like change management and team building. Today, the cost of developing modern software is composed primarily of the cost associated with the developers themselves and not the computers.

Today, object-oriented approaches, which view a system as a collection of self-contained objects that have both data and processes, are the preferred approaches to SAD. This has occurred primarily due to the adoption of the Unified Modeling Language (UML). UML provides a common vocabulary of object-oriented terms and diagramming techniques that is rich enough to model any systems development project from analysis through implementation.

This book captures the dynamic aspects of the field by keeping students focused on doing SAD while presenting the core set of skills that we feel every systems analyst needs to know today and in the future. This book builds on our professional experience as systems analysts and on our experience in teaching SAD in the classroom.

This book will be of particular interest to instructors who have students do a major project as part of their course. Each chapter describes one part of the process, provides clear explanations on how to do it, gives a detailed example, and then has exercises for the students to practice. In this way, students can leave the course with experience that will form a rich foundation for further work as a systems analyst.

OUTSTANDING FEATURES

A Focus on Doing SAD

The goal of this book is to enable students to do SAD—not just read about it, but understand the issues so that they can actually analyze and design systems. The book introduces each major technique, explains what it is, explains how to do it, and presents a set of examples. After reading each chapter, the student will be able to perform that step in the system development process.

Rich Examples of Success and Failure

This book has a running case study (accessible from the student companion website www.wiley.com/go/dennis/systemanalysis6e/casestudy) about a fictitious company called

Patterson Superstore that includes a small health care clinic. Each chapter of the case study demonstrates how the concepts are applied in situations at Patterson Superstore. In this way, the running case serves as a template that students can apply to their own work.

Real World Focus

The skills that students learn in a systems analysis and design course should mirror the work that they ultimately will do in real organizations. We have tried to make this book as "real" as possible by building extensively on our experience as professional systems analysts. Many students who use this book will eventually use the skills on the job in a business environment, and we believe they will have a competitive edge in understanding what successful practitioners feel is relevant in the real world.

Project Approach

We have presented the topics in this book in the order in which an analyst encounters them in a typical project. Although the presentation is necessarily linear (because students have to learn concepts in the way in which they build on each other), we emphasize the incremental and iterative complex nature of SAD as the book unfolds. The presentation of the material should align well with courses that encourage students to work on projects because it presents topics as students need to apply them.

WHAT'S NEW IN THIS EDITION

- Throughout the book, there is a greater emphasis on verifying, validating, and testing, as well as incremental and iterative development. Also, a greater emphasis is on the security nonfunctional requirement.

- In Chapter 1, we have reorganized some of the material to make the chapter flow better. For example, we have moved the Object-Oriented Systems Analysis and Design overview back into the System Development Methodologies section. We have also added a section on the newer DevOps approaches to this section. Finally, we have moved all of the introduction to object orientation (including the material that was in Chapter 8) to a new appendix at the end of this chapter.

- In Chapter 2, we have added a new section within the Project Selection that addresses some of the ethical issues that project managers may face. We have also added Kanban boards as an agile alternative to the standard object-oriented iterative workplans. Also, we have added a section on Tuckman's stages of small group development and a section on meeting management that should aid students in self-managing a semester-long project. Finally, we added a new section on Configuration and Change Management which includes the idea of securing the IT artifacts with a secure development approach and the idea of continuous delivery of DevOps.

- In Chapter 3, we have reorganized the material to increase the flow though the chapter. We have expanded the material dealing with the security nonfunctional requirements, added Fishbone Diagrams to the root cause analysis section, added Givens-Means-Ends analysis to the outcome analysis section, added survey design ideas to questionnaires section, and added journalism and anthropology ideas to the observation section. We also have added a new text analysis section that covers sentence diagramming and ethnographic analysis and we have expanded the User Stories section based the new material on the User Story Lite material. Finally, we have removed the JAD and the Concept Maps sections.

■ In Chapter 4, we have more closely tied the Overview section of the use case description to the use case diagram and the Flow of Events section of the detailed use case description to the activity diagrams. We also have explicitly linked the use case description's primary actor and stakeholders to role-based access controls for the security nonfunctional requirements that are covered in the design chapters.

■ In Chapter 5, we have explicitly linked the CRC card's Associated Use cases list back to the primary actor and stakeholders lists of the use-case description to support the idea of access controls for the security nonfunctional requirement and we have removed the Common Object Lists section. Finally, to increase the incremental and iterative focus in modern information systems development approaches, we moved the Balancing Functional and Structural Models section from Chapter 7 to this chapter. This way, the fact that we may (will) have to iterate back to fix our functional model, based on our more complete understanding of the problem is emphasized.

■ When agile developers "model" the interactions among the actors and classes (objects), they tend to use activity diagrams instead of sequence diagrams. Therefore, in Chapter 6, we have added a section that describes the use of activity diagrams with swimlanes as an approach to model these interactions. We also expanded the sequence diagram section to include examples of calling an "included" or "extended" use case and how iteration can be represented. Also, we removed the communication diagram section. And, we have footnoted the utility of using the more detailed version of the CRUDE matrix to support role-based access controls. Finally, we moved the Balancing Functional and Behavior Models and the Balancing the Structural and Behavioral Models from Chapter 7 to this chapter. Again, this was done to place more attention to the need to always iterate back to previous models to ensure that the evolving model is consistent.

■ In Chapter 7, we moved all of the "Balancing" of the models to Chapters 5 and 6. We also moved the Design Criteria section from Chapter 8 to this chapter.

■ In Chapter 8, besides moving some of the content to Chapters 1 and 7, we have explicitly linked the contracts back to the CRC cards, the primary actors and stakeholders of the associated use cases, and the detailed version of the CRUDE matrix to support the access control security requirements.

■ In Chapter 9, we have expanded the security nonfunctional description by explicitly linking back to CRUDE analysis and CRC cards. We also moved the Optimizing RDBMS-Based Object Storage section to a chapter appendix and have created a new chapter appendix that focuses on converting class diagrams to entity-relationship diagrams.

■ In Chapter 10, we changed the windows layout diagram terminology to wireframe diagram, added a new section that ties the constraints modeled in Chapter 8 to User Interface Design and Implementation, and we explicitly linked the security nonfunctional requirements to the DBMS on the data management layer, Real Use Cases on the human–computer interaction layer, and to the operating system on the physical architecture layer. Finally, we created a new section that addresses the verification and validation of the user interface design. The section contains the old Interface Evaluation section material, along with a description of A/B testing.

■ In Chapter 11, we have greatly expanded the security section. In this section we have described different threats to security, including treating security as an afterthought instead of a major aspect of design. We also added material to the access control section including Capability Lists, Role-Based Access Control, and explicitly linking access controls back to other layers: CRUDE Analysis, CRC Cards,

Contracts-Pre-Conditions, Real Use Cases, and Input Validation. Finally, we added material to the Legal requirements section that addresses software licensing agreements that grant access to corporate and personal data.

■ In Chapter 12, we expanded the Design Tests section to include the ideas of happy paths, sad paths, automatic testing, toggles, and chaos monkey. Also, we included a discussion of how testing can uncover additional functional and nonfunctional requirements. Finally, we added a new section Testing and Security Considerations.

■ In Chapter 13, we expanded the Conversion section to include continuous delivery approach of DevOps and to relate it to the deployment and configuration and change management workflows. We also expanded the Project Assessment section to include the ideas of a Just Culture, blameless post-mortems, and psychological safety.

ORGANIZATION OF THIS BOOK

This book is loosely organized around the phases and workflows of the enhanced Unified Process. Each chapter has been written to teach students specific tasks that analysts need to accomplish over the course of a project, and the deliverables that will be produced from the tasks. As students complete the chapters, they will realize the iterative and incremental nature of the tasks in object-oriented systems development.

Chapter 1 introduces the roles and skills needed for a systems analyst, SDLC, systems development methodologies, the Unified Process, the UML, and an appendix that covers the basic characteristics of object-oriented systems. Chapter 2 presents topics related to the project management workflow of the Unified Process, including project identification, system request, feasibility analysis, project selection, ethical considerations, traditional project management tools (including work breakdown structures, network diagrams, and PERT analysis), project effort estimation using use-case points, evolutionary work breakdown structures, iterative workplans, scope management, timeboxing, risk management, Kanban boards, staffing the project, and meeting management. Chapter 2 also addresses issues related to the Environment and Infrastructure management and the Configuration and Change Management workflows of the Unified Process.

Part One focuses on creating analysis models. Chapter 3 introduces students to an assortment of requirements analysis strategies a variety of requirements-gathering techniques that are used to determine the functional and nonfunctional requirements of the system, and to a system proposal. Chapter 4 focuses on constructing business process and functional models using use-case diagrams, activity diagrams, and use-case descriptions. Chapter 5 addresses producing structural models using CRC cards, class diagrams, and object diagrams. Chapter 6 tackles creating behavioral models using activity diagrams, sequence diagrams, CRUDE analysis and matrices, and behavioral state machines. Chapters 4 through 6 also cover the verification and validation of the models described in each chapter and the balancing of the models across the chapters.

Part Two addresses design modeling. In Chapter 7, students learn to evolve the analysis models into design models via the use of factoring, partitions, and layers and to use package diagrams to support the design models. The students also learn about the design criteria and to create an alternative matrix that can be used to compare custom, packaged, and outsourcing alternatives. Chapter 8 concentrates on specific object design activities and designing the individual classes and their respective methods through the use of contracts and method specifications. Chapter 9 presents the issues involved in designing persistence for objects. These issues include the different storage formats that can be used for object persistence, how to map an object-oriented design into the chosen storage format, and how to design a set of data access and manipulation classes that act as a translator between the classes in the application and the object persistence. This chapter also focuses on the nonfunctional requirements that impact the data management layer. Chapter 10 presents the design of the human–computer interaction layer, where students learn how to design user interfaces using use scenarios, windows navigation diagrams, storyboards, wireframe diagrams, user interface prototypes, real use cases, interface standards, and user interface templates. This chapter also addresses issues related to mobile computing, social media, games, multidimensional information visualizations, immersive environments, and international and cultural issues with regard to user interface design to address nonfunctional requirements such as user interface layout, content awareness, aesthetics, user experience, and consistency. Finally, the students learn how to perform user interface evaluations using heuristic evaluation, walkthrough evaluation, interactive evaluation, formal usability testing, and A/B testing. Chapter 11 focuses on the physical architecture and infrastructure design, which includes deployment diagrams and hardware/software specification. In today's world, this also includes issues related to cloud computing, ubiquitous computing, the Internet of things, and green IT. This chapter, like the previous design chapters, covers the impact that nonfunctional requirements can have on the physical architecture layer.

Part Three provides material that is related to the construction, installation, and operations of the system. Chapter 12 focuses on system construction, where students learn how to build, test, and document the system. Installation and operations are covered in Chapter 13, where students learn about the conversion plan, change management plan, support plan, and project assessment. Additionally, these chapters address the issues related to developing systems in a flat world, where developers and users are distributed throughout the world.

SUPPLEMENTS www.wiley.com/go/dennis/systemanalysis6e

Instructor Book Companion Website

- ■ **Image Gallery:** Instructors can create slides and teaching visuals using the Image Gallery, a complete set of the text figures and art included in the book.
- ■ **Test Bank:** Includes a variety of questions ranging from multiple-choice, true/false, and short answer questions. A computerized, **Respondus** version of the Test Bank is also available.
- ■ **Instructor's Manual:** Provides resources to support the instructor both inside and out of the classroom. The manual includes short experiential exercises that instructors can use to help students experience and understand key topics in each chapter. Short stories have been provided by people working in both corporate and consulting environments for instructors to insert into lectures to make concepts more colorful and real. Additional minicases for every chapter allow students to perform some of the key concepts that were learned in the chapter. Solutions to end of chapter questions and exercises are provided.

Student Book Companion Website

- ■ An online **case study** on an integrated health clinic delivery system is included. It can be accessed at www.wiley.com/go/dennis/systemanalysis6e/casestudy on the student website.
- ■ "Your Turn" and "Concepts in Action" boxes can be accessed on the student companion site.

ACKNOWLEDGMENTS

We would like to thank the students who have taken the ACIS 3515: Information Systems Development I, ACIS 3516: Information Systems Development II, and BIT 4524: Systems Development at Virginia Tech for giving many suggestions over the various editions that drove most of the changes through the text. Also, we would like to acknowledge the conservations that we have had with Gerhard Fischer, Brian Henderson-Sellers, Clayton Lewis, and David Monarchi regarding object-oriented modeling over the years.

Thanks to Elaine Seeman for her work on the online case study. We thank all the people at Wiley who worked with us on this new edition: Lise Johnson, Judy Howarth, Mary Corder, Bharathy Surya Prakash, and Sundar Parkkavan. Our thanks to Dr. Ronny Richardson of the Leven School of Management, Entrepreneurship and Hospitality at Kennesaw State University for the preparation of the Instructor's Manual and Test Bank.

We would also like to thank the following reviewers for their helpful and insightful comments on the first, second, third, fourth, and fifth editions: Evans Adams, Fort Lewis College; Murugan Anandarajon, Drexel University; Ron Anson, Boise State University; Noushin Ashrafi, University of Massachusetts, Boston; Dirk Baldwin, University of Wisconsin-Parkside; Robert Barker, University of Louisville; Qing Cao, University of Missouri–Kansas City; David Champion, DeVry University, Columbus, OH campus; Jeff Cummings, Indiana University; Mohammad Dadashzadeh, Oakland University; Xiaodong Deng, Oakland University; Thomas W. Dillon, James Madison University; Junhua Ding, East Carolina University; Robert Dollinger, University of Wisconsin–Stevens Point; Abhijit Dutt, Carnegie Mellon University; Terry Fox, Baylor University; Ahmad Ghafarian, North Georgia College & State University; Bryan Goda, University of Washington, Tacoma; Donald Golden, Cleveland State University; Cleotilde Gonzalez, Carnegie Melon University; Daniel V. Goulet, University of Wisconsin–Stevens Point; Kathleen S. Hartzel, Duquesne University; Harvey Hayashi, Loyalist College of Applied Arts and Technology; Yujong Hwang, DePaul University; Scott James, Saginaw Valley State University; Zongliang Jiang, North Carolina A&T State University; Rajkumar Kempaiah, Stevens Institute of Technology; Sung-kwan Kim, University of Arkansas at Little Rock; Raymond Kirsch, La Salle University; Rajiv Kishore, State University of New York–Buffalo; Ravindra Krovi, University of Akron; Jean-Piere Kuilboer, University of Massachusetts, Boston; Gilliean Lee, Lander University; Leo Legorreta, California State University Sacramento; Diane Lending, James Madison University; Steve Machon, DeVry University; Fernando Maymí, West Point University; Richard McCarthy, Quinnipiac University; Donald McCracken, Grantham University; Daniel Mittleman, DePaul University; Osama A. Morad, Southern New Hampshire University; Makoto Nakayama, DePaul University; Fred Niederman, Saint Louis University; Parasuraman Nurani, DeVry University; H. Robert Pajkowski, DeVry Institute of Technology, Scarborough, Ontario; June S. Park, University of Iowa; Graham Peace, West Virginia University; Tom Pettay, DeVry Institute of Technology, Columbus, Ohio; Selwyn Piramuthu, University of Florida; Linda Plotnick, Jacksonville State University; J. Drew Procaccino, Rider University; Neil Ramiller, Portland State University; Vladimir V. Riabov, Rivier University; Eliot Rich, University at Albany, State University of New York; Marcus Rothenberger, University of Wisconsin–Milwaukee; Richard Schilhavy, Guilford College; Carl Scott, University of Houston; Tod Sedbrook, University of Northern Colorado; Steven C. Shaffer, Penn State University; Keng Siau, University of Nebraska–Lincoln; Iftikhar Sikder, Cleveland State University; Michael Smith, Georgia Institute of Technology; Jonathan Trower, Baylor University; June Verner, Drexel University; Anna Wachholz, Sheridan College; Bill Watson, Indiana University-Purdue University Indianapolis; Randy S. Weinberg, Carnegie Mellon University; Eli J. Weissman, DeVry Institute of Technology, Long Island City, NY; Heinz Roland Weistroffer, Virginia Commonwealth University; John Wetsch, Southern New Hampshire University; Amy Wilson, DeVry Institute of Technology, Decatur, GA; Amy Woszczynski, Kennesaw State University; Vincent C. Yen, Wright State University; Fan Zhao, Florida Gulf Coast University; and Dan Zhu, Iowa State University.

CONTENTS

■ PART ONE
ANALYSIS MODELING   93

Chapter 3
Requirements Determination   95

Chapter 4
Business Process and Functional Modeling   126

Chapter 8
Class and Method Design 287

Chapter 9
Data Management Layer Design 320

Appendices

Chapter 10
Human–Computer Interaction Layer Design 364

Chapter 11
Physical Architecture Layer Design   414

CHAPTER 1

INTRODUCTION TO SYSTEMS ANALYSIS AND DESIGN

Chapter 1 introduces the systems development life cycle (SDLC), the fundamental four-phase model (planning, analysis, design, and implementation) common to all information systems development projects. It describes the evolution of systems development methodologies and discusses the roles and skills required for a systems analyst. The chapter then overviews the basic characteristics of object-oriented systems and the fundamentals of object-oriented systems analysis and design and closes with a description of the Unified Process and its extensions and the Unified Modeling Language.

OBJECTIVES

- Be familiar with the different roles played by and the skills of a systems analyst.
- Understand the fundamental systems development life cycle and its four phases.
- Understand the evolution of systems development methodologies.
- Be familiar with the fundamental principles of object-oriented systems analysis and design.
- Be familiar with the Unified Process, its extensions, and the Unified Modeling Language.
- Be familiar with the basic characteristics of object-oriented systems.

INTRODUCTION

The *systems development life cycle (SDLC)* is the process of understanding how an information system (IS) can support business needs by designing a system, building it, and delivering it to users. If you have taken a programming class or have programmed on your own, this probably sounds pretty simple. Unfortunately, it is not. A 1996 survey by the Standish Group found that 42 percent of all corporate IS projects were abandoned before completion. A similar study conducted in 1996 by the General Accounting Office found that 53 percent of all U.S. government IS projects were abandoned. Unfortunately, many of the systems that are not abandoned are delivered to the users significantly late, cost far more than planned, and have fewer features than originally planned. For example, IAG Consulting reports that 80 percent of the projects were over time, 72 percent were over budget, and 55 percent contained less than the full functionality; Panorama Consulting Solutions reports that 54 percent of the ERP projects were over time, 56 percent were over budget, and 48 percent delivered less than 50 percent of the initial benefits; and an IBM study reports that 59 percent of the projects missed one or more of on time, within budget, and quality constraints.[1] Although we would

[1] For more information on the problem, see Capers Jones, *Patterns of Software System Failure and Success* (London: International Thompson Computer Press, 1996); and Keith Ellis, *Business Analysis Benchmark: The Impact of Business Requirements on the Success of Technology Projects* (2008). Retrieved May 2014 from IAG Consulting, www.iag.biz; H. H. Jorgensen, L. Owen, and A. Neus, *Making Change Work* (2008). Retrieved May 2014 from IBM, www.ibm. com; Panorama Consulting Solutions, *2012 ERP Report* (2012). Retrieved May 2014 from Panorama-Consulting.com.

like to promote this book as a silver bullet that will keep you from IS failures, we readily admit that a silver bullet that guarantees IS development success simply does not exist. Instead, this book provides you with several fundamental concepts and many practical techniques that you can use to improve the probability of success.

The key person in developing a system is the systems analyst, who analyzes the business situation, identifies opportunities for improvements, and designs an information system to implement them. Being a systems analyst is one of the most interesting, exciting, and challenging jobs around. Systems analysts work with a variety of people and learn how they conduct business. Specifically, they work with a team of systems analysts, programmers, and others on a common mission. Systems analysts feel the satisfaction of seeing systems that they designed and developed make a significant business impact, knowing that they contributed unique skills to make that happen.

However, the primary objective of a systems analyst is not to create a wonderful system; instead, it is to create value for the organization, which for most companies means increasing profits (government agencies and not-for-profit organizations measure value differently). Many failed systems have been abandoned because the analysts tried to build a wonderful system without clearly understanding how the system would fit with an organization's goals, current business processes, and other information systems to provide value. An investment in an information system is like any other investment. The goal is not to acquire the tool, because the tool is simply a means to an end; the goal is to enable the organization to perform work better so that it can earn greater profits or serve its constituents more effectively.

This book introduces the fundamental skills a systems analyst needs. This pragmatic book discusses the best practices in systems development; it does not present a general survey of systems development that covers everything about the topic. By definition, systems analysts do things and challenge the current way that organizations work. To get the most out of this book, you will need to actively apply to your own systems development project the ideas and concepts in the examples. This book guides you through all the steps for delivering a successful information system. By the time you finish the book, you won't be an expert analyst, but you will be ready to start building systems for real.

TYPICAL SYSTEMS ANALYST ROLES AND SKILLS

It is clear during systems development that the project team needs a variety of skills. Project members are *change agents* who identify ways to improve an organization, build an information system to support them, and train and motivate others to use the system. Understanding what to change and how to change it—and convincing others of the need for change—requires a wide range of skills. These skills can be broken down into six major categories: technical, business, analytical, interpersonal, management, and ethical.

Analysts must have the technical skills to understand the organization's existing technical environment, the technology that will make up the new system, and the way both can fit into an integrated technical solution. Business skills are required to understand how IT can be applied to business situations and to ensure that the IT delivers real business value. Analysts are continuous problem solvers at both the project and the organizational levels, and they put their analytical skills to the test regularly.

Analysts often need to communicate effectively one-on-one with users and business managers (who often have little experience with technology) and with programmers (who often have more technical expertise than the analysts). They must be able to give presentations to large and small groups and write reports. Not only do they need to have strong interpersonal abilities, but they also need to manage people with whom they work and they need to manage the pressure and risks associated with unclear situations.

Finally, analysts must deal fairly, honestly, and ethically with other project team members, managers, and system users. Analysts often deal with confidential information or information that, if shared with others, could cause harm (e.g., dissent among employees); it is important to maintain confidence and trust with all people.

In addition to these six general skill sets, analysts require many specific skills associated with roles performed on a project. In the early days of systems development, most organizations expected one person, the analyst, to have all the specific skills needed to conduct a systems development project. Some small organizations still expect one person to perform many roles, but because organizations and technology have become more complex, most large organizations now build project teams containing several individuals with clearly defined responsibilities. Different organizations divide the roles differently. Most IS teams include many other individuals, such as the *programmers*, who actually write the programs that make up the system, and *technical writers*, who prepare the help screens and other documentation (e.g., user manuals and systems manuals).

Business Analyst

A *business analyst* focuses on the business issues surrounding the system. These issues include identifying the business value that the system will create, developing ideas and suggestions for how the business processes can be improved, and designing the new processes and policies in conjunction with the systems analyst. This individual likely has business experience and some type of professional training. He or she represents the interests of the project sponsor and the ultimate users of the system. A business analyst assists in the planning and design phases but is most active during the analysis phase.

Systems Analyst

A *systems analyst* focuses on the IS issues surrounding the system. This person develops ideas and suggestions for how information technology can improve business processes, designs the new business processes with help from the business analyst, designs the new information system, and ensures that all IS standards are maintained. A systems analyst likely has significant training and experience in analysis and design, programming, and even areas of the business. He or she represents the interests of the IS department and works intensively through the project but perhaps less so during the implementation phase.

Infrastructure Analyst

An *infrastructure analyst* focuses on the technical issues surrounding how the system will interact with the organization's technical infrastructure (e.g., hardware, software, networks, and databases). An infrastructure analyst's tasks include ensuring that the new information system conforms to organizational standards and identifying infrastructure changes needed to support the system. This individual probably has significant training and experience in networking, database administration, and various hardware and software products. He or she represents the interests of the organization and IS group that will ultimately have to operate and support the new system once it has been installed. An infrastructure analyst works throughout the project but perhaps less so during planning and analysis phases.

Change Management Analyst

A *change management analyst* focuses on the people and management issues surrounding the system installation. The roles of this person include ensuring that the adequate documentation and support are available to users, providing user training on the new system, and developing strategies to overcome resistance to change. This individual should have significant training and experience in organizational behavior in general and change management in particular. He or she represents the interests of the project sponsor and users for whom the system is being designed. A change management analyst works most actively during the implementation phase but begins laying the groundwork for change during the analysis and design phases.

Project Manager

A *project manager* is responsible for ensuring that the project is completed on time and within budget and that the system delivers all benefits intended by the project sponsor. The role of the project manager includes managing the team members, developing the project plan, assigning resources, and being the primary point of contact when people outside the team have questions about the project. This individual likely has significant experience in project management and has probably worked for many years as a systems analyst beforehand. He or she represents the interests of the IS department and the project sponsor. The project manager works intensely during all phases of the project.

THE SYSTEMS DEVELOPMENT LIFE CYCLE

In many ways, building an information system is similar to building a house. First, the house (or the information system) starts with a basic idea. Second, this idea is transformed into a simple drawing that is shown to the customer and refined (often through several drawings, each improving on the last) until the customer agrees that the picture depicts what he or she wants. Third, a set of blueprints is designed that presents much more detailed information about the house (e.g., the type of water faucets or where the telephone jacks will be placed). Finally, the house is built following the blueprints, often with some changes directed by the customer as the house is erected.

The systems development life cycle (SDLC) has a similar set of four fundamental *phases*: planning, analysis, design, and implementation. Different projects might emphasize different parts of the SDLC or approach the SDLC phases in different ways, but all projects have elements of these four phases. Each *phase* is itself composed of a series of *steps,* which rely upon *techniques* that produce *deliverables* (specific documents and files that provide understanding about the project).

For example, in applying for admission to a university, all students go through the same phases: information gathering, applying, and accepting. Each of these phases has steps; for example, information gathering includes steps such as searching for schools, requesting information, and reading brochures. Students then use techniques (e.g., Internet searching) that can be applied to steps (e.g., requesting information) to create *deliverables* (e.g., evaluations of different aspects of universities).

In many projects, the SDLC phases and steps proceed in a logical path from start to finish. In other projects, the project teams move through the steps consecutively, incrementally, iteratively, or in other patterns. In this section, we describe the phases, the actions, and some of the techniques that are used to accomplish the steps at a very high level.

For now, there are two important points to understand about the SDLC. First, you should get a general sense of the phases and steps through which IS projects move and some of the techniques that produce certain deliverables. Second, it is important to understand that the SDLC is a process of *gradual refinement*. The deliverables produced in the analysis phase provide a general idea of the shape of the new system. These deliverables are used as input to the design phase, which then refines them to produce a set of deliverables that describes in much more detailed terms exactly how the system will be built. These deliverables, in turn, are used in the implementation phase to produce the actual system. Each phase refines and elaborates on the work done previously.

Planning

The *planning phase* is the fundamental process of understanding *why* an information system should be built and determining how the project team will go about building it. It has two steps:

1. During *project initiation,* the system's business value to the organization is identified: How will it lower costs or increase revenues? Most ideas for new systems come from outside the IS area (e.g., from the marketing department and accounting department) in the form of a *system request.* A system request presents a brief summary of a business need, and it explains how a system that supports the need will create business value. The IS department works together with the person or department that generated the request (called the *project sponsor*) to conduct a *feasibility analysis.*

    The system request and feasibility analysis are presented to an information systems *approval committee* (sometimes called a steering committee), which decides whether the project should be undertaken.

2. Once the project is approved, it enters *project management.* During project management, the *project manager* creates a *workplan,* staffs the project, and puts techniques in place to help the project team control and direct the project through the entire SDLC. The deliverable for project management is a *project plan,* which describes how the project team will go about developing the system.

Analysis

The *analysis phase* answers the questions of *who* will use the system, *what* the system will do, and *where* and *when* it will be used. During this phase, the project team investigates any current system(s), identifies opportunities for improvement, and develops a concept for the new system.

This phase has three steps:

1. An *analysis strategy* is developed to guide the project team's efforts. Such a strategy usually includes an analysis of the current system (called the *as-is system*) and its problems and then ways to design a new system (called the *to-be system*).

2. The next step is *requirements gathering* (e.g., through interviews or questionnaires). The analysis of this information—in conjunction with input from the project sponsor and many other people—leads to the development of a concept for a new system. The system concept is then used as a basis to develop a set of business *analysis models,* which describe how the business will operate if the new system is developed.

3. The analyses, system concept, and models are combined into a document called the *system proposal,* which is presented to the project sponsor and other key decision makers (e.g., members of the approval committee) who decide whether the project should continue to move forward.

The system proposal is the initial deliverable that describes what business requirements the new system should meet. Because it is really the first step in the design of the new system, some experts argue that it is inappropriate to use the term "analysis" as the name for this phase; some argue a better name would be "analysis and initial design." Most organizations continue to use the name *analysis* for this phase, however, so we use it in this book as well. Just keep in mind that the deliverable from the analysis phase is both an analysis and a high-level initial design for the new system.

Design

The *design phase* decides *how* the system will operate, in terms of the hardware, software, and network infrastructure; the user interface, forms, and reports; and the specific programs, databases, and files that will be needed. Although most of the strategic decisions about the system were made in the development of the system concept during the analysis phase, the steps in the design phase determine exactly how the system will operate. The design phase has four steps:

1. The *design strategy* is first developed. It clarifies whether the system will be developed by the company's own programmers, whether the system will be outsourced to another firm (usually a consulting firm), or whether the company will buy an existing software package.

2. This leads to the development of the basic *architecture design* for the system, which describes the hardware, software, and network infrastructure to be used. In most cases, the system will add or change the infrastructure that already exists in the organization. The *interface design* specifies how the users will move through the system (e.g., navigation methods such as menus and on-screen buttons) and the forms and reports that the system will use.

3. The *database and file specifications* are developed. These define exactly what data will be stored and where they will be stored.

4. The analyst team develops the *program design*, which defines the programs that need to be written and exactly what each program will do.

This collection of deliverables (architecture design, interface design, database and file specifications, and program design) is the *system specification* that is handed to the programming team for implementation. At the end of the design phase, the feasibility analysis and project plan are reexamined and revised, and another decision is made by the project sponsor and approval committee about whether to terminate the project or continue.

Implementation

The final phase in the SDLC is the *implementation phase*, during which the system is actually built (or purchased, in the case of a packaged software design). This is the phase that usually gets the most attention, because for most systems it is the longest and most expensive single part of the development process. This phase has three steps:

1. System *construction* is the first step. The system is built and tested to ensure that it performs as designed. Because the cost of bugs can be immense, testing is one of the most critical steps in implementation. Most organizations give more time and attention to testing than to writing the programs in the first place.

2. The system is installed. *Installation* is the process by which the old system is turned off and the new one is turned on. One of the most important aspects of conversion is the development of a *training plan* to teach users how to use the new system and help manage the changes caused by the new system.

3. The analyst team establishes a *support plan* for the system. This plan usually includes a formal or informal post-implementation review as well as a systematic way for identifying major and minor changes needed for the system.

SYSTEMS DEVELOPMENT METHODOLOGIES

A *methodology* is a formalized approach to implementing the SDLC (i.e., it is a list of steps and deliverables). There are many different systems development methodologies, and each one is unique, based on the order and focus it places on each SDLC phase. Some methodologies are formal standards used by government agencies, whereas others have been developed by consulting firms to sell to clients. Many organizations have internal methodologies that have been honed over the years, and they explain exactly how each phase of the SDLC is to be performed in that company.

There are many ways to categorize methodologies. One way is by looking at whether they focus on business processes or the data that support the business. A *process-centered methodology* emphasizes process models as the core of the system concept. In Figure 1-1, for example, process-centered methodologies would focus first on defining the processes (e.g., assemble sandwich ingredients). *Data-centered methodologies* emphasize data models as the core of the system concept. In Figure 1-1, data-centered methodologies would focus first on defining the contents of the storage areas (e.g., refrigerator) and how the contents were organized.[2] In contrast, *object-oriented methodologies* attempt to balance the focus between process and data by incorporating both into one model. In Figure 1-1, these methodologies would focus first on defining the major elements of the system (e.g., sandwiches, lunches) and look at the processes and data involved with each element.

Another important factor in categorizing methodologies is the sequencing of the SDLC phases and the amount of time and effort devoted to each.[3] In the early days of computing, programmers did not understand the need for formal and well-planned life-cycle methodologies. They tended to move directly from a very simple planning phase right into the construction step of the implementation phase—in other words, from a very fuzzy, not-well-thought-out system request into writing code. This is the same approach that you sometimes use when writing programs for a programming class. It can work for small programs that require only one programmer, but if the requirements are complex or unclear, you might miss important aspects of the problem and have to start all over again, throwing away part of the program (and the time and effort spent writing it). This approach also makes teamwork difficult because members have little idea about what needs to be accomplished and how to work together to produce a final product. In this section, we describe a set of different classes of systems development methodologies: structured design, rapid application development, object-oriented systems analysis and design, agile development, DevOps, and custom methodologies.

Structured Design

The first category of systems development methodologies is called *structured design*. These methodologies became dominant in the 1980s, replacing the previous ad hoc and undisciplined approach. Structured design methodologies adopt a formal step-by-step approach to the SDLC that moves logically from one phase to the next. Numerous process-centered and data-centered methodologies follow the basic approach of the two structured design categories outlined next.

---

[2] The classic modern process-centered methodology is that by Edward Yourdon, *Modern Structured Analysis* (Englewood Cliffs, NJ: Yourdon Press, 1989). An example of a data-centered methodology is information engineering; see James Martin, *Information Engineering,* vols. 1–3 (Englewood Cliffs, NJ: Prentice Hall, 1989). A widely accepted standardized non-object-oriented methodology that balances processes and data is IDEF; see FIPS 183, *Integration Definition for Function Modeling* (Federal Information Processing Standards Publications, U.S. Department of Commerce, 1993).

[3] A good reference for comparing systems development methodologies is Steve McConnell, *Rapid Development* (Redmond, WA: Microsoft Press, 1996).

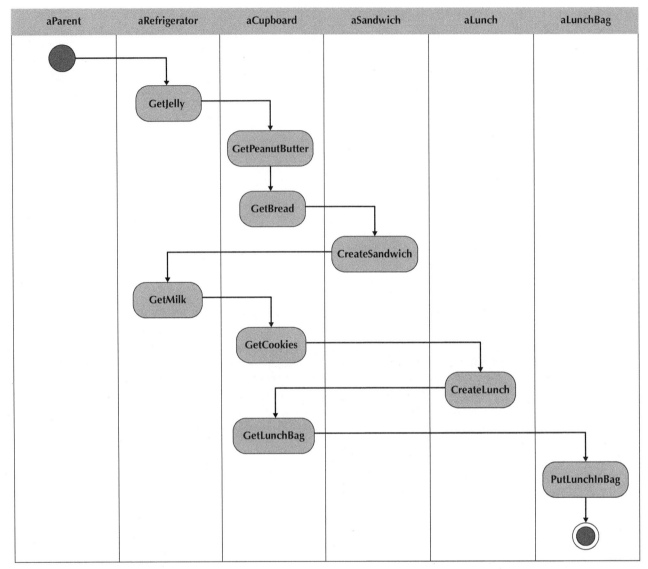

FIGURE 1-1 A Simple Behavioral Model for Making a Simple Lunch

Waterfall Development The original structured design methodology (still used today) is *waterfall development*. With waterfall development-based methodologies, the analysts and users proceed in sequence from one phase to the next. The key deliverables for each phase are typically very long (often hundreds of pages in length) and are presented to the project sponsor for approval as the project moves from phase to phase. Once the sponsor approves the work that was conducted for a phase, the phase ends and the next one begins. This methodology is referred to as waterfall development because it moves forward from phase to phase in the same manner as a waterfall. Although it is possible to go backward in the SDLC (e.g., from design back to analysis), it is extremely difficult (imagine yourself as a salmon trying to swim upstream against a waterfall).

Structured design also introduced the use of formal modeling or diagramming techniques to describe the basic business processes and the data that support them. Traditional structured design uses one set of diagrams to represent the processes and a separate set of diagrams to represent data. Because two sets of diagrams are used, the systems analyst must decide which set to develop first and use as the core of the system: process-model diagrams or data-model diagrams.

The two key advantages of the structured design waterfall approach are that it identifies system requirements long before programming begins and it minimizes changes to the requirements as the project proceeds. The two key disadvantages are that the design must be completely specified before programming begins and that a long time elapses between the completion of the system proposal in the analysis phase and the delivery of the system (usually many months or years). If the project team misses important requirements, expensive post-implementation programming may be needed (imagine yourself trying to design a car on paper; how likely would you be able to remember interior lights that come on when the doors open or to specify the right number of valves on the engine?). A system can also require significant rework because the business environment has changed from the time when the analysis phase occurred.

Parallel Development *Parallel development* methodology attempts to address the problem of long delays between the analysis phase and the delivery of the system. Instead of doing design and implementation in sequence, it performs a general design for the whole system and then divides the project into a series of distinct subprojects that can be designed and implemented in parallel. Once all subprojects are complete, the separate pieces are integrated and the system is delivered.

The primary advantage of this methodology is that it can reduce the time to deliver a system; thus, there is less chance of changes in the business environment causing rework. However, sometimes the subprojects are not completely independent; design decisions made in one subproject can affect another, and the end of the project can require significant integration efforts.

Rapid Application Development (RAD)

A second category of methodologies includes *rapid application development (RAD)*-based methodologies. These are a newer class of systems development methodologies that emerged in the 1990s. RAD-based methodologies attempt to address both weaknesses of structured design methodologies by adjusting the SDLC phases to get some part of the system developed quickly and into the hands of the users. In this way, the users can better understand the system and suggest revisions that bring the system closer to what is needed.[4]

Most RAD-based methodologies recommend that analysts use special techniques and computer tools to speed up the analysis, design, and implementation phases, such as computer-aided software engineering (CASE) tools, joint application design (JAD) sessions, fourth-generation or visual programming languages that simplify and speed up programming, and code generators that automatically produce programs from design specifications. The combination of the changed SDLC phases and the use of these tools and techniques improves the speed and quality of systems development. However, there is one possible subtle problem with RAD-based methodologies: managing user expectations. Owing to the use of the tools and techniques that can improve the speed and quality of systems development, user expectations of what is possible can change dramatically. As a user better understands the information technology (IT), the systems requirements tend to expand. This was less of a problem when using methodologies that spent a lot of time thoroughly documenting requirements.

---

[4] One of the best RAD books is Steve McConnell, *Rapid Development* (Redmond, WA: Microsoft Press, 1996).

Phased Development A *phased development*-based methodology breaks an overall system into a series of *versions* that are developed sequentially. The analysis phase identifies the overall system concept, and the project team, users, and system sponsor then categorize the requirements into a series of versions. The most important and fundamental requirements are bundled into the first version of the system. The analysis phase then leads into design and implementation—but only with the set of requirements identified for version 1.

Once version 1 is implemented, work begins on version 2. Additional analysis is performed based on the previously identified requirements and combined with new ideas and issues that arose from the users' experience with version 1. Version 2 then is designed and implemented, and work immediately begins on the next version. This process continues until the system is complete or is no longer in use.

Phased development-based methodologies have the advantage of quickly getting a useful system into the hands of the users. Although the system does not perform all the functions the users need at first, it does begin to provide business value sooner than if the system were delivered after completion, as is the case with the waterfall and parallel methodologies. Likewise, because users begin to work with the system sooner, they are more likely to identify important additional requirements sooner than with structured design situations.

The major drawback of phased development is that users begin to work with systems that are intentionally incomplete. It is critical to identify the most important and useful features and include them in the first version and to manage users' expectations along the way.

Prototyping A *prototyping*-based methodology performs the analysis, design, and implementation phases concurrently, and all three phases are performed repeatedly in a cycle until the system is completed. With these methodologies, the basics of analysis and design are performed, and work immediately begins on a *system prototype*, a quick-and-dirty program that provides a minimal amount of features. The first prototype is usually the first part of the system that is used. This is shown to the users and the project sponsor, who provide comments. These comments are used to reanalyze, redesign, and reimplement a second prototype, which provides a few more features. This process continues in a cycle until the analysts, users, and sponsor agree that the prototype provides enough functionality to be installed and used in the organization. After the prototype (now called the "system") is installed, refinement occurs until it is accepted as the new system.

The key advantage of a prototyping-based methodology is that it *very* quickly provides a system with which the users can interact, even if it is not ready for widespread organizational use at first. Prototyping reassures the users that the project team is working on the system (there are no long delays in which the users see little progress), and prototyping helps to more quickly refine real requirements.

The major problem with prototyping is that its fast-paced system releases challenge attempts to conduct careful, methodical analysis. Often the prototype undergoes such significant changes that many initial design decisions become poor ones. This can cause problems in the development of complex systems because fundamental issues and problems are not recognized until well into the development process. Imagine building a car and discovering late in the prototyping process that you have to take the whole engine out to change the oil (because no one thought about the need to change the oil until after it had been driven 10,000 miles).

Throwaway Prototyping *Throwaway prototyping*-based methodologies are similar to prototyping-based methodologies in that they include the development of prototypes; however, throwaway prototypes are done at a different point in the SDLC. These prototypes are used for a very different purpose than those previously discussed, and they have a very different appearance.

The throwaway prototyping-based methodologies have a relatively thorough analysis phase that is used to gather information and to develop ideas for the system concept. However, users might not completely understand many of the features they suggest, and there may be challenging technical issues to be solved. Each of these issues is examined by analyzing, designing, and building a *design prototype*. A design prototype is not a working system; it is a product that represents a part of the system that needs additional refinement, and it contains only enough detail to enable users to understand the issues under consideration. For example, suppose users are not completely clear on how an order-entry system should work. In this case, a series of mock-up screens *appear* to be a system, but they really do nothing. Or suppose that the project team needs to develop a sophisticated graphics program in Java. The team could write a portion of the program with pretend data to ensure that they could do a full-blown program successfully.

A system developed using this type of methodology relies on several design prototypes during the analysis and design phases. Each of these prototypes is used to minimize the risk associated with the system by confirming that important issues are understood before the real system is built. Once the issues are resolved, the project moves into design and implementation. At this point, the design prototypes are thrown away, which is an important difference between these methodologies and prototyping methodologies, in which the prototypes evolve into the final system.

Throwaway prototyping-based methodologies balance the benefits of well-thought-out analysis and design phases with the advantages of using prototypes to refine key issues before a system is built. It can take longer to deliver the final system as compared to prototyping-based methodologies, but this type of methodology usually produces more stable and reliable systems.

Object-Oriented Systems Analysis and Design (OOSAD)

A third category of information systems development methodologies is object-oriented analysis and design. Object-oriented approaches to developing information systems, technically speaking, can use any of the traditional methodologies. However, the object-oriented approaches are most associated with a phased development RAD. The primary difference between a traditional approach like structured design and an object-oriented approach is how a problem is decomposed. In traditional approaches, the problem-decomposition process is either process-centric or data-centric. However, processes and data are so closely related that it is difficult to pick one or the other as the primary focus. Based on this lack of congruence with the real world, new *object-oriented methodologies* have emerged that use the RAD-based sequence of SDLC phases but attempt to balance the emphasis between process and data by focusing the analysis of problems on objects that contain both data and processes.

According to the creators of the Unified Modeling Language (UML), Grady Booch, Ivar Jacobson, and James Rumbaugh,[5] any modern object-oriented approach to developing information systems must be use-case driven, architecture-centric, and iterative and incremental.

Use-Case Driven *Use-case driven* means that *use cases* are the primary modeling tools defining the behavior of the system. A use case describes how the user interacts with the system to perform some activity, such as placing an order, making a reservation, or searching for information. The use cases are used to identify and to communicate the requirements of the system to the programmers who must write the system. Use cases are inherently simple because they focus on only one business process at a time. In contrast, the process model diagrams used by

---

[5] Grady Booch, Ivar Jacobson, and James Rumbaugh, *The Unified Modeling Language User Guide* (Reading, MA: Addison-Wesley, 1999).

traditional structured and RAD methodologies are far more complex because they require the systems analyst and user to develop models of the entire system. With traditional methodologies, each system is decomposed into a set of subsystems, which are, in turn, decomposed into further subsystems, and so on. This goes on until no further process decomposition makes sense, and it often requires dozens of pages of interlocking diagrams. In contrast, a use case focuses on only one business process at a time, so developing models is much simpler.[6]

Architecture-Centric Any modern approach to systems analysis and design should be architecture-centric. *Architecture-centric* means that the underlying software architecture of the evolving system specification drives the specification, construction, and documentation of the system. Modern object-oriented systems analysis and design approaches should support at least three separate but interrelated architectural views of a system: functional, static, and dynamic. The *functional*, or *external, view* describes the behavior of the system from the perspective of the user. The *structural*, or *static, view* describes the system in terms of attributes, methods, classes, and relationships. The *behavioral*, or *dynamic, view* describes the behavior of the system in terms of messages passed among objects and state changes within an object.

Iterative and Incremental Modern object-oriented systems analysis and design approaches emphasize *iterative* and *incremental* development that undergoes continuous testing and refinement throughout the life of the project. This implies that the systems analysts develop their understanding of a user's problem by building up the three architectural views little by little. The systems analyst does this by working with the user to create a functional representation of the system under study. Next, the analyst attempts to build a structural representation of the evolving system. Using the structural representation of the system, the analyst distributes the functionality of the system over the evolving structure to create a behavioral representation of the evolving system. As an analyst works with the user in developing the three architectural views of the evolving system, the analyst iterates over each of and among the views. That is, as the analyst better understands the structural and *behavioral views,* the analyst uncovers missing requirements or misrepresentations in the functional view. This, in turn, can cause changes to be cascaded back through the structural and behavioral views. All three architectural views of the system are interlinked and dependent on each other (see Figure 1-2). As each increment and iteration is completed, a more-complete representation of the user's real functional requirements is uncovered.

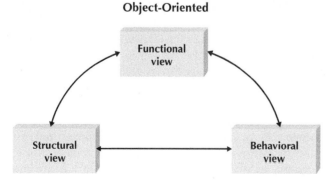

Object-Oriented

FIGURE 1-2 Iterative and Incremental Development

[6] For those of you who have experience with traditional structured analysis and design, this is one of the most unusual aspects of object-oriented analysis and design using UML. Unlike structured approaches, object-oriented approaches stress focusing on just one use case at a time and distributing that single use case over a set of communicating and collaborating objects.

Benefits of Object-Oriented Systems Analysis and Design Concepts in the object-oriented approach enable analysts to break a complex system into smaller, more-manageable modules, work on the modules individually, and easily piece the modules back together to form an information system. This modularity makes systems development easier to grasp, easier to share among members of a project team, and easier to communicate to users, who are needed to provide requirements and confirm how well the system meets the requirements throughout the systems development process. By modularizing systems development, the project team actually is creating reusable pieces that can be plugged into other systems efforts or used as starting points for other projects. Ultimately, this can save time because new projects don't have to start completely from scratch.

Agile Development[7]

A fourth category of systems development methodologies is *agile development*. All agile development methodologies are based on the agile manifesto and a set of twelve principles. The emphasis of the manifesto is to focus the developers on the working conditions of the developers, the working software, the customers, and addressing changing requirements instead of focusing on detailed systems development processes, tools, all-inclusive documentation, legal contracts, and detailed plans. These programming-centric methodologies have few rules and practices, all of which are fairly easy to follow. These methodologies are typically based only on the twelve principles of agile software. These principles include the following:

- Software is delivered early and continuously through the development process, satisfying the customer.
- Changing requirements are embraced regardless of when they occur in the development process.
- Working software is delivered frequently to the customer.
- Customers and developers work together to solve the business problem.
- Motivated individuals create solutions; provide them the tools and environment they need, and trust them to deliver.
- Face-to-face communication within the development team is the most efficient and effective method of gathering requirements.
- The primary measure of progress is working, executing software.
- Both customers and developers should work at a pace that is sustainable. That is, the level of work could be maintained indefinitely without any worker burnout.
- Agility is heightened through attention to both technical excellence and good design.
- Simplicity, the avoidance of unnecessary work, is essential.
- Self-organizing teams develop the best architectures, requirements, and designs.
- Development teams regularly reflect on how to improve their development processes.

Based on these principles, agile methodologies focus on streamlining the systems development process by eliminating much of the modeling and documentation overhead and the time spent on those tasks. Instead, projects emphasize simple, iterative application development.[8] All agile development methodologies follow a simple cycle through the traditional phases of

[7] Three good sources of information on agile development and object-oriented systems are S. W. Ambler, *Agile Modeling: Effective Practices for Extreme Programming and the Unified Process* (New York: Wiley, 2002); C. Larman, *Agile & Iterative Development: A Manager's Guide* (Boston: Addison-Wesley, 2004); R. C. Martin, *Agile Software Development: Principles, Patterns, and Practices* (Upper Saddle River, NJ: Prentice Hall, 2003).

[8] See Agile Alliance, www.agilealliance.com.

the systems development process. Virtually all agile methodologies are used in conjunction with object-oriented technologies.

However, agile methodologies do have critics. One of the major criticisms deals with today's business environment, where much of the actual information systems development is offshored, outsourced, and/or subcontracted. Given agile development methodologies requiring co-location of the development team, this seems to be a very unrealistic assumption. A second major criticism is that if agile development is not carefully managed, and by definition it is not, the development process can devolve into a prototyping approach that essentially becomes a "programmers gone wild" environment where programmers attempt to hack together solutions. A third major criticism, based on the lack of actual documentation created during the development of the software, raises issues regarding the auditability of the systems being created. Without sufficient documentation, neither the system nor the systems-development process can be assured. A fourth major criticism is based on whether agile approaches can deliver large mission-critical systems.

Even with these criticisms, given the potential for agile approaches to address the application backlog and to provide timely solutions to many business problems, agile approaches should be considered in some circumstances. Furthermore, many of the techniques encouraged by attending to the underlying purpose of the agile manifesto and the set of twelve agile principles are very useful in object-oriented systems development. Two of the more popular examples of agile development methodologies are extreme programming (XP) and Scrum.

Extreme Programming[9] *Extreme programming (XP)* is founded on four core values: communication, simplicity, feedback, and courage. These four values provide a foundation that XP developers use to create any system. First, the developers must provide rapid feedback to the end users on a continuous basis. Second, XP requires developers to follow the KISS principle.[10] Third, developers must make incremental changes to grow the system, and they must not only accept change, they must embrace change. Fourth, developers must have a quality-first mentality. XP also supports team members in developing their own skills. Three of the key principles that XP uses to create successful systems are continuous testing, simple coding performed by pairs of developers, and close interactions with end users to build systems very quickly.

Testing and efficient coding practices are the core of XP. Code is tested each day and is placed into an integrative testing environment. If bugs exist, the code is backed out until it is completely free of errors.

An XP project begins with user stories that describe what the system needs to do. Then, programmers code in small, simple modules and test to meet those needs. Users are required to be available to clear up questions and issues as they arise. Standards are very important to minimize confusion, so XP teams use a common set of names, descriptions, and coding practices. XP projects deliver results sooner than even the RAD approaches, and they rarely get bogged down in gathering requirements for the system.

XP adherents claim many strengths associated with developing software using XP. Programmers work closely with all stakeholders, and communication among all stakeholders is improved. Continuous testing of the evolving system is encouraged. The system is developed in an evolutionary and incremental manner, which allows the requirements to evolve as the stakeholders understand the potential that the technology has in providing a solution to

---

[9] For more information, see K. Beck, *eXtreme Programming Explained: Embrace Change* (Reading, MA: Addison-Wesley, 2000); C. Larman, *Agile & Iterative Development: A Manager's Guide* (Boston: Addison-Wesley, 2004); M. Lippert, S. Roock, and H. Wolf, *eXtreme Programming in Action: Practical Experiences from Real World Projects* (New York: Wiley, 2002); www.extremeprogramming.org.

[10] Keep it simple, stupid.

their problem. Estimation is task driven and is performed by the programmer who will implement the solution for the task under consideration. Because all programming is done in pairs, a shared responsibility for each software component develops among the programmers. Finally, the quality of the final product increases during each iteration.

For small projects with highly motivated, cohesive, stable, and experienced teams, XP should work just fine. However, if the project is not small or the teams aren't jelled,[11] the success of an XP development effort is doubtful. This tends to throw into doubt the whole idea of bringing outside contractors into an existing team environment using XP.[12] The chance of outsiders jelling with insiders might simply be too optimistic. XP requires a great deal of discipline, otherwise projects will become unfocused and chaotic. XP is recommended only for small groups of developers—no more than ten developers—and it is not advised for large mission-critical applications. Owing to the lack of analysis and design documentation, there is only code documentation associated with XP, so maintaining large systems built with XP may be impossible. And because mission-critical business information systems tend to exist for a long time, the utility of XP as a business information systems development methodology is in doubt. Finally, the methodology needs a lot of on-site user input, something to which many business units cannot commit.[13] However, some of the techniques associated with XP are useful in object-oriented systems development. For example, user stories, pair programming, and continuous testing are invaluable tools from which object-oriented systems development could benefit.

Scrum[14] *Scrum* is a term that is well known to rugby fans. In rugby, a scrum is used to restart a game. In a nutshell, the creators of the Scrum method believe that no matter how much you plan, as soon as the software begins to be developed, chaos breaks out and the plans go out the window.[15] The best you can do is to react to where the proverbial rugby ball squirts out. You then sprint with the ball until the next scrum. In the case of the Scrum methodology, a sprint lasts thirty working days. At the end of the sprint, a system is delivered to the customer.

Of all systems development approaches, on the surface, Scrum is the most chaotic. To control some of the innate chaos, Scrum development focuses on a few key practices. Teams are self-organized and self-directed. Unlike other approaches, Scrum teams do not have a designated team leader. Instead, teams organize themselves in a symbiotic manner and set their own goals for each sprint (iteration). Once a sprint has begun, Scrum teams do not consider any additional requirements. Any new requirements that are uncovered are placed on a backlog of requirements that still need to be addressed. At the beginning of every workday, a Scrum meeting takes place. At the end of each sprint, the team demonstrates the software to the client. Based on the results of the sprint, a new plan is begun for the next sprint.

[11] A *jelled team* is one that has low turnover, a strong sense of identity, a sense of eliteness, a feeling that they jointly own the product being developed, and enjoyment in working together. For more information regarding jelled teams, see T. DeMarco and T. Lister, *Peopleware: Productive Projects and Teams* (New York: Dorset/House, 1987).

[12] Considering the tendency for offshore outsourcing, this is a major obstacle for XP to overcome. For more information on offshore outsourcing, see P. Thibodeau, "ITAA Panel Debates Outsourcing Pros, Cons," Computerworld Morning Update (September 25, 2003); S. W. Ambler, "Chicken Little Was Right," *Software Development* (October 2003).

[13] Many of the observations on the utility of XP as a development approach were based on conversations with Brian Henderson-Sellers.

[14] For more information, see C. Larman, *Agile & Iterative Development: A Manager's Guide* (Boston: Addison-Wesley, 2004); K. Schwaber and M. Beedle, *Agile Software Development with Scrum* (Upper Saddle River, NJ: Prentice Hall, 2001); R. Wysocki, *Effective Project Management: Traditional, Agile, Extreme*, 5th Ed. (Indianapolis, IN: Wiley Publishing, 2009).

[15] Scrum developers are not the first to question the use of plans. One of President Eisenhower's favorite maxims was, "In preparing for battle I have always found that plans are useless, but planning is indispensable." M. Dobson, *Streetwise Project Management: How to Manage People, Processes, and Time to Achieve the Results You Need* (Avon, MA: F+W Publications, 2003), p. 43.

Scrum meetings are one of the most interesting aspects of the Scrum development process. The team members attend the meetings, but anyone can attend. However, with very few exceptions, only team members may speak. One prominent exception is management providing feedback on the business relevance of the work being performed by a specific team. In this meeting, all team members stand in a circle and report on what they accomplished during the previous day, state what they plan to do today, and describe anything that blocked progress the previous day. To enable continuous progress, any block identified is dealt with within one hour. From a Scrum point of view, it is better to make a "bad" decision about a block at this point in development than to not make a decision. Because the meetings take place each day, a bad decision can easily be undone. Larman[16] suggests that each team member should report any additional requirements that have been uncovered during the sprint and anything that the team member learned that could be useful for other team members to know.

One of the major criticisms of Scrum, as with all agile methodologies, is that it is questionable whether Scrum can scale up to develop very large mission-critical systems. A typical Scrum team size is no more than seven members. The only organizing principle put forth by Scrum followers to address this criticism is to organize a scrum of scrums. Each team meets every day, and after the team meeting takes place, a representative (not leader) of each team attends a scrum-of-scrums meeting. This continues until the progress of entire system has been determined. Depending on the number of teams involved, this approach to managing a large project is doubtful. However, as in XP and other agile development approaches, many of the ideas and techniques associated with Scrum development are useful in object-oriented systems development, such as the focus of a Scrum meeting, the evolutionary and incremental approach to identifying requirements, and the incremental and iterative approach to the development of the system.

DevOps

Another category of systems development methodologies is DevOps.[17] *DevOps* approaches incorporate ideas from both object-oriented approaches to systems development and lean manufacturing into the agile approaches. Two of the more popular approaches are DAD[18] and SAFe.[19] The primary extensions that DevOps approaches support are the inclusion of operations personnel with the development team and continuous deployment.

In earlier approaches, end users were identified as very important stakeholders who should be included in the development team. However, new technology developers realized that including end users, even though necessary, was not sufficient to deliver high quality systems. For example, with cloud technologies concerns related to deployment of the system should be addressed before the development team "throws the system over the wall" to the operations personnel. Consequently, DevOps approaches include operations personnel as members of the development team. In this way, nonfunctional requirements, such as security, can be addressed during the design of the system to be deployed.

---

[16] C. Larman, *Agile & Iterative Development: A Manager's Guide* (Boston: Addison-Wesley, 2004).

[17] For more information, see Gene Kim, Jez Humble, Patrick Debois, and John Willis, *The DevOps Handbook: How to Create World-Class Agility, Reliability, & Security in Technology Organizations* (Portland, OR: IT Revolution Press, 2016), Nicole Forsgren, Jex Humble, and Gene Kim, *The Science Behind DevOps, Accelerate: Building and Scaling High Performing Technology Organizations* (Portland, OR: IT Revolution Press, 2018).

[18] For more information, see Scott W. Ambler and Mark Lines, *Disciplined Agile Delivery: A Practitioner's Guide to Agile Software Delivery in the Enterprise* (Upper Saddle River, NJ: IBM Press, 2012).

[19] For more information, see Richard Knaster and Dean Leffingwell, *SAFe® Distilled: Applying the Scaled Agile Framework® for Lean Software and Systems Engineering* (Boston, MA: Addison-Wesley, 2017); Dean Leffingwell with Alex Yakyma, Richard Knaster, Drew Jemilo, and Inbar Oren, *SAFe® Reference Guide: Scaled Agile Framework® for Lean Software and Systems Engineering* (Boston, MA: Addison-Wesley, 2017).

With both object-oriented and agile approaches, deployment was only performed after a version of the system was completed. In other words, the operations personnel took over the system and deployed it. With DevOps approaches, deployment is completed when a new chunk of software has passed a set of relevant tests. Consequently, deployment of a new version of the system is not performed all at once. Instead, the new version is deployed in pieces over time; this is also referred to as a rolling upgrade. This approach requires quite a bit of automation of the actual deployment pipeline.[20]

Custom Methodologies

This last category of systems development methodologies supports the idea of applying both agile and object-oriented ideas to the systems development methodology itself. The idea behind these approaches is to support the development team in a way that is customized to their specific systems development project. In this case, only a high-level framework is used to create the project-specific method. Two of the approaches that have made progress in this area are based on the work of Brian Henderson-Sellers[21] and of Ivar Jacobson.[22] Both of these groups allow the team to pick and choose different components of a methodology from a component repository to create a custom methodology. Care must be taken to ensure that each component is plug compatible. By that we mean the inputs into a component are compatible with the outputs of the preceding component in the methodology.

THE UNIFIED PROCESS

The Unified Process is a specific methodology that maps out when and how to use the various Unified Modeling Language (UML) techniques for object-oriented analysis and design. The primary contributors were Grady Booch, Ivar Jacobson, and James Rumbaugh. Whereas the UML provides structural support for developing the structure and behavior of an information system, the Unified Process provides the behavioral support. The Unified Process, of course, is use-case driven, architecture-centric, and iterative and incremental. Furthermore, the Unified Process is a two-dimensional systems development process described by a set of phases and workflows. The phases are inception, elaboration, construction, and transition. The workflows include business modeling, requirements, analysis, design, implementation, test, deployment, configuration and change management, project management, and environment.[23] Figure 1-3 depicts the Unified Process.

[20] A good overview of these approaches is described in Len Bass, Ingo Weber, and Liming Zhu, *DevOps: A Software Architect's Perspective* (Upper Saddle River, NJ: Pearson Education, 2015).

[21] For more information, see Ian Graham, Brian Henderson-Sellers, and Houman Younessi, *The OPEN Process Specification* (New York, NY: ACM Press, 1997); Brian Henderson-Sellers, Anthony Simons, and Houman Younessi, *The OPEN Toolbox of Techniques* (New York, NY: ACM Press, 1998); Donald G. Firesmith and Brian Henderson-Sellers, *The OPEN Process Framework* (London, Addison-Wesley, 2002); Brian Henderson-Seller, Jolita Ralyte', Par J. Agerfalk, and Matti Rossi, *Situational Method Engineering* (Berlin: Springer, 2014).

[22] For more information, see Ivar Jaconson, Pan-Wei Ng, Paul E. McMahon, Ian Spence, and Svante Lidman, *The ESSENCE of Software Engineering: Applying the SEMAT Kernel* (Upper Saddle River, NJ: Addison-Wesley, 2013); Ivar Jacobson, Harold "Bud" Lawson, Pan-Wei Ng, Paul E. McMahon, and Michael Goedicke, *The Essentials of Modern Software Engineering: Free the Practices from the Method Prisons!* (ACM Books, 2019).

[23] The material in this section is based on Khawar Zaman Ahmed and Cary E. Umrysh, *Developing Enterprise Java Applications with J2EE and UML* (Boston, MA: Addison-Wesley, 2002); Jim Arlow and Ila Neustadt, *UML and the Unified Process: Practical Object-Oriented Analysis & Design* (Boston, MA: Addison-Wesley, 2002); Peter Eeles, Kelli Houston, and Wojtek Kozacynski, *Building J2EE Applications with the Rational Unified Process* (Boston, MA: Addison-Wesley, 2003); Ivar Jacobson, Grady Booch, and James Rumbaugh, *The Unified Software Development Process* (Reading, MA: Addison-Wesley, 1999); Philippe Kruchten, *The Rational Unified Process: An Introduction,* 2nd Ed. (Boston, MA: Addison-Wesley, 2000); "Rational Unified Process: Best Practices for Software Development Teams," Rational Software White Paper, TP026B, Rev 11/01.

Phases

The *phases* of the Unified Process support an analyst in developing information systems in an iterative and incremental manner. The phases describe how an information system evolves through time. Depending on which development phase the evolving system is currently in, the level of activity varies over the *workflows*. The curve in Figure 1-3 associated with each workflow approximates the amount of activity that takes place during the specific phase. For example, the inception phase primarily involves the business modeling and requirements workflows, while practically ignoring the test and deployment workflows. Each phase contains a set of iterations, and each iteration uses the various workflows to create an incremental version of the evolving system. As the system evolves through the phases, it improves and becomes more complete. Each phase has objectives, a focus of activity over the workflows, and incremental deliverables. Each of the phases is described next.

Inception In many ways, the *inception phase* is very similar to the planning phase of a traditional SDLC approach. In this phase, a business case is made for the proposed system. This includes feasibility analysis that should answer questions such as the following:

> Do we have the technical capability to build it (technical feasibility)?
>
> If we build it, will it provide business value (economic feasibility)?
>
> If we build it, will it be used by the organization (organizational feasibility)?

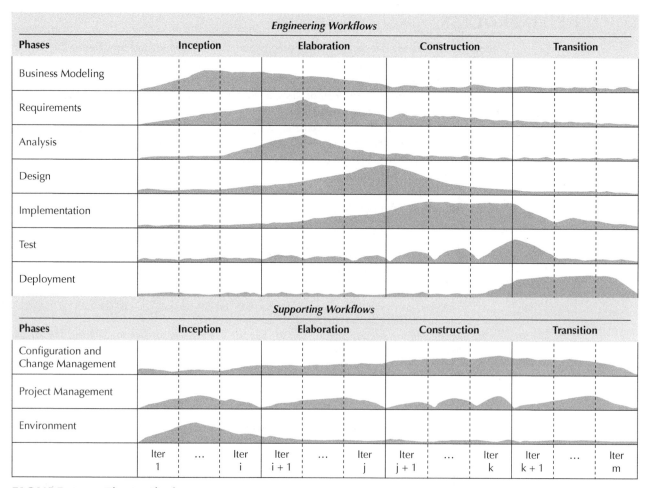

FIGURE 1-3 The Unified Process

To answer these questions, the development team performs work related primarily to the business modeling, requirements, and analysis workflows. In some cases, depending on the technical difficulties that could be encountered during the development of the system, a throwaway prototype is developed. This implies that the design, implementation, and test workflows could also be involved. The project management and environment supporting workflows are very relevant to this phase. The primary deliverables from the inception phase are a vision document that sets the scope of the project; identifies the primary requirements and constraints; sets up an initial project plan; and describes the feasibility of and risks associated with the project, the adoption of the necessary environment to develop the system, and some aspects of the problem domain classes being implemented and tested.

Elaboration When we typically think about object-oriented systems analysis and design, the activities related to the *elaboration phase* of the Unified Process are the most relevant. The *analysis* and *design workflows* are the primary focus during this phase. The elaboration phase continues with developing the vision document, including finalizing the business case, revising the risk assessment, and completing a project plan in sufficient detail to allow the stakeholders to be able to agree with constructing the actual final system. It deals with gathering the requirements, building the UML structural and behavioral models of the problem domain, and detailing how the problem domain models fit into the evolving system architecture. Developers are involved with all but the *deployment engineering workflow* in this phase. As the developers iterate over the workflows, the importance of addressing configuration and change management becomes apparent. Also, the development tools acquired during the inception phase become critical to the success of the project during this phase.[24] The primary deliverables of this phase include the UML structure and behavior diagrams and an executable of a baseline version of the evolving information system. The baseline version serves as the foundation for all later iterations. By providing a solid foundation at this point, the developers have a basis for completing the system in the construction and transition phases.

Construction The *construction phase* focuses heavily on programming the evolving information system. This phase is primarily concerned with the *implementation workflow*. However, the *requirements workflow* and the *analysis* and *design* workflows also are involved with this phase. It is during this phase that missing requirements are identified and the analysis and design models are finally completed. Typically, there are iterations of the workflows during this phase, and during the last iteration, the deployment workflow kicks into high gear. The *configuration and change management workflow*, with its version-control activities, becomes extremely important during the construction phase. At times, an iteration has to be rolled back. Without good version controls, rolling back to a previous version (incremental implementation) of the system is nearly impossible. The primary deliverable of this phase is an implementation of the system that can be released for beta and acceptance testing.

Transition Like the construction phase, the *transition phase* addresses aspects typically associated with the implementation phase of a traditional SDLC approach. Its primary focus is on the testing and deployment workflows. Essentially, the business modeling, requirements, and analysis workflows should have been completed in earlier iterations of the evolving information system. Furthermore, the testing workflow should have been executed during the earlier phases of the evolving system. Depending on the results from the testing workflow, some redesign and programming activities on the design and implementation workflows could be

---

[24] With UML comprising fifteen different, related diagramming techniques, keeping the diagrams coordinated and the different versions of the evolving system synchronized is typically beyond the capabilities of a mere mortal systems developer. These tools typically include project management and CASE tools. We describe the use of these tools in Chapter 2.

necessary, but they should be minimal at this point. From a managerial perspective, the project management, configuration and change management, and environment are involved. Some of the activities that take place are beta and acceptance testing, fine-tuning the design and implementation, user training, and rolling out the final product onto a production platform. Obviously, the primary deliverable is the actual executable information system. The other deliverables include user manuals, a plan to support the users, and a plan for upgrading the information system in the future.

Workflows

The workflows describe the tasks or activities that a developer performs to evolve an information system over time. The workflows of the Unified Process are grouped into two broad categories: engineering and supporting.

Engineering Workflows Engineering workflows include business-modeling, requirements, analysis, design, implementation, test, and deployment workflows. The engineering workflows deal with the activities that produce the technical product (i.e., the information system).

Business Modeling Workflow The *business modeling workflow* uncovers problems and identifies potential projects within a user organization. This workflow aids management in understanding the scope of the projects that can improve the efficiency and effectiveness of a user organization. The primary purpose of business modeling is to ensure that both developer and user organizations understand where and how the to-be-developed information system fits into the business processes of the user organization. This workflow is primarily executed during the inception phase to ensure that we develop information systems that make business sense. The activities that take place on this workflow are most closely associated with the planning phase of the traditional SDLC; however, requirements gathering, and use-case and business process modeling techniques also help us to understand the business situation.

Requirements Workflow In the Unified Process, the *requirements workflow* includes eliciting both functional and nonfunctional requirements. Typically, requirements are gathered from project stakeholders, such as end users, managers within the end user organization, and even customers. The requirements workflow is used the most during the inception and elaboration phases. The identified requirements are very helpful for developing the vision document and the use cases used throughout the development process. Additional requirements tend to be discovered throughout the development process. In fact, only the transition phase tends to have few, if any, additional requirements identified.

Analysis Workflow The *analysis workflow* primarily addresses the creation of an analysis model of the problem domain. In the Unified Process, the analyst begins designing the architecture associated with the problem domain; using the UML, the analyst creates structural and behavior diagrams that depict a description of the problem domain classes and their interactions. The primary purpose of the analysis workflow is to ensure that both the developer and user organizations understand the underlying problem and its domain without overanalyzing. If they are not careful, analysts can create *analysis paralysis*, which occurs when the project becomes so bogged down with analysis that the system is never actually designed or implemented. A second purpose of the analysis workflow is to identify useful reusable classes for class libraries. By reusing predefined classes, the analyst can avoid reinventing the wheel when creating the structural and behavior diagrams. The analysis workflow is predominantly associated with the elaboration phase, but like the requirements workflow, it is possible that additional analysis will be required throughout the development process.

Design Workflow The design workflow transitions the analysis model into a form that can be used to implement the system: the *design model*. Whereas the analysis workflow concentrates on understanding the problem domain, the design workflow focuses on developing a solution that will execute in a specific environment. Basically, the design workflow simply enhances the description of the evolving system by adding classes that address the environment of the system to the evolving analysis model. The design workflow uses activities such as detailed problem domain class design, optimization of the evolving information system, database design, user-interface design, and physical architecture design. The design workflow is associated primarily with the elaboration and construction phases of the Unified Process.

Implementation Workflow The primary purpose of the implementation workflow is to create an executable solution based on the design model (i.e., programming). This includes not only writing new classes but also incorporating reusable classes from executable class libraries into the evolving solution. As with any programming activity, the new classes and their interactions with the incorporated reusable classes must be tested. Finally, in the case of multiple groups performing the implementation of the information system, the implementers also must integrate the separate, individually tested modules to create an executable version of the system. The implementation workflow is associated primarily with the elaboration and construction phases.

Testing Workflow The primary purpose of the *testing workflow* is to increase the quality of the evolving system. Testing goes beyond the simple unit testing associated with the implementation workflow. In this case, testing also includes testing the integration of all modules used to implement the system, user acceptance testing, and the actual alpha testing of the software. Practically speaking, testing should go on throughout the development of the system; testing of the analysis and design models occurs during the elaboration and construction phases, whereas implementation testing is performed primarily during the construction and, to some degree, transition phases. Basically, at the end of each iteration during the development of the information system, some type of testing should be performed.

Deployment Workflow The deployment workflow is most associated with the transition phase of the Unified Process. The *deployment workflow* includes activities such as software packaging, distribution, installation, and beta testing. When actually deploying the new system into a user organization, the developers might have to convert the current data, interface the new software with the existing software, and train the end user to use the new system.

Supporting Workflows The supporting workflows include the project management, configuration and change management, and environment workflows. The supporting workflows focus on the managerial aspects of information systems development.

Project Management Workflow Whereas the other workflows associated with the Unified Process are technically active during all four phases, the *project management workflow* is the only truly cross-phase workflow. The development process supports incremental and iterative development, so information systems tend to grow or evolve over time. At the end of each iteration, a new incremental version of the system is ready for delivery. The project management workflow is quite important owing to the complexity of the two-dimensional development model of the Unified Process (workflows and phases). This workflow's activities include identifying and managing risks, managing scope, estimating the time to complete each iteration and the entire project, estimating the cost of the individual iteration and the whole project, and tracking the progress being made toward the final version of the evolving information system.

Configuration and Change Management Workflow The primary purpose of the configuration and change management workflow is to keep track of the state of the evolving system. In a nutshell, the evolving information system comprises a set of artifacts (e.g., diagrams, source code, and executables). During the development process, these artifacts are modified. A substantial amount of work—and, hence, money—is involved in developing the artifacts. The artifacts themselves should be handled as any expensive asset would be handled—access controls must be put into place to safeguard the artifacts from being stolen or destroyed. Furthermore, because the artifacts are modified on a regular, if not continuous, basis, good version control mechanisms should be established. Finally, a good deal of project management information needs to be captured (e.g., author, time, and location of each modification). The configuration and change management workflow is associated mostly with the construction and transition phases.

Environment Workflow During the development of an information system, the development team needs to use different tools and processes. The *environment workflow* addresses these needs. For example, a CASE tool that supports the development of an object-oriented information system via the UML could be required. Other tools necessary include programming environments, project management tools, and configuration management tools. The environment workflow involves acquiring and installing these tools. Even though this workflow can be active during all of the phases of the Unified Process, it should be involved primarily with the inception phase.

Extensions to the Unified Process

As large and as complex as the Unified Process is, many authors have pointed out a set of critical weaknesses. First, the Unified Process does not address staffing, budgeting, or contract management issues. These activities were explicitly left out of the Unified Process. Second, the Unified Process does not address issues relating to maintenance, operations, or support of the product once it has been delivered. Thus, it is not a complete software process; it is only a development process. Third, the Unified Process does not address cross- or inter-project issues. Considering the importance of reuse in object-oriented systems development and the fact that in many organizations employees work on many different projects at the same time, leaving out inter-project issues is a major omission.

To address these omissions, Ambler and Constantine suggest adding a production phase and two workflows: the operations and support workflow and the infrastructure management workflow (see Figure 1-4).[25] In addition to these new workflows, the test, deployment, and environment workflows are modified, and the project management and the configuration and change management workflows are extended into the production phase. These extensions are based on alternative object-oriented software processes: the OPEN process (Object-oriented Process, Environment, and Notation) and the Object-Oriented Software Process.[26]

[25] S. W. Ambler and L. L. Constantine, *The Unified Process Inception Phase: Best Practices in Implementing the UP* (Lawrence, KS: CMP Books, 2000); S. W. Ambler and L. L. Constantine, *The Unified Process Elaboration Phase: Best Practices in Implementing the UP* (Lawrence, KS: CMP Books, 2000); S. W. Ambler and L. L. Constantine, *The Unified Process Construction Phase: Best Practices in Implementing the UP* (Lawrence, KS: CMP Books, 2000); S. W. Ambler and L. L. Constantine, *The Unified Process Transition and Production Phases: Best Practices in Implementing the UP* (Lawrence, KS: CMP Books, 2002).

[26] S. W. Ambler, *Process Patterns—Building Large-Scale Systems Using Object Technology* (Cambridge, UK: SIGS Books/Cambridge University Press, 1998); S. W. Ambler, *More Process Patterns—Delivering Large-Scale Systems Using Object Technology* (Cambridge, UK: SIGS Books/Cambridge University Press, 1999); I. Graham, B. Henderson-Sellers, and H. Younessi, *The OPEN Process Specification* (Harlow, UK: Addison-Wesley, 1997); B. Henderson-Sellers and B. Unhelkar, *OPEN Modeling with UML* (Harlow, UK: Addison-Wesley, 2000).

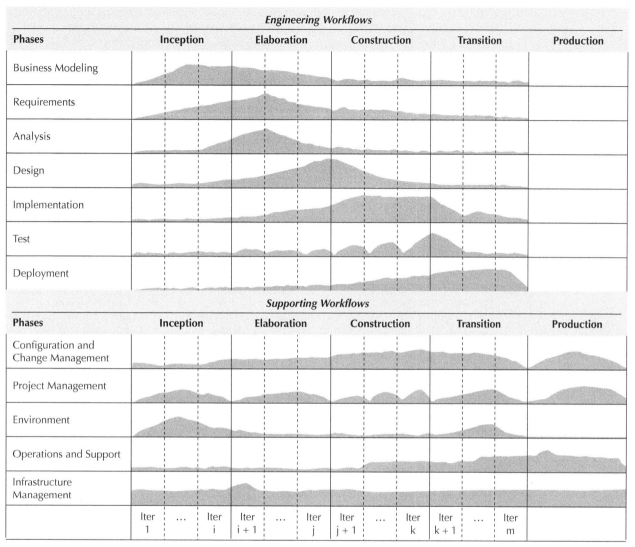

Engineering Workflows					
Phases	**Inception**	**Elaboration**	**Construction**	**Transition**	**Production**
Business Modeling					
Requirements					
Analysis					
Design					
Implementation					
Test					
Deployment					

Supporting Workflows					
Phases	**Inception**	**Elaboration**	**Construction**	**Transition**	**Production**
Configuration and Change Management					
Project Management					
Environment					
Operations and Support					
Infrastructure Management					
	Iter 1 ... Iter i	Iter i + 1 ... Iter j	Iter j + 1 ... Iter k	Iter k + 1 ... Iter m	

FIGURE 1-4 The Enhanced Unified Process

Production Phase The *production phase* is concerned primarily with issues related to the software product after it has been successfully deployed. This phase focuses on issues related to updating, maintaining, and operating the software. Unlike the previous phases, there are no iterations or incremental deliverables. If a new release of the software is to be developed, then the developers must begin a new run through the first four phases. Based on the activities that take place during this phase, no engineering workflows are relevant. The supporting workflows that are active during this phase include the configuration and change management workflow, the project management workflow, the new operations and support workflow, and the infrastructure management workflow.

Operations and Support Workflow The *operations and support workflow*, as you might guess, addresses issues related to supporting the current version of the software and operating the software on a daily basis. Activities include creating plans for the operation and support of the software product once it has been deployed, creating training and user documentation, putting into place necessary backup procedures, monitoring and optimizing the performance of the software, and performing corrective maintenance on the software. This workflow becomes active during the construction phase; its level of activity increases throughout the transition and, finally, the production phase. The workflow finally drops off when the current version of the software is replaced by a new version. Many developers are under the false impression that once the software has been delivered to the customer, their work is finished. In most cases, the work of supporting the software product is much more costly and time consuming than the original development. At that point, the developer's work may have just begun. When considering the newer DevOps approaches, it is obvious that operations personnel should be actively involved with this workflow.

Infrastructure Management Workflow The *infrastructure management workflow's* primary purpose is to support the development of the infrastructure necessary to develop object-oriented systems. Activities such as development and modification of libraries, standards, and enterprise models are very important. When the development and maintenance of a problem-domain architecture model goes beyond the scope of a single project and reuse is going to occur, the infrastructure management workflow is essential. Another very important set of cross-project activities is the improvement of the software development process. Because the activities on this workflow tend to affect many projects and the Unified Process focuses only on a specific project, the Unified Process tends to ignore these activities (i.e., they are simply beyond the scope and purpose of the Unified Process).

Existing Workflow Modifications and Extensions In addition to the workflows that were added to address deficiencies contained in the Unified Process, existing workflows had to be modified and/or extended into the production phase. These workflows include the test, deployment, environment, project management, and configuration and change management workflows.

Test Workflow For high-quality information systems to be developed, testing should be done on every deliverable, including those created during the inception phase. Otherwise, less than high-quality systems will be delivered to the customer.

Deployment Workflow Legacy systems exist in most corporations today, and these systems have databases associated with them that must be converted to interact with the new systems. Owing to the complexity of deploying new systems, the conversion requires significant planning. Therefore, the activities on the deployment workflow need to begin in the inception phase instead of waiting until the end of the construction phase, as suggested by the Unified Process.

Environment Workflow The environment workflow needs to be modified to include activities related to setting up the operations and production environment. The actual work performed is similar to the work related to setting up the development environment that was performed during the inception phase. In this case, the additional work is performed during the transition phase.

Project Management Workflow Even though the project management workflow does not include staffing the project, managing the contracts among the customers and vendors, and managing the project's budget, these activities are crucial to the success of any software development project. We suggest extending project management to include these activities. This workflow should additionally occur in the production phase to address issues such as training, staff management, and client relationship management.

Configuration and Change Management Workflow The configuration and change management workflow is extended into the new production phase. Activities performed during the production phase include identifying potential improvements to the operational system and assessing the potential impact of the proposed changes. Once developers have identified these changes and understood their impact, they can schedule the changes to be made and deployed with future releases.

Figure 1-5 shows the chapters in which the Enhanced Unified Process phases and workflows are covered. Given the offshore outsourcing and automation of information technology,[27] in this textbook, we focus primarily on the elaboration phase and the business modeling, requirements, analysis, design, and project management workflows of the Enhanced Unified Process. However, as Figure 1-5 shows, the other phases and workflows are covered.

Enhanced UP Phases	Chapters
Inception	2–4
Elaboration	3–11
Construction	8, 12
Transition	12–13
Production	13
Enhanced UP Engineering Workflows	**Chapters**
Business Modeling	2–5
Requirements	3–5, 10
Analysis	3–7
Design	7–11
Implementation	9, 12
Test	4–7, 12
Deployment	13
Enhanced UP Supporting Workflows	**Chapters**
Project Management	2, 13
Configuration and Change Management	2, 13
Environment	2
Operations and Support	13
Infrastructure Management	2

FIGURE 1-5   The Enhanced Unified Process and the Textbook Organization

[27] See Thomas L. Friedman, *The World Is Flat: A Brief History of the Twenty-First Century, Updated and Expanded Edition* (New York: Farrar, Straus, and Giroux, 2006); Daniel H. Pink, *A Whole New Mind: Why Right-Brainers Will Rule the Future* (New York: Riverhead Books, 2006).

In many object-oriented systems development environments today, code generation is supported. Thus, from a business perspective, we believe the activities associated with these workflows are the most important.

THE UNIFIED MODELING LANGUAGE

Until 1995, object concepts were popular but implemented in many different ways by different developers. Each developer had his or her own methodology and notation (e.g., Booch, Coad, Moses, OMT, OOSE, and SOMA).[28] Then in 1995, Rational Software brought three industry leaders together to create a single approach to object-oriented systems development. Grady Booch, Ivar Jacobson, and James Rumbaugh worked with others to create a standard set of diagramming techniques known as the *Unified Modeling Language (UML)*. The objective of UML was to provide a common vocabulary of object-oriented terms and diagramming techniques rich enough to model any systems development project from analysis through implementation. In November 1997, the *Object Management Group (OMG)* formally accepted UML as the standard for all object developers. During the following years, the UML has gone through multiple minor revisions. The current version of UML is Version 2.5.

Version 2.5 of the UML defines a set of fifteen diagramming techniques used to model a system. The diagrams are broken into two major groupings: one for modeling the structure of a system and one for modeling behavior. *Structure diagrams* provide a way to represent the data and static relationships in an information system. The structure diagrams include class, object, package, deployment, component, composite structure, and profile diagrams. *Behavior diagrams* provide the analyst with a way to depict the dynamic relationships among the instances or objects that represent the business information system. They also allow modeling of the dynamic behavior of individual objects throughout their lifetime. The behavior diagrams support the analyst in modeling the functional requirements of an evolving information system. The behavior modeling diagrams include activity, sequence, communication, interaction overview, timing, behavior state machine, protocol state machine, and use-case diagrams.[29] Figure 1-6 provides an overview of these diagrams.

Depending on where in the development process the system is, different diagrams play a more important role. In some cases, the same diagramming technique is used throughout the development process. In that case, the diagrams start off very conceptual and abstract. As the system is developed, the diagrams evolve to include details that ultimately lead to

[28] See Grady Booch, *Object-Oriented Analysis and Design with Applications,* 2nd Ed. (Redwood City, CA: Benjamin/Cummings, 1994); Peter Coad and Edward Yourdon, *Object-Oriented Analysis,* 2nd Ed. (Englewood Cliffs, NJ: Yourdon Press, 1991); Peter Coad and Edward Yourdon, *Object-Oriented Design* (Englewood Cliffs, NJ: Yourdon Press, 1991); Brian Henderson-Sellers and Julian Edwards, *Book Two of Object-Oriented Knowledge: The Working Object* (Sydney, Australia: Prentice Hall, 1994); James Rumbaugh, Michael Blaha, William Premerlani, Frederick Eddy, and William Lorensen, *Object-Oriented Modeling and Design* (Englewood Cliffs, NJ: Prentice Hall, 1991); Ivar Jacobson, Magnus Christerson, Patrik Jonsson, and Gunnar Overgaard, *Object-Oriented Software Engineering: A Use Case Approach* (Wokingham, England: Addison-Wesley, 1992); Ian Graham, *Migrating to Object Technology* (Wokingham, England: Addison-Wesley, 1994).

[29] The material contained in this section is based on the *OMG Unified Modeling Language Version 2.5.1, December 2017* (www.uml.org). Additional useful references include Michael Jesse Chonoles and James A. Schardt, *UML 2 for Dummies* (Indianapolis, IN: Wiley, 2003); Hans-Erik Eriksson, Magnus Penker, Brian Lyons, and David Fado, *UML 2 Toolkit* (Indianapolis, IN: Wiley, 2004); Kendall Scott, *Fast Track UML 2.0* (Berkeley, CA: Apress, 2004). For a complete description of all diagrams, see www.uml.org.

Diagram Name	Used to. . .	Primary Phase
Structure Diagrams		
Class	Illustrate the relationships between classes modeled in the system	Analysis, Design
Object	Illustrate the relationships between objects modeled in the system; used when actual instances of the classes will better communicate the model	Analysis, Design
Package	Group other UML elements together to form higher-level constructs	Analysis, Design, Implementation
Deployment	Show the physical architecture of the system; can also be used to show software components being deployed onto the physical architecture	Physical Design, Implementation
Component	Illustrate the physical relationships among the software components	Physical Design, Implementation
Composite Structure Design	Illustrate the internal structure of a class, i.e., the relationships among the parts of a class	Analysis, Design
Profile	Used to develop extensions to the UML itself	None
Behavioral Diagrams		
Activity	Illustrate business workflows independent of classes, the flow of activities in a use case, or detailed design of a method	Analysis, Design
Sequence	Model the behavior of objects within a use case; focuses on the time-based ordering of an activity	Analysis, Design
Communication	Model the behavior of objects within a use case; focus on the communication among a set of collaborating objects of an activity	Analysis, Design
Interaction Overview	Illustrate an overview of the flow of control of a process	Analysis, Design
Timing	Illustrate the interaction among a set of objects and the state changes they go through along a time axis	Analysis, Design
Behavioral State Machine	Examine the behavior of one class	Analysis, Design
Protocol State Machine	Illustrate the dependencies among the different interfaces of a class	Analysis, Design
Use-Case	Capture business requirements for the system and illustrate the interaction between the system and its environment	Analysis

FIGURE 1-6 UML 2.5 Diagram Summary

generating and developing code. In other words, the diagrams move from documenting the requirements to laying out the design. Overall, the consistent notation, integration among the diagramming techniques, and application of the diagrams across the entire development process make the UML a powerful and flexible language for analysts and developers. Later chapters provide more detail on using a subset of the UML in object-oriented systems analysis and design. In particular, these chapters describe activity, use-case, class, sequence, package, and deployment diagrams and the behavior state machines. We also introduce an optional UML diagram, the windows navigation diagram, that is an extension to the behavioral state machine that is used to design user navigation through an information system's user interfaces.

APPLYING THE CONCEPTS AT PATTERSON SUPERSTORE

This course will introduce many new concepts regarding object-oriented analysis and design. To make these concepts more relevant and understandable, we will apply the concepts, introduced in each chapter, to a fictitious company called Patterson Superstore.

Patterson is a retail chain established in Pittsburgh, PA, in 1985. Currently, Patterson uses a mobile application to facilitate prescription order, notification, and auto refill services. This service is widely used by Patterson's client base, and Patterson has leveraged this mobile app to gain an advantage over less technically advanced competitors.

Clients now want to use this technology to access health clinic services. The Vice President of Pharmacy Services, Max Ross, would like to use this opportunity to position Patterson as a leader in the use of technology use for clinic access. The system that he envisions will enable real-time communication with medical personnel (audio, video, and text), mobile appointment scheduling, telehealth assessment, and diagnosis of minor problems through video house calls. Throughout the book, we will revisit Patterson Superstore to see how the concepts introduced in each chapter affect this project.

You can find the rest of the case at www.wiley.com/go/dennis/systemanalysis6e/casestudy.

CHAPTER REVIEW

After reading and studying this chapter, you should be able to:

☐ Explain the different roles played by a systems analyst in the process of developing information systems.
☐ Describe the four primary phases of the Systems Development Life Cycle (SDLC).
☐ Explain the evolution of systems development methodologies from process-centric to data-centric to RAD-based methodologies.
☐ Discuss the three basic characteristics of all object-oriented systems analysis and design approach: use-case driven, architecture-centric, and iterative and incremental development.
☐ Describe the Unified Process.
☐ List and categorize, as to their primary purpose, the different diagrams associated with the Unified Modeling Language (UML).

KEY TERMS

Agile development
Analysis model
Analysis paralysis
Analysis phase
Analysis strategy
Analysis workflow
Approval committee
Architecture-centric
Architecture design
As-is system
Behavior diagram
Behavioral view

Business analyst
Business modeling workflow
Change agent
Change management analyst
Configuration and change management workflow
Construction
Construction phase
Database and file specification
Data-centered methodology
Deliverable
Deployment workflow

Design model
Design phase
Design prototype
Design strategy
Design workflow
DevOps
Dynamic view
Elaboration phase
Engineering workflow
Environment workflow
External view
Extreme programming (XP)

Feasibility analysis
Functional view
Gradual refinement
Implementation phase
Implementation workflow
Inception phase
Incremental
Infrastructure analyst
Infrastructure management workflow
Interface design
Iterative

Methodology	Production phase	Scrum	Technical writer
Object Management Group (OMG)	Program design	Static view	Testing workflow
	Programmer	Structural view	Throwaway prototyping
Object-oriented methodology	Project management	Structure diagram	Training plan
	Project management workflow	Structured design	Transition phase
Operations and support workflow	Project manager	Support plan	Unified Modeling Language (UML)
	Project plan	System proposal	
Parallel development	Project sponsor	System prototype	Use case
Phased development	Prototyping	System request	Use-case driven
Phases	Rapid application development (RAD)	System specification	Version
Planning phase		Systems analyst	Waterfall development
Process-centered methodology	Requirements gathering	Systems development life cycle (SDLC)	Workflows
	Requirements workflow		Workplan

QUESTIONS

1. What are the major roles played by a systems analyst on a project team?
2. Compare and contrast the role of a systems analyst, a business analyst, and an infrastructure analyst.
3. Compare and contrast phases, steps, techniques, and deliverables.
4. Describe the major phases in the SDLC.
5. Which phase in the SDLC is most important? Why?
6. Describe the principal steps in the planning phase. What are the major deliverables?
7. Describe the principal steps in the analysis phase. What are the major deliverables?
8. Describe the principal steps in the design phase. What are the major deliverables?
9. Describe the principal steps in the implementation phase. What are the major deliverables?
10. What are the roles of a project sponsor and the approval committee?
11. What does *gradual refinement* mean in the context of SDLC?
12. Compare and contrast process-centered methodologies with data-centered methodologies.
13. Compare and contrast structured design-based methodologies in general to RAD-based methodologies in general.
14. Describe the major elements in and issues with waterfall development.
15. Describe the major elements in and issues with parallel development.
16. Describe the major elements in and issues with phased development.
17. Describe the major elements in and issues with prototyping.
18. Describe the major elements in and issues with throwaway prototyping.
19. What is a use case?
20. What is meant by use-case driven?
21. Why is it important for an OOSAD approach to be architecture-centric?
22. What does it mean for an OOSAD approach to be incremental and iterative?
23. Describe the major elements and issues with an object-oriented approach to developing information systems.
24. Describe the major elements in and issues with XP.
25. Compare and contrast extreme programming and throwaway prototyping.
26. Describe the major elements in and issues with Scrum.
27. What are the primary differences between a DevOps methodology and an agile or object-oriented methodology?
28. What are the phases and workflows of the Unified Process?
29. Compare the phases of the Unified Process with the phases of the waterfall model.
30. Who is the Object Management Group?
31. What is the Unified Modeling Language?
32. What is the primary purpose of structure diagrams? Give some examples of structure diagrams.
33. For what are behavior diagrams used? Give some examples of behavior diagrams.

EXERCISES

A. Suppose you are a project manager using a waterfall development-based methodology on a large and complex project. Your manager has just read the latest article in *Computerworld* that advocates replacing this methodology with prototyping and comes to you requesting that you switch. What would you say?

B. The basic types of methodologies discussed in this chapter can be combined and integrated to form new hybrid methodologies. Suppose you were to combine throwaway prototyping with the use of waterfall development. What would the methodology look like? How would this new methodology compare to the others?

C. Look on the Web for different kinds of job opportunities that are available for people who want analyst positions. Compare and contrast the skills that the ads ask for to the skills that we presented in this chapter.

D. Think about your ideal analyst position. Write an ad to hire someone for that position. What requirements would the job have? What skills and experience would be required? How would an applicant be able to demonstrate having the appropriate skills and experience?

E. Using your favorite Web search engine, find alternative descriptions of the basic characteristics of object-oriented systems.

F. Investigate IBM's Rational Unified Process (RUP) on the Web. RUP is a commercial version that extends aspects of the Unified Process. Write a brief memo describing how it is related to the Unified Process as described in this chapter.

G. Suppose you are a project manager who typically has been using a waterfall development-based methodology on a large and complex project. Your manager has just read the latest article in *Computerworld* that advocates replacing this methodology with the Unified Process and comes to you requesting you to switch. What do you say?

H. Suppose you are an analyst working for a small company to develop an accounting system. Would you use the Unified Process to develop the system, or would you prefer one of the other approaches? Why?

I. Suppose you are an analyst developing a new information system to automate the sales transactions and manage inventory for each retail store in a large chain. The system would be installed at each store and exchange data with a mainframe computer at the company's head office. Would you use the Unified Process to develop the system, or would you prefer one of the other approaches? Why?

J. Suppose you are an analyst working for a small company to develop an accounting system. What type of methodology would you use? Why?

K. Suppose you are an analyst developing a new executive information system intended to provide key strategic information from existing corporate databases to senior executives to help in their decision making. What type of methodology would you use? Why?

L. Investigate the Unified Modeling Language on the Web. Write a paragraph news brief describing the current state of the UML.

M. Investigate the Object Management Group (OMG) on the Web. Write a report describing the purpose of the OMG and what it is involved with besides the UML.

N. Using the Web, find a set of CASE tools that support the UML. A couple of examples include Poseidon, Rational Rose, and Visual Paradigm. Find at least two more. Write a short report describing how well they support the UML, and make a recommendation as to which one you believe would be the best for a project team to use in developing an object-oriented information system using the UML.

MINICASES

1. Barbara Singleton, manager of western regional sales at the WAMAP Company, requested that the IS department develop a sales force management and tracking system that would enable her to better monitor the performance of her sales staff. Unfortunately, owing to the massive backlog of work facing the IS department, her request was given a low priority.

After six months of inaction by the IS department, Barbara decided to take matters into her own hands. Based on the advice of friends, Barbara purchased simple database software and constructed a sales force management and tracking system on her own.

Although Barbara's system has been "completed" for about six weeks, it still has many features that do not work correctly, and some functions are full of errors. Barbara's assistant is so mistrustful of the system that she has secretly gone back to using her old paper-based system, because it is much more reliable.

Over dinner one evening, Barbara complained to a systems analyst friend, "I don't know what went wrong with this project. It seemed pretty simple to me. Those IS guys wanted me to follow this elaborate set of steps and tasks, but I didn't think all that really applied to a PC-based system. I just thought I could build this system and tweak it around until I got what I wanted without all the fuss and bother of the methodology the IS guys were pushing. I mean, doesn't that just apply to their big, expensive systems?"

Assuming you are Barbara's systems analyst friend, how would you respond to her complaint?

2. Marcus Weber, IS project manager at ICAN Mutual Insurance Co., is reviewing the staffing arrangements for his next major project, the development of an expert system-based underwriter's assistant. This new system will involve a whole new way for the underwriters to perform their tasks. The underwriter's assistant system will function as sort of an underwriting supervisor, reviewing key elements of each application, checking for consistency in the underwriter's decisions, and ensuring that no critical factors have been overlooked. The goal of the new system is to improve the quality of the underwriters' decisions and to improve underwriters' productivity. It is expected that the new system will substantially change the way the underwriting staff do their jobs.

Marcus is dismayed to learn that because of budget constraints, he must choose between one of two available staff members. Barry Filmore has had considerable experience and training in individual and organizational behavior. Barry has worked on several other projects in which the end users had to make significant adjustments to the new system, and Barry seems to have a knack for anticipating problems and smoothing the transition to a new work environment. Marcus had hoped to have Barry's involvement in this project.

Marcus's other potential staff member is Kim Danville. Prior to joining ICAN Mutual, Kim had

considerable work experience with the expert system technologies that ICAN has chosen for this expert system project. Marcus was counting on Kim to help integrate the new expert system technology into ICAN's systems environment, and also to provide on-the-job training and insights to the other developers on this team.

Given that Marcus's budget will only permit him to add Barry or Kim to this project team, but not both, what choice do you recommend for him? Justify your answer.

3. Joe Brown, the president of Roanoke Manufacturing, requested that Jack Jones, the MIS department manager, investigate the viability of selling their products over the Web. Currently, the MIS department is still using an IBM mainframe as their primary deployment environment. As a first step, Jack contacted his friends at IBM to see if they had any suggestions as to how Roanoke Manufacturing could move toward supporting sales in an electronic commerce environment while keeping their mainframe as their main system. His friends explained that IBM now supports Java and Linux on their mainframes. Jack has also learned that IBM owns Rational, the creator of the UML and the Unified Process. Jack's friends suggested that Jack investigate using object-oriented systems as a basis for developing the new system. They also suggested that using the Rational Unified Process (RUP), Java, and virtual Linux machines on his current mainframe as a way to support the move toward a distributed electronic commerce system would protect his current investment in his legacy systems while allowing the new system to be developed in a more modern manner. Even though Jack's IBM friends were very persuasive, Jack is still a little wary about moving his operation from a structured systems approach to this new object-oriented approach. Assuming that you are one of Jack's IBM friends, how would you convince him to move toward using an object-oriented systems development method, such as RUP, and using Java and Linux as a basis for developing and deploying the new system on Roanoke Manufacturing's current mainframe?

BASIC CHARACTERISTICS OF OBJECT-ORIENTED SYSTEMS

Object-oriented systems can be traced back to the Simula and the Smalltalk programming languages. However, until the increase in processor power and the decrease in processor cost that occurred in the 1980s, object-oriented approaches were not practical. Many of the specific details concerning the basic characteristics of object-orientation are language dependent; that is, each object-oriented programming language tends to implement some of the object-oriented basics in a different way. Consequently, we need to know which programming language is going to be used to implement the different aspects of the solution. Otherwise, the system could behave in a manner different than the analyst, designer, and client expect. Today, the C++, Java, Objective-C, Python, and Visual Basic programming languages tend to be the more predominant languages used. In this appendix, we describe the basic characteristics of object-oriented systems, which include classes, objects, methods, messages, encapsulation, information hiding, inheritance, polymorphism, and dynamic binding.

CLASSES AND OBJECTS

A *class* is the general template we use to define and create specific instances, or objects. Every object is associated with a class. For example, all the objects that capture information about patients could fall into a class called Patient, because there are attributes (e.g., name, address, birth date, phone, and insurance carrier) and methods (e.g., make appointment, calculate last visit, change status, and provide medical history) that all patients share (see Figure A1-1).

FIGURE A1-1
Classes and Objects

An *object* is an instantiation of a class. In other words, an object is a person, place, or thing about which we want to capture information. If we were building an appointment system for a doctor's office, classes might include Doctor, Patient, and Appointment. The specific patients, such as Jim Maloney, Mary Wilson, and Theresa Marks, are considered *instances*, or objects, of the patient class (see Figure A1-1).

Each object has *attributes* that describe information about the object, such as a patient's name, birth date, address, and phone number. Attributes are also used to represent relationships between objects; for example, there could be a department attribute in an employee object with a value of a department object that captures in which department the employee object works. Objects also have *state*, which is defined by the value of its attributes and its relationships with other objects at a particular point in time. For example, a patient might have a state of new or current or former.

Each object also has *behaviors*. The behaviors specify what the object can do. For example, an appointment object can probably schedule a new appointment, delete an appointment, and locate the next available appointment. In object-oriented programming, behaviors are implemented as methods (see the next section).

One of the more confusing aspects of object-oriented systems development is the fact that in most object-oriented programming languages, both classes and instances of classes can have attributes and methods. Class attributes and methods tend to be used to model attributes (or methods) that deal with issues related to all instances of the class. For example, to create a new patient object, a message is sent to the Patient class to create a new instance of itself. However, in this book, we focus primarily on attributes and methods of objects and not of classes.

METHODS AND MESSAGES

Methods implement an object's behavior. A method is nothing more than an action that an object can perform. *Messages* are information sent to objects to trigger methods. A message is essentially a function or procedure call from one object to another object. For example, if a patient is new to the doctor's office, the receptionist sends a create message to the application. The Patient class receives the create message and executes its create() method that then creates a new object: aPatient (see Figure A1-2).

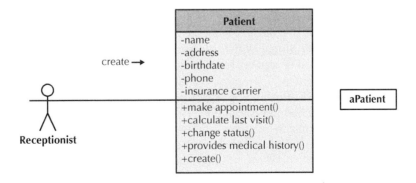

FIGURE A1-2
Messages and
Methods

ENCAPSULATION AND INFORMATION HIDING

The ideas of *encapsulation* and *information hiding* are interrelated in object-oriented systems. However, neither of the terms is new. And, they are different. For example, Python supports encapsulation but does not support information hiding, while C supports information hiding (to a degree) but does not support encapsulation. Encapsulation is simply the combination of process and data into a single object. *Information hiding* suggests that only the information required to use an object be available outside the object; that is, information hiding is related to the *visibility* of the methods and attributes. Typically, this implies that the information required to be passed to the object and the information returned from the object are published. Exactly how the object implements the required functionality is not relevant as long as the object functions correctly. All that is required to use an object are the set of methods and the messages needed to be sent to trigger them. The only communication between objects should be through an object's methods.

The fact that we can use an object by calling methods is the key to reusability because it shields the internal workings of the object from changes in the outside system, and it keeps the system from being affected when changes are made to an object. In Figure A1-2, notice how a message (create) is sent to an object, yet the internal algorithms needed to respond to the message are hidden from other parts of the system. The only information that an object needs to know is the set of operations, or methods, that other objects can perform and what messages need to be sent to trigger them. In object-oriented systems, combining encapsulation with the information-hiding principle supports treating objects as black boxes.

POLYMORPHISM AND DYNAMIC BINDING

Polymorphism means having the ability to take several forms. By supporting polymorphism, object-oriented systems can send the same message to a set of objects, which can be interpreted differently by different classes of objects. For example, inserting a patient means something different than inserting an appointment. Therefore, different pieces of information need to be collected and stored. Based on encapsulation and information hiding, an object does not have to be concerned with *how* something is done when using other objects. We can simply send a message to an object, and that object will be responsible for interpreting the message appropriately. For example, if an artist sent the message Draw yourself to a square object, a circle object, and a triangle object, the results would be very different, even though the message is the same. Notice in Figure A1-3 how each object responds appropriately (and differently) even though the messages are identical.

Polymorphism is made possible through *dynamic binding*. Dynamic, or late, binding is a technique that delays typing the object until run-time. The specific method that is actually called is not chosen by the object-oriented system until the system is running. However, the specific level of support for polymorphism and dynamic binding is language specific. Most object-oriented programming languages support dynamic binding of methods, and some support dynamic binding of attributes. Dynamic binding is in contrast to *static binding*. In a statically bound system, the type of object is determined at compile-time. Therefore, the developer has to choose which method should be called instead of allowing the system to do it. This is why most traditional programming languages have complicated decision logic based on the different types of objects in a system. For example, in a traditional programming language, instead of sending the message Draw yourself to the different types of graphical objects in Figure A1-3, we would have to write decision logic using a case statement or a set of if statements to determine what kind of graphical object we wanted to draw, and we would have to name each draw function differently (e.g., draw square, draw circle,

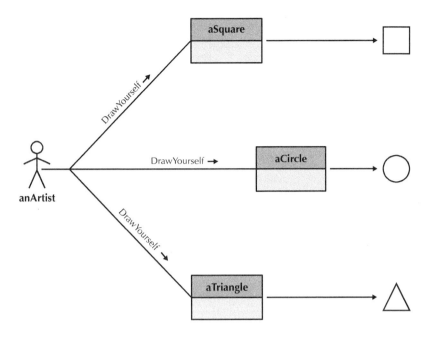

FIGURE A1-3
Polymorphism

or draw triangle). This obviously makes the system much more complicated and difficult to understand.

But polymorphism can be a double-edged sword. Through the use of dynamic binding, there is no way to know before run time which specific object will be asked to execute its method. In effect, there is a decision made by the system that is not coded anywhere.[1] Because all these decisions are made at run time, it is possible to send a message to an object that it does not understand (i.e., the object does not have a corresponding method). This can cause a run-time error that, if the system is not programmed to handle it correctly, can cause the system to abort.[2]

Finally, if the methods are not semantically consistent, the developer cannot assume that all methods with the same name will perform the same generic operation. For example, imagine that you have an array of type person that contains instances of employees and customers (see Figure A1-4). These both implement a compute pay method. An object can send the message to each instance contained in the array to execute the compute pay method for that individual instance. In the case of an instance of employee, the compute pay method computes the amount that the employee is owed by the firm, whereas the compute pay method associated with an instance of a customer computes the amount owed the firm by the customer. Depending on whether the instance is an employee or a customer, a different meaning is associated with the method. Therefore, the semantics of each method must be determined individually. This substantially increases the difficulty of understanding individual objects. The key to controlling the difficulty of understanding object-oriented systems when using polymorphism is to ensure that all methods with the same name implement that same generic operation (i.e., they are semantically consistent).

[1] From a practical perspective, there is an implied case statement. The system chooses the method based on the type of object being asked to execute it and the parameters passed as arguments to the method. This is typically done through message dispatch tables that are hidden from the programmer.

[2] In most object-oriented programming languages, these errors are referred to as exceptions that the system "throws" and must "catch." In other words, the programmer must correctly program the throw and catch or the systems will abort. Again, each programming language can handle these situations in a unique manner.

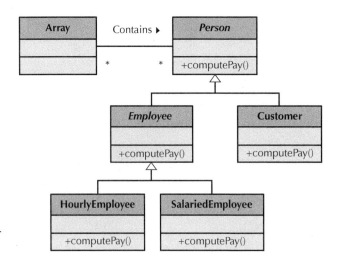

FIGURE A1-4
Example of Polymorphism Misuse

INHERITANCE

Inheritance allows developers to define classes incrementally by reusing classes defined previously as the basis for new classes. Inheritance, as an information systems development characteristic, was first proposed in data modeling in the late 1970s and the early 1980s. The data modeling literature suggests using inheritance to identify higher-level, or more general, classes of objects. Common sets of attributes and methods can be organized into *superclasses*. Typically, classes are arranged in a hierarchy whereby the superclasses, or general classes, are at the top and the *subclasses*, or specific classes, are at the bottom. In Figure A1-5, Person is a superclass to the classes Doctor and Patient. Doctor, in turn, is a superclass to General Practitioner and Specialist. Notice how a class (e.g., Doctor) can serve as a superclass and subclass concurrently. The relationship between the class and its superclass is known as the *a-kind-of* relationship. For example, in Figure A1-5, a General Practitioner is a-kind-of Doctor, which is a-kind-of Person.

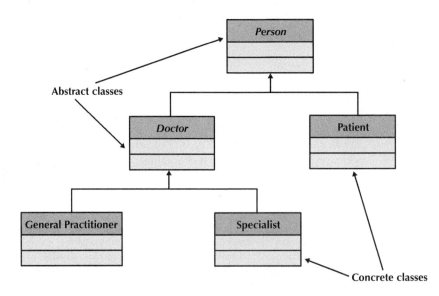

FIGURE A1-5
Class Hierarchy with Abstract and Concrete Classes

Subclasses *inherit* the appropriate attributes and methods from the superclasses above them. That is, each subclass contains attributes and methods from its parent superclass. For example, Figure A1-5 shows that both Doctor and Patient are subclasses of Person and therefore inherit the attributes and methods of the Person class. Inheritance makes it simpler to define classes. Instead of repeating the attributes and methods in the Doctor and Patient classes separately, the attributes and methods that are common to both are placed in the Person class and inherited by the classes below it. Notice how much more efficient inheritance hierarchies of object classes are than the same objects without an inheritance hierarchy (see Figure A1-6).

Most classes throughout a hierarchy lead to instances; any class that has instances is called a *concrete class*. For example, if Mary Wilson and Jim Maloney are instances of the Patient class, Patient would be considered a concrete class (see Figure A1-1). Some classes do not produce instances because they are used merely as templates for other, more-specific classes (especially classes located high up in a hierarchy). These classes are referred to as *abstract classes*. Person is an example of an abstract class. Instead of creating objects from Person, we create instances representing the more-specific classes of Specialist and Patient, both types of Person (see Figure A1-5).

There have been many different types of inheritance mechanisms associated with object-oriented systems.[3] The most common inheritance mechanisms include different forms of single and multiple inheritance. *Single inheritance* allows a subclass to have only a single parent class. Currently, all object-oriented methodologies, databases, and programming languages permit extending the definition of the superclass through single inheritance.

Some object-oriented methodologies, databases, and programming languages allow a subclass to redefine some or all the attributes and/or methods of its superclass. With *redefinition* capabilities, it is possible to introduce an *inheritance conflict* [i.e., an attribute (or method) of a subclass with the same name as an attribute (or method) of a super-class]. For example, in Figure A1-7, Doctor is a subclass of Employee. Both have methods named

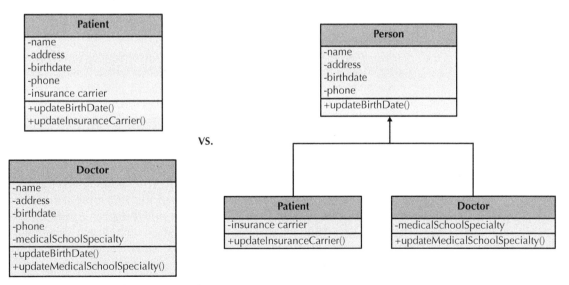

FIGURE A1-6   Inheritance Advantage?

[3] See, for example, M. Lenzerini, D. Nardi, and M. Simi, *Inheritance Hierarchies in Knowledge Representation and Programming Languages* (New York: Wiley, 1991).

FIGURE A1-7
Example of
Redefinition and
Inheritance Conflict

ComputePay(). This causes an inheritance conflict. Furthermore, when the definition of a superclass is modified, all its subclasses are affected. This can introduce additional inheritance conflicts in one (or more) of the superclass's subclasses. For example in Figure A1-7, Employee could be modified to include an additional method, UpdateSchedule(). This would add another inheritance conflict between Employee and Doctor. Therefore, developers must be aware of the effects of the modification not only in the superclass but also in each subclass that inherits the modification.

Finally, through redefinition capabilities, it is possible for a programmer to arbitrarily cancel the inheritance of methods by placing stubs[4] in the subclass that will override the definition of the inherited method. If the cancellation of methods is necessary for the correct definition of the subclass, then it is likely that the subclass has been misclassified (i.e., it is inheriting from the wrong superclass).

As you can see, from a design perspective, inheritance conflicts and redefinition can cause all kinds of problems with interpreting the final design and implementation.[5] However, most inheritance conflicts are due to poor classification of the subclass in the inheritance hierarchy (the generalization a-kind-of semantics are violated), or the actual inheritance mechanism violates the encapsulation and information hiding principle (i.e., subclasses are capable of directly addressing the attributes or methods of a superclass). To address these issues, Jim Rumbaugh and his colleagues suggested the following guidelines:[6]

- ■ Do not redefine query operations.
- ■ Methods that redefine inherited ones should restrict only the semantics of the inherited ones.
- ■ The underlying semantics of the inherited method should never be changed.
- ■ The signature (argument list) of the inherited method should never be changed.

However, many existing object-oriented programming languages violate these guidelines. When it comes to implementing the design, different object-oriented programming languages address inheritance conflicts differently. Therefore, it is important at this point in the development of the system to know what the chosen programming language supports. We must be sure that the design can be implemented as intended. Otherwise, the design needs to be modified before it is turned over to remotely located programmers.

When considering the interaction of inheritance with polymorphism and dynamic binding, object-oriented systems provide the developer with a very powerful, but dangerous, set of tools. Depending on the object-oriented programming language used, this interaction can allow the same object to be associated with different classes at different times. For example, an instance of Doctor can be treated as an instance of Employee or any of its direct and indirect superclasses, such as Salaried Employee and Person, respectively (see Figure A1-7). Therefore, depending on whether static or dynamic binding is supported, the same object may execute different implementations of the same method at different times. Or, if the method is defined only with the Salaried Employee class and it is currently treated as an

---

[4] In this case, a stub is simply the minimal definition of a method to prevent syntax errors from occurring.

[5] For more information, see Ronald J. Brachman, "I Lied about the Trees Or, Defaults and Definitions in Knowledge Representation," *AI Magazine* 5, no. 3 (Fall 1985): 80–93.

[6] J. Rumbaugh, M. Blaha, W. Premerlani, F. Eddy, and W. Lorensen, *Object-Oriented Modeling and Design* (Englewood Cliffs, NJ: Prentice Hall, 1991).

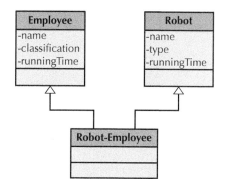

FIGURE A1-8
Additional
Inheritance Conflicts
with Multiple
Inheritance

instance of the Employee class, the instance could cause a run-time error to occur.[7] It is important to know what object-oriented programming language is going to be used so that these kinds of issues can be solved with the design, instead of the implementation, of the class.

With *multiple inheritance*, a subclass may inherit from more than one superclass. In this situation, the types of inheritance conflicts are multiplied. In addition to the possibility of having an inheritance conflict between the subclass and one (or more) of its superclasses, it is now possible to have conflicts between two (or more) superclasses. In this latter case, three different types of additional inheritance conflicts can occur:

- Two inherited attributes (or methods) have the same name (spelling) and semantics.
- Two inherited attributes (or methods) have different names but identical semantics (i.e., they are *synonyms*).
- Two inherited attributes (or methods) have the same name but different semantics (i.e., they are *heteronyms, homographs,* or *homonyms*). This also violates the proper use of polymorphism.

For example, in Figure A1-8, Robot-Employee is a subclass of both Employee and Robot. In this case, Employee and Robot conflict with the attribute name. Which one should Robot-Employee inherit? Because they are the same, semantically speaking, does it really matter? It is also possible that Employee and Robot could have a semantic conflict on the classification and type attributes if they have the same semantics. Practically speaking, the only way to prevent this situation is for the developer to catch it during the design of the subclass. Finally, what if the runningTime attributes have different semantics? In the case of Employee objects, the runningTime attribute stores the employee's time running a mile, whereas the runningTime attribute for Robot objects stores the average time between checkups. Should Robot-Employee inherit both of them? It really depends on whether the robot employees can run the mile or not. With the potential for these additional types of conflicts, there is a risk of decreasing the understandability in an object-oriented system instead of increasing it through the use of multiple inheritance. Our advice is to use great care when using multiple inheritance.

APPENDIX REVIEW

After reading and studying this appendix, you should be able to:

☐ Describe the basic characteristics of object-oriented systems: objects, attributes, methods, messages, encapsulation, information hiding, polymorphism, dynamic binding, and inheritance.

---

[7] This happens with novices quite regularly when using C++.

KEY TERMS

Abstract classes	Dynamic binding	Instance	State
Attribute	Encapsulation	Message	Static binding
Behavior	Information hiding	Method	Subclass
Class	Inherit	Object	Superclass
Concrete classes	Inheritance	Polymorphism	

QUESTIONS

1. What is the difference between classes and objects?
2. What are methods and messages?
3. Why are encapsulation and information hiding important characteristics of object-oriented systems?
4. What is meant by polymorphism when applied to object-oriented systems?
5. Compare and contrast dynamic and static binding.

EXERCISES

A. Look up object-oriented programming in Wikipedia. Write a short report based on its entry.

B. Choose an object-oriented programming language, such as C++, Java, Objective-C, Smalltalk, or VB.Net, and use the Web to find out how the language supports the basic characteristics of object-oriented systems.

C. Assume that you have been assigned the task of creating an object-oriented system that could be used to support students in finding an appropriate apartment to live in next semester. What are the different types of objects (i.e., classes) you would want to include in your system? What attributes or methods would you want to include in their definition? Is it possible to arrange them into an inheritance hierarchy? If so, do it. If not, why not?

D. Create an inheritance hierarchy that could be used to represent the following classes: accountant, customer, department, employee, manager, organization, and salesperson.

CHAPTER 2

PROJECT MANAGEMENT

This chapter primarily describes the project management workflow of the Unified Process. The first step in the process is to identify a project that will deliver value to the business and to create a system request that provides basic information about the proposed system. Second, the analysts perform a feasibility analysis to determine the technical, economic, and organizational feasibility of the system; if appropriate, the system is selected and the development project begins. Third, the project manager estimates the functionality of the project and identifies the tasks that need to be performed. Fourth, the manager staffs the project. Finally, the manager identifies the tools, standards, and processes to be used; identifies opportunities for reuse; determines how the current project fits into the portfolio of projects currently under development; and identifies opportunities to update the overall structure of the firm's portfolio of systems currently in use.

OBJECTIVES

- Understand the importance of linking the information system to business needs.
- Be able to create a system request.
- Understand how to assess technical, economic, and organizational feasibility.
- Be able to perform a feasibility analysis.
- Understand how projects are selected in some organizations.
- Become familiar with work breakdown structures, Gantt charts, and network diagrams.
- Become familiar with use-case–driven effort estimation.
- Be able to create an iterative project workplan.
- Understand how to manage the scope, refine the estimates, and manage the risk of a project.
- Become familiar with the use of Kanban boards for project management.
- Become familiar with how to staff a project.
- Understand how the environment and infrastructure workflows interact with the project management workflow.

INTRODUCTION

Most projects occurring in people's lives, such as weddings or graduation celebrations, require planning and management. Months are spent in advance identifying and performing all the tasks that need to get done, such as sending out invitations and selecting a menu, and time and money are carefully allocated among them. Along the way, decisions are recorded, problems are addressed, and changes are made. The increasing popularity of the party planner, a person whose sole job is to coordinate a party, suggests how tough this job can be. In the end, the success of any party has a lot to do with the effort that went into planning along the way. Systems development projects can be much more complicated than the projects we encounter in our personal lives—usually, more people are involved (e.g., the organization), the costs are higher, and more tasks need to be completed. Owing to the complexity of software and software development, it is virtually impossible to "know" all of the possible things that could happen during systems development projects. Therefore, it is not surprising that "party planners" exist for information systems projects: They are called *project managers*.

Project management is the process of planning and controlling the development of a system within a specified time frame at a minimum cost with the right functionality.[1] In general, a *project* is a set of activities with a starting point and an ending point meant to create a system that brings value to the business. A project manager has the primary responsibility for managing the hundreds of tasks and roles that need to be carefully coordinated. Today, project management is an actual profession, and analysts spend years working on projects before tackling the management of them. However, in many cases, unreasonable demands set by project sponsors and business managers can make project management very difficult. Too often, the approach of the holiday season, the chance at winning a proposal with a low bid, or a funding opportunity pressures project managers to promise systems long before they are able to deliver them. These overly optimistic timetables are thought to be one of the biggest problems that projects face; instead of pushing a project forward faster, they result in delays. Another source is the changing nature of information technology. An innovation in information technology may look so attractive that organizations embrace projects using this technology without assessing whether the technology adds value to the organization; instead the technology itself seems important in its own right. Problems can usually be traced back to the very beginning of the development of the system, where too little attention was given to identifying the business value and understanding the risks associated with the project.

During the inception phase of the Unified Process of a new systems development project, someone—a manager, staff member, sales representative, or systems analyst—typically identifies some business value that can be gained from using information technology. New systems development projects should start from a business need or opportunity. Many ideas for new systems or improvements to existing ones arise from the application of a new technology, but an understanding of technology is usually secondary to a solid understanding of the business and its objectives. This does not mean that technical people should not recommend new systems projects. In fact, the ideal situation is for both IT people (i.e., the experts in systems) and business people (i.e., the experts in business) to work closely to find ways for technology to support business needs. In this way, organizations can leverage the exciting innovative technologies that are available while ensuring that projects are based upon real business objectives, such as increasing sales, improving customer service, and decreasing operating expenses. Ultimately, information systems need to affect the organization's bottom line (in a positive way!). To ensure that a real business need is being addressed, the affected business organization (called the *project sponsor*) proposes the new systems development project using a *system request*. The system request effectively kicks off the inception phase for the new systems development project. The request is forwarded to an

---

[1] For a very good comprehensive description of project management for information systems, see R.K. Wysocki, *Effective Project Management: Traditional, Agile, Extreme*, 5th Ed. (Indianapolis, IN: Wiley Publishing, 2009). Also, the Project Management Institute (www.pmi.org) and the Information Systems Community of Practice of the Project Management Institute (is.vc.pmi.org) have valuable resources on information systems project management. Finally, the following are good books on project management for object-oriented projects: G. Booch, *Object Solutions: Managing the Object-Oriented Project* (Menlo Park, CA: Addison-Wesley, 1996); M. R. Cantor, *Object-Oriented Project Management with UML* (New York: Wiley, 1998); A. Cockburn, *Surviving Object-Oriented Projects: A Manager's Guide* (Reading, MA: Addison-Wesley, 1998); I. Jacobson, G. Booch, and J. Rumbaugh, *The Unified Software Development Process* (Reading, MA: Addison-Wesley, 1999); W. Royce, *Software Project Management: A Unified Framework* (Reading, MA: Addison-Wesley, 1998).

approval committee for consideration. The approval committee reviews the request and makes an initial determination of whether to investigate the proposal or not. If the committee initially approves the request, the systems development team gathers more information to determine the feasibility of the project.

A *feasibility analysis* plays an important role in deciding whether to proceed with an information systems development project. It examines the technical, economic, and organizational pros and cons of developing the system, and it gives the organization a slightly more detailed picture of the advantages of investing in the system as well as any obstacles that could arise. In most cases, the project sponsor works closely with the development team to develop the feasibility analysis. Once the feasibility analysis has been completed, it is submitted to the approval committee, along with a revised system request. The committee then decides whether to approve the project, decline the project, or table it until additional information is available. Projects are selected by weighing risks and returns and by making trade-offs at the organizational level.

Once the committee has approved a project, the development team must carefully plan for the actual development of the system. Because we are following a Unified Process-based approach, the systems development workplan will evolve throughout the development process. Given this evolutionary approach, one critical success factor for project management is to start with a realistic assessment of the work that needs to be accomplished and then manage the project according to that assessment. This can be achieved by carefully creating and managing the workplan, estimating the effort to develop the system, staffing the project, and coordinating project activities.

In addition to covering the above material, this chapter also covers three traditional project management tools that are very useful to manage object-oriented systems development projects (work breakdown structures, Gantt charts, and network diagrams), and we cover a newer approach from agile development (Kanban boards).

PROJECT IDENTIFICATION

A project is identified when someone in the organization identifies a *business need* to build a system. This could occur within a business unit or IT, come from a steering committee charged with identifying business opportunities, or evolve from a recommendation made by external consultants. Examples of business needs include supporting a new marketing campaign, reaching out to a new type of customer, or improving interactions with suppliers. Sometimes, needs arise from some kind of "pain" within the organization, such as a drop in market share, poor customer service levels, or increased competition. Other times, new business initiatives and strategies are created, and a system is required to enable them.

Business needs also can surface when the organization identifies unique and competitive ways of using IT. Many organizations keep an eye on *emerging technology*, which is technology that is still being developed and is not yet viable for widespread business use. For example, if companies stay abreast of technology such as the augmented reality, games, smart cards, and mobile devices, they can develop business strategies that leverage the capabilities of these technologies and introduce them into the marketplace as a *first mover*. Ideally, they can take advantage of this first-mover advantage by making money and continuing to innovate while competitors trail behind.

The *project sponsor* is someone who recognizes the strong business need for a system and has an interest in seeing the system succeed. He or she will work throughout the development process to make sure that the project is moving in the right direction from the perspective of the business. The project sponsor serves as the primary point of contact for the system.

Usually, the sponsor of the project is from a business function, such as marketing, accounting, or finance; however, members of the IT area also can sponsor or cosponsor a project.

The size or scope of a project determines the kind of sponsor needed. A small departmental system might require sponsorship from only a single manager, whereas a large organizational initiative might need support from the entire senior management team and even the CEO. If a project is purely technical in nature (e.g., improvements to the existing IT infrastructure or research into the viability of an emerging technology), then sponsorship from IT is appropriate. When projects have great importance to the business yet are technically complex, joint sponsorship by both the business and IT may be necessary.

The business need drives the high-level *business requirements* for the system. Requirements are what the information system will do, or the *functionality* it will contain. They need to be explained at a high level so that the approval committee and, ultimately, the project team understand what the business expects from the final product. Business requirements are the features and capabilities the information system will have to include, such as the ability to collect customer orders online or the ability for suppliers to receive inventory information as orders are placed and sales are made.

The project sponsor also should have an idea of the *business value* to be gained from the system, both in tangible and intangible ways. *Tangible value* can be quantified and measured easily (e.g., 2 percent reduction in operating costs). An *intangible value* results from an intuitive belief that the system provides important, but hard-to-measure, benefits to the organization (e.g., improved customer service or a better competitive position).

Once the project sponsor identifies a project that meets an important business need and he or she can identify the system's business requirements and value, it is time to formally initiate the project. In most organizations, *project initiation* begins with a document called a *system request*.

System Request

A system request is a document that describes the business reasons for building a system and the value that the system is expected to provide. The project sponsor usually completes this form as part of a formal system project selection process within the organization. Most system requests include five elements: project sponsor, business need, business requirements, business value, and *special issues*. The sponsor describes the person who will serve as the primary contact for the project, and the business need presents the reasons prompting the project. The business requirements of the project refer to the business capabilities that the system will need to have, and the business value describes the benefits that the organization should expect from the system. Special issues are included on the document as a catch-all for other information that should be considered in assessing the project. For example, the project may need to be completed by a specific deadline. Project teams need to be aware of any special circumstances that could affect the outcome of the system. Figure 2-1 shows a template for a system request.

System Request—Name of Project	
Project Sponsor:	Name of project sponsor
Business Need:	Short description of business need
Business Requirements:	Description of business requirements
Business Value:	Expected value that the system will provide
Special Issues or Constraints:	Any additional information that may be relevant to the stakeholders

FIGURE 2-1
System Request
Template

The completed system request is submitted to the approval committee for consideration. This approval committee could be a company steering committee that meets regularly to make information systems decisions, a senior executive who has control of organizational resources, or any other decision-making body that governs the use of business investments. The committee reviews the system request and makes an initial determination, based on the information provided, of whether to investigate the proposal or not. If so, the next step is to conduct a feasibility analysis.

FEASIBILITY ANALYSIS

Once the need for the system and its business requirements have been defined, it is time to create a more detailed business case to better understand the opportunities and limitations associated with the proposed project. Feasibility analysis guides the organization in determining whether or not to proceed with a project. Feasibility analysis also identifies the important *risks* associated with the project that must be addressed if the project is approved. As with the system request, each organization has its own process and format for the feasibility analysis, but most include three types: technical feasibility, economic feasibility, and organizational feasibility. The results of these analyses are combined into a *feasibility study*, which is given to the approval committee (see Figure 2-2).

Although we now discuss feasibility analysis within the context of initiating a project, most project teams will revise their feasibility study throughout the development process and revisit its contents at various checkpoints during the project. If at any point the project's risks and limitations outweigh its benefits, the project team may decide to cancel the project or make necessary improvements.

Technical Feasibility

The first type of feasibility analysis addresses the *technical feasibility* of the project: the extent to which the system can be successfully designed, developed, and installed by the IT group.

FIGURE 2-2
Feasibility Analysis Assessment Factors

Technical Feasibility: Can We Build It?
- Familiarity with Functional area: Less familiarity generates more risk
- Familiarity with Technology: Less familiarity generates more risk
- Project Size: Large projects have more risk
- Compatibility: The harder it is to integrate the system with the company's existing technology, the higher the risk

Economic Feasibility: Should We Build It?
- Development costs
- Annual operating costs
- Annual benefits (cost savings and revenues)
- Intangible costs and benefits

Organizational Feasibility: If We Build It, Will They Come?
- Is the project strategically aligned with the business?
- Project champion(s)
- Senior management
- Users
- Other stakeholders

Technical feasibility analysis is in essence a *technical risk analysis* that strives to answer this question: *Can* we build it?[2]

Many risks can endanger the successful completion of a project. First is the users' and analysts' lack of *familiarity with the functional area*. When analysts are unfamiliar with the business functional area, they have a greater chance of misunderstanding the users or of missing opportunities for improvement. The risk increases dramatically when the users themselves are less familiar with an application, such as with the development of a system to support a business innovation. In general, developing new systems is riskier than producing extensions to an existing system because existing systems tend to be better understood.

Familiarity with the technology is another important source of technical risk. When a system uses technology that has not been used before *within the organization*, there is a greater chance that problems will occur and delays will be incurred because of the need to learn how to use the technology. Risk increases dramatically when the technology itself is new.

Project size is an important consideration, whether measured as the number of people on the development team, the length of time it will take to complete the project, or the number of distinct features in the system. Larger projects present more risk, both because they are more complicated to manage and because there is a greater chance that important system requirements will be overlooked or misunderstood. Furthermore, the extent to which the project is highly integrated with other systems can cause problems because complexity increases when many systems must work together.

Finally, project teams need to consider the *compatibility* of the new system with the technology that already exists in the organization. Systems are rarely built in a vacuum— they are built in organizations that already have numerous systems in place. New technology and applications need to be integrated with the existing environment for many reasons. They might rely on data from existing systems, they might produce data that feed other applications, and they might have to use the company's existing communications infrastructure.

The assessment of a project's technical feasibility is not cut and dried because in many cases, some interpretation of the underlying conditions is needed. One approach is to compare the project under consideration with prior projects undertaken by the organization. Another option is to consult with experienced IT professionals in the organization or external IT consultants; often they are able to judge whether a project is feasible from a technical perspective.

Economic Feasibility

The second element of a feasibility analysis is to perform an *economic feasibility* analysis (also called a *cost–benefit analysis*), which identifies the financial risk associated with the project. It attempts to answer the question, *Should* we build the system? Economic feasibility is determined by identifying costs and benefits associated with the system, assigning values to them, and then calculating the cash flow and return on investment for the project. The more expensive the project, the more rigorous and detailed the analysis should be. Figure 2-3 lists the steps in performing a cost–benefit analysis; each step is described in the following sections.

---

[2] We use *build it* in the broadest sense. Organizations can also choose to buy a commercial software package and install it, in which case, the question might be "Can we select the right package and successfully install it?"

1. Identifing Costs and Benefits	List the tangible costs and benefits for the project. Include both one-time and recurring costs.
2. Assigning Values to Costs and Benefits	Work with business users and IT professionals to create numbers for each of the costs and benefits. Even intangibles should be valued if at all possible.
3. Determining Cash Flow	Project what the costs and benefits will be over a period of time, usually three to five years. Apply a growth rate to the numbers, if necessary.
4. Determining Net Present Value (NPV)	Calculate what the value of future costs and benefits are if measured by today's standards. You will need to select a rate of growth to apply the NPV formula.
5. Determining Return on Investment (ROI)	Calculate how much money the organization will receive in return for the investment it will make using the ROI formula.
6. Determining the Break-Even Point	Find the first year in which the system has greater benefits than costs. Apply the break-even formula using figures from that year. This will help you understand how long it will take before the system creates real value for the organization.
7. Graphing the Break-Even Point	Plot the yearly costs and benefits on a line graph. The point at which the lines cross is the break-even point.

FIGURE 2-3
Steps for Conducting Economic Feasibility

Identifying Costs and Benefits The first task when developing an economic feasibility analysis is to identify the kinds of costs and benefits the system will have and list them along the left-hand column of a spreadsheet. Figure 2-4 lists the examples of costs and benefits that may be included.

Costs and benefits can be broken down into four categories: development costs, operational costs, tangible benefits, and intangibles. *Development costs* are tangible expenses

Development Costs	Operational Costs
Development Team Salaries	Software Upgrades
Consultant Fees	Software Licensing Fees
Development Training	Hardware Repairs
Hardware and Software	Hardware Upgrades
Vendor Installation	Operational Team Salaries
Office Space and Equipment	Communications Charges
Data Conversion Costs	User Training
Tangible Benefits	**Intangible Benefits**
Increased Sales	Increased Market Share
Reductions in Staff	Increased Brand Recognition
Reductions in Inventory	Higher Quality Products
Reductions in IT Costs	Improved Customer Service
Better Supplier Prices	Better Supplier Relations

FIGURE 2-4
Example Costs and Benefits for Economic Feasibility

incurred during the construction of the system, such as salaries for the project team, hardware and software expenses, consultant fees, training, and office space and equipment. Development costs are usually thought of as one-time costs. *Operational costs* are tangible costs required to operate the system, such as the salaries for operations staff, software licensing fees, equipment upgrades, and communications charges. Operational costs are usually thought of as ongoing costs.

Revenues and cost savings are the *tangible benefits* the system enables the organization to collect or the tangible expenses the system enables the organization to avoid. Tangible benefits could include increased sales, reductions in staff, and reductions in inventory. Of course, a project also can affect the organization's bottom line by reaping *intangible benefits* or incurring *intangible costs*. Intangible costs and benefits are more difficult to incorporate into the economic feasibility because they are based on intuition and belief rather than "hard numbers." Nonetheless, they should be listed in the spreadsheet along with the tangible items.

Assigning Values to Costs and Benefits Once the types of costs and benefits have been identified, analysts assign specific dollar values to them. This might seem impossible; how can someone quantify costs and benefits that haven't happened yet? And how can those predictions be realistic? Although this task is very difficult, analysts have to do the best they can to come up with reasonable numbers for all the costs and benefits. Only then can the approval committee make an educated decision about whether or not to move ahead with the project.

The best strategy for estimating costs and benefits is to rely on the people who have the clearest understanding of them. For example, costs and benefits related to the technology or the project itself can be provided by the company's IT group or external consultants, and business users can develop the numbers associated with the business (e.g., sales projections, order levels). Analysts can also consider past projects, industry reports, and vendor information, although these approaches probably will be a bit less accurate. All the estimates will probably be revised as the project proceeds.

Sometimes it is acceptable for analysts to list intangible benefits, such as improved customer service, without assigning a dollar value, whereas other times they have to make estimates regarding the value of an intangible benefit. If at all possible, they should quantify intangible costs or benefits. Otherwise, it will not be apparent whether the costs and benefits have been realized. Consider a system that is supposed to improve customer service. This is intangible, but assume that the greater customer service will decrease the number of customer complaints by 10 percent each year over three years and that $200,000 is spent on phone charges and phone operators who handle complaint calls. Suddenly there are some very tangible numbers with which to set goals and measure the original intangible benefit.

Figure 2-5 shows costs and benefits along with assigned dollar values. Notice that the customer service intangible benefit has been quantified based on fewer customer complaint phone calls. The intangible benefit of being able to offer services that competitors currently offer was not quantified, but it was listed so that the approval committee will consider the benefit when assessing the system's economic feasibility.

Determining Cash Flow A formal cost–benefit analysis usually contains costs and benefits over a selected number of years (usually three to five years) to show cash flow over time (see Figure 2-6). When using this *cash flow method*, the years are listed across the top of the spreadsheet to represent the time period for analysis, and numeric values are entered in the appropriate cells within the spreadsheet's body. Sometimes fixed amounts are entered into

Benefits[a]	
Increased sales	500,000
Improved customer service[b]	70,000
Reduced inventory costs	68,000
Total benefits	**638,000**
Development costs	
2 servers @ $125,000	250,000
Printer	100,000
Software licenses	34,825
Server software	10,945
Development labor	1,236,525
Total development costs	**1,632,295**
Operational costs	
Hardware	54,000
Software	20,000
Operational labor	111,788
Total operational costs	**185,788**
Total costs	**1,818,083**

[a] An important yet intangible benefit will be the ability to offer services that our competitors currently offer.

[b] Customer service numbers have been based on reduced costs for customer complaint phone calls.

FIGURE 2-5
Assigning Values to
Costs and Benefits

the columns. For example, Figure 2-6 lists the same amount for customer complaint calls and inventory costs for all five years. Usually amounts are augmented by some rate of growth to adjust for inflation or business improvements, as shown by the 6 percent increase that is added to the sales numbers in the sample spreadsheet. Finally, totals are added to determine what the overall benefits will be; the higher the overall total, the greater the economic feasibility of the solution.

Determining Net Present Value and Return on Investment There are several problems with the cash-flow method—(1) it does not consider the time value of money (i.e., a dollar today is *not* worth a dollar tomorrow) and (2) it does not show the overall "bang for the buck" that the organization is receiving from its investment. Therefore, some project teams add additional calculations to the spreadsheet to provide the approval committee with a more-accurate picture of the project's worth.

Net present value (NPV) is used to compare the present value of future cash flows with the investment outlay required to implement the project. For example, if you have a friend who owes you a dollar today but instead gives you a dollar three years from now, you've been had! Given a 10 percent increase in value, you'll be receiving the equivalent of 75 cents in today's terms.

NPV can be calculated in many different ways, some of which are extremely complex. Figure 2-7 shows a basic calculation that can be used in your cash flow analysis to get more relevant values. In Figure 2-6, the present value of the costs and benefits are calculated first (i.e., they are shown at a discounted rate). Then, net present value is calculated, and it shows the discounted rate of the combined costs and benefits.

	2015	2016	2017	2018	2019	Total
Increased sales	500,000	530,000	561,800	595,508	631,238	
Reduction in customer complaint calls	70,000	70,000	70,000	70,000	70,000	
Reduced inventory costs	68,000	68,000	68,000	68,000	68,000	
TOTAL BENEFITS:	638,000	668,000	699,800	733,508	769,238	
PV OF BENEFITS:	**619,417**	**629,654**	**640,416**	**651,712**	**663,552**	**3,204,752**
PV OF ALL BENEFITS:	**619,417**	**1,249,072**	**1,889,488**	**2,541,200**	**3,204,752**	
2 Servers @ $125,000	250,000	0	0	0	0	
Printer	100,000	0	0	0	0	
Software licenses	34,825	0	0	0	0	
Server software	10,945	0	0	0	0	
Development labor	1,236,525	0	0	0	0	
TOTAL DEVELOPMENT COSTS:	1,632,295	0	0	0	0	
Hardware	54,000	81,261	81,261	81,261	81,261	
Software	20,000	20,000	20,000	20,000	20,000	
Operational labor	111,788	116,260	120,910	125,746	130,776	
TOTAL OPERATIONAL COSTS:	185,788	217,521	222,171	227,007	232,037	
TOTAL COSTS:	1,818,083	217,521	222,171	227,007	232,037	
PV OF COSTS:	**1,765,129**	**205,034**	**203,318**	**201,693**	**200,157**	**2,575,331**
PV OF ALL COSTS:	**1,765,129**	**1,970,163**	**2,173,481**	**2,375,174**	**2,575,331**	
TOTAL PROJECT BENEFITS AND COSTS:	**(1,180,083)**	**450,479**	**477,629**	**506,501**	**537,201**	
YEARLY NPV:	**(1,145,712)**	**424,620**	**437,098**	**450,019**	**463,395**	**629,421**
CUMULATIVE NPV:	**(1,145,712)**	**(721,091)**	**(283,993)**	**166,026**	**629,421**	
RETURN ON INVESTMENT:	**24.44%**	(629,421/2,575,331)				
BREAK-EVEN POINT:	**3.63 years**	[break-even occurs in year 4; (450,019 − 166,026)/450,019 = 0.63]				
INTANGIBLE BENEFITS:	This service is currently provided by competitors Improved customer satisfaction					

FIGURE 2-6 Cost–Benefit Analysis

The *return on investment* (ROI) is a calculation listed somewhere on the spreadsheet that measures the amount of money an organization receives in return for the money it spends. A high ROI results when benefits far outweigh costs. ROI is determined by finding the total benefits less the costs of the system and dividing that number by the total costs of the system (see Figure 2-7). ROI can be determined per year or for the entire project over a period of time. One drawback of ROI is that it considers only the end points of the investment, not the cash flow in between, so it should not be used as the sole indicator of a project's worth. The spreadsheet in Figure 2-6 shows an ROI figure.

Determining the Break-Even Point If the project team needs to perform a rigorous cost–benefit analysis, it might need to include information about the length of time before the project will break even, or when the returns will match the amount invested in the project.

Calculation	Definition	Formula
Present Value (PV)	The amount of an investment today compared to that same amount in the future, taking into account inflation and time.	$\dfrac{\text{Amount}}{(1+\text{interest rate})^n}$ n = number of years in future
Net Present Value (NPV)	The present value of benefit less the present value of costs.	PV Benefits − PV Costs
Return on Investment (ROI)	The amount of revenues or cost savings results from a given investment.	$\dfrac{\text{Total benefits} - \text{Total costs}}{\text{Total costs}}$
Break-Even Point	The point in time at which the costs of the project equal the value it has delivered.	$\dfrac{\text{Yearly NPV*} - \text{Cumulative NPV}}{\text{Yearly NPV*}}$

* Use the Yearly NPV amount from the first year in which the project has a positive cash flow.
Add the above amount to the year in which the project has a positive cash flow.

FIGURE 2-7 Financial Calculations Used for Cost–Benefit Analysis

The greater the time it takes to break even, the riskier the project. The *break-even point* is determined by looking at the cash flow over time and identifying the year in which the benefits are larger than the costs (see Figure 2-6). Then, the difference between the yearly and cumulative NPV for that year is divided by the yearly NPV to determine how far into the year the break-even point will occur. See Figure 2-7 for the break-even calculation. The break-even point also can be depicted graphically, as shown in Figure 2-8. The cumulative present value of the costs and benefits for each year is plotted on a line graph; the point at which the lines cross is the break-even point.

Organizational Feasibility

The final type of feasibility analysis is to assess the *organizational feasibility* of the system, how well the system ultimately will be accepted by its users and incorporated into the ongoing operations of the organization. There are many organizational factors that can have an effect on the project, and seasoned developers know that organizational feasibility can be the most

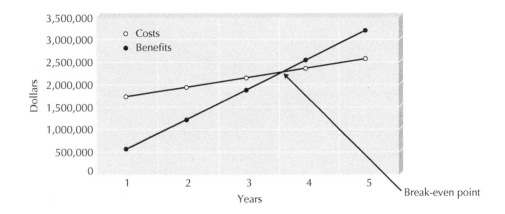

FIGURE 2-8
Break-Even Graph

difficult feasibility dimension to assess. In essence, an organizational feasibility analysis attempts to answer the question, If we build it, will they come?

One way to assess the organizational feasibility of the project is to understand how well the goals of the project align with business objectives. *Strategic alignment* is the fit between the project and business strategy—the greater the alignment, the less risky the project will be from an organizational feasibility perspective. For example, if the marketing department has decided to become more customer focused, then a CRM project that produces integrated customer information would have strong strategic alignment with marketing's goal. Many IT projects fail when the IT department initiates them, because there is little or no alignment with business unit or organizational strategies.

A second way to assess organizational feasibility is to conduct a *stakeholder analysis*.[3] A *stakeholder* is a person, a group, or an organization that can affect (or will be affected by) a new system. In general, the most important stakeholders in the introduction of a new system are the project champion, system users, and organizational management (see Figure 2-9), but systems sometimes affect other stakeholders as well. For example, the IS department can be a stakeholder of a system because IS jobs or roles may be changed significantly after its implementation.

The *champion* is a high-level, noninformation systems executive who is usually the project sponsor who created the system request. The champion supports the project with time, resources (e.g., money), and political support within the organization by communicating the importance of the system to other organizational decision makers. More than one champion is preferable because if the champion leaves the organization, the support could leave as well.

Whereas champions provide day-to-day support for the system, *organizational management* support conveys to the rest of the organization the belief that the system will make a

	Role	Techniques for Improvement
Champion	A champion: • Initiates the project • Promotes the project • Allocates his or her time to project • Provides resources	• Make a presentation about the objectives of the project and the proposed benefits to those executives who will benefit directly from the system • Create a prototype of the system to demonstrate its potential value
Organizational Management	Organizational managers: • Know about the project • Budget enough money for the project • Encourage users to accept and use the system	• Make a presentation to management about the objectives of the project and the proposed benefits • Market the benefits of the system using memos and organizational newsletters • Encourage the champion to talk about the project with his or her peers
System Users	Users: • Make decisions that influence the project • Perform hands-on activities for the project • Ultimately determine whether the project is successful by using or not using the system	• Assign users official roles on the project team • Assign users specific tasks to perform with clear deadlines • Ask for regular feedback from users (e.g., at weekly meetings)

FIGURE 2-9 Some Important Stakeholders for Organizational Feasibility

[3] A good book that presents a series of stakeholder analysis techniques is R. O. Mason and I. I. Mittroff, *Challenging Strategic Planning Assumptions: Theory, Cases, and Techniques* (New York: Wiley, 1981).

valuable contribution and that necessary resources will be made available. Ideally, management should encourage people in the organization to use the system and to accept the many changes that the system will likely create.

A third important group of stakeholders are the *system users* who ultimately use the system once it has been installed in the organization. Too often, the project team meets with users at the beginning of a project and then disappears until after the system is created. In this situation, rarely does the final product meet the expectations and needs of those who are supposed to use it because needs change and users become savvier as the project progresses. User participation should be promoted throughout the development process by getting users involved in the development of the system (e.g., performing tasks, providing feedback, and making decisions). Depending on the type of system being contemplated, from a DevOps approach, operational personnel are also an important group of stakeholders.

Finally, the feasibility study helps organizations make wiser investments by forcing project teams to consider technical, economic, and organizational factors that can affect their projects. It protects IT professionals from criticism by keeping the business units educated about decisions and positioned as the leaders in the decision-making process. Remember, the feasibility study **should be revised** several times during the project at points where the project team makes critical decisions about the system (e.g., before each iteration of the development process).

PROJECT SELECTION

Once the feasibility analysis has been completed, it is submitted to the approval committee, along with a revised system request. The committee then decides whether to approve the project, decline the project, or table it until additional information is available. At the project level, the committee considers the value of the project by examining the business need (found in the system request) and the risks of building the system (presented in the feasibility analysis).

Before approving the project, however, the committee also considers the project from an organizational perspective; it has to keep in mind the company's entire portfolio of projects. This way of managing projects is called *portfolio management*. Portfolio management takes into consideration the different kinds of projects that exist in an organization—large and small, high risk and low risk, and strategic and tactical. (See Figure 2-10 for the different ways of classifying projects.) A good project portfolio has the most appropriate mix of projects for the organization's needs. The committee acts as portfolio manager with the goal of maximizing

Size	What is the size? How many people are needed to work on the project?
Cost	How much will the project cost the organization?
Purpose	What is the purpose of the project? Is it meant to improve the technical infrastructure? Support a current business strategy? Improve operations? Demonstrate a new innovation?
Length	How long will the project take before completion? How much time will go by before value is delivered to the business?
Risk	How likely is it that the project will succeed or fail?
Scope	How much of the organization is affected by the system? A department? A division? The entire corporation?
Return on investment	How much money does the organization expect to receive in return for the amount the project costs?

FIGURE 2-10
Ways to Classify
Projects

the cost–benefit performance and other important factors of the projects in their portfolio. For example, an organization might want to keep high-risk projects to less than 20 percent of its total project portfolio.

The approval committee must be selective about where to allocate resources. This involves *trade-offs* in which the organization must give up something in return for something else to keep its portfolio well balanced. If there are three potentially high-payoff projects, yet all have very high risk, then perhaps only one of the projects will be selected. Also, there are times when a system at the project level makes good business sense, but it does not make sense at the organizational level. Thus, a project may show a very strong ROI and support important business needs for a part of the company, but it is not selected. This could happen for many reasons—because there is no money in the budget for another system, the organization is about to go through some kind of change (e.g., a merger), projects that meet the same business requirements already are under way, or the system does not align well with the current or future corporate strategy.

Ethical Considerations[4]

One final organizational consideration that the approval committee must consider today before approving the project is the societal and humanitarian impact of the project. In other words, what is the ethical responsibility of the organization and development team for the deployment of the proposed project? Even though there are many information systems issues that have an ethical component to them, for example, hacking, whistleblowing, privacy, computer crime, software piracy, and viruses, in this section, we only describe a few issues that are related to the development of a system. These issues include deskilling of the workforce, employee monitoring, technostress, and the health effects of IT.

One of the typical justifications for the development of an information system has always been the potential cost savings and employee productivity improvement. However, from an ethical perspective this implies two things. First, in an economic upturn, the use of IT can make the current employees more productive, hence not requiring the expansion of the workforce. But, in an economic downturn, it implies replacing human employees with IT capital. In other words, potentially firing current employees. Second, it is possible through the use of an IT system to cause the *deskilling of the workforce*. This is especially true with the use of AI-based systems. The upside of this is that the workforce will be less expensive. However, the downside of this is the potential increase of employee stress, boredom, and fatigue, which can lead to a decrease in employee job satisfaction and motivation. And, this can actually cause employee productivity to decrease.

When considering the potential downsides of deskilling and replacing employees, there could be a need to increase *employee monitoring*. Using IT to monitor employees can be both a positive and a negative. Supporters of IT-based monitoring suggest that it can provide a cheap, practical, and accurate set of measures as to employee performance. This is true as long as the measures being used are actually measuring what they purport to measure. However, in the past, this has not always been the case.[5] Consequently, much care must be taken when developing monitoring systems. In the past, some research has shown that employee

---

[4] For more information see M. David Ermann and Michele S. Shauf, *Computers, Ethics, and Society, Third Edition* (Oxford, UK: Oxford University Press, 2003); Tom Forester and Perry Morrison, *Computer Ethics: Cautionary Tales and Ethical Dilemmas in Computing* (Cambridge, MA: MIT Press, 1990); Enid Mumford, *Systems Design: Ethical Tools for Ethical Change* (London, UK: 1996); George Reynolds, *Ethics in Information Technology, Second Edition* (Boston, MA: Thomson Course Technology, 2007).

[5] For example, IT project managers used to count the number of lines of code implemented by a programmer per day and used it as a surrogate for measuring the quality of the programmer. However, any serious programmer realized very quickly that there were a number of ways in which a required function could be implemented. In many cases, the more lines of code written, the less efficient the function would be. Consequently, this productivity type of measure actually encouraged poor code to be written.

monitoring actually improves productivity. However, recent studies have shown that employee monitoring can increase job stress and decrease trust, which can lead to decreases in employee job satisfaction, motivation, and productivity. Furthermore, employee monitoring has been shown to decrease the quality of the work product.

The use of IT-based systems can increase so-called *technostress*. Much of technostress is caused by the increasing expectations that employees must meet. For example, telework has provided benefits to both employees and employers. However, it also has increased the expectation that employees are available 24/7. Some research has shown that some employees disconnecting for downtime would place them at a competitive disadvantage in the workforce. This is especially true in the service industries. Obviously, this type of expectation can increase employee stress, which again can decrease employee job satisfaction, motivation, and productivity. Another example includes the expectation of multitasking. Even though cognitively speaking, humans cannot actually focus their attention on multiple things at a time, the expectation is there. Consequently, employees are expected to constantly switch their attention among the multiple streams of information that they monitor. This not only includes monitoring multiple "open" windows on a desktop, for example in a dashboard, but also having to monitor multiple information sources across multiple devices.

Another unforeseen consequence is the *IT health effects* on the employee. Sitting at a desk and staring at a computer screen all day has been shown to cause health problems. Some of the health problems associated with the use of IT includes eye strain, carpal tunnel syndrome, headaches, neck problems, backaches, sleep deprivation, and fatigue. All of these can drive down employee job satisfaction, motivation, and productivity. Obviously, this is the exact opposite from what organizations desire.

Finally, only considering economic, organizational, and technical feasibility issues are no longer sufficient to determine whether an IT project should be approved or not. In today's world, the above ethical considerations also need to be addressed.

TRADITIONAL PROJECT MANAGEMENT TOOLS

Before we get to actually creating a workplan that is suitable to manage and control an object-oriented systems development project, we need to introduce a set of project management tools that have been used to successfully manage traditional software development projects (and many other types of projects): a work-breakdown structure, a Gantt chart, and a network diagram. To begin with, we must first understand what a task is. A *task* is a unit of work that will be performed by a member or members of the development team, such as feasibility analysis. Each task is described by information such as its name, start and completion dates, person assigned to complete the task, deliverables, completion status, priority, resources needed, estimated time to complete the task, and the actual time it took to complete the task (see Figure 2-11). The first thing a project manager must do is to identify the tasks that need to be accomplished and determine how long each task will take. Tasks and their identification and documentation are the basis of all three of these tools. Once the tasks have been identified and documented, they are organized within a work breakdown structure that is used to drive the creation of Gantt charts and network diagrams that can be used to graphically portray a traditional workplan. These techniques help a project manager understand and manage the project's progress over time.

Work Breakdown Structures

A project manager can use a structured, top-down approach whereby high-level tasks are first defined and then broken down into subtasks. For example, Figure 2-12 shows a list of high-level tasks needed to implement a new IT training class. Some of the main steps in the process include identifying vendors, creating and administering a survey, and building new

Workplan Information	Example
Name of the task	Perform economic feasibility
Start date	Jan 05, 2015
Completion date	Jan 19, 2015
Person assigned to the task	Project sponsor: Mary Smith
Deliverable(s)	Cost–benefit analysis
Completion status	Open
Priority	High
Resources that are needed	Spreadsheet software
Estimated time	16 hours
Actual time	14.5 hours

FIGURE 2-11
Task Information

Task Number	Task Name	Duration (in weeks)	Dependency	Status
1	Identify vendors	2		Complete
2	Review training materials	6	1	Complete
3	Compare vendors	2	2	In Progress
4	Negotiate with vendors	3	3	Open
5	Develop communications information	4	1	In Progress
6	Disseminate information	2	5	Open
7	Create and administer survey	4	6	Open
7.1	Create initial survey	1		Open
7.2	Review initial survey	1	7.1	Open
7.2.1	Review by Director of IT Training	1		Open
7.2.2	Review by Project Sponsor	1		Open
7.2.3	Review by Representative Trainee	1		Open
7.3	Pilot test initial survey	1	7.1	Open
7.4	Incorporate survey changes	1	7.2, 7.3	Open
7.5	Create distribution list	0.5		Open
7.6	Send survey to distribution list	0.5	7.4, 7.5	Open
7.7	Send follow-up message	0.5	7.6	Open
7.8	Collect completed surveys	1	7.6	Open
8	Analyze results and choose vendor	2	4, 7	Open
9	Build new classrooms	11	1	In Progress
10	Develop course options	3	8, 9	Open

FIGURE 2-12
Work Break-down Structure

classrooms. Each step is then broken down in turn and numbered in a hierarchical fashion. There are eight subtasks (i.e., 7.1–7.8) for creating and administering a survey, and there are three subtasks (7.2.1–7.2.3) that make up the review of the initial survey task. A list of tasks hierarchically numbered in this way is called a *work breakdown structure (WBS)*. The number of tasks and level of detail depend on the complexity and size of the project. At a minimum, the WBS must include the duration of the task, the current status of the task (i.e., open, complete), and the *task dependencies*, which occur when one task cannot be performed until another task is completed. For example, Figure 2-12 shows that incorporating changes to the survey (task 7.4) takes a week to perform, but it cannot occur until after the survey is reviewed (task 7.2) and pilot tested (task 7.3). Key *milestones*, or important dates, are also identified on the workplan.

There are two basic approaches to organizing a traditional WBS: by development phase or by product. For example, if a firm decided that it needed to develop a website, the firm could create a WBS based on the inception, elaboration, construction, and transition phases of the Unified Process. In this case, a typical task that would take place during inception would be feasibility analysis. This task would be broken down into the different types of feasibility analysis: technical, economic, and organizational. Each of these would be further broken down into a set of subtasks. Alternatively, the firm could organize the workplan along the lines of the different products to be developed. For example, in the case of a website, the products could include applets, application servers, database servers, the various sets of Web pages to be designed, a site map, and so on. Then these would be further decomposed into the different tasks associated with the phases of the development process. Either way, once the overall structure is determined, tasks are identified and included in the WBS. We return to the topic of WBSs and their use in iterative planning later in this chapter.

Gantt Chart

A *Gantt chart* is a horizontal bar chart that shows the same task information as the project WBS but in a graphical way. Sometimes a picture really is worth a thousand words, and the Gantt chart can communicate the high-level status of a project much faster and easier than the WBS. Creating a Gantt chart is simple and can be done using a spreadsheet package, graphics software, or a project management package.

First, tasks are listed as rows in the chart, and time is listed across the top in increments based on the needs of the projects (see Figure 2-13). A short project may be divided into hours or days, whereas a medium-sized project may be represented using weeks or months. Horizontal bars are drawn to represent the duration of each task; the bar's beginning and end mark exactly when the task will begin and end. As people work on tasks, the appropriate bars are filled in proportionately to how much of the task is finished. For example, task 1 that was assigned to Alan has been completed, while the tasks 2, 5, and 9 have only been partially completed. Too many tasks on a Gantt chart can become confusing, so it's best to limit the number of tasks to around twenty or thirty. If there are more tasks, break them down into subtasks and create Gantt charts for each level of detail.

There are many things a project manager can see quickly by looking at a Gantt chart. In addition to seeing how long tasks are and how far along they are, the project manager also can tell which tasks are sequential, which tasks occur at the same time, and which tasks overlap in some way. He or she can get a quick view of tasks that are ahead of schedule and behind schedule by drawing a vertical line on today's date. If a bar is not filled in and is to the left of the line, that task is behind schedule.

There are a few special notations that can be placed on a Gantt chart. Project milestones are shown using upside-down triangles or diamonds. Arrows are drawn between the task bars to show task dependencies. Sometimes, the names of people assigned to each task are listed next to the task bars to show what human resources have been allocated to the tasks.

Network Diagram

A second graphical way to look at project workplan information is the *network diagram* that lays out the project tasks in a flowchart (see Figure 2-14).

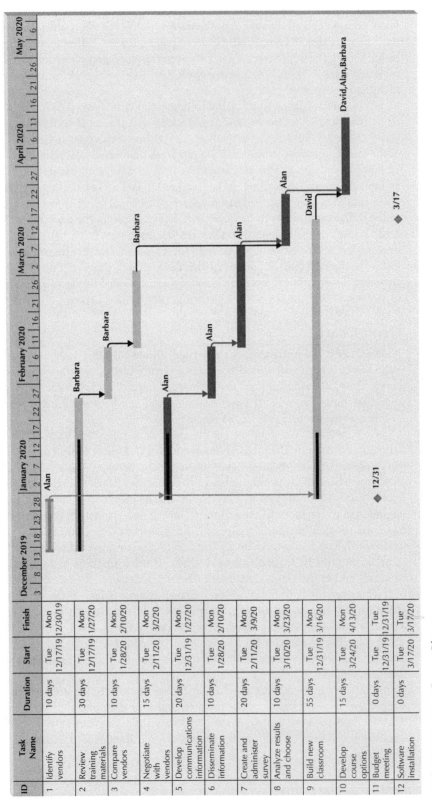

ID	Task Name	Duration	Start	Finish
1	Identify vendors	10 days	Tue 12/17/19	Mon 12/30/19
2	Review training materials	30 days	Tue 12/17/19	Mon 1/27/20
3	Compare vendors	10 days	Tue 1/28/20	Mon 2/10/20
4	Negotiate with vendors	15 days	Tue 2/11/20	Mon 3/2/20
5	Develop communications information	20 days	Tue 12/31/19	Mon 1/27/20
6	Disseminate information	10 days	Tue 1/28/20	Mon 2/10/20
7	Create and administer survey	20 days	Tue 2/11/20	Mon 3/9/20
8	Analyze results and choose	10 days	Tue 3/10/20	Mon 3/23/20
9	Build new classroom	55 days	Tue 12/31/19	Mon 3/16/20
10	Develop course options	15 days	Tue 3/24/20	Mon 4/13/20
11	Budget meeting	0 days	Tue 12/31/19	Tue 12/31/19
12	Software installation	0 days	Tue 3/17/20	Tue 3/17/20

FIGURE 2-13 Gantt Chart

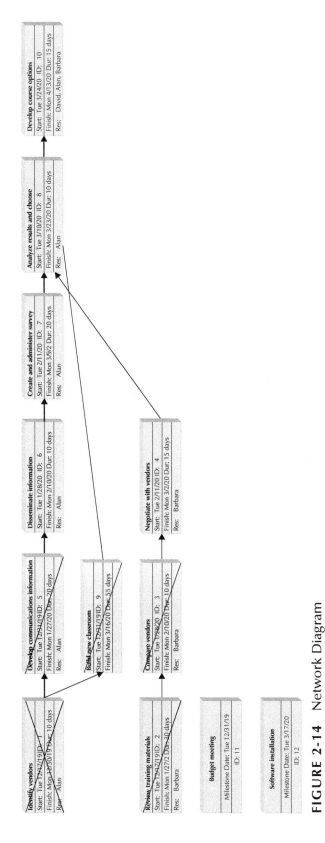

FIGURE 2-14 Network Diagram

Program Evaluation and Review Technique (PERT) is a network analysis technique that can be used when the individual task time estimates are fairly uncertain. Instead of simply putting a point estimate for the duration estimate, PERT uses three time estimates: optimistic, most likely, and pessimistic. It then combines the three estimates into a single weighted average estimate using the following formula:

$$\text{PERT weighted average} = \frac{\text{optimistic estimate} + (4 * \text{most likely estimate}) + \text{pessimistic estimate}}{6}$$

The network diagram is drawn as a node-and-arc type of graph that shows time estimates in the nodes and task dependencies on the arcs. Each *node* represents an individual task, and a line connecting two nodes represents the dependency between two tasks. Partially completed tasks are usually displayed with a diagonal line through the node, for example, Develop communications information, and completed tasks contain crossed lines, for example, Identify vendors.

Network diagrams are the best way to communicate task dependencies because they lay out the tasks in the order in which they need to be completed. The *critical path method* (CPM) simply allows the identification of the critical path in the network. The critical path is the longest path from the project inception to completion. The critical path shows all the tasks that must be completed on schedule for a project as a whole to finish on schedule. If any tasks on the critical path take longer than expected, the entire project will fall behind. Each task on the critical path is a *critical task*, and they are usually depicted in a unique way; in Figure 2-14 they are shown with a gray (actually yellow) filling (see tasks 1, 5, 6, 7, 8, and 10). In some project management software, the critical path also can be highlighted in the Gantt chart. CPM can be used with or without PERT.

PROJECT EFFORT ESTIMATION

The science (or art) of project management is in making *trade-offs* among three important concepts: the functionality of the system, the time to complete the project (when the project will be finished), and the cost of the project. Think of these three things as interdependent levers that the project manager controls throughout the development of the system. Whenever one lever is pulled, the other two levers are affected in some way. For example, if a project manager needs to readjust a deadline to an earlier date, then the solution is either to decrease the functionality of the system or to increase costs by adding more people or having them work overtime. Often, a project manager has to work with the project sponsor to change the goals of the project, such as developing a system with less functionality or extending the deadline for the final system, so that the project has reasonable goals that can be met. In the beginning of the project, the manager needs to estimate each of these levers and then continuously assess how to roll out the project in a way that meets the organization's needs. *Estimation* is the process of assigning projected values for time and effort. The estimates developed at the start of a project are usually based on a range of possible values and gradually become more specific as the project moves forward. That is, the range of values for the inception phase will be much greater than that for the transition phase.

The numbers used to calculate these estimates can be taken from projects with similar tasks and technologies or provided by experienced developers. Generally speaking, the numbers should be conservative. A good practice is to keep track of the actual values for time and effort during the development process so that numbers can be refined along the way and the next project can benefit from real data.

There are a variety of ways to estimate the time required to build a system. Because the Unified Process is use-case driven, we use an approach that is based on use cases: use-case points.[6] *Use-case points*, originally developed by Gustav Karner of Objectory AB,[7] are based on unique features of use cases and object orientation. From a practical point of view, to estimate effort using use-case points, the use cases and the use-case diagram must have been created.[8]

Use-case models have two primary constructs: actors and use cases. An *actor* represents a *role* that a user of the system plays, not a specific user. For example, a role could be secretary or manager. Actors can also represent other systems that will interact with the system under development. For use-case point estimation purposes, actors can be classified as simple, average, or complex. *Simple actors* are separate systems with which the current system must communicate through a well-defined *application program interface (API)*. *Average actors* are separate systems that interact with the current system using standard communication protocols, such as TCP/IP, FTP, and HTTP, or an external database that can be accessed using standard SQL. *Complex actors* are typically end users communicating with the system. Once all of the actors have been categorized as being simple, average, or complex, the project manager counts the number of actors in each category and enters the values into the unadjusted actor-weighting table contained in the use-case point–estimation worksheet (see Figure 2-15). The project manager then computes the *Unadjusted Actor Weight Total (UAW)*. This is computed by summing the individual results that were computed by multiplying the weighting factor by the number of actors of each type. For example, if we assume that the use-case diagram has zero simple, zero average, and four complex actors that interact with the system being developed, the UAW will equal 12 (see Figure 2-16).

A *use case* represents a major business process that the system will perform that benefits the actor(s) in some manner. Depending on the number of unique transactions that the use case must address, a use case can be categorized as being simple, average, or complex. A use case is classified as *simple* if it supports one to three transactions, as *average* if it supports four to seven transactions, or as *complex* if it supports more than seven transactions. Once all of the use cases have been successfully categorized, the project manager enters the number of each type of use case into the unadjusted use-case weighting table contained in the use-case point–estimation worksheet (see Figure 2-15). By multiplying by the appropriate weights and summing the results, we get the value for the *unadjusted use-case weight total (UUCW)*. For example, if we assume that we have three simple use cases, four average use cases, and one complex use case, the value for the unadjusted use-case weight total is 70 (see Figure 2-16). Next, the project manager computes the value of the *unadjusted use-case points (UUCP)* by simply summing the unadjusted actor weight total and the unadjusted use-case weight total. In this case the value of the UUCP equals 82 (see Figure 2-16).

Use-case point-based estimation also has a set of factors that are used to adjust the use-case point value. In this case, there are two sets of factors: *technical complexity factors (TCFs)* and *environmental factors (EFs)*. There are thirteen separate technical factors and eight separate environmental factors. The purpose of these factors is to allow the project as a whole to be evaluated for the complexity of the system being developed and the experience levels of the development staff, respectively. Obviously, these types of factors can affect the effort that a team requires to develop a system. Each of these factors is assigned a value between 0 and 5, 0 indicating that the factor is irrelevant to the system under consideration and 5 indicating that the factor is essential for the system to be successful. The assigned values are then multiplied by their respective weights. These weighted values are then summed up to create a *technical factor value (TFactor)* and an *environmental factor value (EFactor)* (see Figure 2-15).

---

[6] The material in this section is based on descriptions of use-case points contained in Raul R. Reed, Jr., *Developing Applications with Java and UML* (Reading, MA: Addison-Wesley, 2002); Geri Schneider and Jason P. Winters, *Applying Use Cases: A Practical Guide* (Reading, MA: Addison-Wesley, 1998); Kirsten Ribu, "Estimating Object-Oriented Software Projects with Use Cases" (Master's thesis, University of Oslo, 2001).

[7] Objectory AB was acquired by Rational in 1995 and Rational is now part of IBM.

[8] We cover the details of use-case modeling in Chapter 4.

Unadjusted Actor Weighting Table:

Actor Type	Description	Weighting Factor	Number	Result
Simple	External System with well-defined API	1		
Average	External System using a protocol-based interface, e.g., HTTP, TCT/IP, or a database	2		
Complex	Human	3		
		Unadjusted Actor Weight Total (UAW)		

Unadjusted Use-Case Weighting Table:

Use-Case Type	Description	Weighting Factor	Number	Result
Simple	1–3 transactions	5		
Average	4–7 transactions	10		
Complex	>7 transactions	15		
		Unadjusted Use-Case Weight Total (UUCW)		

Unadjusted Use-Case Points (UUCP) = UAW + UUCW

Technical Complexity Factors:

Factor Number	Description	Weight	Assigned Value (0–5)	Weighted Value	Notes
T1	Distributed system	2.0			
T2	Response time or throughput performance objectives	1.0			
T3	End-user online efficiency	1.0			
T4	Complex internal processing	1.0			
T5	Reusability of code	1.0			
T6	Ease of installation	0.5			
T7	Ease of use	0.5			
T8	Portability	2.0			
T9	Ease of change	1.0			
T10	Concurrency	1.0			
T11	Special security objectives included	1.0			
T12	Direct access for third parties	1.0			
T13	Special user training required	1.0			
			Technical Factor Value (TFactor)		

Technical Complexity Factor (TCF) = 0.6 + (0.01 * TFactor)

Environmental Factors:

Factor Number	Description	Weight	Assigned Value (0–5)	Weighted Value	Notes
E1	Familiarity with system development process being used	1.5			
E2	Application experience	0.5			
E3	Object-oriented experience	1.0			
E4	Lead analyst capability	0.5			
E5	Motivation	1.0			
E6	Requirements stability	2.0			
E7	Part-time staff	−1.0			
E8	Difficulty of programming language	−1.0			
			Environmental Factor Value (EFactor)		

Environmental Factor (EF) = 1.4 + (−0.03 * EFactor)
Adjusted Use-Case Points (UCP) = UUCP * TCF * ECF
Effort in Person Hours = UCP * PHM

FIGURE 2-15 Use-Case Point–Estimation Worksheet

Unadjusted Actor Weighting Table:

Actor Type	Description	Weighting Factor	Number	Result
Simple	External system with well-defined API	1	0	0
Average	External system using a protocol-based interface, e.g., HTTP, TCT/IP, or a database	2	0	0
Complex	Human	3	4	12
		Unadjusted Actor Weight Total (UAW)		**12**

Unadjusted Use-Case Weighting Table:

Use-Case Type	Description	Weighting Factor	Number	Result
Simple	1–3 transactions	5	3	15
Average	4–7 transactions	10	4	40
Complex	>7 transactions	15	1	15
		Unadjusted Use-Case Weight Total (UUCW)		**70**

Unadjusted Use-Case Points (UUCP) = UAW + UUCW 82 = 12 + 70

Technical Complexity Factors:

Factor Number	Description	Weight	Assigned Value (0–5)	Weighted Value	Notes
T1	Distributed system	2.0	0	0	
T2	Response time or throughput performance objectives	1.0	5	5	
T3	End-user online efficiency	1.0	3	3	
T4	Complex internal processing	1.0	1	1	
T5	Reusability of code	1.0	1	1	
T6	Ease of installation	0.5	2	1	
T7	Ease of use	0.5	4	2	
T8	Portability	2.0	0	0	
T9	Ease of change	1.0	2	2	
T10	Concurrency	1.0	0	0	
T11	Special security objectives included	1.0	0	0	
T12	Direct access for third parties	1.0	0	0	
T13	Special user training required	1.0	0	0	
		Technical Factor Value (TFactor)		**15**	

*Technical Complexity Factor (TCF) = 0.6 + (0.01 * TFactor)* 0.75 = 0.6 + (0.01 * 15)

Environmental Factors:

Factor Number	Description	Weight	Assigned Value (0–5)	Weighted Value	Notes
E1	Familiarity with system development process being used	1.5	4	6	
E2	Application experience	0.5	4	2	
E3	Object-oriented experience	1.0	4	4	
E4	Lead analyst capability	0.5	5	2.5	
E5	Motivation	1.0	5	5	
E6	Requirements stability	2.0	5	10	
E7	Part-time staff	−1.0	0	0	
E8	Difficulty of programming language	−1.0	4	−4.0	
		Environmental Factor Value (EFactor)		**25.5**	

*Environmental Factor (EF) = 1.4 + (−0.03 * EFactor)* 0.635 = 1.4 + (−0.03 * 25.5)
*Adjusted Use-Case Points (UCP) = UUCP * TCF * ECF* 33.3375 = 70 * 0.75 * 0.635
*Effort in person-hours = UCP * PHM* 666.75 = 20 * 33.3375

FIGURE 2-16 Use-Case Point Estimation for the Appointment System

The technical factors include the following (see Figure 2-15):

- Whether the system is going to be a distributed system
- The importance of response time
- The efficiency level of the end user using the system
- The complexity of the internal processing of the system
- The importance of code reuse
- How easy the installation process has to be
- The importance of the ease of using the system
- How important it is for the system to be able to be ported to another platform
- Whether system maintenance is important
- Whether the system is going to handle parallel and concurrent processing
- The level of special security required
- The level of system access by third parties
- Whether special end user training is to be required.

Assuming the values for the technical factors are T1 (0), T2 (5), T3 (3), T4 (1), T5 (1), T6 (2), T7 (4), T8 (0), T9 (2), T10 (0), T11 (0), T12 (0), and T13 (0), respectively, the *technical factor value (TFactor)* is computed as the weighted sum of the individual technical factors. In this case TFactor equals 15 (see Figure 2-16). Plugging this value into the *technical complexity factor (TCF)* equation (0.6 + (0.01 * TFactor)) of the use-case point worksheet gives a value of 0.75 for the TCF of the system (see Figures 2-15 and 2-16).

The environmental factors include the following (see Figure 2-15):

- The level of experience the development staff has with the development process being used
- The application being developed
- The level of object-oriented experience
- The level of capability of the lead analyst
- The level of motivation of the development team to deliver the system
- The stability of the requirements
- Whether part-time staff have to be included as part of the development team
- The difficulty of the programming language being used to implement the system

Assuming the values for the environmental factors were E1 (4), E2 (4), E3 (4), E4 (5), E5 (5), E6 (5), E7 (0), and E8 (4) gives an *environmental factor value (EFactor)* of 25.5 (see Figure 2-16). Like the TFactor, EFactor is simply the sum of the weighted values. Using the *environmental factor (EF)* equation (1.4 + (−0.03 * EFactor)) of the use-case point worksheet produces a value of 0.635 for the EF of the system (see Figures 2-15 and 2-16). Plugging the TCF and EF values, along with the UUCP value computed earlier, into the adjusted use-case points equation (UUCP * TCF * EF) of the worksheet yields a value of 33.3375 *adjusted use-case points (UCP)* (see Figure 2-16).

Now that we know the estimated size of the system by means of the value of the adjusted use-case points, we are ready to estimate the *effort* required to build the system. In Karner's original work, he suggested simply multiplying the number of use-case points by 20 to estimate the number of person-hours required to build the system. However, based on additional experiences using use-case points, a decision rule to determine the value of the *person-hours multiplier (PHM)* has been created that suggests using either 20 or 28, based on the values assigned to the individual environmental factors. The decision rule is as follows:

> If the sum of (number of EFactors E1 through E6 assigned value < 3) and
> > (number of EFactors E7 and E8 assigned value > 3)
> > > ≤ 2
> > PHM = 20
> Else If the sum of (number of EFactors E1 through E6 assigned value < 3) and
> > (number of EFactors E7 and E8 assigned value > 3)
> > > = 3 or 4
> > PHM = 28
> Else
> > Rethink project; it has too high of a risk for failure

Based on these rules, because none of EFactors E1 through E6 have a value less than 3 and only EFactor E8 has a value greater than 3, the sum of the number of EFactors is 1. Thus, the system should use a PHM of 20. Plugging the values for UCP (33.3375) and PHM (20) into the effort equation (UCP * PHM) gives an estimated number of person-hours of 666.75 hours (see Figures 2-15 and 2-16).

CREATING AND MANAGING THE WORKPLAN

Once a project manager has a general idea of the functionality and effort for the project, he or she creates a *workplan*, which is a dynamic schedule that records and keeps track of all the tasks that need to be accomplished over the course of the project. The workplan lists each task, along with important information about it, such as when it needs to be completed, the person assigned to do the work, and any deliverables that will result. The level of detail and the amount of information captured by the workplan depend on the needs of the project, and the detail usually increases as the project progresses.

The overall objectives for the system should be listed on the system request, and it is the project manager's job to identify all the tasks that need to be accomplished to meet those objectives. This sounds like a daunting task. How can someone know everything that needs to be done to build a system that has never been built before?

One approach for identifying tasks is to get a list of tasks that has already been developed and to modify it. There are standard lists of tasks, or methodologies, that are available for use as a starting point. As we stated in Chapter 1, a *methodology* is a formalized approach to implementing a systems development process (i.e., it is a list of steps and deliverables). A project manager can take an existing methodology, select the steps and deliverables that apply to the current project, and add them to the workplan. If an existing methodology is not available within the organization, methodologies can be purchased from consultants or vendors, or books such as this textbook can serve as a guide. Because most organizations have a methodology they use for projects, using an existing methodology is the most popular way to create a workplan. In our case, because we are using a Unified Process-based methodology, we can use the phases, workflows, and iterations as a starting point to create an evolutionary work breakdown structure and an iterative workplan.

Evolutionary Work Breakdown Structures and Iterative Workplans[9]

Because object-oriented systems approaches to systems analysis and design support incremental and iterative development, any project planning approach for object-oriented systems

---

[9] This material in this section is based on Walker Royce, *Software Project Management: A Unified Framework* (Reading, MA: Addison-Wesley, 1998).

development also requires an incremental and iterative process. In the description of the enhanced Unified Process in Chapter 1, the development process was organized around iterations, phases, and workflows. In many ways, a workplan for an incremental and iterative development process is organized in a similar manner. For each iteration, there are different tasks executed on each workflow. This section describes an incremental and iterative process using evolutionary WBSs for project planning that can be used with object-oriented systems development.

Evolutionary WBSs allow the analyst to develop an *iterative workplan*. First, evolutionary WBSs are organized in a standard manner across all projects: by workflows, phases, and then the specific tasks that are accomplished during an individual iteration. Second, evolutionary WBSs are created in an incremental and iterative manner. This encourages a more realistic view of both cost and schedule estimation. Third, because the structure of an evolutionary WBS is not tied to any specific project, evolutionary WBSs enable the comparison of the current project to earlier projects. This supports learning from past successes and failures.

In the case of the enhanced Unified Process, the workflows are the major points listed in the WBS. Next, each workflow is decomposed along the phases of the enhanced Unified Process. After that, each phase is decomposed along the tasks that are to be completed to create the deliverables associated with an individual iteration contained in each phase (see Figure 1-4). The template for the first two levels of an evolutionary WBS for the enhanced Unified Process would look like that shown in Figure 2-17.

As each iteration through the development process is completed, additional iterations and tasks are added to the WBS (i.e., the WBS evolves along with the evolving information system).[10]

I. Business Modeling	**V.** Implementation	**IX.** Project Management
a. Inception	**a.** Inception	**a.** Inception
b. Elaboration	**b.** Elaboration	**b.** Elaboration
c. Construction	**c.** Construction	**c.** Construction
d. Transition	**d.** Transition	**d.** Transition
b. Production	**e.** Production	**e.** Production
II. Requirements	**VI.** Test	**X.** Environment
a. Inception	**a.** Inception	**a.** Inception
b. Elaboration	**b.** Elaboration	**b.** Elaboration
c. Construction	**c.** Construction	**c.** Construction
d. Transition	**d.** Transition	**d.** Transition
e. Production	**e.** Production	**e.** Production
III. Analysis	**VII.** Deployment	**XI.** Operations and Support
a. Inception	**a.** Inception	**a.** Inception
b. Elaboration	**b.** Elaboration	**b.** Elaboration
c. Construction	**c.** Construction	**c.** Construction
d. Transition	**d.** Transition	**d.** Transition
e. Production	**e.** Production	**e.** Production
IV. Design	**VIII.** Configuration and Change Management	**XII.** Infrastructure Management
a. Inception	**a.** Inception	**a.** Inception
b. Elaboration	**b.** Elaboration	**b.** Elaboration
c. Construction	**c.** Construction	**c.** Construction
d. Transition	**d.** Transition	**d.** Transition
e. Production	**e.** Production	**e.** Production

FIGURE 2-17
Evolutionary WBS Template for the Enhanced Unified Process

[10] Good sources that help explain this approach are Philippe Kruchten, "Planning an Iterative Project," *The Rational Edge* (October 2002); Eric Lopes Cordoza and D. J. de Villiers, "Project Planning Best Practices," *The Rational Edge* (August 2003).

For example, typical activities for the inception phase of the project management workflow would include identifying the project, performing the feasibility analysis, selecting the project, and estimating the effort. The inception phase of the requirements workflow would include determining the requirements gathering and analysis techniques, identifying functional and nonfunctional requirements, interviewing stakeholders, developing a vision document, and developing use cases. Probably no tasks are associated with the inception phase of the operations and support workflow. A sample evolutionary WBS for planning the inception phase of the enhanced Unified Process, based on Figures 1-4 and 2-17, is shown in Figure 2-18. Notice that the last two tasks for the project management workflow are "create workplan for first iteration of the elaboration phase" and "assess the inception phase"; the last two things to do are to plan for the next iteration in the development of the evolving system and to assess the current iteration. As the project moves through later phases, each workflow has tasks added to its iterations. For example, the analysis workflow will have the creation of the functional, structural, and behavioral models during the elaboration phase. Finally, when an iteration includes a lot of complex tasks, traditional tools, such as Gantt charts and network diagrams, can be used to detail the workplan for that specific iteration.

	Duration	Dependency
I. Business Modeling		
a. Inception		
1. Understand current business situation	0.50 days	
2. Uncover business process problems	0.25 days	
3. Identify potential projects	0.25 days	
b. Elaboration		
c. Construction		
d. Transition		
e. Production		
II. Requirements		
a. Inception		
1. Identify appropriate requirements analysis technique	0.25 days	
2. Identify appropriate requirements gathering techniques	0.25 days	
3. Identify functional and nonfunctional requirements		II.a.1, II.a.2
A. Schedule Interview and Observation sessions	3 days	
B. Perform document analysis	5 days	II.a.3.A
C. Conduct interviews		II.a.3.A
1. Interview project sponsor	0.5 days	
2. Interview inventory system contact	0.5 days	
3. Interview special order system contact	0.5 days	
4. Interview ISP contact	0.5 days	
5. Interview CD Selection Web contact	0.5 days	
6. Interview other personnel	1 day	
D. Observe retail store processes	0.5 days	II.a.3.A
4. Analyze current systems	4 days	II.a.1, II.a.2
5. Create requirements definition		II.a.3, II.a.4
A. Determine requirements to track	1 day	
B. Compile requirements as they are elicited	5 days	II.a.5.A
C. Review requirements with sponsor	2 days	II.a.5.B
b. Elaboration		
c. Construction		
d. Transition		
e. Production		

FIGURE 2-18
Evolutionary WBS for a Single Iteration-Based Inception Phase

	Duration	Dependency
III. Analysis		
a. Inception		
1. Identify business processes	3 days	
2. Identify use cases	3 days	III.a.1
b. Elaboration		
c. Construction		
d. Transition		
e. Production		
IV. Design		
a. Inception		
1. Identify potential classes	3 days	III.a
b. Elaboration		
c. Construction		
d. Transition		
e. Production		
V. Implementation		
a. Inception		
b. Elaboration		
c. Construction		
d. Transition		
e. Production		
VI. Test		
a. Inception		
b. Elaboration		
c. Construction		
d. Transition		
e. Production		
VII. Deployment		
a. Inception		
b. Elaboration		
c. Construction		
d. Transition		
e. Production		
VIII. Configuration and Change Management		
a. Inception		
1. Identify necessary access controls for developed artifacts	0.25 days	
2. Identify version control mechanisms for developed artifacts	0.25 days	
b. Elaboration		
c. Construction		
d. Transition		
e. Production		
IX. Project Management		
a. Inception		
1. Create workplan for the inception phase	1 day	
2. Create system request	1 day	
3. Perform feasibility analysis		IX.a.2
A. Perform technical feasibility analysis	1 day	
B. Perform economic feasibility analysis	2 days	
C. Perform organizational feasibility analysis	2 days	

FIGURE 2-18
Continued

	Duration	Dependency
4. Identify project effort	0.50 days	IX.a.3
5. Identify staffing requirements	0.50 days	IX.a.4
6. Compute cost estimate	0.50 days	IX.a.5
7. Create workplan for first iteration of the elaboration phase	1 day	IX.a.1
8. Assess inception phase	1 day	I.a, II.a, III.a IV.a, V.a, VI.a VII.a, VIII.a, IX.a, X.a, XI.a XII.a
b. Elaboration		
c. Construction		
d. Transition		
e. Production		
X. Environment		
a. Inception		
1. Acquire and install CASE tool	0.25 days	
2. Acquire and install programming environment	0.25 days	
3. Acquire and install configuration and change management tools	0.25 days	
4. Acquire and install project management tools	0.25 days	
b. Elaboration		
c. Construction		
d. Transition		
e. Production		
XI. Operations and Support		
a. Inception		
b. Elaboration		
c. Construction		
d. Transition		
e. Production		
XII. Infrastructure Management		
a. Inception		
1. Identify appropriate standards and enterprise models	0.25 days	
2. Identify reuse opportunities, such as patterns, frameworks, and libraries	0.50 days	
3. Identify similar past projects	0.25 days	
b. Elaboration		
c. Construction		
d. Transition		
e. Production		

FIGURE 2-18
Continued

Managing Scope

An analyst may assume that a project will be safe from scheduling problems because he or she carefully estimated and planned the project up front. However, the most common reason for schedule and cost overruns—*scope creep*—occurs after the project is under way. Scope creep happens when new requirements are added to the project after the original project scope was defined and frozen. It can happen for many reasons: Users might suddenly understand the potential of the new system and realize new functionality that would be useful; developers might discover interesting capabilities to which they become very attached; a senior manager might decide to let this system support a new strategy that was developed at a recent board meeting.

Fortunately, using an iterative and incremental development process allows the team to deal with changing requirements in an effective way. However, the more extensive the change becomes, the greater the impact on cost and schedule will be. The keys are to identify the requirements as well as possible in the beginning of the project and to apply analysis techniques effectively. For example, if needs are fuzzy at the project's onset, a combination of intensive meetings with the users and prototyping would allow users to "experience" the requirements and better visualize how the system could support their needs.

Of course, some requirements may be missed no matter what precautions are taken. However, the project manager should allow only absolutely necessary requirements to be added after the project begins. Even at that point, members of the project team should carefully assess the ramifications of the addition and present the assessment to the users. Any change that is implemented should be carefully tracked so that an audit trail exists to measure the impact of the change.

Sometimes changes cannot be incorporated into the present system even though they truly would be beneficial. In this case, these additions should be recorded as future enhancements to the system. The project manager can offer to provide functionality in future releases of the system, thus getting around telling someone "no."

A couple of useful agile techniques to manage the scope of the project while attempting to satisfy the client are daily Scrum meetings and the product backlog used with Scrum. Essentially a daily Scrum meeting is a very short, typically fifteen minutes, meeting that keeps the development team up to date as to the current status of the evolving system. The content of the meeting typically only covers what has been accomplished since the previous meeting, what will be accomplished before the next meeting, and what obstacles could come up that could prevent progress from being made. Also, new requested features could be brought up. However, all proposed additional features are simply added to the product backlog that could be considered during the next iteration or timebox (sprint in Scrum's nomenclature). The product backlog is essentially a prioritized list of the functional requirements that will be completed during the current iteration. In Scrum, only the client is allowed to modify the product backlog. In this manner, the development team always has a list of the current set of critical requirements. As long as the project is relatively small, this approach to scope management is very effective.

Timeboxing

Another approach to scope management is a technique called *timeboxing*. Up until now, we have described task-oriented projects. In other words, we have described projects that have a schedule driven by the tasks that need to be accomplished, so the greater the number of tasks and requirements are, the longer the project will take. Some companies have little patience for development projects that take a long time, and these companies take a time-oriented approach that places meeting a deadline above delivering functionality.

Think about the use of word processing software. For 80 percent of the time, only 20 percent of the features, such as the spelling checker, boldfacing, and cutting and pasting, are used. Other features, such as document merging and creating mailing labels, may be nice to have, but they are not a part of day-to-day needs. The same goes for other software applications; most users rely on only a small subset of their capabilities. Ironically, most developers agree that typically 75 percent of a system can be provided relatively quickly, with the remaining 25 percent of the functionality demanding most of the time.

To resolve this incongruency, the technique of timeboxing has become quite popular, especially when using RAD and agile methodologies. This technique sets a fixed deadline for a project and delivers the system by that deadline no matter what, even if functionality needs to be reduced. Timeboxing ensures that project teams don't get hung up on the final finishing touches that can drag out indefinitely, and it satisfies the business by providing a product within a relatively short time frame.

Several steps are involved in implementing timeboxing on a project. First, set the date of delivery for the proposed goals. The deadline should not be impossible to meet, so it is best to let the project team determine a realistic due date. If you recall from Chapter 1, the Scrum agile methodology sets all of its timeboxes (sprint) to thirty working days. Next, build the core of the system to be delivered; you will find that timeboxing helps create a sense of urgency and helps keep the focus on the most important features. Because the schedule is absolutely fixed, functionality that cannot be completed needs to be postponed. It helps if the team prioritizes a list of features beforehand to keep track of what functionality the users absolutely need. Quality cannot be compromised, regardless of other constraints, so it is important that the time allocated to activities is not shortened unless the requirements are changed (e.g., don't reduce the time allocated to testing without reducing features). At the end of the time period, a high-quality system is delivered, but it is likely that future iterations will be needed to make changes and enhancements. In that case, the timeboxing approach can be used once again.

Refining Estimates

The estimates that are produced during inception need to be refined as the project progresses. This does not mean that estimates were poorly done at the start of the project; rather, it is virtually impossible to develop an exact assessment of the project's schedule at the beginning of the development process. A project manager should expect to be satisfied with broad ranges of estimates that become more and more specific as the project's product becomes better defined.

During planning, when a system is first requested, the project sponsor and project manager attempt to predict how long the development process will take, how much it will cost, and what it will ultimately do when it is delivered (i.e., its functionality). However, the estimates are based on very little knowledge of the system. As the system moves into the elaboration, more information is gathered, the system concept is developed, and the estimates become even more accurate and precise. As the system moves closer to completion, the accuracy and precision increase, until it is delivered.

According to one of the leading experts in software development,[11] a well-done project plan (prepared at the end of inception) has a 100 percent margin of error for project cost and a 25 percent margin of error for schedule time. In other words, if a carefully done project plan estimates that a project will cost $100,000 and take twenty weeks, the project will actually cost between $0 and $200,000 and take between fifteen and twenty-five weeks.

What happens if you overshoot an estimate (e.g., analysis ends up lasting two weeks longer than expected)? There are a number of ways to adjust future estimates. If the project team finishes a step ahead of schedule, most project managers shift the deadlines sooner by the same amount but do not adjust the promised completion date. The challenge, however, occurs when the project team is late in meeting a scheduled date. Three possible responses to missed schedule dates are presented in Figure 2-19. If, early in the project, an estimate proves to be too optimistic, planners should not expect to make up for lost time—very few

[11] Barry W. Boehm et al., "Cost Models for Future Software Life Cycle Processes: COCOMO 2.0," in J. D. Arthur and S. M. Henry (eds.), *Annals of Software Engineering: Special Volume on Software Process and Product Measurement* (Amsterdam: J. C. Baltzer AG Science Publishers, 1995).

Assumptions	Actions	Level of Risk
If you assume the rest of the project is simpler than the part that was late and is also simpler than believed when the original schedule estimates were made, you can make up lost time.	Do not change schedule.	High risk
If you assume the rest of the project is simpler than the part that was late and is no more complex than the original estimate assumed, you can't make up the lost time, but you will not lose time on the rest of the project.	Increase the entire schedule by the total amount of time that you are behind (e.g., if you missed the scheduled date by two weeks, move the rest of the schedule dates to two weeks later). If you included padded time at the end of the project in the original schedule, you might not have to change the promised system delivery date; you'll just use up the padded time.	Moderate risk
If you assume that the rest of the project is as complex as the part that was late (your original estimates were too optimistic), then all the scheduled dates in the future underestimate the real time required by the same percentage as the part that was late.	Increase the entire schedule by the percentage of weeks that you are behind (e.g., if you are two weeks late on part of the project that was supposed to take eight weeks, you need to increase all remaining time estimates by 25 percent). If this moves the new delivery date beyond what is acceptable to the project sponsor, the scope of the project must be reduced.	Low risk

FIGURE 2-19
Possible Actions When a Schedule Date Is Missed

projects end up doing this. Instead, they should change future estimates to include an increase similar to the one that was experienced. For example, if the first phase was completed 10 percent over schedule, planners should increase the rest of their estimates by 10 percent.

Managing Risk

One final facet of project management is *risk management*, the process of assessing and addressing the risks that are associated with developing a project. Many things can cause risks: weak personnel, scope creep, poor design, and overly optimistic estimates. The project team must be aware of potential risks so that problems can be avoided or controlled well ahead of time.

Typically, project teams create a *risk assessment*, or a document that tracks potential risks along with an evaluation of the likelihood of each risk and its potential impact on the project (Figure 2-20). A paragraph or two is also included to explain potential ways that the risk can be addressed. There are many options: The risk could be publicized, avoided, or even eliminated by dealing with its root cause. For example, imagine that a project team plans to use new technology but its members have identified a risk in the fact that its members do not have the right technical skills. They believe that tasks may take much longer to perform because of a high learning curve. One plan of attack could be to eliminate the root cause of the risk—the lack of technical experience by team members—by finding the time and resources needed to provide proper training to the team.

Most project managers keep abreast of potential risks, even prioritizing them according to their magnitude and importance. Over time, the list of risks will change as some items are removed and others surface. The best project managers, however, work hard to keep risks from having an impact on the schedule and costs associated with the project.

	Risk Assessment
RISK 1:	The development of this system likely will be slowed considerably because project team members have not programmed in Java prior to this project.
Likelihood of risk:	High probability of risk.
Potential impact on the project:	This risk will probably increase the time to complete programming tasks by 50 percent.
Ways to address this risk:	

It is very important that time and resources are allocated to up-front training in Java for the programmers who are used for this project. Adequate training will reduce the initial learning curve for Java when programming begins. Additionally, outside Java expertise should be brought in for at least some part of the early programming tasks. This person should be used to provide experiential knowledge to the project team so that Java-related issues (of which novice Java programmers would be unaware) are overcome.

RISK 2: . . .

FIGURE 2-20
Sample Risk
Assessment

AGILE ALTERNATIVES TO ITERATIVE WORKPLANS

Agile development approaches have used variation of the work breakdown structure in the form of a product backlog, Gantt charts, and network diagrams. In this section, we describe the Kanban method,[12] an adaptation from lean manufacturing.

The Kanban method was originally developed as part of the continuous improvement approaches in lean manufacturing. This method is very popular among agile and DevOps approaches to managing IT projects. The *Kanban* method uses lots of sticky notes and a large whiteboard that has a set of labeled columns. The number of columns depends on the complexity and size of the project. A small project could simply have columns for Story, To Do, In Progress, Testing, and Done (see Figure 2-21). For our purposes, a story is similar to a use case.[13] For each story, a sticky note is created and placed in the Story column. Also, a sticky note is created for each and every individual requirement necessary to solve the story. Each requirement should be small enough that a team member would be able to complete in a short period of time, for example, a day or a week. These sticky notes are placed in the To Do column in the same row that the story sticky note was placed. Next, a team member chooses one of the requirements from the To Do column on which they plan to work and places it into the In Progress column. The sticky note remains in the In Progress column until it is either completed and placed into the Testing column or the team member discovers that the requirement is too large. In this case, the team member splits the requirement into a set of subrequirements, creates a sticky note for each subrequirement, and replaces the requirement sticky note with the set of subrequirement sticky notes. The subrequirement sticky notes are then placed in the To Do column. Once a sticky note has been placed into the Testing column, the code that represents the solution to the requirement is tested. If the code passes all of the tests, the sticky note is placed in the Done column. Otherwise, the sticky note is returned to the To Do column. This process is repeated over all stories related to the system until all requirement-based sticky notes are in the Done column.

---

[12] The material in the section is based on David J. Anderson, *Kanban: Successful Evolutionary Change for Your Technology Business* (Sequim, WA: Blue Hole Press, 2010); Eric Brechner, *Agile Project Management with Kanban* (Redmond, WA: Microsoft Press, 2015).

[13] Technically speaking user stories are not the equivalent of a use case. However, we do not cover either use cases or user stories in any detail until Chapters 3 and 4. So, for the purposes of this section, we are treating them the same.

KANBAN

STORIES	TO DO	IN PROGRESS	TESTING	DONE
STORY 1	TASK 5	TASK 3 · TASK 4	TASK 1	TASK 2
STORY 2	TASK 3 · TASK 5	TASK 2 · TASK 4	TASK 1	TASK 6
STORY 3	TASK 3 · TASK 4	TASK 1 · TASK 5	TASK 2	

FIGURE 2-21
Simple Kanban
Board

The Kanban method has a couple of major advantages. First, the method is very simple to implement. All you need are a set of sticky notes and a whiteboard. Second, by simply looking at the board, it is very easy to see the current status of the project. The example board shown in Figure 2-21 is very simple. For larger, more complex projects more columns are used. For example, you could have columns for story, requirements analysis, design, design review, ready for development, development in progress, development completed, build ready, test ready, unit and integration testing, user acceptance testing, release ready, staging, in production, and so on. In other words, larger systems require more management of the development process.

STAFFING THE PROJECT

Staffing the project includes determining how many people should be assigned to the project, matching people's skills with the needs of the project, motivating them to meet the project's objectives, and minimizing the conflict that will occur over time. The deliverables for this part of project management are a staffing plan, which describes the number and kinds of people who will work on the project, the overall reporting structure, and the project charter, which describes the project's objectives and rules. However, before describing the development of a staffing plan, how to motivate people, and how to handle conflict, we describe Tuckman's stages of small group development and a set of characteristics of jelled teams.

Tuckman's Stages of Small Group Development[14]

Agile developers have embraced Tuckman's stages of small group development. The stages include forming, storming, norming, performing, and adjourning. In this section, we describe each of these stages.

[14] The material in the section is based on Bruce W. Tuckman, "Development Sequence in Small Groups," *Psychological Bulletin* 63, No. 6 (1965): 384–399; Bruce W. Tuckman and Mary Ann C. Jensen, "Stages of Small-Group Development Revisited," *Group & Organization Studies* 2, No. 4 (December 1977): 419–427; Denise A. Bonebright, "40 Years of Storming: A Historical Review of Tuckman's Model of Small Group Development," *Human Resource Development International* 13, No. 1 (February 2010): 111–120.

As the name implies, the *forming stage* deals with the startup characteristics that a new team possess. These include members getting to know one another by questioning one another, acting very independent, only being self-motivated, and to some degree attempting to focus on identifying the objectives and purpose of the group.

The *storming stage* sees members attempting to "flex their muscles" in an attempt to demonstrate their individual worth to the group. This stage includes lots of potential for resistance among the group members that can increase the conflict that is natural in a new team. However, as they begin to know one another, group members begin developing group norms and expectations.

As the group evolves into the *norming stage*, the characteristics of the group moves much more toward becoming a team. The group members become much more engaged with one another, anxiety of being in a group begins to subside, members begin to support one another, members become much more accepting of other members' behavior, and the group cohesion becomes a real asset for group performance.

The *performing stage* is the stage that the group becomes a team and not simply a loose connection of individuals working together. The idea of an independent contractor mentality is replaced by an interdependence that supports group decision-making, group problem-solving, and group learning. This stage is most associated with the idea of a "jelled team" (see next section).

The *adjourning stage* is the stage that the team enters once the project has been completed. During this stage a review is typically completed that recognizes both the individual and team efforts that was required to complete the project. If the group actually attained a jelled team status, members of the team will actually be sad that the team is being disbanded.

Characteristics of a Jelled Team[15]

The idea of a jelled team has existed for a long time. Most (if not all) student groups are *not* representative of the idea of a jelled team, and you may have never had the opportunity to appreciate the effectiveness of a true team. In fact, DeMarco and Lister point out that teams are not created; they are grown. Typically, in class projects, students are assigned or asked to form a group, which makes the ability to grow a team very limited. However, growing development teams is crucial in information systems development. The whole set of agile software development approaches hinges on growing jelled teams. Otherwise, agile development approaches would totally fail.

According to DeMarco and Lister,[16] "[a] *jelled team* is a group of people so strongly knit that the whole is greater than the sum of the parts. The production of such a team is greater than that of the same people working in unjelled form." They go on to state that a jelled "team can become almost unstoppable, a juggernaut for success." When is the last time that you worked with a group on a class project that could be described "a juggernaut for success"? Demarco and Lister identify five characteristics of a jelled team.

First, jelled teams have a very low turnover during a project. Typically, members of a jelled team feel a responsibility to the other team members. This responsibility is felt so intensely that for a member to leave the team, the member would feel that they were letting the team down and that they were breaking a bond of trust.

Second, jelled teams have a strong sense of identity. In many classes, when you are part of a group, the group chooses some cute name to identify the group and differentiate it from the

---

[15] The material in the section is based on T. DeMarco and T. Lister, *Peopleware: Productive Projects and Teams*, 2nd Ed. (New York: Dorset House, 1999); P. Lencioni, *The Five Dysfunctions of a Team: A Leadership Fable* (San Francisco: Jossey-Bass, 2002).

[16] T. DeMarco and T. Lister, *Peopleware: Productive Projects and Teams*, 2nd Ed., p. 123.

other groups. However, in this case, it is not simply the choosing of a name. It is instead evolving every member into something that only exists within the team. This can be seen when members of the team tend to do nonwork-related activities together, for example, do lunch together as a team or form a basketball team composed of only members of the development team.

Third, the strong sense of identity tends to lead the team into feeling a sense of eliteness. The members of a jelled development team almost have a swagger about the way they relate to nonteam employees. Good examples that come to mind that possess this sense of eliteness outside of the scope of information systems development teams are certain sports teams, U.S. Navy Seal teams, or big city police force SWAT teams. In all three examples, each team member is highly competent in his or her specialty area, and each other team member knows (not thinks) that he or she can depend on the team members performing his or her individual jobs with a very high-level of skill.

Fourth, during the development process, jelled teams feel that the team owns the information system being developed and not any one individual member. In many ways, you could almost say that jelled teams are a little communistic in nature. By this we mean that the individual contributions to the effort are not important to a true team. The only things that matter are the output of the team. However, this is not to imply that a member who does not deliver his or her fair share will not go unpunished. In a jelled team, any member who is not producing is actually breaking his or her bond of trust with the other team members (see the first characteristic).

The final characteristic of a jelled team is that team members really enjoy (have fun) doing their work. The members actually like to go to work and be with their team members. Much of this can be attributed to the level of challenge they receive. If the project is challenging and the members of the team are going to learn something from completing the project, the members of a jelled team will enjoy tackling the project.

When a team jells, they will avoid the five dysfunctions of a team defined by Lencioni. Lack of trust is the primary cause of a team becoming dysfunctional. Lencioni describes four other causes of a team becoming dysfunctional that can come from the lack of trust. First, dysfunctional teams fear conflict, whereas members of a jelled team never fear conflict.[17] Going to a member of a jelled team and admitting that you do not know how to do something is no big deal. In fact, it provides a method for the team member to help out, which would increase the level of trust between the two members. Second, dysfunctional teams do not have a commitment to the team from the individual members. Instead, they tend to focus on their individual performance instead of the team's performance. This can even be to the detriment of the development team. Obviously, this is not an issue for jelled teams. Third, dysfunctional teams try to avoid accountability. With jelled teams, accountability is not an issue. Members of a jelled team feel a high level of responsibility to the other team members. No team member ever wants to let down the team. Furthermore, owing to the bond that holds jelled teams together, no member has any problem with holding other members accountable for their performance (or lack of performance). Fourth, dysfunctional teams do not pay attention to the team's results. Again, in this case, the cause of this dysfunction is that the individual members only focus on their individual goals. From a team management perspective, the team leader should focus on getting the goals of the team aligned; a jelled team will attain the goals.

Staffing Plan

The first step to staffing is determining the average number of staff needed for the project. To calculate this figure, divide the total person-months of effort by the optimal schedule. So, to

---

[17] When conflict occurs, it is necessary to address it in an effective manner.

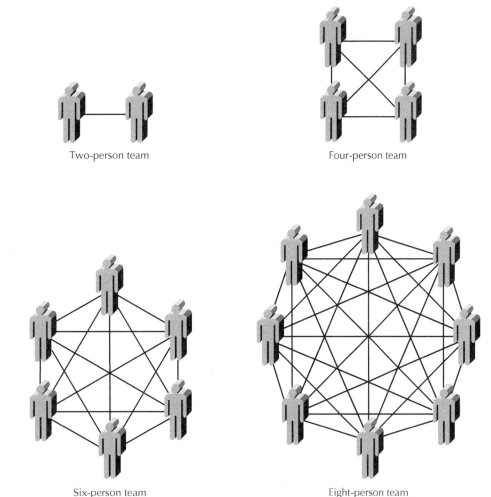

Two-person team

Four-person team

Six-person team

Eight-person team

FIGURE 2-22
Increasing Complexity with Larger Teams

complete a forty-person-month project in ten months, a team should have an average of four full-time staff members, although this may change over time as different specialists enter and leave the team (e.g., business analysts, programmers, technical writers).

Many times, the temptation is to assign more staff to a project to shorten the project's length, but this is not a wise move. Adding staff resources does not translate into increased productivity; staff size and productivity share a disproportionate relationship, mainly because it is more difficult to coordinate a large number of staff members. The more a team grows, the more difficult it becomes to manage. Imagine how easy it is to work on a two-person project team: The team members share a single line of communication. But adding two people increases the number of communication lines to six, and greater increases lead to more dramatic gains in communication complexity. Figure 2-22 illustrates the impact of adding team members to a project team.

One way to reduce efficiency losses on teams is to understand the complexity that is created in numbers and to build in a *reporting structure* that tempers its effects. The general rule is to keep team sizes to fewer than eight to ten people; therefore, if more people are needed, create subteams. In this way, the project manager can keep the communication effective within small teams, which, in turn, communicate to a contact at a higher level in the project.

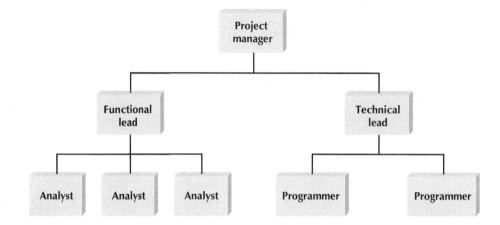

FIGURE 2-23
Possible Reporting
Structure

After the project manager understands how many people are needed for the project, he or she creates a *staffing plan* that lists the roles and the proposed reporting structure that are required for the project. Typically, a project has one project manager who oversees the overall progress of the development effort, with the core of the team comprising the various types of analysts described in Chapter 1. A *functional lead* is usually assigned to manage a group of analysts, and a *technical lead* oversees the progress of a group of programmers and more technical staff members.

There are many structures for project teams; Figure 2-23 illustrates one possible configuration of a project team. After the roles are defined and the structure is in place, the project manager needs to think about which people can fill each role. Often, one person fills more than one role on a project team.

When you make assignments, remember that people have *technical skills* and *interpersonal skills*, and both are important on a project. Technical skills are useful when working with technical tasks (e.g., programming in Java) and in trying to understand the various roles that technology plays in the particular project (e.g., how a Web server should be configured on the basis of a projected number of hits from customers). Interpersonal skills, on the other hand, include interpersonal and communication abilities that are used when dealing with business users, senior management executives, and other members of the project team. They are particularly critical when performing the requirements-gathering activities and when addressing organizational feasibility issues. Each project requires unique technical and interpersonal skills.

Ideally, project roles are filled with people who have the right skills for the job. However, the people who fit the roles best might not be available; they may be working on other projects, or they might not exist in the company. Therefore, assigning project team members really is a combination of finding people with the appropriate skill sets and finding people who are available. When the skills of the available project team members do not match what is actually required by the project, the project manager has several options to improve the situation. First, people can be pulled off other projects, and resources can be shuffled around. This is the most disruptive approach from the organization's perspective. Another approach is to use outside help—such as a consultant or a contractor—to train team members and start them off on the right foot. Mentoring may also be an option; a project team member can be sent to work on another similar project so that he or she can return with skills to apply to the current job.

Motivation

Assigning people to tasks isn't enough; project managers need to motivate the people to ensure a project's success. *Motivation* has been found to be the number one influence on people's performance,[18] but determining how to motivate the team can be quite difficult. You might think that good project managers motivate their staff by rewarding them with money and bonuses, but most project managers agree that this is the last thing that should be done. The more often managers reward team members with money, the more they expect it—and most times monetary motivation won't work. Furthermore, Cougar and Zawacki found that information systems developers had a high need to be able to personally grow in their profession, which would lead to a high level of internal motivations, a high level of quality performance, and a low level of absenteeism.[19] To attain these goals, Pink[20] has suggested a set of principles to follow to motivate individuals in twenty-first century firms. In this section, we adapt his suggestions to information systems development teams.

Pink suggests considering using some form of the 20 percent time rule to motivate individuals. This rule suggests that 20 percent of an employee's time should be spent on some idea in which he or she believes. The project does not have to be related to the project at hand. On the surface, this sounds like a colossal waste of time, but this idea should not be discarded. Google's Gmail and Google News were developed using the 20 percent time rule. If 20 percent sounds too high, Pink suggests that you consider 10 percent to begin with.

He recommends that firms should be willing to fund small "Now That" awards. These awards are given as small signs of appreciation for doing a great job. However, these awards are not given by a manager to an employee but from an employee to a peer of the employee. The awards are monetary, but they are very small, typically $50. As such, they really are not relevant from a monetary perspective. However, they are very relevant because they are given by one of the employee's colleagues to show that some action that the employee did was appreciated.

Pink endorses the idea of applying Robert Reich's (President's Clinton's Secretary of Labor) pronoun test. If an employee (or team member) refers to the firm (the team) as "they," then there is the real possibility that the employee feels disengaged or possibly alienated. On the other hand, when employees refer to the firm as "we," they obviously feel like they are part of the organization. From a team perspective, this could be an indication that the team has begun to jell.

Pink suggests that management should periodically consider giving each employee a day on which he or she can work on anything he or she wants. In some ways, this is related to the 20 percent rule. It does not necessarily require one day a week (20 percent), but it does require some deliverable. The deliverable can be a new utility program that could be used by lots of different projects, it could be a new prototype of a new software product, or it could be an improvement for a business process that is used internally. The goal is to provide team members with the ability to focus on interesting and challenging problems that might (or might not) provide results to the firm's bottom line. Regardless, it demonstrates an amount of trust and respect that the firm has for its employees.

He recommends that managers remove the issue of compensation from the motivation equation. By this, he means that all employees should be paid a sufficient amount so that

[18] Barry W. Boehm, *Software Engineering Economics* (Englewood Cliffs, NJ: Prentice Hall, 1981). One of the best books on managing project teams is that by Tom DeMarco and Timothy Lister, *Peopleware: Productive Projects and Teams* (New York: Dorset House, 1987).

[19] J. Daniel Cougar and Robert A Zawacki, *Motivating and Managing Computer Personnel* (New York, NY: John Wiley & Sons, 1980).

[20] D. H. Pink, *Drive: The Surprising Truth About What Motivates Us* (New York, NY: Riverhead Books, 2009).

compensation awards are not an issue. Technical employees on project teams are much more motivated by recognition, achievement, the work itself, responsibility, advancement, and the chance to learn new skills.[21] Simplistic financial awards, such as raises that are perceived as being unjust, can actually demotivate the overall team and lower overall performance.

He advocates that twenty-first century bosses (team leaders) need to be willing to give up control. Many of the agile development approaches make similar suggestions. Appelo[22] suggests that an open-door policy that is supported by a team leader actually can be self-defeating. In the case of software development teams, an open-door policy implies that the team leader has a door that can be left open, whereas the poor individual team member does not have an office with a door. In this case, Appelo suggests that the team leader move from the office with a door to the same shared space in which the team resides. One of Pink's other ideas is for the team leader to not use controlling language such as telling the team member that he or she "must" do something. Instead, the team leader should ask the team member to "consider" or "think about" the idea. In some ways, a true team leader should never receive credit for any ideas associated with the team. Instead, a team leader should make suggestions and encourage the team members to consider ideas and, most importantly, let the team member and the team receive the credit.

Pink provides evidence that intrinsic motivation is very important for twenty-first century knowledge workers. Pink suggests that intrinsically motivating individuals requires providing them with a degree of autonomy, supporting them in such a way that they can master their area of expertise, and encouraging them to pursue projects with a purpose. Providing team members with autonomy relates to the jelled team concept of trust. Team leaders need to trust the team members to deliver the software for which they are responsible. Supporting team members so that they can master their area of expertise can be as simple as providing support to attend conferences, seminars, and training sessions that deal with the member's area of expertise. It also could imply providing the team member with a high-end development environment. For example, when building information visualization and virtual reality applications, special hardware and software environments can make it much easier to master the technology to develop the application. Finally, today it is very important for team members to feel that what they are doing can make a difference. A team leader should encourage the team members to tackle problems that can impact people's lives. This can easily be accomplished through the use of the 20 percent rule.

Handling Conflict

The third component of staffing is organizing the project to minimize conflict among group members. *Group cohesiveness* (the attraction that members feel to the group and to other members) contributes more to productivity than do project members' individual capabilities or experiences.[23] Clearly defining the roles on the project and holding team members accountable for their tasks are a good way to begin mitigating potential conflict on a project. Some project managers develop a *project charter*, which lists the project's norms and ground rules. For example, the charter may describe when the project team should be at work, when staff meetings will be held, how the group will communicate with each other,

---

[21] F. H. Hertzberg, "One More Time: How Do You Motivate Employees?" *Harvard Business Review* (January–February 1968).

[22] J. Appelo, *Management 3.0: Leading Agile Developers, Developing Agile Leaders* (Upper Saddle River, NJ: Addison-Wesley, 2011).

[23] B. Lakhanpal, "Understanding the Factors Influencing the Performance of Software Development Groups: An Exploratory Group-Level Analysis," *Information and Software Technology* 35, no. 8 (1993): 468–473.

- Clearly define plans for the project.
- Make sure that the team understands how the project is important to the organization.
- Develop detailed operating procedures and communicate these to the team members.
- Develop a project charter.
- Develop schedule commitments ahead of time.
- Forecast other priorities and their possible impact on the project.

Source: H. J. Thamhain and D. L. Wilemon, "Conflict Management in Project Life Cycles," *Sloan Management Review* (Spring 1975).

FIGURE 2-24
Conflict-Avoidance
Strategies

and what are the procedures for updating the workplan as tasks are completed. Figure 2-24 lists additional techniques that can be used at the start of a project to keep conflict to a minimum.

MEETING MANAGEMENT[24]

Possibly the most dreaded aspect of any job is the requirement to attend meetings. In general, many participants consider meetings to be a colossal waste of time. In fact, some research suggests that 60 percent of meeting participants tend to work on other things during meetings and nearly 50 percent of the participants would rather do any other unpleasant activity to avoid attending the meetings. This is especially true when it comes to information systems development team meetings. However, in other research, only 7 percent of meeting participants considered meetings to be unproductive. Based on these divergent results and given the amount of time (money) spent in meetings, we provide a set of recommendations for holding successful, productive meetings.

First, meeting leadership must become an organizational priority. This requires taking meeting management seriously by periodically evaluating meeting leaders as to their effectiveness.

Second, meetings should have an agenda. However, the existence of an agenda is not going to guarantee effective meetings. Effective meetings have a purpose and are focused on only a few goals. Each stated goal must be doable in the allotted time and should be assigned to a participant who is responsible for meeting the goal. One possible meeting agenda/reporting form is portrayed in Figure 2-25.

Third, the length of meetings should be minimized. Even though on the surface it may make sense to have a longer meeting with more goals, longer meetings tend to be less focused and consequently, less effective. Furthermore, do not schedule meetings using a standard amount of time. Only schedule the meeting for the amount of time necessary. For example, if a meeting is only going to have 20 minutes of work to be accomplished, do not schedule it for 30 minutes; schedule it for 20 minutes. Otherwise, the extra 10 minutes will be filled with nonproductive work. This is a waste of resources.

Fourth, only participants that can help reach the goals of the meeting should be invited to participate. Having too many meeting participants can lead to many distractions, freeloading, and multitasking, none of which leads to effective meetings.

Fifth, don't be stuck with the traditional meeting location; sitting around a table in a conference room. A simple way to vary location is to randomly assign seating. Sitting arrangements can affect the effectiveness of a meeting. Two other promising approaches to

[24] Most of this material is adapted from Steven G. Rogelberg, *The Surprising Science of Meetings: How You Can Lead Your Team to Peak Performance* (New York, NY: Oxford University Press, 2019).

Meeting Agenda/Reporting Form

Group Number/Name: _____ **Location:** _____

Date: _____ **Start Time:** _____ **End Time:** _____

Attendees: (List the persons attending the meeting—not everyone needs to attend every meeting.)

Purpose: (Overview description)

Agenda: (What are you planning to do in this meeting? Keep it short and focused on the topic)
1. Announcements and any results/updates regarding previous meeting
2. List Major Goals:
    A.
    B.
    C.
3. Summarize Meeting Accomplishments

Goal A (Do this for each major goal):
    a. Description:

    b. Responsible Member: _____
    c. Required preparation before meeting:
        (List any materials and their location that should be reviewed by participants before the meeting)

    d. Estimated amount of meeting time to be devoted to this goal: _____
    e. Determine action items:

What	Who	By When

Accomplishments of Meeting: (A paragraph or two that relates what happened at the meeting—may include lists of key points discussed, decisions made, and deliverables or action items worked. Take notes during the meeting, write the description immediately after the meeting.)

Unresolved Issues: (List the problems and issues that hinder your progress.)

FIGURE 2-25 Sample Meeting Agenda/Reporting Form

vary location are the standing and walking meetings. A standing meeting is one in which all participants must stand during the entire meeting. Standing tends to speed things along in a meeting. Standing meetings have become very popular with agile development. A walking meeting is one in which the participants go for a walk. Obviously, a walking meeting is only going to be effective for a small number of participants. However, a change of scenery can increase the effectiveness of a meeting.

ENVIRONMENT AND INFRASTRUCTURE MANAGEMENT

The environment and infrastructure management workflows support the development team throughout the development process. The environment workflow primarily deals with choosing the correct set of tools that will be used throughout the development process and identifying the appropriate set of standards to be followed during the development process. Infrastructure management workflow deals with choosing the appropriate level and type of documentation that will be created during the development process. Other activities associated with the infrastructure management workflow include developing, modifying, and reusing predefined components, frameworks, libraries, and patterns. The topic of reuse is discussed in later chapters (see Chapters 5 and 8).

CASE Tools

Computer-aided software engineering (CASE) is a category of software that automates all or part of the development process. Some CASE software packages are used primarily to support the analysis workflow to create integrated diagrams of the system and to store information regarding the system components, whereas others support the design workflow that can be used to generate code for database tables and system functionality. Other CASE tools contain functionality that supports tasks throughout the system-development process. CASE comes in a wide assortment of flavors in terms of complexity and functionality, and many good tools are available in the marketplace to support object-oriented systems development (e.g., ArgoUML, Enterprise Architect, Visual Paradigm, and IBM's Rational Rose).

The benefits of using CASE are numerous. With CASE tools, tasks can be completed and altered faster, development documentation is centralized, and information is illustrated through diagrams, which are typically easier to understand. Potentially, CASE can reduce maintenance costs, improve software quality, and enforce discipline. Some project teams even use CASE to assess the magnitude of changes to the project. Many modern CASE tools that support object-oriented systems development support a development technique known as *round-trip engineering*. Round-trip engineering supports not only code generation but also the reverse engineering of UML diagrams from code. In this way, the system can evolve via diagrams and via code in a round-trip manner.

Of course, like anything else, CASE should not be considered a silver bullet for project development. The advanced CASE tools are complex applications that require significant training and experience to achieve real benefits. Our experience has shown that CASE is a helpful way to support the communication and sharing of project diagrams and technical specifications as long as it is used by trained developers who have applied CASE on past projects. All CASE tools use a *CASE repository* to store diagrams, models, and I/O designs and to ensure consistency across iterations.

Standards

Project team members need to work together, and most project management software and CASE tools support them by providing access privileges to everyone working on the system. However, without set procedures, collaboration can result in confusion. To make matters worse, people sometimes are reassigned in the middle of a project. It is important that their project knowledge does not leave with them and that their replacements can get up to speed quickly.

One way to make certain that everyone is performing tasks in the same way and following the same procedures is to create *standards* that the project team must follow. Standards can include formal rules for naming files, forms that must be completed when

Types of Standards	Examples
Documentation standards	The date and project name should appear as a header on all documentation. All margins should be set to 1 inch. All deliverables should be added to the project binder and recorded in its table of contents.
Coding standards	All modules of code should include a header that lists the programmer, last date of update, and a short description of the purpose of the code. Indentation should be used to indicate loops, if-then-else statements, and case statements. On average, every program should include one line of comments for every five lines of code.
Procedural standards	Record actual task progress in the workplan every Monday morning by 10 AM. Report to project update meeting on Fridays at 3:30 PM. All changes to a requirements document must be approved by the project manager.
Specification requirement standards	Name of program to be created Description of the program's purpose Special calculations that need to be computed Business rules that must be incorporated into the program Pseudocode Due date
User interface design standards	Labels will appear in boldface text, left-justified, and followed by a colon. The tab order of the screen will move from top left to bottom right. Accelerator keys will be provided for all updatable fields.

FIGURE 2-26
A Sampling of
Project Standards

goals are reached, and programming guidelines. Figure 2-26 shows some examples of the types of standards that a project can create. When a team forms standards and then follows them, the project can be completed faster because task coordination becomes less complex.

Standards work best when they are created at the beginning of each major phase of the project and communicated clearly to the entire project team. As the team moves forward, new standards are added when necessary. Some standards (e.g., file naming conventions, status reporting) are applied during the entire development process, whereas others (e.g., programming guidelines) are appropriate only for certain tasks.

Documentation

Finally, during the inception phase of the infrastructure workflow, project teams establish good *documentation* standards that include detailed information about the tasks of the Unified Process. Typically, the standards for the required documentation are set by the development organization. The development team only needs to ascertain which documentation standards are appropriate for the current systems development project. Often, the documentation is stored in a *project binder(s)* that contains all the deliverables and all the internal communication that takes place—the history of the project. The good news is that Unified Process has a set of standard documentation that is expected. The documentation typically includes the system request, the feasibility analysis, the original and later versions of the effort estimation, the evolving workplan, and UML diagrams for the functional, structural, and behavioral models.

A poor project management practice is waiting until the last minute to create documentation; this typically leads to an undocumented system that no one understands. Good project teams learn to document a system's history as it evolves while the details are still fresh in their memory. In most CASE tools that support object-oriented systems development, some of the documentation can be automated. For example, if the programming language chosen to implement the system in is Java, then it is possible to automatically create HTML manual pages that will describe the classes being implemented. This is accomplished through the javadoc[25] tool that is part of the Java development environment. Other tools enable the developer to automatically generate HTML documentation for the UML diagrams.[26] Even though virtually all developers hate creating documentation and documentation takes valuable time, it is a good investment that will pay off in the long run.

CONFIGURATION AND CHANGE MANAGEMENT[27]

This workflow primarily addresses the need of keeping the different parts of the developing system in sync and controlling access to and modification of the different IT artifacts created during the systems development process. These artifacts include the workplans and estimations (this chapter), analysis models (Chapters 4–7), design specifications (Chapters 8–11), source code, and test specifications (Chapters 4–12). With the continuous delivery and deployment of system releases of agile and DevOps approaches, this becomes very critical. Otherwise, the system can be broken easily.

One of the major approaches used to address configuration and change management uses the idea of an artifact library and version controls. The *artifact library* stores all of the artifacts and the relationships among them. For example, a set of CRC cards (Chapter 5) could have a test that specifies that all related use-case scenarios (Chapter 4) should be role-played to ensure the fidelity of the CRC cards to support the use case. In addition to storing the artifacts themselves, the library also would store the relationships among all of the use-case scenarios, the CRC cards, and the role-play test specification. These *dependency relationships* allow the project manager to ensure that all of the artifacts are kept in sync and to support the idea of traceability. *Traceability* refers to the notion of knowing who made the changes to what artifact. This supports the idea of *accountability* where each and every developer is accountable for the work that they have performed. Furthermore, by storing all of these relationships, developers can always trace an artifact back to the requirements (Chapter 3) that it supports.

Version controls supports the rolling back of the system, or part of a system, to a previous version. Consequently, if something is deployed, put into production, and does not work properly, the new version can be removed, the previous version can be deployed, and the new version can be brought back into development. Given that DevOps supports continuous

[25] See Oracle, *Javadoc Tool*. Retrieved May 2014 from www.oracle.com. www.oracle.com/technetwork/java/javase/documentation/index-jsp-135444.html.

[26] For example, see Doc. Composer with the Visual Paradigm Case tool.

[27] See Roger S. Pressman, Bruce R. Maxim, *Software Engineering: A Practitioner's Approach, Eighth Edition* (New York, NY: McGraw-Hill Education, 2015); Jez Humble and David Farley, *Continuous Delivery: Reliable Software Releases Through Build, Test, and Deployment Automation* (Boston, MA: Pearson Education, 2011); Gene Kim, Jez Humble, Patrick Debois, and John Willis, *The DevOps Handbook: How to Create World-Class Agility, Reliability, & Security in Technology Organizations* (Portland, OR: IT Revolution Press, 2016).

PRACTICAL

TIP

Avoiding Classic Planning Mistakes

As Seattle University's David Umphress has pointed out, watching most organizations develop systems is like watching reruns of Gilligan's Island. At the beginning of each episode, someone comes up with a cockamamie scheme to get off the island, and it seems to work for a while, but something goes wrong and the castaways find themselves right back where they started—stuck on the island. Similarly, most companies start new projects with grand ideas that seem to work, only to make a classic mistake and deliver the project behind schedule, over budget, or both. Here we summarize four classic mistakes in the planning and project management aspects of the project and discuss how to avoid them:

1. *Overly optimistic schedule:* Wishful thinking can lead to an overly optimistic schedule that causes analysis and design to be cut short (missing key requirements) and puts intense pressure on the programmers, who produce poor code (full of bugs).

   Solution: Don't inflate time estimates; instead, explicitly schedule slack time at the end of each phase to account for the variability in estimates.

2. *Failing to monitor the schedule:* If the team does not regularly report progress, no one knows if the project is on schedule.

Solution: Require team members to report progress (or the lack of progress) honestly every week. There is no penalty for reporting a lack of progress, but there are immediate sanctions for a misleading report.

3. *Failing to update the schedule:* When a part of the schedule falls behind (e.g., information gathering uses all the slack in item 1 plus 2 weeks), a project team often thinks it can make up the time later by working faster. It can't. This is an early warning that the entire schedule is too optimistic.

   Solution: Immediately revise the schedule and inform the project sponsor of the new end date or use timeboxing to reduce functionality or move it into future versions.

4. *Adding people to a late project:* When a project misses a schedule, the temptation is to add more people to speed it up. This makes the project take longer because it increases coordination problems and requires staff to take time to explain what has already been done.

   Solution: Revise the schedule, use timeboxing, throw away bug-filled code, and add people only to work on an isolated part of the project.

Based upon Steve McConnell, *Rapid Development* (Redmond, WA: Microsoft Press, 1996), pp. 29–50.

delivery and deployment of software, the ability to roll back to a previous version is critical. The ability to deploy software in a continuous manner requires a lot of infrastructure, automation, and a deep level of problem domain understanding. The infrastructure includes the ability to continuously integrate, test, monitor, deliver, and deploy the software in real time. This includes automatically testing, deploying, and sometimes retracting the artifact from production. However, the only way that this can work is if the problem is well understood by time the deployment is to be executed and the actual software being deployed is sufficiently limited.

Another aspect of configuration and change management is the requirement to control who has access to the artifact and the type of access that is granted to the artifact. Not everyone should have access to all of the artifacts. This access can be controlled in the same way as access is controlled to software and data of deployed systems. Typical approaches include capability lists, access control lists, and role-based access controls. Furthermore, authentication of the user and encryption of the artifacts should be supported. We describe these topics in Chapter 11.

APPLYING THE CONCEPTS AT PATTERSON SUPERSTORE

In Chapter 2, we look more closely at the completed system request that Max Ross and his team develop for the Integrated Health Clinic Delivery system, including the business needs, business requirements, and business values and constraints. We will also examine the feasibility analysis that accompanies and justifies the system request. Finally, we will examine how the project effort was estimated, see how the project will be staffed and managed, and look at the Evolutionary Work Breakdown Structure for Version 1 of the Integrated Health Clinic Delivery System.

As we progress through the text, examining how Patterson navigates through the systems analysis and design and development processes will help us understand real-world implementation of the concepts presented.

You can find the rest of the case at www.wiley.com/go/dennis/systemanalysis6e/casestudy.

CHAPTER REVIEW

After reading and studying this chapter, you should be able to:

☐ Explain the ways that projects are identified and initiated.
☐ Explain why it is important to link the information system to business needs of the organization.
☐ Describe the purpose of the systems request and explain the contents of its sections.
☐ Create a systems request for a proposed project.
☐ Discuss the purpose of the feasibility study.
☐ Describe the issues that are considered when evaluating a project's technical feasibility.
☐ Develop an economic feasibility assessment for a project.
☐ Understand and evaluate the organizational feasibility of a project.
☐ Explain how projects are selected.
☐ Describe a task.
☐ Create a standard work breakdown structure, a Gantt chart, and a network diagram.
☐ Perform PERT analysis and identify the critical path.
☐ Estimate the system development effort using use-case points.
☐ Create an evolutionary work breakdown structure.
☐ Describe how iterative and incremental development using timeboxing addresses scope management.
☐ Describe the Kanban method of managing projects.
☐ Describe the Tuckman stages of small group development.
☐ Describe the characteristics of a "jelled" team.
☐ Describe the recommendations for holding effective meetings.
☐ Describe issues relating to motivating software developers.
☐ Describe the importance of CASE tools, standards, and documentation managing software development projects.
☐ Describe the importance of configuration and change management.

KEY TERMS

Accountability
Actor
Adjourning stage
Adjusted use-case points (UCP)
Application program interface (API)
Approval committee
Artifact library
Average actors
Average use case
Break-even point
Business need
Business requirement
Business value
CASE repository
Cash flow method
Champion
Compatibility
Complex actors
Complex use case
Computer-aided software engineering (CASE)
Cost–benefit analysis
Critical path method
Critical task
Dependency relationships
Deskilling of the workforce
Development costs
Documentation
Economic feasibility
Effort

Emerging technology
Employee monitoring
Environmental factor (EF)
Environmental factor value (EFactor)
Estimation
Evolutionary WBS
Familiarity with the functional area
Familiarity with the technology
Feasibility analysis
Feasibility study
First mover
Forming stage
Functional lead
Functionality
Gantt chart
Group cohesiveness
Intangible benefits
Intangible costs
Intangible value
Interpersonal skills
IT health effects
Iterative workplan
Kanban
Methodology
Milestone
Motivation
Net present value (NPV)
Network diagram
Node

Norming stage
Operational costs
Organizational feasibility
Organizational management
Performing stage
Person-hours multiplier (PHM)
Portfolio management
Program evaluation and review technique (PERT)
Project
Project binder
Project charter
Project initiation
Project management
Project manager
Project size
Project sponsor
Reporting structure
Return on investment (ROI)
Risk assessment
Risk management
Risks
Round-trip engineering
Scope creep
Simple actors
Simple use case
Special issues
Staffing plan
Stakeholder
Stakeholder analysis
Standards

Storming stage
Strategic alignment
System request
System users
Tangible benefits
Tangible value
Task
Task dependency
Technical complexity factor (TCF)
Technical factor value (TFactor)
Technical feasibility
Technical lead
Technical risk analysis
Technical skills
Technostress
Timeboxing
Traceability
Trade-offs
Unadjusted actor weight total (UAW)
Unadjusted use-case points (UUCP)
Unadjusted use-case weight total (UUCW)
Use case
Use-case points
Version controls
Work breakdown structure (WBS)
Workplan

QUESTIONS

1. Give three examples of business needs for a system.
2. What is the purpose of an approval committee? Who is usually on this committee?
3. Why should the system request be created by a business person as opposed to an IS professional?
4. What is the difference between intangible value and tangible value? Give three examples of each.
5. What are the purposes of the system request and the feasibility analysis? How are they used in the project selection process?
6. Describe two special issues that may be important to list on a system request.

7. Describe the three techniques for feasibility analysis.
8. Describe a risky project in terms of technical feasibility. Describe a project that would *not* be considered risky.
9. What are the steps for assessing economic feasibility? Describe each step.
10. List two intangible benefits. Describe how these benefits can be quantified.
11. List two tangible benefits and two operational costs for a system. How would you determine the values that should be assigned to each item?

12. Explain the net present value and return on investment for a cost–benefit analysis. Why would these calculations be used?
13. What is the break-even point for the project? How is it calculated?
14. What is stakeholder analysis? Discuss three stakeholders that would be relevant for most projects.
15. Why do many projects end up having unreasonable deadlines? How should a project manager react to unreasonable demands?
16. What are the trade-offs that project managers must manage?
17. Compare and contrast the Gantt chart with the network diagram.
18. Some companies hire consulting firms to develop the initial project plans and manage the project but use their own analysts and programmers to develop the system. Why do you think some companies do this?
19. What is a use-case point? For what is it used?
20. What process do we use to estimate systems development based on use cases?
21. Name two ways to identify the tasks that need to be accomplished over the course of a project.
22. What are the problems associated with conventional WBSs?
23. What is an evolutionary WBS? How does it address the problems associated with a conventional WBS?
24. What is an iterative workplan?
25. What is scope creep, and how can it be managed?
26. What is timeboxing, and why is it used?
27. Create a list of potential risks that could affect the outcome of a project.
28. Describe the Kanban method of managing projects.
29. Describe Tuckman's five stages of small group development.
30. Define the five characteristics of a jelled team.
31. Describe the differences between a technical lead and a functional lead. How are they similar?
32. Describe three technical skills and three interpersonal skills that are very important to have on any project.
33. What are the best ways to motivate a team? What are the worst ways?
34. List three techniques to reduce conflict.
35. Describe how to make meetings more effective.
36. Describe three types of standards and provide examples of each.
37. What belongs in the project binder? How is the project binder organized?

EXERCISES

A. Locate a news article in an IT trade magazine (e.g., *Computerworld*) about an organization that is implementing a new computer system. Describe the tangible and intangible value that the organization is likely to realize from the new system.
B. Car dealers have realized how profitable it can be to sell automobiles using the Web. Pretend that you work for a local car dealership that is part of a large chain such as CarMax. Create a system request you might use to develop a Web-based sales system. Remember to list special issues that are relevant to the project.
C. Suppose that you are interested in buying a new computer. Create a cost–benefit analysis that illustrates the return on investment that you would receive from making this purchase. Computer-related websites (e.g., Apple, Dell, and HP) should have real tangible costs that you can include in your analysis. Project your numbers out to include a three-year period and provide the net present value of the final total.
D. The Amazon.com website originally sold books; then the management of the company decided to extend their Web-based system to include other products. How would you have assessed the feasibility of this venture when the idea first came up? How risky would you have considered the project that implemented this idea? Why?
E. Interview someone who works in a large organization and ask him or her to describe the approval process that exists for approving new development projects. What do they think about the process? What are the problems? What are the benefits?
F. Visit a project management website, such as the Project Management Institute (www.pmi.org). Most have links to project management software products, white papers, and research. Examine some of the links for project management to better understand a variety of Internet sites that contain information related to this chapter.
G. Select a specific project management topic such as CASE, project management software, or timeboxing

and search for information on that topic using the Web. Any search engine (e.g., Bing, Google) can provide a starting point for your efforts.

H. Pretend that the career services office at your university wants to develop a system that collects student résumés and makes them available to students and recruiters over the Web. Students should be able to input their résumé information into a standard résumé template. The information then is presented in a résumé format, and it is also placed in a database that can be queried using an online search form. You have been put in charge of the project. Develop a plan for estimating the project. How long do you think it would take for you and three other students to complete the project? Provide support for the schedule that you propose.

I. Refer to the situation in exercise H. You have been told that recruiting season begins a month from today and that the new system must be used. How would you approach this situation? Describe what you can do as the project manager to make sure that your team does not burn out from unreasonable deadlines and commitments.

J. Consider the system described in exercise H. Create a workplan listing the tasks that will need to be completed to meet the project's objectives. Create a Gantt chart and a network diagram in a project management tool (e.g., Microsoft Project) or using a spreadsheet package to graphically show the high-level tasks of the project.

K. Suppose that you are in charge of the project that is described in exercise H and the project will be staffed by members of your class. Do your classmates have all the right skills to implement such a project? If not, how will you go about making sure that the proper skills are available to get the job done?

L. Complete a use-case point worksheet to estimate the effort to build the system described in exercises H, I, J, and K. You will need to make assumptions regarding the actors, the use cases, and the technical complexity and environmental factors.

M. Consider the application that is used at your school to register for classes. Complete a use-case point worksheet to estimate the effort to build such an application. You will need to make some assumptions about the application's interfaces and the various factors that affect its complexity.

N. Pretend that your instructor has asked you and two friends to create a Web page to describe the course to potential students and provide current class information (e.g., syllabus, assignments, and readings) to current students. You have been assigned the role of leader, so you will need to coordinate your activities and those of your classmates until the project is completed. Describe how you would apply the project management techniques that you have learned in this chapter in this situation. Include descriptions of how you would create a workplan, staff the project, and coordinate all activities—yours and those of your classmates.

O. Select two project management software packages and research them using the Web or trade magazines. Describe the features of the two packages. If you were a project manager, which one would you use to help support your job? Why?

P. In 1997, Oxford Health Plans had a computer problem that caused the company to overestimate revenue and underestimate medical costs. Problems were caused by the migration of its claims processing system from the Pick operating system to a UNIX-based system that uses Oracle database software and hardware from Pyramid Technology. As a result, Oxford's stock price plummeted, and fixing the system became the number one priority for the company. Suppose that you have been placed in charge of managing the repair of the claims processing system. Obviously, the project team will not be in good spirits. How will you motivate team members to meet the project's objectives?

MINICASES

1. The Amberssen Specialty Company is a chain of twelve retail stores that sell a variety of imported gift items, gourmet chocolates, cheeses, and wines in the Toronto area. Amberssen has an IS staff of three people who have created a simple but effective information system of networked point-of-sale registers at the stores and a centralized accounting system at the company headquarters. Harry Hilman, the head of Amberssen's IS group, has just received the following memo from Bill Amberssen, Sales Director (and son of Amberssen's founder).

    Harry—it's time Amberssen Specialty launched itself on the Internet. Many of our competitors are already there, selling to customers without the expense of a retail storefront, and we should be there too. I project that we could double or triple our annual revenues by selling our products on the Internet. I'd like to have this ready by Thanksgiving, in time for the prime holiday gift-shopping season. Bill

After pondering this memo for several days, Harry scheduled a meeting with Bill so that he could clarify Bill's vision of this venture. Using the standard content of a system request as your guide, prepare a list of questions that Harry needs to have answered about this project.

2. The Decker Company maintains a fleet of ten service trucks and crews that provide a variety of plumbing, heating, and cooling repair services to residential customers. Currently, it takes on average about six hours before a service team responds to a service request. Each truck and crew averages twelve service calls per week, and the average revenue earned per service call is $150. Each truck is in service fifty weeks per year. Owing to the difficulty in scheduling and routing, there is considerable slack time for each truck and crew during a typical week.

In an effort to more efficiently schedule the trucks and crews and improve their productivity, Decker management is evaluating the purchase of a prewritten routing and scheduling software package. The benefits of the system will include reduced response time to service requests and more productive service teams, but management is having trouble quantifying these benefits.

One approach is to make an estimate of how much service response time will decrease with the new system, which then can be used to project the increase in the number of service calls made each week. For example, if the system permits the average service response time to fall to four hours, management believes that each truck will be able to make sixteen service calls per week on average—an increase of four calls per week. With each truck making four additional calls per week and the average revenue per call at $150, the revenue increase per truck per week is $600 (4 × $150). With ten trucks in service fifty weeks per year, the average annual revenue increase will be $300,000 ($600 × 10 × 50).

Decker Company management is unsure whether the new system will enable response time to fall to four hours on average or if it will be some other number. Therefore, management has developed the following range of outcomes that may be possible outcomes of

the new system, along with probability estimates of each outcome's occurrence.

New Response Time	# Calls/Truck/Week	Likelihood
2 hours	20	20%
3 hours	18	30%
4 hours	16	50%

Given these figures, prepare a spreadsheet model that computes the expected value of the annual revenues to be produced by using this new system.

3. Emily Pemberton is an IS project manager facing a difficult situation. Emily works for the First Trust Bank, which has recently acquired the City National Bank. Before the acquisition, First Trust and City National were bitter rivals, fiercely competing for market share in the region. Following the acrimonious takeover, numerous staff were laid off in many banking areas, including IS. Key individuals were retained from both banks' IS areas, however, and were assigned to a new consolidated IS department. Emily has been made project manager for the first significant IS project since the takeover, and she faces the task of integrating staffers from both banks on her team. The project they are undertaking will be highly visible within the organization, and the time frame for the project is somewhat demanding. Emily believes that the team can meet the project goals successfully, but success will require that the team become cohesive quickly and that potential conflicts be avoided. What strategies do you suggest that Emily implement in order to help ensure a successfully functioning project team?

4. Tom, Jan, and Julie are IS majors at Great State University. These students have been assigned a class project by one of their professors, requiring them to develop a new Web-based system to collect and update information on the IS program's alumni. This system will be used by the IS graduates to enter job and address information as they graduate and then make changes to that information as they change jobs and/or addresses. Their professor also has a number of queries that she is interested in being able to implement. Based on their preliminary discussions with their professor, the students have determined that the only actor is an IS graduate. They identified one simple use case, four average use cases, and two complex use cases. You need to assign reasonable values to each of the technical complexity and environmental factors. Calculate the effort for this project.

5. In looking for a capstone project for your final MIS course, you found a possible project. The master gardeners in Blint County have created a database of all of the plants in their arboretum. The database is actually a spreadsheet created by one of the volunteers. Along with providing a plant inventory, it is used to print labels of all of the plants that the other master gardeners grow for the annual plant. More than 5,000 plants are supplied each year by 100 gardeners from their home gardens. Because the type and numbers of plants change each year and because the members e-mail the information in varying formats, label printing has become an onerous task. Pam, who prints the labels each year, wants help in making this task manageable. She provided an example of a typical e-mail as well as the type of information she needs.

E-mail
Lilies—labels needed 32–
Lilium lancifolium / lilium tigrinum
Tiger Lily perennial light shade 4′

Ice plant (pink)—labels needed 3
Delosperma cooperi Hardy Ice Plant succulent full sun 2–5″

Information for Labels
Botanical Name
    Common Name
Plant Type
Light Requirement
Height and Width

In order to have this accepted as your project, you need to form a team with the necessary skills and to create a systems request. How would you approach this project? What additional information do you need from Pam in order to begin estimating the scope of this project? Assuming that you have received this information, create a systems request. Also create a list of skills needed, the number of team members required, and a project plan.

PART ONE
ANALYSIS MODELING

Analysis modeling answers the questions of *who* will use the system, *what* the system will do, and *where* and *when* it will be used. During analysis, detailed requirements are identified and a system proposal is created. The team then produces the functional models (use-case diagrams, activity diagrams, and use-case descriptions), structural models (CRC cards and class diagrams, and object diagrams), and behavioral models (activity and sequence diagrams, a CRUDE matrix, and behavioral state machines).

CHAPTER 6 Behavioral Modeling

CHAPTER 3

REQUIREMENTS DETERMINATION

O ne of the first activities of an analyst is to determine the business requirements for a new system. This chapter begins by presenting how to analyze requirements using requirements analysis approaches and how to gather requirements using interviews, questionnaires, observation, and document analysis. The chapter next describes a set of approaches to perform text analysis on all of the material gathered. It then describes the requirements definition, along with user stories, as a way to document the new system's requirements. Finally, the chapter describes the system proposal document that pulls everything together.

OBJECTIVES

- Become familiar with requirements-analysis approaches.
- Understand when to use each requirements-analysis approach.
- Understand how to gather requirements using interviews, questionnaires, observation, and document analysis.
- Understand how sentence diagramming and ethnographic analysis can be used to uncover the actual system requirements.
- Understand how to create a requirements definition.
- Understand the use of user stories as an alternative to a formal requirements definition.
- Be able to begin creating a system proposal.

INTRODUCTION

The systems development process aids an organization in moving from the current system (often called the *as-is system*) to the new system (often called the *to-be system*). The output of planning, discussed in Chapter 2, is the system request, which provides general ideas for the to-be system, defines the project scope, and provides the initial workplan. Analysis takes the general ideas in the system request and refines them into a detailed requirements definition (this chapter), functional models (Chapter 4), structural models (Chapter 5), and behavioral models (Chapter 6) that together form the *system proposal*. The system proposal also includes revised project management deliverables, such as the feasibility analysis and the workplan (Chapter 2).

The output of analysis, the system proposal, is presented to the approval committee, which decides if the project is to continue. If approved, the system proposal moves into design, and its elements (requirements definition and functional, structural, and behavioral models) are used as inputs to the steps in design. This further refines them and defines in much more detail how the system will be built.

The line between analysis and design is very blurry. This is because the deliverables created during analysis are really the first step in the design of the new system. Many of the major design decisions for the new system are found in the analysis deliverables. It is important to remember that the deliverables from analysis are really the first step in the design of the new system.

In many ways, because it is here that the major elements of the system first emerge, the requirements-determination step is the single most critical step of the entire systems development process. During requirements determination, the system is easy to change because little work has been done yet. As the system moves through the systems development process, it becomes harder and harder to return to requirements determination and to make major changes because of all of the rework that is involved. Several studies have shown that more than half of all system failures are due to problems with the requirements.[1] This is why the iterative approaches of object-oriented methodologies are so effective—small batches of requirements can be identified and implemented in incremental stages, allowing the overall system to evolve over time.

REQUIREMENTS DETERMINATION

The purpose of *requirements determination* is to turn the very high-level explanation of the business requirements stated in the system request into a more precise list of requirements that can be used as inputs to the rest of analysis (creating functional, structural, and behavioral models). This expansion of the requirements ultimately leads to the design of the system.

Defining a Requirement

A *requirement* is simply a statement of what the system must do or what characteristic it must have. During analysis, requirements are written from the perspective of the businessperson, and they focus on the "what" of the system. Because they focus on the needs of the business user, they are usually called *business requirements* (and sometimes user requirements). Later in design, business requirements evolve to become more technical, and they describe how the system will be implemented. Requirements in design are written from the developer's perspective, and they are usually called *system requirements*.

We want to stress that there is no black-and-white line dividing a business requirement and a system requirement—and some companies use the terms interchangeably. The important thing to remember is that a requirement is a statement of what the system must do, and requirements will change over time as the project moves from inception to elaboration to construction. Requirements evolve from detailed statements of the business capabilities that a system should have to detailed statements of the technical way the capabilities will be implemented in the new system.

Requirements can be either functional or nonfunctional in nature. A *functional requirement* relates directly to a process a system has to perform or information it needs to contain. For example, requirements stating that a system must have the ability to search for available inventory or to report actual and budgeted expenses are functional requirements. Functional requirements flow directly into the creation of functional, structural, and behavioral models that represent the functionality of the evolving system (see Chapters 4, 5, and 6). Functional requirements are essentially the business requirements uncovered as part of modeling the problem domain.

Nonfunctional requirements refer to behavioral properties that the system must have, such as performance and usability. The ability to access the system using a Web browser is

---

[1] For example, see *The Scope of Software Development Project Failures* (Dennis, MA: The Standish Group, 1995).

considered a nonfunctional requirement. Nonfunctional requirements can influence the rest of analysis (functional, structural, and behavioral models) but often do so only indirectly; nonfunctional requirements are used primarily in design when decisions are made about the database, the user interface, the hardware and software, and the system's underlying physical architecture.

Nonfunctional requirements describe a variety of characteristics regarding the system: operational, performance, security, and cultural and political. Operational requirements address issues related to the physical and technical requirements in which the system will operate. Performance requirements address issues related to the speed, capacity, and reliability of the system. Cultural and political requirements deal with issues related to the cultural and political factors and legal requirements that affect the system. Security requirements deal with issues with regard to who has access to the system, what type of access, and under what specific circumstances. In today's world of cyberwar, denial of service attacks, malware, phishing, ransomware, social engineering, spyware, Trojan horses, and many other types of security threats, the security requirements have become the most important of the nonfunctional requirements. Given that nonfunctional requirements do not describe business processes or information, in many cases, they have been ignored. However, if a system is to be deployed successfully, all of these requirements must be addressed. For pedagogical purposes, we delay addressing these requirements in detail until later in the book when we discuss design (see Chapters 8, 9, 10, and 11) and construction (see Chapter 12).

One area of information systems development that focused on differentiating functional and nonfunctional requirements is *software quality*. There have been many different models proposed to measure the quality of software. However, virtually all of them differentiate functional and nonfunctional requirements. From a quality perspective, *functional* quality is related to the degree that the software meets the functional requirements, that is, how much of the actual problem is solved by the software solution provided, whereas, the nonfunctional requirements are associated with the efficiency, maintainability, portability, reliability, reusability, testability, and usability quality dimensions.

When considering ISO 9000 compliance, quality dimensions are further decomposed into those that the user can see (*external*) and those that the user cannot see (*internal*). The external nonfunctional dimensions include efficiency, reliability, and usability, whereas the internal nonfunctional dimensions include maintainability, portability, reusability, and testability. From a user perspective, the external dimensions are more important. If the system is simply too difficult to use, regardless of how well the system solves the problem, the user will simply not use the system. In other words, from a user's perspective, for an information system to be successful, the system must not only meet the functional specification, but it must also meet the external nonfunctional specifications. From a developer's perspective, the internal dimensions are also important. For example, given that successful systems tend to be long-lived and multiplatform, both the maintainability and portability dimensions can have strategic implications for the system being developed. Also, given the *agile* development approaches being used in industry today, the development of reusable and testable software is crucial.

Three additional topics that have influenced information systems requirements are the Sarbanes–Oxley Act, COBIT (Control OBjectives for Information and related Technology) compliance, and Capability Maturity Model compliance. Depending on the system being considered, these three topics could affect the definition of a system's functional requirements, nonfunctional requirements, or both. The Sarbanes–Oxley Act, for example, mandates additional functional and nonfunctional requirements. These include additional security concerns (nonfunctional) and specific information requirements that management must now provide (functional). When developing financial information systems, information system developers should be sure to include Sarbanes–Oxley expertise in the development team. Moreover, a client could insist on COBIT compliance or that a specific Capability Maturity Model level had been reached in order for the firm to be considered as a possible vendor to supply the system under consideration. Obviously, these types of requirements add to the nonfunctional requirements. Further discussion of these topics is beyond the scope of this book.[2]

Another recent topic that influences requirements for some systems is globalization. For example, a global information supply chain generates a large number of additional nonfunctional requirements. If the necessary operational environments do not exist for a mobile solution to be developed, it is important to adapt the solution to the local environment. Or, it may not be reasonable to expect to deploy a high-technology-based solution in an area that does not have the necessary power and communications infrastructure. In some cases, we may need to consider supporting some parts of the global information supply chain with manual—rather than automated—systems.

Manual systems have an entirely different set of requirements that create different performance expectations and additional security concerns. Furthermore, cultural and political concerns are potentially paramount. A simple example that affects the design of user interfaces is the proper use of color on forms (on a screen or paper). Different cultures interpret different colors differently. In other words, in a global, multicultural business environment, addressing cultural concerns goes well beyond simply having a multilingual user interface. We must be able to adapt the global solution to the local realities. Friedman refers to these concerns as glocalization.[3] Otherwise, we will simply create another example of a failed information systems development project.

Real-World Problems with Requirements Determination

Avison and Fitzgerald provide us with a set of problems that can arise with regard to determining the set of requirements with which to be dealt.[4] First, the analyst might not have access to the correct set of users to uncover the complete set of requirements. This can lead to requirements being missed, misrepresented, and/or over-specified. Second, the specification of the requirements may be inadequate. This can be especially true with the lightweight techniques associated with agile methodologies. Third, some requirements are simply unknowable at the beginning of a development process. However, as the system is developed, the users and analysts will get a better understanding of both the domain issues and the applicable technology. This can cause new functional and nonfunctional requirements to be identified and current requirements to evolve or be canceled. Iterative and incremental-based development methodologies, such as the Unified Process and agile, can help in this case. Fourth, verifying and validating of requirements can be very difficult. We take up this topic in the chapters that deal with the creation of functional (Chapter 4), structural (Chapter 5), and behavioral (Chapter 6) models.

---

[2] A concise discussion of the Sarbanes–Oxley Act is presented in G. P. Lander, *What Is Sarbanes-Oxley?* (New York: McGraw-Hill, 2004). A good reference for Sarbanes–Oxley Act-based security requirements is D. C. Brewer, *Security Controls for Sarbanes-Oxley Section 404 IT Compliance: Authorization, Authentication, and Access* (Indianapolis, IN: Wiley, 2006). For detailed information on COBIT, see www.isaca.org; for ISO 9000, see www.iso.org; and for details on the Capability Maturity Model, see www.sei.cmu.edu/cmmi/.

[3] T. L. Friedman, *The World Is Flat: A Brief History of the Twenty-First Century, Updated and Expanded Edition* (New York: Farrar, Straus, and Giroux, 2006).

[4] See D. Avison and G. Fitzgerald, *Information Systems Development: Methodologies, Techniques, & Tools*, 4th Ed. (London: McGraw-Hill, 2006).

REQUIREMENTS ANALYSIS APPROACHES

Before the project team can determine what requirements are appropriate for a given system, there needs to be a clear vision of the kind of system that will be created and the level of change that it will bring to the organization. The basic process of *analysis* is divided into three steps: understanding the as-is system, identifying improvements, and developing requirements for the to-be system.

Sometimes the first step (i.e., understanding the as-is system) is skipped or is performed in a cursory manner. This happens when no current system exists, if the existing system and processes are irrelevant to the future system, or if the project team is using a RAD or agile development methodology in which the as-is system is not emphasized. Newer RAD, agile, and object-oriented methodologies, such as phased development, prototyping, throwaway prototyping, extreme programming, and Scrum (see Chapter 1), focus almost exclusively on improvements and the to-be system requirements, and they spend little time investigating the current as-is system.

Requirements analysis approaches help the analyst lead users through the analysis steps so that the vision of the system can be developed. Requirements analysis approaches and requirements-gathering techniques go hand in hand. Analysts use requirements-gathering techniques to collect information; requirements analysis approaches drive the kind of information that is gathered and how it is ultimately analyzed. The requirements analysis approaches and requirements gathering happen concurrently and are complementary activities.

To move the users from the as-is system to the to-be system, an analyst needs strong *critical thinking skills*. Critical thinking is the ability to recognize strengths and weaknesses and recast an idea in an improved form, and critical thinking skills are needed to really understand issues and develop new business processes. Analysts must also have strong *systems thinking skills*. One major misunderstanding is that all IT personnel will have systems thinking skills. But this is not so. Systems thinking skills have to do with the ability to see the whole from the different parts of the "system" where a system could be a biological system; not simply an IT system. Furthermore, it refers to the ability to see across different systems to find possible metaphors and analogies that could be useful in the understanding of the current systems development project. These skills are also needed to thoroughly examine the results of requirements gathering, to identify business requirements, and to translate those requirements into a concept for the new system. Both critical and systems thinking skills are so-called twenty-first century skills that are very difficult to automate.[5]

Problem Analysis

The most straightforward (and probably the most commonly used) requirements-analysis approach is *problem analysis*. Problem analysis means asking the users and managers to identify problems with the as-is system and to describe how to solve them in the to-be system. Most users have a very good idea of the changes they would like to see, and most are quite vocal about suggesting them. Most changes tend to solve problems rather than capitalize on opportunities, but the latter is possible as well. Improvements from problem analysis tend to be small and incremental (e.g., provide more space in which to type the customer's address; provide a new report that currently does not exist).

---

[5] For more information see Joseph E. Aoun, *Robot-Proof: Higher Education in the Age of Artificial Intelligence* (Cambridge, MA: MIT Press, 2017); Cathy N. Davidson, *The New Education: How to Revolutionize the University to Prepare Students for a World in Flux* (New York, NY: Basic Books, 2017); and James Bellanca and Ron Brandt (Eds), *21st Century Skills: Rethinking How Students Learn* (Bloomington, IN: Solution Tree Press, 2010).

This type of improvement often is very effective at improving a system's efficiency or ease of use. However, it often provides only minor improvements in business value—the new system is better than the old, but it may be hard to identify significant monetary benefits from the new system.

Root Cause Analysis

The ideas produced by problem analysis tend to be solutions to problems. All solutions make assumptions about the nature of the problem, assumptions that might or might not be valid. In our experience, users (and most people in general) tend to quickly jump to solutions without fully considering the nature of the problem. Sometimes the solutions are appropriate, but many times they address a *symptom* of the problem, not the true problem or *root cause* itself.[6]

For example, suppose a firm notices that its users report inventory stock-outs. The cost of inventory stock-outs can be quite significant. In this case, since they happen frequently, customers could find another source for the items that they are purchasing from the firm. It is in the firm's interest to determine the underlying cause and not simply provide a knee-jerk reaction such as arbitrarily increasing the amount of inventory kept on hand. In the business world, the challenge lies in identifying the root cause—few real-world problems are simple. The users typically propose a set of causes for the problem under consideration. The solutions that users propose can address either symptoms or root causes, but without a careful analysis, it is difficult to tell which one is addressed.

Root cause analysis, therefore, focuses on problems, not solutions. The analyst starts by having the users generate a list of problems with the current system and then prioritize the problems in order of importance. Starting with the most important, the users and/or the analysts then generate all the possible root causes for the problems. Each possible root cause is investigated (starting with the most likely or easiest to check) until the true root causes are identified. If any possible root causes are identified for several problems, those should be investigated first, because there is a good chance they are the real root causes influencing the symptom problems. In our example, there are several possible root causes:

- The firm's supplier might not be delivering orders to the firm in a timely manner.
- There could be a problem with the firm's inventory controls.
- The reorder level and quantities could be set wrong.

Sometimes, using a *fishbone diagram* to represent the causal relationships helps with the analysis. Fishbone diagrams were developed in the quality control area.[7] The causes are shown as "bones" off of the "spine" of the fish while the effect is shown as the "head" of the fish on the far-right side of the diagram. As Figure 3-1 shows, there are many possible root causes that underlie the higher-level causes identified. The key point in root cause analysis is always to challenge the obvious.

Duration Analysis

Duration analysis requires a detailed examination of the amount of time it takes to perform each process in the current as-is system. The analysts begin by determining the total amount of time it takes, on average, to perform a set of business processes for a typical input. They

---

[6] Two good books that discuss the difficulty in finding the root causes to problems are: E. M. Goldratt and J. Cox, *The Goal* (Croton-on-Hudson, NY: North River Press, 1986); and E. M. Goldratt, *The Haystack Syndrome* (Croton-on-Hudson, NY: North River Press, 1990).

[7] Kaoru Ishikawa, *Guide to Quality Control* (Tokyo: 1982)

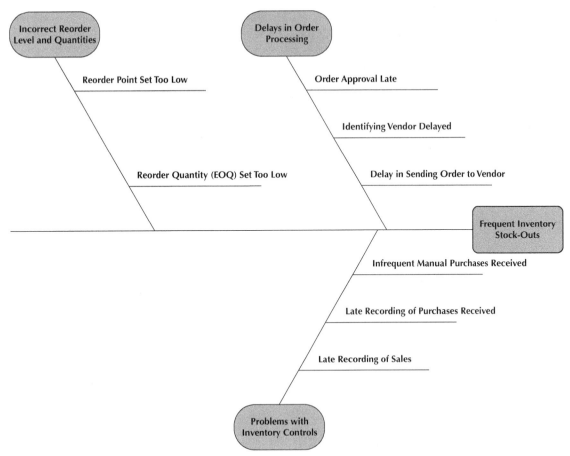

FIGURE 3-1 Root Cause Analysis for Inventory Stock-Outs

then time each of the individual steps (or subprocesses) in the business process. The time to complete the basic step is then totaled and compared to the total for the overall process. A significant difference between the two—and in our experience the total time often can be 10 or even 100 times longer than the sum of the parts—indicates that this part of the process is badly in need of a major overhaul.

For example, suppose that the analysts are working on a home mortgage system and discover that on average, it takes thirty days for the bank to approve a mortgage. They then look at each of the basic steps in the process (e.g., data entry, credit check, title search, and appraisal) and find that the total amount of time actually spent on each mortgage is about eight hours. This is a strong indication that the overall process is badly broken, because it takes thirty days to perform one day's work.

These problems probably occur because the process is badly fragmented. Many different people must perform different activities before the process finishes. In the mortgage example, the application probably sits on many people's desks for long periods of time before it is processed.

Processes in which many different people work on small parts of the inputs are prime candidates for *process integration* or *parallelization*. Process integration means changing the fundamental process so that fewer people work on the input, which often requires changing the processes and retraining staff to perform a wider range of duties. Process parallelization means changing the process so that all the individual steps are performed at the same time. For example, in the mortgage application case, there is probably no reason that the credit check cannot be performed at the same time as the appraisal and title check.

Activity-Based Costing

Activity-based costing is a similar analysis; it examines the cost of each major process or step in a business process rather than the time taken.[8] The analysts identify the costs associated with each of the basic functional steps or processes, identify the most costly processes, and focus their improvement efforts on them.

Assigning costs is conceptually simple. Analysts simply examine the direct cost of labor and materials for each input. Material costs are easily assigned in a manufacturing process, whereas labor costs are usually calculated based on the amount of time spent on the input and the hourly cost of the staff. However, as you may recall from a managerial accounting course, there are indirect costs, such as rent, depreciation, and so on, that also can be included in activity costs.

Informal Benchmarking

Benchmarking refers to studying how other organizations perform a business process in order to learn how your organization can do something better. Benchmarking helps the organization by introducing ideas that employees may never have considered but that have the potential to add value.

Informal benchmarking is fairly common for customer-facing business processes (i.e., processes that interact with the customer). With *informal benchmarking*, the managers and analysts think about other organizations or visit them as customers to watch how the business process is performed. In many cases, the business studied may be a known leader in the industry or simply a related firm.

Outcome Analysis

Outcome analysis focuses on understanding the fundamental outcomes that provide value to customers. Although these outcomes sound as though they should be obvious, they often are not. For example, consider an insurance company. One of its customers has just had a car accident. What is the fundamental outcome from the *customer's* perspective? Traditionally, insurance companies have answered this question by assuming the customer wants to receive the insurance payment quickly. To the customer, however, the payment is only a *means* to the real outcome: a repaired car. The insurance company might benefit by extending its view of the business process past its traditional boundaries to include not paying for repairs but performing the repairs or contracting with an authorized body shop to do them.

With this approach, system analysts encourage the managers and project sponsor to pretend they are customers and to think carefully about what the organization's products and services enable the customers to do—and what they *could* enable the customers to do.

A variation of outcome analysis is *givens-means-ends (GME) analysis*.[9] The primary difference between regular outcome analysis and GME analysis is that GME also considers the givens that the analyst must consider. Effectively, a given is a constraint that cannot be

---

[8] Many books have been written on activity-based costing. Useful ones include K. B. Burk and D. W. Webster, *Activity-Based Costing* (Fairfax, VA: American Management Systems, 1994); D. T. Hicks, *Activity-Based Costing: Making It Work for Small and Mid-sized Companies* (New York: Wiley, 1998). The two books by Eli Goldratt mentioned previously (*The Goal* and *The Haystack Syndrome*) also offer unique insights into costing.

[9] GME analysis has been developed in organizational research with regards to analyzing cognitive maps and in cognitive psychology with research dealing with problem solving and more recently with cognitive load theory.

changed to affect the outcome (end). Only the means can be modified to effect any change in the outcome. For example, if the leadership of an organization cannot change, then the current leadership will either be a positive or negative driver on possible means that can be used to reach the desired goal or end, that is, the leadership is a constraint. Knowing the actual constraints that can affect a solution is useful.

Technology Analysis

Many major changes in business since the turn of the century have been enabled by new technologies. *Technology analysis* starts by having the analysts and managers develop a list of important and interesting technologies. Then the group systematically identifies how every technology could be applied to the business process and identifies how the business would benefit. It is important to note that the technology analysis in no way implies adopting technology for technology's sake. Rather the focus is on using new technologies to meet the goals of the organization.

Activity Elimination

Activity elimination is exactly what it sounds like. The analysts and managers work together to identify how the organization could eliminate each activity in the business process, how the function could operate without it, and what effects are likely to occur. Initially, managers are reluctant to conclude that processes can be eliminated, but this is a force-fit exercise in that they must eliminate each activity. In some cases, the results are silly; nonetheless, participants must address every activity in the business process.

REQUIREMENTS-GATHERING TECHNIQUES

An analyst is very much like a detective (and business users are sometimes like elusive suspects). He or she knows that there is a problem to be solved and therefore must look for clues that uncover the solution. Unfortunately, the clues are not always obvious (and are often missed), so the analyst needs to notice details, talk with witnesses, and follow leads just as Sherlock Holmes would have done. The best analysts thoroughly gather requirements using a variety of techniques and make sure that the current business processes and the needs for the new system are well understood before moving into design. Analysts don't want to discover later that they have key requirements wrong—such surprises late in the development process can cause all kinds of problems.

The requirements-gathering process is used for building political support for the project and establishing trust and rapport between the project team building the system and the users who ultimately will choose to use or not use the system. Involving someone in the process implies that the project teams view that person as an important resource and value his or her opinions. All the key stakeholders (the people who can affect the system or who will be affected by the system) must be included in the requirements-gathering process. The stakeholders might include managers, employees, staff members, operations personnel, and even some customers and suppliers. If a key person is not involved, that individual might feel slighted, which can cause problems during implementation (e.g., How could they have developed the system without my input?).

The second challenge of requirements gathering is choosing the way(s) information is collected. There are many techniques for gathering requirements that vary from asking people questions to watching them work. Some other very useful requirements-gathering and documentation techniques include throwaway prototyping, use cases, and role-playing CRC cards with use-case-based scenarios. Throwaway prototyping was described in Chapter 1. In essence, throwaway prototypes are created to better understand some aspects of the new system.

In many cases, they are used to test out some technical aspects of a nonfunctional requirement, such as connecting a client workstation to a server. If you have never done this before, it will be a lot easier to develop a very small example system to test out the necessary design of the connection from the client workstation to the server instead of trying to do it the first time with the full-blown system. Throwaway prototyping is very useful in designing user interfaces (see Chapter 10). Use cases, as described in Chapter 1, are the fundamental approach that the Unified Process and Unified Modeling Language (UML) use to document and gather functional requirements. We describe them in Chapter 4. Role-playing CRC cards with use-case-based scenarios are very useful when creating functional (see Chapter 4), structural (see Chapter 5), and behavioral (see Chapter 6) models. We describe this approach in Chapter 5.

In this section, we focus on the four most commonly used techniques: interviews, questionnaires, observation, and document analysis. Each technique has its own strengths and weaknesses, many of which are complementary, so most projects use a combination of techniques.[10]

Interviews

An *interview* is the most commonly used requirements-gathering technique. After all, it is natural—if you need to know something, you usually ask someone. In general, interviews are conducted one-on-one (one interviewer and one interviewee), but sometimes, owing to time constraints, several people are interviewed at the same time. There are five basic steps to the interview process: selecting interviewees, designing interview questions, preparing for the interview, conducting the interview, and post-interview follow-up.[11]

1. Select Interviewees

The first step in interviewing is to create an *interview schedule* listing who will be interviewed, when, and for what purpose (see Figure 3-2). The schedule can be an informal list that is used to help set up meeting times or a formal list that is incorporated into the workplan. The people who appear on the interview schedule are selected based on the analyst's information needs. The project sponsor, key business users, and other members of the project team can help the analyst determine who in the organization can best provide important information about requirements. These people are listed on the interview schedule in the order in which they should be interviewed.

People at different levels of the organization have varying perspectives on the system, so it is important to include both managers who manage the processes and staff who actually perform the processes to gain both high-level and low-level perspectives on an issue. Also, the kinds of interview subjects need can change over time. For example, at the start of the project, the analyst has a limited understanding of the as-is business process. It is common to begin by interviewing one or two senior managers to get a strategic view and then to move to midlevel managers who can provide broad, overarching information about the business process and the expected role of the system being developed. Once the analyst has a good understanding of the big picture, lower-level managers and staff members can fill in the exact details of how the process works. Like most other things about systems analysis, this is an iterative process—starting with senior managers, moving to midlevel managers, then staff members, back to midlevel managers, and so on, depending upon what information is needed along the way.

It is quite common for the list of interviewees to grow, often by 50 to 75 percent. As people are interviewed, more information that is needed and additional people who can provide the information will probably be identified.

[10] Some excellent books that address the importance of gathering requirements and various techniques include Alan M. Davis, *Software Requirements: Objects, Functions, & States, Revision* (Englewood Cliffs, NJ: Prentice Hall, 1993); Gerald Kotonya and Ian Sommerville, *Requirements Engineering* (Chichester, England: Wiley, 1998); and Dean Leffingwell and Don Widrig, *Managing Software Requirements: A Unified Approach* (Reading, MA: Addison-Wesley, 2000).

[11] A good book on interviewing is that by Brian James, *The Systems Analysis Interview* (Manchester, England: NCC Blackwell, 1989).

Name	Position	Purpose of Interview	Meeting
Andria McClellan	Director, Accounting	Strategic vision for new accounting system	Mon., March 1 8:00–10:00 AM
Jennifer Draper	Manager, Accounts Receivable	Current problems with accounts receivable process; future goals	Mon., March 1 2:00–3:15 PM
Mark Goodin	Manager, Accounts Payable	Current problems with accounts payable process; future goals	Mon., March 1 4:00–5:15 PM
Anne Asher	Supervisor, Data Entry	Accounts receivable and payable processes	Wed., March 3 10:00–11:00 AM
Fernando Merce	Data Entry Clerk	Accounts receivable and payable processes	Wed., March 3 1:00–3:00 PM

FIGURE 3-2
Sample Interview
Schedule

**2. Design
Interview Questions**

There are three types of interview questions: closed-ended questions, open-ended questions, and probing questions. *Closed-ended questions* are those that require a specific answer. They are similar to multiple-choice or arithmetic questions on an exam (see Figure 3-3). Closed-ended questions are used when an analyst is looking for specific, precise information (e.g., how many credit card requests are received per day). In general, precise questions are the best. For example, rather than asking, Do you handle a lot of requests? it is better to ask, How many requests do you process per day? Closed-ended questions enable analysts to control the interview and obtain the information they need. However, these types of questions don't uncover *why* the answer is the way it is, nor do they uncover information that the interviewer does not think to ask for ahead of time.

Open-ended questions are those that leave room for elaboration on the part of the interviewee. They are similar in many ways to essay questions that you might find on an exam (see Figure 3-3 for examples). Open-ended questions are designed to gather rich information and give the interviewee more control over the information that is revealed during the interview. Sometimes the information that the interviewee chooses to discuss uncovers information that is just as important as the answer (e.g., if the interviewee talks only about other departments when asked for problems, it may suggest that he or she is reluctant to admit his or her own problems).

The third type of question is the *probing question*. Probing questions follow up on what has just been discussed in order to learn more, and they often are used when the interviewer is unclear about an interviewee's answer. They encourage the interviewee to expand on or to confirm information from a previous response, and they signal that the interviewer is listening and is interested in the topic under discussion. Many beginning analysts are reluctant to use probing questions because they are afraid that the interviewee might be offended at being challenged or because they believe it shows that they didn't understand what the interviewee said. When done politely, probing questions can be a powerful tool in requirements gathering.

In general, an interviewer should not ask questions about information that is readily available from other sources. For example, rather than asking what information is used to perform to a task, it is simpler to show the interviewee a form or report (see the section on document analysis) and ask what information on it is used. This helps focus the interviewee on the task and saves time, because the interviewee does not need to describe the information detail—he or she just needs to point it out on the form or report.

No type of question is better than another, and a combination of questions is usually used during an interview. At the initial stage of an IS development project, the as-is process can be unclear, so the interview process begins with *unstructured interviews*, interviews that seek broad and roughly defined information. In this case, the interviewer has a general sense of the information needed but has few closed-ended questions to ask. These are the most challenging interviews to conduct because they require the interviewer to ask open-ended questions and probe for important information on the fly.

As the project progresses, the analyst comes to understand the business process much better and needs very specific information about how business processes are performed (e.g., exactly how a customer credit card is approved). At this time, the analyst conducts *structured interviews*, in which specific sets of questions are developed before the interviews. There usually are more closed-ended questions in a structured interview than in the unstructured approach.

No matter what kind of interview is being conducted, interview questions must be organized into a logical sequence so that the interview flows well. For example, when trying to gather information about the current business process, it can be useful to move in logical order through the process or from the most important issues to the least important.

There are two fundamental approaches to organizing the interview questions: top down or bottom up (see Figure 3-4). With the *top-down interview*, the interviewer starts with broad, general issues and gradually works toward more-specific ones. With the *bottom-up interview*, the interviewer starts with very specific questions and moves to broad questions. In practice, analysts mix the two approaches, starting with broad, general issues, moving to specific questions, and then returning to general issues.

The top-down approach is an appropriate strategy for most interviews (it is certainly the most common approach). The top-down approach enables the interviewee to become accustomed to the topic before he or she needs to provide specifics. It also enables the interviewer to understand the issues before moving to the details because the interviewer might not have sufficient information at the start of the interview to ask very specific questions. Perhaps most importantly, the top-down approach enables the interviewee to raise a set of big-picture issues before becoming enmeshed in details, so the interviewer is less likely to miss important issues.

One case in which the bottom-up strategy may be preferred is when the analyst has already gathered a lot of information about issues and just needs to fill in some holes with details. Bottom-up interviewing may be appropriate if lower-level staff members feel threatened or unable to answer high-level questions. For example, How can we improve customer service? might be too broad a question for a customer service clerk, whereas a specific question is readily answerable (e.g., How can we speed up customer returns?). In any event, all interviews should begin with noncontroversial questions and then gradually move into more contentious issues after the interviewer has developed some rapport with the interviewee.

Types of Questions	Examples
Closed-ended questions	• How many telephone orders are received per day? • How do customers place orders? • What information is missing from the monthly sales report?
Open-ended questions	• What do you think about the current system? • What are some of the problems you face on a daily basis? • What are some of the improvements you would like to see in a new system?
Probing questions	• Why? • Can you give me an example? • Can you explain that in a bit more detail?

FIGURE 3-3
Three Types of
Questions

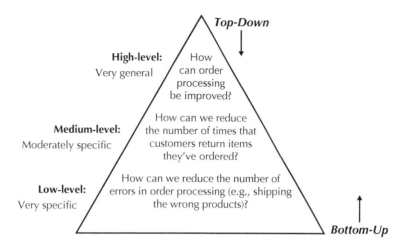

FIGURE 3-4 Top-Down and Bottom-Up Questioning Strategies

3. Prepare for the Interview

It is important to prepare for the interview in the same way that you would prepare to give a presentation. The interviewer should have a general interview plan listing the questions to be asked in the appropriate order, should anticipate possible answers and provide follow-up with them, and should identify segues between related topics. The interviewer should confirm the areas in which the interviewee has knowledge so as not to ask questions that the interviewee cannot answer. Review the topic areas, the questions, and the interview plan, and clearly decide which have the greatest priority in case time runs short.

In general, structured interviews with closed-ended questions take more time to prepare than unstructured interviews. Some beginning analysts prefer unstructured interviews, thinking that they can wing it. This is very dangerous and often counterproductive, because any information not gathered in the first interview will require follow-up efforts, and most users do not like to be interviewed repeatedly about the same issues.

The interviewer should be sure to prepare the interviewee as well. When the interview is scheduled, the interviewee should be told the reason for the interview and the areas that will be discussed far enough in advance so that he or she has time to think about the issues and organize his or her thoughts. This is particularly important when the interviewer is an outsider to the organization and for lower-level employees, who often are not asked for their opinions and who may be uncertain about why they are being interviewed.

4. Conduct the Interview

The first goal is to build rapport with the interviewee, so that he or she trusts the interviewer and is willing to tell the whole truth, not just give the answers that he or she thinks are wanted. The interviewer should appear to be a professional and unbiased independent seeker of information. The interview should start with an explanation of why the interviewer is there and why he or she has chosen to interview the person; then the interviewer should move into the planned interview questions.

It is critical to carefully record all the information that the interviewee provides. In our experience, the best approach is to take careful notes—write down *everything* the interviewee says, even if it does not appear immediately relevant. The interviewer shouldn't be afraid to ask the person to slow down or to pause while writing, because this is a clear indication that the interviewee's information is important. One potentially controversial issue is whether or not to tape-record an interview. Recording ensures that the interviewer does not miss important points, but it can be intimidating for the interviewee. Most organizations have policies or generally accepted practices about the recording of interviews, so they should be determined before an interview. If the interviewer is worried about missing information and cannot tape the interview, then he or she can bring along a second person to take detailed notes.

As the interview progresses, it is important to understand the issues that are discussed. If the interviewer does not understand something, he or she should ask for clarification. The interviewer should not be afraid to ask stupid questions, because the only thing worse than appearing stupid is to be stupid by not understanding something. If the interviewer doesn't understand something during the interview, he or she certainly won't understand it afterward. Jargon should be recognized and defined; any jargon not understood should be clarified. One good strategy to increase understanding during an interview is to periodically summarize the key points that the interviewee is communicating. This avoids misunderstandings and also demonstrates that the interviewer is listening.

Finally, facts should be separated from opinion. The interviewee may say, for example, We process too many credit card requests. This is an opinion, and it is useful to follow this up with a probing question requesting support for the statement (e.g., Oh, how many do you process in a day?). It is helpful to check the facts because any differences between the facts and the interviewee's opinions can point out key areas for improvement. Suppose the interviewee complains about a high or increasing number of errors, but the logs show that errors have been decreasing. This suggests that errors are viewed as a very important problem that should be addressed by the new system, even if they are declining.

As the interview draws to a close, the interviewee should have time to ask questions or provide information that he or she thinks is important but was not part of the interview plan. In most cases, the interviewee has no additional concerns or information, but in some cases this leads to unanticipated, but important, information. Likewise, it can be useful to ask the interviewee if there are other people who should be interviewed. The interview should end on time (if necessary, some topics can be omitted or another interview can be scheduled).

As a last step in the interview, the interviewer should briefly explain what will happen. The interviewer shouldn't prematurely promise certain features in the new system or a specific delivery date, but he or she should reassure the interviewee that his or her time was well spent and very helpful to the project.

One last thing that the interviewer should realize is that an interview is essentially a type of meeting. Consequently, the meeting management issues described in Chapter 2 are relevant.

5. Post-Interview Follow-up

After the interview is over, the analyst needs to prepare an *interview report* that describes the information from the interview (Figure 3-5). The report contains *interview notes*, information that was collected over the course of the interview and is summarized in a useful format. In general, the interview report should be written within forty-eight hours of the interview, because the longer the interviewer waits, the more likely he or she is to forget information.

Often, the interview report is sent to the interviewee with a request to read it and inform the analyst of clarifications or updates. The interviewee needs to be convinced that the interviewer genuinely wants his or her corrections to the report. Usually there are few changes, but the need for any significant changes suggests that a second interview will be required. Never distribute someone's information without prior approval.

Questionnaires

A *questionnaire* is a set of written questions used to obtain information from individuals. Questionnaires are often used when there is a large number of people from whom information and opinions are needed. In our experience, questionnaires are a common technique with systems intended for use outside the organization (e.g., by customers or vendors) or for

Interview Notes Approved by: Linda Estey

Person Interviewed: Linda Estey,
   Director, Human Resources

Interviewer: Barbara Wixom

Purpose of Interview:
- Understand reports produced for Human Resources by the current system
- Determine information requirements for future system

Summary of Interview:
- Sample reports of all current HR reports are attached to this report. The information that is not used and missing information are noted on the reports.
- Two biggest problems with the current system are:
  1. The data are too old (the HR Department needs information within two days of month end; currently, information is provided to them after a three-week delay)
  2. The data are of poor quality (often reports must be reconciled with departmental HR database)
- The most common data errors found in the current system include incorrect job level information and missing salary information.

Open Items:
- Get current employee roster report from Mary Skudrna (extension 4355).
- Verify calculations used to determine vacation time with Mary Skudrna.
- Schedule interview with Jim Wack (extension 2337) regarding the reasons for data quality problems.

Detailed Notes: See attached transcript.

FIGURE 3-5 Interview Report

PRACTICAL	3-1 Developing Interpersonal Skills
TIP	

Interpersonal skills are skills that enable you to develop rapport with others, and they are very important for interviewing. They help you to communicate with others effectively. Some people develop good interpersonal skills at an early age; they simply seem to know how to communicate and interact with others. Other people are less lucky and need to work hard to develop their skills.

Interpersonal skills, like most skills, can be learned. Here are some tips:

- **Don't worry, be happy.** Happy people radiate confidence and project their feelings on others. Try interviewing someone while smiling and then interviewing someone else while frowning and see what happens.
- **Pay attention.** Pay attention to what the other person is saying (which is harder than you might think). See how many times you catch yourself with your mind on something other than the conversation at hand.
- **Summarize key points.** At the end of each major theme or idea that someone explains, repeat the key points back to the speaker (e.g., Let me make sure I

understand. The key issues are. . . ."). This demonstrates that you consider the information important, and it also forces you to pay attention (you can't repeat what you didn't hear).

- **Be succinct.** When you speak, be succinct. The goal in interviewing (and in much of life) is to learn, not to impress. The more you speak, the less time you give to others.
- **Be honest.** Answer all questions truthfully, and if you don't know the answer, say so.
- **Watch body language (yours and theirs).** The way a person sits or stands conveys much information. In general, a person who is interested in what you are saying sits or leans forward, makes eye contact, and often touches his or her face. A person leaning away from you or with an arm over the back of a chair is uninterested. Crossed arms indicate defensiveness or uncertainty, and steepling (sitting with hands raised in front of the body with fingertips touching) indicates a feeling of superiority.

systems with business users spread across many geographic locations. Most people automatically think of paper when they think of questionnaires, but today more questionnaires are being distributed in electronic form, either via e-mail or on the Web. Electronic distribution can save a significant amount of money as compared to distributing paper questionnaires. A good process to use when using questionnaires follows four steps.

1. Select Participants

As with interviews, the first step is to identify the individuals to whom the questionnaire will be sent. However, it is not usual to select every person who could provide useful information. The standard approach is to select a *sample*, or subset, of people who are representative of an entire group. Sampling guidelines are discussed in most statistics books, and most business schools include courses that cover the topic, so we do not discuss it here. The important point in selecting a sample, however, is to realize that not everyone who receives a questionnaire will actually complete it. On average, only 30 to 50 percent of paper and e-mail questionnaires are returned. Response rates for Web-based questionnaires tend to be significantly lower (often only 5 to 30 percent).

2. Designing a Questionnaire[12]

Because the information on a questionnaire cannot be immediately clarified for a confused respondent, developing good questions is critical for questionnaires. Questions on questionnaires must be very clearly written and leave little room for misunderstanding. Given that questionnaires effectively are surveys, issues related to the reliability and validity of the questionnaire must be taken into consideration. For example, if the answers provided by the participants vary widely, then the reliability of the questionnaire is in doubt. Therefore, the results could be useless. Or worse, if the questionnaire has no validity, the results could be misleading. To ensure validity, the questions should be well balanced in that they cover the entire domain of possible answers and the questions are measuring what they intended to measure. For example, does a multiple-choice exam measure the level of knowledge that a student has attained, or does it actually measure how fast a student can read. If it is the latter, then the multiple-choice exam does not measure the knowledge level attained by the student. Finally, given the low response rates stated above, nonresponse bias should be addressed. Depending on the cause of the nonresponse, the results of the questionnaire could again be misleading.

Questions must clearly enable the analyst to separate facts from opinions. Opinion questions often ask respondents the extent to which they agree or disagree (e.g., Are network problems common?), whereas factual questions seek more precise values (e.g., How often does a network problem occur: once an hour, once a day, once a week?). See Figure 3-6 for guidelines on questionnaire design.

Perhaps the most obvious issue—but one that is sometimes overlooked—is to have a clear understanding of how the information collected from the questionnaire will be analyzed and used. This issue must be addressed before the questionnaire is distributed, because it is too late afterward.

Questions should be relatively consistent in style, so that the respondent does not have to read instructions for each question before answering it. It is generally good practice to group related questions together to make them simpler to answer. Some experts suggest that questionnaires should start with questions important to respondents, so that the questionnaire immediately grabs their interest and induces them to answer it. Perhaps the most important step is to have several colleagues review the questionnaire and then pretest it with a few people drawn from the groups to whom it will be sent. It is surprising how often seemingly simple questions can be misunderstood.

---

[12] A good source for questionnaire design is Floyd J. Fowler, Jr., *Survey Research Methods*, 5th Ed. (Thousand Oaks, CA: Sage Publications, 2014).

- Begin with nonthreatening and interesting questions.
- Group items into logically coherent sections.
- Do not put important items at the very end of the questionnaire.
- Do not crowd a page with too many items.
- Avoid abbreviations.
- Avoid biased or suggestive items or terms.
- Number questions to avoid confusion.
- Pretest the questionnaire to identify confusing questions.
- Provide anonymity to respondents.

FIGURE 3-6
Good Questionnaire
Design

3. Administering the Questionnaire

The key issue in administering the questionnaire is getting participants to complete the questionnaire and send it back. Dozens of marketing research books have been written about ways to improve response rates. Commonly used techniques include clearly explaining why the questionnaire is being conducted and why the respondent has been selected, stating a date by which the questionnaire is to be returned, offering an inducement to complete the questionnaire (e.g., a free pen), and offering to supply a summary of the questionnaire responses. Systems analysts have additional techniques to improve response rates inside the organization, such as personally handing out the questionnaire and personally contacting those who have not returned them after a week or two, as well as requesting the respondents' supervisors to administer the questionnaires in a group meeting.

4. Questionnaire Follow-up

It is helpful to process the returned questionnaires and develop a questionnaire report soon after the questionnaire deadline. This ensures that the analysis process proceeds in a timely fashion and that respondents who requested copies of the results receive them promptly.

Observation

Observation, the act of watching processes being performed, is a powerful tool for gathering information about the as-is system because it enables the analyst to see the reality of a situation, rather than listening to others describe it in interviews. Several research studies have shown that many managers really do not remember how they work and how they allocate their time. (Quick, how many hours did you spend last week on each of your courses?) Observation is a good way to check the validity of information gathered from indirect sources such as interviews and questionnaires.

In many ways, the analyst becomes an anthropologist as he or she walks through the organization and observes the business system as it functions. The goal is to keep a low profile, to not interrupt those working, and to not influence those being observed, that is, to become a *fly on the wall*.[13] This implies that the analyst, in many ways, should strive to become simply a part of the environment having no more effect than a new piece of furniture. Nonetheless, it is important to understand that what analysts observe may not be the normal day-to-day routine because people tend to be extremely careful in their behavior when they are being watched. Even though normal practice may be to break formal organizational rules, the observer is unlikely to see this. (Remember how you drove the last time a police car followed you?) Thus, what you see might *not* be what you get.

---

[13] This term was originally applied by journalists, and later by directors in documentaries, to mean that they needed to be able to get to the truth in a manner that did not affect the ones being watched. Given the Hawthorne effect, this is obviously very difficult to attain.

Observation is often used to supplement interview information. The location of a person's office and its furnishings give clues to the person's power and influence in the organization and can be used to support or refute information given in an interview. For example, an analyst might become skeptical of someone who claims to use the existing computer system extensively if the computer is never turned on while the analyst visits. In most cases, observation supports the information that users provide in interviews. When it does not, it is an important signal that extra care must be taken in analyzing the business system.

When doing an observation, it is critical that good field notes are written immediately after the observation session. Otherwise, the memory of what was observed will begin to fade. In ethnographic research, there are different types of observations that can be made. For example, grand and mini tour, focused, and selected observations can be performed. The purpose of the grand and mini tour observations is to simply allow the observer to get a "feel" for the location. Focused observations narrow the scope of the observation task. For example, where a tour-based observation may only deal with issues such as layout of the office and the overall interrelationships among the individuals being observed, a focused observation uses the categories that the tour-based observations uncovered that need to be investigated in a more detailed manner. These categories could include the objects that are being worked on by the employees, the employees themselves, objects that make up the environment in which the employees work, for example, furniture or machines, tasks being performed by the employees, and the processes in which the tasks make up. Finally, a selected observation drills down even further into what is being observed, for example, attempting to observe the individual steps in a task being performed by a specific employee.[14]

Document Analysis

Project teams often use *document analysis* to understand the as-is system. Under ideal circumstances, the project team that developed the existing system will have produced documentation that was then updated by all subsequent projects. In this case, the project team can start by reviewing the documentation and examining the system itself.

Unfortunately, many systems are not well documented because project teams fail to document their projects along the way, and when the projects are over, there is no time to go back and document. Therefore, there might not be much technical documentation about the current systems available, or it might not contain updated information about recent system changes. However, many helpful documents do exist in an organization: paper reports, memorandums, policy manuals, user-training manuals, organizational charts, forms, and, of course, the user interface with the existing system.

But these documents tell only part of the story. They represent the *formal system* that the organization uses. Quite often, the real, or *informal, system* differs from the formal one, and these differences, particularly large ones, give strong indications of what needs to be changed. For example, forms or reports that are never used should probably be eliminated. Likewise, boxes or questions on forms that are never filled in (or are used for other purposes) should be rethought. See Figure 3-7 for an example of how a document can be interpreted.

The most powerful indication that the system needs to be changed is when users create their own forms or add additional information to existing ones. Such changes clearly demonstrate the need for improvements to existing systems. Thus, it is useful to review both blank and completed forms to identify these deviations. Likewise, when users access multiple

---

[14] For more information, see James P. Spradley, *Participant Observation* (New York, NY: Hold, Rinehart and Winston, 1980); Dennis Wixom and Judith Ramey (Eds), *Field Methods Casebook for Software Design* (New York, NY: John Wiley & Sons, 1996).

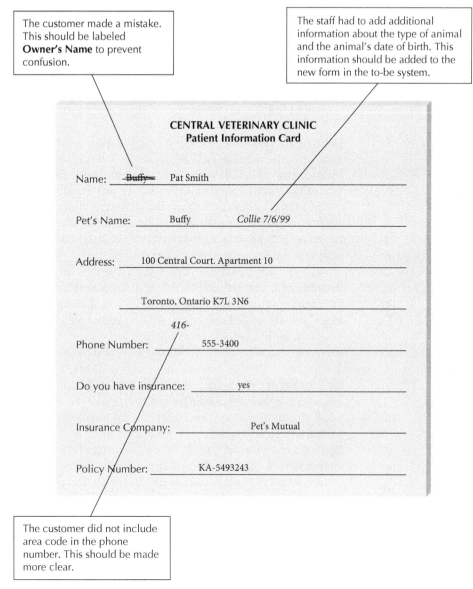

FIGURE 3-7 Performing a Document Analysis

reports to satisfy their information needs, it is a clear sign that new information or new information formats are needed.

Selecting the Appropriate Techniques

Each of the requirements-gathering techniques discussed earlier has strengths and weaknesses. No one technique is always better than the others, and in practice most projects use a combination of techniques. One issue not discussed is that of the analysts' experience. In general, document analysis requires the least amount of training, whereas interviewing, questionnaire development, and observation require extensive training to be effective.

Type of Information The first characteristic is the type of information. Some techniques are more suited for use at different stages of the analysis process, whether understanding the as-is system, identifying improvements, or developing the to-be system. Interviews are commonly used in all three stages. In contrast, document analysis and observation usually are most helpful for understanding the as-is system, although occasionally they provide information about current problems that need to be improved. Questionnaires are often used to gather information about the as-is system as well as general information about improvements.

Depth of Information The depth of information refers to how rich and detailed the information is that the technique usually produces and the extent to which the technique is useful for obtaining not only facts and opinions but also an understanding of *why* those facts and opinions exist. Interviews and observations are very useful for providing a good depth of rich and detailed information and helping the analyst to understand the reasons behind them. At the other extreme, document analysis is useful for obtaining facts, but little beyond that. Questionnaires can provide a medium depth of information, soliciting both facts and opinions with little understanding of why they exist.

Breadth of Information Breadth of information refers to the range of information and information sources that can be easily collected using the chosen technique. Questionnaires and document analysis are both easily capable of soliciting a wide range of information from a large number of information sources. In contrast, interviews and observation require the analyst to visit each information source individually and, therefore, take more time.

Integration of Information One of the most challenging aspects of requirements gathering is integrating the information from different sources. Simply put, different people can provide conflicting information. Combining this information and attempting to resolve differences in opinions or facts is usually very time consuming because it means contacting each information source in turn, explaining the discrepancy, and attempting to refine the information. In many cases, the individual wrongly perceives that the analyst is challenging his or her information, when in fact it is another user in the organization who is doing so. This can make the user defensive and make it hard to resolve the differences. All techniques suffer integration problems to some degree. If two users provide conflicting information, the conflict becomes immediately obvious, as does the source of the conflict.

User Involvement User involvement refers to the amount of time and energy the intended users of the new system must devote to the analysis process. It is generally agreed that as users become more involved in the analysis process, the chance of success increases. However, user involvement can have a significant cost, and not all users are willing to contribute valuable time and energy. Questionnaires, document analysis, and observation place the least burden on users, whereas interviews require the greatest effort.

Cost Cost is always an important consideration. In general, questionnaires, document analysis, and observation are low-cost techniques (although observation can be quite time consuming). The low cost does not imply that they are more or less effective than the other techniques. Interviews generally have moderate costs.

Combining Techniques In practice, requirements gathering combines a series of different techniques. Most analysts start by using interviews with senior manager(s) to gain an understanding of the project and the big-picture issues. From these interviews, it becomes clear whether large or small changes are anticipated. These interviews are often followed with analysis of documents and policies to gain some understanding of the as-is system. Usually interviews come next to gather the rest of the information needed for the as-is picture.

TEXT ANALYSIS

Given that virtually all of the other requirements-gathering techniques produce some type of text report, performing some type of text analysis could be worthwhile. A very useful, but old tool, that can be used to perform some simple text analysis is *sentence diagraming*.[15] This tool was originally designed to aid students to learn English grammar. The tool forces the student to "draw" a sentence using a set of lines that represent the different parts of speech. For example, Figure 3-8 portrays the following sentences as sentence diagrams:

- The patient contacts the office regarding an appointment.
- The receptionist asks the patient for possible appointment times.

By drawing the *sentence diagrams*, it is fairly easy to identify the primary objects of interest. In this case, the objects of interest are patient, office, appointment, and receptionist. We revisit grammar/syntactical text analysis in Chapter 5.

Another useful tool for text analysis is an ethnographic analysis,[16] specifically, performing domain, taxonomic, componential, and theme analysis. The purpose of *domain analysis* is to uncover the objects of interest in the problem domain. Unlike sentence diagramming, which only focuses on the grammar of the text, domain analysis concentrates on the meaning or semantics, and possibly pragmatics, of the objects of interest. Domain analysis begins by trying to identify the semantic relationships among the objects. In most cases, a standard or universal set of semantic relationships is sufficient. Figure 3-9 lists a set of useful universal semantic relationships that can be used as a starting point. However, in some cases these relationships may need to be extended to include problem-domain-specific relationships, for

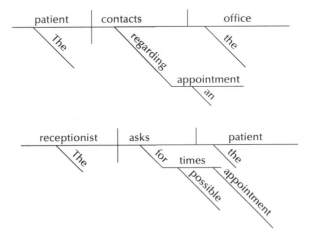

FIGURE 3-8
Sample Sentence
Diagrams

[15] A good reference for sentence diagraming is Cindy L. Vitto, *Grammar by Diagram: Understanding English Grammar Through Traditional Sentence Diagraming* (Peterborough, Ontario: Broadview Press, 2003).

[16] A good reference for this type of analysis is James P. Spradley, *The Ethnographic Interview* (New York, NY: Holt, Rinehart and Winston, 1979).

• Attribution	X is an attribute of Y
• Cause–effect	X is a cause of Y
• Class Inclusion	X is a kind of Y
• Contrasts	X is the opposite of Y
• Means-ends	X is a way to do Y
• Part-Whole	X is a part of Y
• Rationale	X is a reason for doing Y
• Sequence	X is a step in Y
• Similars	X is similar to Y
• Spatial	X is located at Y

Source: James P. Spradley, *The Ethnographic Interview* (New York, NY: Holt, Rinehart and Winston, 1979); Keng Siau, "Relationship Construct in Modeling Information Systems: Identifying Relationships Based on Relation Element Theory," *Journal of Database Management* (Jul–Sep, 2004).

FIGURE 3-9
Sample Universal Semantic Relationships

example, in some problem domains it may be more useful to use a set-theoretic-based relationship instead of the more generic part-whole relationship.

Taxonomic analysis builds up a node and arc type of graph by using the semantic relationships to connect the different objects of interest in the problem domain. Figure 3-10 portrays a partial taxonomy for an appointment system where a doctor is a kind of employee, an appointment is located at the office, the medical history is an attribute of a patient, and so on. By modeling the objects of interest using the semantic relationships, a taxonomy of the problem domain is created.

Where taxonomic analysis focuses on the creation of a taxonomy, *componential analysis* specifically focuses on the attribution semantic relationship. For example, a doctor may have a set of attributes that include first name, last name, home address, office address, and a specialty, among others. Finally, *theme analysis* attempts to identify any underlying themes that were uncovered during the requirements-gathering process. A theme represents any assumptions that are tacit or explicit in the problem domain. In many cases, by reviewing all of the objects of interest and semantic relationships in the taxonomy, themes can be identified by simply reading the various combinations of nodes and arcs in the taxonomy.

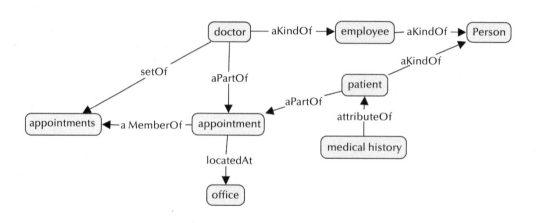

FIGURE 3-10
Sample Taxonomy

REQUIREMENTS DEFINITION

The requirements definition report—usually just called the *requirements definition*—is a straightforward text report that simply lists the functional and nonfunctional requirements in an outline format. Determining requirements for the requirements definition is both a business task and an information technology task. In the early days of computing, there was a presumption that the systems analysts, as experts with computer systems, were in the best position to define how a computer system should operate. Many systems failed because they did not adequately address the true business needs of the users. Gradually, the presumption changed so that the users, as the business experts, were seen as being the best position to define how a computer system should operate. However, many systems failed to deliver performance benefits because users simply automated an existing inefficient system, and they failed to incorporate new opportunities offered by technology.

Therefore, the most effective approach is to have both business people and analysts working together to determine business requirements. Sometimes, however, users don't know exactly what they want, and analysts need to help them discover their needs. By using the requirements analysis approaches described earlier in the chapter, analysts can guide the users in explaining what is wanted from a system. Thus, analysts can help users critically examine the current state of systems and processes (the as-is system), identify exactly what needs to change, and develop a concept for a new system (the to-be system).

Creating a Requirements Definition

Creating a requirements definition is an iterative and ongoing process whereby the analyst collects information with requirements-gathering techniques (e.g., interviews, document analysis), critically analyzes the information to identify appropriate business requirements for the system, and adds the requirements to the requirements definition report. The requirements definition is kept up to date so that the project team and business users can refer to it and get a clear understanding of the new system.

To create a requirements definition, the project team first determines the kinds of functional and nonfunctional requirements that they will collect about the system (of course, these may change over time). These become the main sections of the document. Next, the analysts use a variety of requirements-gathering techniques described earlier to collect information, and they list the business requirements that were identified from that information. Finally, the analysts work with the entire project team and the business users to verify, change, and complete the list and to help prioritize the importance of the requirements that were identified.

This process continues throughout analysis, and the requirements definition evolves over time as new requirements are identified and as the project moves into later phases of the Unified Process. Beware: The evolution of the requirements definition must be carefully managed. The project team cannot keep adding to the requirements definition, or the system will keep growing and growing and never get finished. Instead, the project team carefully identifies requirements and evaluates which ones fit within the scope of the system. When a requirement reflects a real business need but is not within the scope of the current system or current release, it is either added on a list of future requirements or given a low priority. The management of requirements (and system scope) is one of the hardest parts of managing a project.

Figure 3-11 shows a sample requirements definition for an appointment system for a typical doctor's office. Notice it contains both functional and nonfunctional requirements. The functional requirements include managing appointments, producing schedules, and recording the availability of the individual doctors. The nonfunctional requirements include items such as the expected amount of time that it takes to store a new appointment, the need

Nonfunctional Requirements

1. Operational Requirements
  1.1. The system will operate in Windows environment.
  1.2. The system should be able to connect to printers wirelessly.
  1.3. The system should automatically back up at the end of each day.

2. Performance Requirements
  2.1. The system will store a new appointment in 2 seconds or less.
  2.2. The system will retrieve the daily appointment schedule in 2 seconds or less.

3. Security Requirements
  3.1. Only doctors can set their availability.
  3.2. Only a manager can produce a schedule.

4. Cultural and Political Requirements
  4.1. No special cultural and political requirements are anticipated.

Functional Requirements

1. Manage Appointments
  1.1. Patient makes new appointment.
  1.2. Patient changes appointment.
  1.3. Patient cancels appointment.

2. Produce Schedule
  2.1. Office Manager checks daily schedule.
  2.2. Office Manager prints daily schedule.

3. Record Doctor Availability
  3.1. Doctor updates schedule

FIGURE 3-11
Sample Requirements
Definition

to support wireless printing, and which types of employees have access to the different parts of the system.

The requirements are numbered in a legal or outline format so that each requirement is clearly identified. The requirements are first grouped into functional and nonfunctional requirements; within each of those headings, they are further grouped by the type of nonfunctional requirement or by function.

Sometimes business requirements are prioritized on the requirements definition. They can be ranked as having high, medium, or low importance in the new system, or they can be labeled with the version of the system that will address the requirement (e.g., release 1, release 2, release 3). This practice is particularly important when using object-oriented or agile methodologies since they deliver systems in an incremental manner.

The most obvious purpose of the requirements definition is to provide the information needed by the other deliverables in analysis, which include functional, structural, and behavioral models, and to support activities in design. The most important purpose of the requirements definition, however, is to define the scope of the system. The document describes to the analysts exactly what the system needs to end up doing. When discrepancies arise, the document serves as the place to go for clarification.

User Stories[17]

User stories, along with their associated *story cards* and *task lists*, are associated with the agile development approaches. Both story cards and task lists are considered to be lightweight approaches to documenting and gathering requirements. With the agile approaches, the user stories effectively are used as a replacement for the more formal requirements definition (see Figure 3-11) or they can be used as another requirements-gathering technique that acts as an input to the creation of a requirements definition. One major difference between the user story approach and the use-case approach (see Chapter 4) is that the use-case documentation is long-lived, while user stories are typically thrown in the trash once they have been implemented.

User stories have been shown to be very useful in gathering requirements in a nonthreatening manner that respects the user's point of view. They are typically captured using story cards (index cards) and are recorded on a task list (or from a Scrum perspective, on the product backlog). Stories can be used to capture both functional and nonfunctional requirements. A user story typically follows the format of:

> As a <role>,
> I want to <list of functions that the role wants to have the system do>
> so that <list of objectives the role wants to attain>

For example, with regard to the doctor's office appointment example, a functional requirement-based story could be:

> **As a** secretary,
> **I want to** be able to schedule appointments for our patients
> **so that** we can meet our patients' needs.

While an operational nonfunctional requirement-based story could be:

> **As a** secretary,
> **I want to** be able to print the daily schedule using wireless technology
> **so that** all printing can be performed using a shared printer without having to deal with printer cables connecting all of the computers to the printer.

Once the story is written down, a conversation can take place between the user and the developer. The *INVEST criteria* (Independent, Negotiable, Valuable, Estimable, Small, and Testable) has been suggested as a way to ensure that a user story is well written.[18] Each story should be implemented without too many dependencies on other stories, that is, each story should be independent. Each user story should be negotiable between the users and developers.

---

[17] For more information on user stories, see M. Cohn, *User Stories Applied: For Agile Software Development* (Boston, MA: Addison-Wesley, 2004); B. Rinzler, *Telling Stories: A Short Path to Writing Better Software Requirements* (Indianapolis, IN: Wiley, 2009); Jeff Patton and Peter Economy, *User Story Mapping: Discover the Whole Story, Build the Right Product* (Sebastopol, CA: O'Reilly, 2014); M. Lippert, S. Roock, and H. Wolf, *eXtreme Programming in Action: Practical Experiences from Real World Projects* (Chichester, England: Wiley & Sons, Ltd., 2002); C. Larman, *Agile & Iterative Development: A Manager's Guide* (Boston, MA: Addison-Wesley, 2004).

[18] Ivar Jacobson, Harold "Bud" Lawson, Pan-Wei Ng, Paul E. McMahon, and Michael Goedicke, *The Essentials of Modern Software Engineering: Free the Practices from the Method Prisons!* (ACM Books, 2019).

1. Find User Stories

2. Prepare a User Story

3. Split User Stories

4. Accept User Story

FIGURE 3-12 User Story Steps

In other words, both groups should have an understanding as to what is realistic from both perspectives. One thing that is discussed will be to determine the amount of effort it will take to implement it, that is, each story must be estimable. During the discussion, a task list is created for the story. If the story is deemed to be too large—for example, there are too many tasks on the task list—the story is split up into multiple stories each being recorded on its own story card and the tasks are allocated across the new stories. From an agile perspective, a story must be implementable in a single iteration. For example, in Scrum, a single iteration or sprint is limited to thirty days. Finally, a set of acceptance criteria are captured and recorded so that there is no question as to when the user story has been successfully completed. In fact, tests must be defined before the implementation of a user story begins. In many shops, once a set of tasks has been identified with a story, the story and its tasks are taped on a wall together so that all members of the development team can see the requirements. The story can be prioritized by importance by placing a rating on the card. The story can also be evaluated for the level of risk associated with it. The importance level and amount of *risk* associated with the story can be used to help choose which requirements to implement first. The advantage of using story cards and task lists to document requirements is that they are very low tech, high touch, easily updatable, and very portable. From a requirements-gathering and documentation perspective, a typical user story approach is made up of four steps (see Figure 3-12). Typically, user story approaches use Kanban boards (see Chapter 2) to schedule their implementation.

THE SYSTEM PROPOSAL

A *system proposal* brings together into a single comprehensive document the material created during planning and analysis. The system proposal typically includes an executive summary, the system request, the workplan, the feasibility analysis, the requirements definition, and the evolving models that describe the new system. The evolving models include functional models (see Chapter 4), structural models (see Chapter 5), and behavioral models (see Chapter 6).[19]

The executive summary provides all critical information in a very concise form. It can be thought of as a summary of the complete proposal. Its purpose is to allow a busy executive to quickly read through it and determine which parts of the proposal he or she needs to go through more thoroughly. The executive summary normally contains a statement of the problem that the project will address, any background information that is necessary to understand the problem and to understand the proposed solution, a description of any alternative solutions that have been considered and ruled out, and the major points of the proposed solution. The executive summary is typically no more than a single page long. Figure 3-13 provides a template for a system proposal and references to where the other sections of the proposal are described.

[19] Depending on the client, much more detailed specifications may be required; for example the Department of Defense, NASA, IEEE/ANSI, and the Naval Research Laboratory all have very specific formats that must be followed. For more information on these more detailed specifications, see A. M Davis, *Software Requirements, Revision* (Upper Saddle River, NJ: Prentice Hall, 1993); G. Kotonya and I. Sommerville, *Requirements Engineering* (Chichester, England: Wiley, 1998); and R. H. Thayer and M. Dorfman (Eds), *Software Requirements Engineering*, 2nd Ed. (Los Alamitos, CA: IEEE Computer Society Press, 1997).

1. Table of Contents

2. Executive Summary

A summary of all the essential information in the proposal so that a busy executive can read it quickly and decide what parts of the proposal to read in more depth.

3. System Request

The revised system request form (see Chapter 2).

4. Workplan

The original workplan, revised after having completed analysis (see Chapter 2).

5. Feasibility Analysis

A revised feasibility analysis, using the information from analysis (see Chapter 2).

6. Requirements Definition

A list of the functional and nonfunctional business requirements for the system (this chapter).

7. Functional Model

A use-case diagram, a set of activity diagrams, and a set of use-case descriptions that illustrate the basic processes or external functionality that the system needs to support (see Chapter 4).

8. Structural Models

A set of CRC cards, class diagram, and object diagrams that describe the structural aspects of the to-be system (see Chapter 5). This may also include structural models of the current as-is system that will be replaced.

9. Behavioral Models

A set of activity diagrams, sequence diagrams, behavioral-state machines, and a CRUDE matrix that describe the internal behavior of the to-be system (see Chapter 6). This may include behavioral models of the as-is system that will be replaced.

10. Appendices

These contain additional material relevant to the proposal, often used to support the recommended system. This might include results of a questionnaire survey or interviews, industry reports and statistics, and so on.

FIGURE 3-13
System Proposal Template

APPLYING THE CONCEPTS AT PATTERSON SUPERSTORE

Chapter 3 introduced requirements determination for object-oriented systems development projects. Determining the system's requirements is the most important activity in the systems development process. A requirement is WHAT the system must do or WHAT characteristics it must have. If the requirements are not fully or correctly defined, the system developed is unlikely to meet the needs of the user. In other words, if the requirements are wrong, the system will be wrong.

In this chapter's installment of the Patterson Superstore case, we see the requirements analysis and requirements-gathering techniques that the analysts used to determine requirements for Version 1 of the Integrated Health Clinic Delivery System. We also see the functional and nonfunctional requirements that were developed and an initial draft of the developing systems proposal for the project. This systems proposal will be finalized after the functional (Chapter 4), structural (Chapter 5), and behavioral (Chapter 6) modeling of the system has been completed.

You can find the rest of the case at www.wiley.com/go/dennis/systemanalysis6e/casestudy.

CHAPTER REVIEW

After reading and studying this chapter, you should be able to:

- ☐ Differentiate between a functional and a nonfunctional requirement.
- ☐ Discuss the problem analysis requirements approaches.
- ☐ Discuss the root cause analysis requirements approach.
- ☐ Discuss the duration analysis requirements approach.
- ☐ Discuss the activity-based costing analysis requirements approach.
- ☐ Discuss the informal benchmarking analysis requirements approach.
- ☐ Discuss the outcome analysis requirements approach.
- ☐ Discuss the technology analysis requirements approach.
- ☐ Discuss the activity elimination requirements approach.
- ☐ Discuss how to use interviews to gather requirements.
- ☐ Discuss how to use questionnaires to gather requirements.
- ☐ Discuss how to use observation to gather requirements.
- ☐ Discuss how to use document analysis to gather requirements.
- ☐ Discuss how to use text analysis to understand the requirements gathered.
- ☐ Create a requirements definition.
- ☐ Describe how to use story cards and task lists to document requirements.
- ☐ Describe the purpose and contents of system proposal.

KEY TERMS

Activity-based costing	Formal system	Open-ended question	Story cards
Activity elimination	Functional requirements	Outcome analysis	Structured interview
Analysis	Givens-means-ends	Parallelization	System proposal
As-is system	(GME) analysis	Probing question	System requirements
Benchmarking	Informal benchmarking	Problem analysis	Systems thinking
Bottom-up interview	Informal system	Process integration	skills
Business requirements	Interpersonal skills	Questionnaire	Task list
Closed-ended question	Interview	Requirement	Taxonomic analysis
Componential analysis	Interview notes	Requirements definition	Technology analysis
Critical thinking skills	Interview report	Requirements determination	Theme analysis
Document analysis	Interview schedule	Risk	To-be system
Domain analysis	INVEST criteria	Root cause	Top-down interview
Duration analysis	Means	Root cause analysis	Unstructured
Fishbone diagram	Nonfunctional requirements	Sample	interview
Fly on the wall	Observation	Sentence diagram	User stories

QUESTIONS

1. What are the key deliverables that are created during analysis? What is the final deliverable from analysis, and what does it contain?

2. What is the difference between an as-is system and a to-be system?

3. What are the three basic steps of the analysis process? Which step is sometimes skipped or done in a cursory fashion? Why?

4. Compare and contrast problem analysis and root cause analysis. Under what conditions would you use problem analysis? Under what conditions would you use root cause analysis?

5. Compare and contrast duration analysis and activity-based costing.

6. Describe the five major steps in conducting interviews.

7. Explain the differences among a closed-ended question, an open-ended question, and a probing question. When would you use each?
8. Explain the differences between unstructured interviews and structured interviews. When would you use each approach?
9. Explain the difference between a top-down and bottom-up interview approach. When would you use each approach?
10. How can you differentiate between facts and opinions? Why can both be useful?
11. How does designing questions for questionnaires differ from designing questions for interviews?
12. What are typical response rates for questionnaires, and how can you improve them?
13. What are the key aspects of using observation in the information-gathering process?
14. What is document analysis?
15. How does the formal system differ from the informal system? How does document analysis help you understand both?
16. Explain factors that can be used to select information-gathering techniques.
17. Describe the different approaches for text analysis.
18. What is the purpose of the requirements definition?
19. What are some of the advantages of using story cards and task lists as a requirements-gathering and documentation technique?
20. What information is typically included in a system proposal?
21. What is the purpose of the executive summary of the system proposal?

EXERCISES

A. Review the Amazon.com website. Develop the requirements definition for the site. Create a list of functional business requirements that the system meets. What different kinds of nonfunctional business requirements does the system meet? Provide examples for each kind.
B. Suppose you are going to build a new system that automates or improves the interview process for the career services department of your school. Develop a requirements definition for the new system. Include both functional and nonfunctional system requirements. Pretend you will release the system in three different versions. Prioritize the requirements accordingly.
C. Describe in very general terms the as-is business process for registering for classes at your university. Collaborate with another student in your class, and evaluate the process using problem analysis and root cause analysis. Based on your work, list some improvements that you have identified.
D. Describe in very general terms the as-is business process for applying for admission at your university. Collaborate with another student in your class, and evaluate the process using informal benchmarking. Based on your work, list some improvements that you have identified.
E. Describe in very general terms the as-is business process for registering for classes at your university. Collaborate with another student in your class, and evaluate the process using activity elimination. Based on your work, list some improvements that you have identified.
F. Suppose your university is having a dramatic increase in enrollment and is having difficulty finding enough seats in courses for students. Perform a technology analysis to identify new ways to help students complete their studies and graduate.
G. Suppose you are the analyst charged with developing a new system for the university bookstore so that students can order books online and have them delivered to their dorms or off-campus housing. What requirements-gathering techniques will you use? Describe in detail how you would apply the techniques.
H. Suppose you are the analyst charged with developing a new system to help senior managers make better strategic decisions. What requirements-gathering techniques will you use? Describe in detail how you would apply the techniques.
I. Find a partner and interview each other about what tasks each did in the last job you held (full-time, part-time, past, or current). If you haven't worked before, then assume your job is being a student. Before you do this, develop a brief interview plan. After your partner interviews you, identify the type of interview, interview approach, and types of questions used.
J. Find a questionnaire on the Web that has been created to capture customer information. Describe the purpose of the survey, the way questions are worded, and how the questions have been organized. How can it be improved? How will the responses be analyzed?

K. Develop a questionnaire that will help gather information regarding processes at a popular restaurant or the college cafeteria (e.g., ordering, customer service). Give the questionnaire to ten to fifteen students, analyze the responses, and write a brief report that describes the results.

L. Contact the career services department at your university, and find all the pertinent documents designed to help students find permanent and/or part-time jobs. Analyze the documents and write a brief report.

MINICASES

1. The State Firefighter's Association has a membership of 15,000. The purpose of the organization is to provide some financial support to the families of deceased member firefighters and to organize a conference each year bringing together firefighters from all over the state. Members are billed dues and calls annually. Calls are additional funds required to take care of payments made to the families of deceased members. The bookkeeping work for the association is handled by the elected treasurer, Bob Smith, although it is widely known that his wife, Laura, does all the work. Bob runs unopposed each year at the election, because no one wants to take over the tedious and time-consuming job of tracking memberships. Bob is paid a stipend of $8,000 per year, but his wife spends well over twenty hours per week on the job. The organization, however, is not happy with their performance.

A computer system is used to track the billing and receipt of funds. This system was developed about ten years ago by a computer science student and his father using database software that is no longer sold or supported. In fact, the vendor is out of business. The most immediate problem facing the treasurer and his wife is the fact that the software package no longer exists, and there is no one around who knows how to maintain the system. One query, in particular, takes seventeen hours to run. Over the years, they have just avoided running this query, although the information in it would be quite useful. Questions from members concerning their statements cannot easily be answered. Usually Bob or Laura just jots down the inquiry and returns a call with the answer. Sometimes it takes three to five hours to find the information needed to answer the question. Often, they have to perform calculations manually because the system was not programmed to handle certain types of queries. When member information is entered into the system, each field is presented one at a time, which makes it very difficult to return to a field and correct a value that was entered. Sometimes a new member is entered but disappears from the records. The report of membership used in the conference materials does not alphabetize members by city. Only cities are listed in the correct order.

What requirements analysis approach or approaches would you recommend for this situation? Explain your answer.

2. Brian Callahan, IS project manager, is just about ready to depart for an urgent meeting called by Joe Campbell, manager of manufacturing operations. A major project sponsored by Joe recently cleared the approval hurdle, and Brian helped bring the project through project initiation. Now that the approval committee has given the go-ahead, Brian has been working on the project's analysis plan.

One evening, while playing golf with a friend who works in the manufacturing operations department, Brian learned that Joe wants to push the project's time frame up from Brian's original estimate of thirteen months. Brian's friend overheard Joe say, "I can't see why that IS project team needs to spend all that time analyzing things. They've got two weeks scheduled just to look at the existing system! That seems like a real waste. I want that team to get going on building my system."

Because Brian has a little inside knowledge about Joe's agenda for this meeting, he has been considering how to handle Joe. What do you suggest Brian tell Joe?

3. Barry has recently been assigned to a project team that will be developing a new retail store management system for a chain of submarine sandwich shops. Barry has several years of experience in programming, but he has not done much analysis in his career. He was a little nervous about the new work he would be doing, but he was confident he could handle any assignment he was given.

One of Barry's first assignments was to visit one of the submarine sandwich shops and prepare an observation report on how the store operates. Barry planned to arrive at the store around noon, but he chose a store in an area of town he was unfamiliar with, and due to traffic delays and difficulty in finding the store, he did not arrive until 1:30. The store manager was not expecting him and refused to let a stranger behind the counter until Barry had her contact the project sponsor (the director of store management) at company headquarters to verify who he was and what his purpose was.

After finally securing permission to observe, Barry stationed himself prominently in the work area behind the counter so that he could see everything. The staff had to maneuver around him as they went about their tasks, but there were only minor occasional collisions. Barry noticed that the store staff seemed to be going about their work very slowly and deliberately, but he supposed that was because the store wasn't very busy. At first, Barry questioned each worker about what he or she was doing, but the store manager eventually asked him not to interrupt their work so much—he was interfering with their service to the customers.

By 3:30, Barry was a little bored. He decided to leave, figuring he could get back to the office and prepare his report before 5:00 that day. He was sure his team leader would be pleased with his quick completion of his assignment. As he drove, he reflected, "There really won't be much to say in this report. All they do is take the order, make the sandwich, collect the payment, and hand over the order. It's really simple!" Barry's confidence in his analytical skills soared as he anticipated his team leader's praise.

Back at the store, the store manager shook her head, commenting to her staff, "He comes here at the slowest time of day on the slowest day of the week. He never even looked at all the work I was doing in the back room while he was here—summarizing yesterday's sales, checking inventory on hand, making up resupply orders for the weekend . . . plus he never even considered our store-opening and store-closing procedures. I hate to think that the new store management system is going to be built by someone like that. I'd better contact Chuck [the director of store management] and let him know what went on here today."

Evaluate Barry's conduct of the observation assignment.

4. Anne has been given the task of conducting a survey of sales clerks who will be using a new order-entry system being developed for a household products catalog company. The goal of the survey is to identify the clerks' opinions on the strengths and weaknesses of the current system. There are about 50 clerks who work in three different cities, so a survey seemed like an ideal way of gathering the needed information from the clerks.

Anne developed the questionnaire carefully and pretested it on several sales supervisors who were available at corporate headquarters. After revising it based on their suggestions, she sent a paper version of the questionnaire to each clerk, asking that it be returned within one week. After one week, she had only three completed questionnaires returned. After another week, Anne received just two more completed questionnaires. Feeling somewhat desperate, Anne then sent out an e-mail version of the questionnaire, again to all the clerks, asking them to respond to the questionnaire by e-mail as soon as possible. She received two e-mail questionnaires and three messages from clerks who had completed the paper version expressing annoyance at being bothered with the same questionnaire a second time. At this point, Anne has just a 14 percent response rate, which she is sure will not please her team leader. What suggestions do you have that could have improved Anne's response rate to the questionnaire?

CHAPTER 4

BUSINESS PROCESS AND FUNCTIONAL MODELING

Functional models describe business processes and the interaction of an information system with its environment. In object-oriented systems development, two types of models are used to describe the functionality of an information system: use cases and activity diagrams. Use cases are used to describe the basic functions of the information system. Activity diagrams support the logical modeling of business processes and workflows. Both can be used to describe the current as-is system and the to-be system being developed. This chapter describes business process and functional modeling as a means to document and understand requirements and to understand the functional or external behavior of the system.

OBJECTIVES

- Understand the process used to identify business processes and use cases.
- Understand the process used to create use-case diagrams.
- Understand the process used to model business processes with activity diagrams.
- Understand the rules and style guidelines for activity diagrams.
- Understand the process used to create use-case descriptions.
- Understand the rules and style guidelines for use-case descriptions.
- Be able to create functional models of business processes using use-case diagrams, activity diagrams, and use-case descriptions.

INTRODUCTION

The previous chapter discussed popular requirements-gathering techniques, such as interviewing, questionnaires, and observation. Using these techniques, the analyst determined the requirements and created a requirements definition. The requirements definition defined what the system is to do. In this chapter, we focus our attention on use-case driven development. This is in contrast to the typical agile approaches that tend to be more user story driven. One of the major problems with a user story driven approach is that user stories are at such a detailed level that they can become extremely fragmented in their coverage of the requirements. This is similar to the statement that you cannot see the forest for the trees. In fact, in practice, too early of a detailed focus can lead the analysts to be at a knothole level where they cannot even see the tree, let alone the forest. To overcome these situations, much of the scaling up of the agile approaches begin to look more like a Unified Process approach than the original agile approach on which it is based.[1] Because Unified Modeling Language (UML) has

---

[1] For a good comparison of some of these different approaches, see Craig Larman, *Agile & Iterative Development: A Manager's Guide* (Boston, MA: Addison Wesley, 2004); Ivar Jaconson, Pan-Wei Ng, Paul E. McMahon, Ian Spence, and Svante Lidman, *The Essence of Software Engineering: Applying the SEMAT Kernel* (Upper Saddle River, NJ: Addison-Wesley, 2013); Ivar Jacobson, Harold "Bud" Lawson, Pan-Wei Ng, Paul E. McMahon, and Michael Goedicke, *The Essentials of Modern Software Engineering: Free the Practices from the Method Prisons!* (ACM Books, 2019).

been accepted as the standard notation by the Object Management Group (OMG), almost all object-oriented development projects today use these models to document and organize the requirements that are obtained during the analysis workflow.[2] In this chapter, we discuss how the information that is gathered using these techniques is organized and presented in the form of use cases that are modeled and documented using use-case and activity diagrams and use-case descriptions.

As pointed out in Chapter 1, all object-oriented systems development approaches are use-case driven, architecture-centric, and iterative and incremental. A *use case* is a formal way of representing the way a business system interacts with its environment. Essentially, a use case is a high-level overview of the business processes in a business information system. From a practical perspective, use cases represent the entire basis for an object-oriented system. Use cases can document the current system (i.e., as-is system) or the new system being developed (i.e., to-be system). Given that object-oriented systems are use-case driven, use cases also form the foundation for testing (see Chapter 12) and user-interface design (see Chapter 10). Two forms of use-case driven testing are walkthroughs (described later in this chapter) and role-playing (described in Chapter 5).

From an architecture-centric perspective, use-case modeling supports the creation of an external or functional view of a business process in that it shows how the users view the process rather than the internal mechanisms by which the process and supporting systems operate. The structural and behavioral architecture-based views are described in Chapters 5 and 6, respectively. Finally, all object-oriented systems development approaches are developed in an incremental and iterative manner. Even though we present the three architectural views in a sequential manner, this is done primarily for pedagogical reasons. You will find that you will need to not only iterate across the business process and functional models (described in this chapter), you will also have to iterate across all three architectural views to fully capture and represent the requirements for a business information system.

Activity diagrams are typically used to augment our understanding of the business processes and our use-case model. Technically, an activity diagram can be used for any type of process-modeling activity.[3] In this chapter, we describe their use in the context of business process modeling. *Process models* depict how a business system operates. They illustrate the processes or activities that are performed and how objects (data) move among them. A process model can be used to document a current system (i.e., as-is system) or a new system being developed (i.e., to-be system), whether computerized or not. Many different process-modeling techniques are in use today.[4]

Activity diagrams and use cases are *logical models*—models that describe the business domain's activities without suggesting how they are conducted. Logical models are sometimes referred to as *problem domain models*. Reading a use-case or activity diagram, in principle, should not indicate if an activity is computerized or manual, if a piece of information is

---

[2] Other similar techniques that are commonly used in non-UML projects are task modeling and scenario-based design. For task modeling, see Ian Graham, *Migrating to Object Technology* (Reading, MA: Addison-Wesley, 1995); Ian Graham, Brian Henderson-Sellers, and Houman Younessi, *The OPEN Process Specification* (Reading, MA: Addison-Wesley, 1997). For scenario-based design, see John M. Carroll, *Scenario-Based Design: Envisioning Work and Technology in System Development* (New York: Wiley, 1995).

[3] We actually used an activity diagram to describe a simple process in Chapter 1 (see Figure 1-1).

[4] Another commonly used process-modeling technique is IDEF0. IDEF0 is used extensively throughout the U.S. federal government. For more information about IDEF0, see *FIPS 183: Integration Definition for Function Modeling (IDEF0)*, Federal Information Processing Standards Publications (Washington, DC: U.S. Department of Commerce, 1993). From an object-oriented perspective, a good book that uses the UML to address business process modeling is Hans-Erik Eriksson and Magnus Penker, *Business Modeling with UML* (New York: Wiley, 2000). Finally, a new process modeling technique is BPMN (Business Process Modeling Notation). A good book that compares the notation and use of BPMN to UML's activity diagram is Martin Schedlbauer, *The Art of Business Process Modeling: The Business Analysts Guide to Process Modeling with UML & BPMN* (Sudbury, MA: The Cathris Group, 2010).

collected by paper form or via the Web, or if information is placed in a filing cabinet or a large database. These physical details are defined during design when the logical models are refined into *physical models*. These models provide information that is needed to ultimately build the system. By focusing on logical activities first, analysts can focus on how the business should run without being distracted with implementation details.

As a first step, the project team gathers requirements from the users (see Chapter 3). Using the gathered requirements, the project team then identifies the business processes and their environment using use cases and *use-case diagrams*. Next, users work closely with the team to model the business processes in the form of activity diagrams, and the team documents the business processes described in the use-case and activity diagrams by creating a *use-case description* for each use case. Finally, the team verifies and validates the business processes by ensuring that all three models (use-case diagram, activity diagram(s), and use-case descriptions) agree with one another. Once the current understanding of the business processes is documented in the functional models, the team is ready to move on to structural modeling (see Chapter 5).

In this chapter, we first describe business process identification using use cases and use-case diagrams. Second, we describe business process modeling with activity diagrams. Third, we describe use-case descriptions, their elements, and a set of guidelines for creating them. Fourth, we describe the process of verification and validation of the business process and functional models.

BUSINESS PROCESS IDENTIFICATION WITH USE CASES AND USE-CASE DIAGRAMS

In the previous chapter, we learned about approaches and techniques that are useful in identifying the different business processes of a system so that a requirements definition could be created. In this section, we learn how to begin modeling business processes with use cases and the use-case diagram. An analyst can employ use cases to better understand the functionality of the system at a very high level. Typically, a use-case diagram provides a simple, straightforward way of communicating to the users exactly what the system will do. Consequently, a use-case diagram is drawn when gathering and defining requirements of the system and can encourage the users to provide additional high-level requirements. A use-case diagram illustrates in a very simple way the main functions of the system and the different kinds of users that will interact with it. Figure 4-1 describes the basic syntax rules for a use-case diagram. Figure 4-2 presents a use-case diagram for the doctor's office appointment system introduced in the previous chapter. We can see from the diagram that patients, doctors, and management personnel will use the appointment system to manage appointments, record availability, and produce schedules, respectively.

Use cases are the primary drivers for all the UML diagramming techniques. A use case communicates at a high level what the system needs to do, and all the UML diagramming techniques build on this by presenting the use-case functionality in a different way for a different purpose. Use cases are the building blocks by which the system is designed and built.

Use cases capture the typical interaction of the system with the system's users (end users and other systems). These interactions represent the external, or functional, view of the system from the perspective of the user. Each use case describes one and only one function in which users interact with the system. Although a use case may contain several paths that a user can take while interacting with the system, each possible execution path through the use case is referred to as a *scenario*. Another way to look at a scenario is as if a scenario is an instantiation of a specific use case. Scenarios are used extensively in behavioral modeling (see Chapter 6). Finally, by identifying all scenarios and trying to execute them through

An actor: ■ Is a person or system that derives benefit from and is external to the subject. ■ Is depicted as either a stick figure (default) or, if a nonhuman actor is involved, a rectangle with <<actor>> in it (alternative). ■ Is labeled with its role. ■ Can be associated with other actors using a specialization/superclass association, denoted by an arrow with a hollow arrowhead. ■ Is placed outside the subject boundary.	**Actor/Role** **<<actor>>** **Actor/Role**
A use case: ■ Represents a major piece of system functionality. ■ Can extend another use case. ■ Can include another use case. ■ Is placed inside the system boundary. ■ Is labeled with a descriptive verb–noun phrase.	**Use Case**
A subject boundary: ■ Includes the name of the subject inside or on top. ■ Represents the scope of the subject, e.g., a system or an individual business process.	**Subject**
An association relationship: ■ Links an actor with the use case(s) with which it interacts.	* *
An include relationship: ■ Represents the inclusion of the functionality of one use case within another. ■ Has an arrow drawn from the base use case to the used use case.	<<include>> ←---------------
An extend relationship: ■ Represents the extension of the use case to include optional behavior. ■ Has an arrow drawn from the extension use case to the base use case.	<<extend>> ---------------→
A generalization relationship: ■ Represents a specialized use case to a more generalized one. ■ Has an arrow drawn from the specialized use case to the base use case.	↑

FIGURE 4-1 Syntax for Use-Case Diagram

role-playing CRC cards (see Chapter 5), you will be testing the clarity and completeness of your evolving understanding of the system being developed.

Types of Use Cases

There are many different types of use cases. We suggest two separate dimensions on which to classify a use case based on the purpose of the use case and the amount of information that the use case contains: overview versus detail and essential versus real.

An *overview use case* is used to enable the analyst and user to agree on a high-level overview of the requirements. Typically, overview use cases are created very early in the process

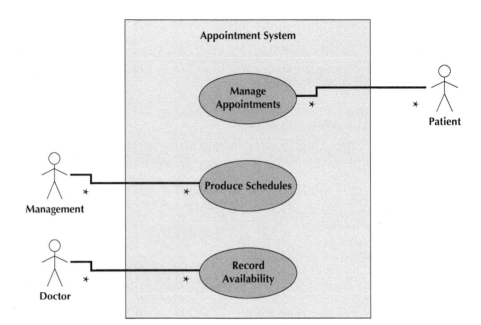

FIGURE 4-2
Use-Case Diagram
for the Appointment
System

of understanding the system requirements, and they document only basic information about the use case, such as its name; ID number; primary actor; type; a brief description; and the relationships among the actors, actors and use cases, and use cases. These can easily be created immediately after the creation of the use-case diagram.

Once the user and the analyst agree upon a high-level overview of the requirements, the overview use cases are converted to detail use cases. A *detail use case* typically documents, as far as possible, all the information needed for the use case. These can be based on the activities and control flows contained in the activity diagrams.

An *essential use case* is one that describes only the minimum essential issues necessary to understand the required functionality. A *real use case* goes farther and describes a specific set of steps. For example, an essential use case in a doctor office might say that the receptionist should attempt to match the patient's desired appointment times with the available times, whereas a real use case might say that the receptionist should look up the available dates on the calendar using Google Calendar to determine if the requested appointment times were available. The primary difference is that essential use cases are implementation independent, whereas real use cases are detailed descriptions of how to use the system once it is implemented. Thus, real use cases tend to be used only in the design, implementation, and testing.

In this chapter, we limit our discussion to overview, essential use-cases and detail, essential use cases. We model and document overview, essential use cases using use case diagrams and overview use case descriptions, while we model and document detail, essential use cases with activity diagrams and detail use case descriptions. Both activity diagrams and use case descriptions are described later in this chapter. Next, we describe and discuss use-case diagrams.

Elements of Use-Case Diagrams

The elements of a use-case diagram include actors, use cases, subject boundaries, and a set of relationships among actors, actors and use cases, and use cases. These relationships consist of association, include, extend, and generalization relationships. Each of these elements is described next.

Actors The stick figures on the diagram represent actors (see Figure 4-1). An *actor* is not a specific user but instead is a role that a user can play while interacting with the system. An actor can also represent another system in which the current system interacts. In this case, the actor optionally can be represented by a rectangle containing <<actor>> and the name of the system. Basically, actors represent the principal elements in the environment in which the system operates. Actors can provide input to the system, receive output from the system, or both. The diagram in Figure 4-2 shows that three actors will interact with the appointment system (a patient, a doctor, and management).

Sometimes an actor plays a specialized role of a more general type of actor. For example, there may be times when a new patient interacts with the system in a way that is somewhat different from a general patient. In this case, a *specialized actor* (i.e., new patient) can be placed on the model, shown using a line with a hollow triangle at the end of the more general actor (i.e., patient). The specialized actor inherits the behavior of the more general actor and extends it in some way (see Figure 4-3).

Association Use cases are connected to actors through association relationships; these relationships show with which use cases the actors interact (see Figure 4-1). A line drawn from an actor to a use case depicts an association. The association typically represents two-way communication between the use case and the actor. If the communication is only one way, then a solid arrowhead can be used to designate the direction of the flow of information. For example, in Figure 4-2 the Patient actor communicates with the Manage Appointments use case. Because there are no arrowheads on the association, the communication is two-way. Finally, it is possible to represent the multiplicity of the association. Figure 4-2 shows an asterisk (*) at either end of the association between the Patient and the Manage Appointments use case. This simply indicates that an individual patient (instance of the Patient actor) executes the Manage Appointments use case as many times as he or she wishes and that it is possible for the appointment part of the Manage Appointments use case to be executed by many different patients. In most cases, this type of many-to-many relationship is appropriate.

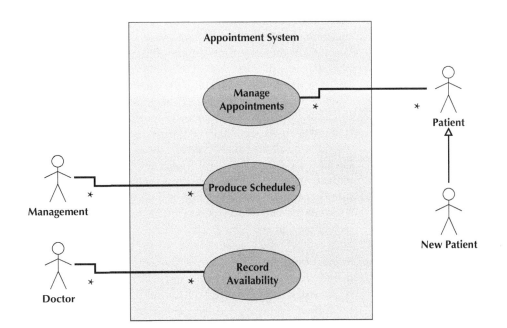

FIGURE 4-3
Use-Case Diagram with a Specialized Actor

However, it is possible to restrict the number of patients who can be associated with the Manage Appointments use case. We discuss the multiplicity issue in detail in the next chapter in regard to class diagrams.

Use Case A use case, depicted by an oval in the UML, is a major process that the system performs and that benefits an actor or actors in some way (see Figure 4-1); it is labeled using a descriptive verb–noun phrase. We can tell from Figure 4-2 that the system has three primary use cases: Manage Appointments, Produce Schedules, and Record Availability.

There are times when a use case includes, extends, or generalizes the functionality of another use case in the diagram. These are shown using include, extend, and generalization relationships. To increase the ease of understanding a use-case diagram, higher-level use cases are normally drawn above the lower-level ones. It may be easier to understand these relationships with the help of examples. Let's assume that every time a patient makes an appointment, the patient is asked to verify payment arrangements. However, it is occasionally necessary to actually make new payment arrangements. Therefore, we may want to have a use case called Make Payment Arrangements that *extends* the Manage Appointments use case to include this additional functionality. That is, the Manage Appointments optionally can call or execute the Make Payment Arrangements use case. In Figure 4-4, an arrow labeled with *extend* was drawn from the Make Payment Arrangements use case to the Manage Appointments use case to denote this special use-case relationship, that is, the extend relationship is drawn from the lower-level use case to the higher level one. In this case, the Make Payment Arrangements use case was drawn lower than the Manage Appointments use case.

Similarly, there are times when a single use case contains common functions that are used by other use cases. For example, suppose there is a use case called Manage Schedule that performs some routine tasks needed to maintain the doctor's office appointment schedule, and the two use cases Record Availability and Produce Schedules both perform the routine tasks. Figure 4-4 shows how we can design the system so that Manage Schedule is a shared use case that is used by others. An arrow labeled with *include* is used to denote the include relationship, and the included use case is drawn below the use cases that contain it. Notice that the arrows are drawn from the Record Availability and Produce Schedules use cases to the common Manage Schedule use case.

Finally, there are times when it makes sense to use a generalization relationship to simplify the individual use cases. For example, in Figure 4-4, the Manage Appointments use case has been specialized to include a use case for an Old Patient and a New Patient. The Make Old Patient Appt use case inherits the functionality of the Manage Appointments use case (including the Make Payment Arrangements use-case extension) and extends its own functionality with the Update Patient Information use case. The Make New Patient Appt use case also inherits all the functionality of the generic Manage Appointments use case and calls the Create New Patient use case, which includes the functionality necessary to create the new patient. The generalization relationship is represented as an unlabeled hollow arrow with the more general use case being higher than the lower use cases. Also, notice that we have added a second specialized actor, Old Patient, and that the Patient actor is now simply a generalization of the Old and New Patient actors.

Subject Boundary The use cases are enclosed within a *subject boundary,* which is a box that defines the scope of the system and clearly delineates what parts of the diagram are external or internal to it (see Figure 4-1). One of the more difficult decisions to make is where to draw the subject boundary. A subject boundary can be used to separate a software system from its environment, a subsystem from other subsystems within the software system, or an individual

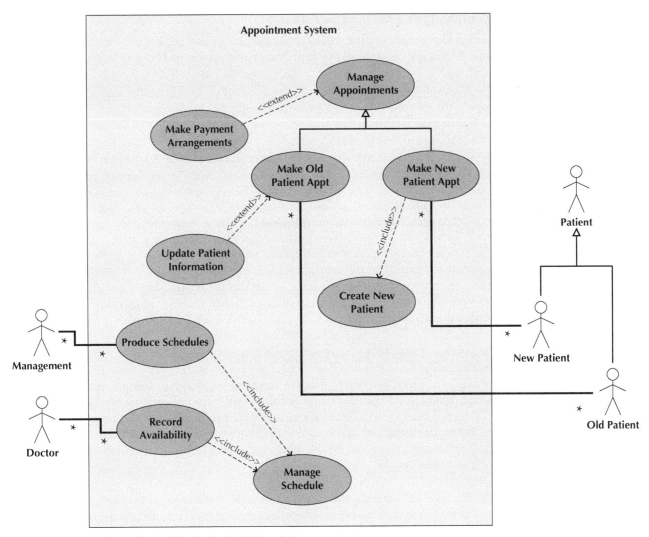

FIGURE 4-4   Extend and Include Relationships

process in a software system. They also can be used to separate an information system, including both software and internal actors, from its environment.

The name of the subject can appear either inside or on top of the box. The subject boundary is drawn based on the scope of the system. In the appointment system, we assumed that the Management and Doctor actors are outside of the scope of the system; that is, they use the system. However, we could have added an internal actor (Receptionist) who captures the interaction between the patients and the respective Make Appt use cases. If we did this, we would add another boundary inside of the current boundary in which the internal actor would reside. Given that including the internal actor starts to include implementation decisions, we have decided not to include the receptionist in the diagram.[5] Care should be taken to decide what the scope of the information system is to be.

[5] In other non-UML approaches to object-oriented systems development, it is possible to represent external actors along with internal actors. In this example, the receptionist would be considered an internal actor (see Graham, *Migrating to Object Technology*; and Graham, Henderson-Sellers, and Younessi, *The OPEN Process Specification*).

Identifying the Major Use Cases

The first step is to review the requirements definition (see Figure 3-11). This helps the analyst to get a complete overview of the underlying business process being modeled.

The second step is to identify the subject's boundaries. This helps the analyst to identify the scope of the system. However, as we work through the development process, the boundary of the system most likely will change.

The third step is to identify the primary actors and their goals. The primary actors involved with the system come from a list of stakeholders and users. Recall that a stakeholder is a person, a group, or an organization that can affect (or will be affected by) a new system, whereas an actor is a role that a stakeholder or user plays, not a specific user (e.g., doctor, not Dr. Jones). The goals represent the functionality that the system must provide the actor for the system to be a success. Identifying the tasks that each actor must perform can facilitate this. For example, does the actor need to create, read, update, delete, or execute (CRUDE)[6] any information currently in the system, are there any external changes of which an actor must inform the system, or is there any information that the system should give the actor? Steps 2 and 3 are intertwined. As actors are identified and their goals are uncovered, the boundary of the system will change.

The fourth step is to simply identify the business processes and major use cases. Rather than jumping into one use case and describing it completely at this point, we only want to identify the major use cases. Identifying only the major use cases at this time prevents the users and analysts from forgetting key business processes and helps the users explain the overall set of business processes for which they are responsible. It is important at this point to understand and define acronyms and jargon so that the project team and others from outside the user group can clearly understand the use cases. Again, the requirements definition is a very useful beginning point for this step.

The fifth step is to carefully review the current set of use cases. It may be necessary to split some of them into multiple use cases or merge some of them into a single use case. Also, based on the current set, a new use case may be identified. You should remember that identifying use cases is an iterative process, with users often changing their minds about what a use case is and what it includes. It is very easy to get trapped in the details at this point, so you need to remember that the goal at this step is to only identify the *major* use cases. For example, in the doctor's office example in Figure 4-2, we defined one use case as Manage Appointments. This use case included the cases for both new patients and existing patients, as well as for when a patient changes or cancels an appointment. We could have defined each of these activities (makes an appointment, changes an appointment, or cancels an appointment) as separate use cases, but this would have created a huge set of small use cases.

The trick is to select the right size and number of use cases such that the problem domain is represented in a semantically sound manner. However, too many use cases may suggest that the use cases are too small or that the system boundary is too large, while too few use cases may imply that the size and complexity of the individual use cases are simply too large. Too large use cases will increase the complexity of the activity diagrams that we use to model the use case details (see later in this chapter). Consequently, the right number of use cases is really a function of the complexity of the problem domain. In other words, from a semantic modeling perspective, we will have to trade off the complexity of the problem domain by

[6] We describe the use of CRUDE analysis and matrices in Chapter 6.

shifting it between the number of use cases on the use case diagram and the detailed modeling of the business process with the activity diagrams. In some situations, the use cases could be grouped together into *packages* (i.e., logical groups of use cases) to make the use case diagrams easier to read and to keep the activity diagrams at a reasonable level of complexity.[7]

Creating a Use-Case Diagram

Basically, drawing the use-case diagram is straightforward once use cases have been detailed. The actual use-case diagram encourages the use of information hiding. The only parts drawn on the use-case diagram are the system boundary, the use cases themselves, the actors, and the various associations between these components. The major strength of the use-case diagram is that it provides the user with an overview of the business processes. However, remember that any time a use case changes, it could affect the use case diagram. There are four major steps in drawing a use-case diagram.

First, we place and draw the use cases on the diagram. These are taken directly from the major use cases previously identified. Special use-case associations (include, extend, or generalization) are also added to the model at this point. Be careful in laying out the diagram. There is no formal order to the use cases, so they can be placed in whatever fashion is needed to make the diagram easy to read and to minimize the number of lines that cross. It often is necessary to redraw the diagram several times with use cases in different places to make the diagram easy to read. Also, for understandability purposes, the number of use cases on the diagram should be balanced with the complexity of the individual activity diagram for each use case. Consequently, there are many possible "correct" use case diagrams for the same problem domain. Correctness of the use case diagram is dependent on the associated activity diagrams.

Second, the actors are placed and drawn on the diagram. To minimize the number of lines that cross on the diagram, the actors should be placed near the use cases with which they are associated.

Third, the subject boundary is drawn. This forms the border of the subject, separating use cases (i.e., the subject's functionality) from actors (i.e., the roles of the external users).

The fourth and last step is to add associations by drawing lines to connect the actors to the use cases with which they interact. No order is implied by the diagram, and the items added along the way do not have to be placed in a particular order; therefore, it might help to rearrange the symbols a bit to minimize the number of lines that cross, making the diagram less confusing.

Campus Housing Example Identify the actors and major use cases for the following high-level business processes in a housing system run by the campus housing service. The campus housing service helps students find apartments. Apartment owners complete information forms about the available rental units (e.g., location, number of bedrooms, and monthly rent). Students can search the available rental units to find apartments that meet their needs (e.g., a two-bedroom apartment for $400 or less per month within a half mile of campus) and contact the apartment owners directly to see the apartment and possibly rent it. Apartment owners call the service to delete their listing when they have rented their apartment(s).

As a first step, we identify the primary actors, major business processes, and major use cases. In this case, the primary actors are the apartment owners and the students. The goal of the primary actors is both sides of a rental transaction, that is, to rent the apartments. The

---

[7] For those familiar with structured analysis and design, packages serve a similar purpose as the leveling and balancing processes used in data flow diagramming. Packages are described in Chapter 7.

major business processes and use cases to allow the actors to realize their goal are to maintain the available rental unit information for the apartment owners and to find appropriate rental units to consider for the students. Using the identified actors and use cases and following the process described above, the use-case diagram in Figure 4-5 was created. Notice that the diagram only includes two use cases and two actors. In this case, the Maintain Available Rental Unit Information use case actually includes two separate subprocesses. The apartment owners can add a rental unit that has become available, and they can delete a rental unit that has been rented and is no longer available. A student can search the Search Available Rental Units use case by using three separate criteria: distance from campus, number of bedrooms, and monthly rent. These criteria can be used individually or by any combination of the three. We will return to this example in the next section of the chapter. However, before we move on, we next describe a slightly more involved system for a university library.

Library Example The functional requirements for an automated university library circulation system include the need to support searching, borrowing, and book-maintenance activities. The system should support searching by title, author, keywords, and ISBN. If the book of interest is currently checked out, a valid borrower should be allowed to request the book to be returned. Once the book has been checked back in, the borrower requesting the book should be notified of the book's availability.

The borrowing activities are built around checking books out and returning books by borrowers. There are three types of borrowers: students, faculty or staff, and guests. Regardless of the type of borrower, the borrower must have a valid ID card. If the borrower is a student, the system is checked with the registrar's office to validate the ID card. If the borrower is a faculty or staff member, the system is checked with the personnel office to validate the ID card. If the borrower is a guest, the ID card is checked against the library's own system. If the ID card is valid, the system must also check to determine whether the borrower has any overdue books or unpaid fines. If the ID card is invalid, the borrower has overdue books, or the borrower has unpaid fines, the system must reject the borrower's request to check out a book, otherwise the borrower's request should be honored. If a book is checked out, the system must update the library's collection to reflect the book's new status.

The book-maintenance activities deal with adding and removing books from the library's book collection. This requires a library manager to both logically and physically add and remove the book. Books being purchased by the library or books being returned in a damaged state typically cause these activities. If a book is determined to be damaged when it is returned and it needs to be removed from the collection, the last borrower will be assessed a fine. However, if the book can be repaired, depending on the cost of the repair, the borrower might not be assessed a fine. Every Monday, the library sends a reminder to borrowers who have

FIGURE 4-5
Campus Housing
Use-Case Diagram

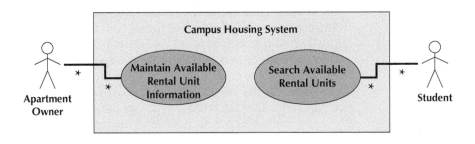

overdue books. If a book is overdue more than two weeks, the borrower is assessed a fine. Depending on how long the book remains overdue, the borrower can be assessed additional fines every Monday.

To begin we need to identify the major use cases and create a use-case diagram that represents the high-level business processes in the business situation just described. Based on the steps to identify the major use cases, we need to review the requirements definition and identify the boundaries (scope) of the problem. Based on the description of the problem, it is obvious that the system to be created is limited to managing the library's book collection. The next thing we need to do is to identify the primary actors and business processes that need to be supported by the system. Based on the functional requirements described, the primary actors are borrowers and librarians, whereas the primary business processes are borrowing books, returning books, searching the book collection, maintaining the book collection, and processing overdue books. Now that we have identified all of the actors and major use cases, we can draw the use-case diagram that represents an overview of the library's book collection management system (see Figure 4-6). Notice the addition of two nonhuman actors (Personnel Office and Registrar Office).

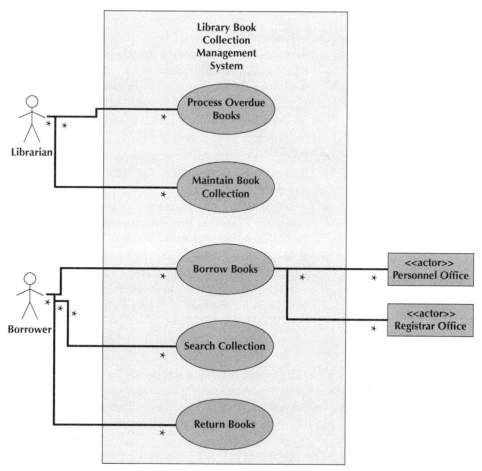

FIGURE 4-6
Library Book
Collection Management
System Use-Case
Diagram

BUSINESS PROCESS MODELING WITH ACTIVITY DIAGRAMS

Business process models describe the different activities that, when combined, support a business process. Business processes typically cut across functional departments (e.g., the creation of a new product involves many different activities that combine the efforts of many employees from many departments). From an object-oriented perspective, these processes cut across multiple objects. Many of the earlier object-oriented systems development approaches tended to ignore business process modeling. However, today we realize that modeling business processes themselves is a very constructive activity that can be used to make sense of the gathered requirements (see Chapter 3). One potential problem of building business process models, from an object-oriented systems development perspective, is that they tend to reinforce a functional decomposition mindset. However, as long as they are used properly, business process models are very powerful tools for communicating the analyst's current understanding of the requirements to the user.

Martin Schedlbauer provides a set of best practices to follow when modeling business processes.[8]

- Be realistic, because it is virtually impossible to identify everything that is included in a business process at this point in the evolution of the system. Even if we could identify everything, everything is not equally important.

- Be agile because even though we might not identify every single feature of a business process, the features that we do identify should be identified in a rigorous manner.

- All modeling is a collaborative/social activity. Therefore, business process modeling must be performed by teams, not by individuals. When an individual creates a model, the chance of mixing up or omitting important tasks is greatly increased.

- Do not use a CASE tool to do the modeling but use whiteboards instead. However, once the process is understood, it is a good idea to use a CASE tool to document the process.

- Process modeling should be done in an iterative manner. As you better understand a business process, you will need to return to the documented version of the process and revise it.

- When modeling a business process, stay focused on that specific process. If tasks associated with other business processes are identified, simply record them on a to-do list and get back to the business process that you are currently modeling.

- Remember that a business process model is an abstraction of reality. By that, we mean that you should not include every minor task in the current description of the business process. Remember, you cannot afford to lose sight of the proverbial forest for the sake of detailed understanding of a single tree. Too many details at this point in the evolution of the system can cause confusion and actually prevent you from solving the underlying problem being addressed by the new system.

In this chapter, activity diagrams are used to model the behavior in a business process independent of objects. Activity diagrams can be used to model everything from a high-level business workflow that involves many different use cases, to the details of an individual use case, all the way down to the specific details of an individual method. In a nutshell, activity

---

[8] Martin Schedlbauer, *The Art of Business Process Modeling: The Business Analysts Guide to Process Modeling with UML & BPMN* (Sudbury, MA: The Cathris Group, 2010).

diagrams can be used to model any type of process.[9] However, in this chapter, we restrict our coverage of activity diagrams to documenting and modeling high-level business processes, that is, we limit the modeling to detail, essential use cases. Consequently, the activity diagrams in this chapter provide a graphical model of the detail use case description described and discussed later in this chapter.

Elements of an Activity Diagram

Activity diagrams portray the primary activities and the relationships among the activities in a process. Figure 4-7 shows the syntax of an activity diagram. Figure 4-8 presents a simple activity diagram that represents the Manage Appointments use case of the appointment system for the doctor's office example.[10]

Actions and Activities *Actions* and *activities* are performed for some specific business reason. Actions and activities can represent manual or computerized behavior. They are depicted in an activity diagram as a rounded rectangle (see Figure 4-7). They should have a name that begins with a verb and ends with a noun (e.g., Get Patient Information or Make Payment Arrangements). Names should be short, yet contain enough information so that the reader can easily understand exactly what they do. The only difference between an action and an activity is that an activity can be decomposed further into a set of activities and/or actions, whereas an action represents a simple nondecomposable piece of the overall behavior being modeled. Typically, only activities are used for business process or workflow modeling. In most cases, each activity is associated with a use case. The activity diagram in Figure 4-8 shows a set of separate but related activities for the Manage Appointments use case (see Figures 4-2–4-4): Get Patient Information, Update Patient Information, Create New Patient, Make Payment Arrangements, Make New Appointment, Change Appointment, and Cancel Appointment. Notice that the Make Payment Arrangements and Make New Appointment activities appear twice in the diagram: once for an "old" patient and once for a "new" patient.

Object Nodes Activities and actions typically modify or transform objects. *Object nodes* model these objects in an activity diagram. Object nodes are portrayed in an activity diagram as rectangles (see Figure 4-7). The name of the class of the object is written inside the rectangle. Essentially, object nodes represent the flow of information from one activity to another activity. The simple appointment system portrayed in Figure 4-8 shows object nodes flowing from the Get Patient Information activity. In most business process–based activity diagrams, object nodes are not included. We have included them in Figure 4-8 for demonstration purposes only.

Control Flows and Object Flows There are two different types of flows in activity diagrams: control and object (see Figure 4-7). *Control flows* model the paths of execution through a

---

[9] Technically speaking, activity diagrams combine process-modeling ideas from many different techniques, including event models, statecharts, and Petri nets. However, UML 2.0's activity diagram has more in common with Petri nets than the other process-modeling techniques. For a good description of using Petri nets to model business workflows, see Wil van der Aalst and Kees van Hee, *Workflow Management: Models, Methods, and Systems* (Cambridge, MA: MIT Press, 2002).

[10] Owing to the actual complexity of the syntax of activity diagrams, we follow a minimalist philosophy in our coverage [see John M. Carrol, *The Nurnberg Funnel: Designing Minimalist Instruction for Practical Computer Skill* (Cambridge, MA: MIT Press, 1990)]. However, the material contained in this section is based on the *OMG Unified Modeling Language: Version 2.5.1, formal/2017-12-05* (www.uml.org). Additional useful references include Michael Jesse Chonoles and James A. Schardt, *UML 2 for Dummies* (Indianapolis, IN: Wiley, 2003); Hans-Erik Eriksson, Magnus Penker, Brian Lyons, and David Fado, *UML 2 Toolkit* (Indianapolis: Wiley, 2004); Kendall Scott, *Fast Track UML 2.0* (Berkeley, CA: Apress, 2004). For a complete description of all diagrams, see www.uml.org.

An action: ■ Is a simple, nondecomposable piece of behavior. ■ Is labeled by its name.	*Action*
An activity: ■ Is used to represent a set of actions. ■ Is labeled by its name.	*Activity*
An object node: ■ Is used to represent an object that is connected to a set of object flows. ■ Is labeled by its class name.	<u>**Class Name**</u>
A control flow: ■ Shows the sequence of execution.	⟶
An object flow: ■ Shows the flow of an object from one activity (or action) to another activity (or action).	⇢
An initial node: ■ Portrays the beginning of a set of actions or activities.	●
A final-activity node: ■ Is used to stop all control flows and object flows in an activity (or action).	◉
A final-flow node: ■ Is used to stop a specific control flow or object flow.	⊗
A decision node: ■ Is used to represent a test condition to ensure that the control flow or object flow only goes down one path. ■ Is labeled with the decision criteria to continue down the specific path.	[Decision Criteria] ◇ [Decision Criteria]
A merge node: ■ Is used to bring back together different decision paths that were created using a decision node.	◇
A fork node: Is used to split behavior into a set of parallel or concurrent flows of activities (or actions)	⊥
A join node: Is used to bring back together a set of parallel or concurrent flows of activities (or actions)	⊤
A swimlane: Is used to break up an activity diagram into rows and columns to assign the individual activities (or actions) to the individuals or objects that are responsible for executing the activity (or action) Is labeled with the name of the individual or object responsible	*Swimlane*

FIGURE 4-7 Syntax for an Activity Diagram

business process. A control flow is portrayed as a solid line with an arrowhead on it showing the direction of flow. Control flows can be attached only to actions or activities. Figure 4-8 portrays a set of control flows through the doctor's office appointment system. *Object flows* model the flow of objects through a business process. Because activities and actions modify or transform objects, object flows are necessary to show the actual objects that flow into and

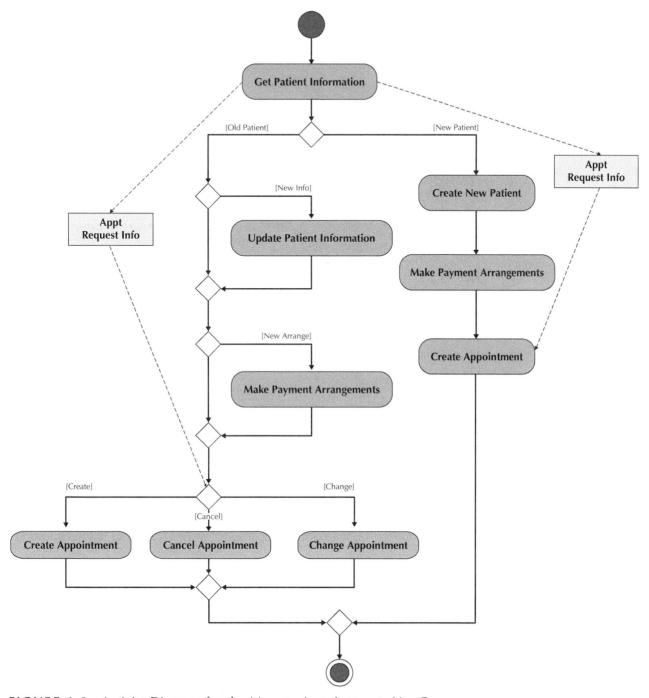

FIGURE 4-8 Activity Diagram for the Manage Appointments Use Case

out of the actions or activities. An object flow is depicted as a dashed line with an arrowhead on it showing the direction of flow. An individual object flow must be attached to an action or activity on one end and an object node on the other end. Figure 4-8 portrays a set of control and object flows through the appointment system of a doctor's office. Like with object nodes, in most business process–based activity diagrams, object flows are not included. We have included them in Figure 4-8 for demonstration purposes only.

Control Nodes There are seven different types of *control nodes* in an activity diagram: initial, final-activity, final-flow, decision, merge, fork, and join (see Figure 4-7). An *initial node* portrays the beginning of a set of actions or activities. An initial node is shown as a small filled-in circle. A *final-activity node* is used to stop the process being modeled. Any time a final-activity node is reached, all actions and activities are ended immediately, regardless of whether they are completed. A final-activity node is represented as a circle surrounding a small, filled-in circle, making it resemble a bull's-eye. A *final-flow* node is similar to a final-activity node, except that it stops a specific path of execution through the business process but allows the other concurrent or parallel paths to continue. A final-flow node is shown as a small circle with an X in it. In most business process–based activity diagrams, it is better to not include them. It is much more difficult to understand a business process that has multiple exit points. Consequently, it is better to always attempt to limit the exit from the business process with a single unifying final-activity node.

The decision and merge nodes support modeling the decision structure of a business process. The *decision node* is used to represent the actual test condition that determines which of the paths exiting the decision node is to be traversed. In this case, each exiting path must be labeled with a guard condition. A *guard condition* represents the value of the test for that particular path to be executed. For example, in Figure 4-8, the decision node immediately below the Get Patient Information activity has two mutually exclusive paths that could be executed: one for old, or previous, patients and the other for new patients. The *merge node* is used to bring back together multiple mutually exclusive paths that have been split based on an earlier decision (e.g., the old- and new-patient paths in Figure 4-8 are brought back together near the bottom of the diagram). However, sometimes, for clarity, it is better not to use a merge node. For example, in Figure 4-9, which of the two activity diagrams, both representing an overview level of an order process, is easier to understand, the one on the left or the one on the right? The one on the left contains a merge node for the More Items on Order question, but the one on the right does not. In a sense, the decision node is playing double duty in the diagram on the right: It also serves as a merge node. Technically speaking, we should not omit the merge node; however, sometimes being technically correct according to the UML's diagramming rules actually causes the diagram to become confusing. From a business process modeling perspective, a good deal of common sense can go a long way.

The fork and join nodes allow parallel and concurrent processes to be modeled (see Figure 4-7). The *fork node* is used to split the behavior of the business process into multiple parallel or concurrent flows. Unlike the decision node, the paths are not mutually exclusive (i.e., both paths are executed concurrently). For example, in Figure 4-10, the fork node is used to show that two concurrent, parallel processes are to be executed. In this case, each process is executed by two separate processors (parents). The purpose of the join node is similar to that of the merge node. The *join node* simply brings back together the separate parallel or concurrent flows in the business process into a single flow.

Swimlanes Activity diagrams can model a business process independent of any object implementation. However, there are times when it helps to break up an activity diagram in such a way that it can be used to assign responsibility to objects or individuals who would actually perform the activity. This is especially useful when modeling a business workflow and is accomplished through the use of *swimlanes*. In Figure 4-10, the swimlanes are used to break up among two parents the making of a school lunch comprising a peanut butter and jelly sandwich, a drink, and dessert. In this case, we use vertical swimlanes. We could also draw the activity diagram using more of a left-to-right orientation instead of a top-down orientation. In that case, the swimlanes are drawn horizontally.

In an actual business workflow, there would be activities that should be associated with roles of individuals involved in the business workflow (e.g., employees or customers) and the

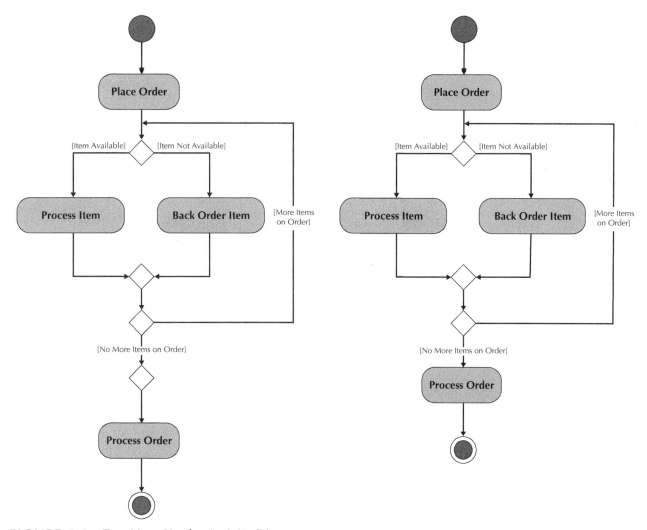

FIGURE 4-9 Two Very Similar Activity Diagrams

activities to be accomplished by the information system being created. This association of activities with external roles, internal roles, and the system is very useful when creating the use-case descriptions described later in this chapter. We will return to the use of swimlanes with activity diagrams when we attempt to assign individual activities to actors (both external and internal) and objects when we create the behavior models (see Chapter 6).

Guidelines for Creating Activity Diagrams

Scott Ambler suggests the following guidelines when creating activity diagrams[11]:

- Because an activity diagram can be used to model any kind of process, you should set the context or scope of the activity being modeled. Once you have determined the scope, you should give the diagram an appropriate title.

[11] The guidelines presented here are based on work done by Scott Ambler. For more details, see Scott W. Ambler, *The Object Primer: The Application Developer's Guide to Object Orientation and the UML,* 2nd Ed. (Cambridge, England: Cambridge University Press/SIGS Books, 2001); and Scott W. Ambler, *The Elements of UML Style* (Cambridge, England: Cambridge University Press, 2003).

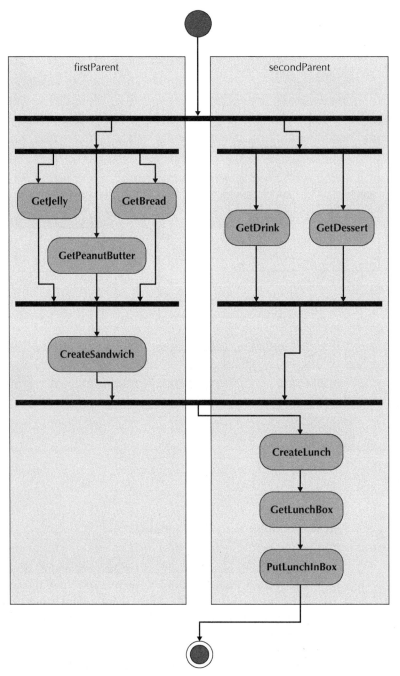

FIGURE 4-10 Activity Diagram for Making a School Box Lunch

- You must identify the activities, control flows, and object flows that occur between the activities.
- You should identify any decisions that are part of the process being modeled.
- You should attempt to identify any prospects for parallelism in the process.
- You should draw the activity diagram.

When drawing an activity diagram, the diagram should be limited to a single initial node that starts the process being modeled. This node should be placed at the top or top left of the diagram, depending on the complexity of the diagram. For most business processes, there should only be a single final-activity node. This node should be placed at the bottom or bottom right of the diagram (see Figures 4-8–4-10). Because most high-level business processes are sequential, not parallel, the use of a final-flow node should be limited.

When modeling high-level business processes or workflows, only the more important decisions should be included in the activity diagrams. In those cases, the guard conditions associated with the outflows of the decision nodes should be mutually exclusive. The outflows and guard conditions should form a complete set (i.e., all potential values of the decision are associated with one of the flows).

As in decision modeling, forks and joins should be included only to represent the more important parallel activities in the process. For example, an alternative version of Figure 4-10 might not include the forks and joins associated with the Get Jelly, Get Bread, Get Peanut Butter, Get Drink, and Get Dessert activities. This would greatly simplify the diagram.[12]

When laying out the activity diagram, line crossings should be minimized to enhance the readability of the diagram. The activities on the diagram should also be laid out in a left-to-right and/or top-to-bottom order based on the order in which the activities are executed. For example, in Figure 4-10, the Create Sandwich activity takes place before the Create Lunch activity.

When creating functional models, swimlanes should be used only to simplify the understanding of an activity diagram. Furthermore, the swimlanes should enhance the readability of a diagram. For example, when using a horizontal orientation for swimlanes, the top swimlane should represent the most important object or individual involved with the process. The order of the remaining swimlanes should be based on minimizing the number of flows crossing the different swimlanes. Also, when there are object flows among the activities associated with the different individuals (swimlanes) executing the activities of the process, it is useful to show the actual object flowing from one individual to another individual by including an object node between the two individuals (i.e., between the two swimlanes). This, of course, affects how the swimlanes should be placed on the diagram.

Finally, any activity that does not have any outflows or any inflows should be challenged. Activities with no outflows are referred to as *black-hole activities*. If the activity is truly an end point in the diagram, the activity should have a control flow from it to a final-activity or final-flow node. An activity that does not have any inflow is known as a *miracle activity*. In this case, the activity is missing an inflow either from the initial node of the diagram or from another activity.

Creating Activity Diagrams

1. Choose a Business Process

There are five steps in creating an activity diagram to document and model a business process. First, you must choose a business process that was previously identified to model. To do this, you should review the requirements definition (see Figure 3-11) and the use-case diagram (see Figures 4-2–4-4) created to represent the requirements. You should also review all of the documentation created during the requirements-gathering process (see Chapter 3), for example, reports created that documented interviews or observations, any analysis of any questionnaires used, and any story cards or task lists created. In most cases, the use cases in the use-case diagram will be the best place to start. For example, in the appointment system, we had identified three primary use cases: Manage Appointments, Produce Schedules, and Record Doctor Availability. We also identified a whole set of minor use cases (these will be useful in identifying the elements of the activity diagram).

[12] In fact, the only reason we depicted the diagram in Figure 4-10 with the multiple fork and join nodes was to demonstrate that it could be done.

Second, identify the set of activities necessary to support the business process. For example, in Figure 3-11, three processes are identified as being part of the Manage Appointments business process. Also, by reviewing the use-case diagram (see Figure 4-4), we see that five minor use cases are associated with the Manage Appointments major use case. Based on this information, we can identify a set of activities. In this case, the activities are Update Patient Information, Make Payment Arrangements, Create New Patient, Create Appointment, Cancel Appointment, and Change Appointment.

Third, identify the control flows and nodes necessary to document the logic of the business process. For example, in Figure 4-4, the Make Payment Arrangements and Update Patient Information use cases are extensions to the Manage Appointments and Make Old Patient Appt use cases. We know that these use cases are executed only in certain circumstances. From this we can infer that the activity diagram must include some decision and merge nodes. Based on the requirements definition (see Figure 3-11), we can infer another set of decision and merge nodes based on the Create Appointment, Cancel Appointment, and Change Appointment activities identified in the previous step.

Fourth, identify the object flows and nodes necessary to support the logic of the business process. Typically, object nodes and flows are not shown on many activity diagrams used to model a business process. The primary exception is if information captured by the system in one activity is used in an activity that is performed later, but *not* immediately after the activity that captured the information. In the appointment example, it is obvious that we need to be able to determine whether the patient is an old or new patient and the type of action that the patient would like to have performed (create, cancel, or change an appointment). It is obvious that a new patient cannot cancel or change an appointment because the patient is by definition a new patient. Obviously, we need to capture this type of information at the beginning of the business process and use it when required. For example, in the appointment problem, we need to have a Get Patient Information activity that captures the appropriate information and makes it available at the appropriate time in the process.

Fifth, lay out and draw the activity diagram to document the business process. For esthetic and understandability reasons, just as when drawing a use-case diagram, you should attempt to minimize potential line crossings. Based on the previous steps and carefully laying out the diagram, the activity diagram in Figure 4-8 was created to document the Manage Appointments business process.

Campus Housing Example The first step in detailing the identified business processes (Maintain Available Rental Unit Information and Search Available Rental Units) is to choose one of them. In this example, we are going to focus on the Maintain Available Rental Unit Information associated with the apartment owners. Based on the earlier description, there are two separate activities (subprocesses): one to add a rental unit and one to delete a rental unit. To add a rental unit, the apartment owner must provide the campus housing service with the location of the apartment, the number of bedrooms in the apartment, and the monthly rent of the apartment. To delete an apartment, the apartment owners must tell the campus housing service that the specific apartment has been rented and is no longer available. Using this information, the activity diagram that represents the logical description of the Maintain Available Rental Unit Information use case is portrayed in Figure 4-11. Notice that there is absolutely no reference to filling out a form, entering the information into a database, or searching the database. There are actually many different potential ways in which the apartment information could be captured, for example, on a manual form, on a computerized form, on a Web form, and via a mobile interface. In fact, we might want to be able to support all of them. Also, there are many different ways in which the information can be stored.

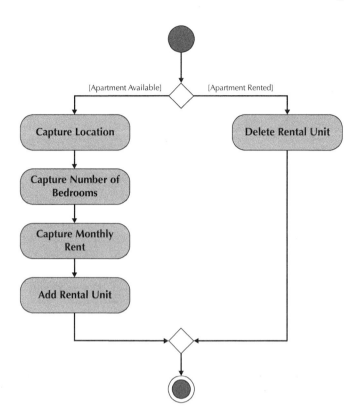

FIGURE 4-11
Campus Housing
Maintain Available
Rental Unit
Information Activity
Diagram

However, at this stage of development, all design and implementation details should be ignored. We are only interested in capturing the functional requirements. Once we have successfully modeled the functional requirements, we can move on to the nonfunctional requirements, design, and implementation details. We will return to this example in the next section of the chapter. However, before we move on, we next describe the activity diagram for the Borrow Books use case of the university library problem.

Library Example As with the Campus Housing example, the first step is to choose a business process to model. In this case, we want to create an activity diagram for the Borrow Books use case (see Figure 4-6). The functional requirements for this use case were:

> The borrowing activities are built around checking books out and returning books by borrowers. There are three types of borrowers: students, faculty or staff, and guests. Regardless of the type of borrower, the borrower must have a valid ID card. If the borrower is a student, having the system check with the registrar's office to validate the ID card. If the borrower is a faculty or staff member, having the system check with the personnel office to validate the ID card. If the borrower is a guest, the ID card is checked against the library's own system. If the ID card is valid, the system must also check to determine whether the borrower has any overdue books or unpaid fines. If the ID card is invalid, the borrower has overdue books, or the borrower has unpaid fines, the system must reject the borrower's request to check out a book, otherwise the borrower's request should be honored.

The second step to model a business process is to identify the activities that make up the process. Based on the requirements for the Borrow Books use case, we can identify three major activities: Validate ID Card, Check for Overdue Books and Fines, and Check Out Books. The

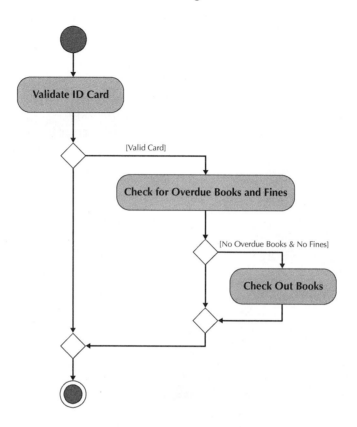

FIGURE 4-12
Activity Diagram
for the Borrow
Books Use Case

third step is to identify the control flows and control nodes necessary to model the decision logic of the business process. In this case, there obviously will have to be an initial node, a final-flow node, and a set of decision and merge nodes for each decision to be made. The fourth step is to identify the object flows and object nodes necessary to complete the description of the business process. In this case, there really is no need to include object nodes and flows. Finally, we can lay out the diagram (see Figure 4-12).

BUSINESS PROCESS DOCUMENTATION WITH USE-CASE DESCRIPTIONS

Use-case diagrams provided a bird's-eye view of the basic functionality of the business processes contained in the evolving system. Activity diagrams, in a sense, open up the black box of each business process by providing a more detailed graphical view of the underlying activities that support each business process. Use-case descriptions provide a means to more fully document the different aspects of each individual use case.[13] The use-case descriptions are based on the identified requirements, use-case diagram, and the activity diagram descriptions of the business processes. Use-case descriptions contain all the information needed to document the functionality of the business processes.[14]

[13] For a more detailed description of use-case modeling, see Alistair Cockburn, Writing Effective Use Cases (Reading, MA: Addison-Wesley, 2001).

[14] Nonfunctional requirements, such as reliability requirements and performance requirements, are often documented outside of the use case through more traditional requirements documents. See Gerald Kotonya and Ian Sommerville, *Requirements Engineering* (Chichester, England: Wiley, 1998); Benjamin L. Kovitz, *Practical Software Requirements: A Manual of Content & Style* (Greenwich, CT: Manning, 1999); Dean Leffingwell and Don Widrig, *Managing Software Requirements: A Unified Approach* (Reading, MA: Addison-Wesley, 2000); and Richard H. Thayer, M. Dorfman, and Sidney C. Bailin (Eds), *Software Requirements Engineering,* 2nd Ed. (Los Alamitos, CA: IEEE Computer Society, 1997).

When creating use-case descriptions, the project team must work closely with the users to fully document the functional requirements. Organizing the functional requirements and documenting them in a use-case description are a relatively simple process, but it takes considerable practice to ensure that the descriptions are complete enough to use in structural (Chapter 5) and behavioral (Chapter 6) modeling. The best place to begin is to review the use-case and activity diagrams. The key thing to remember is that each use case is associated with one and only one *role* that users have in the system.[15] For example, a receptionist in a doctor's office may play multiple roles—he or she can make appointments, answer the telephone, file medical records, welcome patients, and so on. It is possible that multiple users will play the same role. Therefore, use cases should be associated with the roles played by the users and not with the users themselves.

Elements of a Use-Case Description

A use-case description contains all the information needed to build the structural (Chapter 5) and behavioral (Chapter 6) diagrams that follow, but it expresses the information in a less-formal way that is usually simpler for users to understand. Figure 4-13 shows a sample use-case description.[16] A use-case description supports both overview and detail use cases.

Overview Use Case Section The overview use case identifies the use case and provides basic background information about the use case. This section of the use case description is associated with the use case diagram. The *use-case name* should be a verb–noun phrase (e.g., Make Old Patient Appt). The *use-case ID number* provides a unique way to find every use case and also enables the team to trace design decisions back to a specific requirement. The *use-case type* is either overview or detail and essential or real. The *primary actor* is usually the trigger of the use case—the person or thing that starts the execution of the use case. The primary purpose of the use case is to meet the goal of the primary actor. The identification of the primary actor, along with the stakeholders, also provides information that will be useful in addressing role-based access controls that support the security nonfunctional requirements covered in the design and construction chapters later in the book. The *brief description* is typically a single sentence that describes the essence of the use case.

The *importance level* can be used to prioritize the use cases. The importance level enables the users to explicitly prioritize which business functions are most important and need to be part of the first version of the system and which are less important and can wait until later versions if necessary. The importance level can use a fuzzy scale, such as high, medium, and low (e.g., in Figure 4-13 we have assigned an importance level of high to the Make Old Patient Appt use case). It can also be done more formally using a weighted average of a set of criteria. For example, Larman[17] suggests rating each use case over the following criteria using a scale from zero to five:

- The use case represents an important business process.
- The use case supports revenue generation or cost reduction.
- Technology needed to support the use case is new or risky and therefore requires considerable research.

---

[15] For presentation purposes, we defer discussion of role-playing to Chapter 5.

[16] Currently there is no standard set of elements for a use case. The elements described in this section are based on recommendations contained in Alistair Cockburn, *Writing Effective Use Cases* (Reading, MA: Addison-Wesley, 2001); Craig Larman, *Applying UML and Patterns: An Introduction to Object-Oriented Analysis and Design and the Unified Process,* 2nd Ed. (Upper Saddle River, NJ: Prentice Hall, 2002); and Brian Henderson-Sellers and Bhuvan Unhelkar, *OPEN Modeling with UML* (Reading, MA: Addison-Wesley, 2000). Also see Graham, *Migrating to Object Technology.*

[17] Larman, *Applying UML and Patterns: An Introduction to Object-Oriented Analysis and Design.*

Use Case Name:	Make Old Patient Appt		ID:	2	Importance Level:	Low
Primary Actor:	Old Patient		Use Case Type:	Detail, Essential		

Stakeholders and Interests:
Old Patient – wants to make, change, or cancel an appointment
Doctor – wants to ensure patient's needs are met in a timely manner

Brief Description: This use case describes how we make an appointment as well as changing or canceling an appointment for a previously seen patient.

Trigger: Patient calls and asks for a new appointment or asks to cancel or change an existing appointment

Type: External

Relationships:
Association: Old Patient
Include:
Extend: Update Patient Information
Generalization: Manage Appointments

Normal Flow of Events:
1. The Patient contacts the office regarding an appointment.
2. The Patient provides the Receptionist with his or her name and address.
3. If the Patient's information has changed
    Execute the Update Patient Information use case.
4. If the Patient's payment arrangements has changed
    Execute the Make Payments Arrangements use case.
5. The Receptionist asks Patient if he or she would like to make a new appointment, cancel an existing appointment, or change an existing appointment.
    If the patient wants to make a new appointment,
        the S-1: new appointment subflow is performed.
    If the patient wants to cancel an existing appointment,
        the S-2: cancel appointment subflow is performed.
    If the patient wants to change an existing appointment,
        the S-3: change appointment subflow is performed.
6. The Receptionist provides the results of the transaction to the Patient.

SubFlows:
S-1: New Appointment
    1. The Receptionist asks the Patient for possible appointment times.
    2. The Receptionist matches the Patient's desired appointment times with available dates and times and schedules the new appointment.
S-2: Cancel Appointment
    1. The Receptionist asks the Patient for the old appointment time.
    2. The Receptionist finds the current appointment in the appointment file and cancels it.
S-3: Change Appointment
    1. The Receptionist performs the S-2: cancel appointment subflow.
    2. The Receptionist performs the S-1: new appointment subflow.

Alternate/Exceptional Flows:
S-1, 2a1: The Receptionist proposes some alternative appointment times based on what is available in the appointment schedule.
S-1, 2a2: The Patient chooses one of the proposed times or decides not to make an appointment.

FIGURE 4-13 Sample Use-Case Description

- Functionality described in the use case is complex, risky, and/or time critical. Depending on a use case's complexity, it may be useful to consider splitting its implementation over several different versions. For example, we could include the use case point approach based on the number of transactions supported by the use case.
- The use case could increase understanding of the evolving design relative to the effort expended.

A use case may have multiple *stakeholders* that have an interest in the use case. Each use case lists each of the stakeholders with each one's interest in the use case (e.g., Old Patient and Doctor). The stakeholders' list always includes the primary actor (e.g., Old Patient).

Each use case typically has a *trigger*—the event that causes the use case to begin (e.g., Old Patient calls and asks for a new appointment or asks to cancel or change an existing appointment). A trigger can be an *external trigger*, such as a customer placing an order or the fire alarm ringing, or it can be a *temporal trigger*, such as a book being overdue at the library or the need to pay the rent.

Use-case relationships explain how the use case is related to other use cases and users. There are four basic types of *relationships*: association, extend, include, and generalization. An *association relationship* documents the communication that takes place between the use case and the actors that use the use case. An actor is the UML representation for the role that a user plays in the use case. For example, in Figure 4-13, the Make Old Patient Appt use case is associated with the actor Old Patient (see Figure 4-4). In this case, a patient makes an appointment. All actors involved in the use case are documented with the association relationship.

An *include relationship* represents the mandatory inclusion of another use case. The include relationship enables *functional decomposition*—the breaking up of a complex use case into several simpler ones. For example, in Figure 4-4, the Manage Schedule use case was considered to be complex and complete enough to be factored out as a separate use case that could be executed by the Produce Schedules and Record Availability use cases. The include relationship also enables parts of use cases to be reused by creating them as separate use cases.

An *extend relationship* represents the extension of the functionality of the use case to incorporate optional behavior. In Figure 4-13, the Make Old Patient Appt use case conditionally uses the Update Patient Information use case. This use case is executed only if the patient's information has changed.

The *generalization relationship* allows use cases to support *inheritance*. For example, the use case in Figure 4-4, the Manage Appointments use case was specialized so that a new patient would be associated with the Make New Patient Appt and an old patient could be associated with a Make Old Patient Appt. The common, or generalized, behavior of both the Make New Patient Appt and Make Old Patient Appt use cases would be placed in the generalized Manage Appointments use case. In other words, the Make New Patient Appt and Make Old Patient Appt use cases would inherit the common functionality from the Manage Appointments use case. The specialized behavior would be placed in the appropriate specialized use case. For example, the extend relationship to the Update Patient Information use case would be placed with the specialized Make Old Patient Appt use case.

Detail Use Case Section Finally, for detail use cases, individual steps within the business process are described. These steps are associated with the activity diagrams. Three different categories of steps, or *flows of events,* can be documented: normal flow of events, subflows, and alternative, or exceptional, flows:

- The *normal flow of events* includes only steps that normally are executed in a use case. The steps are listed in the order in which they are performed. In Figure 4-13, the patient and the receptionist have a conversation regarding the patient's name, address, and action to be performed.
- In some cases, the normal flow of events should be decomposed into a set of *subflows* to keep the normal flow of events as simple as possible. In Figure 4-13, we have identified three subflows: Create Appointment, Cancel Appointment, and Change Appointment. Each of the steps of these subflows is listed. These subflows are based on the control flow logic in the activity diagram representation of the business process (see Figure 4-7). Alternatively, we could replace a subflow with a separate use case

that could be incorporated via the include relationships (see the earlier discussion). However, this should be done only if the newly created use case makes sense by itself. For example, in Figure 4-13, does it make sense to factor out a Create Appointment, Cancel Appointment, and/or Change Appointment use case? If it does, then the specific subflow(s) should be replaced with a call to the related use case, and the use case should be added to the include relationship list.

■ *Alternative* or *exceptional flows* are ones that do happen but are not considered to be the norm. These must be documented. For example, in Figure 4-13, we have identified two alternative or exceptional flows. The first one simply addresses the situation that occurs when the set of requested appointment time is not available. The second one is simply a second step to the alternative flow. Like the subflows, the primary purpose of separating out alternate or exceptional flows is to keep the normal flow of events as simple as possible. Again, as with the subflows, it is possible to replace the alternate or exceptional flows with separate use cases that could be integrated via the extend relationship (see the earlier discussion).

When should events be factored out from the normal flow of events into subflows? When should subflows and/or alternative or exceptional flows be factored out into separate use cases? Or when should things simply be left alone? The primary criteria should be based on the level of complexity that the use case entails. The more difficult it is to understand the use case, the more likely events should be factored out into subflows, or subflows and/or alternative or exceptional flows should be factored out into separate use cases that are called by the current use case. This, of course, creates more use cases. Therefore, the use-case diagram will become more cluttered. In other words, the choice that the analyst must make is to have a more complex use-case diagram with simpler use cases or have a simpler use-case diagram with more complex use cases. Practically speaking, we must decide which makes more sense. This varies greatly, depending on the problem and the client. Remember, we are trying to represent, in a manner as complete and concise as possible, our understanding of the business processes that we are investigating so that the client can validate the requirements that we are modeling. Therefore, there really is no single right answer. It really depends on the analyst, the client, and the problem.

Optional Characteristics Other characteristics of use cases can be documented by use-case descriptions. These include the level of complexity of the use case; the estimated amount of time it takes to execute the use case; the system with which the use case is associated; specific data flows between the primary actor and the use case; any specific attribute, constraint, or operation associated with the use case; any preconditions that must be satisfied for the use case to execute; or any guarantees that can be made based on the execution of the use case. As we noted at the beginning of this section, there is no standard set of characteristics of a use case that must be captured. We suggest that the information contained in Figure 4-13 is the minimal amount to be captured.

Guidelines for Creating Use-Case Descriptions[18]

The essence of a use case is the flow of events. Writing the flow of events in a manner that is useful for later stages of development generally comes with experience.

First, write each individual step in the form subject–verb–direct object and, optionally, preposition–indirect object. This form is relatively easy to diagram (see sentence diagramming in Chapter 3) and has become known as *SVDPI* sentences. This form of sentence has proved to be useful in identifying classes and operations (see Chapter 5). For example, in

---

[18] These guidelines are based on Cockburn, *Writing Effective Use Cases;* and Graham, *Migrating to Object Technology.*

Figure 4-13, the first step in the normal flow of events, the Patient contacts the office regarding an appointment, suggests the possibility of three classes of objects: Patient, Office, and Appointment. This approach simplifies the process of identifying the classes in the structural model (see Chapter 5). SVDPI sentences cannot be used for all steps, but they should be used whenever possible.

Second, make clear who or what is the initiator of the action and who or what is the receiver of the action in each step. Normally, the initiator should be the subject of the sentence and the receiver should be the direct object of the sentence. For example, in Figure 4-13, the second step, Patient provides the Receptionist with his or her name and address, clearly portrays the Patient as the initiator and the Receptionist as the receiver.

Third, write the step from the perspective of an independent observer. To accomplish this, each step might have to be written first from the perspective of both the initiator and the receiver. Based on the two points of view, the bird's-eye view version can then be written. For example, in Figure 4-13, the Patient provides the Receptionist with his or her name and address, neither the patient's nor the receptionist's perspective is represented.

Fourth, write each step at the same level of abstraction. Each step should make about the same amount of progress toward completing the use case as each of the other steps. In high-level use cases, the amount of progress could be very substantial, whereas in a low-level use case, each step could represent only incremental progress.

Fifth, ensure that the use case contains a sensible set of actions. Each use case should represent a transaction. Therefore, each use case should comprise four parts:

1. The primary actor initiates the execution of the use case by sending a request (and possibly data) to the system.
2. The system ensures that the request (and data) is valid.
3. The system processes the request (and data) and possibly changes its own internal state.
4. The system sends the primary actor the result of the processing.

For example, in Figure 4-13, the patient requests an appointment (steps 1 and 2), the receptionist determines whether any of the patient's information has changed or not (step 3), the receptionist determines whether the patient's payment arrangements have changed or not (step 4), the receptionist sets up the appointment transaction (step 5), and the receptionist provides the results of the transaction to the patient (step 6).

The sixth guideline is the KISS principle. If the use case becomes too complex and/or too long, the use case should be decomposed into a set of use cases. Furthermore, if the normal flow of events of the use case becomes too complex, subflows should be used. For example, in Figure 4-13, the fifth step in the normal flow of events was sufficiently complex to decompose it into three separate subflows. However, care must be taken to avoid the possibility of decomposing too much. Most decomposition should be done with classes (see Chapter 5).

The seventh guideline deals with repeating steps. Normally, in a programming language, we put loop definition and controls at the beginning of the loop. However, because the use-case steps are written in simple English, it is normally better to simply write Repeat steps A through E until some condition is met after step E. It makes the use case more readable to people unfamiliar with programming.

Creating Use Case Descriptions

Use cases provide a bird's-eye view of the business processes contained in the evolving system. The use-case diagram depicts the communication path between the actors and the system, while the activity diagram portrays the underlying logic structure of the use case. Use case description documentation tend to be used to model both the contexts of the system and the detailed requirements of the system. Even though the primary purpose of use cases is to document the functional requirements of the system, they also are used as a basis for testing the evolving system and as a foundation of the user interface design. In this section, we provide a set of steps that can be used to guide the actual creation of a use-case description for each use case in the use-case diagram based on the requirements definition and the use-case and activity diagrams.[19] These steps are performed in order, but of course the analyst often cycles among them in an iterative fashion as he or she moves from one use case to another use case.

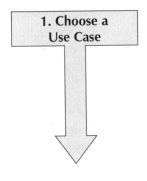

The first step is to choose one of the use cases to document with a use-case description. Using the importance level of the use case can help do this. For example, in Figure 4-13, the Make Old Patient Appt use case has an importance level of high. As such, it should be one of the earlier use cases to be expanded. The criteria suggested by Larman[20] can also be used to set the prioritization of the use cases, as noted earlier. An alternative approach suggests that each use case should be voted on by each member of the development team. In this approach, each team member is given a set of "dots" that they can use to vote on the use cases. They can use all of their dots to vote for a single use case, or they can spread them over a set of use cases. The use cases then can be ranked in order of the number of dots received. Use case descriptions are created for the individual use cases based on the rank order.[21]

The second step is to create an overview description of the use case; that is, name the primary actor, set the type for the use case, list all of the identified stakeholders and their interests in the use case, identify the level of importance of the use case, give a brief description of the use case, give the trigger information for the use case, and list the relationships in which the use case participates. This can be done immediately after the use case diagram has been created.

The third step is to fill in the steps of the normal flow of events required to describe each use case. The steps focus on what the business process does to complete the use case, as opposed to what actions the users or other external entities do. In general, the steps should be listed in the order in which they are performed, from first to last. Remember to write the steps in an SVDPI form whenever possible. In writing the use case, remember the seven guidelines described earlier. The goal at this point is to describe how the chosen use case operates. One of the best ways to begin to understand how an actor works through a use case is to visualize performing the steps in the use case—that is, role play. The techniques of visualizing how to interact with the system and of thinking about how other systems work (informal benchmarking) are important techniques that help analysts and users understand how systems work and how to write a use case. Both techniques (visualization and informal benchmarking) are common in practice. It is important to remember that at this point in the development of a use case, we are interested only in the typical successful execution of the use case. If we try to think of all of the possible combinations of activities that could go on, we will never get anything written. At this point, we are looking only for the three to seven *major* steps. Focus only on performing the typical process that the use case represents. If the activity diagram has been completed, then the activities will serve as a basis for the events. Furthermore, the most likely path through the activity diagram should be the basis for the normal flow of events.

---

[19] The approach in this section is based on the work of Cockburn, *Writing Effective Use Cases*; Graham, *Migrating to Object Technology*; George Marakas and Joyce Elam, "Semantic Structuring in Analyst Acquisition and Representation of Facts in Requirements Analysis," *Information Systems Research* 9, no. 1 (1998): 37–63; and Alan Dennis, Glenda Hayes, and Robert Daniels, "Business Process Modeling with Group Support Systems," *Journal of Management Information Systems* 15, no. 4 (1999): 115–142.

[20] Larman, *Applying UML and Patterns: An Introduction to Object-Oriented Analysis and Design.*

[21] C. Larman, *Agile & Iterative Development: A Manager's Guide* (Boston, MA: Addison-Wesley, 2004).

The fourth step is to ensure that the steps listed in the normal flow of events are not too complex or too long. Each step should be about the same size as the others. For example, if we were writing steps for preparing a meal, steps such as take fork out of drawer and put fork on table are much smaller than prepare cake using mix. If we end up with more than seven steps or steps that vary greatly in size, we should go back and review each step carefully and possibly rewrite the steps.

One good approach to produce the steps for a use case is to have the users visualize themselves actually performing the use case and to have them write down the steps as if they were writing a recipe for a cookbook. In most cases, the users will be able to quickly define what they do in the as-is model. Defining the steps for to-be use cases might take a bit more coaching. In our experience, the descriptions of the steps change greatly as users work through a use case. Our advice is to use a blackboard or whiteboard (or paper with pencil) that can be easily erased to develop the list of steps and then write the list on the use-case form. It should be written on the use-case form only after the set of steps is fairly well defined. As stated above, these steps should be associated with the activities in the activity diagram.

The fifth step focuses on identifying and writing the alternative or exceptional flows. Alternative or exceptional flows are flows of success that represent optional or exceptional behavior. They tend to occur infrequently or as a result of a normal flow failure. They should be labeled so that there is no doubt as to which normal flow of events it is related. For example, in Figure 4-13, alternative/exceptional flow S-1, 2a1 executes when step 2 of subflow S-1 fails (i.e., the requested appointment time was not available). Like the normal flows and subflows, alternative or exceptional flows should be written in the SVDPI form whenever possible.

The sixth step is to carefully review the use-case description and confirm that the use case is correct as written, which means reviewing the use case with the users to make sure each step is correct. The review should look for opportunities to simplify a use case by decomposing it into a set of smaller use cases, merging it with others, looking for common aspects in both the semantics and syntax of the use cases, and identifying new use cases. This is also the time to look into adding the include, extend, and/or generalization relationships between use cases. The most powerful way to confirm a use case is to ask the user to role-play, or execute the process using the written steps in the use case.[22] The analyst hands the user pieces of paper labeled with the major inputs to the use case and has the user follow the written steps like a recipe to make sure that those steps really can produce the outputs defined for the use case using its inputs.

The seventh and final step is to *iterate* the entire set of steps again. Users often change their minds about what is a use case and what it includes. It is very easy to get trapped in the details at this point, so remember that the goal is to just address the major use cases. Therefore, the analyst should continue to iterate these steps until he or she and the users believe that a sufficient number of use cases have been documented to begin identifying candidate classes for the structural model (see Chapter 5). As candidate classes are identified, it is likely that additional use cases will be uncovered.

Campus Housing Example The first step in documenting a use case with a use-case description is to choose a use case. For instructional purposes, we use the same use case used earlier with the activity diagrams; the Maintain Available Rental Unit Information, which is associated with the apartment owners. The next step is to create an Overview Description of the use case. In this case, the primary actor is the apartment owner. Given that the use-case description documents the detailed logic steps for the use case, the type of use case is Detailed and

---

[22] This process is related to role-playing, which is discussed in Chapter 5.

Essential. The Stakeholders include the apartment owners and the campus housing service. Their respective interests are to advertise their available apartments and to provide a service that enables the apartment owners to rent their available apartments. The Brief Description for this use case is "This use case describes how the campus housing service can maintain an up-to-date listing of available apartments." The trigger for the use case is when an apartment owner wants to add or delete an available apartment. As such, the trigger is "fired" from outside of the system. In this case, the apartment owner's action triggers this use case. There is only one Association relationship between this use case and its Primary Actor: Apartment Owner. Figure 4-14 documents this information.

Next, we document and verify the logical steps necessary to successfully execute this use case. That is, we document the normal flow of events, check the normal flow of events (possibly identifying subflows), identify any alternative or exceptional flows, and then carefully review the description to be sure that it is complete. If you recall, in this specific example, the apartment owners provided information to add a rental unit to the available rental units or provided information that identified an available unit that was no longer available and needed to be deleted from the list of available rental units. These two processes were treated as two subprocesses of the Maintain Available Rental Unit Information use case. Now that we have to determine which of these subprocesses is to be treated as the Normal Flow of Events and which is to be treated as an Alternative or Exceptional Flow. However, upon further reflection, the question as to whether these should be separated into two independent use cases or whether they should remain together should be investigated. This is a great example where moving from one representation (activity diagram) to another representation (use case description) in an iterative and incremental manner raises issues that were not readily apparent. In this example, it is probably better to replace the Maintain Available Rental Unit Information use case with two simpler use cases: one for adding a rental unit and one for deleting a rental unit. Consequently, we now have to change the use-case diagram (see Figure 4-15) and create two activity diagrams to replace the earlier ones (see Figure 4-16). And, we must create two use-case descriptions to replace the one that we just begun (see Figures 4-17 and 4-18). We will return to this example in the next chapter when we begin to create a structural model for the campus housing service. However, next we return to the university library problem.

Use Case Name: Maintain Available Rental Unit Information	ID: ___1___	Importance Level: __High__
Primary Actor: Apartment Owner	Use Case Type: Detail, Essential	

Stakeholders and Interests:
Apartment Owner—wants to advertise available apartment
Campus Housing Service—provides a service that enables the apartment owners to rent their available apartments

Brief Description: This use case describes how the campus housing service can maintain an up-to-date listing of available apartments.

Trigger: Apartment Owner wants to add or delete an available apartment

Type: External

Relationships:
Association: Apartment Owner
Include:
Extend:
Generalization:

FIGURE 4-14 Campus Housing Maintain Available Rental Unit Information Overview Use-Case Description

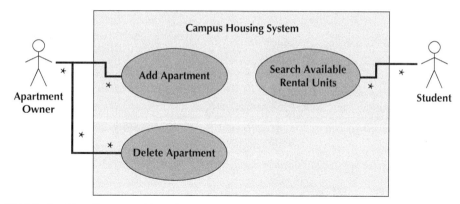

FIGURE 4-15 Campus Housing Use-Case Diagram

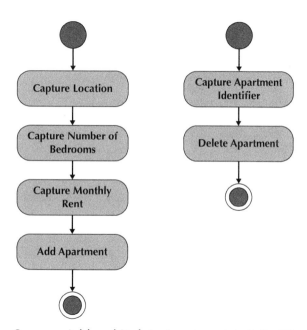

FIGURE 4-16 Campus Add and Delete Apartment Activity Diagrams

Library Example As with the Campus Housing example, the first step to document business processes with use-case descriptions is to choose a use case. Because we previously chose the Borrow Books use case in the Library Collection Management System example, we will stay with it. Next, we need to create the overview description. In this case, we have to go back and look at the use case diagram (see Figure 4-6) that describes the external behavior of the Library Collection Management System and the activity diagram (see Figure 4-12) that describes the functionality of the Borrow Books use case. It is also a good idea to refer back, once again, to the functional requirements that drove the creation of the Borrow Books use case. Here they are:

> The borrowing activities are built around checking books out and returning books by borrowers. There are three types of borrowers: students, faculty or staff, and guests. Regardless of the type of borrower, the borrower must have a valid ID card. If the borrower is a student, having the system check with the registrar's office to validate the ID card. If the borrower is a faculty or staff member, having the system check with

Use Case Name: Add Apartment		ID: 1	Importance Level: High
Primary Actor: Apartment Owner		Use Case Type: Detail, Essential	
Stakeholders and Interests: Apartment Owner—wants to advertise available apartment Campus Housing Service—provides a service that enables the apartment owners to rent their available apartments			
Brief Description: This use case describes how the campus housing service can maintain an up-to-date listing of available apartments.			
Trigger: Apartment Owner wants to add an available apartment			
Type: External			

Relationships:
    Association: Apartment Owner
    Include:
    Extend:
    Generalization:			

Normal Flow of Events:
    1. Capture the location of the apartment.
    2. Capture the number of bedrooms in the apartment.
    3. Capture the monthly rent of the apartment.
    4. Add the apartment to the listing of available apartments.			

SubFlows:			
Alternate/Exceptional Flows:			

FIGURE 4-17 Campus Housing Service Add an Apartment Use-Case Description

the personnel office to validate the ID card. If the borrower is a guest, the ID card is checked against the library's own system. If the ID card is valid, the system must also check to determine whether the borrower has any overdue books or unpaid fines. If the ID card is invalid, the borrower has overdue books, or the borrower has unpaid fines, the system must reject the borrower's request to check out a book, otherwise the borrower's request should be honored.

Based on these three critical pieces of information and using the use-case description template (see Figure 4-13), we can create the overview description of the Borrow Books use case (see Figure 4-19).

By carefully reviewing the functional requirements (above) and the activity diagram (Figure 4-12), we can easily identify the Normal Flow of Events for the Borrow Books use case. Furthermore, it is possible to decide whether any of the events contained in the Normal Flow of Events list should be decomposed using Subflows or other use cases that would need to be included. In the latter case, we would have to modify the Relationships section of the overview description and modify the use-case diagram to reflect this addition. Also, based on the logic structure of the activity diagram, it is possible to identify the alternative exceptional flows to the normal flow of events for the Borrow Books use case. Based on the overall simplicity of the Borrow Books use case, we decided not to decompose the process using either subflows or included use cases. However, due to the logic structure laid out in the activity diagram, there were two alternate/exceptional flows identified. Figure 4-20 depicts the Normal Flow of Events, Subflows, and Alternative/Exceptional Flows sections of the Borrow Books use-case description.

Use Case Name: Delete Apartment	ID: 2	Importance Level: High
Primary Actor: Apartment Owner	Use Case Type: Detail, Essential	

Stakeholders and Interests:
Apartment Owner—wants to delist apartment
Campus Housing Service—provides a service that enables the apartment owners to rent their available apartments

Brief Description: This use case describes how the campus housing service can maintain an up-to-date listing of available apartments.

Trigger: Apartment Owner wants to delete an available apartment

Type: External

Relationships:
    Association: Apartment Owner
    Include:
    Extend:
    Generalization:

Normal Flow of Events:
    1. Capture the apartment identifier.
    2. Delete the apartment from the listing of available apartments.

SubFlows:

Alternate/Exceptional Flows:

FIGURE 4-18 Campus Housing Service Delete an Apartment Use-Case Description

Use Case Name: Borrow Books	ID: 2	Importance Level: High
Primary Actor: Borrower	Use Case Type: Detail, Essential	

Stakeholders and Interests:
Borrower—wants to check outbooks
Librarian—wants to ensure borrower only gets books deserved

Brief Description: This use case describes how books are checked out of the library.

Trigger: Borrower brings books to check out desk.

Type: External

Relationships:
    Association: Borrower, Personnel Office, Registrar's Office
    Include:

    Extend:
    Generalization:

FIGURE 4-19 Overview Description for the Borrow Books Use Case

Normal Flow of Events:
   1. The Borrower brings books to the Librarian at the checkout desk.
   2. The Borrower provides Librarian their ID card.
   3. The Librarian checks the validity of the ID Card.
      If the Borrower is a Student Borrower, Validate ID Card with Registrar's Office.
      If the Borrower is a Faculty/Staff Borrower, Validate ID Card with Personnel Office.
      If the Borrower is a Guest Borrower, Validate ID Card with Library's System.
   4. The Librarian checks whether the Borrower has any overdue books and/or fines.
   5. The Borrower checks out the books.

SubFlows:

Alternate/Exceptional Flows:
   4a. The ID Card is invalid, the book request is rejected.
   5a. The Borrower either has overdue books, fines, or both, the book request is rejected.

FIGURE 4-20   Flow Descriptions for the Borrow Books Use Case

VERIFYING AND VALIDATING THE BUSINESS PROCESSES AND FUNCTIONAL MODELS[23]

Before we move on to structural (Chapter 5) and behavioral (Chapter 6) modeling, we need to verify and validate the current set of functional models to ensure that they faithfully represent the business processes under consideration. This includes testing the fidelity of each model; for example, we must be sure that the activity diagram(s), use-case descriptions, and use-case diagrams all describe the same functional requirements. Before we describe the specific tests to consider, we describe walkthroughs, a manual approach that supports verifying and validating the evolving models.[24]

Verification and Validation through Walkthroughs

A *walkthrough* is essentially a peer review of a product. In the case of the functional models, a walkthrough is a review of the different models and diagrams created during functional modeling. This review typically is completed by a team whose members come from the development team and the client. The purpose of a walkthrough is to thoroughly *test* the fidelity of the functional models to the functional requirements and to ensure that the models are consistent. That is, a walkthrough uncovers *errors* or *faults* in the evolving specification. However, a walkthrough does not correct errors—it simply identifies them. Error correction is to be accomplished by the team after the walkthrough is completed.

Walkthroughs are very interactive. As the presenter walks through the representation, members of the walkthrough team should ask questions regarding the representation. For example, if the presenter is walking through an activity diagram, another member of the team could ask why certain activities or objects were not included. The actual process of simply presenting the representation to a new set of eyes can uncover obvious misunderstandings and omissions. In many cases, the representation creator can get lost in the proverbial trees

---

[23] The material in this section has been adapted from E. Yourdon, *Modern Structured Analysis* (Englewood Cliffs, NJ: Prentice Hall, 1989). Verifying and validating are types of testing.

[24] Even though many modern CASE tools can automate much of the verifying and validating of the analysis models, we feel that it is paramount that systems analysts understand the principles of verification and validation. Furthermore, some tools, such as Visio, that support UML diagramming are only diagramming tools. Regardless, the analyst is expected to perform all diagramming correctly.

and not see the forest.[25] In fact, many times the act of walking through the representation causes a presenter to see the error himself or herself. For psychological reasons, hearing the representation helps the analyst to see the representation more completely.[26] Therefore, the representation creators should regularly do a walkthrough of the models themselves by reading the representations out loud to themselves, regardless of how they think it might make them look.

There are specified roles that different members of the walkthrough team can play. The first is the *presenter* role. This should be played by the person who is primarily responsible for the specific representation being reviewed. This individual presents the representation to the walkthrough team. The second role is *recorder,* or *scribe.* The recorder should be a member of the analysis team. This individual carefully takes the minutes of the meeting by recording all significant events that occur during the walkthrough. In particular, all errors that are uncovered must be documented so that the analysis team can address them. Another important role is to have someone who raises issues regarding maintenance of the representation. Yourdon refers to this individual as a *maintenance oracle.*[27] Owing to the emphasis on reusability in object-oriented development, this role becomes particularly crucial. Finally, someone must be responsible for calling, setting up, and running the walkthrough meetings.

For a walkthrough to be successful, the members of the walkthrough team must be fully prepared. All materials to be reviewed must be distributed with sufficient time for the team members to review them before the actual meeting. All team members should be expected to mark up the representations so that during the walkthrough meeting, all relevant issues can be discussed. Otherwise, the walkthrough will be inefficient and ineffective. During the actual meeting, as the presenter is walking through the representation, the team members should point out any potential errors or misunderstandings. In many cases, the errors and misunderstandings are caused by invalid assumptions that would not be uncovered without the walkthrough.

One potential danger of walkthroughs is when management decides that the results of uncovering errors in the representation are a reflection of an analyst's capability. This must be avoided at all costs. Otherwise, the underlying purpose of the walkthrough—to improve the fidelity of the representation—will be thwarted. Depending on the organization, it may be necessary to omit management from the walkthrough process. If not, the walkthrough process could break down into a slugfest to make some team members to look good by destroying the presenter. To say the least, this is obviously counterproductive.

Functional Model Verification and Validation

We have suggested three different representations for the functional model: activity diagrams, use-case descriptions, and use-case diagrams. In this section, we describe a set of rules to ensure that these three representations are consistent among themselves.

First, when comparing an activity diagram to a use-case description, there should be at least one event recorded in the normal flow of events, subflows, or alternative/exceptional flows of the use-case description for each activity or action that is included in an activity diagram, and each event should be associated with an activity or action. For example, in Figure 4-4, there is an activity labeled Get Patient Information that is associated with the first two events contained in the normal flow of events of the use-case description shown in Figure 4-13.

[25] In many cases, developers can get lost in all of the nitty-gritty detail.
[26] This has to do with using different senses. Because our haptic senses are the most sensitive, touching the representation would be the best. However, it is not clear how one can touch a use case or a class.
[27] See Appendix D of Yourdon, *Modern Structured Analysis.*

Second, all objects portrayed as an object node in an activity diagram must be mentioned in an event in the normal flow of events, subflows, or alternative/exceptional flows of the use-case description. For example, the activity diagram in Figure 4-4 portrays an Appt object, and the use-case description refers to a new appointment and changing or canceling an existing appointment.

Third, sequential order of the events in a use-case description should occur in the same sequential order of the activities contained in an activity diagram. For example, in Figures 4-4 and 4-13, the events associated with the Get Patient Information activity (events 1 and 2) should occur before the events associated with the Make Payment Arrangements activity (event 4).

Fourth, when comparing a use-case description to a use-case diagram, there must be one and only one use-case description for each use case, and vice versa. For example, Figure 4-13 portrays the use-case description of the Make Old Patient Appt use case. However, the use-case diagram shown in Figure 4-4, the activity diagram shown in Figure 4-8, and the use-case description given in Figure 4-13 are inconsistent with each other. In this case, the use-case diagram implies that the Make Payment Arrangements use case is optional regardless of whether the patient is a new or old patient. However, when we review the activity diagram, we see that it is an optional activity for old patients, but a required activity for a new patient. Therefore, only one of the diagrams is correct. In this instance, the use-case diagram needs to be corrected. The new corrected use-case diagram is shown in Figure 4-21.

Fifth, all actors listed in a use-case description must be portrayed on the use-case diagram. Each actor must have an association link that connects it to the use case and must be listed with the association relationships in the use-case description. For example, the Old Patient actor is listed in the use-case description of the Make Old Patient Appt use case (see Figure 4-13), it is listed with the association relationships in the Make Old Patient Appt use-case description, and it is connected to the use case in the use-case diagram (see Figure 4-21).

Sixth, in some organizations, we should also include the stakeholders listed in the use-case description as actors in the use-case diagram. For example, there could have been an association between the Doctor actor and the Make Old Patient Appt use case (see Figures 4-13 and 4-21). However, in this case it was decided not to include this association because the Doctor never participates in the Make Old Patient Appt use case.[28]

Seventh, all other relationships listed in a use-case description (include, extend, and generalization) must be portrayed on a use-case diagram. For example, in Figure 4-13, there is an extend relationship listed with the Update Patient Information use case, and in Figure 4-21, we see that it appears on the diagram between the two use cases.

Finally, there are many diagram-specific requirements that must be enforced. For example, in an activity diagram a decision node can be connected to activity or action nodes only with a control flow, and for every decision node there should be a matching merge node. Every type of node and flow has different restrictions. However, the complete restrictions for all the UML diagrams are beyond the scope of this text.[29]

---

[28] Another possibility, as described earlier in this chapter, could have been to include a Receptionist actor. However, we had previously decided that the Receptionist was in fact part of the Appointment System and not simply a user of the system. If UML supported the idea of internal actors, or actor-to-actor associations, this implicit association could easily be made explicit by having the Patient actor communicate with the Receptionist actor directly, regardless of whether the Receptionist actor was part of the system or not. See footnote 4.

[29] A good reference for these types of restrictions is S.W. Ambler, *The Elements of UML 2.0 Style* (Cambridge, UK: Cambridge University Press, 2005).

FIGURE 4-21 Modified Use-Case Diagram for the Appointment System

APPLYING THE CONCEPTS AT PATTERSON SUPERSTORE

In this chapter, you learned about business processes and functional models. Object-oriented systems are developed in an incremental and iterative manner. This is especially true when the phased approach is used as in the Patterson Superstore case. The team first developed a use-case diagram for the entire Integrated Health Clinic Delivery System. Next, the team moved into modeling the processes of Version 1 of the system by creating an activity diagram and use-case description for Schedule Appointment. You will also see these models revisited and developed in further iterations as more information is uncovered. The three versions of the Integrated Health Clinic Delivery System will each go through individual process and functional modeling as well as structural and behavior modeling with iteration across all of these tasks.

You can find the rest of the case at www.wiley.com/go/dennis/systemanalysis6e/casestudy.

CHAPTER REVIEW

After reading and studying this chapter, you should be able to:

☐ Explain the purpose of a use case in business process and functional modeling.
☐ Describe the different elements of a use-case diagram.
☐ Create use-case diagrams that portray how business information systems interact with their environment.
☐ Explain how to model a specific use case with an activity diagram.
☐ Describe the different elements of an activity diagram.
☐ Create an activity diagram that represents a specific use case.
☐ Document a business process with a use-case description.
☐ Describe the different types of use cases.
☐ Describe the different elements of a use-case description.
☐ Create a use-case description that represents a specific use case.
☐ Verify and validate the evolving functional model using walkthroughs.
☐ Verify and validate the functional model by ensuring the consistency of the three functional representations: use-case diagrams, activity diagrams, and use-case descriptions.

KEY TERMS

Action	Faults	Miracle activity	Stakeholders
Activity	Final-activity node	Normal flow of events	Subflows
Activity diagram	Final-flow node	Object flow	Subject boundary
Actor	Flow of events	Object node	SVDPI
Alternative flows	Fork node	Overview use cases	Swimlanes
Association relationship	Functional decomposition	Packages	Temporal trigger
Black-hole activities	Generalization relationship	Physical model	Test
Brief description	Guard condition	Presenter	Trigger
Control flow	Importance level	Primary actor	Use case
Control node	Include relationship	Process models	Use-case description
Decision node	Inheritance	Real use case	Use-case diagram
Detail use case	Initial node	Recorder	Use-case ID number
Errors	Iterate	Relationships	Use-case name
Essential use case	Join node	Role	Use-case type
Exceptional flows	Logical model	Scenario	Validation
Extend relationship	Maintenance oracle	Scribe	Verification
External trigger	Merge node	Specialized actor	Walkthrough

QUESTIONS

1. Why is business process modeling important?
2. How do you create use cases?
3. Why do we strive to have about three to nine major use cases in a business process?
4. How do you create use-case diagrams?
5. How is use-case diagramming related to functional modeling?
6. Explain the following terms: actor, use case, system boundary, and relationship. Use layperson's language, as though you were describing them to a user.
7. Every association must be connected to at least one _____ and one _____. Why?
8. What are some heuristics for creating a use-case diagram?
9. Why is iteration important in creating use cases?
10. What is the purpose of an activity diagram?
11. What is the difference between an activity and an action?
12. What is the purpose of a fork node?
13. What are the different types of control nodes?

14. What is the difference between a control flow and an object flow?
15. What is an object node?
16. Explain how a detail use case differs from an overview use case. When are each used?
17. How does an essential use case differ from a real use case?
18. What are the major elements of an overview use case?
19. What are the major elements of a detail use case?
20. What is the viewpoint of a use case, and why is it important?
21. What are some guidelines for designing a set of use cases? Give two examples of the extend associations in a use-case diagram. Give two examples for the include associations.

22. Which of the following could be an actor found in a use-case diagram? Why?
    Ms. Mary Smith
    Supplier
    Customer
    Internet customer
    Mr. John Seals
    Data entry clerk
    Database administrator
23. What is a walkthrough? How does it relate to verification and validation?
24. What are the different roles played during a walkthrough? What are their purposes?
25. How are the different functional models related, and how does this affect the verification and validation of the models?

EXERCISES

A. Investigate the UML website at the Object Management Group (www.uml.org). Write a paragraph news brief on the current state of UML (e.g., the current version and when it will be released, future improvements).

B. Investigate the Object Management Group. Write a brief memo describing what it is, its purpose, and its influence on UML and the object approach to systems development. (*Hint:* A good resource is www.omg.org.)

C. Draw a use-case diagram and a set of activity diagrams for the process of buying glasses from the viewpoint of the patient. The first step is to see an eye doctor who will give you a prescription. Once you have a prescription, you go to an optical dispensary, where you select your frames and place the order for your glasses. Once the glasses have been made, you return to the store for a fitting and pay for the glasses.

D. Create a set of detailed use-case descriptions for the process of buying glasses in exercise C.

E. Draw a use-case diagram and a set of activity diagrams for the following dentist's office system. Whenever new patients are seen for the first time, they complete a patient information form that asks their name, address, phone number, and brief medical history, which are stored in the patient information file. When a patient calls to schedule a new appointment or change an existing appointment, the receptionist checks the appointment file for an available time. Once a good time is found for the patient, the appointment is scheduled. If the patient is a new patient, an incomplete entry is made in the patient's file; the full information will be collected when the patient arrives for the appointment. Because appointments are often made far in advance, the receptionist usually mails a reminder postcard to each patient two weeks before the appointment.

F. Create a set of detail use-case descriptions and a use-case point estimation of person hours (see Chapter 2) for the dentist's office system in exercise E.

G. Draw a use-case diagram and a set of activity diagrams for an online university registration system. The system should enable the staff of each academic department to examine the courses offered by their departments, add and remove courses, and change the information about them (e.g., the maximum number of students permitted). It should permit students to examine currently available courses, add and drop courses to and from their schedules, and examine the courses for which they are enrolled. Department staff should be able to print a variety of reports about the courses and the students enrolled in them. The system should ensure that no student takes too many courses and that students who have any unpaid fees are not permitted to register (assume that fees data are maintained by the university's financial office, which the registration system accesses but does not change).

H. Create a set of detailed use-case descriptions and a use-case point estimation of person hours (see Chapter 2) for the online university registration system in exercise G.

I. Draw a use-case diagram and a set of activity diagrams for the following system. A Real Estate Inc. (AREI) sells houses. People who want to sell their houses sign a contract with AREI and provide information about their house. This information is kept in a database by AREI, and a subset of this information is sent to the citywide multiple-listing service used by all real estate agents. AREI works with two types of potential buyers. Some buyers have an interest in one specific house. In this case, AREI prints information from its database, which the real estate agent uses to help show the house to the buyer (a process beyond the scope of the system to be modeled). Other buyers seek AREI's advice in finding a house that meets their needs. In this case, the buyer completes a buyer information form that is entered into a buyer database, and AREI real estate agents use that information to search AREI's database and the multiple-listing service for houses that meet their needs. The results of these searches are printed and used to help the real estate agent show houses to the buyers.

J. Create a set of detailed use-case descriptions and a use-case point estimation of person hours (see Chapter 2) for the real estate system in exercise I.

K. Perform a verification and validation walkthrough of the functional models of the real estate system described in exercises I and J.

L. Draw a use-case diagram and a set of activity diagrams for the following system. A Video Store (AVS) runs a series of fairly standard video stores. Before a video can be put on the shelf, it must be cataloged and entered into the video database. Every customer must have a valid AVS customer card in order to rent a video. Customers rent videos for three days at a time. Every time a customer rents a video, the system must ensure that he or she does not have any overdue videos. If so, the overdue videos must be returned and an overdue fee paid before customer can rent more videos. Likewise, if the customer has returned overdue videos but has not paid the overdue fee, the fee must be paid before new videos can be rented. Every morning, the store manager prints a report that lists overdue videos. If a video is two or more days overdue, the manager calls the customer to remind him or her to return the video. If a video is returned in damaged condition, the manager removes it from the video database and may sometimes charge the customer.

M. Create a set of detailed use-case descriptions and a use-case point estimation of person hours (see Chapter 2) for the video system in exercise L.

N. Perform a verification and validation walkthrough of the functional models of the video store system described in exercises L and M.

O. Draw a use-case diagram and a set of activity diagrams for a gym membership system. When members join the gym, they pay a fee for a certain length of time. Most memberships are for one year, but memberships as short as two months are available. Throughout the year, the gym offers a variety of discounts on their regular membership prices (e.g., two memberships for the price of one for Valentine's day). It is common for members to pay different amounts for the same length of membership. The gym wants to mail out reminder letters to members asking them to renew their memberships one month before their memberships expire. Some members have become angry when asked to renew at a much higher rate than their original membership contract, so the club wants to track the prices paid so that the manager can override the regular prices with special prices when members are asked to renew. The system must track these new prices so that renewals can be processed accurately. One of the problems in the industry is the high turnover rate of members. Although some members remain active for many years, about half of the members do not renew their memberships. This is a major problem, because the gym spends a lot in advertising to attract each new member. The manager wants the system to track each time a member comes into the gym. The system will then identify the heavy users and generate a report so that the manager can ask them to renew their memberships early, perhaps offering them a reduced rate for early renewal. Likewise, the system should identify members who have not visited the gym in more than a month, so the manager can call them and attempt to reinterest them in the gym.

P. Create a set of detailed use-case descriptions and a use-case point estimation of person hours (see Chapter 2) for the system in exercise O.

Q. Perform a verification and validation walkthrough of the functional models of the gym membership system described in exercises O and P.

R. Draw a use-case diagram and a set of activity diagrams for the following system. Picnics R Us (PRU) is a small catering firm with five employees. During a typical summer weekend, PRU caters fifteen picnics with twenty to fifty people each. The business has grown rapidly over the past year, and the owner wants to install a new computer system for managing the ordering and buying process. PRU has a set of ten standard menus. When potential customers call, the receptionist describes the menus to them. If the customer decides to book a picnic, the receptionist records the customer information (e.g., name, address, phone number) and the information about the picnic (e.g., place, date, time, which one of the standard menus, total price) on a contract. The customer is then faxed a copy of the contract and must sign and return it along with a deposit (often a credit card or by debit card) before the picnic is officially booked. The remaining money is collected when the picnic is delivered. Sometimes, the customer wants something special (e.g., birthday cake). In this case, the receptionist takes the information and gives it to the owner, who determines the cost; the receptionist then calls the customer back with the price information. Sometimes the customer accepts the price; other times, the customer requests some changes that have to go back to the owner for a new cost estimate. Each week, the owner looks through the picnics scheduled for that weekend and orders the supplies (e.g., plates) and food (e.g., bread, chicken) needed to make them. The owner would like to use the system for marketing as well. It should be able to track how customers learned about PRU and identify repeat customers, so that PRU can mail special offers to them. The owner also wants to track the picnics for which PRU sent a contract, but the customer never signed the contract and actually booked a picnic.

S. Create a set of detailed use-case descriptions and a use-case point estimation of person hours (see Chapter 2) for the system in exercise R.

T. Perform a verification and validation walkthrough of the functional models of the catering system described in exercises R and S.

U. Draw a use-case diagram and a set of activity diagrams for the following system. Of-the-Month Club (OTMC) is an innovative young firm that sells memberships to people who have an interest in certain products. People pay membership fees for one year and each month receive a product by mail. For example, OTMC has a coffee-of-the-month club that sends members one pound of special coffee each month. OTMC currently has six memberships (coffee, wine, beer, cigars, flowers, and computer games), each of which costs a different amount. Customers usually belong to just one, but some belong to two or more. When people join OTMC, the telephone operator records the name, mailing address, phone number, e-mail address, credit-card information, start date, and membership service(s) (e.g., coffee). Some customers request a double or triple membership (e.g., two pounds of coffee, three cases of beer). The computer game membership operates a bit differently from the others. In this case, the member must also select the type of game (action, arcade, fantasy/science fiction, educational, etc.) and age level. OTMC is planning to greatly expand the number of memberships it offers (e.g., video games, movies, toys, cheese, fruit, and vegetables), so the system needs to accommodate this future expansion. OTMC is also planning to offer three-month and six-month memberships.

V. Create a set of detailed use-case descriptions and a use-case point estimation of person hours (see Chapter 2) for the system in exercise U.

W. Perform a verification and validation walkthrough of the functional models of the Of-the-Month Club system described in exercises U and V.

MINICASES

1. Williams Specialty Company is a small printing and engraving organization. When Pat Williams, the owner, brought computers into the business office five years ago, the business was very small and very simple. Pat was able to use an inexpensive PC-based accounting system to handle the basic information-processing needs of the firm. As time has gone on, however, the business has grown and the work being performed has become significantly more complex. The simple accounting software still in use is no longer adequate to keep track of many of the company's sophisticated deals and arrangements with its customers.

Pat has a staff of four people in the business office who are familiar with the intricacies of the company's record-keeping requirements. Pat recently met with her staff to discuss her plan to hire an IS consulting firm to evaluate the organization's information system needs and recommend a strategy for upgrading its computer system. The staff are excited about the prospect of a new system, because the current system causes them much annoyance. No one on the staff has ever done anything like this before, however, and they are a little wary of the consultants who will be conducting the project.

Assume that you are a systems analyst in the consulting team assigned to the Williams Specialty Co. engagement. At your first meeting with the Williams staff, you want to be sure that they understand the work that your team will be performing and how they will participate in that work.

a. Explain, in clear, nontechnical terms, the goals of the analysis of the project.

b. Explain, in clear, nontechnical terms, how functional models will be used by the project team to model the identified business processes. Explain what these models are, what they represent in the system, and how they will be used by the team.

2. Professional and Scientific Staff Management (PSSM) is a unique type of temporary staffing agency. Many organizations today hire highly skilled technical employees on a short-term, temporary basis to assist with special projects or to provide a needed technical skill. PSSM negotiates contracts with its client companies in which it agrees to provide temporary staff in specific job categories for a specified cost. For example, PSSM has a contract with an oil and gas exploration company in which it agrees to supply geologists with at least a master's degree for $5,000 per week. PSSM has contracts with a wide range of companies and can place almost any type of professional or scientific staff members, from computer programmers to geologists to astrophysicists.

When a PSSM client company determines that it will need a temporary professional or scientific employee, it issues a staffing request against the contract it had previously negotiated with PSSM. When PSSM's contract manager receives a staffing request, the contract number referenced on the staffing request is entered into the contract database. Using information from the database, the contract manager reviews the terms and conditions of the contract and determines whether the staffing request is valid. The staffing request is valid if the contract has not expired, the type of professional or scientific employee requested is listed on the original contract, and the requested fee falls within the negotiated fee range. If the staffing request is not valid, the contract manager sends the staffing request back to the client with a letter stating why the staffing request cannot be filled, and a copy of the letter is filed. If the staffing request is valid, the contract manager enters the staffing request into the staffing request database as an outstanding staffing request. The staffing request is then sent to the PSSM placement department.

In the placement department, the type of staff member, experience, and qualifications requested on the staffing request are checked against the database of available professional and scientific staff. If a qualified individual is found, he or she is marked "reserved" in the staff database. If a qualified individual cannot be found in the database or is not immediately available, the placement department creates a memo that explains the inability to meet the staffing request and attaches it to the staffing request. All staffing requests are then sent to the arrangements department.

In the arrangements department, the prospective temporary employee is contacted and asked to agree to the placement. After the placement details have been worked out and agreed to, the staff member is marked "placed" in the staff database. A copy of the staffing request and a bill for the placement fee is sent to the client. Finally, the staffing request, the "unable-to-fill" memo (if any), and a copy of the placement fee bill are sent to the contract manager. If the staffing request was filled, the contract manager closes the open staffing request in the staffing request database. If the staffing request could not be filled, the client is notified. The staffing request, placement fee bill, and unable-to-fill memo are then filed in the contract office.

a. Create a use-case diagram for the system described here.

b. Create a set of activity diagrams for the business processes described here.

c. For each major use case identified in the use-case diagram, develop both an overview and a detail use-case description.

d. Using the use-case point estimation techniques described in Chapter 2, estimate the number of person hours that it will take to develop this system.

e. Verify and validate the functional models.

CHAPTER 5

STRUCTURAL MODELING

$\mathbf{A}$ structural, or conceptual, model describes the structure of the objects that support the business processes in an organization. During analysis, the structural model presents the logical organization of the objects without indicating how they are stored, created, or manipulated so that analysts can focus on the business, without being distracted by technical details. Later during design, the structural model is updated to reflect exactly how the objects will be stored in databases and files. This chapter describes CRC cards, class diagrams, and object diagrams.

OBJECTIVES

- Understand the rules and style guidelines for creating CRC cards, class diagrams, and object diagrams.
- Understand the processes used to create CRC cards, class diagrams, and object diagrams.
- Be able to create CRC cards, class diagrams, and object diagrams.
- Understand how to verify and validate the structural models.
- Understand how to verify and validate the structural models with the functional models.

INTRODUCTION

During analysis, analysts create business process and functional models to represent how the business system will behave. At the same time, analysts need to understand the information that is used and created by the business system (e.g., customer information and order information). In this chapter, we discuss how the objects underlying the behavior modeled in the business process and functional models are organized and presented.

As pointed out in Chapter 1, all object-oriented systems development approaches are use-case driven, architecture-centric, and iterative and incremental. Use cases, described in Chapter 4, form the foundation on which the business information system is created. From an architecture-centric perspective, structural modeling supports the creation of an internal structural or static view of a business information system in that it shows how the system is structured to support the underlying business processes. Finally, as with business process and functional modeling, you will find that you will need to not only iterate across the structural models (described in this chapter), but you will also have to iterate across all three architectural views (functional, structural, and behavioral) to fully capture and represent the requirements for a business information system.

A *structural model* is a formal way of representing the objects that are used and created by a business system. It illustrates people, places, or things about which information is captured and how they are related to one another. The structural model is drawn using an iterative process in which the model becomes more detailed and less conceptual over time.

In analysis, analysts draw a *conceptual model*, which shows the logical organization of the objects without indicating how the objects are stored, created, or manipulated. Because this model is free from any implementation or technical details, the analysts can focus more easily on matching the model to the real business requirements of the system.

In design, analysts evolve the conceptual structural model into a design model that reflects how the objects will be organized in databases and software. At this point, the model is checked for redundancy, and the analysts investigate ways to make the objects easy to retrieve. The specifics of the design model are discussed in detail in the design chapters.

STRUCTURAL MODELS

Every time a systems analyst encounters a new problem to solve, the analyst must learn the underlying problem domain. The goal of the analyst is to discover the key objects contained in the problem domain and to build a structural model. Object-oriented modeling allows the analyst to reduce the semantic gap between the underlying problem domain and the evolving structural model. However, the real world and the world of software are very different. The real world tends to be messy, whereas the world of software must be neat and logical. Thus, an exact mapping between the structural model and the problem domain may not be possible. In fact, it might not even be desirable.

One of the primary purposes of the structural model is to create a vocabulary that can be used by the analyst and the users. Structural models represent the things, ideas, or concepts contained in the domain of the problem. They also allow the representation of the relationships among the things, ideas, or concepts. By creating a structural model of the problem domain, the analyst creates the vocabulary necessary for the analyst and users to communicate effectively.

It is important to remember that at this stage of development, the structural model does not represent software components or classes in an object-oriented programming language, even though the structural model does contain analysis classes, attributes, operations, and the relationships among the analysis classes. The refinement of these initial classes into programming-level objects comes later. Nonetheless, the structural model at this point should represent the responsibilities of each class and the collaborations among the classes. Typically, structural models are depicted using CRC cards, class diagrams, and object diagrams. However, before describing CRC cards, class diagrams, and object diagrams, we describe the basic elements of structural models: classes, attributes, operations, and relationships.

Classes, Attributes, and Operations

A *class* is a general template that we use to create specific instances, or *objects*, in the problem domain. All objects of a given class are identical in structure and behavior but contain different data in their attributes. There are two general kinds of classes of interest during analysis: concrete and abstract. Normally, when an analyst describes the application domain classes, he or she is referring to concrete classes; that is, *concrete classes* are used to create objects. *Abstract classes* do not actually exist in the real world; they are simply useful abstractions. For example, from an employee class and a customer class, we may identify a generalization of the two classes and name the abstract class *person*. We might not actually instantiate the person class in the system itself, instead creating and using only employees and customers.[1]

---

[1] Because abstract classes are essentially not necessary and are not instantiated, arguments have been made that it would be better not to include any of them in the description of the evolving system at this stage of development [(see J. Evermann and Y. Wand, "Towards Ontologically Based Semantics for UML Constructs," in H. S. Junii, S. Jajodia, and A. Solvberg (Eds) *ER 2001, Lecture Notes in Computer Science 2224* (Berlin: Springer-Verlag, 2001): 354–367)]. However, because abstract classes traditionally have been included at this stage of development, we also include them.

A second classification of classes is the type of real-world thing that a class represents. There are domain classes, user-interface classes, data structure classes, file structure classes, operating environment classes, document classes, and various types of multimedia classes. At this point in the development of our evolving system, we are interested only in domain classes. *Domain classes* represent objects in the problem domain, that is, they are used to represent objects that meet the functional, not nonfunctional requirements. Later in design and implementation, the other types of classes, which represent the nonfunctional requirements, become relevant.

An *attribute* of an analysis class represents a piece of information that is relevant to the description of the class within the application domain of the problem being investigated. An attribute contains information the analyst or user feels the system should keep track of. For example, a possible relevant attribute of an employee class is employee name, whereas one that might not be as relevant is hair color. Both describe something about an employee, but hair color is probably not all that useful for most business applications. Only attributes that are important to the task should be included in the class. Finally, only attributes that are primitive or atomic types (i.e., integers, strings, doubles, date, time, Boolean, etc.) should be added. Most complex or compound attributes are really placeholders for relationships between classes. Therefore, they should be modeled as relationships, not as attributes (see the next section).

The behavior of an analysis class is defined in an *operation* or service. During design, the analyst will convert the operations to *methods*. However, because methods are more related to implementation, at this point in the development we use the term *operation* to describe the actions to which the *instances* of the class are capable of responding. Like attributes, only problem domain–specific operations that are relevant to the functional requirements should be considered. For example, it is normally required that classes provide means of creating instances, deleting instances, accessing individual attribute values, setting individual attribute values, accessing individual relationship values, and removing individual relationship values. However, at this point in the development of the evolving system, the analyst should avoid cluttering up the definition of the class with these basic types of operations and focus only on relevant problem domain–specific operations.

Relationships

There are many different types of relationships that can be defined, but all can be classified into three basic categories of data abstraction mechanisms: generalization relationships, aggregation relationships, and association relationships. These data-abstraction mechanisms allow the analyst to focus on the important dimensions while ignoring nonessential dimensions. As with attributes, the analyst must be careful to include only relationships that address the functional requirements.

Generalization Relationships The generalization relationship is the same relationship as the class inclusion semantic relationship that was used in domain and taxonomic analysis (see Chapter 3). The generalization abstraction enables the analyst to create classes that inherit attributes and operations of other classes. The analyst creates a *superclass* that contains basic attributes and operations that will be used in several *subclasses*. The subclasses inherit the attributes and operations of their superclass and can also contain attributes and operations that are unique just to them. For example, a customer class and an employee class can be generalized into a person class by extracting the attributes and operations both have in common and placing them into the new superclass, *person*. In this way, the analyst can reduce the redundancy in the class definitions so that the common elements are defined once and then reused in the subclasses. Generalization is represented with the *a-kind-of* relationship, so that we say that an employee is a-kind-of person.[2]

2 See Footnote 1.

The analyst also can use the opposite of generalization. *Specialization* uncovers additional classes by allowing new subclasses to be created from an existing class. For example, an employee class can be specialized into a secretary class and an engineer class. Furthermore, generalization relationships between classes can be combined to form generalization hierarchies. Based on the previous examples, a secretary class and an engineer class can be subclasses of an employee class, which in turn could be a subclass of a person class. This would be read as a secretary and an engineer are a-kind-of employee and a customer and an employee are a-kind-of person.

The generalization data abstraction is a very powerful mechanism that encourages the analyst to focus on the properties that make each class unique by allowing the similarities to be factored into superclasses. However, to ensure that the semantics of the subclasses are maintained, the analyst should apply the principle of *substitutability*. By this we mean that the subclass should be capable of substituting for the superclass anywhere that uses the superclass (e.g., anywhere we use the employee superclass, we could also logically use its secretary subclass). By focusing on the a-kind-of interpretation of the generalization relationship, the principle of substitutability is supported.

Aggregation Relationships The aggregation relationship is the same relationship as the part whole semantic relationship that was used in domain and taxonomic analysis (see Chapter 3). Generally speaking, all aggregation relationships relate *parts* to *wholes* or *assemblies*. For our purposes, we use the *a-part-of* or *has-parts* semantic relationship to represent the aggregation abstraction. For example, a door is a-part-of a car, an employee is a-part-of a department, or a department is a-part-of an organization. Like the generalization relationship, aggregation relationships can be combined into aggregation hierarchies. For example, a piston is a-part-of an engine, and an engine is a-part-of a car.

Aggregation relationships are bidirectional. The flip side of aggregation is *decomposition*. The analyst can use decomposition to uncover parts of a class that should be modeled separately. For example, if a door and an engine are a-part-of a car, then a car has-parts door and engine. The analyst can bounce around between the various parts to uncover new parts. For example, the analyst can ask, What other parts are there to a car? or To which other assemblies can a door belong?

Association Relationships There are other types of relationships that do not fit neatly into a generalization (a-kind-of) or aggregation (a-part-of) framework. Technically speaking, these relationships are usually a weaker form of the aggregation relationship. For example, a patient schedules an appointment. It could be argued that a patient is a-part-of an appointment. However, there is a clear semantic difference between this type of relationship and one that models the relationship between doors and cars or even workers and unions. Thus, they are simply considered to be *associations* between instances of classes.

OBJECT IDENTIFICATION

Different approaches have been suggested to aid the analyst in identifying a set of candidate objects for the structural model. The most common approaches are textual analysis, brainstorming, and patterns. Most analysts use a combination of these techniques to make sure that no important objects and object attributes, operations, and relationships have been overlooked.

Textual Analysis

The analyst performs *textual analysis* by reviewing the use-case diagrams and examining the text in the use-case descriptions to identify potential objects, attributes, operations, and relationships. The nouns in the use case suggest candidate classes, and the verbs suggest possible operations. Figure 5-1 presents a summary of useful guidelines. In addition to these guidelines, the text analysis approaches described in Chapter 3, sentence diagramming and domain, taxonomic, componential, and theme analysis, are helpful. The textual analysis of use-case descriptions has been criticized as being too simple, but because its primary purpose is to create an initial rough-cut structural model, its simplicity is a major advantage. For example, if we applied these rules to the Make Old Patient Appt use case described in Chapter 4 (see Figure 5-2), we can easily identify potential objects for an old patient, doctor, appointment, patient, office, receptionist, name, address, patient information, payment, date, and time. We also can easily identify potential operations that can be associated with the identified objects. For example, patient contacts office, makes a new appointment, cancels an existing appointment, changes an existing appointment, matches requested appointment times and dates with requested times and dates, and finds current appointment.

Brainstorming

Brainstorming is a discovery technique that has been used successfully in identifying candidate classes. Essentially, in this context, brainstorming is a process that a set of individuals sitting around a table suggest candidate classes that could be useful for the problem under consideration, that is, that meet the functional requirements. Typically, a brainstorming session is kicked off by a facilitator who asks the set of individuals to address a specific question or a statement that frames the session. For example, using the appointment problem described previously, the facilitator could ask the development team and users to think about their experiences of making appointments and to identify candidate classes based on their past experiences. Notice that this approach does not use the functional models developed earlier. It simply asks the participants to identify the objects with which they have interacted. For example, a potential set of objects that come to mind are doctors, nurses, receptionists, appointment, illness, treatment, prescriptions, insurance card, and medical records. However, if textual analysis has been done previously, the identified candidate classes can be

---

- A common or improper noun implies a class of objects.
- A proper noun or direct reference implies an instance of a class.
- A collective noun implies a class of objects made up of groups of instances of another class.
- An adjective implies an attribute of an object.
- A doing verb implies an operation.
- A being verb implies a classification relationship between an object and its class.
- A having verb implies an aggregation or association relationship.
- A transitive verb implies an operation.
- An intransitive verb implies an exception.
- A predicate or descriptive verb phrase implies an operation.
- An adverb implies an attribute of a relationship or an operation.

Adapted from: These guidelines are based on Russell J. Abbott, "Program Design by Informal English Descriptions," *Communications of the ACM* 26, no. 11 (1983): 882–894; Peter P-S Chen, "English Sentence Structure and Entity-Relationship Diagrams," *Information Sciences: An International Journal* 29, no. 2–3 (1983): 127–149; and Ian Graham, *Migrating to Object Technology* (Reading, MA: Addison Wesley Longman, 1995).

FIGURE 5-1
Textual Analysis
Guidelines

Use Case Name:	Make Old Patient Appt		ID: 2	Importance Level: Low
Primary Actor:	Old Patient		Use Case Type:	Detail, Essential

Stakeholders and Interests:
Old Patient – wants to make, change, or cancel an appointment
Doctor – wants to ensure patient's needs are met in a timely manner

Brief Description: This use case describes how we make an appointment as well as changing or canceling an appointment for a previously seen patient.

Trigger: Patient calls and asks for a new appointment or asks to cancel or change an existing appointment.

Type: External

Relationships:
Association: Old Patient
Include:
Extend: Update Patient Information
Generalization: Manage Appointments

Normal Flow of Events:
1. The Patient contacts the office regarding an appointment.
2. The Patient provides the Receptionist with his or her name and address.
3. If the Patient's information has changed
   Execute the Update Patient Information use case.
4. If the Patient's payment arrangements has changed
   Execute the Make Payment Arrangements use case.
5. The Receptionist asks Patient if he or she would like to make a new appointment, cancel an existing appointment, or change an existing appointment.

> If the patient wants to make a new appointment,
>   the S-1: new appointment subflow is performed.
> If the patient wants to cancel an existing appointment,
>   the S-2: cancel appointment subflow is performed.
> If the patient wants to change an existing appointment,
>   the S-3: change appointment subflow is performed.

6. The Receptionist provides the results of the transaction to the Patient.

SubFlows:
S-1: New Appointment
  1. The Receptionist asks the Patient for possible appointment times.
  2. The Receptionist matches the Patient's desired appointment times with available dates and times and schedules the new appointment.
S-2: Cancel Appointment
  1. The Receptionist asks the Patient for the old appointment time.
  2. The Receptionist finds the current appointment in the appointment file and cancels it.
S-3: Change Appointment
  1. The Receptionist performs the S-2: cancel appointment subflow.
  2. The Receptionist performs the S-1: new appointment subflow.

Alternate/Exceptional Flows:
S-1, 2a1: The Receptionist proposes some alternative appointment times based on what is available in the appointment schedule.
S-1, 2a2: The Patient chooses one of the proposed times or decides not to make an appointment.

TEMPLATE can be found at www.wiley.com/go/dennis/systemanalysis6e

FIGURE 5-2 Use-Case Description (Figure 4-13)

used to seed the brainstorming session. Once a sufficient number of candidate objects have been identified, the participants should discuss and select which of the candidate objects should be considered further. Once these have been identified, further brainstorming can take place to identify potential attributes, operations, and relationships for each of the identified objects.

Bellin and Simone[3] have suggested a set of useful principles to guide a brainstorming session. First, all suggestions should be taken seriously. At this point in the development of the system, it is much better to have to delete something later than to accidentally leave something critical out. Second, all participants should begin thinking fast and furiously. After all ideas are out on the proverbial table, then the participants can be encouraged to ponder the candidate classes they have identified. Third, the facilitator must manage the fast and furious thinking process. Otherwise, the process will be chaotic. Furthermore, the facilitator should ensure that all participants are involved and that a few participants do not dominate the process. To get the most complete view of the problem, we suggest using a round-robin approach wherein participants take turns suggesting candidate classes. Another approach is to use an electronic brainstorming tool that supports anonymity.[4] Fourth, the facilitator can use humor to break the ice so that all participants can feel comfortable in making suggestions.

Patterns

The idea of using patterns is a relatively new area in object-oriented systems development.[5] There have been many definitions of exactly what a pattern is. From our perspective, a *pattern* is simply a useful group of collaborating classes that provide a solution to a commonly occurring problem. Because patterns provide a solution to commonly occurring problems, they are reusable.

An architect, Christopher Alexander, has inspired much of the work associated with using patterns in object-oriented systems development. According to Alexander and his colleagues,[6] it is possible to make very sophisticated buildings by stringing together commonly found patterns, rather than creating entirely new concepts and designs. In a similar manner, it is possible to put together commonly found object-oriented patterns to form elegant object-oriented information systems. For example, many business transactions involve the same types of objects and interactions. Virtually all transactions would require a transaction class, a transaction line item class, an item class, a location class, and a participant class. By reusing these existing patterns of classes, we can more quickly and more completely define the system than if we start with a blank piece of paper.

Many types of patterns have been proposed, ranging from high-level business-oriented patterns to more low-level detailed design patterns. For example, Figure 5-3 depicts a set of useful analysis patterns.[7] Figure 5-4 portrays a class diagram that we created by merging the patterns contained in Figure 5-3 into a single reusable pattern. In this case, we merged the Transaction–Entry–Account pattern (located at the bottom left of Figure 5-3) with the Place–Transaction–Participant–Transaction Line Item–Item pattern (located at the top left of Figure 5-3) on the common Transaction class. Next, we merged the Party–Person–Organization

---

[3] D. Bellin and S. S. Simone, *The CRC Card Book* (Reading, MA: Addison-Wesley, 1997).

[4] A.R. Dennis, J.S. Valacich, T. Connolly, and B.E. Wynne, "Process Structuring in Electronic Brainstorming," *Information Systems Research* 7, no. 2 (June 1996): 268–277.

[5] Many books have been devoted to this topic. For example, see P. Coad, D. North, and M. Mayfield, *Object Models: Strategies, Patterns, & Applications,* 2nd Ed. (Englewood Cliffs, NJ: Prentice Hall, 1997); H.-E. Eriksson and M. Penker, *Business Modeling with UML: Business Patterns at Work* (New York: Wiley, 2000); M. Fowler, *Analysis Patterns: Reusable Object Models* (Reading, MA: Addison-Wesley, 1997); E. Gamma, R. Helm, R. Johnson, and J. Vlissides, *Design Patterns: Elements of Reusable Object-Oriented Software* (Reading, MA: Addison-Wesley, 1995); David C. Hay, *Data Model Patterns: Conventions of Thought* (New York: Dorset House, 1996); and L. Silverston, *The Data Model Resource Book: A Library of Universal Data Models for All Enterprises, Volume 1, Revised Ed.* (New York, NY: Wiley, 2001).

[6] C. Alexander, S. Ishikawa, M. Silverstein, M. Jacobson, I. Fiksdahl-King, and S. Angel, *A Pattern Language* (New York: Oxford University Press, 1977).

[7] The patterns are portrayed using UML Class Diagrams. We describe the syntax of the diagrams later in this chapter. The specific patterns shown have been adapted from patterns described in P. Coad, D. North, and M. Mayfield, *Object Models: Strategies, Patterns, & Applications,* 2nd Ed.; M. Fowler, *Analysis Patterns: Reusable Object Models*; and L. Silverston, *The Data Model Resource Book: A Library of Universal Data Models for All Enterprises, Volume 1, Revised Edition.*

FIGURE 5-3 Sample Patterns

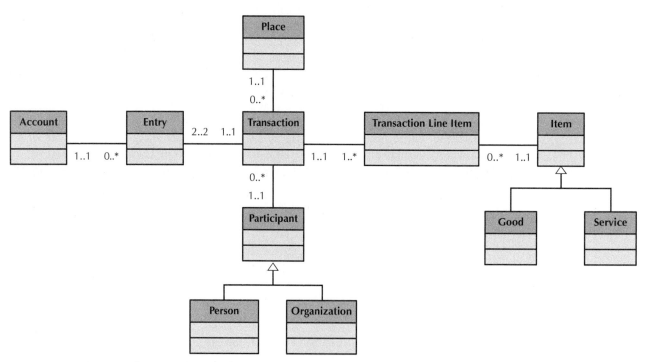

FIGURE 5-4 Sample Integration of Sample Patterns

(located at the top right of Figure 5-3) by merging the Participant and Party classes. Finally, we extended the Item class by merging the Item class with the Product class of the Product–Good–Service pattern (located at the bottom right of Figure 5-3).

In this manner, using patterns from different sources enables the development team to leverage knowledge beyond that of the immediate team members and allows the team to develop more complete and robust models of the problem domain. For example, in the case of the appointment problem, we can look at the objects previously identified through textual analysis and brainstorming and see if it makes sense to map any of them into any predefined reusable patterns. In this specific case, we can look at an appointment as a type of transaction in which a doctor's office participates. By looking at an appointment as a type of transaction, we can apply the pattern we created in Figure 5-4 and discover a set of previously unidentified objects, such as Place, Patient as a type of Participant, and Transaction Line Items that are associated with different types of Items (Goods and/or Services). Discovering these specific additional objects could be useful in developing the billing side of the appointment system. Even though these additional objects could be applicable, they were not uncovered using the other techniques.

Based on this simple example, it is obvious that using patterns to develop structural models can be advantageous. Figure 5-5 lists some common business domains for which patterns

Business Domains	Sources of Patterns
Accounting	3, 4
Actor-Role	2
Assembly-Part	1
Container-Content	1
Contract	2, 4
Document	2, 4
Employment	2, 4
Financial Derivative Contracts	3
Geographic Location	2, 4
Group-Member	1
Interaction	1
Material Requirements Planning	4
Organization and Party	2, 3
Plan	1, 3
Process Manufacturing	4
Trading	3
Transactions	1, 4

1. Peter Coad, David North, and Mark Mayfield, *Object Models: Strategies, Patterns, and Applications*, 2nd Ed. (Englewood Cliffs, NJ: Prentice Hall, 1997).
2. Hans-Erik Eriksson and Magnus Penker, *Business Modeling with UML: Business Patterns at Work* (New York: Wiley, 2000).
3. Martin Fowler, *Analysis Patterns: Reusable Object Models* (Reading, MA: Addison-Wesley, 1997).
4. David C. Hay, *Data Model Patterns: Conventions of Thought* (New York, NY: Dorset House, 1996).

FIGURE 5-5
Useful Patterns

have been developed and their sources. If we are developing a business information system in one of these business domains, then the patterns developed for that domain may be a very useful starting point in identifying needed classes and their attributes, operations, and relationships.

CRC CARDS

CRC (Class–Responsibility–Collaboration) cards are used to document the responsibilities and collaborations of a class. In some object-oriented and agile systems development methodologies, CRC cards are seen to be an alternative competitor to the Unified Process employment of use cases and class diagrams. However, we see them as a useful, low-tech approach that can complement a typical high-tech Unified Process approach that uses CASE tools. We use an extended form of the CRC card to capture all relevant information associated with a class.[8] We describe the elements of our CRC cards later, after we explain responsibilities and collaborations.

Responsibilities and Collaborations

Responsibilities of a class can be broken into two separate types: knowing and doing. *Knowing responsibilities* are those things that an instance of a class must be capable of knowing. An instance of a class typically knows the values of its attributes and its relationships. *Doing responsibilities* are those things that an instance of a class must be capable of doing. In this case, an instance of a class can execute its operations or it can request a second instance, which it knows about, to execute one of its operations on behalf of the first instance.

The structural model describes the objects necessary to support the business processes modeled by the use cases. Most use cases involve a set of several classes, not just one class. These classes form *collaborations*. Collaborations allow the analyst to think in terms of clients, servers, and contracts.[9] A *client* object is an instance of a class that sends a request to an instance of another class for an operation to be executed. A *server* object is the instance that receives the request from the client object. A *contract* formalizes the interactions between the client and server objects. Chapter 8 provides a more-detailed explanation of contracts and examples of their use.

An analyst can use the idea of class responsibilities and client–server–contract collaborations to help identify the classes, along with the attributes, operations, and relationships, involved with a use case. One of the easiest ways to use CRC cards in developing a structural model is through anthropomorphism—pretending that the classes have human characteristics. Members of the development team can either ask questions of themselves or be asked questions by other members of the team. Typically the questions asked are of the form:

> Who or what are you?
> What do you know?
> What can you do?

---

[8] Our CRC cards are based on the works of D. Bellin and S. S. Simone, *The CRC Card Book* (Reading, MA: Addison-Wesley, 1997); I. Graham, *Migrating to Object Technology* (Wokingham, England: Addison-Wesley, 1995); and B. Henderson-Sellers and B. Unhelkar, *OPEN Modeling with UML* (Harlow, England: Addison-Wesley, 2000).

[9] For more information, see K. Beck and W. Cunningham, "A Laboratory for Teaching Object-Oriented Thinking," *Proceedings of OOPSLA, SIGPLAN Notices,* 24, no. 10 (1989): 1–6; B. Henderson-Sellers and B. Unhelkar, *OPEN Modeling with UML* (Harlow, England: Addison-Wesley, 2000); C. Larman, *Applying UML and Patterns: An Introduction to Object-Oriented Analysis and Design* (Englewood Cliffs, NJ: Prentice Hall, 1998); B. Meyer, *Object-Oriented Software Construction* (Englewood Cliffs, NJ: Prentice Hall, 1994); and R. Wirfs-Brock, B. Wilkerson, and L. Wiener, *Designing Object-Oriented Software* (Englewood Cliffs, NJ: Prentice Hall, 1990).

The answers to the questions are then used to add detail to the evolving CRC cards. For example, in the appointment problem, a member of the team can pretend that he or she is an appointment. In this case, the appointment would answer that he or she knows about the doctor and patient who participate in the appointment and they would know the date and time of the appointment. Furthermore, an appointment would have to know how to create itself, delete itself, and to possibly change different aspects of itself. In some cases, this approach will uncover additional objects that have to be added to the evolving structural model.

Elements of a CRC Card

The set of CRC cards contains all the information necessary to build a logical structural model of the problem under investigation. Figure 5-6 shows a sample CRC card. Each CRC card captures and describes the essential elements of a class. The front of the card contains the class name, ID, type, description, associated use cases, responsibilities, and collaborators.

Front:

Class Name: Old Patient	**ID:** 3	**Type:** Concrete, Domain
Description: An individual who needs to receive or has received medical attention		**Associated Use Cases:** 2

Responsibilities	**Collaborators**
Make appointment	Appointment
Calculate last visit	
Change status	
Provide medical history	Medical history

Back:

Attributes:
Amount (double)
Insurance carrier (text)

Relationships:
Generalization (a-kind-of): Person

Aggregation (has-parts): Medical History

Other Associations: Appointment

FIGURE 5-6
Sample CRC Card

The name of a class should be a noun (but not a proper noun, such as the name of a specific person or thing). Just like the use cases, in later stages of development, it is important to be able to trace back design decisions to specific requirements. In conjunction with the list of associated use cases, the ID number for each class can be used to accomplish this. Also, by associating the use cases with the individual classes allows the analyst to be able to track back to determine who the primary actor and stakeholders are. This provides the information required to limit the access to the instances of the class to the individuals who play the roles identified by the primary actors and stakeholders.[10] The description is simply a brief statement that can be used as a textual definition for the class. The responsibilities of the class tend to be the operations that the class must contain (i.e., the doing responsibilities).

The back of a CRC card contains the attributes and relationships of the class. The attributes of the class represent the knowing responsibilities that each instance of the class has to meet. Typically, the data type of each attribute is listed with the name of the attribute (e.g., the amount attribute is double and the insurance carrier is text). Three types of relationships typically are captured at this point: generalization, aggregation, and other associations. In Figure 5-6, we see that a Patient is a-kind-of Person and that a Patient is associated with Appointments.

CRC cards are used to document the essential properties of a class. However, once the cards are filled out, the analyst can use the cards and anthropomorphisms in role-playing (described in the next section) to uncover missing properties by executing the different scenarios associated with the use cases (see Chapter 4). Role-playing also can be used as a basis to test the clarity and completeness of the evolving representation of the system.

Role-Playing CRC Cards with Use Cases[11, 12]

In addition to the object identification approaches described earlier (textual analysis, brainstorming, and patterns), CRC cards can be used in a *role-playing* exercise that has been shown to be useful in discovering additional objects, attributes, relationships, and operations. Furthermore, in addition to walkthroughs, described later in this chapter, role-playing is very useful in testing the fidelity of the evolving structural model. In general, members of the team perform roles associated with the actors and objects previously identified with the different use cases. Technically speaking, the members of the team perform the different steps associated with a specific scenario of a use case. Remember, a scenario is a single, unique execution path through a use case. A useful place to look for the different scenarios of a use case is the activity diagrams (e.g., see Figures 4-8–4-12). A different scenario exists for each time a decision node causes a split in the execution path of the use case. Also, scenarios can be identified from the alternative/exceptional flows in a use-case description. Considering the incremental and iterative nature and that activity diagrams and use-case descriptions should contain the same information, reviewing both representations will ensure that relevant scenarios are not missed.

The first step is to review the use-case descriptions (see Figure 5-2). This allows the team to pick a specific use case to role-play. Even though it is tempting to try to complete as many use cases as possible in a short time, the team should not choose the easiest use cases first. Instead, at this point in the development of the system, the team should choose the use case that is the most important, the most complex, or the least understood.

---

[10] We cover this in more detail in the design and construction portion of the textbook.

[11] This step is related to the verification and validation of the analysis models (functional, structural, and behavioral). Because this deals with verification and validation that take place between the models, in this case functional and structural.

[12] Our role-playing approach is based on the work of D. Bellin and S. S. Simone, *The CRC Card Book* (Reading, MA: Addison-Wesley, 1997).

2. Identify Relevant Actors and Objects

The second step is to identify the relevant roles that are to be played. Each *role* is associated with either an actor or an object. To choose the relevant objects, the team reviews each of the CRC cards and picks the ones that are associated with the chosen use case. For example, in Figure 5-6, we see that the CRC card that represents the Old Patient class is associated with Use Case number 2. So if we were going to role-play the Make Old Patient Appt use case (see Figure 5-2), we would need to include the Old Patient CRC card. By reviewing the use-case description, we can easily identify the Old Patient and Doctor actors (see Primary Actor and Stakeholders section of the use case description in Figure 5-2). By reading the event section of the use-case description, we identify the internal actor role of Receptionist. After identifying all of the relevant roles, we assign each one to a different member of the team.

3. Role-Play Scenarios

The third step is to role-play scenarios of the use case by having the team members perform each one. To do this, each team member must pretend that he or she is an instance of the role assigned to him or her. For example, if a team member was assigned the role of the Receptionist, then he or she would have to be able to perform the different steps in the scenario associated with the Receptionist. In the case of the change appointment scenario, this would include steps 2, 5, 6, S-3, S-1, and S-2. However, when this scenario is performed (role-played), it would be discovered that steps 1, 3, and 4 were incomplete. For example, in Step 1, what actually occurs? Does the Patient make a phone call? If so, who answers the phone? In other words, a lot of information contained in the use-case description is only identified in an implicit, not explicit, manner. When the information is not identified explicitly, there is a lot of room for interpretation, which requires the team members to make assumptions. It is much better to remove the need to make an assumption by making each step explicit. In this case, Step 1 of the Normal Flow of Events should be modified. Once the step has been fixed, the scenario is tried again. This process is repeated until the scenario can be executed to a successful conclusion. Once the scenario has been successfully concluded, the next scenario is performed. This is repeated until all of the scenarios of the use case can be performed successfully.[13]

4. Repeat Steps 1 through 3

The fourth step is to simply repeat steps 1 through 3 for the remaining use cases.

CLASS DIAGRAMS

A *class diagram* is a *static model* that shows the classes and the relationships among classes that remain constant in the system over time. The class diagram depicts classes, which include both behaviors and states, with the relationships between the classes. The following sections present the elements of the class diagram, different approaches that can be used to simplify a class diagram, and an alternative structure diagram: the object diagram.

Elements of a Class Diagram

Figure 5-7 shows a class diagram that was created to reflect the classes and relationships associated with the appointment system. This diagram is based on the classes uncovered through the object identification techniques and the role-playing of the CRC cards described earlier.

Class The main building block of a class diagram is the class, which stores and manages information in the system (see Figure 5-8). Classes support encapsulation by capturing both

---

[13] In some cases, some scenarios are only executed in very rare circumstances. So, from a practical perspective, each scenario could be prioritized individually and only "important" scenarios would have to be implemented for the first release of the system. Only those scenarios would have to be tested at this point in the evolution of the system.

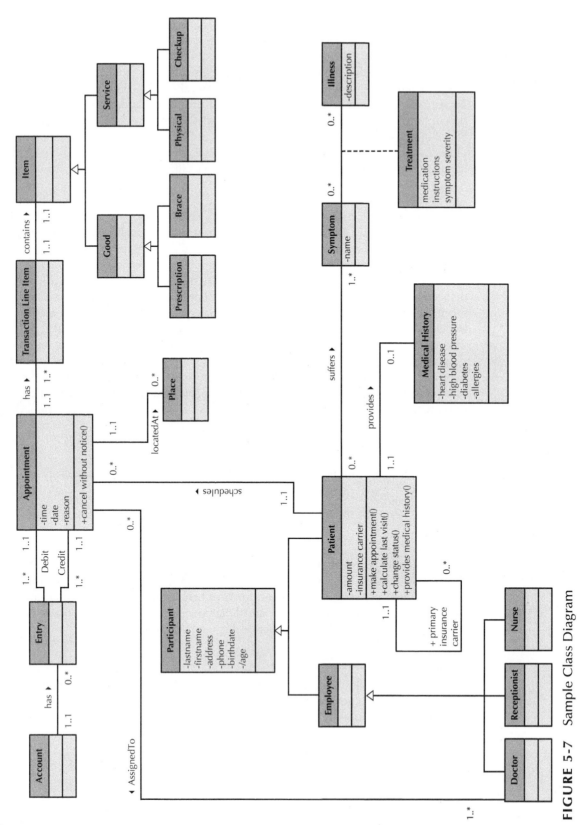

FIGURE 5-7   Sample Class Diagram

A class: • Represents a kind of person, place, or thing about which the system will need to capture and store information. • Has a name typed in bold and centered in its top compartment. • Has a list of attributes in its middle compartment. • Has a list of operations in its bottom compartment. • Does not explicitly show operations that are available to all classes.	**Class1** -Attribute-1 +Operation-1()
An attribute: • Represents properties that describe the state of an object. • Can be derived from other attributes, shown by placing a slash before the attribute's name.	attribute name /derived attribute name
An operation: • Represents the actions or functions that a class can perform. • Can be classified as a constructor, query, update, or destructor operation. • Includes parentheses that may contain parameters or information needed to perform the operation.	operation name ()
An association: • Represents a relationship between multiple classes or a class and itself. • Is labeled using a verb phrase or a role name, whichever better represents the relationship. • Can exist between one or more classes. • Contains multiplicity symbols, which represent the minimum and maximum times a class instance can be associated with the related class instance.	AssociatedWith 0..* 1
A generalization: • Represents a-kind-of relationship between multiple classes.	
An aggregation: • Represents a logical a-part-of relationship between multiple classes or a class and itself. • Is a special form of an association.	0..* IsPartOf ▶ 1 ◇
A composition: • Represents a physical a-part-of relationship between multiple classes or a class and itself • Is a special form of an association.	1..* IsPartOf ▶ 1 ◆

FIGURE 5-8 Class Diagram Syntax

the attributes and operations in a single construct. During analysis, classes refer to the people, places, and things about which the system will capture information. Later, during design and implementation, classes can refer to implementation-specific artifacts such as windows, forms, and other objects used to build the system. Each class is drawn using a three-part rectangle, with the class name at the top, attributes in the middle, and operations at the bottom. We can see that the classes identified earlier, such as Participant, Doctor, Patient, Reception-ist, Medical History, Appointment, and Symptom, are included in Figure 5-7. The value of an object's attributes define the *state* of the object and the behavior of an object is represented by the operations that are defined with the object's class.

Attributes are properties of the class about which we want to capture information (see Figure 5-8). Notice that the Participant class in Figure 5-7 contains the attributes: lastname, firstname, address, phone, and birthdate. At times, you might want to store *derived attributes*, which are attributes that can be calculated or derived; these special attributes are denoted by placing a slash (/) before the attribute's name. Notice how the person class contains a derived attribute called /age, which can be derived by subtracting the patient's birth date from the current date. It is also possible to show the *visibility* of the attribute on the diagram. Visibility relates to the level of *information hiding* to be enforced for the attribute. The visibility of an attribute can be public (+), protected (#), or private (−). A *public* attribute is one that is not hidden from any other object. As such, other objects can modify its value. A *protected* attribute is one that is hidden from all other classes except its immediate subclasses. A *private* attribute is one that is hidden from all other classes. The default visibility for an attribute is normally private.

Operations are actions or functions that a class can perform (see Figure 5-8). The functions that are available to all classes (e.g., create a new instance, return a value for a particular attribute, set a value for a particular attribute, delete an instance) are not explicitly shown within the class rectangle. Instead, only operations unique to the class are included, such as the cancel without notice operation in the Appointment class and the calculate last visit operation in the Patient class in Figure 5-7. Notice that both the operations are followed by parentheses, which contain the parameter(s) needed by the operation. If an operation has no parameters, the parentheses are still shown but are empty. As with attributes, the visibility of an operation can be designated public, protected, or private. The default visibility for an operation is normally public.

There are four types of operations that all classes should contain: constructor, query, update, and destructor. A *constructor operation* creates a new instance of a class. For example, the patient class may have a method called insert (), which creates a new patient instance as patients are entered into the system. As we just mentioned, if an operation implements one of the basic functions (e.g., create a new instance), it is normally not explicitly shown on the class diagram, so typically we do not see constructor methods explicitly on the class diagram.

A *query operation* makes information about the state of an object available to other objects, but it does not alter the object in any way. For instance, the calculate last visit () operation that determines when a patient last visited the doctor's office will result in the object's being accessed by the system, but it will not make any change to its information. If a query method merely asks for information from attributes in the class (e.g., a patient's name, address, phone), then it is not shown on the diagram because we assume that all objects have operations that produce the values of their attributes.

An *update operation* changes the value of some or all the object's attributes, which may result in a change in the object's state. Consider changing the status of a patient from new to current with a method called change status() or associating a patient with a particular appointment with make appointment (appointment). If the result of the operation can change the state of the object, then the operation must be explicitly included on the class diagram. On the other hand, if the update operation is a simple assignment operation, it can be omitted from the diagram.

A *destructor operation* simply deletes or removes the object from the system. For example, if an employee object no longer represents an actual employee associated with the firm, a destructor operation would be used to delete the employee object. However, deleting an object is one of the basic functions and therefore would not be included on the class diagram.

Relationships A primary purpose of a class diagram is to show the relationships, or associations, that classes have with one another. These are depicted on the diagram by drawing lines between classes (see Figure 5-8). When multiple classes share a relationship (or a class shares a relationship with itself), a line is drawn and labeled with either the name of the relationship or the roles that the classes play in the relationship. For example, in Figure 5-7 the two classes patient and appointment are associated with one another whenever a patient schedules an appointment. Thus, a line labeled schedules connects patient and appointment, representing exactly how the two classes are related to each other. Also, notice that there is a small solid triangle beside the name of the relationship. The triangle allows a direction to be associated with the name of the relationship. In Figure 5-7, the schedules relationship includes a triangle, indicating that the relationship is to be read as "patient schedules appointment." Inclusion of the triangle simply increases the readability of the diagram. In Figure 5-9, three additional examples of associations are portrayed: An Invoice is AssociatedWith a Purchase Order (and vice versa), a Pilot Flies an Aircraft, and a Spare Tire IsLocatedIn a Trunk.

Sometimes a class is related to itself, as in the case of a patient being the primary insurance carrier for other patients (e.g., spouse, children). In Figure 5-7, notice that a line was drawn between the patient class and itself and called *primary insurance carrier* to depict the role that the class plays in the relationship. Notice that a plus (+) sign is placed before the label to communicate that it is a role as opposed to the name of the relationship. When labeling an association, we use either a relationship name or a role name (not both), whichever communicates a more thorough understanding of the model.

Relationships also have *multiplicity*, which documents how an instance of an object can be associated with other instances. Numbers are placed on the association path to denote the minimum and maximum instances that can be related through the association in the format minimum number..maximum number (see Figure 5-10). The numbers specify the relationship from the class at the far end of the relationship line to the end with the number. For example, in Figure 5-7, there is a 0..* on the appointment end of the patient schedules appointment relationship. This means that a patient can be associated with zero through many different appointments. At the patient end of this same relationship, there is a 1..1, meaning that an appointment must be associated with one and only one patient. In Figure 5-9, we see that an instance of the Invoice class must be AssociatedWith one instance of the Purchase Order class and that an instance of the Purchase Order class

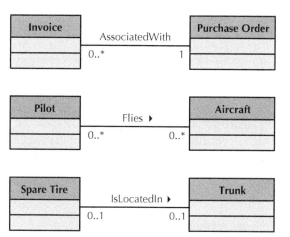

FIGURE 5-9
Sample Association

Exactly one	1	Department ——1—— Boss	A department has one and only one boss.
Zero or more	0..*	Employee ——0..*—— Child	An employee has zero to many children.
One or more	1..*	Boss ——1..*—— Employee	A boss is responsible for one or more employees.
Zero or one	0..1	Employee ——0..1—— Spouse	An employee can be married to zero or one spouse.
Specified range	2..4	Employee ——2..4—— Vacation	An employee can take from two to four vacations each year.
Multiple, disjoint ranges	1..3,5	Employee ——1..3,5—— Committee	An employee is a member of one to three or five committees.

FIGURE 5-10
Multiplicity

may be AssociatedWith zero or more instances of the Invoice class, that an instance of the Pilot class Flies zero or more instances of the Aircraft class, and that an instance of the Aircraft class may be flown by zero or more instances of the Pilot class. Finally, we see that an instance the Spare Tire class IsLocatedIn zero or one instance of the Trunk class, whereas an instance of the Trunk class can contain zero or one instance of the Spare Tire class.

There are times when a relationship itself has associated properties, especially when its classes share a many-to-many relationship. In these cases, a class called an *association class* is formed, which has its own attributes and operations.[14] It is shown as a rectangle attached by a dashed line to the association path, and the rectangle's name matches the label of the association. Think about the case of capturing information about illnesses and symptoms. An illness (e.g., the flu) can be associated with many symptoms (e.g., sore throat, fever), and a symptom (e.g., sore throat) can be associated with many illnesses (e.g., the flu, strep throat, the common cold). Figure 5-7 shows how an association class can capture information about remedies that change depending on the various combinations. For example, a sore throat caused by strep throat requires antibiotics, whereas treatment for a sore throat from the flu or a cold could be throat lozenges or hot tea. Another way to decide when to use an association

[14] For those familiar with data modeling, associative classes serve a purpose similar to the one the associative entity serves in ER diagramming.

class is when attributes that belong to the intersection of the two classes involved in the association must be captured. We can visually think about an association class as a Venn diagram. For example, in Figure 5-11, the Grade idea is really an intersection of the Student and Course classes, because a grade exists only at the intersection of these two ideas. Another example shown in Figure 5-11 is that a job may be viewed as the intersection between a Person and a Company. Most often, classes are related through a normal association; however, there are two special cases of an association that you will see appear quite often: generalization and aggregation.

Generalization and Aggregation Associations A *generalization association* shows that one class (subclass) inherits from another class (superclass), meaning that the properties and operations of the superclass are also valid for objects of the subclass, that is, the generalization association supports the generalization and class inclusion relationships. The generalization path is shown with a solid line from the subclass to the superclass and a hollow arrow pointing at the superclass (see Figure 5-8). For example, Figure 5-7 communicates that doctors, nurses, and receptionists are all kinds of employees and those employees and patients are kinds of participants. Remember that the generalization relationship occurs when you need to use words like "is a kind of" to describe the relationship. Some additional examples of generalization are given in Figure 5-12. For example, Cardinal is a-kind-of Bird, which is a-kind-of Animal; a General Practitioner is a-kind-of Physician, which is a-kind-of Person; and a Truck is a-kind-of Land Vehicle, which is a-kind-of Vehicle.

An *aggregation association* is used when classes actually comprise other classes. The aggregation association supports the aggregation and part–whole relationships. For example, think about a doctor's office that has decided to create health care teams that include doctors, nurses, and administrative personnel. As patients enter the office, they are assigned to a health care team, which cares for their needs during their visits. We could include this new knowledge in Figure 5-7 by adding two new classes (Administrative Personnel and Health Team) and aggregation relationships from the Doctor, the Nurse, and the new Administrative Personnel classes to the new Health Team class. A diamond is placed nearest the class representing the aggregation (health care team), and lines are drawn from the

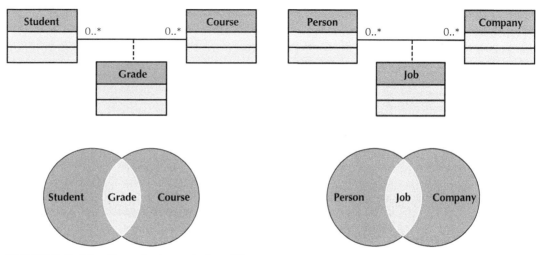

FIGURE 5-11 Sample Association Classes

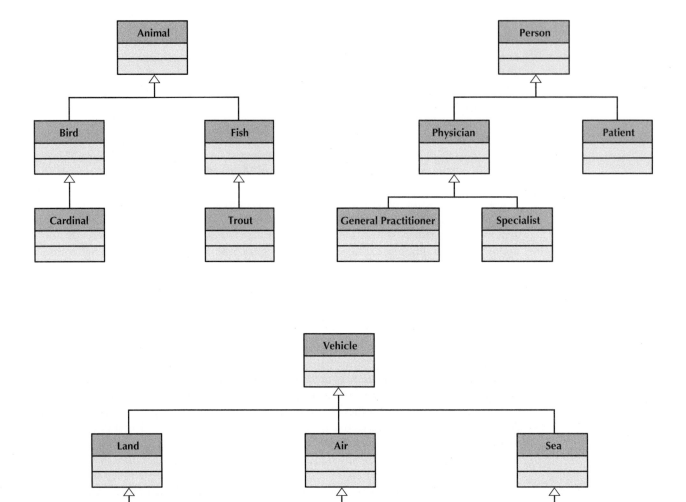

FIGURE 5-12 Sample Generalizations

diamond to connect the classes that serve as its parts (doctors, nurses, and administrative personnel). Typically, you can identify these kinds of associations when you need to use words like "is a part of" or "is made up of" to describe the relationship. However, from a UML perspective, there are two types of aggregation associations: aggregation and composition (see Figure 5-8).

Aggregation is used to portray logical a-part-of relationships and is depicted on a UML class diagram by a hollow or white diamond. For example, in Figure 5-13 three logical aggregations are shown. Logical implies that it is possible for a part to be associated with multiple wholes or that is relatively simple for the part to be removed from the whole. For example, an instance of the Employee class IsPartOf an instance of at least

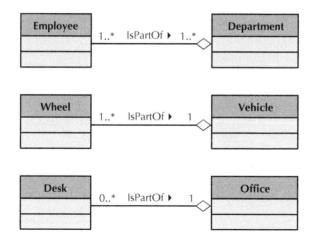

FIGURE 5-13
Sample Aggregation
Associations

one instance of the Department class, an instance of the Wheel class IsPartOf an instance of the Vehicle class, and an instance of the Desk class IsPartOf an instance of the Office class. Obviously, in many cases an employee can be associated with more than one department, and it is relatively easy to remove a wheel from a vehicle or move a desk from an office.

Composition is used to portray a physical part of relationships and is shown by a black diamond. Physical implies that the part can be associated with only a single whole. For example in Figure 5-14, three physical compositions are illustrated: an instance of a door can be a part of only a single instance of a car, an instance of a room can be a part of an instance only of a single building, and an instance of a button can be a part of only a single mouse. However, in many cases, the distinction that you can achieve by including aggregation (white diamonds) and composition (black diamonds) in a class diagram might not be worth the price of adding additional graphical notation for the client to learn. Therefore, many UML experts view the inclusion of aggregation and composition notation to the UML class diagram as simply "syntactic sugar" and not necessary because the same information can always be portrayed by simply using the correct multiplicities with the association syntax.

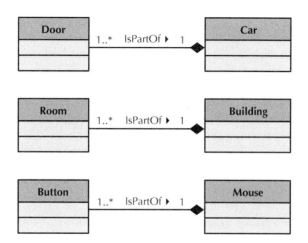

FIGURE 5-14
Sample Composi-
tion Associations

Simplifying Class Diagrams

When a class diagram is fully populated with all the classes and relationships for a real-world system, the class diagram can become very difficult to interpret (i.e., can be very complex). For example, a typical real-world system could have hundreds of classes. Therefore, it is sometimes necessary to simplify the diagram. One way to simplify the class diagram is to show only concrete classes.[15] However, depending on the number of associations that are connected to abstract classes—and thus inherited down to the concrete classes—this particular suggestion could make the diagram more difficult to comprehend.

A second way to simplify the class diagram is through the use of a *view* mechanism. Views were developed originally with relational database management systems to show only a subset of the information contained in the database. In this case, the view would be a useful subset of the class diagram, such as a use-case view that shows only the classes and relationships relevant to a particular use case. A second view could be to show only a particular type of relationship: aggregation, association, or generalization. A third type of view is to restrict the information shown with each class, for example, show only the name of the class, the name and attributes, or the name and operations. These view mechanisms can be combined to further simplify the diagram.

A third approach to simplifying a class diagram is through the use of *packages* (i.e., logical groups of classes). To make the diagrams easier to read and keep the models at a reasonable level of complexity, the classes can be grouped together into packages. Packages are general constructs that can be applied to any of the elements in UML models. In Chapter 4, we introduced the package idea to simplify use-case diagrams. In the case of class diagrams, it is simple to sort the classes into groups based on the relationships that they share.[16]

Object Diagrams

Although class diagrams are necessary to document the structure of the classes, a second type of *static structure diagram*, called an object diagram, can be useful in revealing additional information. An *object diagram* is essentially an instantiation of all or part of a class diagram. *Instantiation* means to create an instance of the class with a set of appropriate attribute values.

Object diagrams can be very useful when trying to uncover details of a class. Generally speaking, it is easier to think in terms of concrete objects (instances) rather than abstractions of objects (classes). For example, in Figure 5-15, a portion of the class diagram in Figure 5-7 has been copied and instantiated. The top part of the figure simply is a copy of a small view of the overall class diagram. The lower portion is the object diagram that instantiates that subset of classes. By reviewing the actual instances involved, John Doe, Appt1, Symptom1, and Dr. Smith, we may discover additional relevant attributes, relationships, and/or operations or possibly misplaced attributes, relationships, and/or operations. For example, an appointment has a reason attribute. Upon closer examination, the reason attribute might have been better modeled as an association with the Symptom class. Currently, the Symptom class is associated with the Patient class. After reviewing the object diagram, this seems to be in error. Therefore, we should modify the class diagram to reflect this new understanding of the problem.

---

[15] See footnote 1.

[16] For those familiar with structured analysis and design, packages serve a purpose similar to the leveling and balancing processes used in data flow diagramming. Packages and package diagrams are described in more detail in Chapter 7.

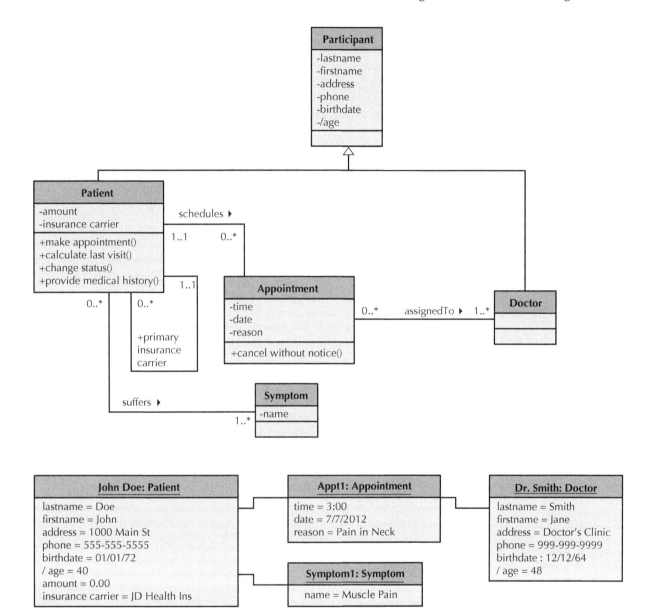

FIGURE 5-15 Sample Object Diagram

STRUCTURAL MODELS USING CRC CARDS AND CLASS DIAGRAMS

Creating a structural model is an incremental and iterative process whereby the analyst makes a rough cut of the model and then refines it over time. Structural models can become quite complex—in fact, there are systems that have hundreds of classes. It is important to remember that CRC cards and class diagrams can be used to describe both the as-is and to-be structural models of the evolving system, but they are most often used for the to-be model. There are many different ways to identify a set of candidate objects and to create CRC cards and class diagrams. Today most object identification begins with the use cases identified for the problem (see Chapter 4). In this section, we describe a use-case–driven process that can be used to create the structural model of a problem domain.

1. Create CRC Cards

We could begin creating the structural model with a class diagram instead of CRC cards. However, owing to the low-tech nature and the ease of role-playing use-case scenarios with CRC cards, we prefer to create the CRC cards first and then transfer the information from the CRC cards into a class diagram later. As a result, the first step of our recommended process is to create CRC cards. Performing textual analysis on the use-case descriptions does this. If you recall, the normal flow of events, subflows, and alternative/exceptional flows of the use-case description were written in a special form called Subject–Verb–Direct object–Preposition–Indirect object (*SVDPI*). By writing the use-case events in this form, it is easier to use the guidelines for textual analysis in Figure 5-1 and the text analysis approaches described in Chapter 3 to identify the objects. Reviewing the primary actors, stakeholders and interests, and brief descriptions of each use case allows additional candidate classes to be identified. It is useful to go back and review the original requirements to look for information that was not included in the text of the use cases. Record all the uncovered information for each candidate object on a CRC card.

2. Review CRC Cards

The second step is to review the CRC cards to determine if additional candidate classes, attributes, operations, and relationships are missing. In conjunction with this review, using the brainstorming approach described earlier can aid the team in identifying missing classes, attributes, operations, and relationships. For example, the team could start a brainstorming session with a set of questions such as follows:

- What are the *tangible things* associated with the problem?
- What are the roles played by the people in the problem domain?
- What incidents and interactions take place in the problem domain?

As you can readily see, by beginning with the use-case descriptions, many of these questions already have partial answers. For example, the primary actors and stakeholders are the roles that are played by the people in the problem domain. However, it is possible to uncover additional roles not thought of previously. This obviously would cause the use-case descriptions, and possibly the use-case diagram, to be modified and possibly expanded. As in the previous step, be sure to record all the uncovered information onto the CRC cards. This includes any modifications uncovered for any previously identified candidate classes and any information regarding any new candidate classes identified.

3. Role-Play the CRC Cards

The third step is to role-play each use-case scenario using the CRC cards. Each CRC card should be assigned to an individual who will perform the operations for the class on the CRC card. As the performers act out their roles, the system tends to break down. When this occurs, additional classes, attributes, operations, or relationships will be identified. Again, as in the previous steps, any time any new information is discovered, new CRC cards are created or modifications to existing CRC cards are made.

4. Create Class Diagram

The fourth step is to create the class diagram based on the CRC cards. Information contained on the CRC cards is transferred to the class diagrams. The responsibilities are transferred as operations; the attributes are drawn as attributes; and the relationships are drawn as generalization, aggregation, or association relationships. However, the class diagram also requires that the visibility of the attributes and operations be known. As a general rule, attributes are private and operations are public. Therefore, unless the analyst has a good reason to change the default visibility of these properties, then the defaults should be accepted. Finally, the analyst should examine the model for additional opportunities to use aggregation or generalization relationships. These types of relationships can simplify the individual class descriptions. As in the previous steps, all changes must be recorded on the CRC cards.

The fifth step is to review the structural model for missing and/or unnecessary classes, attributes, operations, and relationships. Until this step, the focus of the process has been on adding information to the evolving model. At this point, the focus begins to switch from simply adding information to also challenging the reasons for including the information contained in the model. One very useful approach here is to play devil's advocate, where a team member, just for the sake of being a pain in the neck, challenges the reasoning for including all aspects of the model.

The sixth step is to incorporate useful patterns into the evolving structural model. A useful pattern is one that would allow the analyst to more fully describe the underlying domain of the problem being investigated. Looking at the collection of patterns available (Figure 5-5) and comparing the classes contained in the patterns with those in the evolving class diagram enable this. After identifying the useful patterns, the analyst incorporates the identified patterns into the class diagram and modifies the affected CRC cards. This includes adding and removing classes, attributes, operations, and/or relationships.

The seventh and final step is to validate the structural model, including both the CRC cards and the class diagram. We discuss this content in the next section of the chapter and in Chapter 6.

Campus Housing Example

In the previous chapter, we identified a set of use cases (Add an Apartment, Delete an Apartment, and Search Available Rental Units) for the campus housing service that helps students find apartments. By reviewing the use cases, we can easily determine that the campus housing service must keep track of information for each available apartment and its owner. The information to be captured for each apartment is the location of the apartment, the number of bedrooms in the apartment, the monthly rent, and how far the apartment is from the campus. Regarding the owner of the apartment, we need to capture the owner's contact information (e.g., name, address, phone number, and e-mail address). Since students are simply users of the system, there is no need to capture any information regarding them; that is, in this case, students are simply actors. Finally, with regards to relationships among the classes, there is a single, optional, one to many association relationship that links the two classes together. The Apartment Owner CRC card is portrayed in Figure 5-16, and the class diagram for this situation is shown in Figure 5-17.

Library Example

As with the Campus Housing example, the first step is to create the CRC cards that represent the classes in the structural model. In the previous chapter, we used the Library Book Collection Management System example to describe the process of creating the functional models (use-case and activity diagrams and use-case descriptions). In this chapter, we follow the same familiar example. Because we are following a use-case-driven approach to object-oriented systems development, we first review the events described in the use-case descriptions (see Figure 5-18).

Front:

Class Name: Apartment Owner	ID: 1	Type: Concrete, Domain
Description: An apartment owner who has apartments for rent		Associated Use Cases: 2

Responsibilities	Collaborators
Add apartment	Apartment
Delete apartment	Apartment

Back:

Attributes:
Name (string)
Address (address)
Phone number (PhoneNumber)
Email (EmailAddress)

Relationships:
  Generalization (a-kind-of):

  Aggregation (has-parts):

  Other Associations: Apartment

FIGURE 5-16
Campus Housing
Apartment Owner
CRC Card

FIGURE 5-17
Campus Housing
Class Diagram

Apartment Owner		Apartment

0..1   0..*

Next, we perform textual analysis on the events by applying the textual analysis rules described in Figure 5-1. In this case, we can quickly identify the need to include classes for Borrower, Books, Librarian, Check Out Desk, ID Card, Student Borrower, Faculty/Staff Borrower, Guest Borrower, Registrar's Database, Personnel Database, Library's Guest Database, Overdue Books, Fines, and Book Request. We also can easily identify operations to "check the validity" of a book request, to "check out" the books, and to "reject" a book request. Furthermore, the events suggest a "brings" relationship between Borrower and

Normal Flow of Events:
1. The Borrower brings books to the Librarian at the checkout desk.
2. The Borrower provides Librarian their ID card.
3. The Librarian checks the validity of the ID Card.
    If the Borrower is a Student Borrower, Validate ID Card with Registrar's Office.
    If the Borrower is a Faculty/Staff Borrower, Validate ID Card with Personnel Office.
    If the Borrower is a Guest Borrower, Validate ID Card with Library's System.
4. The Librarian checks whether the Borrower has any overdue books and/or fines.
5. The Borrower checks out the books.

SubFlows:

Alternate/Exceptional Flows:
4a. The ID Card is invalid, the book request is rejected.
5a. The Borrower either has overdue books, fines, or both, the book request is rejected.

FIGURE 5-18   Flow Descriptions for the Borrow Books Use Case (Figure 4-20)

Use Case Name: Borrow Books	ID: 2	Importance Level: High
Primary Actor: Borrower	Use Case Type: Detail, Essential	

Stakeholders and Interests:
Borrower—wants to check out books
Librarian—wants to ensure borrower only gets books deserved

Brief Description: This use case describes how books are checked out of the library.

Trigger: Borrower brings books to check out desk.

Type: External

Relationships:
    Association: Borrower, Personnel Office, Registrar's Office
    Include:
    Extend:
    Generalization:

FIGURE 5-19   Overview Description for the Borrow Books Use Case (Figure 4-19)

Books and a "provides" relationship between Borrower and Librarian. This step also suggests that we should review the overview section of the use-case description (see Figure 5-19). In this case, the only additional information gleaned from the use-case description is the possible inclusion of classes for Personnel Office and Registrar's Office. This same process would also be completed for the remaining use cases contained in the functional model: Process Overdue Books, Maintain Book Collection, Search Collection, and Return Books (see Figure 4-6). Since we did not discuss these use cases in the previous chapter, we will review the problem description as a basis for beginning the next step (see Figure 5-20).

The functional requirements for an automated university library circulation system include the need to support searching, borrowing, and book-maintenance activities. The system should support searching by title, author, keywords, and ISBN. If the book of interest is currently checked out, a valid borrower should be allowed to request the book to be returned. Once the book has been checked back in, the borrower requesting the book should be notified of the book's availability.

The borrowing activities are built around checking books out and returning books by borrowers. There are three types of borrowers: students, faculty or staff, and guests. Regardless of the type of borrower, the borrower must have a valid ID card. If the borrower is a student, having the system check with the registrar's office to validate the ID card. If the borrower is a faculty or staff member, having the system check with the personnel office to validate the ID card. If the borrower is a guest, the ID card is checked against the library's own system. If the ID card is valid, the system must also check to determine whether the borrower has any overdue books or unpaid fines. If the ID card is invalid, the borrower has overdue books, or the borrower has unpaid fines, the system must reject the borrower's request to check out a book, otherwise the borrower's request should be honored. If a book is checked out, the system must update the library's collection to reflect the book's new status.

The book-maintenance activities deal with adding and removing books from the library's book collection. This requires a library manager to both logically and physically add and remove the book. Books being purchased by the library or books being returned in a damaged state typically cause these activities. If a book is determined to be damaged when it is returned and it needs to be removed from the collection, the last borrower will be assessed a fine. However, if the book can be repaired, depending on the cost of the repair, the borrower might not be assessed a fine. Every Monday, the library sends a reminder to borrowers who have overdue books. If a book is overdue more than two weeks, the borrower is assessed a fine. Depending on how long the book remains overdue, the borrower can be assessed additional fines every Monday.

FIGURE 5-20
Overview Description
of the Library
Book Collection
Management System

The second step is to review the CRC cards to determine if there is any information missing. In the case of the library system, because we only used the Borrow Books use-case description, some information is obviously missing. By reviewing Figure 5-20, we see that we need to include the ability to search the book collection by title, author, keywords, and ISBN. This obviously implies a Book Collection class with four different search operations: Search By Title, Search By Author, Search By Keywords, and Search By ISBN. Interestingly, the description also implies either a set of subclasses or states for the Book class: Checked Out, Overdue, Requested, Available, and Damaged. We will return to the issue of states versus subclasses in the next chapter. The description implies many additional operations, including Returning Books, Requesting Books, Adding Books, Removing Books, Repairing Books, Fining Borrowers, and Emailing Reminders.

Next, we should use our own library experience to brainstorm potential additional classes, attributes, operations, and relationships that could be useful to include in the Library Book Collection Management System. In our library, there is also the need to Retrieve Books From Storage, Move Books to Storage, Request Books from the Interlibrary Loan System, Return Books to the Interlibrary Loan System, and Deal with E-Books. You also could include classes for Journals, DVDs, and other media. As you can see, many classes, attributes, operations, and relationships can be identified.

The third step, role-playing the CRC cards, requires us to apply the three role-playing steps described earlier:

- Review use cases
- Identify relevant actors and objects
- Role-play scenarios

For our purposes, we will use the Borrow Books use case to demonstrate. The relevant actors include Student Borrowers, Faculty/Staff Borrowers, Guest Borrowers, Librarians, Personnel

Office, and Registrar's Office. These can be easily gleaned from the overview section of the use-case description (see Figure 5-19) and the use-case diagram (see Figure 4-6). The relevant objects seem to include Books, Borrower, and ID Card. Finally, to role-play the scenarios, we need to assign the roles to the different members of the team and try to perform each of the paths through the events of the use-case (see Figure 5-18). Based on the Events of the use case and the use case's activity diagram (see Figure 5-21), we can quickly identify nine scenarios, three for each type of Borrower (Student, Faculty/Staff, and Guest): Valid ID and No Overdue Books and No Fines, Valid ID only, and No Valid ID. When role-playing these scenarios, one question arises: What happens to the books that are requested when the request is rejected? Based on the current functional and structural models, the books are left sitting on the check out desk. That doesn't quite seem right. In reality, the books are reshelved. In fact, the notion of reshelving books is also relevant to when books are checked back in or after books have been repaired. Furthermore, the idea of adding books to the collection should also include the operation of shelving the books. As you should readily see, building structural models will also help uncover behavior that was omitted when building the functional models. Remember, object-oriented systems development is not only use-case driven but also is incremental and iterative.

The fourth step is to put everything together and to draw the class diagram. Figure 5-22 represents the first cut at drawing the class diagram for the Library Book Collection Management System. The classes identified in the previous steps have been linked with other classes via association, aggregation, and generalization relationships. For simplicity purposes, we only show the classes and their relationships, not their attributes, operations, or even the multiplicities on the association relationships.

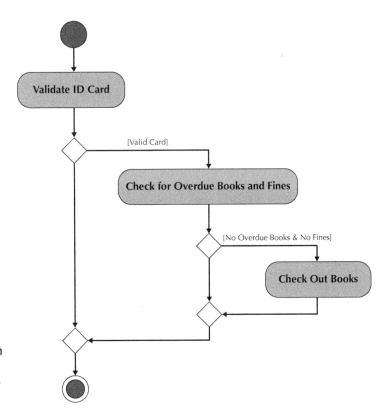

FIGURE 5-21
Activity Diagram for the Borrow Books Use Case (Figure 4-12)

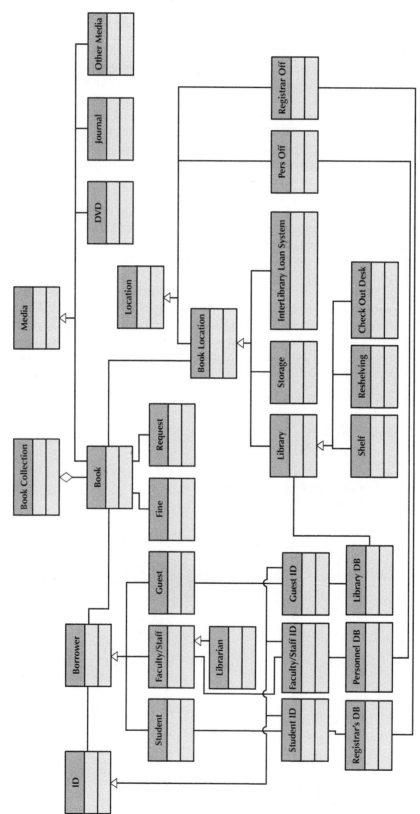

FIGURE 5-22 First-Cut Class Diagram for the Library Book Collection System

The fifth step is to carefully review what has been created. Not only should you look for any missing classes, attributes, operations, and/or relationships, but you should also challenge every aspect of the current model. Specifically, are there classes, attributes, operations, and/or relationships that should be removed from the model? If so, there may be classes on the diagram that should have been modeled as attributes. For example, the Student, Fac/Staff, and Guest IDs should have been attributes with their respective classes. Furthermore, because this is a book collection management system, the inclusion of other media seems to be inappropriate. Finally, the Personnel Office and Registrar's Office are actually only actors in the system, not objects. Based on all of these deletions, a new version of the class diagram was drawn (see Figure 5-23). This diagram is much simpler and easier to understand.

The sixth step, incorporating useful patterns, enables us to take advantage of knowledge that was developed elsewhere. In this case, the pattern used in the library problem includes too many ideas that are not relevant to the current problem. However, by looking back to Figure 5-3, we see that one of the original patterns (the Place, Transaction, Participant, Transaction Line Item, and Item pattern—see the top left of the figure) is relevant. We incorporate that pattern into the class diagram by replacing Place by Check Out Desk, Participant by Borrower, Transaction by Check Out Trans, and Item by Book (Figure 5-24). Technically speaking, each of these replacements is simply a pattern customized to the problem at hand. We also then add the Transaction Line Item class that we had missed in the original structural model.

The seventh step is to review the current state of the structural model. Needless to say, the CRC card version and the class diagram version are no longer in agreement with each other. We return to this step in the next section of the chapter.

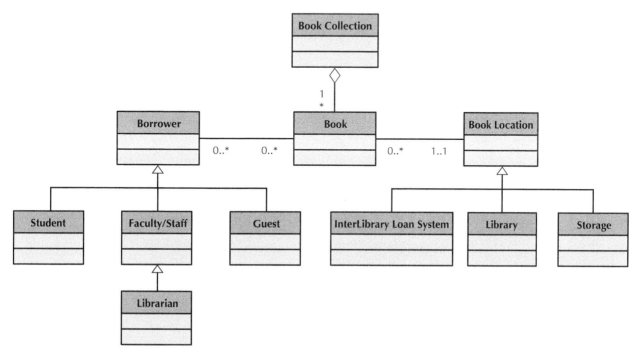

FIGURE 5-23 Second-Cut Class Diagram for the Library Book Collection System

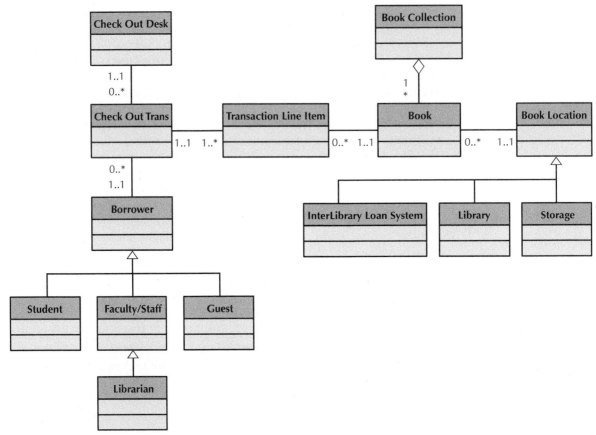

FIGURE 5-24   Class Diagram with Incorporated Pattern for the Library Book Collection System

VERIFYING AND VALIDATING THE STRUCTURAL MODEL[17]

Before we move on to creating behavioral models (see Chapter 6) of the problem domain, we need to verify and validate the structural model. In the previous chapter, we introduced the notion of walkthroughs as a way to verify and validate business processes and functional models. In this chapter, we combine walkthroughs with the power of role-playing as a way to more completely verify and validate the structural model that will underlie the business processes and functional models. In fact, all of the object identification approaches described in this chapter can be viewed as a way to test the fidelity of the structural model. Because we have already introduced the idea of role-playing the CRC cards and object identification, in this section we focus on performing walkthroughs.

In this case, the verification and validation of the structural model are accomplished during a formal review meeting using a walkthrough approach in which an analyst presents the model to a team of developers and users. The analyst walks through the model, explaining each part of the model and all the reasoning behind the decision to include

[17] The material in this section has been adapted from E. Yourdon, *Modern Structured Analysis* (Englewood Cliffs, NJ: Prentice Hall, 1989).

each of the classes in the structural model. This explanation includes justifications for the attributes, operations, and relationships associated with the classes. Each class should be linked back to at least one use case; otherwise, the purpose of including the class in the structural model will not be understood. Also including people outside the development team who produced the model can bring a fresh perspective to the model and uncover missing objects.

Previously, we suggested three representations that could be used for structural modeling: CRC cards, class diagrams, and object diagrams. Because an object diagram is simply an instantiation of some part of a class diagram, we limit our discussion to CRC cards and class diagrams. Similar to how we verified and validated the business process and functional models in the last chapter, we provide a set of rules that will test the consistency within the structural models. For example purposes, we use the appointment problem described in Chapter 4 and in this chapter. An example of the CRC card for the Old Patient class is shown in Figure 5-6, and the associated class diagram is portrayed in Figure 5-7.

First, every CRC card should be associated with a class on the class diagram, and vice versa. In the appointment example, the Old Patient class represented by the CRC card does not seem to be included on the class diagram. However, there is a Patient class on the class diagram (see Figures 5-6 and 5-7). The Old Patient CRC card most likely should be changed to simply Patient.

Second, the responsibilities listed on the front of the CRC card must be included as operations in a class on a class diagram, and vice versa. The make appointment responsibility on the new Patient CRC card also appears as the make appointment() operation in the Patient class on the class diagram. Every responsibility and operation must be checked.

Third, collaborators on the front of the CRC card imply some type of relationship on the back of the CRC card and some type of association that is connected to the associated class on the class diagram. The appointment collaborator on the front of the new Patient CRC card also appears as another association on the back of the CRC card and as an association on the class diagram that connects the Patient class with the Appointment class.

Fourth, attributes listed on the back of the CRC card must be included as attributes in a class on a class diagram, and vice versa. For example, the amount attribute on the new Patient CRC card is included in the attribute list of the Patient class on the class diagram.

Fifth, the object type of the attributes listed on the back of the CRC card and with the attributes in the attribute list of the class on a class diagram implies an association from the class to the class of the object type. For example, technically speaking, the amount attribute implies an association with the double type. However, simple types such as int and double are never shown on a class diagram. Furthermore, depending on the problem domain, object types such as Person, Address, or Date might not be explicitly shown either. However, if we know that messages are being sent to instances of those object types, we probably should include these implied associations as relationships.

Sixth, the relationships included on the back of the CRC card must be portrayed using the appropriate notation on the class diagram. For example in Figure 5-6, in instances of the Patient class are *a-kind-of* Person, it has instances of the Medical History class as part of it, and it has an association with instances of the Appointment class. Thus, the association from the Patient class to the Person class should indicate that the Person class is a generalization of its subclasses, including the Patient class; the association from the Patient class to the Medical History class should be in the form of an aggregation association (a white diamond); and the association between instances of the Patient class and instances of the Appointment class should be a simple association. However, when we review the class diagram in Figure 5-7, this is not what we find. If you recall, we included in the class diagram the transaction pattern portrayed in Figure 5-4. When we did this, many changes were made to the classes contained in the class diagram. All of these changes should have been cascaded back through all of the CRC cards. In this case, the CRC card for the Patient class should show that a Patient is a-kind-of Participant (not Person) and that the relationship from Patient to Medical History should be a simple association (see Figure 5-25).

Seventh, an association class, such as the Treatment class in Figure 5-7, should be created only if there is indeed some unique characteristic (attribute, operation, or relationship) about the intersection of the connecting classes. If no unique characteristic exists, then the association class should be removed and only an association between the two connecting classes should be displayed.

Front:		
Class Name: Patient	**ID:** 3	**Type:** Concrete, Domain
Description: An individual who needs to receive or has received medical attention		**Associated Use Cases:** 2

Responsibilities	**Collaborators**
Make appointment	Appointment
Calculate last visit	
Change status	
Provide medical history	Medical history

Back:

Attributes:
Amount (double)
Insurance carrier (text)

Relationships:
Generalization (a-kind-of): Participant

Aggregation (has-parts):

Other Associations: Appointment, Medical History

FIGURE 5-25
Patient CRC Card

Finally, as in the functional models, specific representation rules must be enforced. For example, a class cannot be a subclass of itself. The Patient CRC card cannot list Patient with the generalization relationships on the back of the CRC card, nor can a generalization relationship be drawn from the Patient class to itself. Again, all the detailed restrictions for each representation are beyond the scope of this book.[18]

Balancing Functional and Structural Models

To balance the functional and structural models, we must ensure that the two sets of models are consistent with each other. That is, the activity diagrams, use-case descriptions, and use-case diagrams must agree with the CRC cards and class diagrams that represent the evolving model of the problem domain. In this case, there are four sets of associations between the models. This gives us a place to begin balancing the functional and structural models.[19]

First, every class on a class diagram and every CRC card must be associated with at least one use case, and vice versa. For example, the CRC card portrayed in Figure 5-25 and its related class contained in the class diagram (see Figure 5-7) are associated with the Make Old Patient Appt use case described in Figure 5-2.

Second, every activity or action contained in an activity diagram and every event contained in a use-case description should be related to one or more responsibilities on a CRC card and one or more operations in a class on a class diagram and vice versa. For example, the Get Patient Information activity on the example activity diagram (see Figure 5-26) and the first two events on the use-case description (see Figure 5-2) are associated with the make appointment responsibility on the CRC card (see Figure 5-25) and the makeAppointment() operation in the Patient class on the class diagram (see Figure 5-7).

Third, every object node on an activity diagram must be associated with an instance of a class on a class diagram (i.e., an object) and a CRC card or an attribute contained in a class and on a CRC card. However, in Figure 5-26, there is an object node, Appt Request Info, that does not seem to be related to any class in the class diagram portrayed in Figure 5-7. Thus, either the activity or class diagram is in error or the object node must represent an attribute. In this case, it does not seem to represent an attribute. We could add a class to the class diagram that creates temporary objects associated with the object node on the activity diagram. However, it is unclear what operations, if any, would be associated with these temporary objects. Therefore, a better solution would be to delete the Appt Request Info object nodes from the activity diagram. In reality, this object node represented only a set of bundled attribute values, that is, data that would be used in the appointment system process (see Figure 5-27).

Fourth, every attribute and association/aggregation relationships contained on a CRC card (and connected to a class on a class diagram) should be related to the subject or object of an event in a use-case description. For example, in Figure 5-2, the second event states: The Patient provides the Receptionist with his or her name and address. By reviewing the CRC card in Figure 5-25 and the class diagram in Figure 5-7, we see that the Patient class is a subclass of the Participant class and hence inherits all the attributes, associations, and operations defined with the Participant class, where name and address attributes are defined.

---

[18] A good reference for these types of restrictions is S.W. Ambler, *The Elements of UML 2.0 Style* (Cambridge, UK: Cambridge University Press, 2005).

[19] Role-playing the CRC cards also can be very useful in verifying and validating the relationships among the functional and structural models.

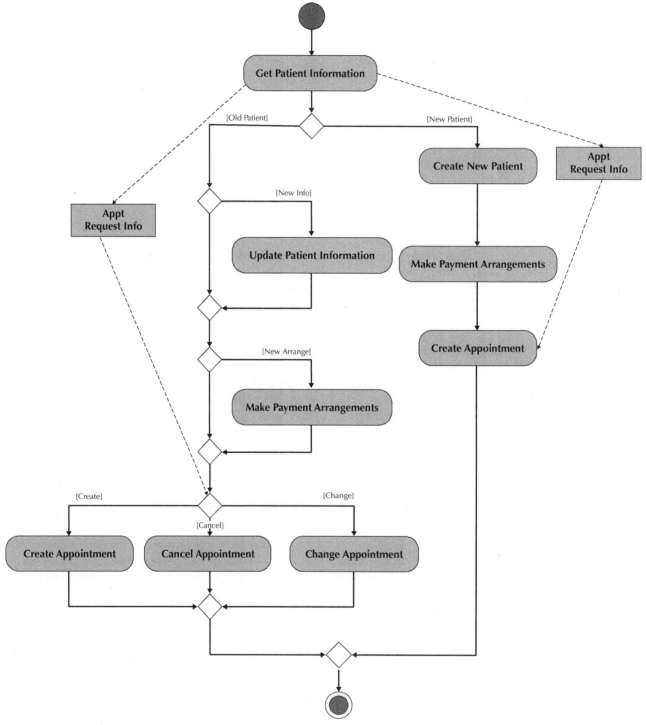

FIGURE 5-26 Activity Diagram for the Manage Appointments Use Case (Figure 4-8)

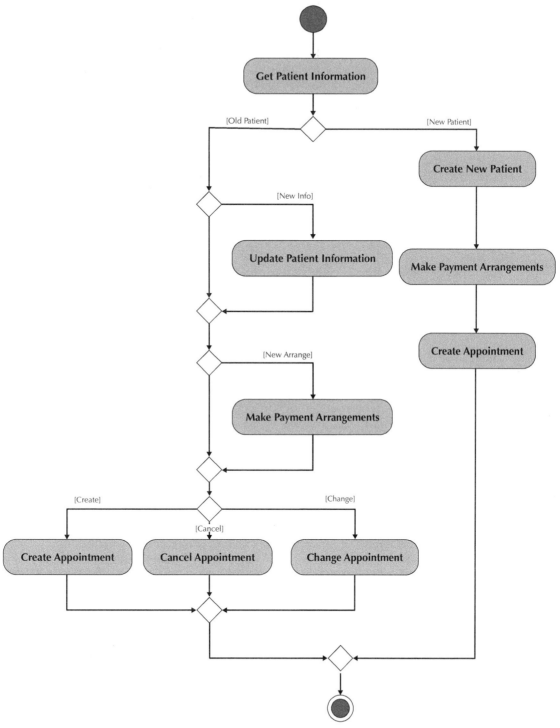

FIGURE 5-27 Corrected Activity Diagram for the Manage Appointments Use Case

---

APPLYING THE CONCEPTS AT PATTERSON SUPERSTORE

In Chapter 4, you learned how the functional models were developed in an iterative manner. After creating the functional model for the Mobile Scheduling (Version 1) of the Integrated Health Clinic Delivery System, the team had a good understanding of the business processes. Now it is time to identify the key data and to develop the structural model of the objects that support those business processes. Structural modeling for Mobile Scheduling (Version 1) involves creating, verifying, and validating CRC cards, class diagram, and object diagrams.

You can find the rest of the case at www.wiley.com/go/dennis/systemanalysis6e/casestudy.

CHAPTER REVIEW

After reading and studying this chapter, you should be able to:

☐ Describe the purpose of a structural model.
☐ Describe the different elements of a structural model.
☐ Explain the difference between abstract and concrete classes.
☐ Describe the three general types of relationships typically used in a structural model.
☐ Create a structural model using textual analysis of use-case descriptions, brainstorming, and patterns.
☐ Explain the purpose of a CRC card in structural modeling.
☐ Create a structural model using CRC cards.
☐ Describe the different elements of a CRC card.
☐ Describe how to role-play CRC cards using use-case scenarios.
☐ Describe the different elements of a class diagram.
☐ Describe the four basic operations that can be represented on a class diagram.
☐ Explain the differences between the types of relationships supported on a class diagram.
☐ Create a class diagram that represents a structural model.
☐ Describe the different elements of an object diagram.
☐ Create an object diagram that represents an instantiation of a portion of a class diagram.
☐ Verify and validate the evolving structural model using role-playing and walkthroughs.
☐ Verify and validate the structural model by ensuring the consistency of the CRC cards and class diagram.
☐ Verify and validate both the structural and functional models by balancing the two.

KEY TERMS

A-kind-of	Brainstorming	Concrete class	Domain classes
A-part-of	Class	Constructor operation	Generalization association
Abstract class	Class diagram	Contract	Has-parts
Aggregation association	Class–Responsibility–	CRC cards	Information hiding
Assemblies	Collaboration (CRC)	Decomposition	Instance
Association	Client	Derived attribute	Instantiation
Association class	Collaboration	Destructor operation	Knowing responsibility
Attribute	Conceptual model	Doing responsibility	Method

Multiplicity
Object
Object diagram
Operation
Package
Parts
Pattern
Private

Protected
Public
Query operation
Responsibility
Role-playing
Roles
Server
Specialization

State
Static model
Static structure
  diagram
Structural model
Subclass
Substitutability
Superclass

SVDPI
Tangible things
Textual analysis
Update operation
View
Visibility
Wholes

QUESTIONS

1. Describe to a businessperson the multiplicity of a relationship between two classes.
2. Why are assumptions important to a structural model?
3. What is an association class?
4. Contrast the following sets of terms: object, class, method, attribute, superclass, subclass, concrete class, abstract class.
5. Give three examples of derived attributes that may exist on a class diagram. How would they be denoted on the class diagram?
6. What are the different types of visibility? How would they be denoted on a class diagram?
7. Draw the relationships that are described by the following business rules. Include the multiplicities for each relationship.

   A patient must be assigned to only one doctor, and a doctor can have one or many patients.
   An employee has one phone extension, and a unique phone extension is assigned to an employee.
   A movie theater shows at least one movie, and a movie can be shown at up to four other movie theaters around town.
   A movie either has one star, two costars, or more than ten people starring together. A star must be in at least one movie.

8. How do you designate the reading direction of a relationship on a class diagram?

9. For what is an association class used in a class diagram? Give an example of an association class that may be found in a class diagram that captures students and the courses that they have taken.
10. Give two examples of aggregation, generalization, and association relationships. How is each type of association depicted on a class diagram?
11. Identify the following operations as constructor, query, or update. Which operations would not need to be shown in the class rectangle?

    Calculate employee raise (raise percent)
    Calculate sick days ()
    Increment number of employee vacation days ()
    Locate employee name ()
    Place request for vacation (vacation day)
    Find employee address ()
    Insert employee ()
    Change employee address ()
    Insert spouse ()

12. How are the different structural models related, and how does this affect verification and validation of the model?
13. How are the different structural models related to the different functional models, and how does this affect verification and validation of the models?

EXERCISES

A. Create a CRC card for each of the following classes: Movie (title, producer, length, director, genre), Ticket (price, adult or child, showtime, movie), and Patron (name, adult or child, age)
B. Create a class diagram based on the CRC cards you created for exercise A.
C. Create a CRC card for each of the following classes. Consider that the entities represent a system for a patient billing system. Include only the attributes that would be appropriate for this context.

   Patient (age, name, hobbies, blood type, occupation, insurance carrier, address, phone)

Insurance carrier (name, number of patients on plan, address, contact name, phone)

Doctor (specialty, provider identification number, golf handicap, age, phone, name)

D. Create a class diagram based on the CRC cards you created for exercise C.

E. Draw a class diagram for each of the following situations:

1. Whenever new patients are seen for the first time, they complete a patient information form that asks their name, address, phone number, and insurance carrier, which are stored in the patient information file. Patients can be signed up with only one carrier, but they must be signed up to be seen by the doctor. Each time a patient visits the doctor, an insurance claim is sent to the carrier for payment. The claim must contain information about the visit, such as the date, purpose, and cost. It would be possible for a patient to submit two claims on the same day.

2. The state of Georgia is interested in designing a system that will track its researchers. Information of interest includes researcher name, title, position, researcher's university name, university location, university enrollment, and researcher's research interests. Researchers are associated with one institution, and each researcher has several research interests.

3. A department store has a wedding registry. This registry keeps information about the customer (usually the bride), the products that the store carries, and the products for which each customer registers. Customers typically register for a large number of products, and many customers register for the same products.

4. Jim Smith's dealership sells Fords, Hondas, and Toyotas. In order to get in touch with these manufacturers easily, the dealership keeps information about each of them. The dealership keeps information about the models of cars from each manufacturer, including dealer price, model name, and series (e.g., Honda, Civic, LX). Additionally, the dealership also keeps all sales information, including buyer's name, address and phone number, car purchased, and amount paid.

F. Examine the class diagrams that you created for exercise E. How would the models change (if at all) based on these new assumptions?

1. Two patients have the same first and last names.

2. Researchers can be associated with more than one institution.

3. The store would like to keep track of purchase items.

4. Many buyers have purchased multiple cars from Jim over time because he is such a good dealer.

G. Visit a website that allows customers to order a product over the Web (e.g., Amazon.com). Create a structural model (CRC cards and class diagram) that the site must need to support its business process. Include classes to show what they need information about. Be sure to include the attributes and operations to represent the type of information they use and create. Finally, draw relationships, making assumptions about how the classes are related.

H. Using the seven-step process described in this chapter, create a structural model (CRC cards and class diagram) for exercise C in Chapter 4.

I. Perform a verification and validation walkthrough for the structural model created for exercise H.

J. Using the seven-step process described in this chapter, create a structural model for exercise E in Chapter 4.

K. Perform a verification and validation walkthrough for the structural model created for exercise J.

L. Using the seven-step process described in this chapter, create a structural model for exercise G in Chapter 4.

M. Perform a verification and validation walkthrough for the structural model created for exercise L.

N. Using the seven-step process described in this chapter, create a structural model for A Real Estate Inc. problem in exercise I in Chapter 4.

O. Perform a verification and validation walkthrough for the structural model created for exercise N.

P. Using the seven-step process described in this chapter, create a structural model for the A Video Store problem in exercise L in Chapter 4.

Q. Perform a verification and validation walkthrough for the structural model created for exercise P.

R. Using the seven-step process described in this chapter, create a structural model for the gym membership problem in exercise O in Chapter 4.

S. Perform a verification and validation walkthrough for the structural model created for exercise R.

T. Using the seven-step process described in this chapter, create a structural model for the Picnics R Us problem in exercise R in Chapter 4.

U. Perform a verification and validation walkthrough for the structural model created for exercise T.

V. Using the seven-step process described in this chapter, create a structural model for Of-the-Month-Club problem in exercise U in Chapter 4.

W. Perform a verification and validation walkthrough for the structural model created for exercise V.

MINICASES

1. West Star Marinas is a chain of twelve marinas that offer lakeside service to boaters; service and repair of boats, motors, and marine equipment; and sales of boats, motors, and other marine accessories. The systems development project team at West Star Marinas has been hard at work on a project that eventually will link all the marina's facilities into one unified, network system.

   The project team has developed a use-case diagram of the current system. This model has been carefully checked. Last week, the team invited a number of system users to role-play the various use cases, and the use cases were refined to the users' satisfaction. Right now, the project manager feels confident that the as-is system has been adequately represented in the use-case diagram.

   The director of operations for West Star is the sponsor of this project. He sat in on the role-playing of the use cases and was very pleased by the thorough job the team had done in developing the model. He made it clear to you, the project manager, that he was anxious to see your team begin work on the use cases for the to-be system. He was a little skeptical that it was necessary for your team to spend any time modeling the current system in the first place but grudgingly admitted that the team really seemed to understand the business after going through that work.

   The methodology you are following, however, specifies that the team should now turn its attention to developing the structural models for the as-is system. When you stated this to the project sponsor, he seemed confused and a little irritated. "You are going to spend even more time looking at the current system? I thought you were done with that! Why is this necessary? I want to see some progress on the way things will work in the future!"

   What is your response to the director of operations? Why do we perform structural modeling? Is there any benefit to developing a structural model of the current system at all? How do the use cases and use-case diagrams help us develop the structural model?

2. Holiday Travel Vehicles sells new recreational vehicles and travel trailers. When new vehicles arrive at Holiday Travel Vehicles, a new vehicle record is created. Included in the new vehicle record are a vehicle serial number, name, model, year, manufacturer, and base cost.

   When a customer arrives at Holiday Travel Vehicles, he or she works with a salesperson to negotiate a vehicle purchase. When a purchase has been agreed upon, a sales invoice is completed by the salesperson. The invoice summarizes the purchase, including full customer information, information on the trade-in vehicle (if any), the trade-in allowance, and information on the purchased vehicle. If the customer requests dealer-installed options, they are listed on the invoice as well. The invoice also summarizes the final negotiated price, plus any applicable taxes and license fees. The transaction concludes with a customer signature on the sales invoice.

   a. Identify the classes described in the preceding scenario (you should find six). Create CRC cards for each class.

   Customers are assigned a customer ID when they make their first purchase from Holiday Travel Vehicles. Name, address, and phone number are recorded for the customer. The trade-in vehicle is described by a serial number, make, model, and year. Dealer-installed options are described by an option code, description, and price.

   b. Develop a list of attributes for each class. Place the attributes onto the CRC cards.

   Each invoice lists just one customer. A person does not become a customer until he or she purchases a vehicle. Over time, a customer may purchase a number of vehicles from Holiday Travel Vehicles.

Every invoice must be filled out by only one salesperson. A new salesperson might not have sold any vehicles, but experienced salespeople have probably sold many vehicles.

Each invoice only lists one new vehicle. If a new vehicle in inventory has not been sold, there will be no invoice for it. Once the vehicle sells, there will be just one invoice for it.

A customer may decide to have no options added to the vehicle or may choose to add many options. An option may be listed on no invoices, or it may be listed on many invoices.

A customer may trade in no more than one vehicle on a purchase of a new vehicle. The trade-in vehicle may be sold to another customer who later trades it in on another Holiday Travel vehicle.

c. Based on the preceding business rules in force at Holiday Travel Vehicles and CRC cards, draw a class diagram and document the relationships with the appropriate multiplicities. Remember to update the CRC cards.

CHAPTER 6

BEHAVIORAL MODELING

Behavioral models describe the internal dynamic aspects of an information system that supports the business processes in an organization. During analysis, behavioral models describe what the internal logic of the processes is without specifying how the processes are to be implemented. Later, in the design and implementation phases, the detailed design of the operations contained in the object is fully specified. In this chapter, we describe three Unified Modeling Language (UML) diagrams that are used in behavioral modeling (activity diagrams, sequence diagrams, and behavioral state machines) and CRUDE (create, read, update, delete, execute) matrices.

OBJECTIVES

- Understand how to use activity diagrams to assign activities to actors and classes.
- Understand the rules and style guidelines for sequence diagrams and behavioral state machines.
- Understand the processes used to create sequence diagrams, CRUDE matrices, and behavioral state machines.
- Be able to create behavioral models using activity diagrams, sequence diagrams, CRUDE matrices, and behavioral state machines.
- Understand how to verify and validate the behavioral models.
- Understand how to verify and validate the behavioral models with the functional and structural models.

INTRODUCTION

The previous two chapters discussed how analysts create both business process and functional and structural models. Systems analysts use business process and functional models to describe the functional or external behavioral view of an information system. And, they use structural models to depict the internal structural or static view of an information system. In this chapter, we discuss how analysts use *behavioral models* to represent the internal behavior or dynamic view of an information system.

By supporting all three views (functional, structural, and behavioral), object-oriented systems analysis and design supports an architecture-centric approach to developing information systems. Furthermore, the behavioral view is driven by the original use cases uncovered during business process and functional modeling. Therefore, as with all object-oriented modeling, behavioral modeling is use case driven. Finally, as with business process and functional and structural modeling, you will find that you will need to not only iterate across the behavioral models (described in this chapter), but you will also have to iterate across all three architectural views (functional, structural, and behavioral) to capture and represent the requirements for a business information system.

There are two types of behavioral models. First, there are behavioral models used to represent the underlying details of a business process portrayed by a use-case model. In UML, activity and sequence are used for this type of behavioral model. Practically speaking, these interaction diagrams allow the analyst to model the distribution of the behavior of the system over the actors and objects in the system. In this way, we can easily see how actors and objects collaborate to provide the functionality defined in a use case. Second, a behavioral model is used to represent the changes that occur in the underlying data. UML uses behavioral state machines for this.

During analysis, analysts use behavioral models to capture a basic understanding of the dynamic aspects of the underlying business process. Traditionally, behavioral models have been used primarily during design, where analysts refine the behavioral models to include implementation details (see Chapter 8). For now, our focus is on *what* the dynamic view of the evolving system is and not on *how* the dynamic aspect of the system will be implemented.

In this chapter, we concentrate on creating behavioral models of the underlying business process. Using the activity and sequence diagrams and behavioral state machines, it is possible to give a complete view of the dynamic aspects of the evolving business information system. We first describe behavioral models and their components. We then describe each of the diagrams, how they are created, and how they are related to the functional and structural models described in Chapters 4 and 5. Finally, we describe CRUDE analysis and the process to verify and validate the behavioral models.

BEHAVIORAL MODELS

When an analyst is attempting to understand the underlying application domain of a problem, he or she must consider both structural and behavioral aspects of the problem. Unlike other approaches to the development of information systems, object-oriented approaches attempt to view the underlying application domain in a holistic manner. By viewing the problem domain as a set of *use cases* that are supported by a set of collaborating objects, object-oriented approaches allow an analyst to minimize the semantic gap between the real-world set of objects and the evolving object-oriented model of the problem domain. However, as we pointed out in the previous chapter, the real world tends to be messy; because software must be logical to work, perfect modeling of the application domain is nearly impossible.

One of the primary purposes of behavioral models is to show how the underlying objects in a problem domain will work together to form a *collaboration* to support each of the *use cases*. Whereas structural models represent the objects and the relationships between them, behavioral models depict the internal view of the business process that a use case describes. The process can be shown by the interaction that takes place between the objects that collaborate to support a use case through the use of activity and sequence diagrams. It is also possible to show the effect that the set of use cases that make up the system has on the objects in the system through the use of behavioral state machines.

Creating behavioral models is an iterative process that iterates not only over the individual behavioral models, but also over the functional (see Chapter 4) and structural (see Chapter 5) models. As the behavioral models are created, it is not unusual to make changes to the functional and structural models. In this chapter, we describe using activity diagrams, sequence diagrams, CRUDE analysis, and behavioral state machines.

INTERACTION DIAGRAMS

One of the primary differences between class diagrams and interaction diagrams, besides the obvious difference that one describes structure and the other behavior, is that the modeling focus on a class diagram is at the class level, whereas the interaction diagrams focus on the object level. In this section, we review objects, operations, and messages and we cover the activity and sequence diagrams that can be used to model the interactions that take place between the objects in an information system.

Objects, Operations, and Messages

An object is an instantiation of a *class*, i.e., an actual person, place, or thing about which we want to capture information. If we were building an appointment system for a doctor's office, classes might include doctor, patient, and appointment. The specific patients, such as Jim Maloney, Mary Wilson, and Theresa Marks, are considered objects—i.e., *instances* of the Patient class.

Each object has *attributes* that describe information about the object, such as a patient's name, birth date, address, and phone number. Each object also has *behaviors*. At this point in the development of the evolving system, the behaviors are described by *operations*. An operation is nothing more than an action that an object can perform. For example, an appointment object can probably schedule a new appointment, delete an appointment, and locate the next available appointment. Later on during the development of the evolving system, the operations will be implemented as *methods*.

Each object also can send and receive messages. *Messages* are information sent to objects to tell an object to execute one of its operations. Essentially, a message is a function or procedure call from one object to another object. For example, if a patient is new to the doctor's office, the system sends an insert message to the application. The patient object receives the instruction (the message) and does what it needs to do to insert the new patient into the system (the behavior).

Activity Diagrams

Before moving on to sequence diagrams, one easy approach to create a model that would aid in assigning the activities to the relevant actors and objects is to modify the *activity diagram* representation of a business process by adding *swimlanes*. In Figure 4-10, the swimlanes were used to break up the making of a school lunch, that included a peanut butter and jelly sandwich, a drink, and dessert, between two parents. Finally, with object-oriented development, activities must be associated with the actors, both external and internal, involved in the business process (e.g., employees or customers) and the objects that realize the process. Furthermore, with agile approaches, when any design process occurs, developers tend to use activity diagrams with swimlanes instead of using sequence diagrams. Consequently, whether the developers use a pure agile approach such as SCRUM or a full-blown enterprise wide approach such as UP, using activity diagrams with swimlanes is useful to associate the activities with the external roles, the internal roles, and the classes (objects) contained in the structural model. In this section, we demonstrate how to "spread" the *activities* contained in a business process or workflow over the actors and objects using the Manage Appointments use case of the appointment system example from Chapters 4 and 5 (see Figures 6-1–6-3).

Only a subset of the entire set of classes in the class diagram (Figure 6-1) will be relevant to the Manage Appointments Use Case (Figures 6-2 and 6-3). By looking at the use case diagram, it is obvious that the Patient actor will be involved in the use case. Also, by looking at the activity and class diagrams, we can easily identify that the Patient and Appointment classes are necessary to support the Manage Appointments use case. Therefore, as a first step in assigning activities to the relevant actors and classes, we should set up three swimlanes; one for the actor and

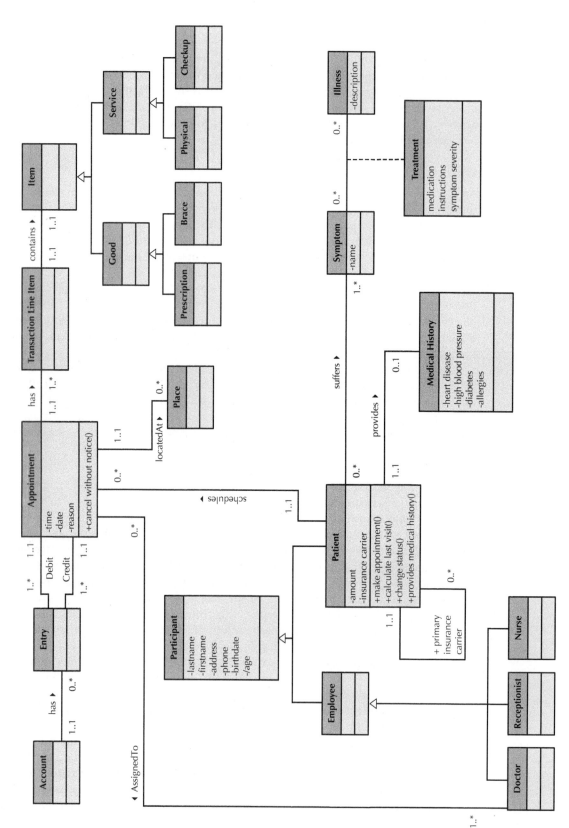

FIGURE 6-1 Appointments System Class Diagram (Figure 5-7)

214

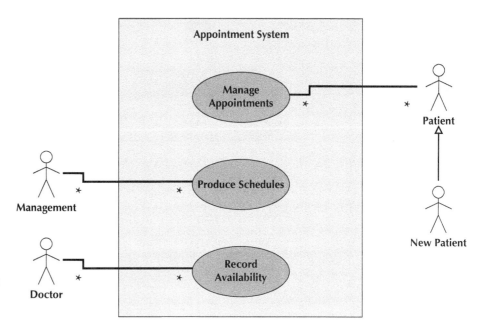

FIGURE 6-2
Appointment System
Use-Case Diagram
(Figure 4-3)

one each for the two classes. For example, given that in object-oriented systems, creating, reading, updating, and deleting operations can only be performed by the object itself, we can quickly assign the Create New Patient, Update Patient Information, and Make Payment Arrangements activities to the Patient class. Furthermore, it is obvious that the Create Appointment, Cancel Appointment, and Change Appointment activities should be assigned to the Appointment class. This leaves us with only trying to assign the Get Patient Information activity to something. Based on the diagrams, we cannot determine who or what should implement this activity. To figure this out, we need to review the use case description. When we do such, we discover that there is another actor involved in the process: Receptionist. The Receptionist actor is an internal actor that is a human part of the system. This is why it does not appear in the use case diagram. Consequently, we need to add another swimlane to our diagram. Furthermore, upon reflection, we realize that the Get Patient Information activity actually is a dialogue between the two actors. Therefore, the Get Patient Information activity is decomposed into different aspects of the overall Get Patient Information activity: Request Appointment, Determine Appointment Type, Get Appointment Times. Based on all of the above, the activity diagram for the Manage Appointments use case is portrayed in Figure 6-4. This figure shows that some of the activities will be performed by actors while others will need to be implemented as operations in classes.

Sequence Diagrams

Like an activity diagram with swimlanes, sequence diagrams illustrate the actors and objects that collaborate in a use case and the messages that pass between them over time for *one* use case. A *sequence diagram* is a *dynamic model* that shows the explicit sequence of messages that are passed between objects in a defined interaction.

The sequence diagram can be a *generic sequence diagram* that shows all possible scenarios[1] for a use case, but usually each analyst develops a set of *instance sequence diagrams*, each of which depicts a single *use case scenario* within the use case. The diagrams are used throughout the analysis and design phases. However, the design diagrams are very implementation specific, often including database objects or specific user interface components as the objects.

---

[1] Remember that a scenario is a single executable path through a use case. Or, it is an instance of the use case.

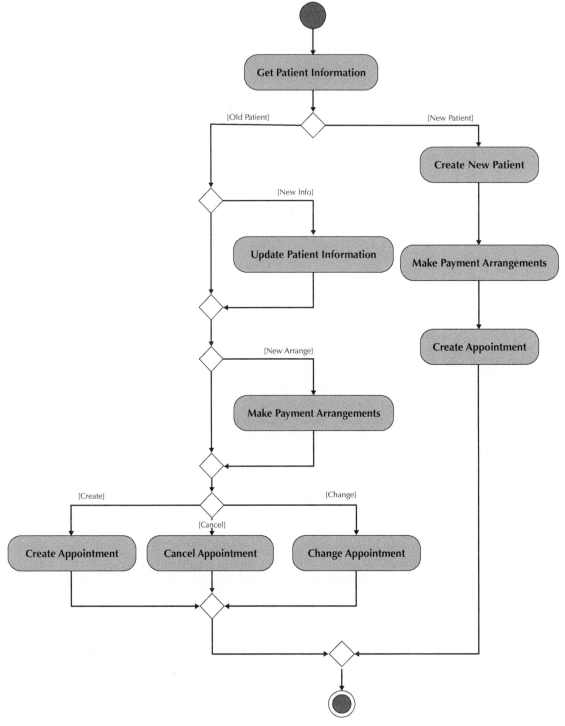

FIGURE 6-3 Activity Diagram for the Manage Appointments Use Case (Figure 5-27)

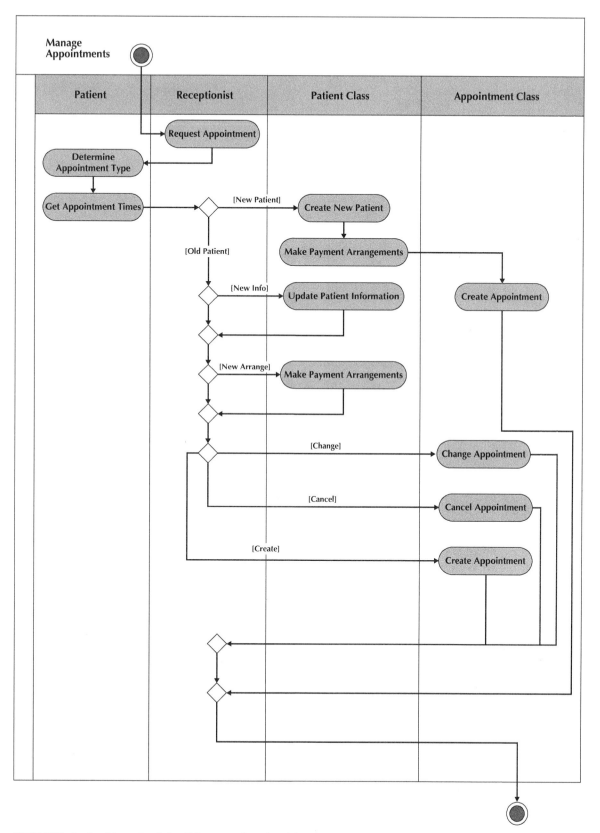

FIGURE 6-4 New Activity Diagram for the Manage Appointments Use Case

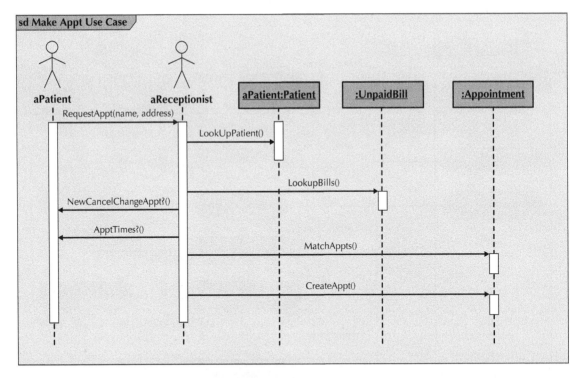

FIGURE 6-5 Example Sequence Diagram

Elements of a Sequence Diagram Figure 6-5 shows an instance sequence diagram that depicts the objects and messages for the Make Old Patient Appt use case, which describes the process by which an existing patient creates a new appointment or cancels or reschedules an appointment for the doctor's office appointment system. In this specific instance, the Make Old Patient Appt process only portrays the successful scenario of creating an appointment.

Actors and *objects* that participate in the sequence are placed across the top of the diagram using actor symbols and object symbols (see Figure 6-2). Notice that the *actors* and objects in Figure 6-5 are aPatient, aReceptionist, aPatient, UnpaidBill, and Appointment.[2] For each of the objects, the name of the class of which they are an instance is given after the object's name (e.g., aPatient means that aPatient is an instance of the Patient class).

A dotted line runs vertically below each actor and object to denote the *lifeline* of the actors and objects over time (see Figure 6-5).[3] Sometimes an object creates a *temporary object*; in this case, an X is placed at the end of the lifeline at the point where the object is destroyed (not shown). For example, think about a shopping cart object for a Web commerce application. The shopping cart is used for temporarily capturing line items for an order, but once the order is confirmed, the shopping cart is no longer needed. In this case, an X would be located at the point at which the shopping cart object is destroyed. When objects continue to exist in the system after they are used in the sequence diagram, then the lifeline continues to the bottom of the diagram (this is the case with all of the objects in Figure 6-5).

A thin rectangular box, called the *execution occurrence*, is overlaid onto the lifeline to show when the classes are sending and receiving messages (see Figure 6-6). A message is a

---

[2] In some versions of the sequence diagram, object symbols are used as surrogates for the actors. However, for clarity, we recommend using actor symbols for actors instead.

[3] Technically speaking, in UML 2.0 the lifeline actually refers to both the object (actor) and the dashed line drawn vertically underneath the object (actor). However, we prefer to use the older terminology because it is more descriptive of what is actually being represented.

Term and Definition	Symbol
An actor: ■ Is a person or system that derives benefit from and is external to the system. ■ Participates in a sequence by sending and/or receiving messages. ■ Is placed across the top of the diagram. ■ Is depicted either as a stick figure (default) or, if a nonhuman actor is involved, as a rectangle with <<actor>> in it (alternative).	anActor **<<actor>>** **anActor**
An object: ■ Participates in a sequence by sending and/or receiving messages. ■ Is placed across the top of the diagram.	anObject : aClass
A lifeline: ■ Denotes the life of an object during a sequence. ■ Contains an X at the point at which the class no longer interacts.	
An execution occurrence: ■ Is a long narrow rectangle placed atop a lifeline. ■ Denotes when an object is sending or receiving messages.	
A message: ■ Conveys information from one object to another one. ■ A operation call is labeled with the message being sent and a solid arrow, whereas a return is labeled with the value being returned and shown as a dashed arrow.	aMessage() ReturnValue
A guard condition: ■ Represents a test that must be met for the message to be sent.	[aGuardCondition]:aMessage()
For object destruction: ■ An X is placed at the end of an object's lifeline to show that it is going out of existence.	X
A frame: ■ Indicates the context of the sequence diagram.	Context

FIGURE 6-6   Sequence Diagram Syntax

communication between objects that conveys information with the expectation that activity will ensue. Many different types of messages can be portrayed on a sequence diagram. However, in the case of using sequence diagrams to model use cases, two types of messages are typically used: operation call and return. *Operation call messages* passed between objects are shown using solid lines connecting two objects with an arrow on the line showing which way the message is being passed. Argument values for the message are placed in parentheses next to the message's name. The order of messages goes from the top to the bottom of the page, so messages located higher on the diagram represent messages that occur earlier on in the sequence, versus the lower messages that occur later. A *return message* is depicted as a dashed line with an arrow on the end of the line portraying the direction of the return. The information being returned is used to label the arrow. However, because adding return messages tends to clutter the diagram, unless the return messages add a lot of information to the diagram, they can be omitted. For example, in Figure 6-5, no return messages are depicted.[4] In Figure 6-5, LookUpPatient() is a message sent from the actor aReceptionist to the object aPatient to determine whether the aPatient actor is a current patient.

At times a message is sent only if a *condition* is met. In those cases, the condition is placed between a set of brackets, [ ]—for example, [aPatient Exists] LookupBills(). The condition is placed in front of the message name. However, when using a sequence diagram to model a specific scenario, conditions are typically not shown on any single sequence diagram. Instead, conditions are implied only through the existence of different sequence diagrams.

An object can send a message to itself, e.g., Create Sandwich in Figure 6-7. This is known as *self-delegation*. Sometimes, an object creates another object. This is shown by the message being sent directly to an object instead of its lifeline.

Figure 6-7 portrays two additional examples of instance-specific sequence diagrams. The first one is related to the Make Lunch use case that was described in the activity diagram portrayed in Figure 4-10. The second one is related to the Place Order use case associated with the activity diagram in Figure 4-9. In both examples, the diagrams simply represent a single scenario. Notice that in the Make Lunch sequence diagram there is a message being sent from an actor to itself [CreateSandwich()]. Depending on the complexity of the scenario being modeled, this particular message could have been eliminated. Obviously, both the process of making a lunch and placing an order can be quite a bit more complex. However, from a learning point of view, you should be able to see how the sequence diagrams and the activity diagrams relate to one another.

Some use cases call other use cases using the extend and include relationship types. In those cases, we need to show the call to the other use case in the related sequence diagram. For example, the Make New Patient Appt use case (Figure 4-21) calls or executes the Make Payment Arrangements and the Create New Patient use cases via the include relationship that points from the parent use case to the two child use cases. To portray this correctly in a sequence diagram requires us to use the frame symbol for each of the two child use cases and to send an execute message to the frame. In Figure 6-8, aReceptionist actor sends the Execute message to each of the two child use cases.

Some use cases contain iterative processes in which a loop should be modeled. For example, Figure 6-9 portrays a sequence diagram that portrays the process that a course registration system might need to model. In this case, the student makes a set of course requests to a registration manager that iterates over a set of classes that are available to enable the student to add courses to their course request. Again, like the previous sequence diagram this is an instant-specific diagram that only portrays the situation in which the courses are available. Notice that the frame not only includes the loop label, but it also includes the condition that terminates the loop: while more courses to request. Other versions of this diagram would be required to portray the situation when a course is not available. For example, the student request could be put onto a waiting list for the courses that were not currently available.

---

[4] However, some CASE tools require the return messages to be displayed. Obviously, when you are using these tools, you have to include the return messages on the diagram.

FIGURE 6-7
Additional
Sample Instance-
Specific Sequence
Diagrams

Guidelines for Creating Sequence Diagrams Ambler[5] provides a set of guidelines when drawing sequence diagrams. In this section, we review six of them.

- Try to have the messages not only in a top-to-bottom order but also, when possible, in a left-to-right order. Given that Western cultures tend to read left to right and top to bottom, a sequence diagram is much easier to interpret if the messages are ordered as much as possible in the same way. To accomplish this, order the actors and objects along the top of the diagram in the order that they participate in the scenario of the use case.
- If an actor and an object conceptually represent the same idea, one inside of the software and the other outside, label them with the same name. In fact, this implies that they exist in both the use-case diagram (as an actor) and in the class diagram (as a class). At first glance, this might seem to lead to confusion. However, if they do

[5] S.W. Ambler, *The Elements of UML 2.0 Style* (Cambridge, England: Cambridge University Press, 2005).

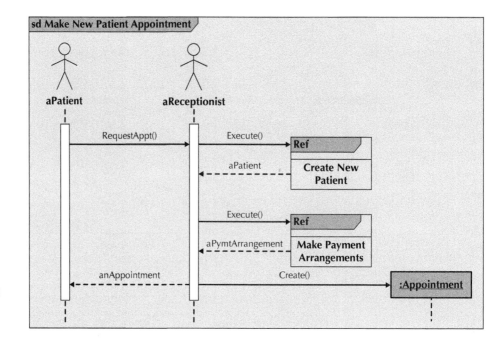

FIGURE 6-8
Example of an Instance-Specific Sequence Diagram Calling "Included" Use Cases

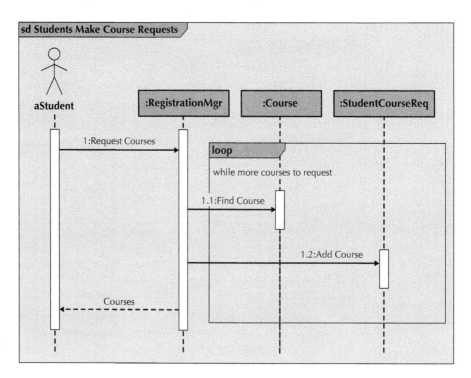

FIGURE 6-9
Example of an Instance-Specific Sequence Diagram that Portrays an Iterative Process

indeed represent the same idea, then they should have the same name. For example, a customer actor interacts with the system and the system stores information about the customer. In this case, they do indeed represent the same conceptual idea.

■ The initiator of the scenario—actor or object—should be the drawn as the farthest left item in the diagram. This guideline is essentially a specialization of the first guideline. In this case, it relates specifically to the actor or object that triggers the scenario.

- When there are multiple objects of the same type, be sure to include a name for the object in addition to the class of the object. For example, in the making a lunch example (see Figure 6-7) there are two objects of type Parent. As such, they should be named. Otherwise, you can simply use the class name. This will simplify the diagram. In this case, the Child object did not have to be named. We could have simply placed a colon in front of the class name instead.

- Show return values only when they are not obvious. Showing all of the returns tends to make a sequence diagram more complex and potentially difficult to comprehend. In many cases, less is more. Only show the returns that actually add information for the reader of the diagram.

- Justify message names and return values near the arrowhead of the message and return arrows, respectively. This makes it much easier to interpret the messages and their return values.

Creating a Sequence Diagram

In this section, we describe a six-step process used to create a sequence diagram.[6] The first step in the process is to determine the context of the sequence diagram. The context of the diagram can be a system, a use case, or a scenario of a use case. The context of the diagram is depicted as a labeled *frame* around the diagram (see Figures 6-5–6-9). Most commonly, it is one use-case scenario. Figure 6-5 portrays the instance sequence diagram for the scenario from the Make Old Patient Appt use case description given in Figure 4-13 for making a new appointment for an existing patient. For each possible scenario for the Make Old Patient Appt use case, a separate instance sequence diagram would be created. On the surface, this seems to be a lot of potentially redundant and useless work. However, at this point in the representation of a system, we are still trying to completely understand the problem. This process of creating instance sequence diagrams for each scenario instead of creating a single generic sequence diagram for the entire use case will enable the developers to attain a more complete understanding of the problem being addressed. For example, the instance sequence diagram in Figure 6-5 is much simpler than the activity diagram in Figure 6-4. Each instance sequence diagram is fairly simple to interpret, whereas a generic sequence diagram can be very complex. The testing of a specific use case is accomplished in a much easier manner by validating and verifying the completeness of the set of instance sequence diagrams instead of trying to work through a single complex generic sequence diagram.

The second step is to identify the actors and objects that participate in the sequence being modeled, i.e., the actors and objects that interact with each other during the use-case scenario. The actors were identified during the creation of the functional model, whereas the objects are identified during the development of the structural model. These are the classes on which the objects of the sequence diagram for this scenario will be based. One very useful approach to identifying all of the scenarios associated with a use case is to role-play the *CRC cards* (see Chapter 5). This can help you identify potentially missing operations that are necessary to support the business process, which the use case is representing, in a complete manner. Also, during role-playing, it is likely that new classes, and hence new objects, will be uncovered.[7] Don't worry too much about identifying all the objects perfectly; remember that the behavioral modeling process is iterative. Usually, the sequence diagrams are revised multiple times during the behavioral modeling processes.

---

[6] The approach described in this section is adapted from Grady Booch, James Rumbaugh, and Ivar Jacobson, *The Unified Modeling Language User Guide* (Reading, MA: Addison-Wesley, 1999).

[7] This obviously will cause you to go back and modify the structural model (see Chapter 5).

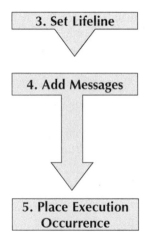

The third step is to set the lifeline for each object. To do this, you need to draw a vertical dotted line below each class to represent the class's existence during the sequence. An X should be placed below the object at the point on the lifeline where the object goes out of existence.

The fourth step is to add the messages to the diagram. This is done by drawing arrows to represent the messages being passed from object to object, with the arrow pointing in the message's transmission direction. The arrows should be placed in order from the first message (at the top) to the last (at the bottom) to show time sequence. Any parameters passed along with the messages should be placed in parentheses next to the message's name. If a message is expected to be returned as a response to a message, then the return message is not explicitly shown on the diagram.

The fifth step is to place the execution occurrence on each object's lifeline by drawing a narrow rectangle box over the lifelines to represent when the classes are sending and receiving messages.

The sixth and final step is to validate the sequence diagram. The purpose of this step is to guarantee that the sequence diagram completely represents the underlying process. This is done by guaranteeing that the diagram depicts all the steps in the process.[8]

Campus Housing Example In Chapters 4 and 5, we created a set of functional and structural models for the campus housing service. In this section, we are going to use those models to create a sequence diagram for the Add Apartment use case. As stated above, the first thing we should do is to set the context, which is in this case the Add Apartment use case. Second, we must identify the actors and objects that will participate in the execution of the use case. To do this, we should review the functional and structural models that were created for the campus housing service problem in Chapters 4 and 5. Figure 6-10 replicates these representations.

Based on the functional and structural representations, we see that the actors involved in the use case are the Apartment Owner and the Campus Housing Service itself. By looking through the Normal Flow of Events and the activity diagram, we see that the only object that seems to be relevant is the instance of the Apartment class that is being added. Given that there are no Alternate/Exceptional Flows or any decisions being made in the Normal Flow of Events, nor are there any decisions in the activity diagram associated with the Add Apartment use case, there is only one scenario to be portrayed. Consequently, there is only one instance sequence diagram to be created. Figure 6-11 depicts the sequence diagram for this use case.

Library Example In the previous chapters, we have demonstrated the diagramming and modeling processes using the Borrow Books use case of the Library Book Collection Management System. When considering instance sequence diagrams, we need to draw one sequence diagram per scenario. In the case of the Borrow Books use case in Chapter 4, there are nine different scenarios. Therefore, for this one use case, there would be nine separate instance sequence diagrams. In this example, we are setting the context of the sequence diagram to only one specific scenario of the Borrow Books use case: Students who have a valid ID and do not have any overdue books or any fines. The other scenarios include Students without a valid ID, Students with a valid ID but who owe fines or have overdue books, and the same three scenarios for the other two types of Borrowers: Faculty/Staff and Guest. In this example, we are only drawing the one sequence diagram for the Students with a valid ID scenario. To begin with, we should review the Flow of Events of the use-case description (see Figure 6-12), the activity diagram (see Figure 6-13), and the use-case diagram (see Figure 6-14).

[8] We describe validation in more detail later in this chapter.

The next step is to identify the actors and objects involved in the scenario. By studying the flow of events and the use-case diagram, we identify students, librarians, and the registrar's office as actors and borrowers, the book collection, and books as the objects. We place the actors and objects across the top of the diagram based on the ordering of their appearance in the normal flow of events. The next step involves simply drawing the lifelines beneath the actors and objects in the scenario. The fourth step is to add the actual messages to the diagram. To do this, we again review the actual steps taken when executing this scenario by reviewing the flow of events (see Figure 6-12) and the activity diagram (see Figure 6-13). We also should review any results from the role-playing of the CRC cards (see Chapter 5). This will help us to properly portray where the functionality is located. For example, in Figure 6-12, the Librarian executes the CheckOutBooks() procedure (the Student sends the message CheckOutBooks () to ask the Librarian to execute the CheckOutBooks () procedure) when the student hands the librarian the books to check out. The Librarian in return asks the Student for the ID card. When the student hands the ID Card to the Librarian, the Librarian asks the Registrar's Office to execute the ValidID() procedure when the Librarian passes the student's ID number over to the Registrar Office system to validate the student's ID number. This continues until the ID Card and Books are returned to the student. Once we have

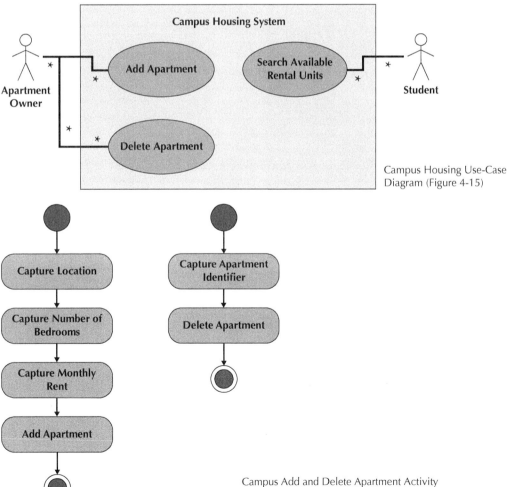

Campus Housing Use-Case Diagram (Figure 4-15)

FIGURE 6-10
Campus Housing Service Functional and Structural Models

Campus Add and Delete Apartment Activity Diagrams (Figure 4-16)

Use Case Name: Add Apartment		ID: 1	Importance Level: High
Primary Actor: Apartment Owner		Use Case Type: Detail, Essential	
Stakeholders and Interests: Apartment Owner—wants to advertise available apartment Campus Housing Service—provides a service that enables the apartment owners to rent their available apartments			
Brief Description: This use case describes how the campus housing service can maintain an up-to-date listing of available apartments.			
Trigger: Apartment Owner wants to add an available apartment			
Type: External			

Relationships:
   Association: Apartment Owner
   Include:
   Extend:
   Generalization:			

Normal Flow of Events:
   1. Capture the location of the apartment.
   2. Capture the number of bedrooms in the apartment.
   3. Capture the monthly rent of the apartment.
   4. Add the apartment to the listing of available apartments.			

SubFlows:			
Alternate/Exceptional Flows:			

Campus Housing Service Add an Apartment Use Case Description (Figure 4-17)

Use Case Name: Delete Apartment		ID: 2	Importance Level: High
Primary Actor: Apartment Owner		Use Case Type: Detail, Essential	
Stakeholders and Interests: Apartment Owner—wants to delist apartment Campus Housing Service—provides a service that enables the apartment owners to rent their available apartments			
Brief Description: This use case describes how the campus housing service can maintain an up-to-date listing of available apartments.			
Trigger: Apartment Owner wants to delete an available apartment			
Type: External			

Relationships:
   Association: Apartment Owner
   Include:
   Extend:
   Generalization:			

Normal Flow of Events:
   1. Capture the apartment identifier.
   2. Delete the apartment from the listing of available apartments.			

SubFlows:			
Alternate/Exceptional Flows:			

Campus Housing Service Delete an Apartment Use Case Description (Figure 4-18)

FIGURE 6-10 *Continued*

Front:

Class Name: Apartment Owner	ID: 1	Type: Concrete, Domain
Description: An apartment owner who has apartments for rent		Associated Use Cases: 2

Responsibilities	Collaborators
Add apartment	Apartment
Delete apartment	Apartment

Back:

Attributes:

Name (string)

Address (address)

Phone number (phone number)

Email (Email address)

Relationships:

    Generalization (a-kind-of):

    Aggregation (has-parts):

    Other Associations: Apartment

Campus Housing Apartment Owner CRC Card (Figure 5-16)

Apartment Owner		Apartment
	0..1 0..*	

FIGURE 6-10
Continued

Campus Housing Class Diagram (Figure 5-17)

decided from whom the messages are to be sent and to whom they are sent, we can place the messages on the diagram. The fifth step then is to add the execution occurrence to the diagrams to show when each actor or object is in the process of executing one of its operations. Next, we must validate the diagram. Finally, we should replicate this process for the other eight scenarios. If we had created an activity diagram with swimlanes, such as the one in Figure 6-4, we could have created this instance sequence diagram by simply following the *control flows* through the diagram. Remember, a scenario is simply a complete execution path through the activity diagram (see Figure 6-15).

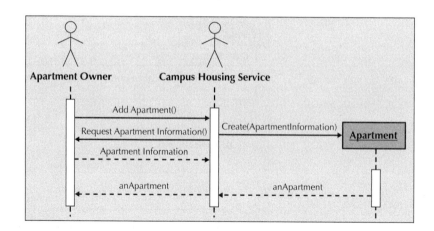

FIGURE 6-11

Sequence Diagram for the Add Apartment Use Case

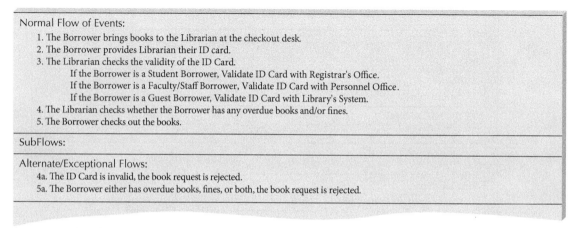

Normal Flow of Events:
1. The Borrower brings books to the Librarian at the checkout desk.
2. The Borrower provides Librarian their ID card.
3. The Librarian checks the validity of the ID Card.
   If the Borrower is a Student Borrower, Validate ID Card with Registrar's Office.
   If the Borrower is a Faculty/Staff Borrower, Validate ID Card with Personnel Office.
   If the Borrower is a Guest Borrower, Validate ID Card with Library's System.
4. The Librarian checks whether the Borrower has any overdue books and/or fines.
5. The Borrower checks out the books.

SubFlows:

Alternate/Exceptional Flows:
   4a. The ID Card is invalid, the book request is rejected.
   5a. The Borrower either has overdue books, fines, or both, the book request is rejected.

FIGURE 6-12   Flow of Events Section of the Use-Case Description of the Borrow Books Use Case (Figure 4-20)

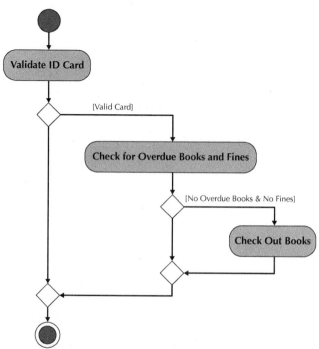

FIGURE 6-13   Activity Diagram of the Borrow Books Use Case (Figure 4-12)

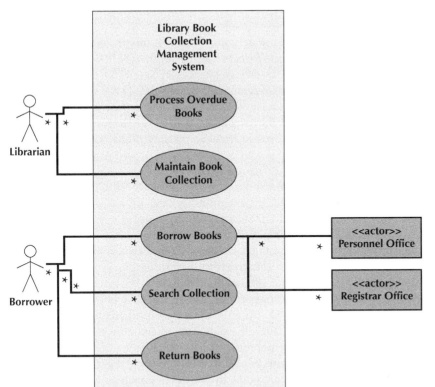

FIGURE 6-14
Use-Case Diagram for the Library
Book Collection Management
System (Figure 4-6)

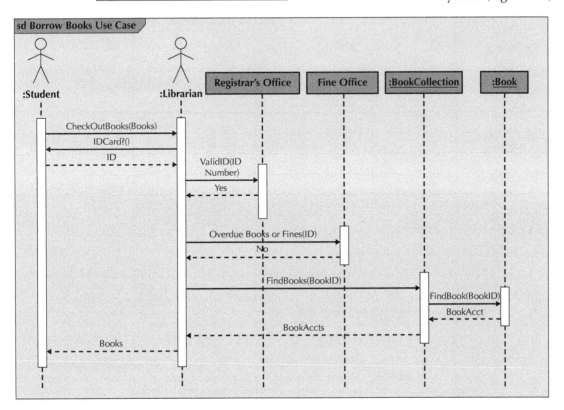

FIGURE 6-15   Sequence Diagram of the Borrow Books Use Case for Students with a Valid ID and No
Overdue Books or Fines

CRUDE ANALYSIS

One useful technique to identify how the underlying objects in the problem domain work together to collaborate in support of the use cases is *CRUDE analysis*.[9] CRUDE analysis uses a *CRUDE matrix*, in which each interaction among objects is labeled with a letter for the type of interaction: C for create, R for read or reference, U for update, D for delete, and E for execute. In an object-oriented approach, a class/actor-by-class/actor matrix is used.[10] Each cell in the matrix represents the interaction between instances of the classes. For example, in Figure 6-5, an instance of the Receptionist actor creates an instance of the Appointment class. Assuming a Row: Column ordering, a C is placed in the cell Receptionist: Appointment. Also, in Figure 6-5, an instance of the Receptionist actor references an instance of the Appointments class. In this case, an R is placed in the Receptionist: Appointments cell. Figure 6-16 shows the CRUDE matrix based on the Make Old Patient Appt use case.

Unlike the interaction diagrams, a CRUDE matrix is most useful as a system-wide representation. Once a CRUDE matrix is completed for the entire system, the matrix can be scanned quickly to ensure that every class can be instantiated. Each type of interaction can be validated for each class. For example, if a class represents only temporary objects, then the column in the matrix should have a D in it somewhere. Otherwise, the instances of the class will never be deleted. Because a data warehouse contains historical data, objects that are to be stored in one should not have any U or D entries in their associated columns. In this way, CRUDE analysis can be used as a way to partially validate the interactions among the objects in an object-oriented system. Finally, the more interactions among a set of classes, the more likely they should be clustered together into a collaboration. However, the number and type of interactions are only an estimate at this point in the development of the system. Care should be taken when using this technique to cluster classes to identify collaborations. We return to this subject in the next chapter when we deal with partitions and collaborations.

	Receptionist	PatientList	Patient	UnpaidBills	Appointments	Appointment
Receptionist		RU	CRUD	R	RU	CRUD
PatientList			R			
Patient						
UnpaidBills						
Appointments						R
Appointment						

FIGURE 6-16 CRUDE Matrix for the Make Old Patient Appt Use Case

[9] CRUD analysis has typically been associated with structured analysis and design [see Alan Dennis, Barbara Haley Wixom and Roberta M. Roth, *Systems Analysis Design*, 3nd Ed. (New York: Wiley, 2006)] and information engineering [see James Martin, *Information Engineering, Book II Planning and Analysis* (Englewood Cliffs, NJ: Prentice Hall, 1990)]. In our case, we have simply adapted it to object-oriented systems development. In the case of object orientation, we have added an E to allow us to document the execution of operations that do not create, read, update, or delete but that instead simply are executed for possible side-effect purposes. Specific details on collaborations are described in Chapter 7.

[10] Another useful but more-detailed form of the CRUDE matrix is a Class/Actor: Operation-by-Class/Actor: Operation matrix. For validation and verification purposes, this more-detailed matrix is more useful. Furthermore, this more detailed matrix is useful to begin identifying role-based access control issues related to the security nonfunctional requirements discussed in the design and construction chapters later in the book. However, for our purposes at this point in our discussion, the Class/Actor-by-Class/Actor matrix is sufficient.

	Apartment Owner Actor	Student Actor	Apartment Owner Class	Apartment Class
Apartment Owner Actor				C,D
Student Actor			R	R
Apartment Owner Class				
Apartment Class				

FIGURE 6-17 Campus Housing Service CRUDE Matrix

CRUDE analysis also can be used to identify complex objects. The more (C)reate, (U)pdate, or (D)elete entries in the column associated with a class, the more likely the instances of the class have a complex life cycle. As such, these objects are candidates for state modeling with a behavioral state machine.

Campus Housing Example

In Chapters 4 and 5, we created a set of functional and structural models for the campus housing service. In this section, we are going to use those models as a basis for performing a CRUDE analysis. The first thing we need to do is to identify all of the actors and the classes that are involved in the campus housing service example. In this case, the actors are apartment owner and student, and the classes are apartment owner and apartment. Given this, our CRUDE matrix is a 4×4 matrix. In this simple example, we only support creating, reading, and deleting instances. Specifically, an apartment owner actor can create and delete instances of apartment, while a student actor can read instances of apartment and apartment owner. Figure 6-17 depicts the CRUDE matrix for the campus housing service.

However, upon review of the matrix, even though instances of apartment owner are read, they are never created or deleted. Unless the instances of apartment owner are created with another system, this is an impossible situation. This is another example of why we follow an iterative and incremental approach in object-oriented systems development. In this case, by creating a CRUDE matrix, we discovered an additional requirement that had previously been overlooked. Consequently, we need to go back and add additional use cases that add and delete apartment owners that are associated with an additional campus housing service staff member actor that executes them (see Figure 6-18). Obviously, at this point in time we should modify the use-case diagram, add activity diagrams, add sequence diagrams, and review the class diagrams, and CRC cards to ensure that they are still correct. We will leave those modifications to you and move on next to the library problem that we have been using in this and the previous chapters.

	Apartment Owner Actor	Student Actor	Staff Member Actor	Apartment Owner Class	Apartment Class
Apartment Owner Actor					C,D
Student Actor				R	R
Staff Member Actor				C,D	
Apartment Owner Class					
Apartment Class					

FIGURE 6-18 Corrected Campus Housing Service CRUDE Matrix

Library Example

The best way to create a CRUDE matrix is to conceptually merge the sequence diagrams that model all of the scenarios of all of the use cases in a system. The easiest way to accomplish this is simply to create an empty class/actor-by-class/actor matrix. In the case of the Library Book Collection Management System, we have six actors (Student, Faculty/Staff, Guest, Librarian, Personnel Office, and Registrar's Office) and eight classes (Book, Book Collection, Student, Faculty/Staff, Guest, Interlibrary Loan System, Library, and Storage). Once this matrix has been laid out, role-playing the scenarios will show which actors and classes interact with each other. Based on the type of interaction, record a C, R, U, D, or E in the appropriate cell of the matrix. Do this repeatedly until all of the scenarios of all of the use cases have been executed. The CRUDE matrix for the Library Book Collection Management System is shown in Figure 6-19. One of the functions that the matrix can serve is to begin the validation process of the entire system. In this case, by quickly reviewing the matrix we can see that absolutely nothing seems to be interacting with the Library and Storage objects. This raises an important question as to whether these objects should exist or not. If nothing calls or uses them and they don't call or use anything, then why are they part of this system? Either they should be removed from the current representation of the system, or we have managed to miss some interaction. Knowing this allows us to go back to the user, in this case the Librarian, and ask what should be done.

BEHAVIORAL STATE MACHINES

Some of the classes in the *class diagrams* represent a set of objects that are quite dynamic in that they pass through a variety of states over the course of their existence. For example, a patient can change over time from being new to current to former based on his or her status with the doctor's office. A *behavioral state machine* is a dynamic model that shows the different states through which a single object passes during its life in response to events, along with its responses and actions. Typically, *behavioral state machines* are not used for all objects; rather, behavioral state machines are used with complex objects to further define them and to help simplify the design of algorithms for their methods. The behavioral state machine shows the different states of the object and what events cause the object to change from one state to another. Behavioral state machines should be used to help understand the dynamic aspects of a single class and how its instances evolve over time[11] unlike interaction diagrams that show how a particular use case or use-case scenario is executed over a set of classes.

In this section, we describe states, events, transitions, actions, and activities. We also explain how behavioral state machines model the state changes through which complex objects pass. As with interaction diagrams, when we create a behavioral state machine for an object, it is possible that we will uncover additional events that need to be included in the functional model (see Chapter 4) and additional operations that need to be included in the structural model (see Chapter 5), so our interaction diagrams might have to be modified again. Because object-oriented development is iterative and incremental, this continuous modification of the evolving models (functional, structural, and behavioral) of the system is to be expected.

States, Events, Transitions, Actions, and Activities

The *state* of an object is defined by the value of its attributes and its relationships with other objects at a particular point in time. For example, a patient might have a state of new, current,

---

[11] Some authors refer to this as modeling an object's life cycle.

	Student Actor	Faculty/ Staff Actor	Guest Actor	Librarian Actor	Personnel Office Actor	Registrar's Office Actor	Book	Book Collection	Student Class	Faculty/ Staff Class	Guest Class	Interlibrary Loan System	Library	Storage
Student Actor				E			R,E	R				E		
Faculty/ Staff Actor				E			R,E	R				E		
Guest Actor				E			R,E	R				E		
Librarian Actor		E	E		R,E	R,E	C,R,U,D,E	R,U,E	R,U	R,U	C,R,U,D,E	R,E		
Personnel Office Actor														
Registrar's Office Actor														
Book														
Book Collection														
Student Class														
Faculty/ Staff Class														
Guest Class														
Interlibrary Loan System														
Library														
Storage														

FIGURE 6-19 CRUDE Matrix for the Library Book Collection Management System

or former. The attributes or properties of an object affect the state that it is in, however, not all attributes or attribute changes will make a difference. For example, think about a patient's address. Those attributes make very little difference to changes in a patient's state. However, if states were based on a patient's geographic location (e.g., in-town patients were treated differently than out-of-town patients), changes to the patient's address would influence state changes.

An *event* is something that takes place at a certain point in time and changes a value or values that describe an object, which, in turn, changes the object's state. It can be a designated condition becoming true, the receipt of the call for a method by an object, or the passage of a designated period of time. The state of the object determines exactly what the response will be.

A *transition* is a relationship that represents the movement of an object from one state to another state. Some transitions have a guard condition. A *guard condition* is a Boolean expression that includes attribute values, which allows a transition to occur only if the condition is true. An object typically moves from one state to another based on the outcome of an action triggered by an event. All transitions are associated with an event that must be implemented as an operation with the object's class. Consequently, if there is a transition in a behavioral state machine that is not associated with an operation, then either the transition is in error or an operation is missing.

Elements of a Behavioral State Machine

Figure 6-20 presents an example of a behavioral state machine representing the patient class in the context of a hospital environment. From this diagram, we can tell that a patient enters a hospital and is admitted after checking in. If a doctor finds the patient to be healthy, he or she is released and is no longer considered a patient after two weeks elapse. If a patient is found to be unhealthy, he or she remains under observation until the diagnosis changes.

A *state* is a set of values that describes an object at a specific point in time and represents a point in an object's life in which it satisfies some condition, performs some action, or waits for something to happen (see Figure 6-21). In Figure 6-20 states include entering, admitted, released, and under observation. A state is depicted by a *state symbol*, which is a rectangle with rounded corners with a descriptive label that communicates a particular state. There are two exceptions. An *initial state* is shown using a small, filled-in circle, and an object's *final state* is shown as a circle surrounding a small, filled-in circle. These exceptions depict when an object is created and when an object is deleted, respectively.

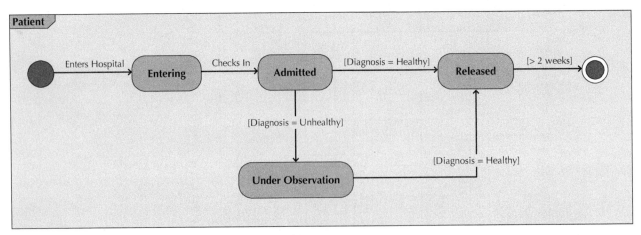

FIGURE 6-20 Sample Behavioral State Machine Diagram

Term and Definition	Symbol
A state: ■ Is shown as a rectangle with rounded corners. ■ Has a name that represents the state of an object.	aState
An initial state: ■ Is shown as a small, filled-in circle. ■ Represents the point at which an object begins to exist.	●
A final state: ■ Is shown as a circle surrounding a small, filled-in circle (bull's-eye). ■ Represents the completion of activity.	◉
An event: ■ Is a noteworthy occurrence that triggers a change in state. ■ Can be a designated condition becoming true, the receipt of an explicit signal from one object to another, or the passage of a designated period of time. ■ Is used to label a transition.	anEvent
A transition: ■ Indicates that an object in the first state will enter the second state. ■ Is triggered by the occurrence of the event labeling the transition. ■ Is shown as a solid arrow from one state to another, labeled by the event name.	⟶
A frame: ■ Indicates the context of the behavioral state machine.	Context

FIGURE 6-21   Behavioral State Machine Diagram Syntax

Arrows are used to connect the state symbols, representing the transitions between states. Each arrow is labeled with the appropriate event name and any parameters or conditions that may apply. For example, the two transitions from admitted to released and under observation contain guard conditions. As in the other behavioral diagrams, in many cases it is useful to explicitly show the context of the behavioral state machine using a frame.

Figure 6-22 depicts two additional behavioral state machines. The first one is for the lunch object that was associated with the Make Lunch use-case scenario of Figure 6-7. In this case, there is obviously additional information that has been captured about the lunch object. For example, the scenario of Figure 6-7 did not include information regarding the lunch being taken out of the box or being eaten. This implies additional use cases and/or use-case scenarios that would have to be included in a system dealing with lunch processing. The second behavioral state machine deals with the life cycle of an order. The order object is associated with the submit order use-case scenario described in Figures 6-7. As in the lunch example, there is quite a bit of additional information contained in this behavioral state machine. For an order-processing system, additional sequence diagrams would be necessary to completely represent all the processing associated with an order object. Obviously, because

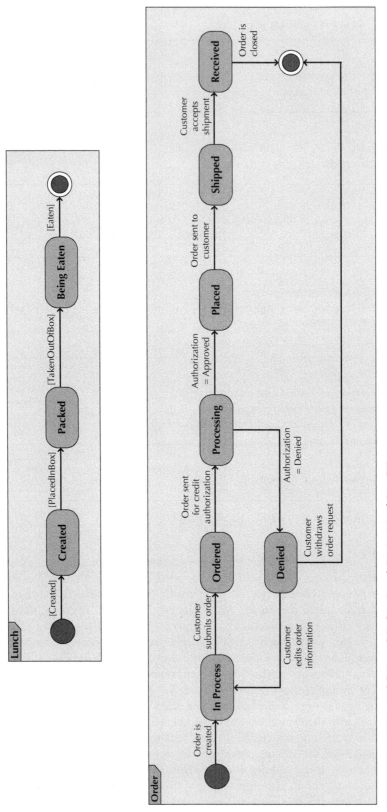

FIGURE 6-22 Additional Behavioral State Machine Diagrams

behavioral state machines can uncover additional processing requirements, they can be very useful in filling out the complete description of an evolving system.

Sometimes, states and subclasses can be confused. For example, in Figure 6-23, are the classes Freshman, Sophomore, Junior, and Senior subclasses of the class Undergraduate or are they states that an instance of the Undergraduate class goes through during its lifetime? In this case, the latter is the better answer. When trying to identify all potential classes during structural modeling (see Chapter 5), you might actually identify states of the relevant super-class instead of subclasses. This is another example of how tightly intertwined the functional,

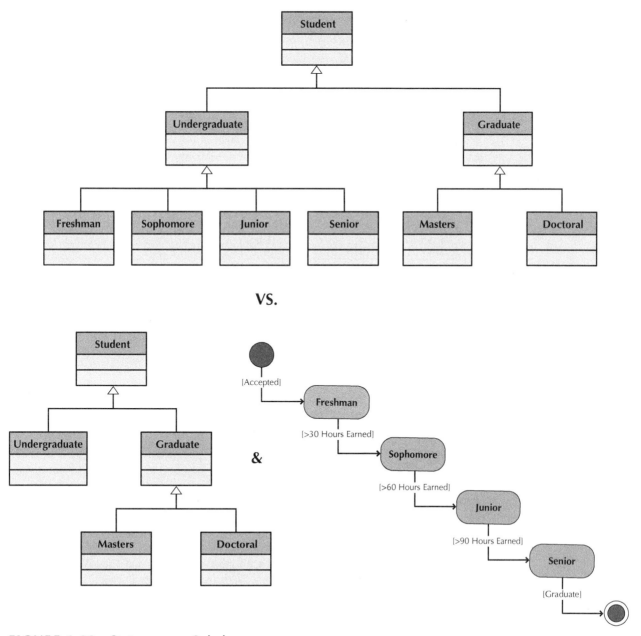

FIGURE 6-23 States versus Subclasses

structural, and behavioral models can be. From a modeling perspective, although we eventually removed the Freshman, Sophomore, Junior, and Senior subclasses from the structural model, capturing that information during structural modeling and removing it based on discoveries made during behavioral modeling were preferable to omitting it and taking a chance of missing a crucial piece of information about the problem domain. Remember, object-oriented development is iterative and incremental. As we progress to a correct model of the problem domain, we will make many mistakes.

Guidelines for Creating Behavioral State Machines

As with the sequence diagrams, Amble suggests a set of guidelines when drawing behavior state machines. In this case, we consider six of his recommendations.[12]

- Create a behavioral state machine for objects whose behavior changes based on the state of the object. In other words, do not create a behavioral state machine for an object whose behavior is always the same regardless of its state. These objects are too simple.

- To adhere to the left-to-right and top-to-bottom reading conventions of Western cultures, the initial state should be drawn in the top left corner of the diagram and the final state should be drawn in the bottom right of the diagram.

- Make sure that the names of the states are simple, intuitively obvious, and descriptive. For example, in Figure 6-20, the state names of the Patient object are Entering, Admitted, Under Observation, and Released.

- Question black hole and miracle states. These types of states are problematic for the same reason black hole and miracle activities are a problem for activity diagrams (see Chapter 4). *Black hole states*, states that an object goes into and never comes out of, most likely are actually final states. *Miracle states*, states that an object comes out of but never went into, most likely are initial states.

- Be sure that all guard conditions are mutually exclusive (not overlapping). For example, in Figure 6-20, the guard condition [Diagnosis = Healthy] and the guard condition [Diagnosis = Unhealthy] do not overlap. However, if you created a guard condition of [x >= 0] and a second guard condition [x <= 0], the guard conditions overlap when x = 0, and it is not clear to which state the object would transition. This would obviously cause confusion.

- All transitions should be associated with a message and an operation. Otherwise, the state of the object could never change. Even though this may be stating the obvious, there have been numerous times that analysts forget to go back and ensure that this is indeed true.

Creating a Behavioral State Machine

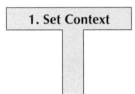

Behavioral state machines are drawn to depict an instance of a single class from a class diagram. Typically, the classes are very dynamic and complex, requiring a good understanding of their states over time and events triggering changes. You should examine your class diagram to identify which classes undergo a complex series of state changes and draw a diagram for each of them. In this section, we describe a five-step process used to build a behavioral state machine.[13] Like the other behavioral models, the first step in the process is determining

---

[12] S.W. Ambler, *The Elements of UML 2.0 Style* (Cambridge, England: Cambridge University Press, 2005).

[13] The approach described in this section is adapted from Booch, Rumbaugh, and Jacobson, *The Unified Modeling Language User Guide*.

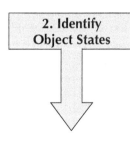

2. Identify Object States

the context of the behavioral state machine, which is shown in the label of the frame of the diagram. The context of a behavioral state machine is usually a class. However, it also could be a set of classes, a subsystem, or an entire system.

The second step is to identify the various states that an object will have over its lifetime. This includes establishing the boundaries of the existence of an object by identifying the initial and final states of an object. The information necessary to perform this is gleaned from reading the use-case descriptions, talking with users, and relying on the requirements-gathering techniques that you learned about in Chapter 3. An easy way to identify the states of an object is to write the steps of what happens to an object over time, from start to finish, similar to how the normal flow of events section of a use-case description would be created.

3. Lay Out Diagram

The third step is to determine the sequence of the states that an object will pass through during its lifetime. Using this sequence, the states are placed onto the behavioral state machine in a left-to-right order.

4. Add Transitions

The fourth step is to identify the transitions between the states of the objects and to add the events, actions, and guard conditions associated with the transitions. The events are the *triggers* that cause an object to move from one state to the next state. In other words, an event causes an action to execute that changes the value(s) of an object's attribute(s) in a significant manner. The actions are typically operations contained within the object. Also, guard conditions can model a set of test conditions that must be met for the transition to occur. At this point in the process, the transitions are drawn between the relevant states and labeled with the event, action, or guard condition.

5. Validate

The fifth step is to validate the behavioral state machine by making sure that each state is reachable and that it is possible to leave all states except for final states. Obviously, if an identified state is not reachable, either a transition is missing or the state was identified in error. Only final states can be a dead end from the perspective of an object's life cycle.

Campus Housing Example

Based on the functional and structural models for the campus housing service (see Figure 6-10), and the sequence diagram for the Add Apartment use case (see Figure 6-11), in this section, we are going to create a behavioral state machine for the Apartment class. By reviewing all of the representations, it is obvious that the behavioral state machine will be very simple. In this case, an apartment comes into existence when it is added and goes out of existence when it is deleted. Its only state is For Rent. Figure 6-24 depicts the behavioral state machine for this class. Given the simplicity of this diagram, in most cases it would be removed from the behavioral model. However, the exercise of creating the behavioral state machine for this object is still worthwhile.

FIGURE 6-24
Behavioral State Machine for the Apartment Class

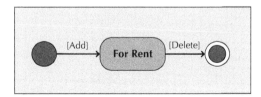

Library Example

The first step in drawing a behavioral state machine is to set the context. For our purposes, the context typically is an instance of a class that has multiple states and whose behavior depends upon the state in which it currently resides. As suggested earlier, we should review the class diagram (see Figure 6-25) to identify the "interesting" classes. In the case of the Library Book Collection Management System, the obvious class to consider is the Book class.

The next step is to identify the different states through which an instance of the Book class can traverse during its lifetime. Good places to look for possible state changes are the use-case descriptions (see Figure 6-12), the activity diagrams (see Figure 6-13), and the sequence diagrams (see Figure 6-15). In the case of a book, even though the states may be similar, you must be careful in identifying the states associated with an instance of the Book class and not the states associated with the physical book itself. In Chapter 5, we observed that there were a number of implied states to consider. These included Checked Out, Overdue, Requested, Available, and Damaged. If the book is damaged, the book could either be repaired and put back into circulation or it could be too damaged to repair and be removed from circulation instead. Even though a Borrower could be fined for an overdue or damaged book, being fined is not a state of a book, it is a state of a borrower.

Next, we lay out the diagram by ordering the states in a sequential manner based on the life cycle of a book. For example, it probably makes no sense to have a book to go from a repaired state to a damaged state. However, going from a damaged state to a repaired state makes sense. Nor does it make sense for a book to go from an available state directly to an

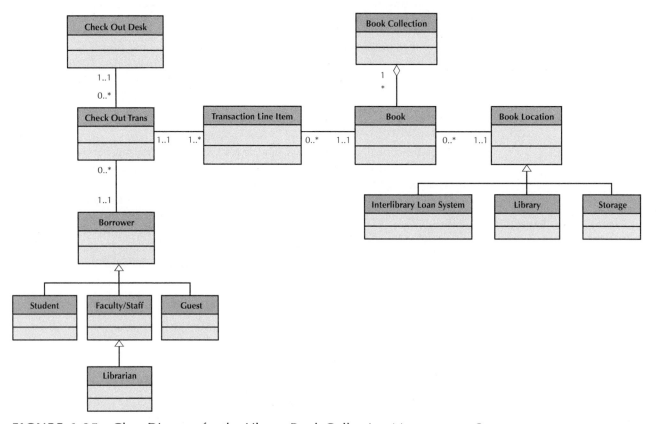

FIGURE 6-25 Class Diagram for the Library Book Collection Management System

FIGURE 6-26 Behavioral State Machine for an Instance of the Book Class in the Library Book Collection Management System

overdue state. However, the converse makes sense. The states we identified for a book object include Available, Checked Out, Overdue, Requested, Damaged, and Being Repaired. Next, we added the transitions between the states and labeled them with the appropriate guard conditions. The behavioral state machine for an instance of the Book class is portrayed in Figure 6-26.

Finally, we validate the diagram by checking for missing states or transitions and ensuring that there are no black hole or miracle states.

VERIFYING AND VALIDATING THE BEHAVIORAL MODEL[14]

In this chapter, we described three different diagrams (activity diagram, sequence diagram, and behavioral state machine) and CRUDE matrices that could be used to represent the behavioral model. The activity and sequence diagrams modeled the interaction among the actors and classes that work together to support the business processes included in a system, the CRUDE matrix represented a system-level overview of the interactions among the objects in the system, and the behavioral state machine described the state changes through which an object traverses during its lifetime. In this chapter, we combine walkthroughs with CRUDE matrices to more completely verify and validate the behavioral models. Since we covered CRUDE analysis and matrices in the previous section, we focus only on walkthroughs in this section. We also describe the process in balancing the behavioral models with the functional and structural models. We again use the appointment system and focus on Figures 6-5, 6-16, and 6-20 to describe a set of rules that can be used to ensure that the behavioral model is internally consistent.

First, all transitions contained in a behavior state machine must be associated with a message being sent on a sequence diagram, and it must be classified as a (C)reate, (U)pdate, or (D)elete message in a CRUDE matrix. For example, in Figure 6-20 the Checks In transition

[14] The material in this section has been adapted from E. Yourdon, *Modern Structured Analysis* (Englewood Cliffs, NJ: Prentice Hall, 1989).

must be associated with a message in the corresponding sequence diagrams. Furthermore, it should be associated with an (U)pdate entry in the CRUDE matrix associated with the hospital patient system.

Second, all entries in a CRUDE matrix imply a message being sent from an actor or object to another actor or object. If the entry is a (C)reate, (U)pdate, or (D)elete and the execution of the related operation changes the state of the object, then there must be an associated transition in a behavioral state machine that represents the instances of the receiving class. For example, in Figure 6-16 the R and U entries in the Receptionist row and Appointments column imply that instances of the Receptionist actor will read and update instances of the Appointments class. Thus, there should be read and update messages on the sequence diagrams corresponding with the appointments processes. Reviewing Figure 6-5, we see that there is a message, Match Appts(), from the aReceptionist actor to the Appointments object. However, based on this review, it is unclear whether the Match Appts() message represents a read, an update, or both. Therefore, additional analysis is required.[15] Because there is an (U)pdate message involved a transition on a behavioral state machine that portrays the life cycle of an Appointments object could be required.

Finally, many representation-specific rules have been proposed. However, as in the other models, these rules are beyond the scope of this section on verification and validation.[16]

Balancing Functional and Behavioral Models

As in balancing the functional and structural models, we must ensure the consistency of the two sets of models. In this case, the activity diagrams, use-case descriptions, and use-case diagrams must agree with the sequence diagrams, behavioral state machines, and CRUDE matrix.

First, sequence diagrams must be associated with a use case on the use-case diagram and a use-case description. For example, the sequence diagram in Figure 6-5 is related to scenarios of the Make Old Patient Appt use case that appears in the use-case description in Figure 6-27 and the use-case diagram in Figure 6-28.

Second, actors on sequence diagrams and/or CRUDE matrices must be associated with actors on the use-case diagram or referenced in the use-case description, and vice versa. For example, the aPatient actor in the sequence diagram in Figure 6-5, and the Patient row and column in the CRUDE matrix in Figure 6-16 appears in the use-case diagram in Figure 6-28 and the use-case description in Figure 6-27. However, the aReceptionist does not appear in the use-case diagram but is referenced in the events associated with the Make Old Patient Appt use-case description. In this case, the aReceptionist actor is obviously an internal actor, which cannot be portrayed on UML's use-case diagram.

Third, messages on sequence diagrams, transitions on behavioral state machines, and entries in a CRUDE matrix must be related to activities and actions on an activity diagram and events listed in a use-case description, and vice versa. For example, the CreateAppt() message on the sequence diagram (see Figure 6-5) is related to the CreateAppointment activity (see Figure 6-29) and the S-1: New Appointment subflow on the use-case description (see Figure 6-28). The C entry in the Receptionist Appointment cell of the CRUDE matrix is also associated with these messages, activity, and subflow.

---

[15] We have delayed the description of designing operations and methods until Chapter 8. Therefore, the detailed information required to understand a specific message has not been created yet. However, in many cases, enough information will already have been created to validate many of the transitions in behavioral state machines and CRUDE matrices.

[16] A good reference for these types of restrictions is S.W. Ambler, *The Elements of UML 2.0 Style* (Cambridge, England: Cambridge University Press, 2005).

Use-Case Name: Make Old Patient Appt		ID: 2	Importance Level: Low
Primary Actor: Old Patient		Use Case Type: Detail, Essential	

Stakeholders and Interests:
Old patient - wants to make, change, or cancel an appointment
Doctor - wants to ensure patient's needs are met in a timely manner

Brief Description: This use case describes how we make an appointment as well as changing or canceling an appointment for a previously seen patient.

Trigger: Patient calls and asks for a new appointment or asks to cancel or change an existing appointment

Type: External

Relationships:
    Association: Old Patient
    Include:
    Extend: Update Patient Information
    Generalization: Manage Appointments

Normal Flow of Events:
1. The Patient contacts the office regarding an appointment.
2. The Patient provides the Receptionist with his or her name and address.
3. If the Patient's information has changed
    Execute the Update Patient Information use case.
4. If the Patient's payment arrangements has changed
    Execute the Make Payment Arrangements use case.
5. The Receptionist asks Patient if he or she would like to make a new appointment, cancel an existing appointment, or change an existing appointment.

    If the patient wants to make a new appointment,
      the S-1: new appointment subflow is performed.
    If the patient wants to cancel an existing appointment,
      the S-2: cancel appointment subflow is performed.
    If the patient wants to change an existing appointment,
      the S-3: change appointment subflow is performed.
6. The Receptionist provides the results of the transaction to the Patient.

SubFlows:
  S-1: New Appointment
    1. The Receptionist asks the Patient for possible appointment times.
    2. The Receptionist matches the Patient's desired appointment times with available dates and times and schedules the new appointment.
  S-2: Cancel Appointment
    1. The Receptionist asks the Patient for the old appointment time.
    2. The Receptionist finds the current appointment in the appointment file and cancels it.
  S-3: Change Appointment
    1. The Receptionist performs the S-2: cancel appointment subflow.
    2. The Receptionist performs the S-1: new appointment subflow.

Alternate/Exceptional Flows:
  S-1, 2a1: The Receptionist proposes some alternative appointment times based on what is available in the appointment schedule.
  S-1, 2a2: The Patient chooses one of the proposed times or decides not to make an appointment.

FIGURE 6-27 Use-Case Description for the Make Old Patient Appt Use Case (Figure 4-13)

Fourth, all complex objects represented by an object node in an activity diagram must have a behavioral state machine that represents the object's lifecycle, and vice versa. As stated previously, complex objects tend to be very dynamic and pass through a variety of states during their lifetimes. However, in this case because we no longer have any object nodes in the activity diagram (see Figure 6-29), there is no necessity for a behavioral state machine to be created based on the activity diagram.

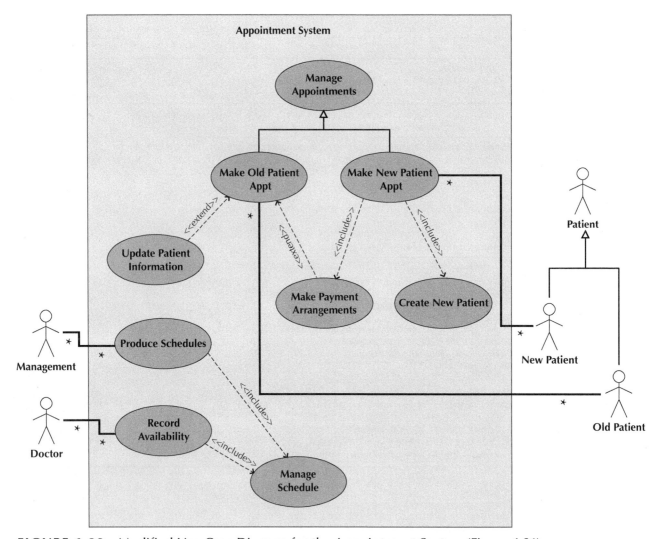

FIGURE 6-28 Modified Use-Case Diagram for the Appointment System (Figure 4-21)

Balancing Structural and Behavioral Models

When considering the structural and behavioral models, there are five areas in which we must ensure the consistency between the models.[17] First, objects that appear in a CRUDE matrix must be associated with classes that are represented by CRC cards and appear on the class diagram, and vice versa. For example, the Patient class in the CRUDE matrix in Figure 6-16 is associated with the CRC card in Figure 6-30 and the Patient class in the class diagram in Figure 6-1.

Second, because behavioral state machines represent the life cycle of complex objects, they must be associated with instances (objects) of classes on a class diagram and with a CRC card that represents the class of the instance. For example, the behavioral state machine that describes an instance of a Patient class in Figure 6-20 implies that a Patient class exists on a related class diagram (see Figure 6-1) and that a CRC card exists for the related class (see Figure 6-30).

---

[17] Role-playing (see Chapter 5) and CRUDE analysis also can be very useful in this undertaking.

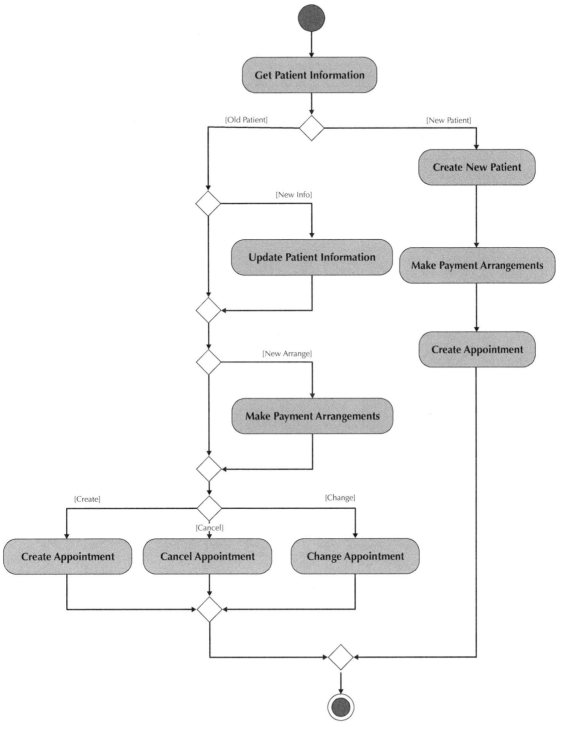

FIGURE 6-29 Corrected Activity Diagram for the Manage Appointments Use Case (Figure 5-27)

Front:

Class Name: Patient	ID: 3	Type: Concrete, Domain
Description: An individual who needs to receive or has received medical attention		Associated Use Cases: 2

Responsibilities	Collaborators
Make appointment	Appointment
Calculate last visit	
Change status	
Provide medical history	Medical history

Back:

Attributes:
Amount (double)
Insurance carrier (text)

Relationships:
Generalization (a-kind-of): Participant

Aggregation (has-parts):

Other Associations: Appointment, Medical History

FIGURE 6-30
Patient CRC Card
(Figure 5-25)

Third, the objects on a sequence diagram must be an instantiation of a class that is represented by a CRC card and is located on a class diagram. For example, Figure 6-5 has an anAppt object that is an instantiation of the Appointment class. Therefore, the Appointment class must exist in the class diagram (see Figure 6-1), and a CRC card should exist that describes it. However, when an object on a sequence diagram that is not associated with a class that exists on the class diagram, e.g., UnpaidBill, the analyst must decide to either modify the class diagram by adding these classes or rethink the sequence diagram. In this case, it is better to add the class to the class diagram (see Figure 6-31).

Fourth, messages contained on the sequence diagrams, transitions on behavioral state machines, and cell entries on a CRUDE matrix must be associated with responsibilities and associations on CRC cards and operations in classes and associations connected to the classes on class diagrams. For example, the CreateAppt() message on the sequence diagram in Figure 6-5 relates to the makeAppointment operation of the Patient class and the schedules

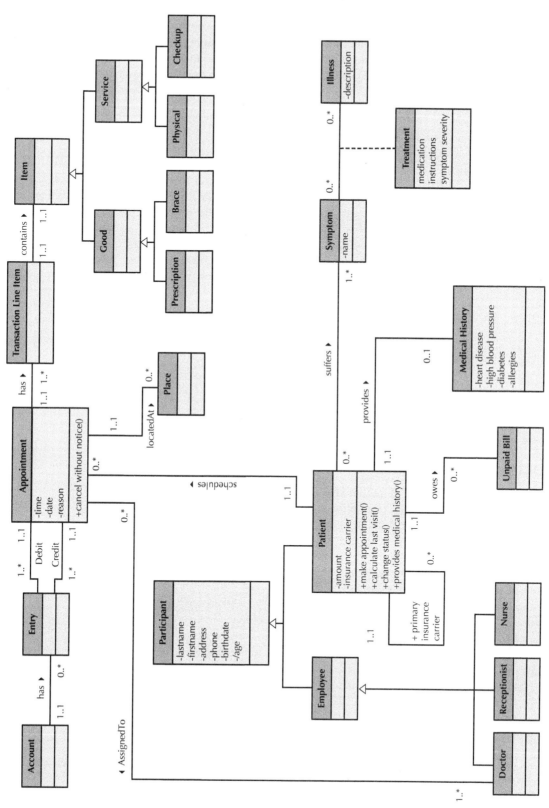

FIGURE 6-31   Corrected Appointment System Class Diagram

247

association between the Patient and Appointment classes on the class diagram (see Figure 6-31).

Fifth, the states in a behavioral state machine must be associated with different values of an attribute or set of attributes that describe an object. For example, the behavioral state machine for the hospital patient object implies that there should be an attribute, possibly current status, which needs to be included in the definition of the class.

APPLYING THE CONCEPTS AT PATTERSON SUPERSTORE

After developing the functional and structural models, the project manager, Ruby Ross, tasked the team with developing the behavioral models for the Mobile Scheduling (Version 1) of the Integrated Health Clinic Delivery System. The behavioral models include the interactions diagram (activity and sequence) as well as the behavioral state machine. In addition, the team created a CRUDE matrix to analyze the collaboration between the objects identified during structural modeling. While the structural model depicted the static aspects of the system, behavioral models show the internal dynamic aspects of the system. By modeling both the static (structural) and dynamic (behavioral) aspects of a system, object-oriented systems analysis and design attempts to view the underlying problem domain in a holistic way.

You can find the rest of the case at www.wiley.com/go/dennis/systemanalysis6e/casestudy.

CHAPTER REVIEW

After reading and studying this chapter, you should be able to:

☐ Describe the purpose of the behavioral models.
☐ Describe the purpose of the interaction diagrams.
☐ Describe the different elements of the sequence diagrams.
☐ Create a behavioral model using a sequence diagram.
☐ Explain the purpose of a behavioral state machine.
☐ Describe the purpose of CRUDE analysis.
☐ Create a behavioral model using a CRUDE matrix.
☐ Verify and validate the evolving behavioral model using CRUDE analysis and walkthroughs.
☐ Describe the different elements of the behavioral state machines.
☐ Create a behavioral model using a behavioral state machine.
☐ Verify and validate the functional model by ensuring the consistency of the behavioral model representations: activity diagrams, sequence diagrams, a CRUDE matrix, and behavioral state machines.
☐ Verify and validate both the behavioral models with the functional and structural models by balancing them.

KEY TERMS

Activity	Attributes	Black hole states	Collaboration
Activity diagram	Behavior	Class	Condition
Actor	Behavioral state machines	Class diagram	Control flow

CRC cards	Generic sequence diagram	Miracle states	State symbol
CRUDE analysis	Guard condition	Object	Swimlanes
CRUDE matrix	Initial state	Operation	Temporary object
Dynamic model	Instance	Operation call message	Transition
Event	Instance sequence diagram	Return message	Trigger
Execution occurrence	Lifeline	Self-delegation	Use case
Final state	Messages	Sequence diagram	Use case scenario
Frame	Methods	State	

QUESTIONS

1. How is behavioral modeling related to functional and structural modeling?
2. Describe how the use of activity diagrams with swimlanes are helpful in behavioral modeling.
3. What is the difference between an external and internal actor?
4. How does a use case relate to an activity diagram?
5. How does a use case scenario relate to an activity diagram?
6. How does a use case relate to a generic sequence diagram?
7. How does a use case scenario relate to an instance sequence diagram?
8. Contrast the following sets of terms: state, behavior, class, object, action, and activity.
9. Why is iteration important when creating a behavioral model?
10. What are the main building blocks for the sequence diagram? How are they represented on the model?
11. How do you show that a temporary object is to go out of existence on a sequence diagram?
12. Do lifelines always continue down the entire page of a sequence diagram? Explain.

13. Describe the steps used to create a sequence diagram.
14. When drawing a sequence diagram, what guidelines should you follow?
15. Are states always depicted using rounded rectangles on a behavioral state machine? Explain.
16. What is CRUDE analysis, and what is it used for?
17. What kinds of events can lead to state transitions on a behavioral state machine?
18. What are the steps in building a behavioral state machine?
19. When drawing a behavioral state machine, what guidelines should you follow?
20. How are guard conditions shown on a behavioral state machine?
21. Describe the type of class that is best represented by a behavioral state machine. Give two examples of classes that would be good candidates for a behavioral state machine.
22. Identify the models that contain each of the following components: actor, association, class, extends, association, final state, guard condition, initial state, links, message, multiplicity, object, state, transition, and update operation.

EXERCISES

A. Think about sending a first-class letter to an international pen pal. Describe the process that the letter goes through to get from your initial creation of the letter to being read by your friend, from the letter's perspective. Draw a behavioral state machine that depicts the states that the letter moves through.

B. Draw a behavioral state machine that describes the various states that a travel authorization can have through its approval process. A travel authorization form is used in most companies to approve travel expenses for employees. Typically, an employee fills out a blank form and sends it to his or her boss for a signature. If the amount is fairly small (<$300), then the boss signs the form and routes it to accounts payable to be input into the accounting system. The system cuts a check that is sent to the employee for the right amount, and after the check is cashed, the form is filed away with the canceled check. If the check is not cashed within 90 days, the travel form expires. When the amount of the travel voucher is a large amount (>$300), then the boss signs the form and sends it to the CFO, along with a paragraph explaining the purpose of the travel; the CFO signs the form and passes it along to accounts payable. Of course, the boss and the CFO can reject the travel authorization form if they do not feel that the expenses are reasonable. In this case, the employee can change the form to include more explanation or decide to pay the expenses.

C. Think about the system that handles student admissions at your university. The primary function of the system should be able to track a student from the request for information through the admissions process until the student is either admitted to the school or rejected.

1. Write a use-case description that can describe an Admit Student use case.

Assume that applicants who are children of alumni are handled differently from other applicants. Also, assume that a generic Update Student Information use case is available for your system to use.

2. Create a use-case diagram that includes all of the above use cases.

Assume that an admission form includes the contents of the form, SAT information, and references. Additional information is captured about children of alumni, such as their parent's graduation year, contact information, and college major.

3. Create a class diagram for the use cases identified with questions 1 and 2. Also, be sure to include the above information.

Assume that a temporary student object is used by the system to hold information about people before they send in an admission form. After the form is sent in, these people are considered students.

4. Create an activity diagram with swimlanes for the above use cases.

5. Create instance sequence diagrams for the scenarios of the above use cases.

6. Perform a CRUDE analysis to show the interactivity of the objects in the system.

7. Create a behavioral state machine to depict a person as he or she moves through the admission process.

8. Perform a verification and validation walkthrough of the problem.

D. For the A Real Estate Inc. problems in Chapters 4 (exercises I, J, and K) and 5 (exercises N and O)

1. Create an activity diagram with swimlanes for one of the use cases.

2. Choose one use case and, for each scenario, create a sequence diagram.

3. Perform a CRUDE analysis to show the interactivity of the objects in the system.

4. Create a behavioral state machine to depict one of the classes on the class diagram you created for Chapter 5, exercise N.

5. Perform a verification and validation walkthrough of the problem.

E. For the A Video Store problems in Chapters 4 (exercises L, M, and N) and 5 (exercises P and Q):

1. Create an activity diagram with swimlanes for one of the use cases.

2. Choose one use case and, for each scenario, create a sequence diagram.

3. Perform a CRUDE analysis to show the interactivity of the objects in the system.

4. Create a behavioral state machine to depict one of the classes on the class diagram you created for Chapter 5, exercise P.

5. Perform a verification and validation walkthrough of the problem.

F. For the gym membership problems in Chapters 4 (exercises O, P, and Q) and 5 (exercises R and S):

1. Create an activity diagram with swimlanes for one of the use cases.

2. Choose one use case and, for each scenario, create a sequence diagram.

3. Perform a CRUDE analysis to show the interactivity of the objects in the system.

4. Create a behavioral state machine to depict one of the classes on the class diagram you created for Chapter 5, exercise R.

5. Perform a verification and validation walkthrough of the problem.

G. For the Picnics R Us problems in Chapters 4 (exercises R, S, and T) and 5 (exercises T and U):

1. Create an activity diagram with swimlanes for one of the use cases.

2. Choose one use case and, for each scenario, create a sequence diagram.

3. Perform a CRUDE analysis to show the interactivity of the objects in the system.

4. Create a behavioral state machine to depict one of the classes on the class diagram you created for Chapter 5, exercise T.

5. Perform a verification and validation walkthrough of the problem.

H. For the Of-the-Month-Club problems in Chapters 4 (exercises U, V, and W) and 5 (exercises V and W):

    1. Create an activity diagram with swimlanes for one of the use cases.

    2. Choose one use case and, for each scenario, create a sequence diagram.

    3. Perform a CRUDE analysis to show the interactivity of the objects in the system.

    4. Create a behavioral state machine to depict one of the classes on the class diagram you created for Chapter 5, exercise V.

    5. Perform a verification and validation walkthrough of the problem.

MINICASES

1. Refer to the functional model (use-case diagram, activity diagrams, and use-case descriptions) you prepared for the Professional and Scientific Staff Management (PSSM) Minicase in Chapter 4. Based on your performance, PSSM was so satisfied that it wanted you to develop both the structural and behavioral models so that it could more fully understand both the interaction that would take place between the users and the system and the system itself in greater detail.

    a. Create both CRC cards and a class diagram based on the functional models created in Chapter 4.

    b. Modify the activity diagrams created in Chapter 4 to include swimlanes for each of the use cases.

    c. Create a sequence diagram for each scenario of each use case identified in the functional model.

    d. Perform a CRUDE analysis to show the interactivity of the objects in the system.

    e. Create a behavioral state machine for each of the complex classes in the class diagram.

    f. Perform a verification and validation walkthrough of each model: functional, structural, and behavioral.

2. Refer to the structural model (CRC cards and class diagram) that you created for the Holiday Travel Vehicles Minicase in Chapter 5. Based on your performance, Holiday Travel Vehicles was so satisfied that it wanted you to develop both the functional and behavioral models so that it could more fully understand both the interaction that would take place between the users and the system and the system itself in greater detail.

    a. Based on the structural model you created in Chapter 5 and the problem description in Chapter 5, create a functional model (use case diagram, activity diagrams, and use case descriptions) for the business processes associated with the Holiday Travel Vehicles sales system. Be sure to include swimlanes with the activity diagrams.

    b. Create a sequence diagram for each scenario of each use case identified in the functional model.

    c. Perform a CRUDE analysis to show the interactivity of the objects in the system.

    d. Create a behavioral state machine for each of the complex classes in the class diagram.

    e. Perform a verification and validation walkthrough of each model: functional, structural, and behavioral.

PART TWO
DESIGN MODELING

Whereas analysis modeling concentrates on the functional requirements of the evolving system, design modeling incorporates the nonfunctional requirements. That is, design modeling focuses on *how* the system will operate. First, the project team verifies and validates the analysis models (functional, structural, and behavioral). Next, a set of factored and partitioned analysis models are created. The class and method designs are illustrated using the class specifications (using CRC cards and class diagrams), contracts, and method specifications. Next, the data management layer is addressed by designing the actual database or file structure to be used for object persistence, and a set of classes that will map the class specifications into the object persistence format chosen. Concurrently, the team produces the human–computer interaction layer design using use scenarios, windows navigation diagrams, real use cases, interface templates, storyboards, wireframe diagrams, and user interface prototypes. The physical architecture layer design is created using deployment diagrams and hardware software specifications. This collection of deliverables represents the system specification that is handed to the programming team for implementation.

CHAPTER 7 Moving on to Design
Verifying and Validating the Analysis Models
Evolving the Analysis Models into Design Models
Packages and Package Diagrams
Design Criteria
Design Strategies
Selecting an Acquisition Strategy

CHAPTER 8 Class and Method Design
Object Design Activities
Constraints and Contracts
Method Specification
Verifying and Validating Class and Method Design

CHAPTER 9 Data Management Layer Design
Object Persistence Formats
Mapping Problem Domain Objects to Object Persistence Formats

MOVING ON TO DESIGN

Object-oriented system development uses the requirements that were gathered during analysis to create a blueprint for the future system. A successful object-oriented design builds upon what was learned in earlier phases and leads to a smooth implementation by creating a clear, accurate plan of what needs to be done. This chapter describes the initial transition from analysis to design and presents three ways to approach the design for the new system.

OBJECTIVES

- Understand the verification and validation of the analysis models.
- Understand the transition from analysis to design.
- Understand the use of factoring, partitions, and layers.
- Be able to create package diagrams.
- Become familiar with the design criteria of coupling, cohesion, and connascence.
- Be familiar with the custom, packaged, and outsource design alternatives.
- Be able to create an alternative matrix.

INTRODUCTION

The purpose of analysis is to figure out what the business needs are. The purpose of design is to decide how to build the system. The major activity that takes place during *design* is evolving the set of analysis representations into design representations.

Throughout design, the project team carefully considers the new system with respect to the current environment and systems that exist within the organization as a whole. Major considerations in determining how the system will work include environmental factors, such as integrating with existing systems, converting data from legacy systems, and leveraging skills that exist in-house. Although the planning and analysis are undertaken to develop a possible system, the goal of design is to create a blueprint for a system that can be implemented.

An important initial part of design is to examine several design strategies and decide which will be used to build the system. Systems can be built from scratch, purchased and customized, or outsourced to others, and the project team needs to investigate the viability of each alternative. This decision influences the tasks that are to be accomplished during design.

At the same time, detailed design of the individual classes and methods that are used to map out the nuts and bolts of the system and how they are to be stored must still be completed. Techniques such as CRC cards, class diagrams, contract specification, method specification, and database design provide the final design details in preparation for the construction phase, and they ensure that programmers have sufficient information to build the right system efficiently. These topics are covered in Chapters 8 and 9.

Design also includes activities such as designing the user interface, system inputs, and system outputs, which involve the ways that the user interacts with the system. Chapter 10 describes these three activities in detail, along with techniques such as storyboarding and prototyping, which help the project team design a system that meets the needs of its users and is satisfying to use.

Finally, physical architecture decisions are made regarding the hardware and software that will be purchased to support the new system and the way that the processing of the system will be organized. For example, the system can be organized so that its processing is centralized at one location, distributed, or both centralized and distributed, and each solution offers unique benefits and challenges to the project team. Because global issues and security influence the implementation plans that are made, they need to be considered along with the system's technical architecture. Physical architecture, security, and global issues are described in Chapter 11.

The many steps of design are highly interrelated and, as with the steps in analysis, the analysts often go back and forth among them. For example, prototyping in the interface design step often uncovers additional information that is needed in the system. Alternatively, a system that is being designed for an organization that has centralized systems might require substantial hardware and software investments if the project team decides to change to a system in which all the processing is distributed.

PRACTICAL TIP **Avoiding Classic Design**

*I*n Chapter 2, we discussed several classic mistakes and how to avoid them. Here, we summarize four classic mistakes in design and discuss how to avoid them.

1. *Reducing design time:* If time is short, there is a temptation to reduce the time spent in "unproductive" activities such as design so that the team can jump into "productive" programming. This results in missing important details that have to be investigated later at a much higher time and cost (usually at least ten times higher).

   Solution: If time pressure is intense, use timeboxing to eliminate functionality or move it into future versions.

2. *Feature creep:* Even if you are successful at avoiding scope creep, about 25 percent of system requirements will still change. And, changes—big and small—can significantly increase time and cost.

   Solution: Ensure that all changes are vital and that the users are aware of the impact on cost and time. Try to move proposed changes into future versions.

3. *Silver bullet syndrome:* Analysts sometimes believe the marketing claims for some design tools that claim to solve all problems and magically reduce time and costs. No *one* tool or technique can eliminate overall time or costs by more than 25 percent (although some can reduce individual steps by this much).

   Solution: If a design tool has claims that appear too good to be true, just say no.

4. *Switching tools midproject:* Sometimes analysts switch to what appears to be a better tool during design in the hopes of saving time or costs. Usually, any benefits are outweighed by the need to learn the new tool. This also applies even to minor upgrades to current tools.

   Solution: Don't switch or upgrade unless there is a compelling need for *specific* features in the new tool, and then explicitly *increase* the schedule to include learning time.

Based upon material from Steve McConnell, *Rapid Development* (Redmond, WA: Microsoft Press, 1996).

VERIFYING AND VALIDATING THE ANALYSIS MODELS

Before we evolve our analysis representations into design representations, we need to verify and validate the current set of analysis models to ensure that they faithfully represent the problem domain under consideration. This includes testing the fidelity of each model; for example, we must be sure that the activity diagram(s), use-case descriptions, and use-case diagrams all describe the same functional requirements. It also involves testing the fidelity between the models; for instance, transitions on a behavioral state machine are associated with operations contained in a class diagram. Figure 7-1 portrays the fact that the object-oriented analysis models are highly interrelated. This figure reinforces the fact that all modern systems should be built in a use case driven, architecture centric, and incremental and iterative manner. However, if we have completed all of the verifying and validating of the models as described in Chapters 4–6, we will have successfully balanced them. However, given the importance of testing, we thought we would bring it up again.[1]

EVOLVING THE ANALYSIS MODELS INTO DESIGN MODELS

Now that we have successfully verified and validated our analysis models, we need to begin evolving them into appropriate design models. The purpose of the analysis models was to represent the underlying business problem domain as a set of collaborating objects. In other words, the analysis activities defined the functional requirements. To achieve this, the analysis activities ignored nonfunctional requirements such as performance and the system environment issues (e.g., distributed or centralized processing, user-interface issues, and database issues). In contrast, the primary purpose of the design models is to increase the likelihood of successfully delivering a system that implements the functional requirements in a manner that is affordable and easily maintainable. Therefore, in systems design, we address both the functional and nonfunctional requirements.

From an object-oriented perspective, system design models simply refine the system analysis models by adding system environment (or solution domain) details to them and refining the problem domain information already contained in the analysis models. When evolving the analysis model into the design model, you should first carefully review the use cases and the current set of classes (their operations and attributes and the relationships between them). Are all the classes necessary? Are there any missing classes? Are the classes fully defined? Are any attributes or methods missing? Do the classes have any unnecessary attributes and methods? Is the current representation of the evolving system optimal?

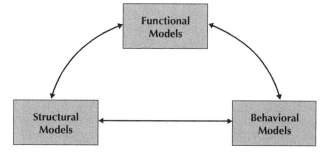

FIGURE 7-1
Object-Oriented
Analysis Models

[1] In fact, we return to testing in both the follow-on design chapters (Chapters 9, 10, and 11) and the construction chapter (Chapter 12).

Obviously, if we have already verified and validated the analysis models, quite a bit of this has already taken place. Yet, given that object-oriented systems development is both incremental and iterative, we must review the analysis models again. However, this time we begin looking at the models of the problem domain through a design lens. In this step, we make modifications to the problem domain models that will enhance the efficiency and effectiveness of the evolving system.

In the following sections, we introduce factoring, partitions and collaborations, and layers as a way to evolve problem domain-oriented analysis models into optimal solution domain-oriented design models. From an enhanced Unified Process perspective (see Figure 1-4), we are moving from the analysis workflow to the design workflow, and we are moving further into the Elaboration phase and partially into the Construction phase.

Factoring

Factoring is the process of separating out a *module* into a stand-alone module. The new module can be a new *class* or a new *method*. For example, when reviewing a set of classes, it may be discovered that they have a similar set of attributes and methods. Thus, it might make sense to factor out the similarities into a separate class. Depending on whether the new class should be in a superclass relationship to the existing classes or not, the new class can be related to the existing classes through a *generalization (a-kind-of)* or possibly through an *aggregation (has-parts)* relationship. Using the appointment system example, if the Employee class had not been identified, we could possibly identify it at this stage by factoring out the similar methods and attributes from the Nurse, Receptionist, and Doctor classes. In this case, we would relate the new class (Employee) to the existing classes using the generalization (a-kind-of) relationship. Obviously, by extension we also could have created the Participant class if it had not been previously identified.

Abstraction and *refinement* are two processes closely related to factoring. Abstraction deals with the creation of a higher-level idea from a set of ideas. Identifying the Employee class is an example of abstracting from a set of lower classes to a higher one. In some cases, the abstraction process identifies *abstract classes*, whereas in other situations, it identifies additional *concrete classes*.[2] The refinement process is the opposite of the abstraction process. In the appointment system example, we could identify additional subclasses of the Employee class, such as Secretary and Bookkeeper. Of course we would add the new classes only if there were sufficient differences among them. Otherwise, the more general class, Employee, would suffice.

Partitions and Collaborations

Based on all the factoring, refining, and abstracting that can take place to the evolving system, the sheer size of the system representation can overload the user and the developer. At this point in the evolution of the system, it might make sense to split the representation into a set of *partitions*. A partition is the object-oriented equivalent of a subsystem,[3] where a subsystem is a decomposition of a larger system into its component systems (e.g., an accounting information system could be functionally decomposed into an accounts-payable system, an

---

[2] See Chapter 5 for the differences between abstract and concrete classes.

[3] Some authors refer to partitions as subsystems [e.g., see R. Wirfs-Brock, B. Wilkerson, and L. Weiner, *Designing Object-Oriented Software* (Englewood Cliffs, NJ: Prentice Hall, 1990)], whereas others refer to them as layers [e.g., see I. Graham, *Migrating to Object Technology* (Reading, MA: Addison-Wesley, 1994)]. However, we have chosen to use the term *partition* [C. Larman, *Applying UML and Patterns: An Introduction to Object-Oriented Analysis and Design* (Englewood Cliffs, NJ: Prentice Hall, 1998)] to minimize confusion between subsystems in a traditional systems development approach and layers associated with Rational's Unified Approach.

accounts-receivable system, a payroll system, etc.). From an object-oriented perspective, partitions are based on the pattern of activity (messages sent) among the objects in an object-oriented system. We describe an easy approach to model partitions and collaborations later in this chapter: packages and package diagrams.

If you recall, an individual class can support multiple use cases. Therefore, an individual class can participate in multiple use-case-based collaborations. In cases where classes are supporting multiple use cases, the collaborations should be merged. The class diagram should be reviewed to see how the different classes are related to one another. For example, if attributes of a class have complex object types, such as Person, Address, or Department, and these object types were not modeled as associations in the class diagram, we need to recognize these implied associations. Creating a diagram that combines the class diagram with the message passing on the sequence diagrams can be very useful to show to what degree the classes are coupled.[4] The greater the coupling between classes, the more likely the classes should be grouped together in a collaboration or partition. By looking at a CRUDE matrix, we can use CRUDE analysis (see Chapter 6) to identify potential classes on which to merge collaborations.

One of the easiest techniques to identify the classes that could be grouped to form a collaboration is through the use of cluster analysis or multiple dimensional scaling. These statistical techniques enable the team to objectively group classes together based on their affinity for each other. The affinity can be based on semantic relationships, different types of messages being sent between them (e.g., create, read, update, delete, or execute), or some weighted combination of both. There are many different similarity measures and many different algorithms on which the clusters can be based, so one must be careful when using these techniques. Always make sure that the collaborations identified using these techniques make sense from the problem domain perspective. Just because a mathematical algorithm suggests that the classes belong together does not make it so. However, this is a good approach to create a first-cut set of collaborations.

Depending on the complexity of the merged collaboration, it may be useful in decomposing the collaboration into multiple partitions. In this case, in addition to having collaborations between objects, it is possible to have collaborations among partitions. The general rule is the more messages sent between objects, the more likely the objects belong in the same partition. The fewer messages sent, the less likely the two objects belong together.

Another useful approach to identifying potential partitions is to model each collaboration between objects in terms of clients, servers, and contracts. A *client* is an instance of a *class* that sends a *message* to an instance of another class for a *method* to be executed; a *server* is the instance of a class that receives the message; and a *contract* is the specification that formalizes the interactions between the client and server objects (see Chapters 5 and 8). This approach allows the developer to build up potential partitions by looking at the contracts that have been specified between objects. In this case, the more contracts there are between objects, the more likely that the objects belong in the same partition. The fewer contracts, the less chance there is that the two classes belong in the same partition.

Remember, the primary purpose of identifying collaborations and partitions is to determine which classes should be grouped together in design.

Layers

Until this point in the development of our system, we have focused only on the problem domain; we have totally ignored the system environment (data management, user interface, and physical architecture). To successfully evolve the analysis model of the system into a

---

[4] We describe the concept of coupling later in this chapter.

design model of the system, we must add the system environment information. One useful way to do this, without overloading the developer, is to use *layers*. A layer represents an element of the software architecture of the evolving system. We have focused only on one layer in the evolving software architecture: the problem domain layer. There should be a layer for each of the different elements of the system environment (e.g., data management, user interface, and physical architecture). Like partitions and collaborations, layers also can be portrayed using packages and package diagrams (see the following section).

The idea of separating the different elements of the architecture into separate layers can be traced back to the MVC architecture of *Smalltalk*.[5] When Smalltalk was first created,[6] the authors decided to separate the application logic from the logic of the user interface. In this manner, it was possible to easily develop different user interfaces that worked with the same application. To accomplish this, they created the *Model–View–Controller (MVC)* architecture, where *Models* implemented the application logic (problem domain) and *Views* and *Controllers* implemented the logic for the user interface. Views handled the output, and Controllers handled the input. Because graphical user interfaces were first developed in the Smalltalk language, the MVC architecture served as the foundation for virtually all graphical user interfaces that have been developed today (including the Mac interfaces, the Windows family, and the various Unix-based GUI environments).

Based on Smalltalk's innovative MVC architecture, many different software layers have been proposed.[7] We suggest the following layers on which to base software architecture: foundation, problem domain, data management, human–computer interaction, and physical architecture (see Figure 7-2). Each layer limits the types of classes that can exist on it (e.g., only user interface classes may exist on the human–computer interaction layer).

Layers	Examples	Relevant Chapters
Foundation	Date, Enumeration	7, 8
Problem Domain	Employee, Customer	4, 5, 6, 7, 8
Data Management	DataInputStream, FileInputStream	8, 9
Human–Computer Interaction	Button, Panel	8, 10
Physical Architecture	ServerSocket, URLConnection	8, 11

FIGURE 7-2
Layers and
Sample Classes

---

[5] See S. Lewis, *The Art and Science of Smalltalk: An Introduction to Object-Oriented Programming Using Visual-Works* (Englewood Cliffs, NJ: Prentice Hall, 1995).

[6] Smalltalk was invented in the early 1970s by a software-development research team at Xerox PARC. It introduced many new ideas into the area of programming languages (e.g., object orientation, windows-based user interfaces, reusable class library, and the development environment). In many ways, Smalltalk is the parent of all object-based and object-oriented languages, such as Visual Basic, C++, and Java.

[7] For example, Problem Domain, Human Interaction, Task Management, and Data Management [P. Coad and E. Yourdon, *Object-Oriented Design* (Englewood Cliffs, NJ: Yourdon Press, 1991)]; Domain, Application, and Interface [I. Graham, *Migrating to Object Technology* (Reading, MA: Addison-Wesley, 1994)]; Domain, Service, and Presentation [C. Larman, *Applying UML and Patterns: An Introduction to Object-Oriented Analysis and Design* (Englewood Cliffs, NJ: Prentice Hall, 1998)]; Business, View, and Access [A. Bahrami, *Object-Oriented Systems Development using the Unified Modeling Language* (New York: McGraw-Hill, 1999)]; Application-Specific, Application-General, Middleware, System-Software [I. Jacobson, G. Booch, and J. Rumbaugh, *The Unified Software Development Process* (Reading, MA: Addison-Wesley, 1999)]; Foundation, Architecture, Business, and Application [M. Page-Jones, *Fundamentals of Object-Oriented Design in UML* (Reading, MA: Addison-Wesley, 2000)].

Foundation The *foundation layer* is, in many ways, a very uninteresting layer. It contains classes that are necessary for any object-oriented application to exist. They include classes that represent fundamental data types (e.g., integers, real numbers, characters, and strings), classes that represent fundamental data structures, sometimes referred to as container classes (e.g., lists, trees, graphs, sets, stacks, and queues), and classes that represent useful abstractions, sometimes referred to as utility classes (e.g., date, time, money). These classes are rarely, if ever, modified by a developer. They are simply used. Today, the classes found on this layer are typically included with the object-oriented development environments.

Problem Domain The *problem-domain layer* is what we have focused our attention on up until now. The focus of the problem-domain layer was the functional requirements. At this stage in the development of our system, we need to further detail the classes so that we can implement them in an effective and efficient manner. In other words, we need to begin switching our focus from optimizing the user's perspective and start optimizing for the machine's perspective. Many issues need to be addressed when designing classes such that they will be implemented in an efficient manner. For example, there are criteria that are useful in evaluating the "goodness" of the design described in this chapter and there are various design activities that are useful in optimizing the design for the machine described in Chapter 8.

Data Management The *data management layer* addresses the issues involving the persistence of the objects contained in the system. The types of classes that appear in this layer deal with how objects can be stored and retrieved. The classes contained in this layer are called the Data Access and Manipulation (DAM) classes. The DAM classes allow the problem domain classes to be independent of the storage used and, hence, increase the portability of the evolving system. Some of the issues related to this layer include choice of the storage format and optimization. There is a plethora of different options in which to choose to store objects. These include sequential files, random access files, relational databases, object/relational databases, object-oriented databases, and NoSQL data stores. Each of these options has been optimized to provide solutions for different access and storage problems. Today, from a practical perspective, there is no single solution that optimally serves all applications. The correct solution is most likely some combination of the different storage options. A complete description of all the issues related to the *data management layer* is well beyond the scope of this book.[8] However, we do present the fundamentals in Chapter 9.

Human–Computer Interaction The *human–computer interaction layer* contains classes associated with the View and Controller idea from Smalltalk. The primary purpose of this layer is to keep the specific user-interface implementation separate from the problem domain classes. This increases the portability of the evolving system. Typical classes found on this layer include classes that can be used to represent buttons, windows, text fields, scroll bars, check boxes, drop-down lists, and many other classes that represent user-interface elements.

When designing the user interface for an application, many issues must be addressed: How important is consistency across different user interfaces? What about differing levels of user experience? How is the user expected to be able to navigate through the system? What

---

[8] There are many good database design books that are relevant to this layer; see, for example, M. Gillenson, *Fundamentals of Database Management Systems* (Hoboken, NJ: John Wiley & Sons, 2005); F. R. McFadden, J. A. Hoffer, and Mary B. Prescott, *Modern Database Management*, 4th Ed. (Reading, MA: Addison-Wesley, 1998); M. Blaha and W. Premerlani, *Object-Oriented Modeling and Design for Database Applications* (Englewood Cliffs, NJ: Prentice Hall, 1998); and R. J. Muller, *Database Design for Smarties: Using UML for Data Modeling* (San Francisco: Morgan Kaufmann, 1999).

about help systems and online manuals? What types of input elements should be included? What types of output elements should be included? Other questions that must be addressed are related to the platform on which the software will be deployed. For example, is the application going to run on a stand-alone computer, is it going to be distributed, or is the application going mobile? If it is expected to run on mobile devices, what type of platform: notebooks, tablets, or phones? Will it be deployed using Web technology, which runs on multiple devices, or will it be created using apps that are based on Android from Google, iOS from Apple, or Windows from Microsoft? Depending on the answer to these questions, different types of user interfaces are possible.

With the advent of social networking platforms, such as Facebook, Twitter, blogs, YouTube, and LinkedIn, the implications for the user interface can be mind boggling. Depending on the application, different social networking platforms may be appropriate for different aspects of the application. Furthermore, each of the different social networking platforms enables (or prevents) consideration of different types of user interfaces. Finally, with the potential audience of your application being global, many different cultural issues will arise in the design and development of culturally aware user interfaces (such as multilingual requirements). Obviously, a complete description of all the issues related to human–computer interaction is beyond the scope of this book.[9] However, from the user's perspective, the user interface is the system. We present the basic issues in user interface design in Chapter 10.

Physical Architecture The *physical architecture layer* addresses how the software will execute on specific computers and networks. This layer includes classes that deal with communication between the software and the computer's operating system and the network. For example, classes that address how to interact with the various ports on a specific computer are included in this layer.

Unlike in the foundation layer, many design issues must be addressed before choosing the appropriate set of classes for this layer. These design issues include the choice of a computing or network architecture (such as the various client-server architectures), the actual design of a network, hardware and server software specification, and security issues. Other issues that must be addressed with the design of this layer include computer hardware and software configuration (choice of operating systems, such as Linux, Mac OSX, and Windows; processor types and speeds; amount of memory; data storage; and input/output technology), standardization, virtualization, grid computing, distributed computing, and Web services. This then leads us to one of the proverbial gorillas on the corner. What do you do with the cloud? The cloud is essentially a form of distributed computing. In this case, the cloud allows you to treat the platform, infrastructure, software, and even business processes as remote services that can be managed by another firm. In many ways, the cloud allows much of IT to be outsourced (see the discussion of outsourcing later in this chapter). Also as brought up with the human–computer interaction layer, the whole issue of mobile computing is very relevant to this layer. In particular, the different devices, such as phones and tablets, are relevant and the way they will communicate with each other, such as through cellular networks or WiFi is also important.

Finally, given the amount of power that IT requires today, the whole topic of Green IT must be addressed. Topics that need to be addressed related to Green IT are the location of

---

[9] Books on user interface design that address these issues include B. Schheiderman, *Designing the User Interface: Strategies for Effective Human Computer Interaction*, 3rd Ed. (Reading, MA: Addison-Wesley, 1998); J. Tidwell, *Designing Interfaces: Patterns for Effective Interaction Design*, 2nd Ed. (Sebastopol, CA: O'Reilly Media, 2010); S. Krug, *Don't Make Me Think: A Common Sense Approach to Web Usability* (Berkeley, CA: New Riders Publishing, 2006); and N. Singh and A. Pereira, *The Culturally Customized Web Site: Customizing Web Sites for the Global Marketplace* (Oxford, UK: Elsevier, 2005).

the data center, data center cooling, alternative power sources, reduction of consumables, the idea of a paperless office, Energy Star compliance, and the potential impact of virtualization, the cloud, and mobile computing. Like the data management and human–computer interaction layers, a complete description of all the issues related to the physical architecture is beyond the scope of this book.[10] However, we do present the basic issues in Chapter 11.

PACKAGES AND PACKAGE DIAGRAMS

In UML, collaborations, partitions, and layers can be represented by a higher-level construct: a package.[11] In fact, a package serves the same purpose as a folder on your computer. When packages are used in programming languages such as Java, packages are actually implemented as folders. A *package* is a general construct that can be applied to any of the elements in UML models. In Chapter 4, we introduced the idea of packages as a way to group use cases together to make the use-case diagrams easier to read and to keep the models at a reasonable level of complexity. In Chapter 5, we did the same thing for class diagrams. In this section, we describe a *package diagram*: a diagram composed only of packages.

The symbol for a package is similar to a tabbed folder (see Figure 7-3). Depending on where a package is used, packages can participate in different types of relationships. For example, in a class diagram, packages represent groupings of classes. Therefore, aggregation and association relationships are possible.

In a package diagram, it is useful to depict a new relationship, the *dependency relationship*. A dependency relationship is portrayed by a dashed arrow (see Figure 7-3). A dependency relationship represents the fact that a modification dependency exists between two packages. That is, it is possible that a change in one package could cause a change to be required in another package. Figure 7-4 portrays the dependencies among the different layers (foundation, problem domain, data management, human–computer interaction, and physical architecture). For example, if a change occurs in the problem domain layer, it most likely will cause changes to occur in the human–computer interaction, physical architecture, and data management layers. Notice that these layers point to the problem domain layer and

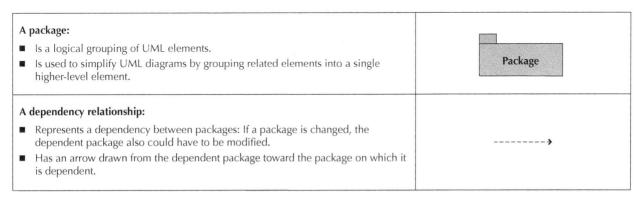

A package: ■ Is a logical grouping of UML elements. ■ Is used to simplify UML diagrams by grouping related elements into a single higher-level element.	Package
A dependency relationship: ■ Represents a dependency between packages: If a package is changed, the dependent package also could have to be modified. ■ Has an arrow drawn from the dependent package toward the package on which it is dependent.	- - - - - - - →

FIGURE 7-3 Syntax for Package Diagram

[10] Some books that cover these topics include S. D. Burd, *Systems Architecture*, 6th Ed. (Boston: Course Technology, 2011); I. Englander, *The Architecture of Computer Hardware, Systems Software, & Networking: An Information Technology Approach* (Hoboken, NJ: Wiley, 2009); and K. K. Hausman and S. Cook, *IT Architecture for Dummies* (Hoboken, NJ: Wiley Publishing, 2011).

[11] This discussion is based on material in Chapter 7 of M. Fowler with K. Scott, *UML Distilled: A Brief Guide to the Standard Object Modeling Language*, 3rd Ed. (Reading, MA: Addison-Wesley, 2004).

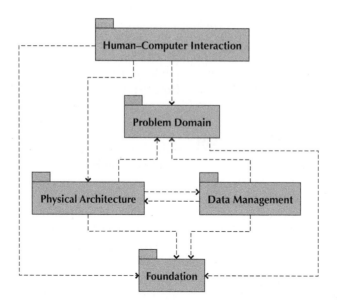

FIGURE 7-4
Package Diagram
of Dependency
Relationships
among Layers

therefore are dependent on it. However, the reverse is not true.[12] Also note that all layers are dependent upon the foundation layer. This is due to the contents of the foundation layer being the fundamental classes from which all other classes will be built. Consequently, any changes made to this layer could have ramifications to all other layers.

At the class level, there could be many causes for dependencies among classes. For example, if the signature for a method is changed, then this causes the interface for all objects of this class to change. In other words, the contract has been modified. Therefore, all classes that have objects that send messages to the instances of the modified class might have to be modified. Capturing dependency relationships among the classes and packages helps the organization in maintaining object-oriented information systems.

Collaborations, partitions, and layers are modeled as packages in UML. Collaborations are normally factored into a set of partitions, which are typically placed on a layer. Partitions can be composed of other partitions. Also, it is possible to have classes in partitions, which are contained in another partition, which is placed on a layer. All these groupings are represented using packages in UML. Remember that a package is simply a generic grouping construct used to simplify UML models through the use of composition.[13]

A simple package diagram, based on the appointment system example from the previous chapters, is shown in Figure 7-5. This diagram portrays only a very small portion of the entire system. In this case, we see that the Patient UI, Patient-DAM, and Patient Table classes depend on the Patient class. Furthermore, the Patient-DAM class depends on the Patient Table class. The same can be seen with the classes dealing with the actual appointments. By isolating the Problem Domain classes (such as the Patient and Appt classes) from the actual object persistence classes (such as the Patient Table and Appt Table classes) through the use of the intermediate Data Management classes (Patient-DAM and Appt-DAM classes), we isolate the Problem Domain classes from the actual storage medium.[14] This greatly simplifies

---

[12] A useful side effect of the dependencies among the layers is that the project manager can divide the project team up into separate subteams: one for each design layer. This is possible because each of the design layers is dependent on the problem domain layer, which has been the focus of analysis. In design, the team can gain some productivity-based efficiency by working on the different layer designs in parallel.

[13] For those familiar with traditional approaches, such as structured analysis and design, packages serve a similar purpose as the leveling and balancing processes used in data flow diagramming.

[14] These issues are described in more detail in Chapter 9.

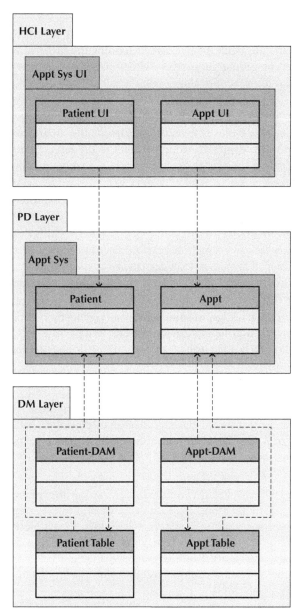

FIGURE 7-5 Partial
Package Diagram
of the Appointment
System

the maintenance and increases the reusability of the Problem Domain classes. Of course, in a complete description of a real system, there would be many more dependencies.

Guidelines for Creating Package Diagrams

As with the UML diagrams described in the earlier chapters, we provide a set of guidelines that we have adapted from Ambler to create package diagrams.[15] In this case, we offer the following six guidelines:

■ Use package diagrams to logically organize designs. Specifically, use packages to group classes together when there is an inheritance, aggregation, or composition relationship between them or when the classes form a collaboration.

[15] S. W. Ambler, *The Elements of UML 2.0 Style* (Cambridge, UK: Cambridge University Press, 2005).

- In some cases, inheritance, aggregation, or association relationships exist between packages. In those cases, for readability purposes, try to support inheritance relationships vertically, with the package containing the superclass being placed above the package containing the subclass. Use horizontal placement to support aggregation and association relationships, with the packages being placed side by side.

- When a dependency relationship exists on a diagram, it implies that there is at least one semantic relationship between elements of the two packages. The direction of the dependency is typically from the subclass to the superclass, from the whole to the part, and with contracts, from the client to the server. In other words, a subclass is dependent on the existence of a superclass, a whole is dependent upon its parts existing, and a client can't send a message to a nonexistent server.

- When using packages to group use cases together, be sure to include the actors and the associations that they have with the use cases grouped in the package. This will allow the diagram's user to better understand the context of the diagram.

- Give each package a simple, but descriptive name to provide the package diagram user with enough information to understand what the package encapsulates. Otherwise, the user will have to drill-down or open up the package to understand the package's purpose.

- Be sure that packages are cohesive. For a package to be cohesive, the classes contained in the package, in some sense, belong together. A simple, but not perfect, rule to follow when grouping classes together in a package is that the more the classes depend on each other, the more likely they belong together in a package.

Creating Package Diagrams

1. Set Context

In this section, we describe a simple five-step process to create package diagrams. The first step is to set the context for the package diagram. Remember, packages can be used to model partitions and/or layers. Revisiting the appointment system again, let's set the context as the problem domain layer.

2. Cluster Classes

The second step is to cluster the classes together into partitions based on the relationships that the classes share. The relationships include generalization, aggregation, the various associations, and the message sending that takes place between the objects in the system. To identify the packages in the appointment system, we should look at the different analysis models [e.g., the class diagram (see Figure 7-6), the sequence diagrams (see Figure 7-7)], and the CRUDE matrix (see Figure 7-8). If at all possible, classes in a generalization hierarchy should be kept together in a single partition.

3. Create Packages

The third step is to place the clustered classes together in a partition and model the partitions as packages. Figure 7-9 portrays five packages in the PD Layer: Account Pkg, Participant Pkg, Patient Pkg, Appointment Pkg, and Treatment Pkg.

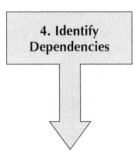

4. Identify Dependencies

The fourth step is to identify the dependency relationships among the packages. We accomplish this by reviewing the relationships that cross the boundaries of the packages to uncover potential dependencies. In the appointment system, we see association relationships that connect the Account Pkg with the Appointment Pkg (via the associations between the Entry class and the Appointment class), the Participant Pkg with the Appointment Pkg (via the association between the Doctor class and the Appointment class), the Patient Pkg, which is contained within the Participant Pkg, with the Appointment Pkg (via the association between the Patient and Appointment classes), and the Patient Pkg with the Treatment Pkg (via the association between the Patient and Symptom classes).

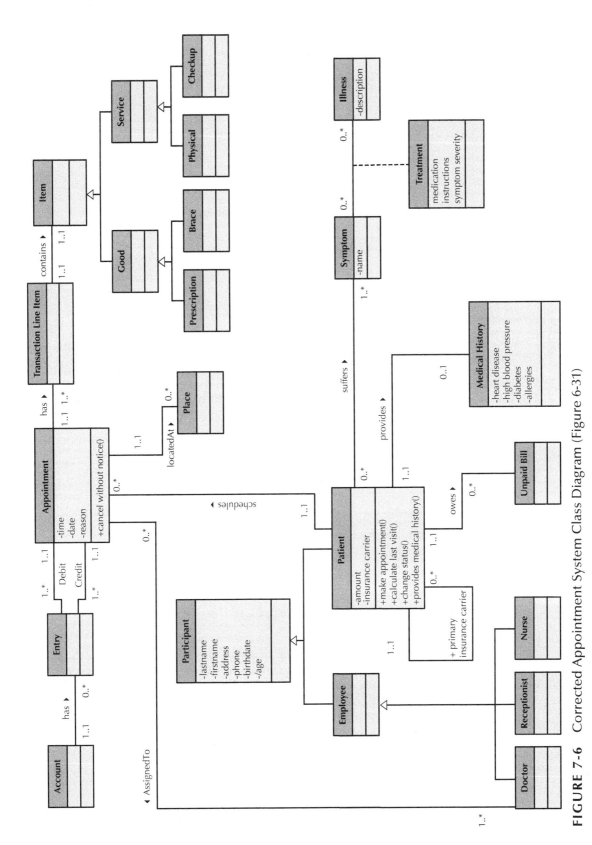

FIGURE 7-6 Corrected Appointment System Class Diagram (Figure 6-31)

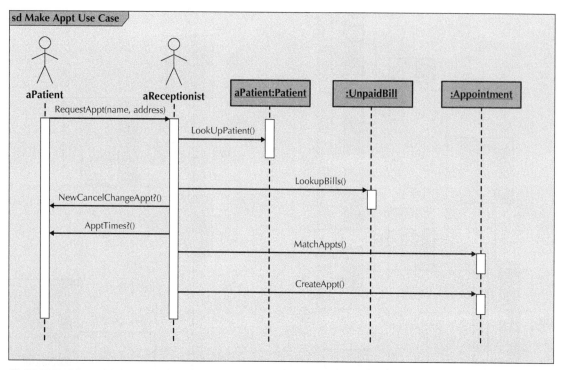

FIGURE 7-7 Sequence Diagram for a Scenario of the Make Old Patient Appt Use Case (Figure 6-5)

	Receptionist	PatientList	Patient	UnpaidBills	Appointments	Appointment
Receptionist		RU	CRUD	R	RU	CRUD
PatientList			R			
Patient						
UnpaidBills						
Appointments						R
Appointment						

FIGURE 7-8 CRUDE Matrix for the Make Old Patient Appt Use Case (Figure 6-16)

5. Lay Out and Draw Diagram

The fifth step is to lay out and draw the diagram. Using the guidelines, place the packages and dependency relationships in the diagram. In the case of the Appointment system, there are dependency relationships between the Account Pkg and the Appointment Pkg, the Participant Pkg and the Appointment Pkg, the Patient Pkg and the Appointment Pkg, and the Patient Pkg and the Treatment Pkg. To increase the understandability of the dependency relationships among the different packages, a pure package diagram that shows only the dependency relationships among the packages can be created (see Figure 7-10).

Verifying and Validating Package Diagrams

Like all the previous models, package diagrams need to be verified and validated. In this case, the package diagrams were derived primarily from the class diagram, the sequence diagrams, and the CRUDE matrix. Only two areas need to be reviewed.

FIGURE 7-9 Package Diagram of the PD Layer of the Appointment Problem

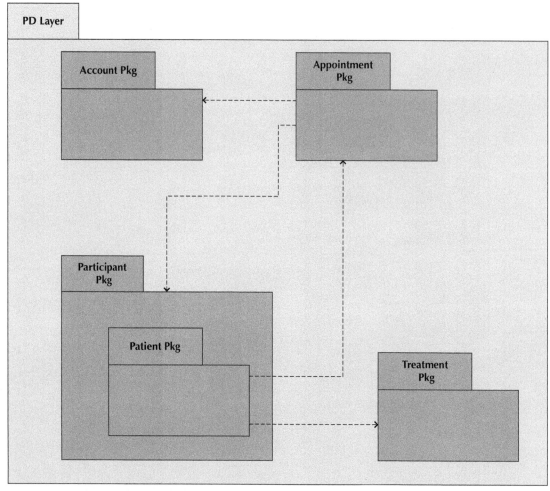

FIGURE 7-10 Overview Package Diagram of the PD Layer for the Appointment System

First, the identified packages must make sense from a problem domain or functional requirements point of view. For example, in the context of an appointment system, the packages in Figure 7-10 (Participant, Patient, Appt, Account, and Treatment) seem to be reasonable.

Second, all dependency relationships must be based on message-sending relationships on the sequence diagrams, cell entries in the CRUDE matrix, and associations on the class diagram. In the case of the appointment system, the identified dependency relationships are reasonable (see Figures 7-6, 7-7, 7-8, and 7-10).

DESIGN CRITERIA

When considering the design of an object-oriented system, a set of criteria exists that can be used to determine whether the design is a good one or a bad one. According to Coad and Yourdon,[16] "A good design is one that balances trade-offs to minimize the total cost of the system over its entire lifetime." These criteria include coupling, cohesion, and connascence.

---

[16] Peter Coad and Edward Yourdon, *Object-Oriented Design* (Englewood Cliffs, NJ: Yourdon Press, 1991), p. 128.

Coupling

Coupling refers to how interdependent or interrelated the modules (classes, objects, and methods) are in a system. The higher the interdependency, the more likely changes in part of a design can cause changes to be required in other parts of the design. For object-oriented systems, Coad and Yourdon[17] identified two types of coupling to consider: interaction and inheritance.

Interaction coupling deals with the coupling among methods and objects through message passing. Lieberherr and Holland put forth the *law of Demeter* as a guideline to minimize this type of coupling.[18] Essentially, the law minimizes the number of objects that can receive messages from a given object. The law states that an object should send messages only to one of the following:

- Itself (For example, in Figure 7-11a, Object1 can send Message1 to itself. In other words, a method associated with Object1 can use other methods associated with Object1.[19])

- An object that is contained in an attribute of the object or one of its superclasses (For example, in Figure 7-11b, the PO1 instance of the Purchase Order class should be able to send messages using its Customer, State, and Date attributes.)

- An object that is passed as a parameter to the method (For example, in Figure 7-11c, the aPatient instance sends the message Request Appt(name, address) to the aReceptionist instance, which is allowed to send messages to the instances contained in the name and address parameters.)

- An object that is created by the method (For example, in Figure 7-11c, the method Request Appt associated with the aReceptionist instance creates an instance of the Appointment class. The Request Appt method is allowed to send messages to that instance.)

- An object that is stored in a global variable[20]

Even though the law of Demeter attempts to minimize interaction coupling among methods and objects, each of the above allowed forms of message sending in fact increases coupling. For example, the coupling increases between the objects if the calling method passes attributes to the called method or if the calling method depends on the value being returned by the called method.

Inheritance coupling, as its name implies, deals with how tightly coupled the classes are in an inheritance hierarchy. Most authors tend to say simply that this type of coupling is desirable. However, depending on the issues raised previously in the appendix of Chapter 1 with inheritance—inheritance conflicts, redefinition capabilities, and dynamic binding—a high level of inheritance coupling might not be a good thing. For example, in Figure 7-12, should Method2() defined in Subclass be allowed to call Method1() defined in Superclass? Or, should Method2() defined in Subclass refer to Attribute1 defined in Superclass? Or, even more confusing, assuming that Superclass is an abstract class, can a Method1() call Method2() or use Attribute2 defined in Subclass? Obviously, the first two examples have

---

[17] Ibid.

[18] Karl J. Lieberherr and Ian M. Holland, "Assuring Good Style for Object-Oriented Programs," *IEEE Software* 6, no. 5 (September, 1989): 38–48; Karl J. Lieberherr, *Adaptive Object-Oriented Software: The Demeter Method with Propagation Patterns* (Boston, MA: PWS Publishing, 1996).

[19] Obviously, this is stating what is expected.

[20] From a design perspective, global variables should be avoided. Most pure object-oriented programming languages do not explicitly support global variables, and we do not address them any further.

(a)

(b)

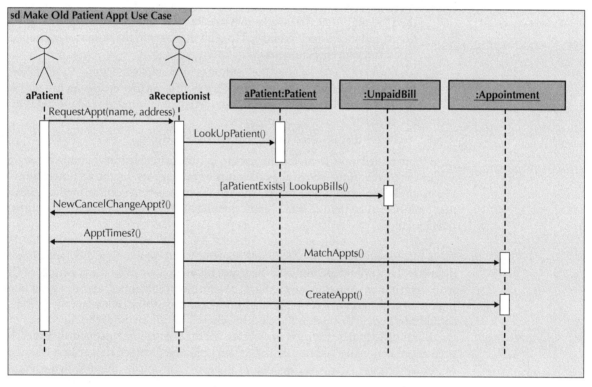

(c)

FIGURE 7-11 Examples of Interaction Coupling

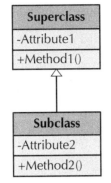

FIGURE 7-12
Example of Inherit-ance Coupling

some intuitive sense. Using the properties of a superclass is the primary purpose of inheriting from it in the first place. On the other hand, the third example is somewhat counterintuitive. However, owing to the way that different object-oriented programming languages support dynamic binding, polymorphism, and inheritance, all these examples could be possible.

As Snyder has pointed out, most problems with inheritance involve the ability within the object-oriented programming languages to violate the encapsulation and information-hiding principles.[21] From a design perspective, the developer needs to optimize the trade-offs of violating the encapsulation and information-hiding principles and increasing the desirable coupling between subclasses and its superclasses. The best way to solve this conundrum is to ensure that inheritance is used only to support generalization/specialization (a-kind-of) semantics and the principle of substitutability (see Chapter 5). All other uses should be avoided.

Cohesion

Cohesion refers to how single-minded a module (class, object, or method) is within a system. A class or object should represent only one thing, and a method should solve only a single task. Three general types of cohesion have been identified by Coad and Yourdon for object-oriented systems: method, class, and generalization/specialization.[22]

Method cohesion addresses the cohesion within an individual method (i.e., how single-minded a method is). Methods should do one and only one thing. A method that actually performs multiple functions is more difficult to understand—and, therefore, to implement and maintain—than one that performs only a single function.

Class cohesion is the level of cohesion among the attributes and methods of a class (i.e., how single-minded a class is). A class should represent only one thing, such as an employee, a department, or an order. All attributes and methods contained in a class should be required for the class to represent the thing. For example, an employee class should have attributes that deal with a social security number, last name, first name, middle initial, addresses, and benefits, but it should not have attributes such as door, engine, or hood. Furthermore, there should be no attributes or methods that are never used. In other words, a class should have only the attributes and methods necessary to fully define instances for the problem at hand. In this case, we have *ideal class cohesion*. Glenford Meyers suggested that a cohesive class[23] should have these attributes:

- It should contain multiple methods that are visible outside the class (i.e., a single-method class rarely makes sense).
- Each visible method performs only a single function.

[21] Alan Snyder, "Encapsulation and Inheritance in Object-Oriented Programming Languages," in N. Meyrowitz (Ed.), *OOPSLA '86 Conference Proceedings, ACM SigPlan Notices* 21, no. 11 (November 1986); Alan Snyder, "Inheritance and the Development of Encapsulated Software Components," in B. Shriver and P. Wegner (Eds), *Research Directions in Object-Oriented Programming* (Cambridge, MA: MIT Press, 1987).

[22] Coad and Yourdon, *Object-Oriented Design.*

[23] We have adapted his informational-strength module criteria from structured design to object-oriented design. [See Glenford J. Myers, *Composite/Structured Design* (New York, NY: Van Nostrand Reinhold, 1978).]

- All methods reference only attributes or other methods defined within the class or one of its superclasses (i.e., if a method is going to send a message to another object, the remote object must be the value of one of the local object's attributes).[24]

Generalization/specialization cohesion addresses the sensibility of the inheritance hierarchy. How are the classes in the inheritance hierarchy related? Are the classes related through a generalization/specialization (a-kind-of) semantics? Or, are they related via some association, aggregation, or membership type of relationship that was created for simple reuse purposes? Recall all the issues raised previously on the use of inheritance. For example, in Figure 7-13, the subclasses Classrooms and Staff inherit from the superclass Department. Obviously, instances of the Classrooms and Staff classes are not a-kind-of Department. However, in the early days of object-oriented programming, this use of inheritance was quite common. When a programmer saw that there were some common properties that a set of classes shared, the programmer would create an artificial abstraction that defined the commonalities. This was potentially useful in a reuse sense, but it turned out to cause many maintenance nightmares. In this case, instances of the Classrooms and Staff classes are associated with or a-part-of an instance of Department. Today we know that highly cohesive inheritance hierarchies should support only the semantics of generalization and specialization (a-kind-of) and the principle of substitutability.

Connascence

Connascence[25] generalizes the ideas of cohesion and coupling, and it combines them with the arguments for encapsulation. To accomplish this, three levels of encapsulation have been identified. Level-0 encapsulation refers to the amount of encapsulation realized in an individual line of code, level-1 encapsulation is the level of encapsulation attained by combining lines of code into a method, and level-2 encapsulation is achieved by creating classes that contain both methods and attributes. Method cohesion and interaction coupling address primarily level-1 encapsulation. Class cohesion, generalization/specialization cohesion, and inheritance coupling address only level-2 encapsulation. Connascence, as a generalization of cohesion and coupling, addresses both level-1 and level-2 encapsulation.

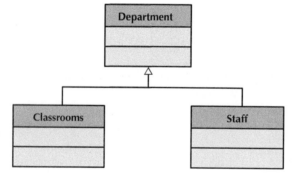

FIGURE 7-13
Generalization/
Specialization vs.
Inheritance Abuse

[24] This restricts messages passing to only the first, second, and fourth conditions supported by the law of Demeter. For example, in Figure 7-11c, aReceptionist must have attributes associated with it that contains objects for Patients, Unpaid Bills, and Appointments. Furthermore, once an instance of Appointment is created, aReceptionist must have an attribute with the instance as its value to send any additional messages.

[25] See Meilir Page-Jones, "Comparing Techniques by Means of Encapsulation and Connascence," *Communications of the ACM* 35, no. 9 (September 1992): 147–151.

But what exactly is connascence? Connascence literally means to be born together. From an object-oriented design perspective, it really means that two modules (classes or methods) are so intertwined that if you make a change in one, it is likely that a change in the other will be required. On the surface, this is very similar to coupling and, as such, should be minimized. However, when you combine it with the encapsulation levels, it is not quite that simple. In this case, we want to minimize overall connascence by eliminating any unnecessary connascence throughout the system; minimize connascence across any encapsulation boundaries, such as method boundaries and class boundaries; and maximize connascence within any encapsulation boundary.

Based on these guidelines, a subclass should never directly access any hidden attribute or method of a superclass [i.e., a subclass should not have special rights to the properties of its superclass(es)]. If direct access to the nonvisible attributes and methods of a superclass by its subclass is allowed—and is permitted in most object-oriented programming languages—and a modification to the superclass is made, then owing to the connascence between the subclass and its superclass, it is likely that a modification to the subclass also is required.[26] In other words, the subclass has access to something across an encapsulation boundary (the class boundary between the subclass and the superclass). Practically speaking, you should maximize the cohesion (connascence) within an encapsulation boundary and minimize the coupling (connascence) between the encapsulation boundaries.

DESIGN STRATEGIES

Until now, we have assumed that the system will be built and implemented by the project team; however, there are actually three ways to approach the creation of a new system: developing a custom application in-house, buying and customizing a packaged system, and relying on an external vendor, developer, or service provider to build the system. Each of these choices has strengths and weaknesses, and each is more appropriate in different scenarios. The following sections describe each design choice in turn, and then we present criteria that you can use to select one of the three approaches for your project.

Custom Development

Many project teams assume that *custom development*, or building a new system from scratch, is the best way to create a system. For one thing, teams have complete control over the way the system looks and functions. Custom development also allows developers to be flexible and creative in the way they solve business problems. Additionally, a custom application is easier to change to include components that take advantage of current technologies that can support such strategic efforts.

Building a system in-house also builds technical skills and functional knowledge within the company. As developers work with business users, their understanding of the business grows and they become better able to align IS with strategies and needs. These same developers climb the technology learning curve so that future projects applying similar technology require much less effort.

Custom application development, however, requires dedicated effort that involves long hours and hard work. Many companies have a development staff who already is overcommitted

---

[26] Based on these guidelines, the use of the protected visibility, as supported in Java and C++, should be minimized, if not avoided. "Friends" as defined in C++ also should be minimized or avoided. Owing to the level of dependencies these language features create, any convenience afforded to a programmer is more than offset in potential design, understandability, and maintenance problems. These features must be used with great caution and must be fully documented.

to filling huge backlogs of systems requests and just does not have time for another project. Also, a variety of skills—technical, interpersonal, functional, project management, and modeling—must be in place for the project to move ahead smoothly. IS professionals, especially highly skilled individuals, are quite difficult to hire and retain.

The risks associated with building a system from the ground up can be quite high, and there is no guarantee that the project will succeed. Developers could be pulled away to work on other projects, technical obstacles could cause unexpected delays, and the business users could become impatient with a growing timeline.

Packaged Software

Many business needs are not unique, and because it makes little sense to reinvent the wheel, many organizations buy *packaged software* that has already been written rather than developing their own custom solution. In fact, there are thousands of commercially available software programs that have already been written to serve a multitude of purposes. Think about your own need for a word processor—did you ever consider writing your own word processing software? That would be very silly considering the number of good software packages available that are relatively inexpensive.

Similarly, most companies have needs that can be met quite well by packaged software, such as payroll or accounts receivable. It can be much more efficient to buy programs that have already been created, tested, and proven. Moreover, a packaged system can be bought and installed in a relatively short time when compared with a custom system. Plus, packaged systems incorporate the expertise and experience of the vendor who created the software.

Packaged software can range from reusable components to small, single-function tools to huge, all-encompassing systems such as *enterprise resource planning (ERP)* applications that are installed to automate an entire business. Implementing ERP systems is a process in which large organizations spend millions of dollars installing packages by companies such as SAP or Oracle and then change their businesses accordingly. Installing ERP software is much more difficult than installing small application packages because benefits can be harder to realize and problems are much more serious.

However, there are problems related to packaged software. For example, companies buying packaged systems must accept the functionality that is provided by the system, and rarely is there a perfect fit. If the packaged system is large in scope, its implementation could mean a substantial change in the way the company does business. Letting technology drive the business can be dangerous.

Most packaged applications allow *customization*, or the manipulation of system parameters to change the way certain features work. For example, the package might have a way to accept information about your company or the company logo that would then appear on input screens. Or an accounting software package could offer a choice of various ways to handle cash flow or inventory control so that it can support the accounting practices in different organizations. If the amount of customization is not enough and the software package has a few features that don't quite work the way the company needs it to work, the project team can create workarounds.

A *workaround* is a custom-built add-on program that interfaces with the packaged application to handle special needs. It can be a nice way to create needed functionality that does not exist in the software package. But workarounds should be a last resort for several reasons. First, workarounds are not supported by the vendor who supplied the packaged software, so upgrades to the main system might make the workaround ineffective. Also, if problems arise, vendors have a tendency to blame the workaround as the culprit and refuse to provide support.

Although choosing a packaged software system is simpler than custom development, it too can benefit from following a formal methodology, just as if a custom application were being built.

Systems integration refers to the process of building new systems by combining packaged software, existing legacy systems, and new software written to integrate these. Many consulting firms specialize in systems integration, so it is not uncommon for companies to select the packaged software option and then outsource the integration of a variety of packages to a consulting firm. (Outsourcing is discussed in the next section.)

The key challenge in systems integration is finding ways to integrate the data produced by the different packages and legacy systems. Integration often hinges on taking data produced by one package or system and reformatting it for use in another package or system. The project team starts by examining the data produced by and needed by the different packages or systems and identifying the transformations that must occur to move the data from one to the other. In many cases, this involves fooling the different packages or systems into thinking that the data were produced by an existing program module that the package or system expects to produce the data rather than the new package or system that is being integrated.

A third approach is through the use of an *object wrapper*.[27] An object wrapper is essentially an object that "wraps around" a legacy system, enabling an object-oriented system to send messages to the legacy system. Effectively, object wrappers create an application program interface (API) to the legacy system. The creation of an object wrapper protects the corporation's investment in the legacy system.

Outsourcing

The design choice that requires the least amount of in-house resources is *outsourcing*—hiring an external vendor, developer, or service provider to create the system. Outsourcing has become quite popular in recent years. Some estimate that as many as 50 percent of companies with IT budgets of more than $5 million are currently outsourcing or evaluating the approach.

With outsourcing, the decision making and/or management control of a business function is transferred to an outside supplier. This transfer requires two-way coordination, exchange of information, and trust between the supplier and the business. From an IT perspective, IT outsourcing can include hiring consultants to solve a specific problem, hiring contract programmers to implement a solution, hiring a firm to manage the IT function and assets of a company, or actually outsourcing the entire IT function to a separate firm. Today, through the use of application service providers (ASPs), Web services technology, and cloud services, it is possible to use a pay-as-you-go approach for a software package.[28] Essentially, IT outsourcing involves hiring a third party to perform some IT function that traditionally would be performed in-house.

There can be great benefit to having someone else develop a company's system. The outside company may be more experienced in the technology or have more resources, such as experienced programmers. Many companies embark upon outsourcing deals to reduce costs, whereas others see it as an opportunity to add value to the business.

For whatever reason, outsourcing can be a good alternative for a new system. However, it does not come without costs. If you decide to leave the creation of a new system in the hands of someone else, you could compromise confidential information or lose control over future development. In-house professionals are not benefiting from the skills that could be learned from the project; instead, the expertise is transferred to the outside organization. Ultimately, important skills can walk right out the door at the end of the contract. Furthermore, when offshore outsourcing is being considered, we must also be cognizant of language issues, time-zone differences, and cultural differences (e.g., acceptable business practices as understood in

[27] Ian Graham, *Object-Oriented Methods: Principles & Practice*, 3rd Ed. (Reading, MA: Addison-Wesley, 2001).

[28] For an economic explanation of how this could work, see H. Baetjer, *Software as Capital: An Economic Perspective on Software Engineering* (Los Alamitos, CA: IEEE Computer Society Press, 1997).

one country that may be unacceptable in another). All these concerns, if not dealt with properly, can prevail over any advantage that outsourcing or offshore outsourcing could realize.

Most risks can be addressed if a company decides to outsource, but two are particularly important. First, the company must thoroughly assess the requirements for the project—a company should never outsource what is not understood. If rigorous planning and analysis has occurred, then the company should be well aware of its needs. Second, the company should carefully choose a vendor, developer, or service with a proven track record with the type of system and technology that its system needs.

Three primary types of contracts can be drawn to control the outsourcing deal. A *time-and-arrangements contract* is very flexible because a company agrees to pay for whatever time and expenses are needed to get the job done. Of course, this agreement could result in a large bill that exceeds initial estimates. This works best when the company and the outsourcer are unclear about what it is going to take to finish the job.

A company will pay no more than expected with a *fixed-price contract* because if the outsourcer exceeds the agreed-upon price, it will have to absorb the costs. Outsourcers are much more careful about defining requirements clearly up front, and there is little flexibility for change.

The type of contract gaining in popularity is the *value-added contract*, whereby the outsourcer reaps some percentage of the completed system's benefits. The company has very little risk in this case, but it must expect to share the wealth once the system is in place.

Creating fair contracts is an art because flexibility must be carefully balanced with clearly defined terms. Often, needs change over time. Therefore, the contract should not be so specific and rigid that alterations cannot be made. Think about how quickly mobile technology has changed. It is difficult to foresee how a project might evolve over a long period of time. Short-term contracts help leave room for reassessment if needs change or if relationships are not working out the way both parties expected. In all cases, the relationship with the outsourcer should be viewed as a partnership where both parties benefit and communicate openly.

Managing the outsourcing relationship is a full-time job. Thus, someone needs to be assigned full time to manage the outsourcer, and the level of that person should be appropriate for the size of the job (a multimillion dollar outsourcing engagement should be handled by a high-level executive). Throughout the relationship, progress should be tracked and measured against predetermined goals. If a company does embark upon an outsourcing design strategy, it should be sure to get adequate information. Many books have been written that provide much more detailed information on the topic.[29] Figure 7-14 summarizes some guidelines for outsourcing.

Outsourcing
• Keep the lines of communication open between you and your outsourcer.
• Define and stabilize requirements before signing a contact.
• View the outsourcing relationship as a partnership.
• Select the vendor, developer or service provider carefully.
• Assign a person to managing the relationship.
• Don't outsource what you don't understand.
• Emphasize flexible requirements, long-term relationships and short-term contracts.

FIGURE 7-14
Outsourcing
Guidelines

---

[29] For more information on outsourcing, we recommend M. Lacity and R. Hirschheim, *Information Systems Outsourcing: Myths, Metaphors, and Realities* (New York, NY: Wiley, 1993); L. Willcocks and G. Fitzgerald, *A Business Guide to Outsourcing Information Technology* (London: Business Intelligence, 1994); E. Carmel, *Offshoring Information Technology: Sourcing and Outsourcing to a Global Workforce* (Cambridge, England: Cambridge University Press, 2005); J. K. Halvey and B. M. Melby, *Information Technology Outsourcing Transactions: Process, Strategies, and Contracts*, 2nd Ed. (Hoboken, NJ: Wiley, 2005); and T. L. Friedman, *The World Is Flat: A Brief History of the Twenty-First Century, Updated and Expanded Edition* (New York: Farrar, Straus, and Giroux, 2006).

Selecting a Design Strategy

Each of the design strategies just discussed has its strengths and weaknesses, and no one strategy is inherently better than the others. Thus, it is important to understand the strengths and weaknesses of each strategy and when to use each. Figure 7-15 summarizes the characteristics of each strategy.

Business Need If the business need for the system is common and technical solutions already exist that can meet the business need of the system, it makes little sense to build a custom application. Packaged systems are good alternatives for common business needs. A custom alternative should be explored when the business need is unique or has special requirements. Usually, if the business need is not critical to the company, then outsourcing is the best choice—someone outside of the organization can be responsible for the application development.

In-house Experience If in-house experience exists for all the functional and technical needs of the system, it will be easier to build a custom application than if these skills do not exist. A packaged system may be a better alternative for companies that do not have the technical skills to build the desired system. For example, a project team that does not have mobile technology skills might want to consider outsourcing those aspects of the system.

Project Skills The skills that are applied during projects are either technical (e.g., Java, SQL) or functional (e.g., security), and different design alternatives are more viable, depending on how important the skills are to the company's strategy. For example, if certain functional and technical expertise that relates to mobile application development is important to an organization because it expects mobile to play an important role in its sales over time, then it makes sense for the company to develop mobile applications in-house, using company employees so that the skills can be developed and improved. On the other hand, some skills, such as network security, may be beyond the technical expertise of employees or not of interest to the company's strategists—it is just an operational issue that needs to be addressed. In this case, packaged systems or outsourcing should be considered so that internal employees can focus on other business-critical applications and skills.

	Use Custom Development When. . .	Use a Packaged System When. . .	Use Outsourcing When. . .
Business Need	The business need is unique.	The business need is common.	The business need is not core to the business.
In-house Experience	In-house functional and technical experience exists.	In-house functional experience exists.	In-house functional or technical experience does not exist.
Project Skills	There is a desire to build in-house skills.	The skills are not strategic.	The decision to outsource is a strategic decision.
Project Management	The project has a highly skilled project manager and a proven methodology.	The project has a project manager who can coordinate the vendor's efforts.	The project has a highly skilled project manager at the level of the organization that matches the scope of the outsourcing deal.
Time Frame	The time frame is flexible.	The time frame is short.	The time frame is short or flexible.

FIGURE 7-15 Design Strategy Characteristics

Project Management Custom applications require excellent project management and a proven methodology. So many things, such as funding obstacles, staffing holdups, and overly demanding business users, can push a project off-track. Therefore, the project team should choose to develop a custom application only if it is certain that the underlying coordination and control mechanisms will be in place. Packaged and outsourcing alternatives also need to be managed; however, they are more shielded from internal obstacles because the external parties have their own objectives and priorities (e.g., it may be easier for an outside contractor to say no to a user than it is for a person within the company). Typically, packaged and outsourcing alternatives have their own methodologies, which can benefit companies that do not have an appropriate methodology to use.

Time Frame When time is a factor, the project team should probably start looking for a system that is already built and tested. In this way, the company will have a good idea of how long the package will take to put in place and what the final result will contain. The time frame for custom applications is hard to pin down, especially when you consider how many projects end up missing important deadlines. If a company must choose the custom development alternative and the time frame is very short, it should consider using techniques such as timeboxing to manage this problem. The time to produce a system using outsourcing really depends on the system and the outsourcer's resources. If a service provider has services in place that can be used to support the company's needs, then a business need could be implemented quickly. Otherwise, an outsourcing solution could take as long as a custom development initiative.

SELECTING AN ACQUISITION STRATEGY

Once the project team has a good understanding of how well each design strategy fits with the project's needs, it must begin to understand exactly *how* to implement these strategies. For example, what tools and technology would be used if a custom alternative were selected? What vendors make packaged systems that address the project's needs? What service providers would be able to build this system if the application were outsourced? This information can be obtained from people working in the IS department and from recommendations by business users. Alternatively, the project team can contact other companies with similar needs and investigate the types of systems that they have put in place. Vendors and consultants usually are willing to provide information about various tools and solutions in the form of brochures, product demonstrations, and information seminars. However, a company should be sure to validate the information it receives from vendors and consultants. After all, they are trying to make a sale. Therefore, they may stretch the capabilities of their tool by focusing on only the positive aspects of the tool while omitting the tool's drawbacks.

It is likely that the project team will identify several ways that a system could be constructed after weighing the specific design options. For example, the project team might have found three vendors that make packaged systems that potentially could meet the project's needs. Or the team may be debating over whether to develop a system using Java as a development tool and the database management system from Oracle or to outsource the development effort to a consulting firm such as Accenture or CGI. Each alternative has pros and cons associated with it that need to be considered, and only one solution can be selected in the end.

To aid in this decision, additional information should be collected. Project teams employ several approaches to gather additional information that is needed. One helpful tool is the *request for proposal (RFP)*, a document that solicits a formal proposal from a potential vendor, developer, or service provider. RFPs describe in detail the system or service that is needed, and vendors respond by describing in detail how they could supply those needs.

Although there is no standard way of writing an RFP, it should include certain key facts that the vendor requires, such as a detailed description of needs, any special technical needs or circumstances, evaluation criteria, procedures to follow, and a timetable. In a large project, the RFP can be hundreds of pages long, since it is essential that all required project details are included.

The RFP is not just a way to gather information. Rather, it results in a vendor proposal that is a binding offer to accomplish the tasks described in the RFP. The vendor proposal includes a schedule and a price for which the work is to be performed. Once the winning vendor proposal is chosen, a contract for the work is developed and signed by both parties.

For smaller projects with smaller budgets, the *request for information (RFI)* may be sufficient. An RFI is a shorter, less detailed request that is sent to potential vendors to obtain general information about their products and services. Sometimes, the RFI is used to determine which vendors have the capability to perform a service. It is often then followed up with an RFP to the qualified vendors.

When a list of equipment is so complete that the vendor need only provide a price, without any analysis or description of what is needed, the *request for quote (RFQ)* may be used. For example, if twenty long-range RFID tag readers are needed from the manufacturer on a certain date at a certain location, the RFQ can be used. If an item is described, but a specific manufacturer's product is not named, then extensive testing will be required to verify fulfillment of the specifications.

Alternative Matrix

An *alternative matrix* can be used to organize the pros and cons of the design alternatives so that the best solution will be chosen in the end (see Figure 7-16). This matrix is created using the same steps as the feasibility analysis, which was presented in Chapter 2. The only difference is that the alternative matrix combines several feasibility analyses into one matrix so that the alternatives can easily be compared. An alternative matrix is a grid that contains the

Evaluation Criteria	Relative Importance (Weight)	Alternative 1: Custom Application Using VB.NET	Score (1–5)*	Weighted Score	Alternative 2: Custom Application Using Java	Score (1–5)*	Weighted Score	Alternative 3: Packaged Software Product ABC	Score (1–5)*	Weighted Score
Technical Issues:										
Criterion 1	20		5	100		3	60		3	60
Criterion 2	10		3	30		3	30		5	50
Criterion 3	10		2	20		1	10		3	30
Economic Issues:										
Criterion 4	25	Supporting	3	75	Supporting	3	75	Supporting	5	125
Criterion 5	10	Information	3	30	Information	1	10	Information	5	50
Organizational Issues:										
Criterion 6	10		5	50		5	50		3	30
Criterion 7	10		3	30		3	30		1	10
Criterion 8	5		3	15		1	5		1	5
TOTAL	100			350			270			360

* This denotes how well the alternative meets the criteria. 1 = poor fit; 5 = perfect fit.

FIGURE 7-16 Sample Alternative Matrix Using Weights

technical, budget, and organizational feasibilities for each system candidate, pros and cons associated with adopting each solution, and other information that is helpful when making comparisons. Sometimes weights are provided for different parts of the matrix to show when some criteria are more important to the final decision.

To create the alternative matrix, draw a grid with the alternatives across the top and different criteria (e.g., feasibilities, pros, cons, and other miscellaneous criteria) along the side. Next, fill in the grid with detailed descriptions about each alternative. This becomes a useful document for discussion because it clearly presents the alternatives being reviewed and comparable characteristics for each one.

Sometimes, weights and scores are added to the alternative matrix to create a weighted alternative matrix that communicates the project's most important criteria and the alternatives that best address them. A scorecard is built by adding a column labeled "weight" that includes a number depicting how much each criterion matters to the final decision. Typically, analysts take 100 points and spread them out across the criteria appropriately. If five criteria were used and all mattered equally, then each criterion would receive a weight of 20. However, if costs were the most important criterion for choosing an alternative, it might receive 60 points, and the other four criteria might get only 10 points each.

Then, the analysts add to the matrix a column called "Score" that communicates how well each alternative meets the criteria. Usually, number ranges like 1 to 5 or 1 to 10 are used to rate the appropriateness of the alternatives by the criteria. So, for the cost criterion, the least expensive alternative may receive a 5 on a 1-to-5 scale, whereas a costly alternative would receive a 1. Weighted scores are computed with each criterion's weight multiplied by the score it was given for each alternative. Then, the weighted scores are totaled for each alternative. The highest weighted score achieves the best match for our criteria. When numbers are used in the alternative matrix, project teams can make decisions quantitatively and on the basis of hard numbers.

It should be pointed out, however, that the score assigned to the criteria for each alternative is nothing more than a subjective assignment. Consequently, it is entirely possible for an analyst to skew the analysis according to his or her own biases. In other words, the weighted alternative matrix can be made to support whichever alternative you prefer and yet retains the appearance of an objective, rational analysis. To avoid the problem of a biased analysis, each analyst on the team could develop ratings independently; then, the ratings could be compared and discrepancies resolved in an open team discussion.

The final step, of course, is to decide which solution to design and implement. The decision should be made by a combination of business users and technical professionals after the issues involved with the different alternatives are well understood. Once the decision is finalized, design can continue as needed, based on the selected alternative.

APPLYING THE CONCEPTS AT PATTERSON SUPERSTORE

The team had one major task to complete before moving into design. After developing and verifying the functional, structural, and behavioral models, they now had to validate that the functional, structural, and behavioral models developed in analysis agreed with each other. In other words, they needed to balance the functional, structural, and behavioral models. As you will see, this activity revealed inconsistencies and uncovered new information about the system that they hope to implement. After creating corrected iterations of each of the three types of models, the team explored design alternatives and determined a design strategy.

You can find the rest of the case at www.wiley.com/go/dennis/systemanalysis6e/casestudy.

CHAPTER REVIEW

After reading and studying this chapter, you should be able to:

- ☐ Describe the purpose of balancing the analysis models.
- ☐ Describe the purpose of the factoring, refinement, and abstraction processes.
- ☐ Describe the purpose of partitions and collaborations.
- ☐ Name and describe the layers.
- ☐ Explain the purpose of a package diagram.
- ☐ Describe the different elements of the package diagram.
- ☐ Create a package diagram to model partitions and layers.
- ☐ Verify and validate package diagrams using walkthroughs.
- ☐ Describe the law of Demeter.
- ☐ Describe the different types of cohesion and why cohesion should be maximized.
- ☐ Describe connascence and how it is related to cohesion and coupling.
- ☐ Describe the pros and cons of the three basic design strategies.
- ☐ Describe the basis of selecting a design strategy.
- ☐ Explain how and when to use RFPs, RFIs, and RFQs to gather information from vendors.
- ☐ Describe how to use a weighted alternative matrix to select an acquisition strategy.

KEY TERMS

Abstract classes	Data management layer	Interaction coupling	Physical architecture layer
Abstraction	Dependency relationship	Law of Demeter	Problem domain layer
Aggregation	Enterprise resource	Layer	Refinement
A-kind-of	planning (ERP)	Message	Request for information (RFI)
Alternative matrix	Factoring	Method	Request for proposal (RFP)
Class	Fixed-price contract	Method cohesion	Request for quote (RFQ)
Class cohesion	Foundation layer	Model	Server
Client	Generalization	Model–View–	Smalltalk
Cohesion	Generalization/	Controller (MVC)	Systems integration
Concrete classes	specialization	Module	Time-and-arrangements
Connascence	cohesion	Object wrapper	contract
Contract	Has-parts	Outsourcing	Value-added contract
Controller	Human–computer	Package	View
Coupling	interaction layer	Package diagram	Workaround
Custom development	Ideal class cohesion	Packaged software	
Customization	Inheritance coupling	Partition	

QUESTIONS

1. Explain the primary difference between an analysis model and a design model.
2. What are the interrelationships among the functional, structural, and behavioral models that need to be tested?
3. What does factoring mean? How is it related to abstraction and refinement?
4. What is a partition? How does a partition relate to a collaboration?
5. What is a layer? Name the different layers.
6. What is the purpose of the different layers?
7. Describe the different types of classes that can appear on each of the layers.
8. What issues or questions arise on each of the different layers?
9. What is a package? How are packages related to partitions and layers?
10. What is a dependency relationship? How do you identify them?

11. What are the five steps for identifying packages and creating package diagrams?
12. What needs to be verified and validated in package diagrams?
13. When drawing package diagrams, what guidelines should you follow?
14. What is the law of Demeter?
15. Describe the difference between inheritance and interaction coupling.
16. Describe method cohesion.
17. What is meant by class cohesion? What are the characteristics of ideal class cohesion?
18. Define connascence. How is it related to the ideas of encapsulation, coupling, and cohesion?
19. What situations are most appropriate for a custom development design strategy?

20. What are some problems with using a packaged software approach to building a new system? How can these problems be addressed?
21. Why do companies invest in ERP systems?
22. What are the pros and cons of using a workaround?
23. When is outsourcing considered a good design strategy? When is it not appropriate?
24. What is an object wrapper?
25. What is systems integration? Explain the challenges.
26. What are the differences between the time-and-arrangements, fixed-price, and value-added contracts for outsourcing?
27. How are the alternative matrix and feasibility analysis related?
28. What is an RFP? How is this different from an RFI?

EXERCISES

A. Describe the difference in meaning between the following two class diagrams. Which is a better model? Why?

B. From a cohesion, coupling, and connascence perspective, is the following class diagram a good model? Why or why not?

C. From a cohesion, coupling, and connascence perspectives, are the following class diagrams good models? Why or why not?

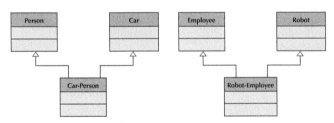

D. For the A Real Estate Inc. problem in Chapters 4 (exercises I, J, and K), 5 (exercises N and O), and 6 (exercise D):
   1. Using the sequence diagrams and the CRUDE matrix, create a package diagram of the problem domain layer.
   2. Perform a verification and validation walkthrough of the package diagram.
   3. Based on the analysis models that have been created and your current understanding of the firm's position, what design strategy would you recommend? Why?

E. For the A Video Store problem in Chapters 4 (exercises L, M, and N), 5 (exercises P and Q), and 6 (exercise E):

1. Using the sequence diagrams and the CRUDE matrix, create a package diagram of the problem domain layer.

2. Perform a verification and validation walkthrough of the package diagram.

3. Based on the analysis models that have been created and your current understanding of the firm's position, what design strategy would you recommend? Why?

F. For the gym membership problem in Chapters 4 (exercises O, P, and Q), 5 (exercises R and S), and 6 (exercise F):

1. Using the sequence diagrams and the CRUDE matrix, create a package diagram of the problem domain layer.

2. Perform a verification and validation walkthrough of the package diagram.

3. Based on the analysis models that have been created and your current understanding of the firm's position, what design strategy would you recommend? Why?

G. For the Picnics R Us problem in Chapters 4 (exercises R, S, and T), 5 (exercises T and U), and 6 (exercise G):

1. Using the sequence diagrams and the CRUDE matrix, create a package diagram of the problem domain layer.

2. Perform a verification and validation walkthrough of the package diagram.

3. Based on the analysis models that have been created and your current understanding of the firm's

position, what design strategy would you recommend? Why?

H. For the Of-the-Month-Club problem in Chapters 4 (exercises U, V, and W), 5 (exercises V and W), and 6 (exercise H):

1. Using the sequence diagrams and the CRUDE matrix, create a package diagram of the problem domain layer.

2. Perform a verification and validation walkthrough of the package diagram.

3. Based on the analysis models that have been created and your current understanding of the firm's position, what design strategy would you recommend? Why?

I. Suppose you are leading a project that will implement a new course-enrollment system for your university. You are thinking about either using a packaged course-enrollment application or outsourcing the job to an external consultant. Create an outline for an RFP to which interested vendors and consultants could respond.

J. Suppose you and your friends are starting a small business painting houses in the summertime. You need to buy a software package that handles the financial transactions of the business. Create an alternative matrix that compares three packaged systems (e.g., Quicken, MS Money, Quickbooks). Which alternative appears to be the best choice?

MINICASES

1. Susan, president of MOTO, Inc., a human resources management firm, is reflecting on the client management software system her organization purchased four years ago. At that time, the firm had just gone through a major growth spurt, and the mixture of automated and manual procedures that had been used to manage client accounts became unwieldy. Susan and Nancy, her IS department head, researched and selected the package that is currently used. Susan had heard about the software at a professional conference she attended, and, at least initially, it worked fairly

well for the firm. Some of their procedures had to change to fit the package, but they expected that and were prepared for it.

Since that time, MOTO, Inc., has continued to grow, not only through an expansion of the client base but also through the acquisition of several smaller employment-related businesses. MOTO, Inc., is a much different business than it was four years ago. Along with expanding to offer more diversified human resources management services, the firm's support staff has also expanded. Susan and Nancy are particularly proud of the IS department they have built up over the years. Using strong ties with a local university, an attractive compensation package, and a good working environment, the IS department is well staffed with competent, innovative people, plus a steady stream of college interns that keeps the department fresh and lively. One of the IS teams pioneered the use of the Internet to offer MOTO's services to a whole new market segment, an experiment that has proved very successful.

It seems clear that a major change is needed in the client-management software, and Susan has already begun to plan financially to undertake such a project. This software is a central part of MOTO's operations, and Susan wants to be sure that a high-quality system is obtained this time. She knows that the vendor of their current system has made some revisions and additions to its product line. A number of other software vendors also offer products that may be suitable. Some of these vendors did not exist when the purchase was made four years ago. Susan is also considering Nancy's suggestion that the IS department develop a custom software application.

  a. Outline the issues that Susan should consider that would support the development of a custom software application in-house.

  b. Outline the issues that Susan should consider that would support the purchase of a software package.

  c. Within the context of a systems-development project, when should the decision of make-versus-buy be made? How should Susan proceed? Explain your answer.

2. Refer to Minicase 1 (West Star Marinas) in Chapter 5. After all the analysis models (both the as-is and to-be models) for West Star Marinas were completed, the director of operations finally understood why it was important to understand the as-is system before delving into the development of the to-be system.

However, you now tell him that the to-be models are only the problem-domain portion of the design. He is now very confused. After explaining to him the advantages of using a layered approach to developing the system, he says, "I don't care about reusability or maintenance. I only want the system to be implemented as soon as possible. You IS types are always trying to pull a fast one on the users. Just get the system completed."

What is your response to the Director of Operations? Do you jump into implementation as he seems to want? What do you do next?

3. Refer to the analysis models that you created for professional and scientific staff management (PSSM) for Minicase 2 in Chapter 4 and for Minicase 1 in Chapter 6.

  a. Using the sequence diagrams and the CRUDE matrix, create a package diagram of the problem domain layer.

  b. Perform a verification and validation walkthrough of the package diagram.

  c. Based on the analysis models that have been created and your current understanding of the firm's position, what design strategy would you recommend? Why?

4. Refer to the analysis models that you created for Holiday Travel Vehicles for Minicase 2 in Chapter 5 and for Minicase 2 in Chapter 6.

  a. Using the sequence diagrams and the CRUDE matrix, create a package diagram of the problem domain layer.

  b. Perform a verification and validation walkthrough of the package diagram.

  c. Based on the analysis models that have been created and your current understanding of the firm's position, what design strategy would you recommend? Why?

CHAPTER 8

CLASS AND METHOD DESIGN

$\mathbf{T}$he most important step of the design phase is designing the individual classes and methods. Object-oriented systems can be quite complex, so analysts need to create instructions and guidelines for programmers that clearly describe what the system must do. This chapter presents a set of activities and techniques used to design classes and methods. Together they are used to ensure that the object-oriented design communicates how the system needs to be coded.

OBJECTIVES

- Be able to specify, restructure, and optimize object designs.
- Be able to identify the reuse of predefined classes, libraries, frameworks, and components.
- Be able to specify constraints and contracts.
- Be able to create a method specification.

INTRODUCTION

WARNING: *This material may be hazardous to your mental stability*. Not really, but now that we have your attention, you must realize that this material is fairly technical in nature and that it is extremely important in today's "flat" world. Today, much of the actual implementation will be done in a different geographic location than where the analysis and design are performed. We must ensure that the design is specified in a "correct" manner and that there is no, or at least minimal, ambiguity in the design specification.

In today's flat world, the common language spoken among developers is very likely to be UML and some object-oriented language, such as Java, and not English. English has always been and always will be ambiguous. Furthermore, to what variety of English do we refer? As both Oscar Wilde and George Bernard Shaw independently pointed out, the United States and England are divided by a common language.

Practically speaking, Class and Method design is where all the work actually gets done during design. No matter on which layer you are focusing, the classes, which will be used to create the system objects, must be designed. Some people believe that with reusable class libraries and off-the-shelf components, this type of low-level, or detailed, design is a waste of time and that we should jump immediately into the "real" work: coding the system. However, past experience shows that low-level, or detailed, design is critical despite the use of libraries and components. Detailed design is still very important for three reasons. First, with today's modern CASE tools, quite a bit of the actual code can be generated by the tool from the detailed design. Second, even preexisting classes and components need to be understood, organized, and pieced together. Third, it is still common for the project team to have to write some code and produce original classes that support the application logic of the system.

Jumping right into coding will guarantee disastrous results. For example, even though the use of layers can simplify the individual classes, they can increase the complexity of the interactions between them. If the classes are not designed carefully, the resulting system can be very inefficient. Or worse, the instances of the classes (i.e., the objects) will not be capable of communicating with each other, which will result in the system's not working properly.

In an object-oriented system, changes can take place at different levels of abstraction. These levels include variable, method, class/object, package,[1] library, and/or application/ system levels (see Figure 8-1). The changes that take place at one level can affect other levels (e.g., changes to a class can affect the package level, which can affect both the system level and the library level, which in turn can cause changes back down at the class level). Finally, changes can occur at different levels at the same time.

The good news is that the detailed design of the individual classes and methods is fairly straightforward. The interactions among the objects on the problem-domain layer have been designed, in some detail, during analysis (see Chapters 4 through 6). The other layers (data management, human–computer interaction, and physical architecture) are highly dependent on the problem-domain layer. Therefore, if the problem-domain classes are designed correctly, the design of the classes on the other layers will fall into place, relatively speaking.

That being said, it has been our experience that many project teams are much too quick at jumping into writing code for the classes without first designing them. Some of this has been caused by the fact that object-oriented systems analysis and design has evolved from object-oriented programming. Furthermore, with the growing popularity of agile approaches and their focus on the idea that the code is the design, this problem could become overwhelming. Until recently there has been a general lack of accepted guidelines on how to design and

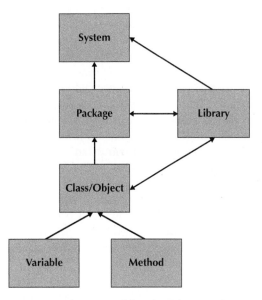

FIGURE 8-1
Levels of Abstraction in Object-Oriented Systems

Source: Based on material from David P. Tegarden, Steven D. Sheetz, and David E. Monarchi, "A Software Complexity Model of Object-Oriented Systems," *Decision Support Systems* 13 (March 1995): 241–262.

[1] Other names for a package include cluster, partition, pattern, subject, and subsystem.

develop effective object-oriented systems. However, with the acceptance of UML as a standard object notation, standardized approaches based on work of many object methodologists have begun to emerge.[2]

OBJECT DESIGN ACTIVITIES

The design activities for classes and methods are really an extension of the analysis and evolution activities presented previously (see Chapters 4 through 7). In this case, we expand the descriptions of the partitions, layers, and classes. Practically speaking, the expanded descriptions are created through the activities that take place during the detailed design of the classes and methods. The activities used to design classes and methods include additional specification of the current model, identifying opportunities for reuse, restructuring the design, optimizing the design, and, finally, mapping the problem-domain classes to an implementation language. Of course, any changes made to a class on one layer can cause the classes on the other layers that are coupled to it to be modified as well.

Adding Specifications

At this point in the development of the system, it is crucial to review the current set of functional, structural, and behavioral models. First, we should ensure that the classes on the problem-domain layer are both necessary and sufficient to solve the underlying problem. To do this, we need to be sure that there are no missing attributes or methods and no extra or unused attributes or methods in each class. Furthermore, are there any missing or extra classes? If we have done our job well during analysis, there will be few, if any, attributes, methods, or classes to add to the models. And it is unlikely that we have any extra attributes, methods, or classes to delete from the models. However, we still need to ensure that we have factored, abstracted, and refined the evolving models and created the relevant partitions and collaborations (see Chapter 7).

Second, we need to finalize the *visibility* (hidden or visible) of the attributes and methods in each class. Depending on the object-oriented programming language used, this could be predetermined. [For example, in Smalltalk, attributes are hidden and methods are visible. Other languages allow the programmer to set the visibility of each attribute or method. For example, in C++ and Java, you can set the visibility to private (hidden), public (visible), or protected (visible to subclasses, but not to other classes).[3]] By default, most object-oriented analysis and design approaches assume Smalltalk's approach.

Third, we need to decide on the signature of every method in every class. The *signature* of a method comprises three parts: the name of the method, the parameters or arguments that must be passed to the method, including their object type, and the type of value that the method will return to the calling method. The signature of a method, also known as the method's *protocol*, is related to the method's *contract*.[4]

Fourth, we need to define any *constraints* that must be preserved by the objects (e.g., an attribute of an object that can have values only in a certain range). There are three different types of constraints: preconditions, postconditions, and invariants.[5] These are captured in the

[2] For example, OPEN [I. Graham, B. Henderson-Seller, and H. Yanoussi, *The Open Process Specification* (Reading, MA: Addison-Wesley, 1997)], RUP [P. Kruchten, *The Rational Unified Process: An Introduction*, 2nd Ed. (Reading, MA: Addison-Wesley, 2000)], and the Enhanced Unified Process (see Chapter 1).

[3] It is also possible to control visibility through packages and friends.

[4] Contracts were introduced in Chapter 5, and they are described in detail later in this chapter.

[5] Constraints are described in more detail later in this chapter.

form of contracts and assertions added to the CRC cards and class diagrams. We also must decide how to handle a violation of a constraint. Should the system simply abort? Should the system automatically undo the change that caused the violation? Should the system let the end user determine the approach to correct the violation? In other words, the designer must design the errors that the system is expected to handle. It is best not to leave these types of design decisions for the programmer to solve. Violations of a constraint are known as *exceptions* in languages such as C++ and Java.

Even though we have described these activities in the context of the problem-domain layer, they are also applicable to the other layers: data management (Chapter 9), human–computer interaction (Chapter 10), and physical architecture (Chapter 11).

Identifying Opportunities for Reuse

Previously, we looked at possibly employing reuse in our models in analysis through the use of *patterns* (see Chapter 5). In design, in addition to using analysis patterns, there are opportunities for using design patterns, frameworks, libraries, and components. The opportunities vary depending on which layer is being reviewed. For example, it is doubtful that a class library will be of much help on the problem-domain layer, but a class library could be of great help on the foundation layer.

Like analysis patterns, *design patterns* are simply useful grouping of collaborating classes that provide a solution to a commonly occurring problem. The primary difference between analysis and design patterns is that design patterns are useful in solving "a general design problem in a particular context,"[6] whereas analysis patterns tended to aid in filling out a problem-domain representation. For example, a useful design pattern is the Whole-Part pattern (see Figure 8-2a). The Whole-Part pattern explicitly supports the Aggregation and Composition relationships within the UML. Another useful design pattern is the Iterator pattern (see Figure 8-2b). The primary purpose of the Iterator pattern is to provide the designer with a standard approach to support traversing different types of collections. By using this pattern, regardless of the collection type (Concrete Aggregate), the designer knows that the collection will need to create an iterator (Concrete Iterator) that customizes the standard operations used to traverse the collection: first(), next(), isDone(), and currentItem(). Given the number of collections typically found in business applications, this pattern is one of the more useful ones. For example, in Figure 8-3a, we replicate a portion of both the Appointment and Library problems discussed in previous chapters, and in Figure 8-3b we show how the Iterator pattern can be applied to those sections of their evolving designs. Finally, some of the design patterns support different physical architectures (see Chapter 11). For example, the Forwarder-Receiver pattern (see Figure 8-2c) supports a peer-to-peer architecture. Many design patterns are available in C++ or Java source code.

A *framework* is composed of a set of implemented classes that can be used as a basis for implementing an application. Most frameworks allow us to create subclasses to inherit from classes in the framework. There are object-persistence frameworks that can be purchased and used to add persistence to the problem-domain classes, which would be helpful on the data management layer. Of course, when inheriting from classes in a framework, we are creating a dependency (i.e., increasing the inheritance coupling from the subclass to the superclass). Therefore, if we use a framework and the vendor makes changes to the framework, we will have to at least recompile the system when we upgrade to the new version of the framework.

A *class library* is similar to a framework in that it typically has a set of implemented classes that were designed for reuse. However, frameworks tend to be more domain specific.

---

[6] Erich Gamma, Richard Helm, Ralph Johnson, and John Vlissides, *Design Patterns: Elements of Reusable Object-Oriented Software* (Reading, MA: Addison-Wesley, 1995).

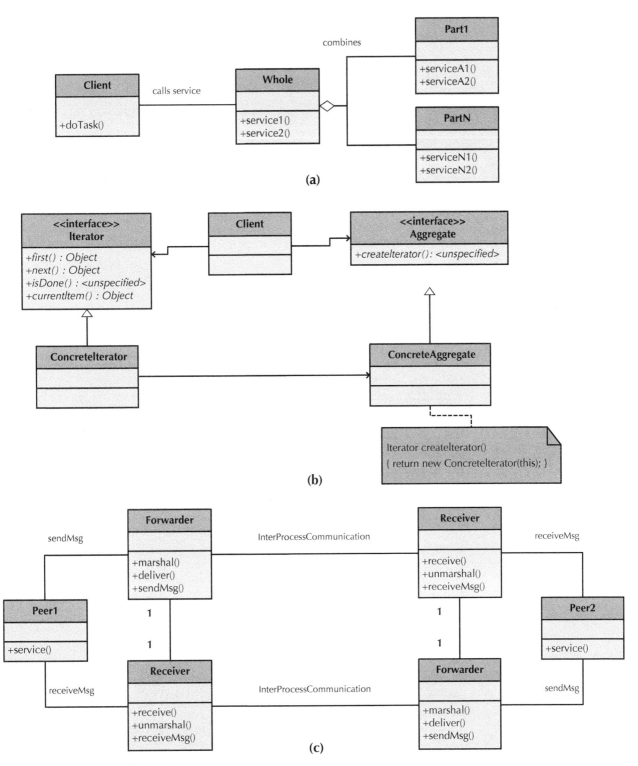

FIGURE 8-2 Sample Design Patterns

Sources: Based upon material from F. Buschmann, R. Meunier, H. Rohnert, P. Sommerlad, and M. Stal, *Pattern-Oriented Software Architecture: A System of Patterns* (Chichester, UK: Wiley, 1996); and E. Gamma, R. Helm, R. Johnson, and J. Vlissides, *Design Patterns: Elements of Reusable Object-Oriented Software* (Reading, MA: Addison-Wesley, 1995).

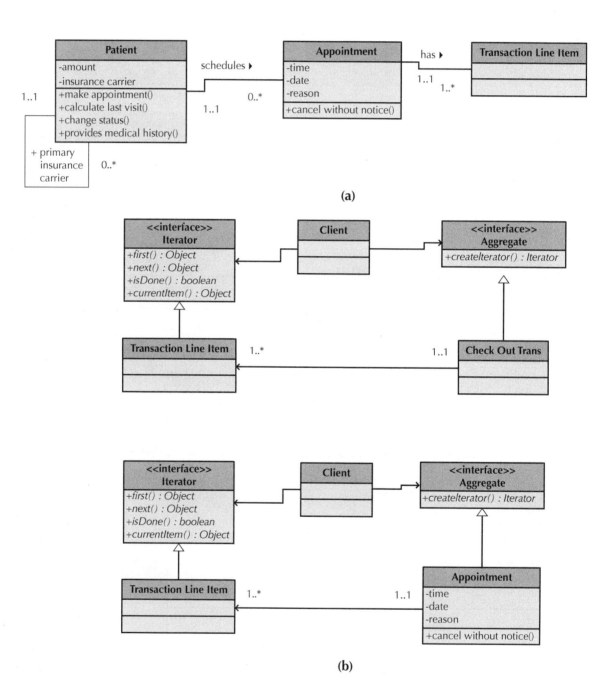

FIGURE 8-3 Iterator Design Pattern Applied to Library and Appointment Problems

In fact, frameworks may be built using a class library. A typical class library could be purchased to support numerical or statistical processing, file management (data management layer), or user interface development (human–computer interaction layer). In some cases, instances of classes contained in the class library can be created, and in other cases, classes in the class library can be extended by creating subclasses based on them. As with frameworks, if we use inheritance to reuse the classes in the class library, we will run into all the issues dealing with inheritance coupling and connascence. If we directly instantiate classes in the class library, we will create a dependency between our object and the library object based on the signatures of the methods in the library object. This increases the interaction coupling between the class library object and our object.

A *component* is a self-contained, encapsulated piece of software that can be plugged into a system to provide a specific set of required functionalities. Today, there are many components available for purchase. A component has a well-defined *API (application program interface)*. An API is essentially a set of method interfaces to the objects contained in the component. The internal workings of the component are hidden behind the API. Components can be implemented using class libraries and frameworks. However, components also can be used to implement frameworks. Unless the API changes between versions of the component, upgrading to a new version normally requires only linking the component back into the application. As such, recompilation typically is not required.

Which of these approaches should we use? It depends on what we are trying to build. In general, frameworks are used mostly to aid in developing objects on the physical architecture, human–computer interaction, or data management layers; components are used primarily to simplify the development of objects on the problem-domain and human–computer interaction layers; and class libraries are used to develop frameworks and components and to support the foundation layer. Whichever of these reuse approaches you use, you must remember that reuse brings many potential benefits and possible problems. For example, the software has previously been verified and validated, which should reduce the amount of testing required for our system. However as stated before, if the software on which we are basing our system changes, then most likely, we will also have to change our system. Furthermore, if the software is from a third-party firm, we are creating a dependency from our firm (or our client's firm) to the third-party vendor. Consequently, we need to have some confidence that the vendor will be in business for a while.

Restructuring the Design

Once the individual classes and methods have been specified and the class libraries, frameworks, and components have been incorporated into the evolving design, we should use factoring to restructure the design. *Factoring* (Chapter 7) is the process of separating out aspects of a method or class into a new method or class to simplify the overall design. For example, when reviewing a set of classes on a particular layer, we might discover that a subset of them shares a similar definition. In that case, it may be useful to factor out the similarities and create a new class. Based on the issues related to cohesion, coupling, and connascence, the new class may be related to the old classes via inheritance (generalization) or through an aggregation or association relationship.

Another process that is useful for restructuring the evolving design is *normalization*. Normalization is described in Chapter 9 in relation to relational databases. However, normalization can be useful at times to identify potential classes that are missing from the design. Also related to normalization is the requirement to implement the actual association and aggregation relationships as attributes. Virtually no object-oriented programming language differentiates between attributes and association and aggregation relationships. Therefore, all association and aggregation relationships must be converted to attributes in the classes. For example in Figure 8-4a, the Customer and State classes are associated with the Order class. Furthermore, the Product-Order association class is associated with both the Order and Product classes. One of the first things that must be done is to convert the Product Order Association class to a normal class. Notice the multiplicity values for the new associations between the Order and the Product Order classes and the Product Order and Product classes (see Figure 8-4b). Next, we need to convert all associations to attributes that represent the relationships between the affected classes. In this case, the Customer class must have an Orders attribute added to represent the set of orders that an instance of the Customer class may possess; the Order class must add attributes to reference instances of the Customer, State, and Product Order classes; the State class must have an attribute added to it to reference all of the instances of the Order class that is associated with that particular state; the new Product Order class must have attributes that allow an instance of the Product Order class to reference which instance of the Order class and which instance of the Product class is relevant to it; and, finally, the Product class must add an attribute that references the relevant instances of the Product Order class (see Figure 8-4c). As you can see, even in this very small example, many changes need to be made to ready the design for implementation.

Finally, all inheritance relationships should be challenged to ensure that they support only a generalization/specialization (a-kind-of) semantics. Otherwise, all the problems mentioned previously with inheritance coupling, class cohesion, and generalization/specialization cohesion will come to pass.

Optimizing the Design[7]

Up until now, we have focused our energy on developing an understandable design. With all the classes, patterns, collaborations, partitions, and layers designed and with all the class libraries, frameworks, and components included in the design, understandability has been our primary focus. However, increasing the understandability of a design typically creates an inefficient design. Conversely, focusing on efficiency issues will deliver a design that is more difficult to understand. A good practical design manages the inevitable trade-offs that must occur.[8]

The first optimization to consider is to review the access paths between objects. In some cases, a message from one object to another has a long path to traverse (i.e., it goes through many objects). If the path is long and the message is sent frequently, a redundant path should be considered. Adding an attribute to the calling object that will store a direct connection to the object at the end of the path can accomplish this.

A second optimization is to review each attribute of each class. It should be determined which methods use the attributes and which objects use the methods. If the only methods that use an attribute are read and update methods and only instances of a single class send messages to read and update the attribute, then the attribute may belong with the calling class instead of the called class. Moving the attribute to the calling class will substantially speed up the system.

A third optimization is to review the direct and indirect fan-out of each method. *Fan-out* refers to the number of messages sent by a method. The direct fan-out is the number of

---

[7] The material contained in this section is based on James Rumbaugh, Michael Blaha, William Premerlani, Frederick Eddy, and William Lorensen, *Object-Oriented Modeling and Design* (Englewood Cliffs, NJ: Prentice Hall, 1991); Bernd Brugge and Allen H. Dutoit, *Object-Oriented Software Engineering: Conquering Complex and Changing Systems* (Englewood Cliffs, NJ: Prentice Hall, 2000).

[8] The optimizations described here are only suggestions. In all cases, the decision to implement one or more of these optimizations really depends on the problem domain of the system and the environment on which the system will reside, i.e., the data management layer (see Chapter 9), the human–computer interaction layer (see Chapter 10), and the physical architecture layer (see Chapter 11).

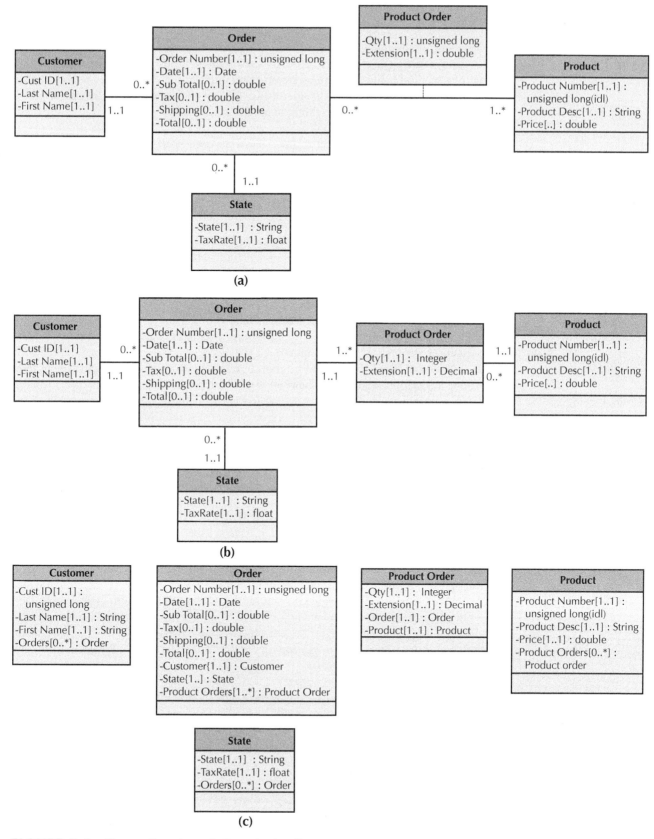

FIGURE 8-4 Converting Associations to Attributes

295

messages sent by the method itself, whereas the indirect fan-out also includes the number of messages sent by the methods called by the other methods in a message tree. If the fan-out of a method is high relative to the other methods in the system, the method should be optimized. One way to do this is to consider adding an index to the attributes used to send the messages to the objects in the message tree.

A fourth optimization is to look at the execution order of the statements in often-used methods. In some cases, it is possible to rearrange some of the statements to be more efficient. For example, if based on the objects in the system, it is known that a search routine can be narrowed by searching on one attribute before another one, then the search algorithm should be optimized by forcing it to always search in a predefined order.

A fifth optimization is to avoid recomputation by creating a *derived attribute* (or *active value*) (e.g., a total that stores the value of the computation). This is also known as *caching computational results*, and it can be accomplished by adding a *trigger* to the attributes contained in the computation (i.e., attributes on which the derived attribute is dependent). This would require a recomputation to take place only when one of the attributes that go into the computation is changed. Another approach is to simply mark the derived attribute for recomputation and delay the recomputation until the next time the derived attribute is accessed. This last approach delays the recomputation as long as possible. In this manner, a computation does not occur unless it must occur. Otherwise, every time a derived attribute needs to be accessed, a computation will be required.

A sixth optimization that should be considered deals with objects that participate in a one-to-one association; that is, they both must exist for either to exist. In this case, it might make sense, for efficiency purposes, to collapse the two defining classes into a single class. However, this optimization might need to be reconsidered when storing the "fatter" object in a database. Depending on the type of object persistence used (see Chapter 9), it can actually be more efficient to keep the two classes separate. Alternatively, it could make more sense for the two classes to be combined on the problem-domain layer but kept separate on the data management layer.

Mapping Problem-Domain Classes to Implementation Languages[9]

Up until this point, it has been assumed that the classes and methods in the models would be implemented directly in an object-oriented programming language. However, now it is important to map the current design to the capabilities of the programming language used. For example, if we have used multiple inheritance in our design but we are implementing in a language that supports only single inheritance, then the multiple inheritance must be factored out of the design. If the implementation is to be done in an object-based language, one that does not support inheritance,[10] or a non-object-based language, such as C, we must map the problem-domain objects to programming constructs that can be implemented using the chosen implementation environment.

Implementing Problem Domain Classes in a Single-Inheritance Language The only issue associated with implementing problem-domain objects is the factoring out of any multiple inheritance—i.e., the use of more than one superclass—used in the evolving design. For example, if you were to implement the solution in Java, Smalltalk, or Visual

---

[9] The mapping rules presented in this section are based on material in Coad and Yourdon, *Object-Oriented Design*.

[10] In this case, we are talking about implementation inheritance, not the interface inheritance. Interface inheritance supported by Visual Basic and Java supports only inheriting the requirements to implement certain methods, not any implementation. Java and Visual Basic.net also support single inheritance as described in this text.

Basic.net, you must factor out any multiple inheritance. The easiest way to do this is to use the following rule:

> **RULE 1a:** Convert the additional inheritance relationships to association relationships. The multiplicity of the new association from the subclass to the superclass should be 1..1. If the additional superclasses are concrete, that is, they can be instantiated themselves, then the multiplicity from the superclass to the subclass is 0..1. Otherwise, it is 1..1. Furthermore, an exclusive-or (XOR) constraint must be added between the associations. Finally, you must add appropriate methods to ensure that all information is still available to the original class.

or

> **RULE 1b:** Flatten the inheritance hierarchy by copying the attributes and methods of the additional superclass(es) down to all of the subclasses and remove the additional superclass from the design.[11]

Figure 8-5 demonstrates the application of these rules. Figure 8-5a portrays a simple example of multiple inheritance where Flying Car inherits from both Airplane and Car, and Amphibious Car inherits from both Car and Boat. Assuming that Car is concrete, we apply Rule 1a to part a, and we end up with the diagram in part b, where we have added the association between Flying Car and Car and the association between Amphibious Car and Boat. The multiplicities have been added correctly, and the XOR constraint has been applied. If we apply Rule 1b to part a, we end up with the diagram in part c, where all the attributes of Car have been copied down into Flying Car and Amphibious Car. In this latter case, you might have to deal with the effects of inheritance conflicts.

The advantage of Rule 1a is that all problem-domain classes identified during analysis are preserved. This allows maximum flexibility of maintenance of the design of the problem domain layer. However, Rule 1a increases the amount of message passing required in the system, and it has added processing requirements involving the XOR constraint, thus reducing the overall efficiency of the design. Accordingly, our recommendation is to limit Rule 1a to be applied only when dealing with "extra" superclasses that are concrete because they have an independent existence in the problem domain. Use Rule 1b when they are abstract because they do not have an independent existence from the subclass.

Implementing Problem Domain Objects in an Object-Based Language If we are going to implement our solution in an *object-based language* (i.e., a language that supports the creation of objects but does not support implementation inheritance), we must factor out all uses of inheritance from the problem-domain class design. Applying the preceding rule to all superclasses enables us to restructure our design without any inheritance.

Figure 8-6 demonstrates the application of the preceding rules. Figure 8-6a shows the same simple example of multiple inheritance portrayed in Figure 8-5, where Flying Car inherits from both Airplane and Car, and Amphibious Car inherits from both Car and Boat. Assuming that Airplane, Car, and Boat are concrete, we apply Rule 1a to part a and we end up with the diagram in part b, where we have added the associations, the multiplicities, and the XOR constraint. If we apply Rule 1b to part a, we end up with the diagram in part c, where all the attributes of the superclasses have been copied down into Flying Car and Amphibious Car. In this latter case, you might have to deal with the effects of inheritance conflicts.

---

[11] It is also a good idea to document this modification in the design so that in the future, modifications to the design can be maintained easily.

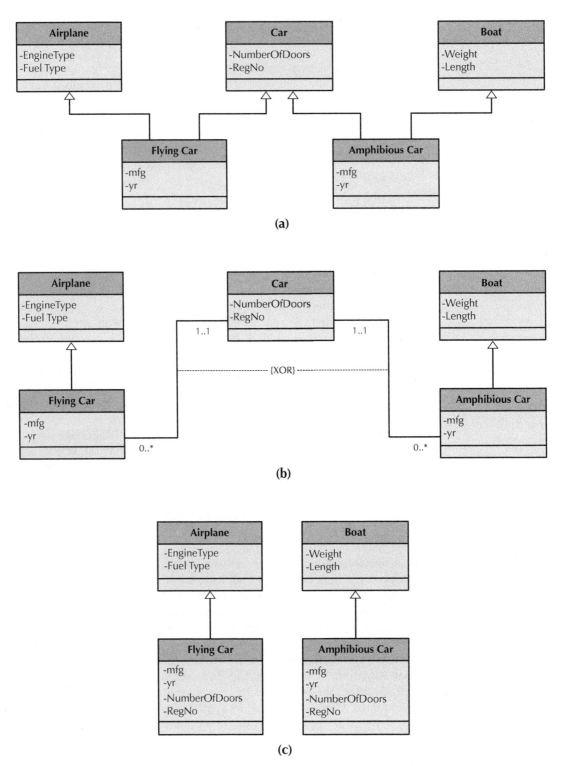

FIGURE 8-5 Factoring Out Multiple-Inheritance Effect for a Single-Inheritance Language

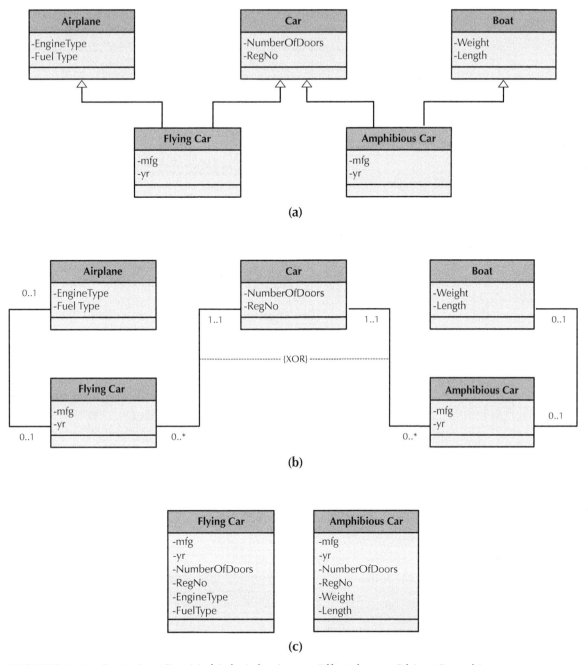

FIGURE 8-6 Factoring Out Multiple Inheritance Effect for an Object-Based Language

Implementing Problem-Domain Objects in a Traditional Language From a practical perspective, we are much better off implementing an object-oriented design in an object-oriented programming language, such as C++, Java, Objective-C, or Visual Basic.net. Practically speaking, the gulf between an object-oriented design and a traditional programming language is simply too great for mere mortals to be able to cross. The best advice that we can give about implementing an object-oriented design in a traditional programming language is to run away as fast and as far as possible from the project. However, if we are brave (foolish?) enough to attempt this, we must realize that in addition to factoring out inheritance from the design, we have to factor out all uses of polymorphism, dynamic binding, encapsulation, and information hiding. This is quite a bit of additional work to be accomplished. The way we factor these object-oriented features out of the detailed design of the system tends to be language dependent. Therefore, this is beyond the scope of this text.

CONSTRAINTS AND CONTRACTS

Contracts were introduced in Chapter 5 in association with collaborations. A contract formalizes the interactions between the client and server objects, where a *client* (*consumer*) object is an instance of a class that sends a message to a *server* (*supplier*) object that executes one of its methods in response to the request. Contracts are modeled on the legal notion of a contract, where both parties, client and server objects, have obligations and rights. Practically speaking, a contract is a set of constraints and guarantees. If the constraints are met, then the server object guarantees certain behavior.[12] Constraints can be written in a natural language (e.g., English), a semiformal language (e.g., *Structured English*[13]), or a formal language (e.g., UML's Object Constraint Language). Given the need for precise, unambiguous specification of constraints, we recommend using UML's Object Constraint Language.

The *Object Constraint Language (OCL)*[14] is a complete language designed to specify constraints. In this section, we provide a short overview of some of the more useful constructs contained in the language (see Figure 8-7). Essentially, all OCL expressions are simply a declarative statement that evaluates to either being true or false. If the expression evaluates to true, then the constraint has been satisfied. For example, if a customer had to have a less than a one hundred dollar balance owed to be allowed to place another credit order, the OCL expression would be:

balance owed <= 100.00

OCL also has the ability to traverse relationships between objects, e.g., if the amount on a purchase order is required to be the sum of the values of the individual purchase order lines, this can be modeled as:

amount = OrderLine.sum(getPrice())

OCL also provides the ability to model more-complex constraints with a set of logical operators: and, or, xor, and not. For example, if customers were to be given a discount only if they were a senior citizen or a "prime" customer, OCL could be used to model the constraint as:

age > 65 or customerType = "prime"

OCL provides many other constructs that can be used to build unique constraints. These include math-oriented operators, string operators, and relationship traversal operators. For

---

[12] The idea of using contracts in design evolved from the "Design by Contract" technique developed by Bertrand Meyer. See Bertrand Meyer, *Object-Oriented Software Construction* (Englewood Cliffs, NJ: Prentice Hall, 1988).

[13] We describe Structured English with Method Specification later in this chapter.

[14] For a complete description of the object constraint language, see Jos Warmer and Anneke Kleppe, *The Object Constraint Language: Precise Modeling with UML* (Reading, MA: Addison-Wesley, 1999).

Operator Type	Operator	Example
Comparison	=	a = 5
	<	a < 100
	<=	a <= 100
	>	a > 100
	>=	a >= 100
	<>	a <> 100
Logical	and	a and b
	or	a or b
	xor	a xor b
	not	not a
Math	+	a + b
	−	a − b
	*	a * b
	/	a / b
String	concat	a = b.concat(c)
Relationship Traversal	.	relationshipAttributeName.b
	::	superclassName::propertyName
Collection	size	a.size
	count(object)	a.count(b)
	includes(object)	a.includes(b)
	isEmpty	a.isEmpty
	sum()	a.sum(b,c,d)
	select(expression)	a.select(b > d)

FIGURE 8-7
Sample OCL
Constructs

example, if the printed name on a customer order should be the concatenation of the customer's first name and last name, then OCL could represent this constraint as:

printedName = firstName.concat(lastName)

We already have seen an example of the "." operator being used to traverse a relationship from Order to OrderLine above. The "::" operator allows the modeling of traversing inheritance relationships.

OCL also provides a set of operations that are used to support constraints over a collection of objects. For example, we demonstrated the use of the sum() operator above where we wanted to guarantee that the amount was equal to the summation of all of the prices of the items in the collection. The size operation returns the number of items in the collection. The count operation returns the number of occurrences in the collection of the specific object passed as its argument. The includes operation tests whether the object passed to it is already included in the collection. The isEmpty operation determines whether the collection is empty or not. The select operation provides support to model the identification of a subset of the collection based on the expression that is passed as its argument. Obviously, OCL provides a rich set of operators and operations in which to model constraints.

Types of Constraints

Three different types of constraints are typically captured in object-oriented design: preconditions, postconditions, and invariants.

Contracts are used primarily to establish the preconditions and postconditions for a method to be able to execute properly. A *precondition* is a constraint that must be met for a method to execute. For example, the parameters passed to a method must be valid for the method to execute. Otherwise, an exception should be raised. A *postcondition* is a constraint that must be met after the method executes, or the effect of the method execution must be undone. For example, the method cannot make any of the attributes of the object take on an invalid value. In this case, an exception should be raised, and the effect of the method's execution should be undone.

Whereas preconditions and postconditions model the constraints on an individual method, *invariants* model constraints that must always be true for all instances of a class. Examples of invariants include domains or types of attributes, multiplicity of attributes, and the valid values of attributes. This includes the attributes that model association and aggregation relationships. For example, if an association relationship is required, an invariant should be created that will enforce it to have a valid value for the instance to exist. Invariants are normally attached to the class. We can attach invariants to the CRC cards or class diagram by adding a set of assertions to them.

In Figure 8-8, the back of the CRC card constrains the attributes of an Order to specific types. For example, Order Number must be an unsigned long, and Customer must be an instance of the Customer class. Furthermore, additional invariants were added to four of the attributes. For example, Cust ID must not only be an unsigned long, but it also must have one and only one value [i.e., a multiplicity of (1..1)], and it must have the same value as the result of the GetCustID() message sent to the instance of Customer stored in the Customer attribute. Also shown is the constraint for an instance to exist, an instance of the Customer class, an instance of the State class, and at least one instance of the Product class must be associated with the Order object (see the Relationships section of the CRC card where the multiplicities are 1..1, 1..1, and 1..*, respectively). Figure 8-9 portrays the same set of invariants on a class diagram. However, if all invariants are placed on a class diagram, the diagram becomes very difficult to understand. Consequently, we recommend either extending the CRC card to document the invariants instead of attaching them all to the class diagram or creating a separate text document that contains them (see Figure 8-10).

Elements of a Contract

Contracts document the message passing that takes place between objects. Technically speaking, a contract should be created for each message sent and received by each object, one for each interaction. However, there would be quite a bit of duplication if this were done. In practice, a contract is created for each method that can receive messages from other objects (i.e., one for each visible method).

A contract should contain the information necessary for a programmer to understand what a method is to do (i.e., they are declarative in nature). This information includes the method name, class name, ID number, client objects, associated use cases, description, arguments received, type of data returned, and the pre- and postconditions.[15] Contracts do not have a detailed algorithmic description of how the method is to work. Detailed algorithmic

---

[15] Currently, there is no standard format for a contract. The contract in Figure 8-11 is based on material contained in Ian Graham, *Migrating to Object Technology* (Reading, MA: Addison-Wesley, 1995); Craig Larman, *Applying UML and Patterns: An Introduction to Object-Oriented Analysis and Design* (Englewood Cliffs, NJ: Prentice Hall, 1998); Meyer, *Object-Oriented Software Construction;* R. Wirfs-Brock, B. Wilkerson, and L. Wiener, *Designing Object-Oriented Software* (Englewood Cliffs, NJ: Prentice Hall, 1990).

Front:

Class Name: Order	**ID:** 2	**Type:** Concrete, Domain
Description: An Individual who needs to receive or has received medical attention		**Associated Use Cases:** 3

Responsibilities	Collaborators
Calculate subtotal	
Calculate tax	
Calculate shipping	
Calculate total	

(a)

Back:

Attributes:

Order Number (1..1) (unsigned long)

Date (1..1) (Date)

Sub Total (0..1) (double) {Sub Total = ProductOrder. sum(GetExtension())}

Tax (0..1) (double) (Tax = State.GetTaxRate() * Sub Total)

Shipping (0..1) (double)

Total (0..1) (double)

Customer (1..1) (Customer)

Cust ID (1..1) (unsigned long) {Cust ID = Customer. GetCustID()}

State (1..1) (State)

StateName (1..1) (String) {State Name = State. GetState()}

Relationships:

Generalization (a-kind-of):

Aggregation (has-parts):

Other Associations: Customer {1..1} State {1..1}Product {1..*}

FIGURE 8-8
Invariants on a CRC Card

(b)

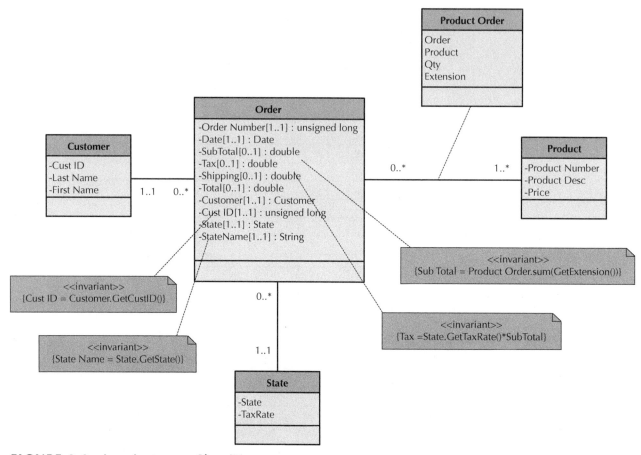

FIGURE 8-9 Invariants on a Class Diagram

FIGURE 8-10
Invariants in a Text
File

Order class invariants:

Cust ID = Customer.GetCustID()

State Name = Sate.GetState()

Sub Total = ProductOrder.sum(GetExtension())

Tax = State.GetTaxRate() * Sub Total

descriptions typically are documented in a method specification (as described later in this chapter). In other words, a contract is composed of the information required for the developer of a client object to know what messages can be sent to the server objects and what the client can expect in return. Figure 8-11 shows a sample format for a contract.

Because each contract is associated with a specific method and a specific class, the contract must document them. The ID number of the contract is used to provide a unique identifier for every contract. The Clients (Consumers) element of a contract is a list of classes and methods that send a message to this specific method. This list is determined by reviewing the sequence diagrams associated with the server class.[16] The Associated Use Cases element is a

---

[16] The Clients (Consumers) list can also be derived from the more detailed form of the CRUDE matrix (Class/Actor: Operation-by-Class/Actor: Operation). Furthermore, this more detailed matrix is useful to begin identifying role-based access control issues related to the security nonfunctional requirements discussed in the later in the book.

Method Name:	Class Name:		ID:
Clients (Consumers):			
Associated Use Cases:			
Description of Responsibilities:			
Arguments Received:			
Type of Value Returned:			
Pre-Conditions:			
Post-Conditions:			

FIGURE 8-11
Sample Contract Form

list of use cases in which this method is used to realize the implementation of the use case. The use cases listed here can be found by reviewing the server class's CRC card and the associated sequence diagrams. Also, as described in Chapter 5, by associating the use cases with the individual classes allows the analyst to be able to track back to determine who the primary actor and stakeholders are. This provides the information required to limit the access to the instances of the class to the individuals who play the roles identified by the primary actors and stakeholders. Between the Clients (Consumers) and the Associated Use Cases list, the information to support role-based access control to address the security nonfunctional requirements can be identified. We cover security issues in more detail in Chapters 9–12.

The Description of Responsibilities provides an informal description of what the method is to perform, not how it is to do it. The arguments received are the data types of the parameters passed to the method, and the value returned is the data type of the value that the method returns to its clients. Together with the method name, they form the signature of the method.

The pre- and postcondition elements are where the pre- and postconditions for the method are recorded. Recall that pre- and postconditions can be written in a natural language, a semiformal language, or a formal language. As with invariants, we recommend that you use UML's Object Constraint Language.[17]

Example

In this example, we return to the order example shown in Figures 8-4, 8-8, 8-9, and 8-10. In this case, we limit the discussion to the design of the addOrder method for the Customer class. The first decision we must make is how to specify the design of the relationship from

---

[17] See Warmer and Kleppe, *The Object Constraint Language: Precise Modeling with UML.*

Customer to Order. By reviewing Figures 8-4, 8-8, and 8-9, we see that the relationship has a multiplicity of 0..* which means that an instance of customer may exist without having any orders or an instance of customer could have many orders. As shown in Figure 8-4c, the relationship has been converted to an attribute that can contain many instances of the Order class.

However, an important question that would not typically come up during analysis is whether the order objects should be kept in sorted order or not. Another question that is necessary to have answered for design purposes is how many orders could be expected by a customer. The answers to these two questions will determine how we should organize the orders from the customer object's perspective. If the number of orders is going to be relatively small and the orders don't have to be kept in sorted order, then using a built-in programming language construct such as a vector is sufficient. However, if the number of orders is going to be large or the orders must be kept in sorted order, then some form of a sorted data structure, such as a linked list, is necessary. For example purposes, we assume that a customer's orders will need to be kept in sorted order and that there will be a large number of them. Therefore, instead of using a vector to contain the orders, we use a sorted singly linked list.

To keep the design of the Customer class as close to the problem domain representation as possible, the design of the Customer class is based on the Iterator pattern in Figure 8-2. For simplicity purposes, we assume that an order is created before it is associated with the specific customer. Otherwise, given the additional constraints of the instance of State class and the instance of the Product Order class existing before an instance of Order can be created would also have to be taken into consideration. This assumption allows us to ignore the fact that an instance of State can have many orders, an instance of Order can have many instances of Product Order associated with it, and an instance of Product can have many instances of Product Order associated with it, which would require us to design many additional containers (vectors or other data structures).

Based on all of the above, a new class diagram fragment was created that represents a linked list-based relationship between instances of the Customer class and instances of the Order class (see Figure 8-12). By carefully comparing Figures 8-4 and 8-12, we see that the Iterator pattern idea has been included between the Customer and Order classes. The domain of the Orders relationship-based attribute of the Customer class has been replaced with OrderList to show that the list of orders will be contained in a list data structure. Figure 8-13 portrays how the relationship between a customer instance and a set of order instances is stored in a sorted singly linked list data structure. In this case, we see that a Customer object has an OrderList object associated with it, each OrderList object could have N OrderNode objects, and each OrderNode object will have an Order object. We see that each Order object is associated with a single Customer object. By comparing Figures 8-4 and 8-13, we see that the intention of the multiplicity constraints of the Orders attribute of Customer, where a customer can have many orders, and the multiplicity constraints of the Customer attribute of Orders is being modeled correctly. Finally, notice that one of the operations contained in the OrderList class is a private method. We will return to this specific point in the next section that addresses method specification.

Using Figures 8-11–8-13, contracts for the addOrder method of the Customer class and the insertOrder method for the OrderList class can be specified (see Figure 8-14). In the case of the addOrder method of the Customer class, we see that only instances of the Order class use the method (see Clients section), that the method only implements part of the logic that supports the addCustomerOrder use case (see Associated Use Cases section), and that the contract includes a short description of the methods responsibilities. We also see that the method receives a single argument of type Order and that it does not return anything (void). Finally, we see that both a precondition and a postcondition were specified.

Customer

-Cust ID[1..1] : unsigned long
-Last Name[1..1] : String
-First Name[1..1] : String
-Orders[1..1] : OrderList
-createOrderList() : OrderList
+addOrder(in anOrder : Order) : void

OrderList

-FirstNode[0..1] : OrderNode
-CurrentNode[0..1] : OrderNode
-LastNode[0..1] : OrderNode
+advance() : void
+begOfList?() : boolean
+endOfList?() : boolean
+emptyList?() : boolean
+resetList() : void
+getCurrentOrderNode() : OrderNode
-middleListInsert(in newOrderNode : OrderNode) : void
+insertOrder(in anOrder : Order) : void

OrderNode

-NextNode[0..1] : OrderNode
-Order[1..1] : Order
+OrderNode(in anOrder : Order)
+getOrder() : Order
+getNextOrderNode() : OrderNode
+setNextOrderNode(in anOrderNode : OrderNode) : void

Order

-Order Number[1..1] : unsigned long
-Date[1..1] : Date
-SubTotal[0..1] : double
-Tax[0..1] : double
-Shipping[0..1] : double
-Total[0..1] : double
-Customer[1..1] : Customer
-State[1..1] : State
-Product Orders[1..*] : Product Order

FIGURE 8-12 Class Diagram Fragment of the Customer to Order Relationship Modeled as a Sorted Singly Linked List

307

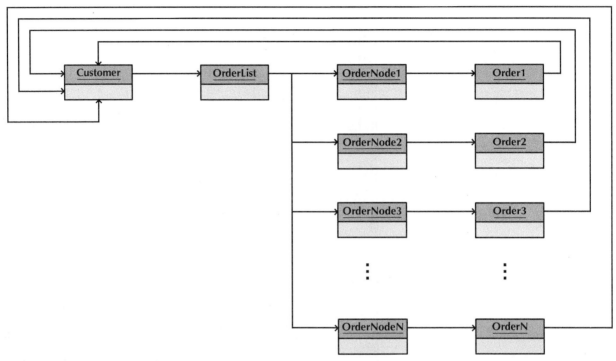

FIGURE 8-13 Object Diagram of the Customer to Order Relationship Modeled as a Sorted Singly Linked List

The precondition simply states that the new Order object cannot be a member of the current list of Orders; that is, the order cannot have previously been associated with this customer. The postcondition, on the other hand, specifies that the new list of orders must be equal to the old list of orders (@pre) plus the new order object (including).

The contract for the insertOrder method for the OrderList class is somewhat simpler than the addOrder method's contract. From a practical perspective, the insertOrder method implements part of the addOrder method's logic. Specifically speaking, it implements that actual insertion of the new order object into the specific data structure chosen to manage the list of Order objects associated with the specific Customer object. Consequently, because we already have specified the precondition and postcondition for the addOrder method, we do not have to further specify the same constraints for the insertOrder method. However, this does implicitly increase the dependence of the Customer objects on the implementation chosen for the list of customer orders. This is a good example of moving from the problem domain to the solution domain. While we were focusing on the problem domain during analysis, the actual implementation of the list of orders was never considered. However, because we now are designing the implementation of the relationship between the Customer objects and the Order objects, we have had to move away from the language of the end user and toward the language of the programmer. During design, the focus moves toward optimizing the code to run faster on the computer and not worrying about the end user's ability to understand the inner workings of the system; from an end user's perspective, the system should become more of a black box with which they interact. As we move farther into the detailed design of the implementation of the problem domain classes, some solution domain classes, such as the approach to implement relationships, will creep into the specification of the problem domain layer. In this particular example, the OrderList and OrderNode classes

Method Name:	addOrder	Class Name:	Customer	ID:	36

Clients (consumers): Order

Associated Use Cases:
addCustomerOrder

Description of Responsibilities:
Implement the necessary behavior to add a new order to an existing customer keeping the orders in sorted order by the order's order number.

Arguments Received:
anOrder:Order

Type of Value Returned: void

Pre-Conditions:
not orders.includes(anOrder)

Post-Conditions:
Orders = Orders@pre.including(anOrder)

Method Name:	insertOrder	Class Name:	OrderList	ID:	123

Clients (consumers): Customer

Associated Use Cases:
addCustomerOrder

Description of Responsibilities:
Implement inserting an Order object into an OrderNode object and manage the insertion of the OrderNode object into the current location in the sorted singly linked list of orders.

Arguments Received:
anOrder:Order

Type of Value Returned: void

Pre-Conditions:
None.

Post-Conditions:
None.

FIGURE 8-14
Sample Contract for the add Order Method of the Customer Class and the insert Order Method of the Order List Class

also could be used to implement the relationships from State objects to Order objects, from Order objects to ProductOrder objects, and from Product objects to ProductOrder objects (see Figure 8-4). Given our simple example, one can clearly see that specifying the design of the problem domain layer could include many additional solution domain classes to be specified on the problem domain layer.

METHOD SPECIFICATION

Once the analyst has communicated the big picture of how the system needs to be put together, he or she needs to describe the individual classes and methods in enough detail so that programmers can take over and begin writing code. Methods on the CRC cards, class diagram, and contracts are described using *method specifications*. Method specifications are written documents that include explicit instructions on how to write the code to implement the method. Typically, project team members write a specification for each method and then pass them all along to programmers who write the code during implementation of the project. However, with agile development approaches, the creation of method specifications is never done. Instead, given that the developers are programmers, the developers simply write the code and skip the specifications. Specifications need to be very clear and easy to understand, or programmers will be slowed down trying to decipher vague or incomplete instructions.

There is no formal syntax for a method specification, so every organization uses its own format, often using a form like the one in Figure 8-15. Typical method specification forms contain four components that convey the information that programmers will need for writing the appropriate code: general information, events, message passing, and algorithm specification.

General Information

The top of the form in Figure 8-15 contains general information, such as the name of the method, name of the class in which this implementation of the method will reside, ID number, Contract ID (which identifies the contract associated with this method implementation), programmer assigned, the date due, and the target programming language. This information is used to help manage the programming effort.

Events

The second section of the form is used to list the events that trigger the method. An *event* is a thing that happens or takes place. Clicking the mouse generates a mouse event, pressing a key generates a keystroke event—in fact, almost everything the user does generates an event.

In the past, programmers used procedural programming languages that contained instructions that were implemented in a predefined order, as determined by the computer system, and users were not allowed to deviate from the order. Many programs today are *event driven* (e.g., programs written in languages such as Visual Basic, Objective C, C++, or Java), and event-driven programs include methods that are executed in response to an event initiated by the user, system, or another method. After initialization, the system waits for an event to occur. When it does, a method is fired that carries out the appropriate task, and then the system waits once again.

We have found that many programmers still use method specifications when programming in event-driven languages, and they include the event section on the form to capture when the method will be invoked. Other programmers have switched to other design tools that capture event-driven programming instructions, such as the behavioral state machine described in Chapter 6.

Method Name:	Class Name:	ID:
Contract ID:	Programmer:	Date Due:

Programming Language:

❏ Visual Basic ❏ Smalltalk ❏ C++ ❏ Java

Triggers/Events:

Arguments Received: Data Type:	Notes:

Messages Sent & Arguments Passed: ClassName.MethodName:	Data Type:	Notes:

Arguments Returned: Data Type:	Notes:

Algorithm Specification:

Misc. Notes:

FIGURE 8-15
Method Specification Form

Message Passing

The next sections of the method specification describe the message passing to and from the method, which are identified on the sequence diagrams. Programmers need to understand what arguments are being passed into, passed from, and returned by the method because the arguments ultimately translate into attributes and data structures within the actual method.

Algorithm Specifications

Algorithm specifications can be written in Structured English or some type of formal language.[18] Structured English is simply a formal way of writing instructions that describe the steps of a process. Because it is the first step toward the implementation of the method, it looks much like a simple programming language. Structured English uses short sentences that clearly describe exactly what work is performed on what data. There are many versions of Structured English because there are no formal standards; each organization has its own type of Structured English. Figure 8-16 shows some examples of commonly used Structured English statements.

Action statements are simple statements that perform some action. An If statement controls actions that are performed under different conditions, and a For statement (or a While statement) performs some actions until some condition is reached, i.e., these support the iteration or looping constructs of programming languages. A Case statement is an advanced form of an If statement that has several mutually exclusive branches.

If the algorithm of a method is complex, a tool that can be useful for algorithm specification is UML's *activity diagram* (Chapters 4 and 6). Recall that activity diagrams can be used to specify any type of process. Obviously, an algorithm specification represents a process. However, owing to the nature of object orientation, processes tend to be highly distributed over many little methods over many objects. Needing to use an activity diagram to specify the algorithm of a method can, in fact, hint at a problem in the design. For example, the method should be further decomposed or there could be missing classes.

The last section of the method specification provides space for other information that needs to be communicated to the programmer, such as calculations, special business rules, calls to subroutines or libraries, and other relevant issues. This also can point out changes or

Common Statements	Example
Action Statement	Profits = Revenues − Expenses Generate Inventory-Report
If Statement	IF Customer Not in the Customer Object Store THEN Add Customer record to Customer Object Store ELSE Add Current-Sale to Customer's Total-Sales Update Customer record in Customer Object Store

For Statement	FOR all Customers in Customer Object Store DO
	    Generate a new line in the Customer-Report
	    Add Customer's Total-Sales to Report-Total

Case Statement	CASE
	    IF Income < 10,000: Marginal-tax-rate = 10 percent
	    IF Income < 20,000: Marginal-tax-rate = 20 percent
	    IF Income < 30,000: Marginal-tax-rate = 31 percent
	    IF Income < 40,000: Marginal-tax-rate = 35 percent
	    ELSE Marginal-Tax-Rate = 38 percent
	ENDCASE

FIGURE 8-16
Structured English

---

[18] For our purposes, Structured English will suffice. However, there has been some work with the Catalysis, Fusion, and Syntropy methodologies to include formal languages, such as VDM and Z, into specifying object-oriented systems.

improvements that will be made to any of the other design documentation based on problems that the analyst detected during the specification process.[19]

Example

This example continues the addition of a new order for a customer described in the previous section (see Figure 8-17). Even though in most cases, because there are libraries of data structure

Method Name: insertOrder	Class Name: OrderList	ID: 100
Contract ID: 123	Programmer: J. Doe	Date Due: 1/1/12

Programming Language:

❑ Visual Basic ❑ Smalltalk ❑ C++ ❑ Java

Triggers/Events:

Customer places an order

Arguments Received: Data Type:	Notes:
Order	The new customer's new order.

Messages Sent & Arguments Passed: ClassName.MethodName:	Data Type:	Notes:
OrderNode.new()	Order	
OrderNode.getOrder()		
Order.getOrderNumber()		
OrderNode.setNextNode()	OrderNode	
self.middleListInsert()	OrderNode	

Arguments Returned: Data Type:	Notes:
void	

Algorithm Specification:

See Figures 8-30 and 8-31.

Misc. Notes:

None.

FIGURE 8-17   Method Specification for the insertOrder Method

[19] Remember that the development process is very incremental and iterative. Therefore, changes could be cascaded back to any point in the development process (e.g., to use-case descriptions, use-case diagrams, CRC cards, class diagrams, object diagrams, sequence diagrams, activity diagrams, behavioral state machines, and package diagrams).

```
Create new OrderNode with the new Order
IF emptyList?()
    FirstNode = LastNode = CurrentNode = newOrderNode
ELSE IF newOrderNode.getOrder().getOrderNumber() < FirstNode.getOrder().getOrderNumber()
    newOrderNode.setNextNode(FirstNode)
    FirstNode = newOrderNode
ELSE IF newOrderNode.getOrder().getOrderNumber() > LastNode.getOrder().getOrderNumber()
    LastNode.setNextNode(newOrderNode)
    LastNode = newOrderNode
ELSE
    middleListInsert(newOrderNode)
```

FIGURE 8-18
Structured English–
Based Algorithm
Specification for the
insertOrder Method

classes available that you could simply reuse and therefore would not need to specify the algorithm to insert into a sorted singly linked list, we use it as an example of how method specification can be accomplished. The general information section of the specification documents the method's name, its class, its unique ID number, the ID number of its associated contract, the programmer assigned, the date that its implementation is due, and the programming language to be used. Second, the trigger/event that caused this method to be executed is identified. Third, the data type of the argument passed to this method is documented (Order). Fourth, owing to the overall complexity of inserting a new node into the list, we have factored out one specific aspect of the algorithm into a separate private method (middleListInsert()) and we have specified that this method will be sending messages to instances of the OrderNode class and the Order class. Fifth, we specify the type of return value that insertOrder will produce. In this case, the insertOrder method will not return anything (void). Finally, we specify the actual algorithm. In this example, for the sake of completeness, we provide both a Structured English–based (see Figure 8-18) and an activity diagram–based algorithm specification (see Figure 8-19). Previously, we stated that we had factored out the logic of inserting into the middle of the list into a separate private method: middleListInsert(). Figure 8-20 shows the logic of this method. Imagine collapsing this logic back into the logic of the insert Order method, i.e., replace the middleListInsert(newOrderNode) activity in Figure 8-19 with the contents of Figure 8-20. Obviously, the insertOrder method would be more complex.

VERIFYING AND VALIDATING CLASS AND METHOD DESIGN

Like all of the previous problem domain models, the constraints, contracts, and method specifications need to be verified and validated. Given that we are primarily dealing with the problem domain in this chapter, the constraints and contracts were derived from the functional requirements and the problem domain representations. However, they are applicable to the other layers. In that case, they would be derived from the solution domain representations associated with the data management (see Chapter 9), human–computer interaction (see Chapter 10), and system architecture (see Chapter 11) layers. Given all of the issues described earlier with the design criteria (see Chapter 7), additional specifications, reuse opportunities, design restructuring and optimization, and mapping to implementation languages, it is likely that many modifications have taken place to the analysis representations of the problem domain. Consequently, virtually everything must be re-verified and re-validated.

First, we recommend that a walkthrough of all of the evolved problem domain representations be performed. That is, all functional models must be consistent; all structural models must be consistent; all behavioral models must be consistent; and the functional, structural, and behavioral models must be balanced.

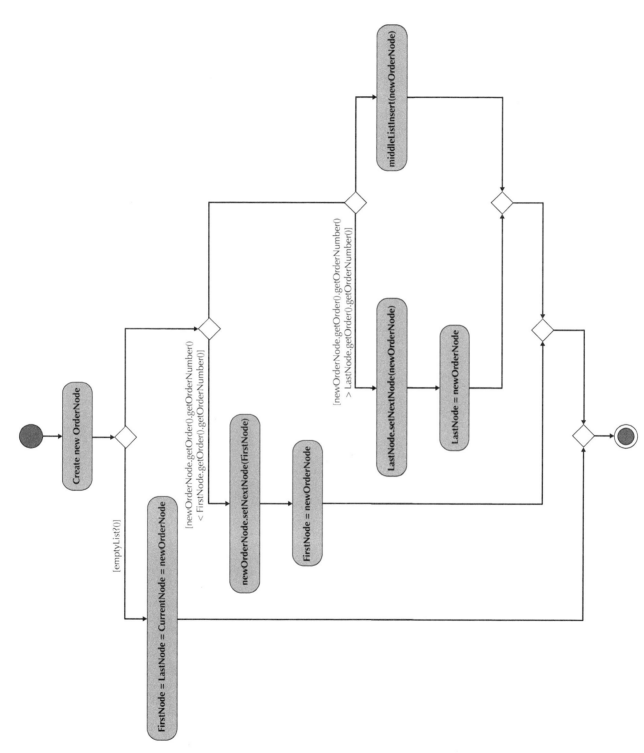

FIGURE 8-19 Activity Diagram–Based Algorithm Specification for the insertOrder Method

315

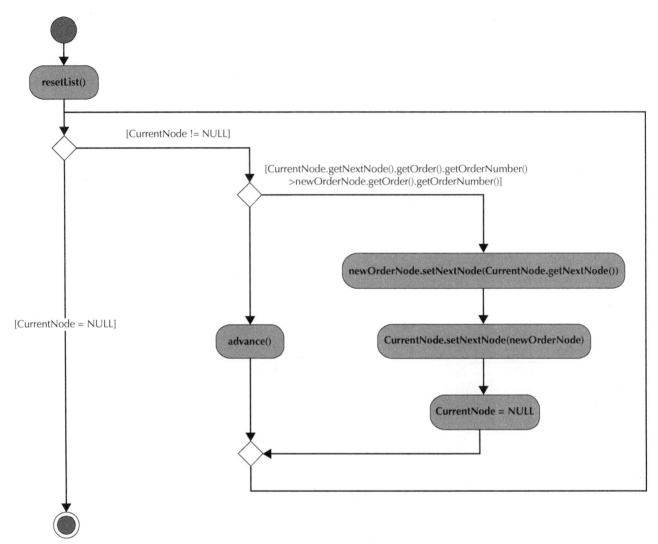

FIGURE 8-20 Activity Diagram–based Algorithm Specification for the middleListInsert Method

Second, all constraints, contracts, and method specifications must be tested. The best way to do this is to role-play the system using the different scenarios of the use cases. In this case, we must enforce the invariants on the evolved CRC cards (see Figure 8-8), the pre- and post-conditions on the contract forms (see Figures 8-11 and 8-14), and the design of each method specified with the method specification forms (see Figures 8-15 and 8-17) and algorithm specifications (see Figures 8-18–8-20).

Given the amount of verifying and validating of the models that we have performed previously on the evolving system, it might seem like overkill to perform the above again. However, given the pure volume of changes that can take place during design, it is crucial to thoroughly test the models again before the system is implemented. In fact, testing is so important to the agile development approaches, testing forms the virtual backbone of those methodologies. Without thorough testing, there is no guarantee that the system being implemented will address the problem being solved. Once the system has been implemented, testing becomes even more important (see Chapter 12).

APPLYING THE CONCEPTS AT PATTERSON SUPERSTORE

In this installment of the Patterson Superstore case, Ruby and her team have shifted their focus from capturing the requirements, behavior, and structure of the evolving system to the design of the individual classes and method for the system. First, they had to return once more to the functional, structural, and behavior models to ensure that the classes defined in analysis (the problem domain layer) are both sufficient and necessary. They then moved to designing the contracts and method specifications.

You can find the rest of the case at www.wiley.com/go/dennis/systemanalysis6e/casestudy.

CHAPTER REVIEW

After reading and studying this chapter, you should be able to:

☐ Identify opportunities for reuse through the use of patterns, frameworks, class libraries, and components.
☐ Optimize a design.
☐ Map the problem domain classes to a single-inheritance language.
☐ Map the problem domain classes to an object-based language.
☐ Understand the difficulties in implementing an object-oriented design in a traditional programming language.
☐ Use the OCL to define precondition, postcondition, and invariant constraints.
☐ Create contracts to specify the interaction between client and server objects.
☐ Specify methods using the method specification form.
☐ Specify the logic of a method using Structured English and activity diagrams.
☐ Understand how to verify and validate both the design of the classes and the design of their methods.

KEY TERMS

Active value
Activity diagram
API (application program interface)
Caching computational results
Class library
Client
Component
Constraint
Consumer
Contract
Derived attribute
Design pattern
Event
Event driven
Exceptions
Factoring
Fan-out
Framework
Invariant
Method specification
Normalization
Object-based language
Object constraint language (OCL)
Patterns
Postcondition
Precondition
Protocol
Server
Signature
Structured English
Supplier
Trigger
Visibility

QUESTIONS

1. When designing a specific class, what types of additional specification for a class could be necessary?
2. What are exceptions?
3. What are constraints? What are the three different types of constraints?
4. What are patterns, frameworks, class libraries, and components? How are they used to enhance the evolving design of the system?
5. How are factoring and normalization used in designing an object system?

6. What are the different ways to optimize an object system?
7. What is the typical downside of system optimization?
8. What is the purpose of a contract? How are contracts used?
9. What is the Object Constraint Language? What is its purpose?
10. What is the Structured English? What is its purpose?
11. What is an invariant? How are invariants modeled in a design of a class? Give an example of an invariant for an hourly employee class using the Object Constraint Language.
12. Create a contract for a compute pay method associated with an hourly employee class. Specify the preconditions and postconditions using the Object Constraint Language.
13. How do you specify a method's algorithm? Give an example of an algorithm specification for a compute pay method associated with an hourly employee class using Structured English.
14. How do you specify a method's algorithm? Give an example of an algorithm specification for a compute pay method associated with an hourly employee class using an activity diagram.
15. How are methods specified? Give an example of a method specification for a compute pay method associated with an hourly employee class.

EXERCISES

A. For the A Real Estate Inc. problem in Chapters 4 (exercises I, J, and K), 5 (exercises N and O), 6 (exercise D), and 7 (exercise D):

1. Choose one of the classes and create a set of invariants for attributes and relationships and add them to the CRC card for the class.
2. Choose one of the methods in the class that you chose and create a contract and a method specification for it. Use OCL to specify any pre- or postcondition and use both Structured English and an activity diagram to specify the algorithm.

B. For the A Video Store problem in Chapters 4 (exercises L, M, and N), 5 (exercises P and Q), 6 (exercise E), and 7 (exercise E):

1. Choose one of the classes and create a set of invariants for attributes and relationships and add them to the CRC card for the class.
2. Choose one of the methods in the class that you chose and create a contract and a method specification for it. Use OCL to specify any pre- or postcondition and use both Structured English and an activity diagram to specify the algorithm.

C. For the gym membership problem in Chapters 4 (exercises O, P, and Q), 5 (exercises R and S), 6 (exercise F), and 7 (exercise F):

1. Choose one of the classes and create a set of invariants for attributes and relationships and add them to the CRC card for the class.

2. Choose one of the methods in the class that you chose and create a contract and a method specification for it. Use OCL to specify any pre- or postcondition and use both Structured English and an activity diagram to specify the algorithm.

D. For the Picnics R Us problem in Chapters 4 (exercises R, S, and T), 5 (exercises T and U), 6 (exercise G), and 7 (exercise G):

1. Choose one of the classes and create a set of invariants for attributes and relationships and add them to the CRC card for the class.
2. Choose one of the methods in the class that you chose and create a contract and a method specification for it. Use OCL to specify any pre- or postcondition and use both Structured English and an activity diagram to specify the algorithm.

E. For the Of-the-Month-Club problem in Chapters 4 (exercises U, V, and W), 5 (exercises V and W), 6 (exercise H), and 7 (exercise H):

1. Choose one of the classes and create a set of invariants for attributes and relationships and add them to the CRC card for the class.
2. Choose one of the methods in the class that you chose and create a contract and a method specification for it. Use OCL to specify any pre- or postcondition and use both Structured English and an activity diagram to specify the algorithm.

MINICASES

1. Your boss has been in the software development field for 30 years. He has always prided himself on his ability to adapt his skills from one approach to developing software to the next approach. For example, he had no problem learning structured analysis and design in the early 1980s and information engineering in the early 1990s. He even understands the advantage of rapid application development. But the other day, when you and he were talking about the advantages of object-oriented approaches, he became totally confused. He thought that characteristics such as polymorphism and inheritance were an advantage for object-oriented systems. However, when you explained the problems with inheritance conflicts, redefinition capabilities, and the need for semantic consistency across different implementations of methods, he was ready to simply give up. To make matters worse, you then went on to explain the importance of contracts in controlling the development of the system. At this point in the conservation, he basically threw in the towel. As he walked off, you heard him say something like "I guess it's true, it's too hard to teach an old dog new tricks."

   Being a loyal employee and friend, you decided to write a short tutorial to give your boss on object-oriented systems development. As a first step, create a detailed outline for the tutorial. As a subtle example, use good design criteria, such as coupling and cohesion, in the design of your tutorial outline.

2. You have been working with the professional and scientific management (PSSM) problem for quite a while. You should go back and refresh your memory about the problem before attempting to solve this situation. Refer back to your solutions to Minicase 3 in Chapter 7.
   a. For each class in the structural model, using OCL, create a set of invariants for attributes and relationships and add them to the CRC cards for the classes.
   b. Choose one of the classes in the structural model. Create a contract for each method in that class. Be sure to use OCL to specify the preconditions and the postconditions. Be as complete as possible.
   c. Create a method specification for each method in the class you chose for question b. Use both Structured English and activity diagrams for the algorithm specification.

3. You have been working with the Holiday Travel Vehicle problem for quite a while. You should go back and refresh your memory about the problem before attempting to solve this situation. Refer back to your solutions to Minicase 4 in Chapter 7.

In the new system for Holiday Travel Vehicles, the system users follow a two-stage process to record complete information on all of the vehicles sold. When an RV or trailer first arrives at the company from the manufacturer, a clerk from the inventory department creates a new vehicle record for it in the computer system. The data entered at this time include basic descriptive information on the vehicle such as manufacturer, name, model, year, base cost, and freight charges. When the vehicle is sold, the new vehicle record is updated to reflect the final sales terms and the dealer-installed options added to the vehicle. This information is entered into the system at the time of sale when the salesperson completes the sales invoice.

When it is time for the clerk to finalize the new vehicle record, the clerk selects a menu option from the system, which is called Finalize New Vehicle Record. The tasks involved in this process are described below.

When the user selects Finalize New Vehicle Record from the system menu, the user is immediately prompted for the serial number of the new vehicle. This serial number is used to retrieve the new vehicle record for the vehicle from system storage. If a record cannot be found, the serial number is probably invalid. The vehicle serial number is then used to retrieve the option records that describe the dealer-installed options that were added to the vehicle at the customer's request. There may be zero or more options. The cost of the option specified on the option record(s) is totaled. Then, the dealer cost is calculated using the vehicle's base cost, freight charge, and total option cost. The completed new vehicle record is passed back to the calling module.
   a. Update the structural model (CRC cards and class diagram) with this additional information.
   b. For each class in the structural model, using OCL, create a set of invariants for attributes and relationships and add them to the CRC cards for the classes.
   c. Choose one of the classes in the structural model. Create a contract for each method in that class. Be sure to use OCL to specify the preconditions and the postconditions. Be as complete as possible.
   d. Create a method specification for each method in the class you chose for question b. Use both Structured English and activity diagrams for the algorithm specification.

CHAPTER 9

DATA MANAGEMENT
LAYER DESIGN

$\mathbf{A}$ project team designs the data management layer of a system using a three-step process: selecting the format of the storage, mapping the problem domain classes to the selected format, and then designing the necessary data access and manipulation classes. This chapter describes the different ways objects can be stored and several important characteristics that should be considered when choosing among object persistence formats. It describes a problem domain class to object persistence format mapping process for the most important object persistence formats. Next, the chapter describes how to design data access and manipulation classes and describes how to ensure the fidelity of the data management layer. We describe the effect that nonfunctional requirements have on the data-management layer. Finally, since the most popular storage format today is the relational database and that most database administrators use the entity-relationship diagram to represent the relational database design, the chapter provides an appendix on the optimization of relational databases from both storage and access perspectives and a description of how to map the class diagram based design of the relational database to an entity relationship diagram.

OBJECTIVES

- Become familiar with several object persistence formats.
- Be able to map problem domain objects to different object persistence formats.
- Be able to design the data access and manipulation classes.
- Understand the effect of nonfunctional requirements on the data management layer.
- Understand how to verify and validate the data management layer.
- Be able to optimize storage efficiency and speed of a relational database used for object storage and access.
- Be able to estimate the size of a relational database.

INTRODUCTION

Applications are of little use without the data that they support. How useful is a multimedia application that can't support images or sound? Why would someone log into a system to find information if it took him or her less time to locate the information manually? One of the leading complaints by end users is that the final system is too slow, so to avoid such complaints project team members must allow time during design to carefully make sure that the file or database performs as fast as possible. At the same time, the team must keep hardware costs down by minimizing the storage space that the application will require. The goals of maximizing access to the objects and minimizing the amount of space taken to store objects can conflict, and designing object persistence efficiency usually requires trade-offs.

The design of the *data management layer* addresses these concerns. It includes both the design of data access and manipulation classes and the actual data storage. The design of the data access and manipulation classes should ensure the independence of the problem domain classes from the data storage format. As such, the data access and manipulation classes handle all communication with the database. In this manner, the problem domain is decoupled from the object storage, allowing the object storage to be changed without affecting the problem domain classes.

The data storage component manages how data are stored and handled by the programs that run the system. The data storage component is composed of a set of object persistence classes. Effective object persistence design decreases the chances of ending up with inefficient systems, long system response times, and users who cannot get to the information that they need in the way that they need it—all of which can affect the success of the project. From a practical perspective, there are five basic types of formats that can be used to store objects for application systems: files (sequential and random), object-oriented databases, object-relational databases, relational databases, and NoSQL data stores.[1] Each type has certain characteristics that make it more appropriate for some types of systems over others. Once the object persistence format is selected to support the system, the problem domain objects need to drive the design of the actual object storage. Then the object storage needs to be designed to optimize its processing efficiency.

OBJECT PERSISTENCE FORMATS

Each of the *object persistence* types is described in this section. *Files* are electronic lists of data that have been optimized to perform a particular transaction. For example, Figure 9-1 shows a customer order file with information about customers' orders, in the form in which it is used, so that the information can be accessed and processed quickly by the system.

A *database* is a collection of groupings of information, each of which is related to each other in some way (e.g., through common fields). Logical groupings of information could include such categories as customer data, information about an order, product information, and so on. A *database management system (DBMS)* is software that creates and manipulates these databases (see Figure 9-2 for a relational database example). Such *end-user DBMSs* as Microsoft Access support small-scale databases that are used to enhance personal productivity, whereas *enterprise DBMSs*, such as DB2, Versant, and Oracle, can manage huge volumes of data and support applications that run an entire company. An end-user DBMS is significantly less expensive and easier for novice users to use than its enterprise counterpart, but it does not have the features or capabilities that are necessary to support mission-critical or large-scale systems.

Sequential- and Random-Access Files

From a practical perspective, most object-oriented programming languages support sequential- and random-access files as part of the language.[2] In this section, we describe what sequential- and random-access files are.[3] We also describe how sequential- and random-access files are used to support an application. For example, they can be used to support master files, look-up files, transaction files, audit files, and history files.

Sequential-access files allow only sequential file operations to be performed (e.g., read, write, and search). Sequential-access files are very efficient for sequential operations that process all of the objects consecutively, such as report writing. However, for random operations,

---

[1] There are other types of files, such as relative, indexed sequential, and multi-indexed sequential, and databases, such as hierarchical, network, and multidimensional. However, these formats typically are not used for object persistence.

[2] For example, see the FileInputStream, FileOutputStream, and RandomAccessFile classes in the java.io package.

[3] For a more complete coverage of issues related to the design of files, see Owen Hanson, *Design of Computer Data Files* (Rockville, MD: Computer Science Press, 1982).

Order Number	Date	Cust ID	Last Name	First Name	Amount	Tax	Total	Prior Customer	Payment Type
234	11/23/00	2242	DeBerry	Ann	$ 90.00	$5.85	$ 95.85	Y	MC
235	11/23/00	9500	Chin	April	$ 12.00	$0.60	$ 12.60	Y	VISA
236	11/23/00	1556	Fracken	Chris	$ 50.00	$2.50	$ 52.50	N	VISA
237	11/23/00	2242	DeBerry	Ann	$ 75.00	$4.88	$ 79.88	Y	AMEX
238	11/23/00	2242	DeBerry	Ann	$ 60.00	$3.90	$ 63.90	Y	MC
239	11/23/00	1035	Black	John	$ 90.00	$4.50	$ 94.50	Y	AMEX
240	11/23/00	9501	Kaplan	Bruce	$ 50.00	$2.50	$ 52.50	N	VISA
241	11/23/00	1123	Williams	Mary	$120.00	$9.60	$129.60	N	MC
242	11/24/00	9500	Chin	April	$ 60.00	$3.00	$ 63.00	Y	VISA
243	11/24/00	4254	Bailey	Ryan	$ 90.00	$4.50	$ 94.50	Y	VISA
244	11/24/00	9500	Chin	April	$ 24.00	$1.20	$ 25.20	Y	VISA
245	11/24/00	2242	DeBerry	Ann	$ 12.00	$0.78	$ 12.78	Y	AMEX
246	11/24/00	4254	Bailey	Ryan	$ 20.00	$1.00	$ 21.00	Y	MC
247	11/24/00	2241	Jones	Chris	$ 50.00	$2.50	$ 52.50	N	VISA
248	11/24/00	4254	Bailey	Ryan	$ 12.00	$0.60	$ 12.60	Y	AMEX
249	11/24/00	5927	Lee	Diane	$ 50.00	$2.50	$ 52.50	N	AMEX
250	11/24/00	2242	DeBerry	Ann	$ 12.00	$0.78	$ 12.78	Y	MC
251	11/24/00	9500	Chin	April	$ 15.00	$0.75	$ 15.75	Y	MC
252	11/24/00	2242	DeBerry	Ann	$132.00	$8.58	$140.58	Y	MC
253	11/24/00	2242	DeBerry	Ann	$ 72.00	$4.68	$ 76.68	Y	AMEX

FIGURE 9-1 Customer Order File

such as finding or updating a specific object, they are very inefficient. On the average, 50 percent of the contents of a sequential-access file will have to be searched before finding the specific object of interest in the file. They come in two flavors: ordered and unordered.

An *unordered sequential access file* is basically an electronic list of information stored on disk. Unordered files are organized serially (i.e., the order of the file is the order in which the objects are written to the file). Typically, new objects simply are added to the file's end.

Ordered sequential access files are placed into a specific sorted order (e.g., in ascending order by customer number). There is overhead associated with keeping files in a particular sorted order. The file designer can keep the file in sorted order by always creating a new file each time a delete or addition occurs, or he or she can keep track of the sorted order via the use of a *pointer*, which is information about the location of the related record. A pointer is placed at the end of each record, and it "points" to the next record in a series or set. The underlying data/file structure in this case is the *linked list*[4] data structure demonstrated in the previous chapter.

Random-access files allow only random or direct file operations to be performed. This type of file is optimized for random operations, such as finding and updating a specific object.

[4] For more information on various data structures, see Ellis Horowitz and Sartaj Sahni, *Fundamentals of Data Structures* (Rockville, MD: Computer Science Press, 1982); Michael T. Goodrich and Roberto Tamassia, *Data Structures and Algorithms in Java* (New York: Wiley, 1998).

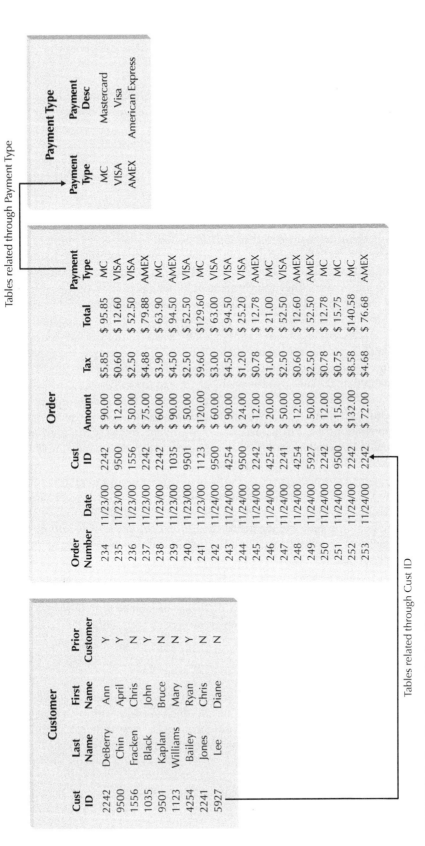

Tables related through Payment Type

Payment Type

Payment Type	Payment Desc
MC	Mastercard
VISA	Visa
AMEX	American Express

Order

Order Number	Date	Cust ID	Amount	Tax	Total	Payment Type
234	11/23/00	2242	$ 90.00	$5.85	$ 95.85	MC
235	11/23/00	9500	$ 12.00	$0.60	$ 12.60	VISA
236	11/23/00	1556	$ 50.00	$2.50	$ 52.50	VISA
237	11/23/00	2242	$ 75.00	$4.88	$ 79.88	AMEX
238	11/23/00	2242	$ 60.00	$3.90	$ 63.90	MC
239	11/23/00	1035	$ 90.00	$4.50	$ 94.50	AMEX
240	11/23/00	9501	$ 50.00	$2.50	$ 52.50	VISA
241	11/23/00	1123	$120.00	$9.60	$129.60	MC
242	11/24/00	9500	$ 60.00	$3.00	$ 63.00	VISA
243	11/24/00	4254	$ 90.00	$4.50	$ 94.50	VISA
244	11/24/00	9500	$ 24.00	$1.20	$ 25.20	VISA
245	11/24/00	2242	$ 12.00	$0.78	$ 12.78	AMEX
246	11/24/00	4254	$ 20.00	$1.00	$ 21.00	MC
247	11/24/00	2241	$ 50.00	$2.50	$ 52.50	VISA
248	11/24/00	4254	$ 12.00	$0.60	$ 12.60	AMEX
249	11/24/00	5927	$ 50.00	$2.50	$ 52.50	AMEX
250	11/24/00	2242	$ 12.00	$0.78	$ 12.78	MC
251	11/24/00	9500	$ 15.00	$0.75	$ 15.75	MC
252	11/24/00	2242	$132.00	$8.58	$140.58	MC
253	11/24/00	2242	$ 72.00	$4.68	$ 76.68	AMEX

Customer

Cust ID	Last Name	First Name	Prior Customer
2242	DeBerry	Ann	Y
9500	Chin	April	Y
1556	Fracken	Chris	N
1035	Black	John	Y
9501	Kaplan	Bruce	N
1123	Williams	Mary	N
4254	Bailey	Ryan	Y
2241	Jones	Chris	N
5927	Lee	Diane	N

Tables related through Cust ID

FIGURE 9-2 Customer Order Database

Random-access files typically have a faster response time to find and update operations than any other type of file. However, because they do not support sequential processing, applications such as report writing are very inefficient. The various methods to implement random-access files are beyond the scope of this book.[5]

There are times when it is necessary to be able to process files in both a sequential and random manner. One simple way to do this is to use a sequential file that contains a list of the keys (the field in which the file is to be kept in sorted order) and a random-access file for the actual objects. This minimizes the cost of additions and deletions to a sequential file while allowing the random file to be processed sequentially by simply passing the key to the random file to retrieve each object in sequential order. It also allows fast random processing to occur by using only the random-access file, thus optimizing the overall cost of file processing. However, if a file of objects needs to be processed in both a random and sequential manner, the developer should consider using a database instead.

There are many different application types of files—e.g., master files, lookup files, transaction files, audit files, and history files. *Master files* store core information that is important to the business and, more specifically, to the application, such as order information or customer mailing information. They usually are kept for long periods of time, and new records are appended to the end of the file as new orders or new customers are captured by the system. If changes need to be made to existing records, programs must be written to update the old information.

Lookup files contain static values, such as a list of valid ZIP codes or the names of the U.S. states. Typically, the list is used for validation. For example, if a customer's mailing address is entered into a master file, the state name is validated against a lookup file that contains U.S. states to make sure that the operator entered the value correctly.

A *transaction file* holds information that can be used to update a master file. The transaction file can be destroyed after changes are added, or the file may be saved in case the transactions need to be accessed again in the future. Customer address changes, for one, would be stored in a transaction file until a program is run that updates the customer address master file with the new information.

For control purposes, a company might need to store information about how data change over time. For example, as human resources clerks change employee salaries in a human resources system, the system should record the person who made the changes to the salary amount, the date, and the actual change that was made. An *audit file* records before and after images of data as they are altered so that an audit can be performed if the integrity of the data is questioned.

Sometimes files become so large that they are unwieldy, and much of the information in the file is no longer used. The *history file* (or archive file) stores past transactions (e.g., old customers, past orders) that are no longer needed by system users. Typically, the file is stored off-line, yet it can be accessed on an as-needed basis. Other files, such as master files, can then be streamlined to include only active or very recent information.

Relational Databases

A relational database is the most popular kind of database for application development today. A relational database is based on collections of tables with each table having a *primary key*—a field or fields whose values are unique for every row of the table. The tables are related to one another by placing the primary key from one table into the related table as a *foreign key* (see Figure 9-3). Most *relational database management systems (RDBMS)* support *referential*

---

[5] For a more-detailed look at the underlying data and file structures of the different types of files, see Mary E. S. Loomis, *Data Management and File Structures*, 2nd Ed. (Englewood Cliffs, NJ: Prentice Hall, 1989); and Michael J.Folk and Bill Zoeellick, *File Structures: A Conceptual Toolkit* (Reading, MA: Addison-Wesley, 1987).

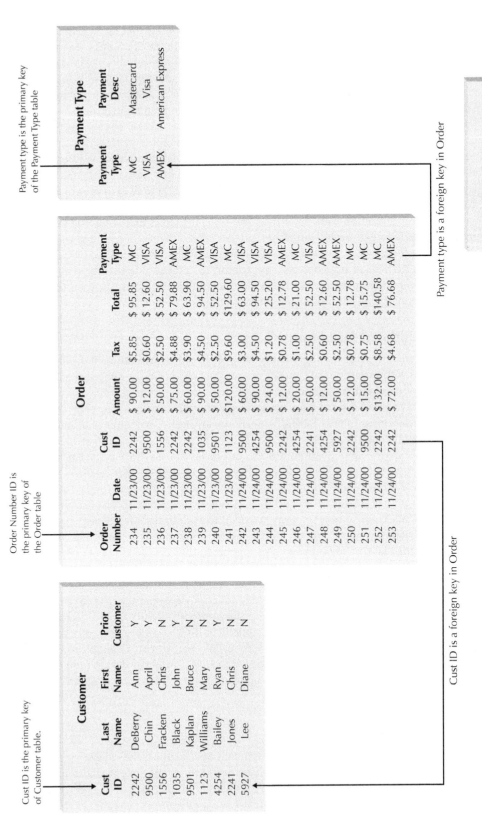

Payment type is the primary key of the Payment Type table

Payment Type

Payment Type	Payment Desc
MC	Mastercard
VISA	Visa
AMEX	American Express

Order Number ID is the primary key of the Order table

Order

Order Number	Date	Cust ID	Amount	Tax	Total	Payment Type
234	11/23/00	2242	$ 90.00	$5.85	$ 95.85	MC
235	11/23/00	9500	$ 12.00	$0.60	$ 12.60	VISA
236	11/23/00	1556	$ 50.00	$2.50	$ 52.50	VISA
237	11/23/00	2242	$ 75.00	$4.88	$ 79.88	AMEX
238	11/23/00	2242	$ 60.00	$3.90	$ 63.90	MC
239	11/23/00	1035	$ 90.00	$4.50	$ 94.50	AMEX
240	11/23/00	9501	$ 50.00	$2.50	$ 52.50	VISA
241	11/23/00	1123	$120.00	$9.60	$129.60	MC
242	11/24/00	9500	$ 60.00	$3.00	$ 63.00	VISA
243	11/24/00	4254	$ 90.00	$4.50	$ 94.50	VISA
244	11/24/00	9500	$ 24.00	$1.20	$ 25.20	VISA
245	11/24/00	2242	$ 12.00	$0.78	$ 12.78	AMEX
246	11/24/00	4254	$ 20.00	$1.00	$ 21.00	MC
247	11/24/00	2241	$ 50.00	$2.50	$ 52.50	VISA
248	11/24/00	4254	$ 12.00	$0.60	$ 12.60	AMEX
249	11/24/00	5927	$ 50.00	$2.50	$ 52.50	AMEX
250	11/24/00	2242	$ 12.00	$0.78	$ 12.78	MC
251	11/24/00	9500	$ 15.00	$0.75	$ 15.75	MC
252	11/24/00	2242	$132.00	$8.58	$140.58	MC
253	11/24/00	2242	$ 72.00	$4.68	$ 76.68	AMEX

Payment type is a foreign key in Order

Cust ID is a foreign key in Order

Cust ID is the primary key of Customer table.

Customer

Cust ID	Last Name	First Name	Prior Customer
2242	DeBerry	Ann	Y
9500	Chin	April	Y
1556	Fracken	Chris	N
1035	Black	John	Y
9501	Kaplan	Bruce	N
1123	Williams	Mary	N
4254	Bailey	Ryan	Y
2241	Jones	Chris	N
5927	Lee	Diane	N

Referential Integrity:

- All payment type values in Order must exist first in the Payment Type table
- All Cust ID values in order must exist first in the Customer table

FIGURE 9-3 Relational Database

integrity, or the idea of ensuring that values linking the tables together through the primary and foreign keys are valid and correctly synchronized. For example, if an order-entry clerk using the tables in Figure 9-3 attempted to add order 254 for customer number 1111, he or she would have made a mistake because no customer exists in the Customer table with that number. If the RDBMS supported referential integrity, it would check the customer numbers in the Customer table, discover that the number 1111 is invalid, and return an error to the entry clerk. The clerk would then go back to the original order form and recheck the customer information.

Tables have a set number of columns and a variable number of rows that contain occurrences of data. *Structured query language (SQL)* is the standard language for accessing the data in the tables. SQL operates on complete tables, as opposed to the individual rows in the tables. Thus, a query written in SQL is applied to all the rows in a table all at once, which is different from a lot of programming languages, which manipulate data row by row. When queries must include information from more than one table, the tables first are *joined* based on their primary key and foreign key relationships and treated as if they were one large table. Examples of RDBMS software are Microsoft SQL Server, Oracle, DB2, and MySQL.

To use a RDBMS to store objects, objects must be converted so that they can be stored in a table. From a design perspective, this entails mapping a UML class diagram to a relational database schema.

Object-Relational Databases

Object-relational database management systems (ORDBMSs) are relational database management systems with extensions to handle the storage of objects in the relational table structure. This is typically done through the use of user-defined types. For example, an attribute in a table could have a data type of map, which would support storing a map. This is an example of a complex data type. In pure RDBMSs, attributes are limited to simple or atomic data types, such as integers, floats, or chars.

ORDBMSs, because they are simply extensions to their RDBMS counterparts, also have very good support for the typical data management operations that business has come to expect from RDBMSs, including an easy-to-use query language (SQL), authorization, concurrency-control, and recovery facilities. However, because SQL was designed to handle only simple data types, it too has been extended to handle complex object data. Currently, vendors deal with this issue in different manners. For example, DB2, Informix, and Oracle all have extensions that provide some level of support for objects.

Many of the ORDBMSs on the market still do not support all of the object-oriented features that can appear in an object-oriented design (e.g., inheritance). As described in Chapter 1, one of the problems in supporting inheritance is that inheritance support is language dependent. For example, the way Smalltalk supports inheritance is different from C^{++}'s approach, which is different from Java's approach. Thus, vendors currently must support many different versions of inheritance, one for each object-oriented language, or decide on a specific version and force developers to map their object-oriented design (and implementation) to their approach. Like RDBMSs, a mapping from a UML class diagram to an object-relational database schema is required.

Object-Oriented Databases

The next type of database management system that we describe is the *object-oriented database management systems (OODBMS)*. There have been two primary approaches to supporting object persistence within the OODBMS community: adding persistence extensions to an object-oriented programming language and creating an entirely separate database management system.

With an OODBMS, collections of objects are associated with an extent. An *extent* is simply the set of instances associated with a particular class (i.e., it is the equivalent of a table in a RDBMS). Technically speaking, each instance of a class has a unique identifier assigned to it by the OODBMS: the *Object ID*. However, from a practical point of view, it is still a good idea to have a semantically meaningful primary key (even though from an OODBMS perspective this is unnecessary). Referential integrity is still very important. In an OODBMS, from the user's perspective, it looks as if the object is contained within the other object. However, the OODBMS actually keeps track of these relationships through the use of the Object ID, and therefore foreign keys are not technically necessary.[6]

OODBMSs provide support for some form of inheritance. However, as already discussed, inheritance tends to be language dependent. Currently, most OODBMSs are tied closely to either a particular *object-oriented programming language (OOPL)* or a set of OOPLs. Originally, most OODBMSs supported either Smalltalk or C++. Today, many of the commercially available OODBMSs provide support for C++, Java, and Smalltalk.

OODBMSs also support the idea of *repeating groups* (fields) or *multivalued attributes*. These are supported through the use of *attribute sets* and *relationship sets*. RDBMSs do not explicitly allow multivalued attributes or repeating groups. This is considered to be a violation of the first normal form (discussed in the appendix to this chapter) for relational databases. Some ORDBMSs do support repeating groups and multivalued attributes.

Until recently, OODBMSs have mainly been used to support multimedia applications or systems that involve complex data (e.g., graphics, video, sound). Application areas, such as computer-aided design and manufacturing (CAD/CAM), financial services, geographic information systems, health care, telecommunications, and transportation, have been the most receptive to OODBMSs. They are also becoming popular technologies for supporting electronic commerce, online catalogs, and large Web multimedia applications. Examples of pure OODBMSs include Gemstone, Objectivity, and Versant.

Although pure OODBMS exist, most organizations currently invest in *ORDBMS* technology. The market for OODBMS is expected to grow, but its ORDBMS and RDBMS counterparts dwarf it. One reason for this situation is that there are many more experienced developers and tools in the RDBMS arena. Furthermore, relational users find that using an OODBMS comes with a fairly steep learning curve.

NoSQL Data Stores[7]

NoSQL data stores are the newest type of object persistence available. Depending on whom you talk to, NoSQL either stands for No SQL or Not Only SQL. Regardless, the data stores that are described as NoSQL typically do not support SQL. Currently, there is no standard for NoSQL data stores. Most NoSQL data stores were created to address problems associated with storing large amounts of distributed data in RDBMSs. NoSQL data stores tend to support very fast queries. However, when it comes to updating, NoSQL data stores normally do not support a locking mechanism, and consequently, all copies of a piece of data are not required to be consistent at all times. Instead they tend to support an eventually consistent based model. Therefore, it is technically possible to have different values for different copies of the same object stored in different locations in a distributed system. Depending on the

[6] Depending on the storage and updating requirements, it usually is a good idea to use a foreign key in addition to the Object ID. The Object ID has no semantic meaning. Therefore, in the case of needing to rebuild relationships between objects, Object IDs are difficult to validate. Foreign keys, by contrast, should have some meaning outside of the DBMS.

[7] For a more complete description of NoSQL data stores see Pramod J. Sadalage and Martin Fowler, *NoSQL Distilled: A Brief Guide to the Emerging World of Polyglot Persistence* (Upper Saddle River, NJ: Addison Wesley, 2013).

application, this could cause problems for decision makers. Therefore, their applicability is limited and are not applicable to most traditional business transaction processing systems. Some of the better known NoSQL data stores include Bigtable, Dynamo, HBase, CouchDB, and Cassandra. There are many different types of NoSQL data stores, including key-value stores, document stores, column-oriented stores, and object databases. Besides object databases, which are either ORDBMSs or OODBMSs (see previous sections), we describe each NoSQL data store type below.

Key-value data stores essentially provide a distributed index (primary key) to where a BLOB (binary large object) is stored. A BLOB treats a set of attributes as one large object. A good example of this type of NoSQL data store is Dynamo. Dynamo provides support for many of the core services for Amazon. Obviously, as one of the largest e-commerce sites in the world, Amazon needed a solution for object persistence that was scalable, distributable, and reliable. Typical RDBMS-based solutions would not work for some of these applications. Applications that typically use key-value data stores are Web-based shopping carts, product catalogs, and bestseller lists. These types of applications do not require updating the underlying data. For example, you do not update the title of a book in your shopping cart when you are making a purchase at Amazon. Given the scale and distributed nature of this type of system, there are bound to be many failures across the system. Being fault tolerant and temporarily sacrificing some consistency across all copies of an object is a reasonable trade-off.

Document data stores, as the name suggests, are built around the idea of documents. The idea of document databases has been around for a long time. These types of stores are considered to be schema free. By that we mean there is no detailed design of the database. A good example of an application that would benefit from this type of approach is a business card database. In a relational database, multiple tables would need to be designed. In a document data store, the design is done more in a "just in time" manner. As new business cards are input into the system, attributes not previously included are simply added to the evolving design. Previously entered business cards would simply not have those attributes associated with them. One major difference between key-value data stores and document data stores is that the "document" has structure and can be easily searched based on the non-key attributes contained in the document, whereas the key-value data store simply treats the "value" as one big monolithic object. CouchDB is a good example of this type of data store.

Columnar data stores organize the data into columns instead of rows. However, there seems to be some confusion as to what this actually implies. In the first approach to columnar data stores, the rows represent the attributes and the columns represent the objects. In contrast, relational databases represent attributes in columns and represent objects in rows. This type of columnar data store is very effective in business intelligence, data mining, and data warehousing applications where the data are fairly static and many computations are performed over a single or a small subset of the available attributes. In comparison to a relational database where you would have to select a set of attributes from all rows, with this type of data store, you would simply have to select a set of rows. This should be a lot faster than with a relational database. A few good examples of this type of columnar data store include Oracle's Retail Predictive Application Server, Vertica, and SAP IQ. The second approach to columnar data stores, which includes HBase, Cassandra, and Bigtable, is designed to handle very large data sets (petabytes of data) that can be accessed as if the data are stored in columns. However, in this case, the data are actually stored in a three-dimensional map composed of object ID, attribute name, timestamp, and value instead of using columns and rows. This approach is highly scalable and distributable. These types of data stores support social applications such as Twitter and Facebook and support search applications such as Google Maps, Earth, and Analytics.

Given the popularity of social computing, business intelligence, data mining, data warehousing, e-commerce, and their need for highly scalable, distributable, and reliable data storage,

NoSQL data stores are an area that should be considered as part of an object persistence solution. However, given the overall diversity and complexity of NoSQL data stores and their limited applicability to traditional business applications, we do not consider them any further in this text.

Selecting an Object Persistence Format

Each of the file and database storage formats that have been presented has its strengths and weaknesses, and no one format is inherently better than the others. In fact, sometimes a project team chooses multiple formats (e.g., a relational database for one, a file for another, and an object-oriented database for a third). Thus, it is important to understand the strengths and weaknesses of each format and when to use each one. Figure 9-4 presents a summary of the characteristics of each and the characteristics that can help identify when each type of format is more appropriate.

Major Strengths and Weaknesses The major strengths of files include the following: Some support for sequential- and random-access files is normally part of an OOPL, files can be designed to be very efficient, and they are a good alternative for temporary or short-term storage. However, all file manipulation must be done through the OOPL. Files do not have any form of access control beyond that of the underlying operating system. Finally, in most cases, if files are used for permanent storage, redundant data most likely will result. This can cause many update anomalies.

	Sequential and Random Access Files	Relational DBMS	Object Relational DBMS	Object-Oriented DBMS	NoSQL data store
Major Strengths	Usually part of an object-oriented programming language Files can be designed for fast performance Good for short-term data storage	Leader in the database market Can handle diverse data needs	Based on established, proven technology, e.g., SQL Able to handle complex data	Able to handle complex data Direct support for object orientation	Able to handle complex data
Major Weaknesses	Redundant data Data must be updated using programs, i.e., no manipulation or query language No access control	Cannot handle complex data No support for object orientation Impedance mismatch between tables and objects	Limited support for object orientation Impedance mismatch between tables and objects	Technology is still maturing Skills are hard to find	Technology is still maturing Skills are hard to find
Data Types Supported	Simple and Complex	Simple	Simple and Complex	Simple and Complex	Simple and Complex
Types of Application Systems Supported	Transaction processing	Transaction processing and decision making	Transaction processing and decision making	Transaction processing and decision making	Primarily decision making
Existing Storage Formats	Organization dependent	Organization dependent	Organization dependent	Organization dependent	Organization dependent
Future Needs	Poor future prospects	Good future prospects	Good future prospects	Good future prospects	Good future prospects

FIGURE 9-4 Comparison of Object Persistence Formats

RDBMSs bring with them proven commercial technology. They are the leaders in the DBMS market. Furthermore, they can handle very diverse data needs. However, they cannot handle complex data types, such as images. Therefore, all objects must be converted to a form that can be stored in tables composed of atomic or simple data. They provide no support for object orientation. This lack of support causes an *impedance mismatch* between the objects contained in the OOPL and the data stored in the tables. An impedance mismatch refers to the amount of work done by both the developer and DBMS and the potential information loss that can occur when converting objects to a form that can be stored in tables.

Because ORDBMSs are typically object-oriented extensions to RDBMSs, they inherit the strengths of RDBMSs. They are based on established technologies, such as SQL, and unlike their predecessors, they can handle complex data types. However, they provide only limited support for object orientation. The level of support varies among the vendors; therefore, ORDBMSs may also suffer from the impedance mismatch problem.

OODBMSs support complex data types and have the advantage of directly supporting object orientation. Therefore, they do not suffer from the impedance mismatch that the previous DBMSs do. However, the OODBMS community is still maturing. Therefore, this technology might still be too risky for some firms. The other major problems with OODBMS are the lack of skilled labor and the perceived steep learning curve of the RDBMS community.

NoSQL data stores support complex data types. However, they can suffer from some forms of impedance mismatch. The primary problems with NoSQL data stores are their lack of maturity and the lack of skilled labor who knows how to effectively use them.

Data Types Supported The first issue is the type of data that will need to be stored in the system. Most applications need to store simple data types, such as text, dates, and numbers. All files and DBMSs are equipped to handle this kind of data. The best choice for simple data storage, however, is usually the RDBMS because the technology has matured over time and has continuously improved to handle simple data very effectively. Increasingly, applications are incorporating complex data, such as video, images, or audio. ORDBMSs, OODBMSs, or NoSQL data stores are best able to handle data of this type. Complex data stored as objects can be manipulated much faster than with other storage formats. However, one possibility to handle data that includes both simple and complex data is to use a combination of object persistence formats.

Type of Application System There are many different kinds of application systems that can be developed. *Transaction-processing systems* are designed to accept and process many simultaneous requests (e.g., order entry, distribution, payroll). In transaction-processing systems, the data are continuously updated by a large number of users, and the queries that these systems require typically are predefined or targeted at a small subset of records (e.g., List the orders that were backordered today or What products did customer #1234 order on May 12, 2020?).

Another set of application systems is the set designed to support decision making, such as *decision support systems (DSS)*, *management information systems (MIS)*, *executive information systems (EIS)*, and *expert systems (ES)*. These decision-making support systems are built to support users who need to examine large amounts of read-only historical data. The questions that they ask are often ad hoc, and include hundreds or thousands of records at a time (e.g., List all customers in the West region who purchased a product costing more than $500 at least three times, or What products had increased sales in the summer months that have not been classified as summer merchandise?).

Transaction-processing systems and DSSs thus have very different data storage needs. Transaction-processing systems need data storage formats that are tuned for a lot of data updates and fast retrieval of predefined, specific questions. Files, relational databases, object-relational databases, and object-oriented databases can all support these kinds of requirements. By contrast, systems to support decision making are usually only reading data (not updating it), often in ad hoc ways. The best choices for these systems usually are RDBMSs because these formats can be configured specially for needs that may be unclear and less apt to change the data. However, depending on the type of data needed to support the decision-making application, RDBMSs may not be appropriate. In that case, ORDBMS, OODBMS, a NoSQL data store, or some combination of object persistence formats may be the better solution.

Existing Storage Formats The storage format should be selected primarily on the basis of the kind of data and application system being developed. However, project teams should consider the existing storage formats in the organization when making design decisions. In this way, they can better understand the technical skills that already exist and how steep the learning curve will be when the storage format is adopted. For example, a company that is familiar with RDBMS will have little problem adopting a relational database for the project, whereas an OODBMS or a NoSQL data store might require substantial developer training.

Future Needs Not only should a project team consider the storage technology within the company, but it should also be aware of current trends and technologies that are being used by other organizations. A large number of installations of a specific type of storage format suggest that skills and products are available to support the format. Therefore, the selection of that format is safe. For example, it would probably be easier and less expensive to find RDBMS expertise when implementing a system than to find help with an OODBMS or a NoSQL data store.

Other Miscellaneous Criteria Other criteria that should be considered include cost, licensing issues, concurrency control, ease of use, security and access controls, version management, storage management, lock management, query management, language bindings, and APIs. We also should consider performance issues, such as cache management, insertion, deletion, retrieval, and updating of complex objects. Finally, the level of support for object orientation (such as objects, single inheritance, multiple inheritance, polymorphism, encapsulation and information hiding, methods, multivalued attributes, and repeating groups) is critical.

MAPPING PROBLEM DOMAIN OBJECTS TO OBJECT PERSISTENCE FORMATS

There are many different formats from which to choose to support object persistence. Each of the formats can have some conversion requirements. Regardless of the object persistence format chosen, we suggest supporting primary keys and foreign keys by adding them to the problem domain classes at this point. However, this does imply that some additional processing will be required. The developer has to set the value for the foreign key when adding the relationship to an object. From a practical perspective, file formats are used mostly for temporary storage. Thus, we do not consider them further.

We also recommend that data management functionality specifics, such as retrieval and updating of data from the object storage, be included only in classes contained in the data management layer. This will ensure that the data management classes are dependent on the problem domain classes and not vice versa. This allows the design of problem domain classes to be independent of any specific object persistence environment, thus increasing their portability and their potential for reuse. Like our previous recommendation, this also implies additional processing.

Mapping Problem Domain Objects to an OODBMS Format

If we support object persistence with an OODBMS, the mappings between the problem domain objects and the OODBMS tend to be fairly straightforward. As a starting point, we suggest that each concrete problem domain class should have a corresponding object persistence class in the OODBMS. There will also be a data access and manipulation (DAM) class (described later in this chapter) that contains the functionality required to manage the interaction between the object persistence class and the problem domain layer. For example, using the appointment system example from the previous chapters, the Patient class is associated with an OODBMS class (see Figure 9-5). The Patient class essentially will be unchanged from analysis. The Patient-OODBMS class will be a new class that is dependent on the Patient class, whereas the Patient-DAM class will be a new class that depends on both the Patient class and the Patient-OODBMS class. The Patient-DAM class must be able to read from and write to the OODBMS. Otherwise, it will not be able to store and retrieve instances of the Patient class. Even though this does add over-head to the installation of the system, it allows the problem domain class to be independent of the OODBMS being used. If at a later time another OODBMS or object persistence format is adopted, only the DAM classes will have to be modified. This approach increases both the portability and the potential for reuse of the problem domain classes.

Even though we are implementing the DAM layer using an OODBMS, a mapping from the problem domain layer to the OODBMS classes in the data access and management layer may be required. If multiple inheritance is used in the problem domain but not supported by the OODBMS, then the multiple inheritance must be factored out of the OODBMS classes. For each case of multiple inheritance (i.e., more than one superclass), the following rules can be used to factor out the multiple inheritance effects in the design of the OODBMS classes.[8]

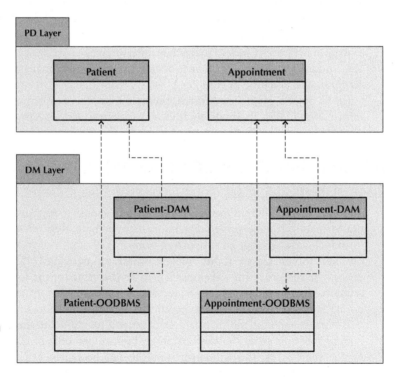

FIGURE 9-5
Appointment System Problem-Domain and DM Layers

[8] The rules presented in this section are based on material in Ali Bahrami, *Object-Oriented Systems Development Using the Unified Modeling Language* (New York: McGraw-Hill, 1999); Michael Blaha and William Premerlani, *Object-Oriented Modeling and Design for Database Applications* (Upper Saddle River, NJ: Prentice Hall, 1998); Akmal B. Chaudri and Roberto Zicari, *Succeeding with Object Databases: A Practical Look at Today's Implementations with Java and XML* (New York: Wiley, 2001); Peter Coad and Edward Yourdon, *Object-Oriented Design* (Upper Saddle River, NJ: Yourdon Press, 1991); and Paul R. Read, Jr., *Developing Applications with Java and UML* (Boston: Addison-Wesley, 2002).

Rule 1a: Add a column(s) to the OODBMS class(es) that represents the subclass(es) that will contain an Object ID of the instance stored in the OODBMS class that represents the "additional" superclass(es). This is similar in concept to a foreign key in an RDBMS. The multiplicity of this new association from the subclass to the "superclass" should be 1..1. Add a column(s) to the OODBMS class(es) that represents the superclass(es) that will contain an Object ID of the instance stored in the OODBMS class that represents the subclass(es). If the superclasses are concrete, that is, they can be instantiated themselves, then the multiplicity from the superclass to the subclass is 0..1, otherwise, it is 1..1. An exclusive-or (XOR) constraint must be added between the associations. Do this for each "additional" superclass.

or

Rule 1b: Flatten the inheritance hierarchy of the OODBMS classes by copying the attributes and methods of the additional OODBMS superclass(es) down to all of the OODBMS subclasses and remove the additional superclass from the design.[9]

These multiple inheritance rules are very similar to those described in Chapter 8. Figure 9-6 demonstrates the application of these rules. The right side of the figure portrays the same problem domain classes that were in Chapter 8: Airplane, Car, Boat, FlyingCar, and AmphibiousCar. FlyingCar inherits from both Airplane and Car, and AmphibiousCar inherits from both Car and Boat. Figure 9-6a portrays the mapping of multiple inheritance relationships into a single inheritance-based OODBMS using Rule 1a. Assuming that Car is concrete, we apply Rule 1a to the Problem Domain classes, and we end up with the OODBMS classes on the left side of Part a, where we have:

- Added a column (attribute) to FlyingCar-OODBMS that represents an association with Car-OODBMS;
- Added a column (attribute) to AmphibiousCar-OODBMS that represents an association with Car-OODBMS;
- Added a pair of columns (attributes) to Car-OODBMS that represents an association with FlyingCar-OODBMS and AmphibiousCar-OODBMS and for completeness sake;
- Added associations between AmphibiousCar-OODBMS and Car-OODBMS and FlyingCar-OODBMS and Car-OODBMS that have the correct multiplicities and the XOR constraint explicitly shown.

We also display the dependency relationships from the OODBMS classes to the problem domain classes. Furthermore, we illustrate the fact that the association between FlyingCar-OODBMS and Car-OODBMS and the association between AmphibiousCar-OODBMS and Car-OODBMS are based on the original factored-out inheritance relationships in the problem domain classes by showing dependency relationships from the associations to the inheritance relationships.

On the other hand, if we apply Rule 1b to map the Problem Domain classes to a single inheritance-based OODBMS, we end up with the mapping in Figure 9-6b, where all the attributes of Car have been copied into the FlyingCar-OODBMS and AmphibiousCar-OODBMS classes. In this latter case, you may have to deal with the effects of inheritance conflicts (see Chapter 1).

---

[9] It is also a good idea to document this modification in the design so that in the future, modifications to the design can be easily maintained.

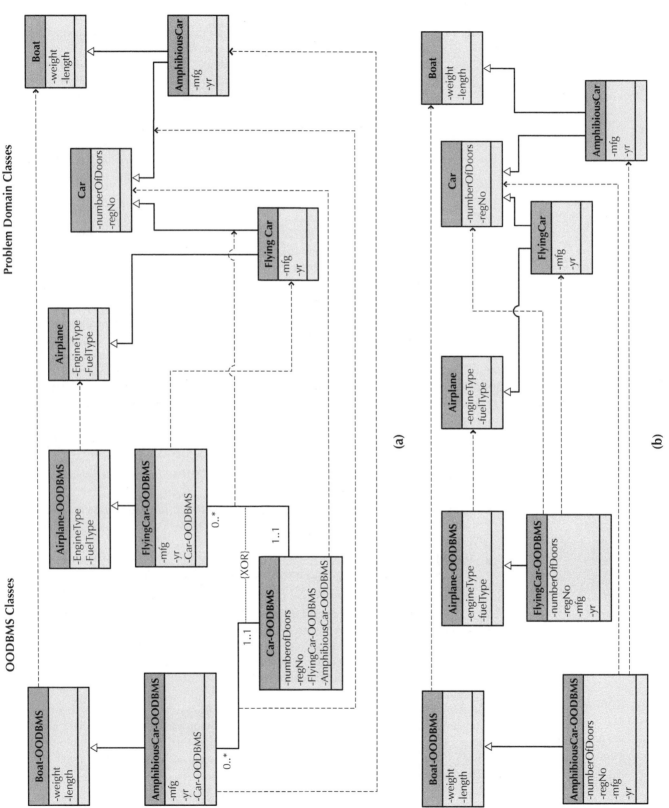

FIGURE 9-6 Mapping Problem Domain Objects to a Single Inheritance-Based OODBMS

The advantage of Rule 1a is that all problem domain classes identified during analysis are preserved in the database. This allows maximum flexibility of maintenance of the design of the data management layer. However, Rule 1a increases the amount of message passing required in the system, and it has added processing requirements involving the XOR constraint, thus reducing the overall efficiency of the design. Our recommendation is to limit Rule 1a to be applied only when dealing with "extra" superclasses that are concrete because they have an independent existence in the problem domain. Use Rule 1b when they are abstract because they do not have an independent existence from the subclass.

In either case, additional processing will be required. In the first case, cascading of deletes will work, not only from the individual object to all its elements but also from the superclass instances to all the subclass instances. In the second case, there will be a lot of copying and pasting of the structure of the superclass to the subclasses. In the case that a modification of the structure of the superclass is required, the modification must be cascaded to all of the subclasses. However, multiple inheritance is rare in most business problems. In most situations, the preceding rules will never be necessary.

When instantiating problem domain objects from OODBMS objects, additional processing will be required also. The additional processing will be in the retrieval of the OODBMS objects and taking their elements to create a problem domain object. Also, when storing the problem domain object, the conversion to a set of OODBMS objects is required. Basically speaking, any time that an interaction takes place between the OODBMS and the system, if multiple inheritance is involved and the OODBMS supports only single inheritance, a conversion between the two formats will be required.

Mapping Problem Domain Objects to an ORDBMS Format

If we support object persistence with an ORDBMS, then the mapping from the problem domain objects to the data management objects is much more involved. Depending on the level of support for object orientation, different mapping rules are necessary. For our purposes, we assume that the ORDBMS supports Object IDs, multivalued attributes, and stored procedures. However, we assume that the ORDBMS does not provide any support for inheritance. Based on these assumptions, Figure 9-7 lists a set of rules that can be used to design the mapping from the Problem Domain objects to the tables of the ORDBMS-based data management layer.

First, all concrete Problem Domain classes must be mapped to the tables in the ORDBMS. For example in Figure 9-8, the Patient class has been mapped to Patient-ORDBMS table. Notice that the Participant class has also been mapped to an ORDBMS table. Even though the Participant class is abstract, this mapping was done because in the complete class diagram (see Figure 7-6), the Participant class had multiple direct subclasses (Employee and Patient).

Second, single-valued attributes should be mapped to columns in the ORDBMS tables. Again, referring to Figure 9-8, we see that the amount attribute of the Patient class has been included in the Patient Table class.

Third, depending on the level of support of stored procedures, the methods and derived attributes should be mapped either to stored procedures or program modules.

Fourth, single-valued (one-to-one) aggregation and association relationships should be mapped to a column that can store an Object ID. This should be done for both sides of the relationship.

Fifth, multivalued attributes should be mapped to columns that can contain a set of values. For example in Figure 9-8, the insurance carrier attribute in the Patient class may contain multiple values because a patient may have more than one insurance carrier. Thus, in the Patient table, a multiplicity has been added to the insurance carrier attribute to portray this fact.

Rule 1: Map all concrete Problem Domain classes to the ORDBMS tables. Also, if an abstract problem domain class has multiple direct subclasses, map the abstract class to an ORDBMS table.

Rule 2: Map single-valued attributes to columns of the ORDBMS tables.

Rule 3: Map methods and derived attributes to stored procedures or to program modules.

Rule 4: Map single-valued aggregation and association relationships to a column that can store an Object ID. Do this for both sides of the relationship.

Rule 5: Map multivalued attributes to a column that can contain a set of values.

Rule 6: Map repeating groups of attributes to a new table and create a one-to-many association from the original table to the new one.

Rule 7: Map multivalued aggregation and association relationships to a column that can store a set of Object IDs. Do this for both sides of the relationship.

Rule 8: For aggregation and association relationships of mixed type (one-to-many or many-to-one), on the single-valued side (1..1 or 0..1) of the relationship, add a column that can store a set of Object IDs. The values contained in this new column will be the Object IDs from the instances of the class on the multivalued side. On the multivalued side (1..,* or 0..*), add a column that can store a single Object ID that will contain the value of the instance of the class on the single-valued side.

For generalization/inheritance relationships:

Rule 9a: Add a column(s) to the table(s) that represents the subclass(es) that will contain an Object ID of the instance stored in the table that represents the superclass. This is similar in concept to a foreign key in an RDBMS. The multiplicity of this new association from the subclass to the "superclass" should be 1..1. Add a column(s) to the table(s) that represents the superclass(es) that will contain an Object ID of the instance stored in the table that represents the subclass(es). If the superclasses are concrete, that is, they can be instantiated themselves, then the multiplicity from the superclass to the subclass is 0..1, otherwise, it is 1..1. An exclusive-or (XOR) constraint must be added between the associations. Do this for each superclass.

or

Rule 9b: Flatten the inheritance hierarchy by copying the superclass attributes down to all of the subclasses and remove the superclass from the design.*

*It is also a good idea to document this modification in the design so that in the future, modifications to the design can be maintained easily.

FIGURE 9-7 Schema for Mapping Problem Domain Objects to ORDBMS

The sixth mapping rule addresses repeating groups of attributes in a problem domain object. In this case, the repeating group of attributes should be used to create a new table in the ORDBMS. It can imply a missing class in the problem domain layer. Normally, when a set of attributes repeats together as a group, it implies a new class. Finally, we must create a one-to-many association from the original table to the new one.

The seventh rule supports mapping multivalued (many-to-many) aggregation and association relationships to columns that can store a set of Object IDs. Basically, this is a combination of the fourth and fifth rules. Like the fourth rule, this should be done for both sides of the relationships. For example, in Figure 9-8, the Symptom table has a multivalued attribute (Patients) that can contain multiple Object IDs to Patient Table objects, and Patient table has a multivalued attribute (Symptoms) that can contain multiple Object IDs to Symptom Table objects.

The eighth rule combines the intentions of Rules 4 and 7. In this case, the rule maps one-to-many and many-to-one relationships. On the single-valued side (1..1 or 0..1) of the relationship, a column that can store a set of Object IDs from the table on the multivalued side (1..* or 0..*) of the relationship should be added. On the multivalued side, a column should be added to the table that can store an Object ID from an instance stored in the table on the single-valued side of the relationship. For example, in Figure 9-8, the Patient table has a multivalued attribute (Appts) that can contain multiple Object IDs to Appointment Table objects, whereas the Appointment table has a single-valued attribute (Patient) that can contain an Object ID to a Patient Table object.

The ninth, and final, rule deals with the lack of support for generalization and inheritance. In this case, there are two different approaches. These approaches are virtually identical

ORDBMS Tables   **Problem Domain Classes**

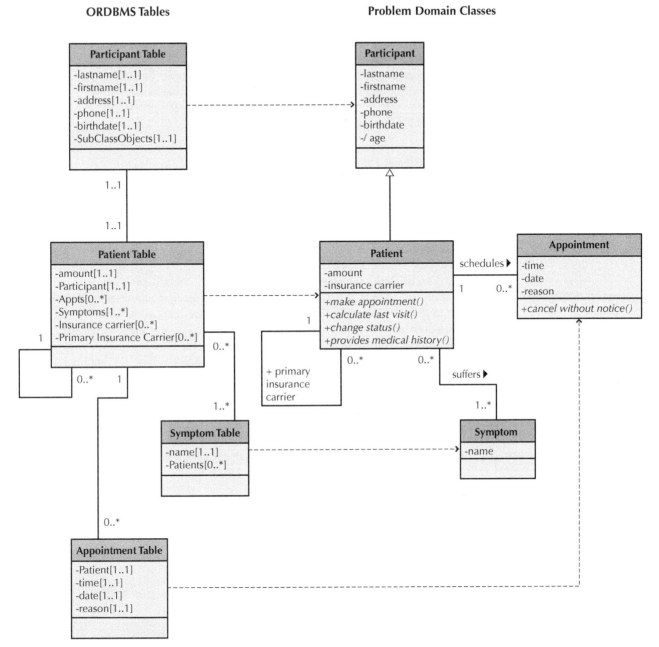

FIGURE 9-8   Example of Mapping Problem Domain Objects to ORDBMS Schema

to the rules described with the preceding OODBMS object persistence formats. For example, in Figure 9-8, the Patient table contains an attribute (Participant) that can contain an Object ID for a Participant Table object, and the Participant table contains an attribute (SubClassObjects) that contains an Object ID for an object, in this case, stored in the Patient table. In the other case, the inheritance hierarchy is flattened.

Of course, additional processing is required any time an interaction takes place between the database and the system. Every time an object must be created or retrieved from the database, updated, or deleted, the ORDBMS object(s) must be converted to the problem domain object, or vice versa. The only other choice is to modify the problem domain objects. However, such a modification can cause problems between the problem domain layer and the physical architecture and human–computer interface layers. Generally speaking, the cost of conversion between the ORDBMS and the problem domain layer should be more than offset by the savings in development time associated with the interaction between the problem domain and physical architecture and human–computer interaction layers and the ease of maintenance of a semantically clean problem domain layer.

Mapping Problem Domain Objects to a RDBMS Format

If we support object persistence with an RDBMS, then the mapping from the problem domain objects to the RDBMS tables is similar to the mapping to an ORDBMS. However, the assumptions made for an ORDBMS are no longer valid. Figure 9-9 lists a set of rules that can be used to design the mapping from the problem domain objects to the RDBMS-based data management layer tables.

The first four rules are basically the same set of rules used to map problem domain objects to ORDBMS-based data management objects. First, all concrete problem domain classes must be mapped to tables in the RDBMS. Second, single-valued attributes should be mapped to columns in the RDBMS table. Third, methods should be mapped to either stored procedures or program modules, depending on the complexity of the method. Fourth, single-valued (one-to-one) aggregation and association relationships are mapped to columns that can store the foreign keys of the related tables. This should be done for both sides of the relationship. For example, in Figure 9-10, we needed to include tables in the RDBMS for the Participant, Patient, Symptom, and Appointment classes.

Rule 1: Map all concrete-problem domain classes to the RDBMS tables. Also, if an abstract Problem Domain class has multiple direct subclasses, map the abstract class to a RDBMS table.

Rule 2: Map single-valued attributes to columns of the tables.

Rule 3: Map methods to stored procedures or to program modules.

Rule 4: Map single-valued aggregation and association relationships to a column that can store the key of the related table, i.e., add a foreign key to the table. Do this for both sides of the relationship.

Rule 5: Map multivalued attributes and repeating groups to new tables and create a one-to-many association from the original table to the new ones.

Rule 6: Map multivalued aggregation and association relationships to a new associative table that relates the two original tables together. Copy the primary key from both original tables to the new associative table, i.e., add foreign keys to the table.

Rule 7: For aggregation and association relationships of mixed type, copy the primary key from the single-valued side (1..1 or 0..1) of the relationship to a new column in the table on the multivalued side (1..* or 0..*) of the relationship that can store the key of the related table, i.e., add a foreign key to the table on the multivalued side of the relationship.

For generalization/inheritance relationships:

Rule 8a: Ensure that the primary key of the subclass instance is the same as the primary key of the superclass. The multiplicity of this new association from the subclass to the "superclass" should be 1..1. If the superclasses are concrete, that is, they can be instantiated themselves, then the multiplicity from the superclass to the subclass is 0..1, otherwise, it is 1..1. Furthermore, an exclusive-or (XOR) constraint must be added between the associations. Do this for each superclass.

or

Rule 8b: Flatten the inheritance hierarchy by copying the superclass attributes down to all of the subclasses and remove the superclass from the design.*

*It is also a good idea to document this modification in the design so that in the future, modifications to the design can be maintained easily.

FIGURE 9-9 Schema for Mapping Problem Domain Objects to RDBMS

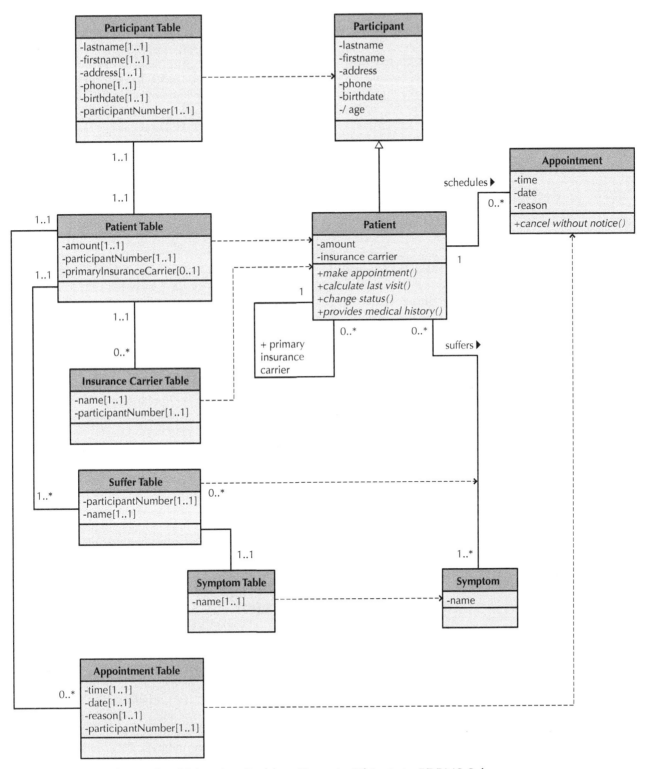

FIGURE 9-10 Example of Mapping Problem Domain Objects to RDBMS Schema

The fifth rule addresses multivalued attributes and repeating groups of attributes in a problem domain object. In these cases, the attributes should be used to create new tables in the RDBMS. As in the ORDBMS mappings, repeating groups of attributes can imply missing classes in the Problem Domain layer. In that case, a new problem domain class may be required. Finally, we should create a one-to-many or zero-to-many association from the original table to the new one. For example, in Figure 9-10, we needed to create a new table for insurance carrier because it was possible for a patient to have more than one insurance carrier.

The sixth rule supports mapping multivalued (many-to-many) aggregation and association relationships to a new table that relates the two original tables. In this case, the new table should contain foreign keys back to the original tables. For example, in Figure 9-10, we needed to create a new table that represents the suffer association between the Patient and Symptom problem domain classes.

The seventh rule addresses one-to-many and many-to-one relationships. With these types of relationships, the multivalued side (0..* or 1..*) should be mapped to a column in its table that can store a foreign key back to the single-valued side (0..1 or 1..1). It is possible that we have already taken care of this situation because we earlier recommended inclusion of both primary and foreign key attributes in the problem domain classes. In the case of Figure 9-10, we had already added the primary key from the Patient class to the Appointment class as a foreign key (see participantNumber). However, in the case of the reflexive relationship, primary insurance carrier, associated with the Patient class, we need to add a new attribute (primaryInsuranceCarrier) to be able to store the relationship.

The eighth, and final, rule deals with the lack of support for generalization and inheritance. As in the case of an ORDBMS, there are two different approaches. These approaches are virtually identical to the rules described with OODBMS and ORDBMS object persistence formats given earlier. The first approach is to add a column to each table that represents a subclass for each of the concrete superclasses of the subclass. Essentially, this ensures that the primary key of the subclass is the same as the primary key for the superclass. If we had previously added the primary and foreign keys to the problem domain objects, as we recommended, then we do not have to do anything else. The primary keys of the tables will be used to rejoin the instances stored in the tables that represent each of the pieces of the problem domain object. Conversely, the inheritance hierarchy can be flattened and the rules (Rules 1 through 7) can be reapplied.

As in the case of the ORDBMS approach, additional processing will be required any time that an interaction takes place between the database and the system. Every time an object must be created, retrieved from the database, updated, or deleted, the mapping between the problem domain and the RDBMS must be used to convert between the two different formats. In this case, a great deal of additional processing will be required.

DESIGNING DATA ACCESS AND MANIPULATION CLASSES

The final step in developing the data management layer is to design the *data access and manipulation classes* that act as a translator between the object persistence and the problem domain objects. Thus, they should always be capable of at least reading and writing both the object persistence and problem domain objects. As described earlier, the object persistence classes are derived from the concrete problem domain classes, whereas the data access and manipulation classes depend on both the object persistence and problem domain classes.

Depending on the application, a simple rule to follow is that there should be one data access and manipulation class for each concrete problem domain class. In some cases, it might make sense to create data access and manipulation classes associated with the human–computer interaction classes (see Chapter 10). However, this creates a dependency from the data management layer to the human–computer interaction layer. Adding this additional complexity to the design of the system normally is not recommended.

Returning to the ORDBMS solution for the Appointment system example (see Figure 9-8), we see that we have four problem domain classes and four ORDBMS tables. Following the previous rule, the DAM classes are rather simple. They have to support only a one-to-one translation between the concrete problem domain classes and the ORDBMS tables (see Figure 9-11). Because the Participant problem domain class is an abstract class, only three data access and manipulation classes are required: Patient-DAM, SymptomDAM, and Appointment-DAM. However, the process to create an instance of the Patient problem domain class can be fairly complicated. The Patient-DAM class might have to be able to retrieve information from all four ORDBMS tables. To accomplish this, the Patient-DAM class retrieves the information from the Patient table. Using the Object-IDs stored in the attribute values associated with the Participant, Appts, and Symptoms attributes, the remaining information required to create an instance of Patient is easily retrieved by the Patient-DAM class.

In the case of using an RDBMS to provide persistence, the data access and manipulation classes tend to become more complex. For example, in the Appointment system, there are still four problem domain classes, but, owing to the limitations of RDBMSs, we have to support six RDBMS tables (see Figure 9-10). The data access and manipulation class for the Appointment problem domain class and the Appointment RDBMS table is no different from those supported for the ORDBMS solution (see Figures 9-11 and 9-12). However, owing to the multivalued attributes and relationships associated with the Patient and Symptom problem domain classes, the mappings to the RDBMS tables were more complicated. Consequently, the number of dependencies from the data access and manipulation classes (Patient-DAM and Symptom-DAM) to the RDBMS tables (Patient table, Insurance Carrier table, Suffer table, and the Symptom table) has increased. Furthermore, because the Patient problem domain class is associated with the other three problem domain classes, the actual retrieval of all information necessary to create an instance of the Patient class could involve joining information from all six RDBMS tables. To accomplish this, the Patient-DAM class must first retrieve information from the Patient table, Insurance Carrier table, Suffer table, and the Appointment table. Because the primary keys of the Patient table and the Participant table are identical, the Patient-DAM class can either directly retrieve the information from the Participant table, or the information can be joined using the participantNumber attributes of the two tables, which act as both primary and foreign keys. Finally, using the information contained in the Suffer table, the information in the Symptom table can also be retrieved. Obviously, the farther we get from the object-oriented problem domain class representation, the more work must be performed. However, as in the case of the ORDBMS example, notice that absolutely no modifications were made to the problem domain classes. Therefore, the data access and manipulation classes again have prevented data management functionality from creeping into the problem domain classes.

One specific approach that has been suggested to support the implementation of data access and manipulation classes is to use an object-relational mapping library such as Hibernate.[10] Hibernate, developed within the JBoss community, allows the mapping of

---

[10] For more information on Hibernate, see www.hibernate.org.

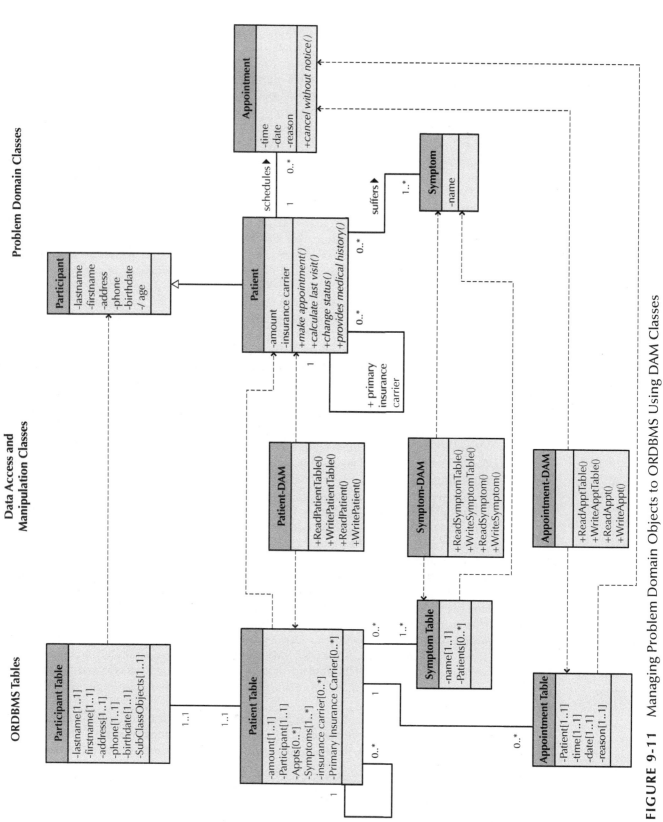

FIGURE 9-11 Managing Problem Domain Objects to ORDBMS Using DAM Classes

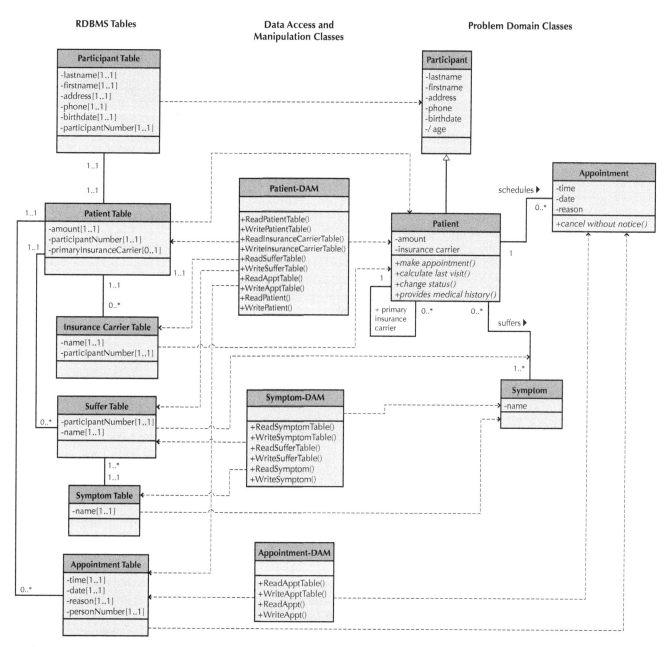

FIGURE 9-12   Mapping Problem Domain Objects to RDBMS Using DAM Classes

objects written in Java that are to be stored in an RDBMS. Instead of using an object-oriented programming language to implement the data access and manipulation classes, with Hibernate, they are implemented in XML files that contain the mapping. As in the above approach, modeling the mapping in an XML file prevents the details on data access and manipulation from sneaking into the problem domain representation.

NONFUNCTIONAL REQUIREMENTS AND DATA MANAGEMENT LAYER DESIGN[11]

Recall that nonfunctional requirements refer to behavioral properties that the system must have. These properties include issues related to performance, security, ease of use, operational environment, and reliability. In this text, we have grouped nonfunctional requirements into four categories: operational, performance, security, and cultural and political requirements. We describe each of these in relation to the data management layer.

The *operational requirements* for the data management layer include issues that deal with the technology being used to support object persistence. However, the choice of the *hardware and operating system* limits the choice of the technology and format of the object persistence available. This is especially true when you consider mobile computing. Given the limited memory and storage available on these devices, the choices to support object persistence are limited. One possible choice to support object persistence that works both on Google's Android and Apple's iOS-based platforms is SQLite. SQLite is a lightweight version of SQL that supports RDBMS. However, there are many different approaches to support object persistence that are more platform dependent; for example, Android supports storing objects with shared preferences (a key-value pair-based NoSQL approach), internal storage, on an SD card, in a local cache, or on a remote system. This, in turn, determines which set of the mapping rules described earlier will have to be used. Another operational requirement could be the ability to import and export data using XML. Again, this could limit the object stores under consideration.

The primary *performance requirements* that affect the data management layer are speed and capacity. As described before, depending on the anticipated—and, afterwards, actual—usage patterns of the objects being stored, different indexing and caching approaches may be necessary. When considering distributing objects over a network, speed considerations can cause objects to be replicated on different nodes in the network. Thus, multiple copies of the same object may be stored in different locations on the network. This raises the issue of update anomalies. Depending on the application being built, NoSQL data stores that support an eventually consistent update model may be appropriate. Also, depending on the estimated size and growth of the system, different DBMSs may need to be considered. An additional requirement that can affect the design of the data management layer deals with the availability of the objects being stored. It might make sense to limit the availability to different objects based on the time of day. For example, one class of users may be allowed to access a set of objects only from 8 to 12 in the morning and a second set of users may be able to access them only from 1 to 5 in the afternoon. Through the DBMS, these types of restrictions could be set.

The *security requirements* deal primarily with access controls, encryption, and backup. Through a modern DBMS, different types of access can be set (e.g., Create, Read, Update, or Delete) granting access only to users (or class of users) who have been authorized. Furthermore, *access control* can be set to guarantee that only users with "administrator" privileges are allowed to modify the object storage schema or access controls.[12] Much of the required information to support access controls for this layer is contained in the CRUDE matrices and CRC cards used during analysis. For example, the CRC cards refer to the associated use cases which contain the list of roles (primary actors and stakeholders) that should have access to the data stored in the DBMS. Furthermore, the more detailed version of the CRUDE matrix (see footnote 10 in Chapter 6), allows the specific type of access that should be granted to each role. Encryption requirements on this layer deal with whether the object

---

[11] Because the vast majority of nonfunctional requirements affect the physical architecture layer, we provide additional details in Chapter 11.

[12] We cover access controls in more detail in Chapter 11.

should be stored in an encrypted format or not. Even though encrypted objects are more secure than unencrypted objects, the process of encrypting and decrypting the objects will slow down the system. Depending on the physical architecture being used, the cost of encryption may be negligible. For example, if we plan on encrypting the objects before transmitting them over a network, there may be no additional cost of storing them in the encrypted format. Backup requirements deal with ensuring that the objects are routinely copied and stored in case the object store becomes corrupted or unusable. Having a backup copy made on a periodic basis and storing the updates that have occurred since the last backup copy was made ensure that the updates are not lost and the object store can be reconstituted by running the copies of the updates against the backup copy to create a new current copy.

There are few *political and cultural requirements* that can affect the data management layer. These include issues related to the expected number of characters that should be allocated for a data field, the format of a data field, and the issues related to security. For example, how many characters should be allocated for a last name field that is part of an Employee object, what format should a date be stored, or where will the data be physically located—different parts of the world have different laws regarding the protection of data. Finally, there could be a corporate IT bias toward different hardware and software platforms. If so, this could limit the type of object store available.

VERIFYING AND VALIDATING THE DATA MANAGEMENT LAYER

Like the models on the problem domain layer, the specifications for the data management layer need to be verified and validated. By now, it might seem a little heavy handed to insist on more verifying and validating. However, depending on the object persistence chosen, the changes that have been applied to the design of the evolving system may be very substantial. Consequently, it is crucial to thoroughly test the fidelity of the design again before the system is implemented. Without thoroughly testing the data management layer, there is no guarantee that an efficient and effective system will be implemented. Verifying and validating the design of the data management layer fall into three basic groups.

First, we recommend verifying and validating any changes made to the problem domain by performing walkthroughs of the modified functional, structural, and behavioral models. Furthermore, all of the models must be consistent and balanced. And, if any problem domain class was modified that was associated with a use-case scenario, that scenario should be tested again through role-playing.

Second, the dependency of the object persistence instances on the problem domain must be enforced. For example, all invariants associated with a problem domain class need to be verified and validated. For example, if a name data field is specified in a problem domain class as being thirty-five characters long and as being a required field, then similar constraints must be enforced when the field is stored.

Third, the design of the data access and manipulation classes need to be tested to ensure that they are dependent on the problem domain classes and the object persistence format, not the other way around. For example, in Figure 9-11, we see that the Patient-DAM class is dependent on both the Patient problem domain class and the Patient table.

Once the system has been implemented, testing of the data management layer becomes even more important. One issue that should be addressed is the testing of the nonfunctional requirements. In this case, tests must be designed and performed for each of the nonfunctional requirements. For example, for the performance requirements, load testing must be performed to identify possible performance bottlenecks in the database. We will return to this topic in Chapter 12.

> ## APPLYING THE CONCEPTS AT PATTERSON SUPERSTORE
>
> Ben Joseph, the data specialist, led the team in designing the model for the data management layer for the first phase of the Integrated Health Clinic Delivery System. Their first step was to choose the object persistence format that the system would use. Then they mapped the problem domain to the object persistence classes. Finally, they designed the Data Access and Manipulation (DAM) classes.
>
> You can find the rest of the case at www.wiley.com/go/dennis/systemanalysis6e/casestudy.

CHAPTER REVIEW

After reading and studying this chapter, you should be able to:

- [ ] Describe the different types of object persistence formats.
- [ ] Select the appropriate object persistence format based on its strengths and weaknesses.
- [ ] Map a set of problem domain objects to an OODBMS format.
- [ ] Map a set of problem domain objects to an ORDBMS format.
- [ ] Map a set of problem domain objects to an RDBMS format.
- [ ] Create a set of data access and manipulation classes that act as a communication layer between the problem domain layer and the actual object persistence used.
- [ ] Describe why the operational and performance nonfunctional requirements of the object persistence format are constrained by decisions made regarding the physical architecture layer.
- [ ] Describe how the nonfunctional requirements of the object persistence format may influence the actual design of the data management layer; these include both the object persistence format and the data access and manipulation classes.
- [ ] Understand how to verify and validate both the design of both the object persistence format and the data access and manipulation classes.

KEY TERMS

Access control
Attribute sets
Audit file
Columnar data stores
Data access and
   manipulation classes
Database
Database management
   system (DBMS)
Data management layer
Decision support systems (DSS)
Document data stores
End-user DBMS
Enterprise DBMS
Executive information
   systems (EIS)

Expert system (ES)
Extent
File
Foreign key
Hardware and
   operating system
History file
Impedance mismatch
Join
Key-value data stores
Linked list
Lookup file
Management information
   system (MIS)
Master file
Multivalued attributes (fields)

NoSQL data stores
Object ID
Object-oriented database management system (OODBMS)
Object-oriented programming language (OOPL)
Object persistence
Object-relational database management system (ORDBMS)
Operational requirements
Ordered sequential access file
Performance requirements
Pointer
Political and cultural requirements

Primary key
Random-access files
Referential integrity
Relational database management system (RDBMS)
Relationship sets
Repeating groups
Security requirements
Sequential-access files
Structured query language (SQL)
Transaction file
Transaction-processing systems
Unordered sequential access file

QUESTIONS

1. Describe the steps in object persistence design.
2. How are a file and a database different from each other?
3. What is the difference between an end-user database and an enterprise database? Provide an example of each one.
4. What are the differences between sequential- and random-access files?
5. Name five types of files and describe the primary purpose of each type.
6. What is the most popular kind of database today? Provide three examples of products that are based on this database technology.
7. What is referential integrity and how is it implemented in an RDBMS?
8. List some of the differences between an ORDBMS and an RDBMS.
9. What are the advantages of using an ORDBMS over an RDBMS?
10. List some of the differences between an ORDBMS and an OODBMS.
11. What are the advantages of using an ORDBMS over an OODBMS?
12. What are the advantages of using an OODBMS over an RDBMS?
13. What are the advantages of using an OODBMS over an ORDBMS?
14. What are the factors in determining the type of object persistence format that should be adopted for a system? Why are these factors so important?
15. Why should you consider the storage formats that already exist in an organization when deciding upon a storage format for a new system?
16. When implementing the object persistence in an ORDBMS, what types of issues must you address?
17. When implementing the object persistence in an RDBMS, what types of issues must you address?
18. What are some of the nonfunctional requirements that can influence the design of the data management layer?
19. What is the primary purpose of the data access and manipulation classes?
20. Why should the data access and manipulation classes be dependent on the problem domain classes instead of the other way around?
21. Why should the object persistence classes be dependent on the problem domain classes instead of the other way around?

EXERCISES

A. Using the Web or other resources, identify a product that can be classified as an end-user database and a product that can be classified as an enterprise database. How are the products described and marketed? What kinds of applications and users do they support? In what kinds of situations would an organization choose to implement an end-user database over an enterprise database?
B. Visit a commercial website (e.g., Amazon.com). If files were being used to store the data supporting the application, what types of files would be needed? What access type would be required? What data would they contain?
C. Using the Web, review one of the following products. What are the main features and functions of the software? In what companies has the DBMS been implemented, and for what purposes? According to the information that you found, what are three strengths and weaknesses of the product?
   1. Relational DBMS
   2. Object-relational DBMS
   3. Object-oriented DBMS
D. What is the most popular kind of database today? Provide three examples of products that are based on this database technology.
E. What is referential integrity and how is it implemented in an RDBMS?
F. When implementing the object persistence in an RDBMS, what types of issues must you address?
G. Jim Smith's dealership sells Fords, Hondas, and Toyotas. The dealership keeps information about each car manufacturer with whom it deals so that the dealership can get in touch with them easily. The dealership also keeps information about the models of cars that it carries from each manufacturer. It keeps information such as list price, the price the dealership paid to obtain the model, and the model name and series (e.g., Honda Civic LX). It also keeps information about all sales that it has made (e.g., it records a buyer's name, the car bought, and the amount paid for the car). To contact the buyers in the future, contact information is also kept (e.g., address, phone number).

1. Create a problem-domain class diagram for this situation.
2. Create a class diagram that shows the mapping of the problem domain classes to a RDBMS for format.
3. Add the DAM classes between the problem-domain classes and the RDBMS classes.

H. For the A Real Estate Inc. problem in Chapter 4 (exercises I, J, and K), Chapter 5 (exercises N and O), Chapter 6 (exercise D), Chapter 7 (exercise D), and Chapter 8 (exercise A):
   1. Create a class diagram that shows the mapping of the problem domain classes to a RDBMS for format.
   2. Add the DAM classes between the problem-domain classes and the RDBMS classes.

I. For the A Video Store problem in Chapter 4 (exercises L, M, and N), Chapter 5 (exercises P and Q), Chapter 6 (exercise E), Chapter 7 (exercise E), and Chapter 8 (exercise B):
   1. Create a class diagram that shows the mapping of the problem domain classes to a RDBMS for format.
   2. Add the DAM classes between the problem-domain classes and the RDBMS classes.

J. For the gym membership problem in Chapter 4 (exercises O, P, and Q), Chapter 5 (exercises R and S), Chapter 6 (exercise F), Chapter 7 (exercise F), and Chapter 8 (exercise C):
   1. Create a class diagram that shows the mapping of the problem domain classes to a RDBMS for format.
   2. Add the DAM classes between the problem-domain classes and the RDBMS classes.

K. For the Picnics R Us problem in Chapter 4 (exercises R, S, and T), Chapter 5 (exercises T and U), Chapter 6 (exercise G), Chapter 7 (exercise G), and Chapter 8 (exercise D):
   1. Create a class diagram that shows the mapping of the problem domain classes to a RDBMS for format.
   2. Add the DAM classes between the problem-domain classes and the RDBMS classes.

L. For the Of-the-Month-Club problem in Chapter 4 (exercises U, V, and W), Chapter 5 (exercises V and W), Chapter 6 (exercise H), Chapter 7 (exercise H), and Chapter 8 (exercise E):
   1. Create a class diagram that shows the mapping of the problem domain classes to a RDBMS for format.
   2. Add the DAM classes between the problem-domain classes and the RDBMS classes.

MINICASES

1. Refer to the Professional and Scientific Staff Management (PSSM) minicases in Chapters 4, 6, 7, and 8.
   a. Create a class diagram that shows the mapping of the problem domain classes to a RDBMS for format.
   b. Add the DAM classes between the problem-domain classes and the RDBMS classes.

2. Refer to the Holiday Travel minicases in Chapters 5–8.
   a. Create a class diagram that shows the mapping of the problem domain classes to a RDBMS for format.
   b. Add the DAM classes between the problem-domain classes and the RDBMS classes.

APPENDICES

APPENDIX 9-1: OPTIMIZING RDBMS-BASED OBJECT STORAGE

Once the object persistence format is selected, the object persistence should be optimized for processing efficiency. The methods of optimization vary based on the format that you select; however, the basic concepts remain the same. Once you understand how to optimize a particular type of object persistence, you will have some idea as to how to approach the optimization of other formats. This section focuses on the optimization of the most popular storage format: relational databases.

There are two primary dimensions in which to optimize a relational database: for storage efficiency and for speed of access. Unfortunately, these two goals often conflict because the best design for access speed may take up a great deal of storage space as compared to other, less-speedy designs. Ultimately, the project team will go through a series of trade-offs until the ideal balance is reached.

Optimizing Storage Efficiency

The most efficient tables in a relational database in terms of storage space have no redundant data and very few null values. The presence of null values suggests that space is being wasted (and more data to store means higher data storage hardware costs). For example, the table in Figure A9-1 repeats customer information, such as name and state, each time a customer places an order, and it contains many null values in the product-related columns. These nulls occur whenever a customer places an order for fewer than three items (the maximum number on an order).

In addition to wasting space, redundancy and null values also allow more room for error and increase the likelihood that problems will arise with the integrity of the data. What if customer 1035 moved from Maryland to Georgia? In the case of Figure A9-1, a program must be written to ensure that all instances of that customer are updated to show Georgia as the new state of residence. If some of the instances are overlooked, then the table will contain an *update anomaly*, whereby some of the records contain the correctly updated value for state and other records contain the old information.

Nulls threaten data integrity because they are difficult to interpret. A blank value in the Order table's product fields could mean the customer did not want more than one or two products on his or her order, the operator forgot to enter in all three products on the order, or the customer canceled part of the order and the products were deleted by the operator. It is impossible to be sure of the actual meaning of the nulls.

For both these reasons—wasted storage space and data integrity threats—project teams should remove redundancy and nulls from the table. During design, the class diagram is used to examine the design of the RDBMS tables (e.g., see Figure 9-12) and to optimize it for storage efficiency. If you follow the modeling instructions and guidelines that were presented in Chapter 5, you will have little trouble creating a design that is highly optimized in this way because a well-formed logical data model does not contain redundancy or many null values.

Sample Records:

Order

-Order Number : unsigned long
-Date : Date
-Cust ID : unsigned long
-Last Name : String
-First Name : String
-State : String
-Tax Rate : float
-Product 1 Number : unsigned long
-Product 1 Desc. : String
-Product 1 Price : double
-Product 1 Qty. : unsigned long
-Product 2 Number : unsigned long
-Product 2 Desc. : String
-Product 2 Price : double
-Product 2 Qty. : unsigned long
-Product 3 Number : unsigned long
-Product 3 Desc. : String
-Product 3 Price : double
-Product 3 Qty. : unsigned long

Redundant Data

Null Cells

Order Number	Date	Cust ID	Last Name	First Name	State	Tax Rate	Prod. 1 Number	Prod. 1 Desc.	Prod. 1 Price	Prod. 1 Qty.	Prod. 2 Number	Prod. 2 Desc.	Prod. 2 Price	Prod. 2 Qty.	Prod. 3 Number	Prod. 3 Desc.	Prod. 3 Price	Prod. 3 Qty.
239	11/23/00	1035	Black	John	MD	0.05	555	Cheese Tray	$45.00	2								
260	11/24/00	1035	Black	John	MD	0.05	444	Wine Gift Pack	$60.00	1								
273	11/27/00	1035	Black	John	MD	0.05	222	Bottle Opener	$12.00	1								
241	11/23/00	1123	Williams	Mary	CA	0.08	444	Wine Gift Pack	$60.00	2								
262	11/24/00	1123	Williams	Mary	CA	0.08	222	Bottle Opener	$12.00	2								
287	11/27/00	1123	Williams	Mary	CA	0.08	222	Bottle Opener	$12.00	2								
290	11/30/00	1123	Williams	Mary	CA	0.08	555	Cheese Tray	$45.00	3								
234	11/23/00	2242	DeBerry	Ann	DC	0.065	555	Cheese Tray	$45.00	2								
237	11/23/00	2242	DeBerry	Ann	DC	0.065	111	Wine Guide	$15.00	1	444	Wine Gift Pack	$60.00	1				
238	11/23/00	2242	DeBerry	Ann	DC	0.065	444	Wine Gift Pack	$60.00	1								
245	11/24/00	2242	DeBerry	Ann	DC	0.065	222	Bottle Opener	$12.00	1								
250	11/24/00	2242	DeBerry	Ann	DC	0.065	222	Bottle Opener	$12.00	1								
252	11/24/00	2242	DeBerry	Ann	DC	0.065	222	Bottle Opener	$12.00	1	444	Wine Gift Pack	$60.00	2				
253	11/24/00	2242	DeBerry	Ann	DC	0.065	222	Bottle Opener	$12.00	1	444	Wine Gift Pack	$60.00	1				
297	11/30/00	2242	DeBerry	Ann	DC	0.065	333	Jams & Jellies	$20.00	2								
243	11/24/00	4254	Bailey	Ryan	MD	0.05	555	Cheese Tray	$45.00	2								
246	11/24/00	4254	Bailey	Ryan	MD	0.05	333	Jams & Jellies	$20.00	3								
248	11/24/00	4254	Bailey	Ryan	MD	0.05	222	Bottle Opener	$12.00	1	333	Jams & Jellies	$20.00	2	111	Wine Guide	$15.00	1
235	11/23/00	9500	Chin	April	KS	0.05	222	Bottle Opener	$12.00	3								
242	11/23/00	9500	Chin	April	KS	0.05	333	Jams & Jellies	$20.00	3								
244	11/24/00	9500	Chin	April	KS	0.05	222	Bottle Opener	$12.00	2								
251	11/24/00	9500	Chin	April	KS	0.05	111	Wine Guide	$15.00	2								

FIGURE A9-1 Optimizing Storage

Sometimes, however, a project team needs to start with a model that was poorly constructed or with one that was created for files or a nonrelational type of format. In these cases, the project team should follow a series of steps that serve to check the model for storage efficiency. These steps make up a process called normalization.[1] *Normalization* is a process whereby a series of rules are applied to the RDBMS tables to assess the efficiency of the tables (see Figure A9-2). These rules help analysts identify tables that are not represented correctly. Here, we describe three normalization rules that are applied regularly in practice. Figure A9-1 shows a model in 0 Normal Form, which is an unnormalized model before the normalization rules have been applied.

A model is in *first normal form (1NF)* if it does not lead to multivalued fields, fields that allow a set of values to be stored, or repeating fields, which are fields that repeat within a table to capture multiple values. The rule for 1NF says that all tables must contain the same number of columns (i.e., fields) and that all the columns must contain a single value. Notice that the model in Figure A9-1 violates 1NF because it causes product number, description, price, and quantity to repeat three times for each order in the table. The resulting table has many records that contain nulls in the product-related columns, and orders are limited to three products because there is no room to store information for more.

A much more efficient design (and one that conforms to 1NF) leads to a separate table to hold the repeating information; to do this, we create a separate table on the model to capture

0 Normal Form

Do any tables have repeating fields? Do some records have a different number of columns from other records?	Yes: Remove the repeating fields. Add a new table that contains the fields that repeat.
	No: The data model is in 1NF

First Normal Form

Is the primary key made up of more than one field? If so, do any fields depend on only a part of the primary key?	Yes: Remove the partial dependency. Add a new table that contains the fields that are partially dependent.
	No: The data model is in 2NF

Second Normal Form

Do any fields depend on another nonprimary key field?	Yes: Remove the transitive dependency. Add a new table that contains the fields that are transitively dependent.
	No: The data model is in 3NF

Third Normal Form

FIGURE A9-2
The Steps of
Normalization

[1] Normalization also can be performed on the problem domain layer (see Chapter 8). However, the normalization process should be used on the problem domain layer only to uncover missing classes. Otherwise, optimizations that have nothing to do with the semantics of the problem domain can creep into the problem domain layer.

product order information. A zero-to-many relationship would then exist between the two tables. As shown in Figure A9-3, the new design eliminates nulls from the Order table and supports an unlimited number of products that can be associated with an order.

Second normal form (2NF) requires first that the data model is in 1NF and second that the data model leads to tables containing fields that depend on a whole *primary key*. This means that the primary key value for each record can determine the value for all the other fields in the record. Sometimes fields depend on only part of the primary key (i.e., *partial dependency*), and these fields belong in another table.

For example, in the new Product Order table that was created in Figure A9-3, the primary key is a combination of the order number and product number, but the product description and price attributes are dependent only upon product number. In other words, by knowing product number, we can identify the product description and price. However, knowledge of the order number and product number is required to identify the quantity. To rectify this violation of 2NF, a table is created to store product information, and the description and price attributes are moved into the new table. Now, product description is stored only once for each instance of a product number as opposed to many times (every time a product is placed on an order).

A second violation of 2NF occurs in the Order table: customer first name and last name depend only upon the customer ID, not the whole key (Cust ID and Order number). As a result, every time the customer ID appears in the Order table, the names also appear. A much more economical way of storing the data is to create a Customer table with the Customer ID as the primary key and the other customer-related fields (i.e., last name and first name) listed only once within the appropriate record. Figure A9-4 illustrates how the model would look when placed in 2NF.

Third normal form (3NF) occurs when a model is in both 1NF and 2NF and, in the resulting tables, none of the fields depend on nonprimary key fields (i.e., *transitive dependency*). Figure A9-4 contains a violation of 3NF: The tax rate on the order depends upon the state to which the order is being sent. The solution involves creating another table that contains state abbreviations serving as the primary key and the tax rate as a regular field. Figure A9-5 presents the end results of applying the steps of normalization to the original model from Figure A9-1.

Optimizing Data Access Speed

After you have optimized the design of the object storage for efficiency, the end result is that data are spread out across a number of tables. When data from multiple tables need to be accessed or queried, the tables must be first joined. For example, before a user can print out a list of the customer names associated with orders, first the Customer and Order tables need to be joined, based on the customer number field (see Figure A9-5). Only then can both the order and customer information be included in the query's output. *Joins* can take a lot of time, especially if the tables are large or if many tables are involved.

Consider a system that stores information about 10,000 different products, 25,000 customers, and 100,000 orders, each averaging three products per order. If an analyst wanted to investigate whether there were regional differences in music preferences, he or she would need to combine all the tables to be able to look at products that have been ordered while knowing the state of the customers placing the orders. A query of this information would result in a huge table with 300,000 rows (i.e., the number of products that have been ordered) and 11 columns (the total number of columns from all of the tables combined).

The project team can use several techniques to try to speed up access to the data, including denormalization, clustering, and indexing.

Revised Model:

Note: Order Number will serve as part of the primary key of Order

Note: Cust ID also will serve as part of the primary key of Order

Note: Order Number will serve as part of the primary key of Product Order

Note: Product Number will serve as part of the primary key of Product Order

Note: Order Number also will serve as a foreign key in Product Order

(a)

Sample Records:

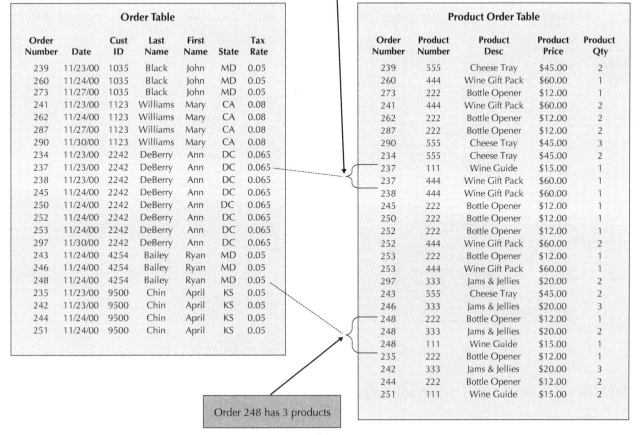

(b)

FIGURE A9-3   1NF: Remove Repeating Fields

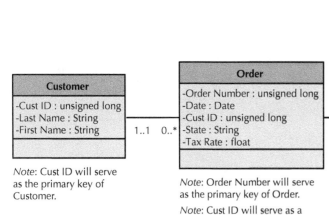

Product Order

-Order Number : unsigned long
-Product Number : unsigned long
-Qty : unsigned long

Customer

-Cust ID : unsigned long
-Last Name : String
-First Name : String

Order

-Order Number : unsigned long
-Date : Date
-Cust ID : unsigned long
-State : String
-Tax Rate : float

Product

-Product Number : unsigned long
-Product Desc : String
-Price : double

0..*   1..*

1..1   0..*

Note: Cust ID will serve as the primary key of Customer.

Note: Order Number will serve as the primary key of Order.

Note: Cust ID will serve as a foreign key in Order.

Note: Order Number will serve as part of the primary key of Product Order.

Note: Order Number also will serve as a foreign key in Product Order.

Note: Product Number will serve as part of the primary key in Product Order.

Note: Product Number also will serve as a foreign key in Product Order.

Note: Product Number will serve as part of the primary key of Product Order.

Sample Records:

Customer Table

Cust ID	Last Name	First Name
1035	Black	John
1123	Williams	Mary
2242	DeBerry	Ann
4254	Bailey	Ryan
9500	Chin	April

Last Name and First Name was moved to the Customer table to eliminate redundancy

Order Table

Order Number	Date	Cust ID	State	Tax Rate
239	11/23/00	1035	MD	0.05
260	11/24/00	1035	MD	0.05
273	11/27/00	1035	MD	0.05
241	11/23/00	1123	CA	0.08
262	11/24/00	1123	CA	0.08
287	11/27/00	1123	CA	0.08
290	11/30/00	1123	CA	0.08
234	11/23/00	2242	DC	0.065
237	11/23/00	2242	DC	0.065
238	11/23/00	2242	DC	0.065
245	11/24/00	2242	DC	0.065
250	11/24/00	2242	DC	0.065
252	11/24/00	2242	DC	0.065
253	11/24/00	2242	DC	0.065
297	11/30/00	2242	DC	0.065
243	11/24/00	4254	MD	0.05
246	11/24/00	4254	MD	0.05
248	11/24/00	4254	MD	0.05
235	11/23/00	9500	KS	0.05
242	11/23/00	9500	KS	0.05
244	11/24/00	9500	KS	0.05
251	11/24/00	9500	KS	0.05

Product Order Table

Order Number	Product Number	Product Qty
239	555	2
260	444	1
273	222	1
241	444	2
262	222	2
287	222	2
290	555	3
234	555	2
237	111	1
237	444	1
238	444	1
245	222	1
250	222	1
252	222	1
252	444	2
253	222	1
253	444	1
297	333	2
243	555	2
246	333	3
248	222	1
248	333	2
248	111	1
235	222	1
242	333	3
244	222	2
251	111	2

Product Table

Product Number	Product Desc	Product Price
111	Wine Guide	$15.00
222	Bottle Opener	$12.00
333	Jams & Jellies	$20.00
444	Wine Gift Pack	$60.00
555	Cheese Tray	$45.00

Product Desc and Price was moved to the Product table to eliminate redundancy

FIGURE A9-4 2NF Partial Dependencies Removed

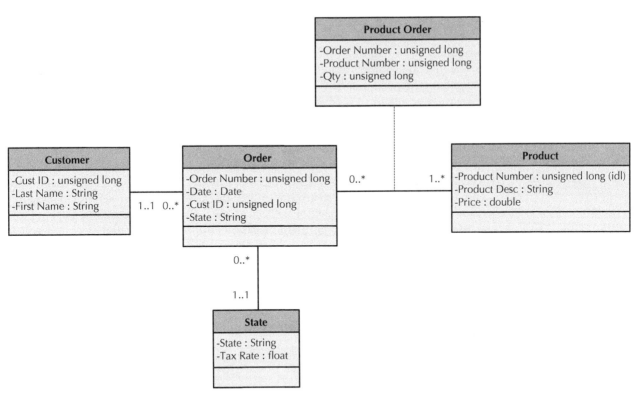

FIGURE A9-5   3NF Normalized Field

Denormalization   After the object storage is optimized, the project team may decide that increased data retrieval speed is more important than storage efficiency or data update speed and elect to denormalize or add redundancy back into the design. *Denormalization* reduces the number of joins that need to be performed in a query, thus speeding up access. Figure A9-6 shows a denormalized model for customer orders. The customer last name was added back into the Order table because the project team learned during analysis that queries about orders usually require the customer last name field. Instead of joining the Order table repeatedly to the Customer table, the system now needs to access only the Order table because it contains all of the relevant information needed to solve the music preference question posed above.

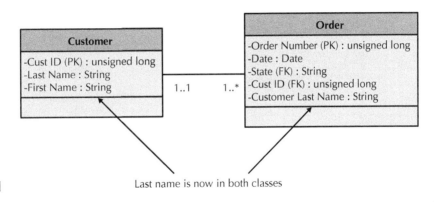

FIGURE A9-6
Denormalized
Physical Data Model

Last name is now in both classes

Denormalization is ideal in situations in which information is queried frequently but updated rarely. However, due to the additional storage required and the potential update anomalies, denormalization should be applied sparingly. There are three cases in which you may rely upon denormalization to reduce joins and improve performance. First, denormalization can be applied in the case of look-up tables, which are tables that contain descriptions of values (e.g., a table of product descriptions or a table of payment types). Because descriptions of codes rarely change, it may be more efficient to include the description along with its respective code in the main table to eliminate the need to join the look-up table each time a query is performed (see Figure A9-7a).

Second, one-to-one relationships are good candidates for denormalization. Although logically two tables should be separated, from a practical standpoint the information from both tables may regularly be accessed together. Think about an order and its shipping information. Logically, it might make sense to separate the attributes related to shipping into a separate table, but as a result the queries regarding shipping will probably always need a join to the Order table. If the project team finds that certain shipping information, such as state and shipping method, is needed when orders are accessed, they may decide to combine the tables or include some shipping attributes in the Order table (see Figure A9-7b).

Third, at times it is more efficient to include a parent entity's attributes in its child entity on the physical data model. For example, consider the Customer and Order tables in Figure A9-6, which share a one-to-many relationship, with Customer as the parent and Order

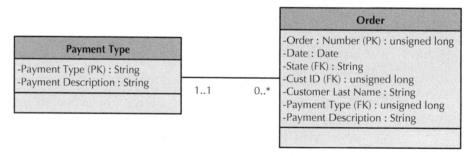

Notice that the payment description field
appears in both Payment Type and Order.

(a)

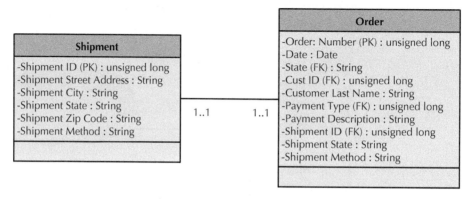

FIGURE A9-7
Denormalization
Situations (FK,
foreign key; PK,
primary key)

Notice that the shipment state and shipment method
are included in both Shipment and Order.

(b)

as the child. If queries regarding orders continuously require customer information, the most popular customer fields can be placed in Order to reduce the required joins to the Customer table, as was done with Customer Last Name.

Clustering Speed of access also is influenced by the way that the data are retrieved. Think about shopping in a grocery store. If you have a list of items to buy but you are unfamiliar with the store's layout, you need to walk down every aisle to make sure that you don't miss anything from your list. Likewise, if records are arranged in no particular order (or in an order that is irrelevant to your data needs), then any query of the records results in a *table scan* in which the DBMS has to access every row in the table before retrieving the result set. Table scans are the most inefficient of data retrieval methods.

One way to improve access speed is to reduce the number of times that the storage medium needs to be accessed during a transaction. One method is to *cluster* records together physically so that similar records are stored close together. With *intrafile clustering*, like records in the table are stored together in some way, such as in order by primary key or, in the case of a grocery store, by item type. Thus, whenever a query looks for records, it can go directly to the right spot on the disk (or other storage medium) because it knows in what order the records are stored, just as we can walk directly to the bread aisle to pick up a loaf of bread. *Interfile clustering* combines records from more than one table that typically are retrieved together. For example, if customer information is usually accessed with the related order information, then the records from the two tables may be physically stored in a way that preserves the customer-order relationship. Returning to the grocery store scenario, an inter-file cluster would be similar to storing peanut butter, jelly, and bread next to each other in the same aisle because they are usually purchased together, not because they are similar types of items. Of course, each table can have only one clustering strategy because the records can be arranged physically in only one way.

Indexing A familiar time saver is an index located in the back of a textbook, which points directly to the page or pages that contain a topic of interest. Think of how long it would take to find all the times that relational database appears in this textbook without the index to rely on! An *index* in data storage is like an index in the back of a textbook; it is a minitable that contains values from one or more columns in a table and the location of the values within the table. Instead of paging through the entire textbook, we can move directly to the right pages and get the information we need. Indexes are one of the most important ways to improve database performance. Whenever there are performance problems, the first place to look is an index.

A query can use an index to find the locations of only those records that are included in the query answer, and a table can have an unlimited number of indexes. Figure A9-8 shows an index that orders records by payment type. A query that searches for all the customers who used American Express can use this index to find the locations of the records that contain American Express as the payment type without having to scan the entire Order table.

Project teams can make indexes perform even faster by placing them into the main memory of the data storage hardware. Retrieving information directly from memory is much faster than retrieving it from a hard disk—Think about how much faster it is to retrieve a memorized phone number versus one that must be looked up in a phone book. Similarly, when a database has an index in memory, it can locate records very, very quickly.

Of course, indexes require overhead in that they take up space on the storage medium. Also, they need to be updated as records in tables are inserted, deleted, or changed. Thus, although indexes lead to faster access to the data, they slow down the update process. In general, we should create indexes sparingly for transaction systems or systems that require a lot

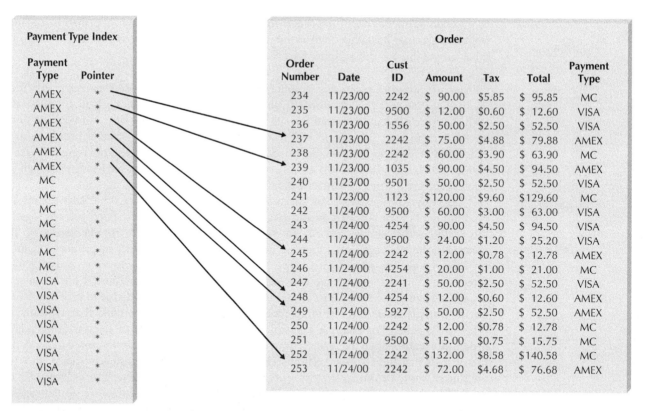

FIGURE A9-8 Payment Type Index

of updates, but we should apply indexes generously when designing systems for decision support (see Figure A9-9).

Estimating Data Storage Size

Even if we have denormalized our physical data model, clustered records, and created indexes appropriately, the system will perform poorly if the database server cannot handle its volume of data. Therefore, one last way to plan for good performance is to apply *volumetrics*, which means estimating the amount of data that the hardware will need to support. You can incorporate your estimates into the database server hardware specification to make sure that the database hardware is sufficient for the project's needs. The size of the database is based on the amount of raw data in the tables and the overhead requirements of the DBMS. To estimate size, you will need to have a good understanding of the initial size of your database as well as its expected growth rate over time.

Raw data refers to all the data that are stored within the tables of the database, and it is calculated based on a bottom-up approach. First, write down the estimated average width for

FIGURE A9-9
Guidelines for
Creating Indexes

> Use indexes sparingly for transaction systems.
>
> Use many indexes to increase response times in decision support systems.
>
> For each table, create a unique index that is based on the primary key.
>
> For each table, create an index that is based on the foreign key to improve the performance of joins.
>
> Create an index for fields that are used frequently for grouping, sorting, or criteria.

Field	Average Size
Order Number	8
Date	7
Cust ID	4
Last Name	13
First Name	9
State	2
Amount	4
Tax Rate	2
Record Size	49
Overhead	30%
Total Record Size	63.7
Initial Table Size	50,000
Initial Table Volume	3,185,000
Growth Rate/Month	1,000
Table Volume @ 3 years	5,478,200

FIGURE A9-10
Calculating
Volumetrics

each column (field) in the table and sum the values for a total record size (see Figure A9-10). For example, if a variable-width Last Name column is assigned a width of 20 characters, you can enter 13 as the average character width of the column. In Figure A9-10, the estimated record size is 49.

Next, calculate the *overhead* for the table as a percentage of each record. Overhead includes the room needed by the DBMS to support such functions as administrative actions and indexes, and it should be assigned based on past experience, recommendations from technology vendors, or parameters that are built into software that was written to calculate volumetrics. For example, your DBMS vendor might recommend that you allocate 30 percent of the records' raw data size for overhead storage space, creating a total record size of 63.7 in Figure A9-10 example.

Finally, record the number of initial records that will be loaded into the table, as well as the expected growth per month. This information should have been collected during analysis. According to Figure A9-10, the initial space required by the first table is 3,185,000, and future sizes can be project based on the growth figure. These steps are repeated for each table to get a total size for the entire database.

Many CASE tools provide you with database-size information based on how you set up the object persistence, and they calculate volumetrics estimates automatically. Ultimately, the size of the database needs to be shared with the design team so that the proper technology can be put in place to support the system's data and potential performance problems can be addressed long before they affect the success of the system.

APPENDIX 9-2: CONVERTING CLASS DIAGRAMS TO ENTITY-RELATIONSHIP DIAGRAMS

The *entity-relationship diagram (ERD)* is the primary diagram used to design databases. The ERD was originally created to provide a semantically sound way to perform *data modeling*. Specifically, it was created as a means to semantically model and design relational databases. In this book, we used the class diagram both as our structural modeling and our database design tool. Like the class diagram, the ERD is a static model. However, unlike the class diagram, the ERD can only model data. Consequently, anything that can be done with an ERD can be done with a class diagram; but not vice versa. In this appendix, we introduce the syntax of the ERD and we describe how to map a class diagram to an ERD.

The ERD was created by Peter Chen to provide an easy, but yet comprehensive, way to model/design a relational database that represented the data and their relationships in a problem domain.[2] AN ERD is made up of entities and relationships. An *entity* is the data equivalent of a *class* , while *relationships* are the equivalent of *associations*. Where an association has *multiplicities*, relationships have *cardinalities*. However, unlike the multiplicities associated with the class diagram, cardinalities cannot show specified range of connections, e.g., 2..4, nor can show a multiple disjoint relationships, e.g., 1..3,5. Figure A9-11 compares the class

[2] P. Chen, "The Entity-Relationship Model – Toward a Unified View of Data." *ACM Transactions on Database Systems*, 1, 1976, 9–36.

Class Diagram Syntax		Entity-Relationship Diagram Syntax	
Class	ClassName -attributeName -methodName	Entity	Entity Name attribute name attribute name
Associations and Multiplicities		**Relationships and Cardinalities**	
0..* 1		≫○————‖—	
1..* 1		≻‖————‖—	
0..* 0..1		≫○————○‖	
1..* 0..1		≻‖————○‖	

FIGURE A9-11   Class Diagram and ERD Syntax Comparison

diagram and ERD syntax. With the class diagram, the multiple ends were shown with an *, the optional association was shown as a 0, and a mandatory or required association is shown by a 1. Notice, with the ERD, the multiple end is shown as a "crows foot," the optional relationship is shown with a 0 on the line, and a required relationship is shown by a vertical line crossing the relationship line. Finally, to convert a class diagram to an ERD, you simply follow the rules for mapping a problem domain class diagram to the RDBMS tables described in Figure 9-9. Once this is done, then simply convert all classes to entities, all associations to relationships, and all multiplicities to cardinalities by using Figure A9-11. Figure A9-12 portrays the results of this process of converting the RDBMS Tables portion of the class diagram in Figures 9-10 and 9-12 to an ERD. In this case, we are showing the entities with their name only. Optionally, we could have also shown the attributes.

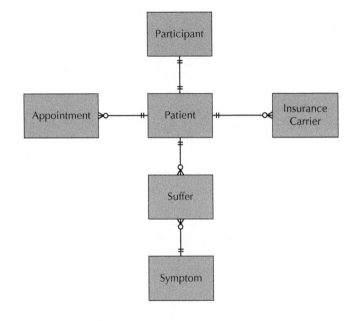

FIGURE A9-12
ERD equivalent
of RDBMS Tables
in Figures 9-10
and 9-12

APPENDIX REVIEW

After reading and studying this appendix, you should be able to:

☐ Use normalization to minimize update anomalies and to increase storage efficiency.
☐ Describe the first three normal forms.
☐ Describe when to use denormalization, clustering, and indexing to increase the speed of data access.
☐ Describe why denormalization, clustering, and indexing can slow down updating.
☐ Apply volumetrics to estimate the amount of data storage required.
☐ Map a class diagram to an entity-relationship diagram.

KEY TERMS

Association
Cardinality
Class
Cluster
Data modeling
Denormalization
Entity

Entity-relationship
  diagram (ERD)
First normal form (1NF)
Index
Interfile clustering
Intrafile clustering
Join

Multiplicity
Normalization
Overhead
Partial dependency
Primary key
Raw data
Relationship

Second normal form (2NF)
Table scan
Third normal form (3NF)
Transitive dependency
Update anomaly
Volumetrics

QUESTIONS

1. Name three ways null values can be interpreted in a relational database. Why is this problematic?
2. What are the two dimensions in which to optimize a relational database?
3. What is the purpose of normalization?
4. How does a model meet the requirements of third normal form?
5. Describe three situations that can be good candidates for denormalization.
6. Describe several techniques that can improve performance of a database.

7. What is the difference between interfile and intrafile clustering? Why are they used?
8. What is an index and how can it improve the performance of a system?
9. Describe what should be considered when estimating the size of a database.
10. Why is it important to understand the initial and projected size of a database during design?

EXERCISES

A. You have been given a file that contains the following fields relating to CD information. Using the steps of normalization, create a model that represents this file in third normal form. The fields include:

Musical group name	CD title 2
Musicians in group	CD title 3
Date group was formed	CD 1 length
Group's agent	CD 2 length
CD title 1	CD 3 length

Assumptions:
- Musicians in group contain a list of the members of the people in the musical group.
- Musical groups can have more than one CD, so both group name and CD title are needed to uniquely identify a particular CD.

B. For Jim Smith dealership problem in exercise G:
1. Describe how you would denormalize the model that you created. Draw the new class diagram based on your suggested changes. How would performance be affected by your suggestions?

2. Examine the model that you created. Develop a clustering and indexing strategy for this model. Describe how your strategy will improve the performance of the database.

3. Calculate the size of the database. Provide size estimates for the initial size of the database as well as for the database in one year's time. Assume that the dealership sells ten models of cars from each manufacturer to approximately 20,000 customers a year. The system will be set up initially with one year's worth of data.

4. Create an ERD based on the class diagram you created in 1.

C. For the A Real Estate Inc. problem in exercise H:

1. Apply the rules of normalization to the class diagram to check the diagram for processing efficiency.

2. Develop a clustering and indexing strategy for this model. Describe how your strategy will improve the performance of the database.

3. Create an ERD based on the class diagram you created in 1.

D. For the A Video Store problem in exercise I:

1. Apply the rules of normalization to the class diagram to check the diagram for processing efficiency.

2. Develop a clustering and indexing strategy for this model. Describe how your strategy will improve the performance of the database.

3. Create an ERD based on the class diagram you created in 1.

E. For the gym membership problem in exercise J:

1. Apply the rules of normalization to the class diagram to check the diagram for processing efficiency.

2. Develop a clustering and indexing strategy for this model. Describe how your strategy will improve the performance of the database.

3. Create an ERD based on the class diagram you created in 1.

F. For the Picnics R Us problem in exercise K:

1. Apply the rules of normalization to the class diagram to check the diagram for processing efficiency.

2. Develop a clustering and indexing strategy for this model. Describe how your strategy will improve the performance of the database.

3. Create an ERD based on the class diagram you created in 1.

G. For the Of-the-Month-Club problem in exercise L:

1. Apply the rules of normalization to the class diagram to check the diagram for processing efficiency.

2. Develop a clustering and indexing strategy for this model. Describe how your strategy will improve the performance of the database.

3. Create an ERD based on the class diagram you created in 1.

MINICASES

1. The system development team at the Wilcon Company is working on developing a new customer order entry system. In the process of designing the new system, the team has identified the following class and its attributes:

Inventory Order
Order Number (PK)
Order Date
Customer Name
Street Address
City
State
Zip
Customer Type
Initials
District Number
Region Number

1 to 22 occurrences of:
Item Name
Quantity Ordered
Item Unit
Quantity Shipped
Item Out
Quantity Received

a. State the rule that is applied to place a class in first normal form. Based on the above class, create a class diagram that will be in 1NF.

b. State the rule that is applied to place a class into second normal form. Revise the class diagram for the Wilcon Company using the class and attributes described (if necessary) to place it in 2NF.

c. State the rule that is applied to place a class into third normal form. Revise the class diagram to place it in 3NF.

d. When planning for the physical design of this database, can you identify any likely situations where the project team might choose to denormalize the class diagram? After going through the work of normalizing, why would this be considered?

2. In the new system under development for Holiday Travel Vehicles, seven tables will be implemented in the new relational database. These tables are: New Vehicle, Trade-in Vehicle, Sales Invoice, Customer, Salesperson, Installed Option, and Option. The expected average record size for these tables and the initial record count per table are given here.

Table Name	Average Record Size	Initial Table Size (records)
New Vehicle	65 characters	10,000
Trade-in Vehicle	48 characters	7,500
Sales Invoice	76 characters	16,000
Customer	61 characters	13,000
Salesperson	34 characters	100
Installed Option	16 characters	25,000
Option	28 characters	500

a. Perform a volumetrics analysis for the Holiday Travel Vehicle system. Assume that the DBMS that will be used to implement the system requires 35 percent overhead to be factored into the estimates. Also, assume a growth rate for the company of 10 percent per year. The systems development team wants to ensure that adequate hardware is obtained for the next three years.

b. Map the class diagram that you have created for the Holiday Travel Vehicle system to an ERD.

3. Refer to the Professional and Scientific Staff Management (PSSM) minicases in Chapters 4, 6, 7, and 8.

a. Apply the rules of normalization to the class diagram to check the diagram for processing efficiency.

b. Develop a clustering and indexing strategy for this model. Describe how your strategy will improve the performance of the database.

c. Create an ERD based on the class diagram you created for question 3a.

CHAPTER 10

HUMAN–COMPUTER
INTERACTION LAYER DESIGN

A user interface is the part of the system with which the users interact. From the user's point of view, the user interface is the system. It includes the screen displays that provide navigation through the system, the screens and forms that capture data, and the reports that the system produces (whether on paper, on the screen, or via some other medium). This chapter introduces the basic principles and processes of interface design and discusses how to design the interface structure and standards, navigation design, input design, and output design. The chapter introduces the issues related to designing user interfaces for the mobile computing environment, social media, games, multidimensional information visualizations, and immersive environments. It also introduces the issues that need to be considered when designing user interfaces for a global audience. Finally, the chapter describes the effect of the nonfunctional requirements on designing the human–computer interaction layer.

OBJECTIVES

- Understand several fundamental user interface design principles.
- Understand the process of user interface design.
- Understand how to design the user interface structure.
- Understand how to design the user interface standards.
- Understand commonly used principles and techniques for navigation design.
- Understand commonly used principles and techniques for input design.
- Understand commonly used principles and techniques for output design.
- Be able to design a user interface.
- Understand the unique design issues for user interface design for mobile computing, social media, games, multidimensional information visualization, and immersive applications.
- Understand the issues that need to be addressed when designing user interfaces for international and multicultural audiences.
- Understand the effect of nonfunctional requirements on the human–computer interaction layer.

INTRODUCTION

Interface design is the process of defining how a system will interact with external entities (e.g., customers, suppliers, and other systems). In this chapter, we focus on the design of *user interfaces*, but it is also important to remember that there are sometimes *system interfaces*, which exchange information with other systems. System interfaces are typically designed as part of a systems integration effort. They are defined in general terms as part of the physical architecture and data management layers. The human–computer interaction layer defines the way in which the users interact with the system and the nature of the inputs and outputs that the system accepts and produces.

Up until now, the entire development process has been focused on getting the problem domain layer and its storage on the data management layer right. However, from the user's point of view, the user interface on the human–computer interaction layer is the system. Users do not really care about how the problem domain objects are stored. But, they do care about how they can use the system to support them in their activities. Based on our layered based design approach, the user interface of the human–computer interaction layer is independent of the data management layer. But it is dependent on both the problem domain and physical architecture layers. Depending on the type of device that the human–computer interaction layer is deployed on will set both opportunities and constraints as to what user interface features can be included. For example, deploying the human computer interaction layer on both a smartphone and a desktop computer will cause two different user interfaces to be designed.

Even though there are command-line user interfaces (e.g., Terminal on Mac OSX), we are only focusing on *graphical user interfaces (GUI)* that use windows, menus, icons, etc.[1] Today, GUI-based interfaces are the most common type of interfaces that we use.[2] Regardless of the underlying hardware being used, a GUI-based user interface comprises three fundamental parts. The first is the *navigation mechanism*, the way in which the user gives instructions to the system and tells it what to do (e.g., buttons, menus). The second is the *input mechanism*, the way in which the system captures information (e.g., forms for adding new customers). The third is the *output mechanism*, the way in which the system provides information to the user or to other systems (e.g., reports, Web pages). Each of these is conceptually different, but they are closely intertwined. All GUI-based displays contain navigation mechanisms, and most contain input and output mechanisms. Therefore, navigation design, input design, and output design are tightly coupled and must be performed in an incremental and iterative manner.

In this chapter, even though we focus primarily on designing user interfaces that run in a laptop or desktop type of environment, we also provide general guidelines for mobile computing, social media applications, advanced technology interfaces, such as 3D augmented and virtual reality applications, and finally, issues related to going global with the user interface.

PRINCIPLES FOR USER INTERFACE DESIGN

In many ways, user interface design is an art. The goal is to make the interface pleasing to the eye and simple to use while minimizing the effort the users need to accomplish their work. The system is never an end in itself; it is merely a means to accomplish the business of the organization.

---

[1] Many people attribute the origin of GUI interfaces to Apple or Microsoft. Some people know that Microsoft copied from Apple, which, in turn, "borrowed" the whole idea from a system developed at the Xerox Palo Alto Research Center (PARC) in the 1970s. Very few know that the Xerox system was based on a system developed by Doug Engelbart of Stanford that was first demonstrated at the Western Computer Conference in 1968. Around the same time, he also invented the mouse, desktop video conferencing, groupware, and a host of other things we now take for granted. Doug is a legend in the computer science community and has won too many awards to count but is relatively unknown by the general public.

[2] A set of good books on GUI design include Jennifer Tidwell, *Designing Interfaces*, 2nd Ed. (Sebastopol, CA: O'Reilly Media, 2010); Ben Shneiderman, *Designing the User Interface: Strategies for Effective Human–Computer Interaction*, 3rd Ed. (Reading, MA: Addison-Wesley, 1998); Alan Cooper, *About Face 3: The Essentials of Interaction Design* (Indianapolis, IN: Wiley, 2007).

We have found that the greatest problem facing experienced designers is using space effectively. Simply put, often there is much more information that needs to be presented on a screen or report or form than will fit comfortably. Analysts must balance the need for simplicity and pleasant appearance against the need to present the information across multiple pages or screens, which decreases simplicity. In this section, we discuss some fundamental interface design principles, which are common for navigation design, input design, and output design[3] (see Figure 10-1).

Layout

The first element of design is the basic *layout* of the screen, form, or report. Most software designed for personal computers follows the standard Windows or Macintosh approach for screen design. The *screen* is divided into three boxes. The top box is the navigation area, through which the user issues commands to navigate through the system. The bottom box is the status area, which displays information about what the user is doing. The middle—and largest—box is used to display reports and present forms for data entry.

This use of multiple layout areas also applies to inputs and outputs. Data areas on reports and forms are often subdivided into subareas, each of which is used for a different type of information. These areas are almost always rectangular, although sometimes space constraints require odd shapes. Nonetheless, the margins on the edges of the screen should be consistent. Each of the areas within the report or form is designed to hold different information. For example, on an order form (or order report), one part may be used for customer information (e.g., name, address), one part for information about the order in general (e.g., date, payment information), and one part for the order details (e.g., how many units of which items at what price each). Each area is self-contained so that information in one area does not run into another.

The areas and information within areas should have a natural intuitive flow to minimize the users' movement from one area to the next. People in Westernized nations (e.g., United

Principle	Description
Layout	The interface should be a series of areas on the screen that are used consistently for different purposes—for example, a top area for commands and navigation, a middle area for information to be input or output, and a bottom area for status information.
Content Awareness	Users should always be aware of where they are in the system and what information is being displayed.
Aesthetics	Interfaces should be functional and inviting to users through careful use of white space, colors, and fonts. There is often a trade-off between including enough white space to make the interface look pleasing without losing so much space that important information does not fit on the screen.
User Experience	Although ease of use and ease of learning often lead to similar design decisions, sometimes there is a trade-off between the two. Novice or infrequent users of software prefer ease of learning, whereas frequent users prefer ease of use.
Consistency	Consistency in interface design enables users to predict what will happen before they perform a function. It is one of the most important elements in ease of learning, ease of use, and aesthetics.
Minimal User Effort	The interface should be simple to use. Most designers plan on having no more than three mouse clicks from the starting menu until users perform work.

FIGURE 10-1
Principles of User
Interface Design

---

[3] A good book on the design of interfaces is Susan Weinschenk, Pamela Jamar, and Sarah Yeo, *GUI Design Essentials* (New York: Wiley, 1997).

States, Canada, and Mexico) tend to read left-to-right, top-to-bottom, so related information should be placed so that it is used in this order (e.g., address lines, followed by city, state or province, and then ZIP code or postal code). Sometimes the sequence is in chronological order, or from the general to the specific, or from most frequently to least frequently used. In any event, before the areas are placed on a form or report, the analyst should have a clear understanding of what arrangement makes the most sense for how the form or report will be used. The flow between sections should also be consistent, whether horizontal or vertical. Ideally, the areas will remain consistent in size, shape, and placement for the forms used to enter information (whether paper or on screen) and the reports used to present it.

Content Awareness

Content awareness refers to the ability of an interface to make the user aware of the information it contains with the least amount of effort on the user's part. All parts of the interface, whether navigation, input, or output, should provide as much content awareness as possible, but it is particularly important for forms or reports that are used quickly or irregularly. Content awareness applies to the interface in general. All interfaces should have titles (on the screen frame, for example). Menus should show where the user is and, if possible, where the user came from to get there.

Content awareness also applies to the areas within forms and reports. All areas should be clear and well-defined so that it is difficult for the user to become confused about the information in any area. Then users can quickly locate the part of the form or report that is likely to contain the information they need. Sometimes the areas are marked by lines, colors, or headings; in other cases, the areas are only implied.

Content awareness also applies to the *fields* within each area. Fields are the individual elements of data that are input or output. The *field labels* that identify the fields on the interface should be short and specific—objectives that often conflict. There should be no uncertainty about the format of information within fields, whether for entry or display. For example, a date of 10/5/21 is different depending on whether you are in the United States (October 5, 2021) or in Canada (May 10, 2021). Any fields for which there is the possibility of uncertainty or multiple interpretations should provide explicit explanations.

Content awareness also applies to the information that a form or report contains. In general, all forms and reports should contain a preparation date (i.e., the date printed or the date completed) so that the age of information is obvious. Likewise, all printed forms and software should provide version numbers so that users, analysts, and programmers can identify outdated materials.

Aesthetics

Aesthetics refers to designing interfaces that are pleasing to the eye. Interfaces do not have to be works of art, but they do need to be functional and inviting to use. In most cases, less is more, meaning that a simple, minimalist design is the best.

Space is usually at a premium on forms and reports, and often there is the temptation to squeeze as much information as possible onto a page or a screen. Unfortunately, this can make a form or report so unpleasant that users do not want to use it. In general, all forms and reports need a minimum amount of *white space* that is intentionally left blank.

In general, novice or infrequent users of an interface, whether on a screen or on paper, prefer interfaces with low density, often one with a density of less than 50 percent (i.e., less than 50 percent of the interface occupied by information). More-experienced users prefer higher densities, sometimes approaching 90 percent occupied, because they know where information is located and high densities reduce the amount of physical movement through the interface.

The design of text is equally important. As a general rule, all text should be in the same font and about the same size. Fonts should be no smaller than 8 points, but 10 points is often preferred, particularly if the interface will be used by older people. Changes in font and size are used to indicate changes in the type of information that is presented (e.g., headings, status indicators). In general, italics and underlining should be avoided because they make text harder to read.

Serif fonts (i.e., those having letters with serifs, or tails, such as Times Roman) are the most readable for printed reports, particularly for small letters. Sans serif fonts (i.e., those without serifs, such as Helvetica or Arial) are the most readable for computer screens and are often used for headings in printed reports. Never use all capital letters, except possibly for titles.

Color and patterns should be used carefully and sparingly and only when they serve a purpose. (About 10 percent of men are color blind, so the improper use of color can impair their ability to read color text.) A quick trip around the Web will demonstrate the problems caused by indiscriminate use of colors and patterns. Remember, the goal is pleasant readability, not art; color and patterns should be used to strengthen the message, not overwhelm it. Color is best used to separate and categorize items, such as showing the difference between headings and regular text, or to highlight important information. Therefore, colors with high contrast should be used (e.g., black and white). In general, black text on a white background is the most readable, and blue on red is the least readable. Also, when it comes to the proper use of color, cultural issues come into play. We discuss this later in the chapter.

User Experience

User experience can essentially be broken down into two levels: those with experience and those without. Interfaces should be designed for both types of users. Novice users usually are most concerned with *ease of learning*—how quickly they can learn new systems. Expert users are usually most concerned with *ease of use*—how quickly they can use the system once they have learned how to use it. Often these two are complementary and lead to similar design decisions, but sometimes there are trade-offs. Novices, for example, often prefer menus that show all available system functions, because these promote ease of learning. Experts, on the other hand, sometimes prefer fewer menus organized around the most commonly used functions.

Research shows that expert and novice users have different requirements and behavior patterns in some cases. For example, novices virtually never look at the bottom area of a screen that presents status information, whereas experts refer to the status bar when they need information. Most systems should be designed to support frequent users, except for systems designed to be used infrequently or when many new users or occasional users are expected. Likewise, systems that contain functionality that is used only occasionally must contain a highly intuitive interface or an interface that contains clear, explicit guidance regarding its use. The balance of quick access to commonly used and well-known functions and guidance through new and less-well-known functions is challenging to the interface designer, and this balance often requires elegant solutions.

Systems that will end up being used by many people on a daily basis are more likely to have a majority of expert users (e.g., order-entry systems). Although interfaces should try to balance ease of use and ease of learning, these types of systems should put more emphasis on ease of use rather than ease of learning. Users should be able to access the commonly used functions quickly, with few keystrokes or a small number of menu selections. In many other systems (e.g., decision-support systems), most people remain occasional users for the lifetime of the system. In this case, greater emphasis may be placed on ease of learning rather than ease of use.

Consistency

Consistency in design is probably the single most important factor in making a system simple to use because it enables users to predict what will happen. When interfaces are consistent, users can interact with one part of the system and then know how to interact with the rest, aside from elements unique to those parts. Consistency usually refers to the interface within one computer system, so that all parts of the same system work in the same way. Ideally, the system should also be consistent with other computer systems in the organization and with commercial software that is used. Many software development tools support consistent system interfaces by providing standard interface objects (e.g., list boxes, pull-down menus, and radio buttons).

Consistency occurs at many different levels. Consistency in the *navigation controls* conveys how actions in the system should be performed. For example, using the same icon or command to change an item clearly communicates how changes are made throughout the system. Consistency in terminology is also important. This refers to using the same words for elements on forms and reports (e.g., not customer in one place and client in another). We also believe that consistency in report and form design is important, although a study suggests that being *too* consistent can cause problems.[4] When reports and forms are very similar except for very minor changes in titles, users sometimes mistakenly use the wrong form and either enter incorrect data or misinterpret its information. The implication for design is to make the reports and forms similar but give them some distinctive elements (e.g., color, size of titles) that enable users to immediately detect differences.

Minimizing User Effort

Interfaces should be designed to minimize the amount of effort needed to accomplish tasks. This means using the fewest possible mouse clicks or keystrokes to move from one part of the system to another. Most interface designers follow the *three-clicks rule*: Users should be able to go from the start or main menu of a system to the information or action they want in no more than three mouse clicks or three keystrokes. However, with regard to this point, you need to be aware of Krug's principles (discussed later).

USER INTERFACE DESIGN PROCESS

User interface design is a use-case driven, incremental, and iterative process. Analysts often move back and forth between the different parts (navigation, input, and output) of the user interface, rather than proceeding sequentially from one part to another part. Given that the design process is use case driven, the analysts begin the user interface design process by examining the *use cases* (see Chapter 4) and their associated *activity* and *sequence diagrams* (see Chapter 6) developed in analysis. Analysts then typically set down with users to develop use scenarios that describe commonly employed patterns of actions the users will perform so that the interface enables users to quickly and smoothly perform these scenarios. In some cases, additional requirements are uncovered. Depending on the importance of the newly uncovered requirements, this can cause the problem domain layer to be modified, which in turn can cause the data management layer to be modified. However, many times, these new requirements can be delayed until the next iteration of the system. With agile approaches, user interface design and requirements modeling is so intertwined that new requirements are uncovered on a regular basis. Consequently, depending on the stability of the modeling of the

---

[4] John Satzinger and Lorne Olfman, "User Interface Consistency Across End-User Application: The Effects of Mental Models," *Journal of Management Information Systems* (Spring 1998): 167–193.

problem domain, user interface design could occur concurrently with functional modeling. Even though functional and behavioral modeling is associated with the analysis workflow and user interface design is associated with the design workflow, the level of activity associated with the two workflows overlaps (see Figures 1-3 and 1-4). As such, performing user interface design alongside of functional and behavioral modeling is compatible with both the Unified Process and the Enhanced Unified Process.

Once a basic set of use scenarios have been developed, the actual user interface is designed. As we stated earlier, all GUI-based user interfaces comprise three parts: navigation, input, and output. To some degree, all three parts tend to be designed together. Consequently, the user interface design process tends to follow a prototyping style of development (see Chapter 1) wherein the analyst and user will incrementally build a design by iterating across all three parts of the user interface using different design tools. For example, when designing the structure of the navigation, a windows navigation diagram (WND) is very useful; when designing the layout of the user interface, a wireframe diagram is very useful; and when attempting to try and tie the navigation, input, and output designs together, storyboards and user interface prototypes are very useful. Another useful idea when developing a user interface is to have a set of accepted interface standards that can be used across multiple applications. For example, a standard set of menus, icons, and user interface templates simplify the entire design of the human computer interaction layer. Once the basic design has been completed for a specific use case, then the *essential use case* developed in functional modeling should be converted to a *real use case* that, along with the other tools used to design the interface, can be used as a basis for documentation, training, and testing.

Use Scenario Development

A *use scenario* is an outline of the steps that the users perform to accomplish some part of their work. A use scenario is one path through an essential use case. For example, Figure 10-2 shows the use-case diagram for the Appointment System. This figure shows that the Create New Patient use case is distinct from the Make Payment Arrangements use case. We model these two use cases separately because they represent separate processes that are used by the Make New Patient Appt use case.

The use-case diagram was designed to model all possible uses of the system—its complete functionality or all possible paths through the use case at a fairly high level of abstraction. In one use scenario, a patient makes a request with the receptionist regarding an appointment with the doctor. The receptionist looks up the patient and checks to see if the patient has any bills to be paid. The receptionist then asks the patient whether he or she wants to set up a new appointment, cancel an existing appointment, or change an existing appointment. If the patient wants to make a new appointment, the receptionist asks the patient for some suggested appointment times, which the receptionist matches against potential times available. The receptionist finally creates a new appointment (see Figures 6-4 and 6-5).

In another use scenario, a patient simply wants to cancel an appointment. In this case, the receptionist looks up the patient and checks to see if the patient has any bills to be paid. The receptionist then asks the patient for the time of the appointment to be canceled. Finally, the receptionist deletes the appointment.

Use scenarios are presented in a simple narrative description that is tied to the essential use cases developed during analysis (see Chapter 4). Figure 10-3 shows the two use scenarios just described. The key point with using use cases for interface design is *not* to document all possible use scenarios within a use case. The goal is to document two or three of the most common use scenarios so that the interface can be designed to enable the most common uses to be performed simply and easily.

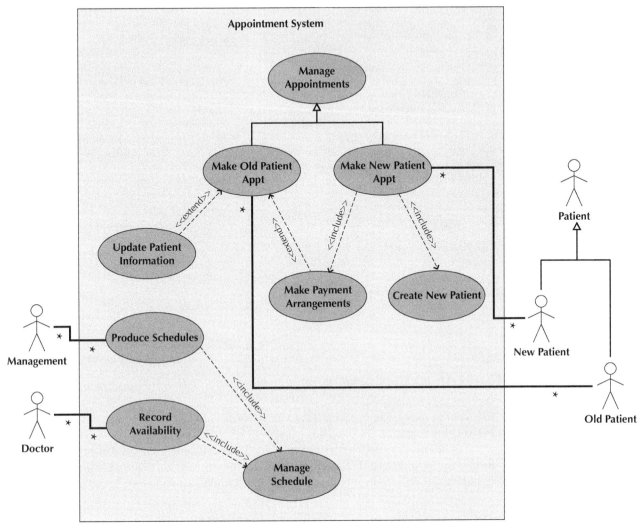

FIGURE 10-2 Appointment System Use-Case Diagram (see Figures 4-21 and 6-28)

Navigation Structure Design

The navigation structure defines the basic components of the interface and how they work together to provide functionality to users. A *windows navigation diagram (WND)*[5] is used to show how all the screens, forms, and reports used by the system are related and how the user moves from one to another. Most systems have several WNDs, one for each major part of the system.

A WND is very similar to a behavioral state machine (see Chapter 6), in that they both model state changes. A behavioral state machine typically models the *state* changes of an object, whereas a WND models the state changes of the user interface. In a WND, each state of the user interface is represented as a box. A box typically corresponds to a user interface component, such as a *window, form, button,* or *report*. For example, in Figure 10-4, there are

---

[5] A WND is based on the behavioral state machine and object diagrams [see Meilir Page-Jones, *Fundamentals of Object-Oriented Design in UML* (New York: Dorset House, 2000)].

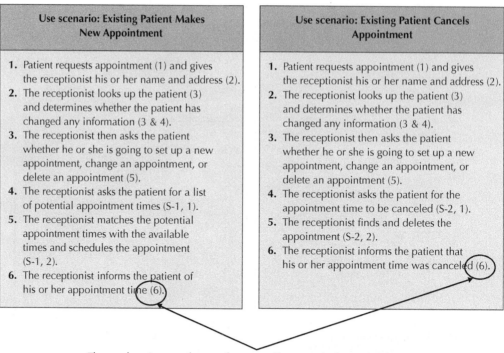

The numbers in parentheses refer to specific events in the essential use case.

FIGURE 10-3 Use Scenarios

five separate states: Client Menu, Find Client Form, Add Client Form, Client List, and Client Information Report.

Transitions are modeled as either a single-headed or double-headed arrow. A single-headed arrow indicates that a return to the calling state is not required, whereas a double-headed arrow represents a required return. For example in Figure 10-4, the transition from

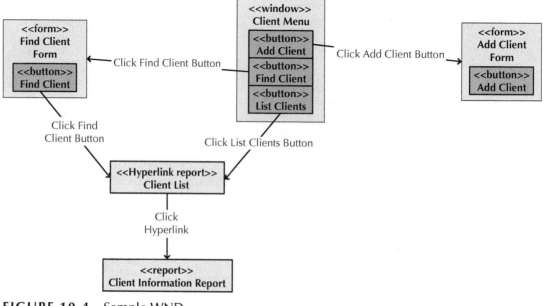

FIGURE 10-4 Sample WND

the Client Menu state to the Find Client Form state does not require a return. The arrows are labeled with the action that causes the user interface to move from one state to another. For example, in Figure 10-4, to move from the Client Menu state to the Find Client Form state, the user must click the Find Client Button on the Client Menu.

The last item to be described in a WND is the *stereotype*. A stereotype is modeled as a text item enclosed within guillemets or angle brackets (<< >>). The stereotype represents the type of user interface component of a box on the diagram. For example, the Client Menu is a window, whereas Find Client Form is a form.

The basic navigation structure of an interface follows the basic structure of the business process itself, as defined in the use cases and behavioral model. The analyst starts with the essential use cases and develops the fundamental flow of control of the system as it moves from object to object. The analyst then examines the use scenarios to see how well the WND supports them. Quite often, the use scenarios identify paths through the WND that are more complicated than they should be. The analyst then reworks the WND to simplify the ability of the interface to support the use scenarios, sometimes by making major changes to the menu structure, sometimes by adding shortcuts.

Interface Standards Design

Interface standards are the basic design elements that are common across the individual screens, forms, and reports within the system. Depending on the application, there may be several sets of interface standards for different parts of the system (e.g., one for Web screens, one for mobile screens, one for paper reports, and one for input forms). For example, the part of the system used by data entry operators might mirror other data entry applications in the company, whereas a Web interface for displaying information from the same system might adhere to some standardized Web format. Likewise, each individual interface might not contain all of the elements in the standards (e.g., a report screen might not have an edit capability), and they might contain additional characteristics beyond the standard ones, but the standards serve as the touchstone that ensures the interfaces are consistent across the system. The following sections discuss some of the main areas in which interface standards should be considered: metaphors, objects, actions, icons, and templates.

Interface Metaphor First of all, the analysts must develop the fundamental interface metaphor(s) that defines how the interface will work. An *interface metaphor* is a concept from the real world that is used as a model for the computer system. The metaphor helps the user understand the system and enables the user to predict what features the interface might provide, even without actually using the system. Sometimes systems have one metaphor, whereas in other cases there are several metaphors in different parts of the system.

Often, the metaphor is explicit. Quicken, for example, uses a checkbook metaphor for its interface, even to the point of having the users type information into an on-screen form that looks like a real check. In other cases, the metaphor is implicit or unstated, but it is there, nonetheless. Many Windows systems use the paper form or table as a metaphor.

In some cases, the metaphor is so obvious that it requires no thought. For example, most online stores use a shopping cart metaphor to temporarily store the items that the customer is considering purchasing. In other cases, a metaphor is hard to identify. In general, it is better not to force a metaphor that really doesn't fit a system, because an ill-fitting metaphor will confuse users by promoting incorrect assumptions.

Interface Templates An *interface template* defines the general appearance of all screens in the information system and the paper-based forms and reports that are used. The template design, for example, specifies the basic layout of the screens (e.g., where the navigation area(s), status area, and form/report area(s) will be placed) and the color scheme(s) that will be applied. It defines whether windows will replace one another on the screen or will cascade over the top of each other. The template defines a standard placement and order for common interface actions (e.g., File Edit View rather than File View Edit). In short, the template draws together the other major interface design elements: metaphors, objects, actions, and icons.

Interface Objects The template specifies the names that the interface will use for the major *interface objects*, the fundamental building blocks of the system, such as the classes. In many cases, the object names are straightforward, such as calling the shopping cart the "shopping cart." In other cases, it is not so simple. For example, Amazon.com sells much more than books. In some cases, the user might not know whether he or she is looking for a book, CD, DVD, or Kindle download. In those cases, the user can use a catchall search item: All Departments. In the case that the user knows the type of item that he or she wants to buy, the user can limit the search by specifying more-specific types of search items, such as Apps for Android, Books, Kindle Store, or Music. Obviously, the object names should be easily understood and help promote the interface metaphor.

In general, in cases of disagreements between the users and the analysts over names, whether for objects or actions (discussed later), the users should win. A more understandable name always beats a more precise or more accurate one.

Interface Actions The template also specifies the navigation and command language style (e.g., menus) and grammar (e.g., object-action order; see the navigation design section later in this chapter). It gives names to the most commonly used *interface actions* in the navigation design (e.g., buy versus purchase or modify versus change).

Interface Icons The interface objects and actions and their status (e.g., deleted or overdrawn) may be represented by *interface icons*. Icons are pictures that appear on command buttons as well as in reports and forms to highlight important information. Icon design is very challenging because it means developing a simple picture less than half the size of a postage stamp that needs to convey an often-complex meaning. The simplest and best approach is to simply adopt icons developed by others (e.g., a blank page to indicate create a new file, a diskette to indicate save).[6] This has the advantage of quick icon development, and the icons might already be well understood by users because they have seen them in other software.

Commands are actions that are especially difficult to represent with icons because they are in motion, not static. Many icons have become well known from widespread use, but icons are not as well understood as first believed. Use of icons can sometimes cause more confusion than insight. Icon meanings become clearer with use, but sometimes a picture is not worth even one word; when in doubt, use a word, not a picture.

Interface Design Prototyping

An *interface design prototype* is a mock-up or a simulation of a computer screen, form, or report. A prototype is prepared for each interface in the system to show the users and the programmers how the system will perform. In the "old days," an interface design prototype was usually specified on a paper form that showed what would be displayed on each part of the screen. Paper forms are still used today, but more and more interface design prototypes are being built using computer tools instead of paper. The most common approaches to interface design prototyping are wireframe diagrams, storyboards, and language prototypes.

---

[6] However, given that diskettes are rarely used anymore, the value of using the diskette icon may be fading away.

Wireframe Diagram A *wireframe diagram* is simply a picture that resembles the actual user interface that the user will gradually receive. Typically, it is created using a tool such as Microsoft's Visio or Google's Lucidchart. Using this type of tool, the designer can quickly drag and drop the user interface components onto the canvas to lay out the design of the user interface. For example, Figure 10-5 portrays a simple wireframe diagram. Even though there is no executable capability associated with a wireframe diagram, it does allow the user to quickly get a feel for the look of the user interface that will be delivered.

Storyboard At its simplest, an interface design prototype is a paper-based *storyboard*. The storyboard shows hand-drawn pictures of what the screens will look like and how they flow from one screen to another, in the same way a storyboard for a cartoon shows how the action will flow from one scene to the next (see Figure 10-6). Storyboards are the simplest technique because all they require is paper (often a flip chart) and a pen—and someone with some artistic ability. Storyboards also combine both the navigation information of the windows navigation diagram and to some degree the layout information of the wireframe diagram. However, with today's graphics tools, the designer can work effectively with a set of users to design both the look and feel of the evolving system without having to actually implement anything, by combining the wireframe diagrams with the windows navigation diagram into a single better storyboard type of diagram (see Figure 10-7).

User Interface Prototypes With today's programming environments, such as Visual Studio and NetBeans, it is fairly easy to develop executable *user interface prototypes* (see Figure 10-8) that would allow the user to be able to interact with the user interface by clicking on buttons and entering pretend data into forms (but because there is no system behind the pages, the data are never processed). The different parts of the user interface are linked together so that as the user clicks on buttons, the requested part of the system appears. These executable prototypes take longer to develop than windows navigation diagrams, wireframe diagrams, and storyboards but have the distinct advantage of showing *exactly* what the screens will look like. The user does not have to guess about the shape or position of the elements on the screen. However, one of the potential issues that can arise when developing user interface prototypes is that the user's expectations of when the systems will be completed can become unrealistic. To actually connect the prototype up to the problem domain such that the system actually works is not a trivial problem. So, user expectations need to be carefully managed. Otherwise, a system that meets all of its specifications could end up being considered a failure.

FIGURE 10-5
Sample Wireframe Diagram

FIGURE 10-6 Sample Storyboard

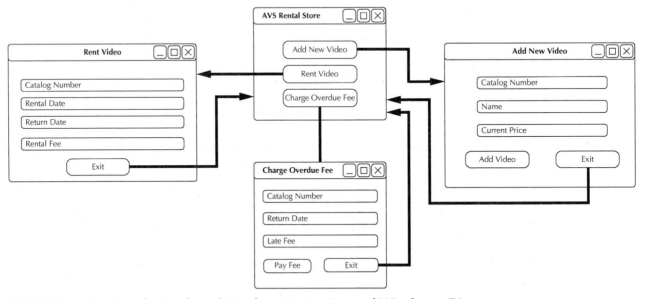

FIGURE 10-7 Sample Combined Windows Navigation and Wireframe Diagrams

Selecting the Appropriate Techniques Projects often use a combination of different interface design prototyping techniques for different parts of the system. Storyboarding is the fastest and least expensive but provides the least amount of detail. Wireframe diagrams provide more of a feel that the user will experience, while remaining fairly inexpensive to

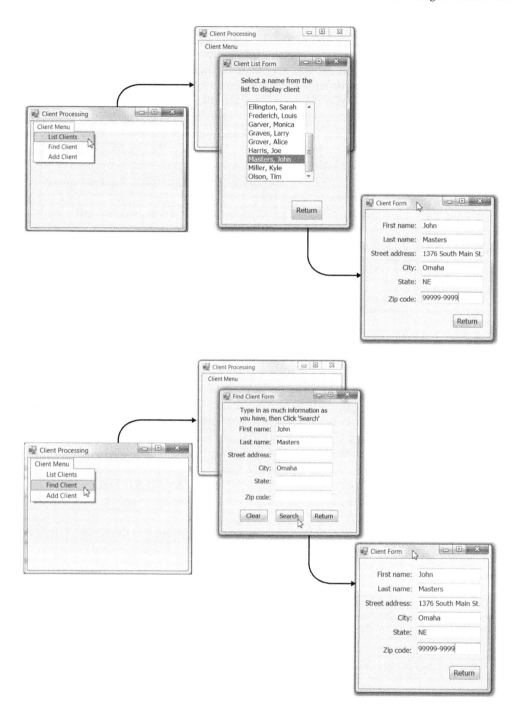

FIGURE 10-8
Sample User
Interface Prototype

develop. User interface prototypes are the slowest, most expensive, and most detailed approach. Therefore, storyboarding is used for parts of the system in which the interface is well understood and when more-expensive prototypes are thought to be unnecessary. However, in most cases it is probably worth the additional cost of developing wireframe diagrams in addition to storyboards. User interface prototypes are used for parts of the system that are critical, yet not well understood.

Common Sense Approach to User Interface Design

When you consider all of the above material, creating an effective user interface design can be a daunting and very time-consuming task. An interesting book by Steve Krug,[7] however, provides us with a set of guiding principles for Web usability. In this section, we adapt his principles to general user interface design.

First, the user should never have to think about how to navigate the user interface. As Krug puts it, "Don't make me think." Cognitively speaking, any time the user has to stop and figure out how to use the user interface, the creator of the user interface has failed. That might seem a little harsh, but it is true. From the user's perspective, the user interface is the system. If the developers have done their homework, the user interface should be intuitive to use. From a practical perspective, we should study how the user really uses the system. Based on Krug's observations of users, he found that users do not read Web pages; instead, they tend to scan them. As a general user interface design guideline, we suggest that you make it easy for users to identify the different parts of the user interface so that they simply scan the screen to see the section of the interface that is applicable to the problem that they are solving. Given the user's tendency to simply scan the user interface, Krug suggests that we should consider studying billboards for inspiration. Billboards are designed to be "read" at 70 mph as you drive down the highway. Obviously, the most relevant information must catch your attention for the billboard advertisement to work. He suggests that we should use the set of conventions with which we are familiar. For example, when looking at a newspaper you know that it is organized into different sections. In the case of the *Wall Street Journal,* you know that the front page acts as an index into the rest of the paper. Consequently, we should look for conventions that we can employ to aid the user.

Second, he suggests that the number of clicks that a user must perform to complete the task is somewhat irrelevant. Instead, building on his first guiding principle, the important thing is to design the user interface such that the choices (clicks) to be made are unambiguous. Making a lot of obvious choices is a lot quicker and easier than a few vague and ambiguous ones. Consequently, don't worry about the number of screens that the user must work through. However, like any other rule, this can be taken to an extreme. Too many clicks is still too many clicks. The overall goal is to minimize the user's effort. Simply focus on making it easier for the user to complete the task.

Third, minimize the number of words on the screen. Given that users scan the screen to find for what they are searching, make it easier by not cluttering the screen with lots of noise. He suggests that in the case of Web interfaces, 50 to 75 percent of the words can be eliminated without losing any information contained on the screen. Obviously, this may be somewhat extreme, but it does suggest that following the KISS[8] principle is critical when designing effective user interfaces.

NAVIGATION DESIGN

The navigation component of the interface enables the user to enter commands to navigate through the system and perform actions to enter and review information it contains. The navigation component also presents messages to the user about the success or failure of his or her actions. The goal of the navigation system is to make the system as simple as possible to use. A good navigation component is one the user never really notices. It simply functions the

---

[7] Steve Krug, *Don't Make Me Think: A Common Sense Approach to Web Usability,* 2nd Ed. (Berkeley, CA: New Riders, 2006).

[8] Keep it simple, stupid!

way the user expects, and thus the user gives it little thought. In other words, keep Krug's three guiding principles in mind as you work through the next three sections of the text.

Basic Principles

One of the hardest things about using a computer system is learning how to manipulate the navigation controls to make the system do what you want. Analysts should assume that users have not read the manual, have not attended training, and do not have external help readily at hand. All controls should be clear and understandable and placed in an intuitive location on the screen. Ideally, the controls should anticipate what the user will do and simplify his or her efforts. For example, many setup programs are designed so that for a typical installation, the user can simply keep pressing the Next button.

Prevent Mistakes The first principle of designing navigation controls is to prevent the user from making mistakes. A mistake costs time and causes frustration. Worse still, a series of mistakes can cause the user to discard the system. Mistakes can be reduced by labeling commands and actions appropriately and by limiting choices. Too many choices can confuse the user, particularly when the choices are similar and hard to describe in the short space available on the screen. When there are many similar choices on a menu, consider creating a second menu level or a series of options for basic commands.

Never display a command that cannot be used. Many Windows applications gray out commands that cannot be used; they are displayed on pull-down menus in a very light-colored font, but they cannot be selected. This shows that they are available but cannot be used in the current context. It also keeps all menu items in the same place.

When the user is about to perform a critical function that is difficult or impossible to undo (e.g., deleting a file), it is important to confirm the action with the user (and make sure the selection was not made by mistake). Having the user respond to a confirmation message, which explains what the user has requested and asks the user to confirm that this action is correct, usually does this.

Simplify Recovery from Mistakes No matter what the system designer does, users will make mistakes. The system should make it as easy as possible to correct these errors. Ideally, the system has an Undo button that makes mistakes easy to override; however, writing the software for such buttons can be very complicated.

Use Consistent Grammar Order One of the most fundamental decisions is the *grammar order*. Most commands require the user to specify an object (e.g., file, record, word), and the action to be performed on that object (e.g., copy, delete). The interface can require the user to first choose the object and then the action (an *object–action order*) or first choose the action and then the object (an *action–object order*). Most Windows applications use an object–action grammar order (e.g., think about copying a block of text in your word processor).

The grammar order should be consistent throughout the system, both at the data element level and at the overall menu level. Experts debate about the advantages of one approach over the other, but because most users are familiar with the object–action order, most systems today are designed using that approach.

Types of Navigation Controls

There are two traditional hardware devices that can be used to control the user interface: the keyboard and a pointing device such as a mouse, trackball, or touch screen. Today, depending on the hardware being used, voice recognition systems can also be used to control the user interface. There are three basic software approaches for defining user commands: languages, menus, and direct manipulation.

Languages With a *command language*, the user enters commands using a special language developed for the computer system (e.g., UNIX and SQL both use command languages). Command languages sometimes provide greater flexibility than other approaches because the user can combine language elements in ways not predetermined by developers. However, they put a greater burden on users because users must learn syntax and type commands rather than select from a well-defined, limited number of choices. Systems today use command languages sparingly, except in cases where there is an extremely large number of command combinations that make it impractical to try to build all combinations into a menu (e.g., SQL queries for databases).

Natural language interfaces are designed to understand the user's own language (e.g., English, French, Spanish). These interfaces attempt to interpret what the user means, and often they present back to the user a list of interpretations from which to choose. An example of the use of natural language is Google's search engine. Google's search engine enables users to use free-form text to search the Web for topics of interest.

Menus The most common type of navigation system today is the *menu*. A menu presents a user with a list of choices, each of which can be selected. Menus are easier to learn than languages because a limited number of available commands are presented to the user in an organized fashion. Clicking on an item with a pointing device or pressing a key that matches the menu choice (e.g., a function key) takes very little effort. Therefore, menus are usually preferred to languages.

Menus need to be designed with care because the submenus behind a main menu are hidden from users until they click on the menu item. It is better to make menus broad and shallow (i.e., each menu containing many items with only one or two layers of menus) rather than narrow and deep (i.e., each menu containing only a few items, but each leading to three or more layers of menus). A broad and shallow menu presents the user with the most information initially so that he or she can see many options and requires only a few mouse clicks or keystrokes to perform an action. A narrow and deep menu makes users hunt for items hidden behind menu items and requires many more clicks or keystrokes to perform an action.

Research suggests that in an ideal world, any one menu should contain no more than eight items, and it should take no more than two mouse clicks or keystrokes from any menu to perform an action (or three from the main menu that starts a system).[9] However, analysts sometimes must break this guideline in the design of complex systems by grouping menu items separated by a horizontal line. Often menu items have *hot keys* that enable experienced users to quickly invoke a command with keystrokes in lieu of a menu choice (e.g., on a Windows machine, across many applications, Ctrl-F tends to invoke the Find command; on a Mac, you use Command-F instead).

Menus should put together like items so that the user can intuitively guess what each menu contains. Most designers recommend grouping menu items by interface objects (e.g., customers, purchase orders, inventory) rather than by interface actions (e.g., new, update, format), so that all actions pertaining to one object are in one menu, all actions for another object are in a different menu, and so on. However, this is highly dependent on the specific interface. Some of the more common types of menus include *menu bars, drop-down menus, pop-up menus, tab menus,* and *toolbars.*

[9] Kent L. Norman, *The Psychology of Menu Selection* (Norwood, NJ: Ablex Publishing Corp., 1991).

Direct Manipulation With *direct manipulation*, the user enters commands by working directly with interface objects. For example, users can change the size of objects in Microsoft PowerPoint by clicking on them and moving their sides, or they can move files in Windows Explorer by dragging the filenames from one folder to another. Direct manipulation can be simple, but it suffers from two problems. First, users familiar with language- or menu-based interfaces don't always expect it. Second, not all commands are intuitive. [How do you copy (not move) files in Windows Explorer? On the Macintosh, why does moving a folder to the trash delete the file if it is on the hard disk, but eject the DVD if the file is on a DVD?]

Messages

Messages are the way the system responds to a user and informs him or her of the status of the interaction. There are many different types of messages, such as *error messages*, *confirmation messages*, *acknowledgment messages*, *delay messages*, and *help messages*. In general, messages should be clear, concise, and complete, which are sometimes conflicting objectives. All messages should be grammatically correct and free of jargon and abbreviations (unless they are the users' jargon and abbreviations). Avoid negatives because they can be confusing (e.g., replace "Are you sure you do not want to continue?" with "Do you want to quit?"). Likewise, avoid humor, because it wears off quickly after the same message appears dozens of times.

Messages should require the user to acknowledge them (by clicking, for example), rather than being displayed for a few seconds and then disappearing. The exceptions are messages that inform the user of delays in processing, which should disappear once the delay has passed. In general, messages are text, but sometimes, standard icons are used. For example, Windows displays an hourglass when the system is busy. All messages should be carefully crafted, but error and help messages require particular care. Messages (and especially error messages) should always explain the problem in polite, succinct terms (e.g., what the user did incorrectly) and explain corrective action as clearly and as explicitly as possible so that the user knows exactly what needs to be done. In the case of complicated errors, the error message should display what the user entered, suggest probable causes for the error, and propose possible user responses. When in doubt, provide either more information than the user needs or the ability to get additional information. Error messages should provide a message number. Message numbers are not intended for users, but their presence makes it simpler for help desks and customer support lines to identify problems and help users because many messages use similar wording.

Navigation Design Documentation

The design of the navigation for a system is done through the use of WNDs and real use cases. Real use cases are derived from the essential use cases (see Chapter 4), use scenarios, and WNDs. Recall that an essential use case is one that describes only the minimum essential issues necessary to understand the required functionality. A real use case describes a specific set of steps that a user performs to use a specific part of a system. Hence, real use cases are very useful when developing role-based access controls to support the security nonfunctional requirements (see Chapter 11), the documentation of the system (see Chapter 12), and when designing the tests (Chapter 12) and user training (see Chapter 13). However, since real use cases are implementation dependent, there may need to be customized versions for each platform on which the system is to be deployed.

To evolve an essential use case into a real use case, two changes must be made. First, the use-case type must be changed from essential to real. Second, all events must be specified in terms of the actual user interface. And, given the peculiarities of different platforms, e.g., desktops, tablets, and smartphones, real-use cases will need to be developed for each platform on which the use case is being deployed. Therefore, the normal flow of events, subflows, and alternative/exceptional flows must be modified. The normal flow of events, subflows, and alternative/exceptional flows for the real use case associated with the storyboard user interface prototype given in Figure 10-6 is shown in Figure 10-9. For example, step 2 of the

---

Use-Case Name: Maintain Client List	ID: 12	Importance Level: High

Primary Actor: Sales Rep	Use-Case Type: Detail, Real

Stakeholders and Interests: Sales Rep - wants to add, find, or list clients

Brief Description: This use case describes how sales representatives can search and maintain the client list.

Trigger: Patient calls and asks for a new appointment or asks to cancel or change an existing appointment.

Type: External

Relationships:

                                        Association: Sales Rep
                                        Include:
                                        Extend:

    Generalization:

Normal Flow of Events:

1. The Sales Rep starts up the system.
2. The System provides the Sales Rep with the Main Menu for the System.
3. The System asks Sales Rep if he or she would like to Add a client. Find an existing Client, or to List all existing clients.
   If the Sales Rep wants to add a client, he or she clicks on the Add Client Link and execute S-1: New Client.
   If the Sales Rep wants to find a client, he or she clicks on the Find Client Link and execute S-2: Find Client.
   If the Sales Rep wants to list all clients, he or she clicks on the List Client Link and execute S-3: List Clients.
4. The System returns the Sales Rep to the Main Menu of the System.

Subflows:

S-1: New Client
    1. The System asks the Sales Rep for relevant information.
    2. The Sales Rep types in the relevant information into the Form.
    3. The Sales Rep submits the information to the System.
S-2: Find Client
    1. The System asks the Sales Rep for the search information.
    2. The Sales Rep types in the search information into the Form.
    3. The Sales Rep submits the information to the System.
    4. If the System finds a single Client that meets the search information,
        the System produces a Client Information report and returns the Sales Rep to the Main Menu of the System
      Else
        If the System f inds a list of Clients that meet the search information. The System executes S-3: List Clients.
S-3: List Clients
    1. If this Subflow is executed from Step 3
        The System creates a List of All clients
      Else
        The System creates a List of clients that matched the S-2: Find Client search criteria.
    2. The Sales Rep selects a client.
    3. The System produces a Client Information report.

Alternate/Exceptional Flows:
    S-2 4a.   The System produces an Error Message.

FIGURE 10-9
Real Use-Case
Example

normal flow of events states that "The System provides the Sales Rep with the Main Menu for the System," which allows the Sales Rep to interact with the Maintain Client List aspect of the system.

INPUT DESIGN

Inputs facilitate the entry of data into the computer system, whether highly structured data, such as order information (e.g., item numbers, quantities, costs) or unstructured information (e.g., comments). Input design means designing the screens used to enter the information as well as any forms on which users write or type information (e.g., timecards, expense claims).

Basic Principles

The goal of the input mechanism is to simply and easily capture accurate information for the system. The fundamental principles for input design reflect the nature of the inputs (whether batch or online) and ways to simplify their collection.

Online versus Batch Processing There are two general formats for entering inputs into a computer system: online processing and batch processing. With *online processing* (sometimes called *transaction processing*), each input item (e.g., a customer order, a purchase order) is entered into the system individually, usually at the same time as the event or transaction prompting the input. For example, when you check a book out from the library, buy an item at the store, or make an airline reservation, the computer system that supports that process uses online processing to immediately record the transaction in the appropriate database(s). Online processing is most commonly used when it is important to have *real-time information* about the business process. For example, when you reserve an airline seat, the seat is no longer available for someone else to use.

With *batch processing*, all the inputs collected over some time period are gathered together and entered into the system at one time in a batch. Some business processes naturally generate information in batches. For example, most hourly payrolls are done using batch processing because time cards are gathered together in batches and processed at once. Batch processing is also used for transaction processing systems that do not require real-time information. For example, most stores send sales information to district offices so that new replacement inventory can be ordered. This information can be sent in real time as it is captured in the store so that the district offices are aware within a second or two that a product is sold. If stores do not need this up-to-the-second real-time data, they will collect sales data throughout the day and transmit it every evening in a batch to the district office. This batching simplifies the data communications process and often saves in communications costs, but it does mean that inventories are not accurate in real time but rather are accurate only at the end of the day after the batch has been processed.

Capture Data at the Source Perhaps the most important principle of input design is to capture the data in an electronic format at its original source or as close to the original source as possible. In the early days of computing, computer systems replaced traditional manual systems that operated on paper forms. As these business processes were automated, many of the original paper forms remained, either because no one thought to replace them or because it was too expensive to do so. Instead, the business process continued to contain manual forms that were taken to the computer center in batches to be typed into the computer system by a *data entry operator*.

Many business processes still operate this way today. For example, most organizations have expense claim forms that are completed by hand and submitted to an accounting department, which approves them and enters them into the system in batches. There are three problems with this approach. First, it is expensive because it duplicates work (the form is filled out twice, once by hand, once by keyboard). Second, it increases processing time because the paper forms must be physically moved through the process. Third, it increases the cost and probability of error, because it separates the entry from the processing of information; someone might misread the handwriting on the input form, data may be entered incorrectly, or the original input could contain an error that invalidates the information.

Most transaction-processing systems today are designed to capture data at its source. *Source data automation* refers to using special hardware devices to automatically capture data without requiring anyone to type it. Stores commonly use *bar-code readers* that automatically scan products and enter data directly into the computer system. No intermediate formats such as paper forms are used. Similar technologies include *optical character recognition*, which can read printed numbers and text (e.g., on checks), *magnetic stripe readers*, which can read information encoded on magnetic strip (e.g., credit cards), and *smart cards*, which contain microprocessors, memory chips, and batteries (much like credit card–sized calculators). As well as reducing the time and cost of data entry, these systems reduce errors because they are far less likely to capture data incorrectly. Today, portable computers and scanners allow data to be captured at the source even in mobile settings (e.g., air courier deliveries, use of rental cars).

These automatic systems are not capable of collecting a lot of information, so the next-best option is to capture data immediately from the source using a trained entry operator. Many airline and hotel reservations, loan applications, and catalog orders are recorded directly into a computer system, while the customer provides the operator with answers to questions. Some systems eliminate the operator altogether and allow users to enter their own data. For example, most universities no longer accept paper-based applications for admissions; all applications are typed by students into electronic forms.

The forms for capturing information (on a screen, on paper, etc.) should support the data source. That is, the order of the information on the form should match the natural flow of information from the data source, and data-entry forms should match paper forms used to initially capture the data.

Minimize Keystrokes Another important principle is to minimize keystrokes. Keystrokes cost time and money, whether they are performed by a customer, user, or trained data-entry operator. The system should never ask for information that can be obtained in another way (e.g., by retrieving it from a database or by performing a calculation). Likewise, a system should not require a user to type information that can be selected from a list; selecting reduces errors and speeds entry.

In many cases, some fields have values that recur often. These frequent values should be used as the *default value* for the field so that the user can simply accept the value and not have to retype it time and time again. Examples of default values are the current date, the area code held by the majority of a company's customers, and a billing address, which is based on the customer's residence. Most systems permit changes to default values to handle data-entry exceptions as they occur.

Types of Inputs

Each data item that has to be input is linked to a field on the form into which its value is typed. Each field also has a field label, which is the text beside, above, or below the field that tells the user what type of information belongs in the field. Often the field label is similar to the name of the data element, but they do not have to have identical words. In some cases, a field displays a template over the entry box to show the user exactly how data should be typed. There are many different types of inputs, in the same way that there are many different types of fields.

Text As the name suggests, a *text box* is used to enter text. Text boxes can be defined to have a fixed length or can be scrollable and can accept a virtually unlimited amount of text. In either case, boxes can contain single or multiple lines of textual information. We never use a text box if we can use a selection box.

Text boxes should have field labels placed to the *left* of the entry area, their size clearly delimited by a box (or a set of underlines in a non-GUI interface). If there are multiple text boxes, their field labels and the left edges of their entry boxes should be aligned. Text boxes should permit standard GUI functions, such as cut, copy, and paste.

Numbers A *number box* is used to enter numbers. Some software can automatically format numbers as they are entered, so that 3452478 becomes $34,524.78. Dates are a special form of numbers that sometimes have their own type of number box. Never use a number box if you can use a selection box.

Selection Box A *selection box* enables the user to select a value from a predefined list. The items in the list should be arranged in some meaningful order, such as alphabetical for long lists or in order of most frequently used. The default selection value should be chosen with care. A selection box can be initialized as unselected. However, it is better to start with the most commonly used item already selected.

Input Validation

All data entered into the system need to be validated to ensure their accuracy. Input *validation* (also called *edit checks*) can take many forms. Ideally, computer systems should not accept data that fail any important validation check to prevent invalid information from entering the system. However, even though this can be very difficult and invalid data can sometimes slip past data-entry operators and the users providing the information, enforcing the constraints discussed in Chapter 8 is a good place to start. Remember, there are three types of constraints that must be captured: *invariants*, *preconditions*, and *postconditions*. By reviewing the *contracts* and *assertions* that captured the constraints, most, if not all, data validation issues can be identified.

There are six different types of validation checks: *completeness check*, *format check*, *range check*, *check digit check*, *consistency check*, and *database check* (see Figure 10-10). Every system should use at least one validation check on all entered data and, ideally, perform all appropriate checks where possible. One thing that we should remember, in many cases the data that comes into a program via a user interface is typically formatted as a string. Consequently, the system must perform a format check on the string contents before any of the other validation checks can be performed. If the value is not the right data type, then none of the other tests will matter. For example, if an invariant states that the value of an attribute must be an integer, then a format check of the string value must test whether the value passed into the system can be cast to an integer or not. Only after it is shown that the value can be cast to an integer can the other checks be performed.

Type of Validation	When to Use	Notes
Completeness check Ensures all required data have been entered	When several fields must be entered before the form can be processed	If required information is missing, the form is returned to the user unprocessed.
Format check Ensures data are of the right type (e.g., numeric) and in the right format (e.g., month, day, year)	When fields are numeric or contain coded data	Ideally, numeric fields should not permit users to type text data, but if this is not possible, the entered data must be checked to ensure it is numeric. Some fields use special codes or formats (e.g., license plates with three letters and three numbers) that must be checked.
Range check Ensures numeric data are within correct minimum and maximum values	With all numeric data, if possible	A range check permits only numbers between correct values. Such a system can also be used to screen data for "reasonableness"—e.g., rejecting birthdates prior to 1880 because people do not live to be a great deal over 100 years old (most likely, 1980 was intended).
Check digit check Check digits are added to numeric codes	When numeric codes are used	Check digits are numbers added to a code as a way of enabling the system to quickly validate correctness. For example, U.S. Social Security numbers and Canadian Social Insurance numbers assign only eight of the nine digits in the number. The ninth number—the check digit—is calculated using a mathematical formula from the first eight numbers. When the identification number is typed into a computer system, the system uses the formula and compares the result with the check digit. If the numbers don't match, then an error has occurred.
Consistency checks Ensure combinations of data are valid	When data are related	Data fields are often related. For example, someone's birth year should precede the year in which he or she was married. Although it is impossible for the system to know which data are incorrect, it can report the error to the user for correction.
Database checks Compare data against a database (or file) to ensure they are correct	When data are available to be checked	Data are compared against information in a database (or file) to ensure they are correct. For example, before an identification number is accepted, the database is queried to ensure that the number is valid. Because database checks are more expensive than the other types of checks (they require the system to do more work), most systems perform the other checks first and perform database checks only after the data have passed the previous checks.

FIGURE 10-10 Types of Input Validation

OUTPUT DESIGN

Outputs are what the system produces, whether on the screen, on paper, or in other media, such as the Web. Outputs are perhaps the most visible part of any system because a primary reason for using an information system is to access the information that it produces.

Basic Principles

The goal of the output mechanism is to present information to users so that they can accurately understand it with the least effort. The fundamental principles for output design reflect how the outputs are used and ways to make it simpler for users to understand them.

Understand Report Usage The first principle in designing reports is to understand how they are used. Reports can be used for many different purposes. In some cases—but not very often—reports are read cover to cover because all information is needed. In most cases, reports are used to identify specific items or used as references to find information, so the order in which items are sorted on the report or grouped within categories is critical. This is particularly important for the design of electronic or Web-based reports. Web reports that are intended to be read from start to finish should be presented in one long scrollable page, whereas reports that are used primarily to find specific information should be broken into multiple pages, each with a separate link. Page numbers and the date on which the report was prepared are also important for reference reports.

The frequency of the report can also play an important role in its design and distribution. *Real-time reports* provide data that are accurate to the second or minute at which they were produced (e.g., stock market quotes). *Batch reports* are those that report historical information that may be months, days, or hours old, and they often provide additional information beyond the reported information (e.g., totals, summaries, historical averages).

There are no inherent advantages to real-time reports over batch reports. The only advantages lie in the time value of the information. If the information in a report is time critical (e.g., stock prices, air-traffic control information), then real-time reports have value. This is particularly important because real-time reports are often expensive to produce; unless they offer some clear business value, they might not be worth the extra cost.

Manage Information Load Most managers get too much information, not too little (i.e., the *information load* that the manager must deal with is too great). The goal of a well-designed report is to provide all the information needed to support the task for which it was designed. This does not mean that the report needs to provide all the information available on the subject—just what the users decide they need in order to perform their jobs. In some cases, this can result in the production of several different reports on the same topics for the same users because they are used in different ways. This is not a bad design.

For users in Westernized countries, the most important information should always be presented first in the top-left corner of the screen or paper report. Information should be provided in a format that is usable without modification. The user should not need to re-sort the report's information; instead critical information should be highlighted so that users can find it more easily amid a mass of data, or perform additional mathematical calculations.

Minimize Bias No analyst sets out to design a biased report. The problem with bias is that it can be very subtle; analysts can introduce it unintentionally. *Bias* can be introduced by the way lists of data are sorted because entries that appear first in a list can receive more attention than those later in the list. Data are often sorted in alphabetical order, making those entries starting with the letter *A* more prominent. Data can be sorted in chronological order (or reverse chronological order), placing more emphasis on older (or most recent) entries. Data may be sorted by numeric value, placing more emphasis on higher or lower values. For example, consider a monthly sales report by state. Should the report be listed in alphabetical order by state name, in descending order by the amount sold, or in some other order (e.g., geographic region)? There are no easy answers to this, except to say that the order of presentation should match the way the information is used.

Graphical displays and reports can present particularly challenging design issues.[10] The scale on the axes in graphs is particularly subject to bias. For most types of graphs, the scale should always begin at zero; otherwise, comparisons among values can be misleading. For example, have sales increased by very much since year 1 (see Figures 10-11a and b)? The numbers in both charts

---

[10] Two of the best books on the design of charts and graphical displays are by Edward R. Tufte, *The Visual Display of Quantitative Information, Envisioning Information* (Cheshire, CT: Graphics Press, 2001) and *Visual Explanations: Images and Quantities, Evidence and Narrative* (Cheshire, CT: Graphics Press, 1997). Another good book is by William Cleveland, *Visualizing Data* (Summit, NJ: Hobart Press, 1993).

are the same, but the visual images the two present are quite different. A glance at Figure 10-11a would suggest only minor changes, whereas a glance at Figure 10-11b might suggest that there have been some significant increases. In fact, sales have increased by a total of 15 percent over five years, or 3 percent per year. Figure 10-11a presents the most accurate picture; Figure 10-11b is biased because the scale starts very close to the lowest value in the graph and misleads the eye into inferring that there have been major changes. You should also beware of the so-called 3D effects. For example, the pie charts in Figures 10-11c and d represent the same data; in fact the data itself are constant. However, owing to the "3D" pie chart, the slices nearer the front look bigger.

Types of Outputs

There are many different types of reports, such as *detail reports*, *summary reports*, *exception reports*, *turnaround documents*, and *graphs* (see Figure 10-12). Classifying reports is challenging because many reports have characteristics of several different types. For example, some detail reports also produce summary totals, making them summary reports.

Media

Many different types of media are used to produce reports. Today, most organizations have moved toward "printing" reports electronically. One popular format is Adobe's pdf. These "reports" are stored in electronic format on file servers or Web servers so that users can easily access them. Often the reports are available in more predesigned formats than their

(a) Unbiased graph with scale starting at 0

(b) Biased graph with scale starting at 94

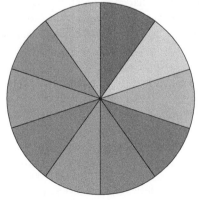

(c) Unbiased graph in 2D

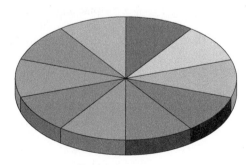

(d) Biased graph in 3D

FIGURE 10-11
Bias in Graphs

Type of Report	When to Use	Notes
Detail report Lists detailed information about all the items requested	When user needs full information about the items	This report is usually produced only in response to a query about items matching some criteria.
		This report is usually read cover to cover to aid understanding of one or more items in depth.
Summary report Lists summary information about all items	When user needs brief information on many items	This report is usually produced only in response to a query about items matching some criteria, but it can be a complete database.
		This report is usually read for the purpose of comparing several items to each other.
		The order in which items are sorted is important.
Turnaround document Outputs that "turn around" and become inputs	When a user (often a customer) needs to return an output to be processed	Turnaround documents are a special type of report that are both outputs and inputs. For example, most bills sent to consumers (e.g., credit-card bills) provide information about the total amount owed and also contain a form that consumers fill in and return with payment.
Graphs Charts used in addition to and instead of tables of numbers	When users need to compare data among several items	Well-done graphs help users compare two or more items or understand how one has changed over time.
		Graphs are poor at helping users recognize precise numeric values and should be replaced by or combined with tables when precision is important.
		Bar charts tend to be better than tables of numbers or other types of charts when it comes to comparing values between items (but avoid three-dimensional charts that make comparisons difficult).
		Line charts make it easier to compare values over time, whereas scatter charts make it easier to find clusters or unusual data.
		Pie charts show proportions or the relative shares of a whole.

FIGURE 10-12   Types of Reports

paper-based counterparts because the cost of producing and storing different formats is minimal. Electronic reports also can be produced on demand as needed, and they enable the user to more easily search for certain words. Furthermore, electronic reports can provide a means of supporting ad hoc reports, where users customize the contents of the report at the time the report is generated. Some users still print the electronic report on their own printers, but the reduced cost of electronic delivery over distance and the ease of enabling more users to access the reports than when they were only in paper form usually offset the cost of local printing.

MOBILE COMPUTING AND USER INTERFACE DESIGN[11]

From a user interface design perspective, going mobile is both exciting and challenging. Obviously, with today's smartphones, such as the iPhone™, there are many possibilities. However, just because these phones have the ability to surf the Web doesn't mean that a

[11] Obviously, in a short section we cannot cover all of the issues related to developing mobile applications. For anyone who is seriously considering developing mobile applications, we recommend that you begin by looking at books that deal with the specific devices on which you will be deploying your application. For example, Donn Felker, *Android*™ *Application Development for Dummies*™ (Hoboken, NJ: Wiley, 2011); Neal Goldstein and Tony Bove, *iPhone*™ *Application Development All-In-One for Dummies*™ (Hoboken, NJ: Wiley, 2010); Neal Goldstein and Tony Bove, *iPad*™ *Application Development for Dummies*™ (Hoboken, NJ: Wiley, 2010); and Chris Stevens, *Designing for the iPad*™: *Building Applications that Sell* (Chichester, UK: Wiley, 2011).

simple Web interface is the answer. These devices have limited screen space and have capabilities, such as *touch screens* and *haptic feedback* (such as vibration or pulses), which regular computers do not. Consequently, you really need to focus on designing the interface for the device and not simply porting the Web interface over to it. Furthermore, you need to realize that a *tablet*, such as the iPad™, is not a big *smartphone*; it is in its own category with its own challenges and capabilities. Consequently, you really need to design the interface for *mobile devices* from the ground up. In this section, we discuss some challenges and provide some guidelines to develop effective mobile interfaces. However, before we begin, you should realize that all of the material described previously is still applicable. It's just that when you are dealing with these devices, additional issues must be considered.

Tidwell[12] identifies six challenges that a mobile user interface designer must face. The screen of a phone is small. There simply is not a lot of "real estate" available to use. Not only are the screens small, but they come in different sizes. What works on one screen might not work on another screen. Some screens have haptic abilities: They respond to touch and orientation, and in some case, they vibrate. Obviously, these abilities are not available on all mobile devices. However, they do provide interesting possibilities for user interface design. Virtual and actual physical keypads are tiny. Consequently, too much typing can be challenging for the user to input the right information. People use their mobile devices, especially their phones, in all kinds of environments. They use them in dark places (like a poorly lit classroom). They use them in bright sunlight. They use them in quiet places (like the library or movie theater) and they use them in noisy places (such as at a football game). These devices are simply used everywhere today. Because these devices are used everywhere, the users can be easily distracted from the device. For example, have you ever texted someone when you aren't supposed to be using your phone, like during class? Or, what about out on a date? In other words, users are typically multitasking while using their phone. They do not want to spend a lot of energy on trying to navigate your mobile site or app. Consequently, Krug's three design principles described earlier are very important, especially his first one: Don't make me think!

Based on these challenges, Tidwell provides a set of suggestions that you should follow in designing a user interface for these devices. First, given the mobile context, you really need to focus on what the user needs and not what the user might want. In other words, you really should go back to business process and functional modeling (Chapter 4). In this case, only focus on the tasks that users need to perform when they are in the mobile context. This is a good example of a nonfunctional requirement (mobile computing) affecting the possible functional requirements.

Second, if you are porting an application or website to a mobile device, remove all "fluff" from the site: Strip the site down to its bare essentials. If the user needs access to the full site, be sure to provide a link to it in an obvious location. Alternatively, you could provide a complete mobile version of the application or website to the user. Obviously, the design of the user interface will be different, but the functionality should be the same.

Third, whenever possible, take advantage of the unique capabilities built into these devices. Some of the devices have *GPS* built in. Depending on your application, knowing where the user is could change the results. In other cases, the device has an accelerometer that allows the app to "know" the orientation of the device. Many of these devices have speech recognition capabilities, cameras that can be used for scanning, touch screens that allow sophisticated gestures to be used, and haptic feedback, such as bumps and vibrations. All of

---

[12] Jenifer Tidwell, *Designing Interfaces: Patterns for Effective Design,* 2nd Ed. (Sebastopol, CA: O'Reilly, 2010).

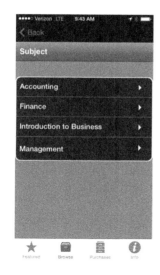

FIGURE 10-13
Linearization
Example, Wiley
Business Study
Center, used
with permission

these capabilities could prove useful in developing different mobile applications.

Fourth, when considering a phone, you tend to have a limited width from which to work. Consequently, you should try to linearize the content of the application (see Figure 10-13). By that we mean, take advantage of vertical scrolling and try to minimize, if not eliminate, horizontal scrolling. It is simply more natural for users to scroll up and down instead of left to right on these devices.

Fifth, optimize your mobile application for the user. This includes minimizing the number of times the device must interact with a server to download or upload information with a server. Not everyone has access to 4G, alone 5G, networks. In many cases, uploading and downloading are still very slow. Optimization also includes the user's interaction with the device. Instead of using a lot of typing, scrolling, and taps on a touch screen, consider using the speech recognition capability. It's a lot easier to speak slowly to a smartphone than it is to have to type a lot into a virtual or physical keyboard.

Tidwell also provides a set of reusable patterns that have been customized for mobile devices. These include things such as a vertical stack, filmstrip, and bottom navigation.[13]

In addition to the general suggestions that Tidwell provides, the whole area of interaction must be designed. With traditional GUI-based interfaces, the interactions tended to be limited to typing on a keyboard; using a mouse to click, scroll, or zoom in an interface; or using a combination of keyboard and the mouse to rotate part of the content in the interface. Overall, it is a fairly limited set of interactions. However, with the new mobile devices that have speech recognition, voice generation, touch screens, haptic feedback (via vibration), accelerometers that allow the device to know its orientation, and cameras that can be used for scanning input, the number of options for designing the navigation and input and output parts of the user interface have increased substantially. From our perspective, we are just now detecting the tip of the proverbial iceberg of possibilities with these devices. However, the general prototyping approach suggested earlier in the chapter works. Just the number of options to consider has increased substantially.

When it comes to the navigation part of the user interface, the primary additional option is the use of the touchscreen.[14] In fact, there is an entire vocabulary when it comes to the way users interact with touchscreens. Today, the designer needs to consider tapping, pinching, spreading, flicking, scrolling (one-finger vs. two-finger), and dragging to name a few. For example:

- Tapping can be used to open or activate an app, to select an object in the interface, or to stop an action, such as scrolling.
- Pinching is used to shrink or zoom out.
- Spreading is used to enlarge or zoom in.
- Flicking can be used to move an object or for interacting with a slider to scroll.

---

[13] pttrns.com and www.mobile-patterns.com provide many good patterns to use when developing mobile applications.

[14] A good reference to gestural design is Dan Saffer, *Designing Gestural Interfaces* (Sebastopol, CA: O'Reilly, 2008).

- Scrolling can be accomplished by using a single finger on a scroll bar or by using two fingers on anywhere on the interface.
- Move an object on the screen by placing a finger on the object and dragging it to another location. This is similar to using a mouse to drag an object to another location.

Different mobile devices may implement each of these slightly differently. Obviously, the number of choices to support navigation has greatly expanded.

For the input part of the user interface, the primary additional options to consider are the use of the camera as a device to scan items; microphone as a speech input device; and accelerometer to detect acceleration, orientation, and vibrations. For example, Google Maps™ supports a voice recognition interface to find a location. Also, there are numerous apps that use the accelerometer to detect acceleration and vibration (e.g., Wavefront Labs' Accelerometer Data Pro™). Furthermore, many games available on mobile devices use the accelerometer as an input device.

The primary additional options to consider for the output part of the user interface include voice generation and haptic feedback. For example, Google Maps™ and Waze™ support a voice generation capability that provides driving directions. Additionally, virtually all smartphones support a vibrate option when the phone rings and when alerts or text messages arrive.

SOCIAL MEDIA AND USER INTERFACE DESIGN[15]

Given the impact that Facebook™ and Twitter™, e.g., the Arab uprising, have had in today's world, developing applications for *social media* has obviously come to the forefront. In many ways, mobile computing and social media have grown up together. Like mobile computing, each social media platform has its own capabilities and challenges. Social media platforms range from sites that allow you to simply upload material to them, such as Instagram™ and YouTube™, to sites that support a virtual existence in the metaverse, such as Second Life™. During your career, you might need to develop applications for a specific social media platform, such as Facebook™ or Twitter™, or possibly develop your own social media site.

When developing your own social media presence, you must understand who is your target audience. Is the audience employees of your firm, or is the audience outside of the firm? In this section, we only focus on an external audience. Once you know who the audience is, you need to know what they are saying about the firm. In many ways, social media is nothing more than another channel for marketing the firm's products and capabilities. Before you can deploy a social media presence, you really need to understand what the users' needs (desires) are. In other words, back to requirements determination. In this case, the problem is that the users are "out there" somewhere, so typical approaches to gathering requirements, such as interviews and observation, don't work. Instead, you need to hunt through the Web to root out your requirements. Some of the more useful places to look are blogs or other social media outlets that address issues that would be of interest to your firm. When all else fails, you can always use a search engine such as Google™. Regardless, you obviously have to understand the functional requirements before you can design your social media presence.

Once you understand your functional requirements, you need to determine what type of social media presence is necessary to address the requirements effectively. Each social media platform has its own niche. Consequently, you might need to deploy many different applications across different platforms to effectively meet the firm's social media presence requirements. Also, you must look at your social media site as a means for your firm to build and

---

[15] Much of the material in this section has been based upon material from Jenifer Tidwell, *Designing Interfaces: Patterns for Effective Design,* 2nd Ed. (Sebastopol, CA: O'Reilly, 2010).

maintain a positive image or brand. Therefore, the social media site must contain material that your potential customers want to consume. You must remember that the underlying purpose of marketing is to "manufacture" wants and then "convert" the wants into needs. Given that your social media site is effectively another marketing channel, your site must be able to draw in new customers and to get current customers to regularly return. In this section, we provide some general guidelines for developing your own social media site so that both new customers visit and current customers return.[16]

First, you really need to post to your site regularly. If the content of the site becomes stagnant, no one will want to visit. The content of the site should contain a mixture of media: videos, podcasts, sound clips, and so on. The site's material should include a mixture of firm-driven material, material from customers, and links to relevant content that is located on other sites. Also, be sure to include ways for visitors to join in a "conversation" with the firm, such as Facebook™ comments or Twitter™ Tweets.

Second, make sure that you understand the difference between *push* and *pull* approaches. If the user must come to you to find out something, then you are using a pull-based approach. On the other hand, if you put the information out to the user, then you are using a push-based approach. When it comes to social media, you really need to use a combination of the approaches. For example, in Facebook™ if someone posts on your wall or sends you a request, Facebook™ will send you an e-mail message to try and entice you back to the Facebook™ site. The act of posting to your site was a pull-based action, and the e-mail message sent to you is a push-based action. In a nutshell, you want to focus on more of a push-based approach. You want your content to get to your customers in as an effective manner as possible. You don't want them to have to come looking for you. Encourage them to opt in for update notifications to come to them in a form that they prefer. Some might prefer e-mail notifications, and others might prefer you post to their Facebook™ or Twitter™ accounts. Also, be sure to include links to your social media sites on your home page. But be sure not to overwhelm the customer. Not every customer wants to know every tidbit regarding the firm. Only give the customer what the customer wants. Remember, Krug's first principle: Don't make me think! A corollary to this principle for social media would be: Don't make me work! Make it easy for the customer to find only what they want (or maybe what we want them to want).

Third, be sure that your home page and your social media sites are all synced together so that when one is updated, the other sites "know" about the update. This makes your job of maintaining the different sites much easier, and it allows your customers to have a consistent experience across all sites. However, don't overdo this. It is obvious that different sites have different media and, potentially, different audiences. You aren't going to use Facebook™ in the same way you would use Twitter™, YouTube™, or a blog. Be sure to include crosslinks among the different sites. This enables your customer to easily navigate through your different sites.

Fourth, enable the customers to share the great content that you have created. You can include buttons that allow them to email the content to their closest "friends" or other followers in their own social network. You also should provide a means to gather feedback from your customers regarding your content. One way is to include the ability for customers to make and share comments regarding your content. Another way is to provide a voting or "like" mechanism to encourage the customer to become engaged with your site.

---

[16] Two good books devoted to developing applications for social media in general are Erin Malone, *Designing Social Interfaces* (Sebastopol, CA: O'Reilly, 2009) and Gavin Bell, *Building Social Web Applications: Establishing Community at the Heart of Your Site* (Sebastopol, CA: O'Reilly, 2009). There are a couple of books devoted to two specific social media platforms. Two good books are Jesse Stay, *Facebook™ Application Development for Dummies™* (Hoboken, NJ: Wiley, 2011) and Dusty Reagan, *Twitter™ Application Development for Dummies™* (Hoboken, NJ: Wiley, 2010).

Fifth, be sure to design your sites so that not only your customers can easily find the material for which they are searching, but also search engines can find the material. Search engines are at least as likely to bring new customers to your sites as other customers. Design the site so that once the customer lands on your site, he or she stays there for a while. One way that you can accomplish this is by providing the customer with links to "related" material. If you decided to include a voting or "like" mechanism, be sure to enable the customer to see the "best" or, at least, the most popular material first. Another possibility is to create a leaderboard that displays the most shared material. You need to leverage the information gained by implementing the fourth guideline.

Sixth, one of the more difficult things to accomplish is to have your sites become a place that your customers feel that they belong. You want your customers to feel that they are members of something; you want to try to build a feeling of community. The more they feel that they belong, the more likely they will recommend your site to their friends. One way to accomplish this is to encourage employees, at least the "right" employees, to author their own "independent" sites that discuss topics of interest to your customers. This will give a more personal feel to the firm and possibly entice customers to stick around on the site longer.

Finally, in most cases, your customers visit your sites using a variety of hardware platforms. The platforms range from the desktop to the notebook to the tablet to the smartphone. Consequently, all of the material related to general user interface design and to mobile computing is applicable. Because you have a global audience, you need to be sure to take into account international and cultural issues in your design.

GAMES, MULTIDIMENSIONAL INFORMATION VISUALIZATIONS, AND IMMERSIVE ENVIRONMENTS[17]

With the advent of games and multidimensional information visualizations being used in business and the potential of applying immersive technologies, such as the Oculus Rift™, to solve business problems using augmented and virtual reality, the design of the human computer interaction layer is becoming even more important in information systems development. In many ways, user interface design for games, multidimensional information visualizations, and immersive environments is very similar to designing a user interface for more traditional application areas. However, in other ways, it is very different.

Games, Gamification, and User Interface Design

Games have been around for a very, very long time. They have been very successful in many different areas because they are fun and engaging.[18] When applying games to business situations, there are two general approaches to consider: development of games that support business processes and gamification of business processes. The development of games to solve business problems is relatively new. Traditionally, they have been used primarily with academic simulations. However, given the popularity of games in our culture, business games are

---

[17] Obviously, in a short section we cannot cover all of the issues related to developing games, multidimensional information visualizations, or using immersive environments to solve business applications. However, in this section we provide with an overview of the types of issues that you may run into when using these technologies. We also provide pointers to many references that have been useful in our development efforts.

[18] Jane McGonigal, *Reality Is Broken: Why Games Make Us Better and How They Can Change the World* (New York: Penguin Books, 2011); James Paul Gee, *Why Video Games Are Good for Your Soul* (Champaign, IL: Common Ground Publishing, 2005); Bernard Suits, *The Grasshopper: Games, Life, and Utopia* (Ontario, CA: Broadview Press, 2005).

being developed and deployed to increase customer and employee engagement.[19] *Gamification* deals with applying gaming mechanics to non-gaming situations. Gamification has been used to redesign classrooms and to support learning, and, like games, it too has been used to increase customer and employee engagement.[20]

In both using games and gamification, the secret to success deals with motivating the customer and/or employee to remain engaged with the business process. Even though traditional motivation approaches have worked to motivate employees in the past, due to the nature of the changing types of work performed, they no longer function in an efficient or effective manner (see Chapter 2). Traditional approaches typically used a "stick and carrot" approach to motivation. If an individual (child, student, or employee) did something undesired, he or she was punished. On the other hand, if they did something desired, they were rewarded. In other words, motivation was based entirely on extrinsic benefits. Games and gamification focus primarily on intrinsic benefits; not extrinsic benefits.[21] Typically, you play games because you enjoy the game. When was the last time that you played a game because you had to and not wanted to? Did you play it for money? Was it so that you could please someone else? Or, was it so that you could be part of something larger than yourself? How enjoyable was it? Are you motivated to play it again? Why? Chances are that money was not a sufficient motivator to play it again. But, playing a game for the fun of it will probably motivate you to play it over and over again. In fact, depending on your gaming personality type, playing a game to please someone else or to be part of something larger than yourself may motivate you to play it again.[22]

Given the success of business game development and the gamification of business processes, there are a few things that we can learn to improve user interfaces. One of the first things is that games are designed explicitly to be fun.[23] Typically, when we design business information systems, one of the last things we think about is whether the system is fun to use or not. When was the last time you considered using an accounting information system as being fun? However, in this case, the fun component of a business information system deals specifically with how engaging the user interface is.[24] Therefore, there are a few things that we can apply from games to develop more engaging user interfaces.[25]

First, games are about creating a user experience. Obviously, when creating an experience, the user interface designer must pay close attention to all of the issues that we have described earlier. Otherwise, not only will the experience be light on the engagement factor, but it could create a negative experience instead of the positive one that we hope for.

---

[19] Jesse Schell, *The Art of Game Design: A Book of Lenses* (Boca Raton, FL: CRC Press, 2008); Jon Radoff, *Game On: Energize Your Business with Social Media Games* (Indianapolis, IN: Wiley, 2011); and Bryon Reeves and J. Leighton Read, *Total Engagement: Using Games and Virtual Worlds to Change the Way People Work and Businesses Compete* (Boston, MA: Harvard Business Press, 2009).

[20] Lee Sheldon, *The Multiplayer Classroom: Designing Coursework as a Game* (Boston, MA: Course Technology, 2012); Rajat Paharia, *Loyalty 3.0: How Big Data and Gamification Are Revolutionizing Customer and Employee Engagement* (New York: McGraw-Hill, 2013); Gabe Zichermann and Joselin Linder, *The Gamification Revolution: How Leaders Leverage Game Mechanics to Crush the Competition* (New York: McGraw-Hill, 2013); and Kris Duggin and Kate Shoup, *Business Gamification for Dummies* (Hoboken, NJ: Wiley, 2013).

[21] Kevin Werbach and Dan Hunter, *For the Win: How Game Thinking Can Revolutionize Your Business* (Philadelphia, PA: Wharton Digital Press, 2012).

[22] Ralph Koster, *A Theory of Fun for Game Design,* 2nd Ed. (Sebastopol, CA: O'Reilly Media, 2014); Jesse Schell, *The Art of Game Design: A Book of Lenses* (Boca Raton, FL: CRC Press, 2008); and Kevin Werbach and Dan Hunter, *For the Win: How Game Thinking Can Revolutionize Your Business* (Philadelphia, PA: Wharton Digital Press, 2012).

[23] Ralph Koster, *A Theory of Fun for Game Design,* 2nd Ed. (Sebastopol, CA: O'Reilly Media, 2014).

[24] Jon Radoff, *Game On: Energize Your Business with Social Media Games* (Indianapolis, IN: Wiley, 2011); and Bryon Reeves and J. Leighton Read, *Total Engagement: Using Games and Virtual Worlds to Change the Way People Work and Businesses Compete* (Boston, MA: Harvard Business Press, 2009).

[25] Jesse Schell, *The Art of Game Design: A Book of Lenses* (Boca Raton, FL: CRC Press, 2008).

Second, game experiences are all about the ideas and themes woven throughout the game. In our case, the ideas of storytelling (see Chapter 3) and use cases (see Chapter 4) provide a basis to design and develop the user(s)' engagement experience.

Third, game developers worry a lot about the player (user). This brings a better focus to the roles (actors) that the users play in our system (see Chapter 3). When it comes to game design, not only do we have to worry about the tasks in which the user will be engaged, but we also have to start thinking about the individual psychological and cognitive differences among the different users.[26] This applies both to different types of customers and employees.

Fourth, game developers also tend to try and build a community around the game. In this way, users have a built-in support mechanism. Schell[27] suggests a set of tips to develop a strong community that can be applied to general business information systems development. He suggests that we should foster friendships by encouraging the users to talk with each other about the system and we should try to create community property by having the users (and developers) take joint responsibility for the system. However, one of his more relevant suggestions is to support multiple levels of users based on their level of experience. By having the system detect the level of expertise of the user in using the system, the system can introduce features, such as short cuts, once a specific "level" has been reached. This is associated with "leveling up" in games. This would help in addressing the trade-offs between ease of learning and ease of use when developing a user interface. This could also encourage users to "buy in" to the system.

Fifth, when it comes to successful game design, you must consider the aesthetics. As such, without a focus on aesthetics, the experience that you want the customer or employee to incur may be less than desirable. In fact, it could discourage them from returning to your site.

Multidimensional Information Visualization Design

There have been many different types of *multidimensional information visualizations* that have been used in business.[28] However, the different types fall into two basic categories: multidimensional information visualizations in *2D space* and multidimensional information visualizations in *nonimmersive 3D space*. Those visualizations that are displayed in 2D space include the basic business charts and graphs you would find in a spreadsheet or statistics package, e.g., heat maps, maps, node-link diagrams, parallel coordinates, radar charts, scatterplots, and treemaps.[29] The primary issue related to the use of these types of charts and diagrams deals with the potential of bias creeping into the display (see earlier in the chapter). However, when considering visualizations that are displayed in nonimmersive 3D space, additional issues are raised.[30]

---

[26] Chaomei Chen, *Information Visualization and Virtual Environments* (London: Springer-Verlag, 1999); and Howard Gardner, *Frames of Mind: The Theory of Multiple Intelligences* (New York: Basic Books, 1983).

[27] Jesse Schell, *The Art of Game Design: A Book of Lenses* (Boca Raton, FL: CRC Press, 2008).

[28] David Tegarden, "Business Information Visualization," *Communications of the Association for Information Systems*, Vol. 1, Article 4 (1999) (http://aisel.aisnet.org/cais/vol1/iss1/4).

[29] A set of good books that address these types of information visualizations are: Ben Fry, *Visualizing Data* (Sebastopol, CA: O'Reilly Media, 2008); Derek L. Hansen, Ben Shneiderman, and Marc A. Smith, *Analyzing Social Media Networks with NodeXL: Insights from a Connected World* (Burlington, MA: Morgan Kaufmann, 2011); Nathan Yau, *Visualize This: The FlowingData Guide to Design, Visualization, and Statistics* (Indianapolis, IN: Wiley, 2011); and Nathan Yau, *Data Points: Visualization That Means Something* (Indianapolis, IN: Wiley, 2013).

[30] A set of good books that address these types of information visualizations are: Judith R. Brown, Rae Earnshaw, Mikael Jern, and John Vince, *Visualization: Using Computer Graphics to Explore Data and Present Information* (New York: Wiley, 1995); Robert Spence, *Information Visualization* (Harlow England: ACM Press, 2001); Chaomei Chen, *Information Visualization: Beyond the Horizon*, 2nd Ed. (London: Springer-Verlag, 2004); and Usama Fayyad, Georges Grinstein, and Andreas Wierse (Eds), *Information Visualization in Data Mining and Knowledge Discovery* (San Francisco: Morgan Kaufmann, 2002).

FIGURE 10-14
Multidimensional
Surface Chart in
3D Space

FIGURE 10-15
Multidimensional
Bar Chart in
3D Space

FIGURE 10-16
Multidimensional
Bar Chart on
Floors and Walls
in 3D Space

The first issue that comes up is the issue of being able to determine a specific value that is being represented. For example, in Figure 10-14, which portrays a multidimensional surface chart, it is virtually impossible to determine specific values represented in the 3D space. In this case, there are four separate values being plotted: one for the X-axis, one for the Y-axis, one for the Z-axis, and one that uses the color of the surface. Only the last value, due to the legend, can be easily determined. Another example of this problem is portrayed in Figure 10-15 that shows a multidimensional bar chart. Again, four separate values are depicted. There are two basic approaches used to address this problem: being able to rotate and zoom the visualization and providing a *drill-down capability* that allows the specific values to be displayed (see Figure 10-16).

Another issue that comes up when displaying data in 3D space is *occlusion*; that is, when viewing data in 3D, some of the visualization may be covered up, hidden, by other parts of the visualization. For example, in Figure 10-15, the values drawn at the "back" of the visualization cannot be easily determined. In Figure 10-16, the negative values are drawn below the surface of the floor of the visualization. As such, the negative values cannot be seen. However, by rotating the visualization "up" and being able to click on a specific value, the values associated with that observation can be drilled down into and displayed in a semi-transparent window. In Figure 10-17, the visualization displays the basic values on the floor. With this visualization, in addition to supporting displays on the walls, the user can also use a slicing plane that "cuts through" the visualization to help better understand the data being visualized. These types of visualizations have been used quite extensively in supporting business decision making.

There are many more types of multidimensional information visualizations that have been used in business, e.g., volumes, floors and walls, maps, and surfaces. Each has its own strengths, weaknesses, and challenges. Furthermore, today there are many specialized tools that can be used to aid in designing and developing these types of visualizations. However, the basic design process is essentially the same user interface design process described earlier. You still have to design the navigation controls, the input mechanisms, and the output. To begin with, you will have to understand the underlying problem domain and the tasks that the user needs to perform. Next, you will need to choose the type of visualization to be

FIGURE 10-17
Multidimensional
Bar Chart on Floor
with Line Graphs on
Walls in 3D Space

designed based on the task that the user needs supported. This is still an art form. Our recommendation is to sit down with the user and go through different types of information visualizations to try and determine which of the information visualizations are reasonable. This decision should be based on whether the mapping of the data to the visualization is "intuitive" from the user's perspective or not. Also, remember that just because you can implement a complex, multidimensional information visualization does not mean that you should do it. In many cases, simple business charts and graphics are more than sufficient. Like game design, be sure to focus on aesthetics. If the visualization is not pleasing to the eye of the user, then it is probably the wrong visualization. Finally, given that visualization design is more of an art than a science, testing the visualization's effectiveness with many users is critical.

User Interface Design and Immersive Environments

Augmented and virtual reality using immersive technologies, such the Oculus Rift™, is among the latest and exciting application areas being utilized to solve business problems. Where *virtual reality (VR)* technologies completely immerse the user into an artificial simulated digital environment, *augmented reality (AR)* technologies are used to augment or enhance the view of the real world. There are both opportunities and challenges with deploying both of these technologies.

AR has primarily been used in advertising, real world navigation, room design, games, social networking, and medical applications.[31] If you happen to watch the NFL™ on TV, you have already experienced augmented reality: Think of the "first down" line that magically appears on the screen. The typical hardware used is a smartphone or tablet. One of the primary challenges in AR is the ability to use the camera to see and the software to interpret the real-world landscape that is being augmented by the system. This is known as *object recognition*. This especially is a problem when using AR browsers that "connects" the real world with content on the Web. In this case, a browser must recognize where it is physically located and add "links" to allow the user to look up additional information about the locations that it sees. To do this, the browser must use the camera, the GPS, and the accelerometer of the smartphone. Another major issue with regard to AR is of a social nature. For example, using AR devices while talking with someone can raise issues about privacy, such as are you paying attention to the other person or are you looking at the information being displayed and what exactly is the information being displayed. There are also apps available today that support facial recognition, which obviously raises even more issues with privacy. However, there are all kinds of possible benefits from using this technology, e.g., think about the advertising that takes place in the movie *Minority Report*. Using AR could allow you to see information that has been personalized about the locations around you as you walk down the street.

A prototyping approach, similar to the user interface design approach described earlier is used to design AR applications.[32] All of the issues related to traditional user interface design, game design, and multidimensional information visualization design are relevant and

[31] A good book to get a basic overview of augmented reality is Gregory Kipper and Joseph Rampolla, *Augmented Reality: An Emerging Technologies Guide to AR* (Waltham, MA: Syngress, 2013).

[32] Tony Mullen, *Prototyping Augmented Reality* (Indianapolis, IN: Syngress, 2011).

must be addressed, e.g., imagine using a heads-up display while driving your car to provide information about your location. Are you focusing on the road or are you simply experiencing another form of distraction? Consequently, testing the AR system in real-world situations is essential.

VR has been both overhyped and underutilized. Even though today VR has primarily been associated with games, it has been used in business for a long time.[33] It has been used in areas such as derivatives trading, financial risk management, industrial process control, marketing analysis, network modeling, operations management, organizational modeling, portfolio management, product design and manufacturing, room layout design, sensitivity analysis, simulated meetings, stock market analysis, and training. However, from a user interface design perspective, VR raises additional issues that need to be addressed.

It is believed that VR attains its power by captivating the user's attention and inducing a sense of *immersion*, the feeling of being present in the space being simulated. The challenge of creating the feeling of immersion has two primary dimensions: sensory and affective. In the sensory dimension, the combination of stimuli employed must be of sufficient vividness that an individual's automatic perceptual processes are triggered, resulting in the simulation being perceived as life-like. In the affective dimension, the user should be cast in an interactive, exploratory role. When considering these dimensions, one should remember that virtual reality resides in an individual's consciousness and, therefore, the relative contribution of each of these dimensions in creating a sense of immersion will vary across individuals. Thus, immersion is a function of both technology and perceiver. This raises the issue of individual psychological and cognitive differences.[34]

Interaction with a virtual world may take the form of *wayfinding* through the virtual space, rearranging existing, or creating new, 3D objects, or communicating with another agent (person or automaton) sharing the same virtual space. Visitors to large virtual worlds are often unable to comprehend the overall topological structure of the space. They may wander aimlessly when attempting to find a particular location for the first time and may subsequently have difficulty finding their way back to locations already visited. Wayfinding tasks require the user to be able to conceptualize the virtual space as a whole and to develop a *cognitive map* of it.[35] A cognitive map consists of not only spatial relationships, but also of auditory, sensory, and emotional impressions. In games, a map is typically provided to help with understanding where one is in the virtual space and from where one has come. Like the immersion issue, wayfinding also raises issues related to individual psychological and cognitive differences.

The last challenge with regard to using VR as a user interface platform deals with collaboration. When considering multiuser, distributed VR systems, such as many of today's video games, occlusion can become a very large problem. Not only can objects in the VR space hide other VR objects, but they can hide other users. Also, it is possible for one user to see something of interest that the other users may not. In this case, the issue of wayfinding comes back up. For example, if user A finds an interesting piece of information, then user A must

[33] David Tegarden, "Business Information Visualization," *Communications of the Association for Information Systems*, Vol. 1, Article 4 (1999) (http://aisel.aisnet.org/cais/vol1/iss1/4); Alan Wexelblat (Ed.), *Virtual Reality: Applications and Explorations* (Boston, MA: Academic Press, 1993); Dimitris Chorafas and Heinrich Steinmann, *Virtual Reality: Practical Applications in Business and Industry* (Englewood Cliffs, NJ: Prentice Hall, 1995); and Robert Thierauf, *Virtual Reality Systems for Business* (Westport, CN: Quorum Books, 1995).

[34] Chaomei Chen, *Information Visualization and Virtual Environments* (London: Springer-Verlag, 1999); and Howard Gardner, *Frames of Mind: The Theory of Multiple Intelligences* (New York: Basic Books, 1983).

[35] Reginald Golledge (Ed.), *Wayfinding Behavior: Cognitive Mapping and Other Spatial Processes* (Baltimore, MD: The John Hopkins University Press, 1999); and Rob Kitchin and Scott Freundschuh, *Cognitive Mapping: Past, Present and Future* (London: Routledge, 2000).

communicate how to navigate to a location in which the other users will be able to observe the finding. There are multiple possibilities here, including providing wayfinding directions from a specified "viewpoint," "teleporting" the other users from their individual current locations to the current location of user A, having user A go find the other users and bring them to the appropriate location, or having user A simply "drive" all other users to the appropriate location by taking over their ability to navigate through the visualization. Furthermore, once the other users are at the appropriate location, how do they return to their previous location?

Obviously, designing effective and efficient VR applications is very difficult.[36] Again, the overall design process is similar to the general user interface design process described earlier. However, given the potential for VR to support business decision making by combining gaming and information visualization technologies into a single seamless distributed environment and that the investment in specialized hardware and software is dropping, VR could provide large payoffs.

INTERNATIONAL AND CULTURAL ISSUES AND USER INTERFACE DESIGN[37]

With the World Wide Web, virtually any firm can have a global presence. With this capability, a firm must be cognizant of a set of international and cultural issues. These issues include multilingual requirements, color, and cultural differences.

Multilingual Requirements

The first and most obvious difference between applications used in one region and those designed for global use is language. Global applications often have *multilingual requirements*, which means that they have to support users who speak different languages and write using non-English letters (e.g., those with accents, Cyrillic, Japanese). One of the most challenging aspects in designing global systems is getting a good translation of the original language messages into a new language. Words often have similar meanings but can convey subtly different meanings when they are translated, so it is important to use translators skilled in translating technical words. A few rules that you should follow are to:

- Keep the writing short and simple. It is much easier to avoid mistranslations.
- Avoid humor, jargon, slang, clichés, puns, analogies, and metaphors. These tend to be too culturally specific. Consequently, the underlying point being made will most likely be lost in translation.
- Use good grammar. Be sure to punctuate everything correctly. Even though you might be tempted to ignore grammar and punctuation rules to try to make a point, it makes translating more difficult, especially for automated translation systems. Don't depend on automated spelling and grammar checkers to enforce this.

Another challenge is often screen space. In general, English-language messages usually take 20 percent to 30 percent fewer letters than their French or Spanish counterparts. Designing

---

[36] A recent book that tackles how to design a VR system is Ann Lantham Cudworth, *Virtual World Design* (Boca Raton, FL: CRC Press, 2014).

[37] A set of books that provide a good introduction to building information systems for a multicultural audience include Elisa M. del Galdo and Jakob Nielsen, *International User Interfaces* (New York, NY: Wiley, 1996); Nitish Singh and Arun Pereira, *The Culturally Customized Web Site: Customizing Web Sites for the Global Marketplace* (Oxford, UK: Elsevier Butterworth Heinemann, 2005); and John Yunker, *Beyond Borders: Web Globalization Strategies* (Berkley, CA: New Riders, 2003).

global systems requires allocating more screen space to messages than might be used in the English-language version.

Some systems are designed to handle multiple languages on the fly so that users in different countries can use different languages concurrently; that is, the same system supports several different languages simultaneously (a concurrent multilingual system). Other systems contain separate parts that are written in each language and must be reinstalled before a specific language can be used; that is, each language is provided by a different version of the system so that any one installation will use only one language (i.e., a discrete multilingual system). Either approach can be effective, but this functionality must be designed into the system well in advance of implementation.

Finally, one other consideration that must be considered is reading direction. In most Western societies, readers read from left to right and top to bottom. This is not true for many cultures. For example, in Arabic countries, readers typically read right to left and top to bottom.

Color

To begin with, color is not black and white. The meaning associated with a *color* is totally culturally dependent. In fact, black and white isn't necessarily black and white; they could be white and black. In most Western cultures, black is associated with death, mourning, and grief or with respect and formality. For example, in the United States, we typically wear black to a funeral, or you would expect to see religious leaders in black (think about the robes typically worn by a Catholic priest). In many Eastern cultures, on the other hand, white is associated with death or the color of robes worn by religious leaders. In an example reported by Singh and Pereira, when senior citizens in the United States and India were asked to "visualize the following statement: A lady dressed in white, in a place of worship," the results that came back were as near to the opposite as one could get. In India, the lady would be a widow, but in the United States she would be expected to be a bride.[38]

Other colors that have meanings that are culturally driven include green, blue, red, yellow, and purple. In the United States, red implies excitement, spice, passion, sex, and even anger; in Mexico, it indicates religion; in the United Kingdom, it indicates authority, power, and government; in Scandinavian countries, it indicates strength; and in China, it means communism, joy, and good luck. Blue is associated with holiness in Israel; cleanliness in Scandinavia; love and truth in India; loyalty in Germany; and trust, justice, and "official" business in the United States. In Ireland, green signifies nationalism and Catholicism, and in the United States it denotes health, environmentalism, safety, greed, and envy. Green is a very confusing color for Americans. In the Arab Middle East green is a sign of holiness, in France it represents criminality, and in Malaysia it signifies danger and disease. Yellow also has many culturally dependent meanings. In the United States, it is associated with caution and cowardice; in Scandinavia, warmth; in Germany, envy; and in India, commerce. Purple signifies death, nobility, or the Church in Latin America, the United States, and Italy, respectively. Obviously, when building a website for a global audience, colors must be chosen carefully; otherwise, unintentional messages will be sent.

Cultural Differences

The *New York Times* columnist Tom Friedman talks about the need for a firm to use its own local capabilities as a basis for competitive advantage in a global market. He refers to this

---

[38] Nitish Singh and Arun Pereira, *The Culturally Customized Web Site: Customizing Web Sites for the Global Marketplace* (Oxford, UK: Elsevier Butterworth Heinemann, 2005).

process as *glocalization*. In some ways, when developing a website for an international audience, you need to consider the opposite of glocalization. You need to think about what message needs to be sent to a local culture from your global organization to achieve the business goals of the firm. Consequently, you need to be able to understand the *cultural differences* among the possible users of your system when designing the user interface. Cultural issues have been studied at both organizational and national levels. Different researchers have emphasized different dimensions on which to focus our attention. In this section, we limit our discussion to cultural issues that affect designing effective user interfaces. In particular, we only address the research of Edward Hall and Geert Hofstede.[39]

Hall identified three dimensions that are directly relevant to user interface design: speed of messages, context, and time. The *speed of messages* dimension deals with how fast a member of a culture is expected to understand a message and how "deep" the content of a typical message will be in a culture. The deeper the message content, the longer it will take for a member of a culture to understand the message. For example, two different approaches to describe a historical event would be a news headline (fast and shallow) and a documentary (slow and deep). According to Hall, different cultures have different expectations of the content of and response to a message. This particular dimension has implications for the content of the message contained in the user interface. Krug's third design principle turns out to be culturally driven. For a Western audience, minimizing the number of words contained in a user interface makes sense. Westerners prefer to get to the point as fast as possible. However, this is not true for Eastern cultures.[40] Consequently, for a firm like Amazon.com, providing detailed reviews and short excerpts from a book provides support for a slow and deep culture, while providing bullet point types of comments supports the fast and shallow culture. By providing both, Amazon.com addresses both needs.

The second dimension, *context*, deals with the level of implicit information that is used in the culture versus the information needing to be made explicit. In *high-context* cultures, most information is known intrinsically and does not have to be made explicit. Therefore, the actual content of the message is fairly limited. However, in *low-context* cultures, everything must be spelled out explicitly to avoid any ambiguity, and therefore the message needs to be very detailed. You will find this dimension causing problems when attempting to close a business deal. In most Western societies, the lawyers want everything spelled out. In contrast, in most Eastern societies, it may, in fact, be considered insulting to have to spell everything out. From a website design perspective, a high-context culture would want the design to focus on aesthetics, politeness, and humility to produce an effective website, but in a low-context culture, things such as the terms and conditions of a purchase, the "rank" of the product and firm, and the use of superlatives in describing the product and firm are critical attributes of a successful website.

Hall's third dimension, *time*, addresses how a culture deals with many different things going on simultaneously. In a *polychronic time* culture, members of the culture tend to do many things at the same time but are easily distracted and view time commitments as very flexible. With *monochronic time* cultures, members of the culture solve many things by focusing on one thing at a time, are single-minded, and consider time commitments as something that is set in stone. When designing for a polychronic culture, the liberal use of "pop-up" messages might be fun and engaging, while in a monochronic culture, pop-up messages

---

[39] See Geert Hofstede, *Culture's Consequences: Comparing Values, Behaviors, Institutions and Organizations across Nations*, 2nd Ed. (Thousand Oaks, CA: Sage, 2001); Geert Hofstede, Gert Jan Hofstede, and Michael Minkov, *Cultures and Organizations: Software of the Mind*, 3rd Ed. (New York: McGraw-Hill, 2010); and Edward T. Hall, *Beyond Culture* (New York: Anchor Books, 1981).

[40] See Richarde E. Nisbett, *The Geography of Thought: How Asians and Westerners Think Differently . . . And Why* (New York: Free Press, 2003).

simply annoy the user. In the past, Northern Hemisphere cultures have been monochronic and Southern Hemisphere cultures have been polychronic. However, with the use of e-mail interruptions and text messaging, this could change over time. Regardless, allowing interruptions to occur does in fact distract the users from their current task. Depending on the culture, this could be a good or bad thing to support.

Hofstede also has identified cultural dimensions that are relevant to the user interface. These include power distance, uncertainty avoidance, individualism versus collectivism, and masculinity versus femininity. The first dimension, *power distance*, addresses how the distribution of social power is dealt with in the culture. In cultures with a high power distance, members of the culture believe in the authority of the social hierarchy. In cultures with low power distance, members of the culture believe that power should be more equally distributed. Consequently, in cultures with a high power distance, emphasis on the "greatness" of the leaders of the firm, the use of "proper titles" for members of the firm, and the posting of testimonials on behalf of the firm by "prominent" members of society is important. International awards won by the firm, its members, or its products should also be posted prominently on the website.

The second dimension, *uncertainty avoidance*, addresses to what degree a culture is comfortable with uncertainty. In a culture with a high uncertainty avoidance, members avoid taking risks, value tradition, and are much more comfortable in a rule-driven society. In cultures that score high on uncertainty avoidance, more customer service needs to be provided, more important "local" contacts need to be available, the firm's and product's history and tradition need to be provided on the website, and, in the case of software, the use of free trials and downloads is critical. In other words, you need to build trust and reduce perceived risk between the customer and the firm. This can be supported through product seals of approval or the use of WebTrust™ certifications for the website.[41] Merely translating a website from a low uncertainty avoidance culture to a high uncertainty avoidance culture is not sufficient. You also need to point out relationships between the local culture and the firm's products.

The third dimension, *individualism* versus *collectivism*, is based on the level of emphasis the culture places on the individual or the collective, or group. In North America and Europe, individualism is rewarded. However, in East Asia, it is believed that by focusing on optimizing the group, the individual will be most successful. In other words, it is the group that is the most important. In a collective society, presenting information on how the firm "gives back" to the community; supports "member" clubs, "loyalty" programs, and "chat" facilities; and provides links to "local" sites of interest are very important characteristics for a website. In contrast, in an individualistic society, providing support for personalization of the user's experience with the website, emphasizing the uniqueness of the products that the user is viewing, and emphasizing the privacy policy of the site are critical.

Hofstede's fourth dimension, *masculinity* versus *femininity*, does not mean how men and women are treated by the culture. But, instead this dimension addresses how well masculine and feminine characteristics are valued by the culture. For example, in a masculine culture, characteristics such as being assertive, ambitious, aggressive, and competitive are valued, whereas in a feminine culture, characteristics such as being encouraging, compassionate, thoughtful, gentle, and cooperative are valued. In masculine cultures, a focus on the effectiveness of the firm's products is essential. Also, clearly separating male- and female-oriented topics and placing them on different sections of a website can be critical. Relative to male cultures, feminine cultures value a focus on aesthetics and using more of a soft-sell approach,

[41] See https://www.cpacanada.ca/en/business-and-accounting-resources/audit-and-assurance/overview-of-webtrust-services.

where the focus on more affective, intangible aspects of the firm, its members, and its products is more appropriate.

Obviously, operationalizing Hall's and Hofstede's dimensions for effective user interface design is not easy. Furthermore, given all of the different platforms on which a user interface can be deployed, the level of complexity and difficulty in designing effective and efficient user interfaces that take into consideration the global and multicultural world in which we live is increasing. However, in a global market, ignoring cultural issues in user interface design, whether it is for an internal system used only by employees of the firm or an external system that is used by customers, will most certainly cause a system to fail.

NONFUNCTIONAL REQUIREMENTS AND HUMAN–COMPUTER INTERACTION LAYER DESIGN

The human–computer interaction layer is heavily influenced by nonfunctional requirements. In this chapter, we dealt with issues such as layout of the user interface, awareness of content, aesthetics, user experience, and consistency. We also have provided information on how to design the navigation, inputs, and outputs of the user interface. Finally, we have considered mobile computing, social media, immersive and multidimensional environments, and international and cultural issues in user-interface design. None of these have anything to do with the functional requirements of the system. However, if they are ignored, the system can be unusable. As with the data management layer, there are four primary types of nonfunctional requirements that can be important in designing the human–computer interaction layer: operational, performance, security, and cultural and political requirements.

Operational requirements, such as choice of hardware and software platforms, influence the design of the human–computer interaction layer. For example, something as simple as the number of buttons on a mouse (one, two, three, or more) changes the interaction that the user will experience. Other operational nonfunctional requirements that can influence the design of the human–computer interaction layer include system integration and portability. In these cases, a Web-based solution may be required, which can affect the design; not all features of a user interface can be implemented efficiently and effectively on the Web. This can require additional user interface design. Obviously, the entire area of mobile computing can affect the success or failure of the system.

Performance requirements, over time, have become less of an issue for this layer. However, speed requirements are still paramount, especially with mobile computing. Most users do not care for hitting return or clicking the mouse and having to take a coffee break while they are waiting for the system to respond, so efficiency issues must be still addressed. Depending on the user interface toolkit used, different user interface components may be required. Furthermore, the interaction of the human–computer interaction layer with the other layers must be considered. For example, if the system response is slow, incorporating more-efficient data structures with the problem domain layer, including indexes in the tables with the data management layer, and/or replicating objects across the physical architecture layer could be required.

Security requirements affecting the human–computer interaction layer deal primarily with the access controls implemented to protect the objects from unauthorized access, the authorization controls that support limiting log-ins, and the possibility of encrypting any and all data that is transmitted between the user interface and the system. Most of the information necessary to support these controls can be derived from the real use case descriptions and the CRC cards and CRUDE matrices referenced in previous chapters. However, most of these controls are enforced through the DBMS on the data management layer (Chapter 9) and the operating system on the physical architecture layer (Chapter 11). However, through the expansion of the validation of inputs to the system to include the security requirements, the design of this layer can be critical.[42]

In addition to the international and cultural issues described previously, unstated norms effect the cultural and political requirements that can affect the design of the human–computer interaction layer. Unstated norm requirements include having the date displayed in the appropriate format (MM/DD/YYYY versus DD/MM/YYYY). For a system to be truly useful in a global environment, the user interface must be customizable to address local cultural requirements.

VERIFYING AND VALIDATING THE HUMAN–COMPUTER INTERACTION LAYER[43]

In addition to performing input validation, verifying and validating the human–computer interaction layer design is necessary to understand how to improve the user interface before the system is complete. Most interface designers intentionally or unintentionally design an interface that meets their personal preferences, which might or might not match the preferences of the users. The key message, therefore, is to have as many people as possible evaluate the interface, and the more users the better. Most experts recommend involving at least ten potential users in the evaluation process.

Interface evaluations almost always identify improvements, so the interface design process is repeated in a cyclical process until no new improvements are identified. In practice, most analysts interact closely with the users during the interface design process so that users have many chances to see the interface as it evolves, rather than waiting for one overall interface evaluation at the end of the interface design process. It is better for all concerned (both analysts and users) if changes are identified sooner rather than later. For example, if the interface structure or standards need improvements, it is better to identify changes before most of the screens that use the standards have been designed.[44] Ideally, interface evaluation should be performed while the system is being designed—before it is built—so that any major design problems can be identified and corrected before the time and cost of programming have been spent on a weak design. It is not uncommon for the system to undergo one or two major changes after the users see the first interface design prototype because they identify problems that are overlooked by the project team. However, many organizations save interface evaluation for the very last step in the systems development before the system is installed.

As with interface design prototyping, interface evaluation can take many different forms, each with different costs and different amounts of detail. In addition to all of the types of input validation described earlier, there are five common approaches to interface evaluation: heuristic evaluation, walkthrough evaluation, interactive evaluation, A/B testing, and formal usability testing. As with interface design prototyping, the different parts of a system can be evaluated using different techniques.

---

[42] We describe security requirements in more detail in Chapter 11.

[43] Verifying and validation approaches, in general, were described in Chapters 4 through 7. Also, further approaches to testing the evolving system are described in Chapter 12. In this section, we describe approaches that have been customized to the human–computer interaction layer.

[44] A good source for more information on user interface evaluation is Deborah Hix and H. Rex Hartson, *Developing User Interfaces, Ensuring Usability Through Product & Process* (New York: Wiley, 1993).

A *heuristic evaluation* examines the interface by comparing it to a set of heuristics or principles for interface design. The project team develops a checklist of interface design principles—from the list at the start of this chapter, for example, as well as the list of principles in the navigation, input, and output design sections later in this chapter. At least three members of the project team then individually work through the interface design prototype, examining every interface to ensure that it satisfies each design principle on a formal checklist. After each has gone through the prototype separately, they meet as a team to discuss their evaluations and identify specific improvements that are required.

An interface design *walkthrough evaluation* is a meeting conducted with the users who ultimately have to operate the system. The project team presents the prototype to the users and walks them through the various parts of the interface. The project team shows the storyboard and wireframe diagrams or actually demonstrates the user interface prototype and explains how the interface will be used. The users identify improvements to each of the interfaces that are presented.

With an *interactive evaluation*, the users themselves actually work with the user interface prototype in a one-person session with member(s) of the project team (an interactive evaluation cannot be used with a storyboard or wireframe diagrams). As the user works with the prototype (often by going through the use scenarios, using the real use cases described earlier in this chapter, or just navigating at will through the system), he or she tells the project team member(s) what he or she likes and doesn't like and what additional information or functionality is needed. As the user interacts with the prototype, team member(s) records the cases when he or she appears to be unsure of what to do, makes mistakes, or misinterprets the meaning of an interface component. If the pattern of uncertainty, mistakes, or misinterpretations reoccurs across several of the users participating in the evaluation, it is a clear indication that those parts of the interface need improvement.

A/B testing is a form of interactive evaluation. These techniques were originally developed in marketing to ascertain which marketing campaign would be the best. In our case, multiple user interface prototypes are created instead of different marketing campaigns. Potential users are assigned to the different versions of the user interface. The effectiveness of the user interfaces are tested and statistically analyzed to determine which of the user interfaces should be further developed and deployed.

Formal *usability testing* is commonly done with commercial software products and products developed by large organizations that will be widely used through the organization. As the name suggests, it is a very formal—almost scientific—process that can be used only with language prototypes (and systems that have been completely built awaiting installation or shipping).[45] As with interactive evaluation, usability testing is done in one-person sessions in which a user works directly with the software. However, it is typically done in a special lab equipped with video cameras and special software that records every keystroke and mouse operation so that they can be replayed to understand exactly what the user did.

The user is given a specific set of tasks to accomplish (usually the use scenarios), and after some initial instructions, the project team's members are not permitted to interact with the user to provide assistance. The user must work with the software without help, which can be hard on the users if they become confused with the system. It is critical that users understand that the goal is to test the interface, not their abilities, and if they are unable to complete the task, the interface—not the user—has failed the test.

Formal usability testing is very expensive, because each one-user session can take one to two days to analyze depending on the volume of detail collected in the computer logs and

[45] A good source for usability testing is Jakob Nielsen and Robert Mack (Eds), *Usability Inspection Methods* (New York: Wiley, 1994). See also www.useit.com/papers.

videos. Sessions typically last one to two hours. Most usability testing involves five to ten users, because if there are fewer than five users, the results depend too much on the specific individual users who participated, and more than ten users are often too expensive to justify (unless a large commercial software developer is involved).

APPLYING THE CONCEPTS AT PATTERSON SUPERSTORE

The design of the human–computer interaction layer is particularly important because to the user, the interface is the system. The challenge for the team was ensuring that the interface will display accurately on devices of various sizes. Next, they developed the WND for the Mobile Scheduling phase of the system and developed the design proto-types for the interface. After completing these tasks, the team developed the navigation documentation artifacts.

You can find the rest of the case at www.wiley.com/go/dennis/systemanalysis6e/casestudy.

CHAPTER REVIEW

After reading and studying this chapter, you should be able to:

- ☐ Describe the six basic principles of user interface design.
- ☐ Apply the use-case driven process described to design a user interface.
- ☐ Describe the purpose of use scenarios in user interface design.
- ☐ Describe how to use windows navigation diagrams, wireframe diagrams, storyboards, and user interface prototypes during the design of a user interface.
- ☐ Describe the difference between essential and real use cases.
- ☐ Describe the importance and use of interface standards in user interface design.
- ☐ Discuss the relationship between user interface design and requirements determination.
- ☐ Design efficient and effective navigation controls that are easy to use, prevent users from making mistakes, support obvious approaches for users to recover from mistakes, and use a consistent grammar order.
- ☐ Design efficient and effective input mechanisms that capture the necessary information for the system.
- ☐ Design efficient and effective output that supports the users in their tasks.
- ☐ Describe the unique issues related to designing user interfaces for mobile computing platforms.
- ☐ Describe the unique navigation controls, input mechanisms, and outputs that mobile computing platforms possess.
- ☐ Describe the unique issues related to designing user interfaces for social applications.
- ☐ Describe the unique issues related to designing user interfaces for immersive and multidimensional applications.
- ☐ Discuss the international and cultural issues that can affect the design of the human–computer interaction layer.
- ☐ Describe how nonfunctional requirements may influence the actual design of the human–computer interaction layer.
- ☐ Describe the five common approaches used to evaluate user interfaces.

KEY TERMS

A/B testing	Action-object order	Assertions	Batch processing
Acknowledgment message	Activity diagrams	Augmented reality (AR)	Batch report
	Aesthetics	Bar-code reader	Bias

Button
Check digit check
Cognitive map
Collectivism
Color
Combo box
Command language
Completeness check
Confirmation message
Consistency
Consistency check
Content awareness
Context
Contractions
Cultural differences
2D space
Database check
Data-entry operator
Default value
Delay message
Detail report
Direct manipulation
Drill-down capability
Drop-down menu
Ease of learning
Ease of use
Edit check
Error message
Essential use case
Exception report
Femininity
Field
Field label

Form
Format check
Gamification
GPS
Grammar order
Graph
Graphical user interface (GUI)
Haptic feedback
Help message
Heuristic evaluation
High-context
Hot key
Immersion
Individualism
Information load
Input mechanism
Interactive evaluation
Interface action
Interface design prototype
Interface evaluation
Interface icon
Interface metaphor
Interface object
Interface standards
Interface template
Invariants
Layout
Low context
Magnetic stripe readers
Masculinity
Menu
Menu bar
Mobile device

Monochronic time
Multidimensional information
  visualization
Multilingual requirements
Natural language
Navigation controls
Navigation mechanism
Nonimmersive 3D space
Number box
Object-action order
Object recognition
Occlusion
Online processing
Optical character recognition
Output mechanism
Polychronic time
Pop-up menu
Postcondition
Power distance
Precondition
Pull
Push
Range check
Real-time information
Real-time report
Real use case
Report
Screen
Selection box
Sequence diagrams
Smart card
Smartphone
Social media

Source data automation
Speed of messages
State
Stereotype
Storyboard
Summary report
System interface
Tablet
Tab menu
Text box
Three-clicks rule
Time
Toolbar
Touch screens
Transaction processing
Transition
Turnaround document
Uncertainty avoidance
Usability testing
Use case
User experience
User interface
User interface prototype
Use scenario
Validation
Virtual reality (VR)
Walkthrough evaluation
Wayfinding
White space
Window
Window navigation
  diagram (WND)
Wireframe diagram

QUESTIONS

1. Explain three important user interface design principles.
2. What are three fundamental parts of most user interfaces?
3. Why is content awareness important?
4. What is white space, and why is it important?
5. Under what circumstances should densities be low? High?
6. How can a system be designed to be used by both experienced and first-time users?
7. Why is consistency in design important? Why can too much consistency cause problems?
8. How can different parts of the interface be consistent?
9. Describe the basic process of user interface design.
10. What are use cases, and why are they important?
11. What is a WND, and why is it used?

12. Why are interface standards important?
13. Explain the purpose and contents of interface metaphors, interface objects, interface actions, interface icons, and interface templates.
14. Why do we prototype the user interface design?
15. What are Krug's three design principles?
16. Describe three basic principles of navigation design.
17. How can you prevent mistakes?
18. Explain the differences between object-action order and action-object order.
19. Describe four types of navigation controls.
20. Why are menus the most commonly used navigation control?
21. Compare and contrast four types of menus.
22. Under what circumstances would you use a drop-down menu versus a tab menu?

23. Under what circumstances would you use an image map versus a simple list menu?
24. Describe five types of messages.
25. What are the key factors in designing an error message?
26. What is context-sensitive help? Does your word processor have context-sensitive help?
27. How do an essential use case and a real use case differ?
28. What is the relationship between essential use cases and use scenarios?
29. What is the relationship between real use cases and use scenarios?
30. Explain three principles in the design of inputs.
31. Compare and contrast batch processing and online processing. Describe one application that would use batch processing and one that would use online processing.
32. Why is capturing data at the source important?
33. Describe four devices that can be used for source data automation.
34. Describe five types of inputs.
35. Why is input validation important?
36. Describe five types of input validation methods.
37. Describe how invariants, preconditions, and postconditions are useful in input validation.
38. Explain three principles in the design of outputs.
39. Describe five types of outputs.
40. What do you think are three common mistakes that novice analysts make in navigation design?
41. What do you think are three common mistakes that novice analysts make in input design?
42. What do you think are three common mistakes that novice analysts make in output design?
43. What are the six challenges you face when developing mobile applications?
44. What are the six suggestions to address the mobile computing challenges?
45. What are the unique navigation controls, input mechanisms, and outputs that mobile computing supports?

46. With regard to social media, what is the difference between "push" and "pull" approaches to interacting with customers?
47. Why is it important to keep your social media sites synced?
48. How can you keep your customers engaged with your social media sites?
49. Why do people play games?
50. What is gamification?
51. What is occlusion? Why is it an issue when developing multidimensional information visualizations? Augmented reality systems? Virtual reality systems?
52. What is augmented reality?
53. Name some of potential business applications of augmented reality.
54. What is virtual reality?
55. Name some of potential business applications of virtual reality.
56. When developing a virtual reality system, what are some of the issues that need to be addressed?
57. What is a cognitive map?
58. What are some of the multilingual issues that you may face when developing for a global audience?
59. How important is the proper use of color when developing websites for a global audience? Give some examples of potential pitfalls that you could run into.
60. Name the three cultural dimensions that are relevant to user interface design identified by Hall. Why are they relevant?
61. Name the four cultural dimensions that are relevant to user interface design identified by Hofstede. Why are they relevant?
62. What are some of the nonfunctional requirements that can influence the design of the human–computer interaction layer?
63. Why is it important to perform an interface evaluation before the system is built?
64. Compare and contrast the five types of interface evaluation.
65. Under what conditions is heuristic evaluation justified?

EXERCISES

A. Develop two use scenarios for a website that sells some retail products (e.g., books, music, clothes).
B. Create a storyboard for a website that sells some retail products (e.g., books, music, clothes).
C. Draw a WND for a website that sells some retail products (e.g., books, music, clothes).

D. Create a wireframe diagram for the home page of a website that sells some retail products (e.g., books, music, clothes).
E. Describe the primary components of the interface standards for a website that sells some retail products (metaphors, objects, actions, icons, and template).

F. Using the Web, identify a set of games that are useful in some aspect of business, e.g., advertising or training.

G. Using the Web, identify a set of multidimensional information visualizations that are used to support business decision-making.

H. Using the Web, find businesses that are currently using augmented and virtual reality systems.

I. For the A Real Estate Inc. problem in Chapter 4 (exercises I, J, and K), Chapter 5 (exercises N and O), Chapter 6 (exercise D), Chapter 7 (exercise D), Chapter 8 (exercise A), and Chapter 9 (exercise H):
  1. Develop two use scenarios.
  2. Draw a WND.
  3. Design a storyboard.

J. Based on your solution to exercise I:
  1. Create wireframe diagrams for the interface design.
  2. Develop a real use case.

K. For the A Video Store problem in Chapter 4 (exercises L, M, and N), Chapter 5 (exercises P and Q), Chapter 6 (exercise E), Chapter 7 (exercise E), Chapter 8 (exercise B), and Chapter 9 (exercise I):
  1. Develop two use scenarios.
  2. Draw a WND.
  3. Design a storyboard.

L. Based on your solution to exercise K:
  1. Create wireframe diagrams for the interface design.
  2. Develop a real use case.

M. For the gym membership problem in Chapter 4 (exercises O, P, and Q), Chapter 5 (exercises R and S), Chapter 6 (exercise F), Chapter 7 (exercise F), Chapter 8 (exercise C), and Chapter 9 (exercise J):
  1. Develop two use scenarios.
  2. Draw a WND.
  3. Design a storyboard.

N. Based on your solution to exercise M:
  1. Create wireframe diagrams for the interface design.
  2. Develop a real use case.

O. For the Picnics R Us problem in Chapter 4 (exercises R, S, and T), Chapter 5 (exercises T and U), Chapter 6 (exercise G), Chapter 7 (exercise G), Chapter 8 (exercise D), and Chapter 9 (exercise K):
  1. Develop two use scenarios.
  2. Draw a WND.
  3. Design a storyboard.

P. Based on your solution to exercise O:
  1. Create wireframe diagrams for the interface design.
  2. Develop a real use case.

Q. For the Of-the-Month-Club problem in Chapter 4 (exercises U, V, and W), Chapter 5 (exercises V and W), Chapter 6 (exercise H), Chapter 7 (exercise H), Chapter 8 (exercise E), and Chapter 9 (exercise L):
  1. Develop two use scenarios.
  2. Draw a WND.
  3. Design a storyboard.

R. Based on your solution to exercise Q:
  1. Create wireframe diagrams for the interface design.
  2. Develop a real use case.

S. Create a user interface design for a mobile solution for the:
  1. A Real Estate Inc. problem.
  2. A Video Store problem.
  3. Gym membership problem.
  4. Picnics R Us problem.
  5. Of-the-Month-Club problem.

T. How would your answers change to exercises I through S if you were developing for a global marketplace?

MINICASES

1. Tots to Teens is a catalog retailer specializing in children's clothing. A project has been under way to develop a new order entry system for the company's catalog clerks. The old system had a character-based user interface that corresponded to the system's COBOL underpinnings. The new system will feature a graphical user interface more in keeping with up-to-date PC products in use today. The company hopes that this new user interface will help reduce the turnover it has experienced with its order entry clerks. Many newly hired order entry staff found the old system very difficult to learn and were overwhelmed by the numerous mysterious codes that had to be used to communicate with the system.

A user interface walkthrough evaluation was scheduled for today to give the user a first look at the new system's interface. The project team was careful to invite several key users from the order entry department.

In particular, Norma was included because of her years of experience with the order entry system. Norma was known to be an informal leader in the department; her opinion influenced many of her associates. Norma had let it be known that she was less than thrilled with the ideas she had heard for the new system. Owing to her experience and good memory, Norma worked very effectively with the character-based system and was able to breeze through even the most convoluted transactions with ease. Norma had trouble suppressing a sneer when she heard talk of such things as "icons" and "buttons" in the new user interface.

Cindy was also invited to the walkthrough because of her influence in the order entry department. Cindy has been with the department for just one year, but she quickly became known because of her successful organization of a sick child daycare service for the children of the department workers. Sick children are the number-one cause of absenteeism in the department, and many of the workers could not afford to miss workdays. Never one to keep quiet when a situation needed improvement, Cindy has been a vocal supporter of the new system.

   a. Drawing upon the design principles presented in the text, describe the features of the user interface that will be most important to experienced users like Norma.

   b. Drawing upon the design principles presented in the text, describe the features of the user interface that will be most important to novice users like Cindy.

2. The members of a systems development project team have gone out for lunch together, and as often happens, the conversation turns to work. The team has been working on the development of the user interface design, and so far, work has been progressing smoothly. The team should be completing work on the interface prototypes early next week. A combination of storyboards and language prototypes has been used in this project. The storyboards depict the overall structure and flow of the system, but the team developed language prototypes of the actual screens because they felt that seeing the actual screens would be valuable for the users.

   Chris (the youngest member of the project team): I read an article last night about a really cool way to evaluate a user interface design. It's called usability testing, and it's done by all the major software vendors. I think we should use it to evaluate our interface design.

   Heather (systems analyst): I've heard of that, too, but isn't it really expensive?

   Mark (project manager): I'm afraid it is expensive and I'm not sure we can justify the expense for this project.

   Chris: But we really need to know that the interface works. I thought this usability testing technique would help us prove we have a good design.

   Amy (systems analyst): It would, Chris, but there are other ways too. I assumed we'd do a thorough walkthrough with our users and present the interface to them at a meeting. We can project each interface screen so that the users can see it and give us their reaction. This is probably the most efficient way to get the users' response to our work.

   Heather: That's true, but I'd sure like to see the users sit down and work with the system. I've always learned a lot by watching what they do, seeing where they get confused, and hearing their comments and feedback.

   Ryan (systems analyst): It seems to me that we've put so much work into this interface design that all we really need to do is review it ourselves. Let's just make a list of the design principles we're most concerned about and check it ourselves to make sure we've followed them consistently. If we have, we should be fine. We want to get moving on the implementation, you know.

   Mark: These are all good ideas. It seems like we've all got a different view of how to evaluate the interface design. Let's try to sort out the technique that's best for our project.

   Develop a set of guidelines that can help a project team like this one select the most appropriate interface evaluation technique for their project.

3. The menu structure for Holiday Travel Vehicle's existing character-based system is shown here. Develop and prototype a new interface design for the system's functions using a graphical user interface. Also, develop a set of real use cases for your new interface. Assume the new system will need to include the same functions as those shown in the menus provided. Include any messages that will be produced as a user interacts with your interface (error, confirmation, status, etc.). Also, prepare a written summary that describes how your interface implements the principles of good interface design as presented in the textbook.

```
                Holiday Travel Vehicles

                      Main Menu

                 1 Sales Invoice
                 2 Vehicle Inventory
                 3 Reports
                 4 Sales Staff

        Type number of menu selection here:____
```

```
                Holiday Travel Vehicles

                 Sales Staff Maintenance Menu

                 1 Add Salesperson Record
                 2 Change Salesperson Record
                 3 Delete Salesperson Record

        Type number of menu selection here:____
```

```
                Holiday Travel Vehicles

                   Sales Invoice Menu

                 1 Create Sales Invoice
                 2 Change Sales Invoice
                 3 Cancel Sales Invoice

        Type number of menu selection here:____
```

```
                Holiday Travel Vehicles

                  Vehicle Inventory Menu

                 1 Create Vehicle Inventory Record
                 2 Change Vehicle Inventory Record
                 3 Delete Vehicle Inventory Record

        Type number of menu selection here:____
```

```
                Holiday Travel Vehicles

                     Reports Menu

                 1 Commission Report
                 2 RV Sales by Make Report
                 3 Trailer Sales by Make Report
                 4 Dealer Options Report

        Type number of menu selection here:____
```

4. One aspect of the new system under development at Holiday Travel Vehicles will be the direct entry of the sales invoice into the computer system by the salesperson as the purchase transaction is being completed. In the current system, the salesperson fills out a paper form (shown below).

Design and prototype an input screen that will permit the salesperson to enter all the necessary information for the sales invoice. The following information may be helpful in your design process. Assume that Holiday Travel Vehicles sells recreational vehicles and trailers from four different manufacturers. Each manufacturer has a fixed number of names and models of RVs and trailers.

For the purposes of your prototype, use this format:

Mfg-A	Name-1 Model-X
Mfg-A	Name-1 Model-Y
Mfg-A	Name-1 Model-Z
Mfg-B	Name-1 Model-X
Mfg-B	Name-1 Model-Y
Mfg-B	Name-2 Model-X
Mfg-B	Name-2 Model-Y
Mfg-B	Name-2 Model-Z
Mfg-C	Name-1 Model-X
Mfg-C	Name-1 Model-Y
Mfg-C	Name-1 Model-Z
Mfg-C	Name-2 Model-X
Mfg-C	Name-3 Model-X
Mfg-D	Name-1 Model-X
Mfg-D	Name-2 Model-X
Mfg-D	Name-2 Model-Y

Also, assume there are ten different dealer options that could be installed on a vehicle at the customer's request. The company currently has ten salespeople on staff.

Holiday Travel Vehicles
Sales Invoice

Invoice #: _____
Invoice Date: _____

Customer Name: _____
Address: _____
City: _____
State: _____
Zip: _____
Phone: _____

New RV/TRAILER
(circle one)

Name: _____
Model: _____
Serial #: _____ Year: _____
Manufacturer: _____

Trade-in RV/TRAILER
(circle one)

Name: _____
Model: _____
Year: _____
Manufacturer: _____

Options:	Code	Description	Price
	_____	_____	_____
	_____	_____	_____
	_____	_____	_____
	_____	_____	_____

Vehicle Base Cost: _____
Trade-in Allowance: _____   _____
Total Options: _____   (Salesperson Name)
Tax: _____
License Fee: _____   _____
Final Cost: _____   (Customer Signature)

5. Refer to the Professional and Scientific Staff Management (PSSM) minicases in Chapters 4, 6, 7, 8, and 9.
   a. Develop two use scenarios, draw a WND, and design a storyboard.
   b. Based on your answers to part a, create wireframe diagrams for the user interface and develop a set of real use cases for the user interface.
   c. How would your user interface design have to be modified if you were to deploy it on a tablet? What about a smartphone?
   d. What, if any, social media sites should PSSM consider?
   e. How would your answers change if you were developing the system for a global audience?

CHAPTER 11

PHYSICAL ARCHITECTURE
LAYER DESIGN

$\mathbf{A}$n important component of the design of an information system is the design of the physical architecture layer, which describes the system's hardware, software, and network environment. The physical architecture layer design flows primarily from the nonfunctional requirements, such as operational, performance, security, cultural, and political requirements. The deliverable from the physical architecture layer design includes the architecture and the hardware and software specification.

OBJECTIVES

- Understand the different physical architecture components.
- Understand server-based, client-based, and client–server physical architectures.
- Be familiar with cloud computing, ubiquitous computing and the Internet of things (IoT), and Green IT.
- Be able to create a network model using a deployment diagram.
- Be familiar with how to create a hardware and software specification.
- Understand how operational, performance, security, cultural, and political requirements affect the design of the physical architecture layer.

INTRODUCTION

In today's environment, most information systems are spread across multiple computers. A Web-based system, for example, runs in the browser on a desktop computer but interacts with the Web server (and possibly other computers) over the Internet. A system that operates completely inside a company's network may have a Visual Basic program installed on one computer but interact with a database server elsewhere on the network. Therefore, an important step of design is the creation of the physical architecture layer design, the plan for how the system will be distributed across the computers, and what hardware and software will be used for each computer.

Designing the physical architecture layer can be quite difficult; therefore, many organizations hire expert consultants or assign very experienced analysts to the task.[1] In this chapter, we examine the key factors in physical architecture layer design, but it is important to remember that it takes lots of experience to do it well. The nonfunctional requirements developed

---

[1] For more information on the physical architecture layer, see Irv Englander, *The Architecture of Computer Hardware and Systems Software: An Information Technology Approach*, 5th Ed. (Hoboken, NJ: Wiley, 2014); and Kalani Kirk Hausman and Susan L. Cook, *IT Architecture for Dummies*^{TM} (Hoboken, NJ: Wiley, 2011).

during analysis (see Chapter 3) play a key role in physical architecture layer design. These requirements are reexamined and refined into more-detailed requirements that influence the system's architecture.

ELEMENTS OF THE PHYSICAL ARCHITECTURE LAYER

The objective of designing the physical architecture layer is to determine what parts of the application software will be assigned to what hardware. Although there are numerous ways the software components can be placed on the hardware components, we describe three of the principal application architectures in use today: *server-based architectures*, *client-based architectures*, and *client–server architectures*.

Architectural Components

The major *architectural components* of any system are the software and the hardware. The major software components of the system being developed have to be identified and then allocated to the various hardware components on which the system will operate. Each of these components can be combined in a variety of different ways.

All software systems can be divided into four basic functions. The first is *data storage* (associated with the object persistence located on the data management layer—see Chapter 9). Most application programs require data to be stored and retrieved, whether the information is a small file such as a memo produced by a word processor or a large database that stores an organization's accounting records. These are the data documented in the structural model (CRC cards and class diagrams). The second function is *data access logic* (associated with the data access and manipulation classes located on the data management layer—see Chapter 9), the processing required to access data, which often means database queries in *SQL (structured query language)*. The third function is the *application logic* (located on the problem domain layer—see Chapters 4 through 8), which can be simple or complex, depending on the application. This is the logic documented in the functional (activity diagrams and use cases) and behavioral models (activity, sequence, and behavioral state machines). The fourth function is the *presentation logic* (located on the human–computer interaction layer—see Chapter 10), the presentation of information to the user, and the acceptance of the user's commands (the user interface). These four functions (data storage, data access logic, application logic, and presentation logic) are the basic building blocks of any application.

The three primary hardware components of a system are *client computers*, *servers*, and the *network* that connects them. Client computers are the input/output devices employed by the user and are usually desktop or laptop computers, but they can also be handheld devices, cell phones, special-purpose terminals, and so on. Servers are typically larger computers that are used to store software and hardware that can be accessed by anyone who has permission. The network that connects the computers can vary in speed from a slow cell phone, to medium-speed always-on frame relay networks, to fast always-on broadband connections such as cable modem, DSL, or T1 circuits, to high-speed always-on ethernet, T3, or ATM circuits.[2]

[2] For more information on networks, see Alan Dennis, *Networking in the Internet Age* (New York: Wiley, 2002).

FIGURE 11-1
Server-Based
Architecture

Server-Based Architectures

The very first computing architectures were server-based architectures, with the server performing all four functions. The clients enabled users to send and receive messages to and from the server. The clients merely captured keystrokes and sent them to the server for processing and accepted instructions from the server on what to display (see Figure 11-1).

This very simple architecture often works very well. Application software is developed and stored on one computer, and all data are on the same computer. There is one point of control, because all messages flow through the one central server. The fundamental problem with server-based networks is that the server must process all messages. As the demands for more and more applications grow, many server computers become overloaded and unable to quickly process all the users' demands. Response time becomes slower, and network managers are required to spend increasingly more money to upgrade the server computer. Unfortunately, upgrades come in large increments and are expensive; it is difficult to upgrade "a little."

Client-Based Architectures

With client-based architectures, the clients are personal computers on a local area network (LAN), and the server computer is a server on the same network. The application software on the client computers is responsible for the presentation logic, the application logic, and the data access logic; the server simply stores the data (see Figure 11-2).

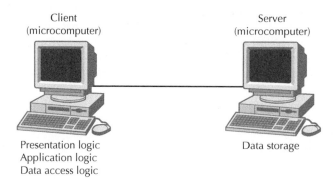

FIGURE 11-2
Client-Based
Architectures

This simple architecture also often works well. However, as the demands for more and more network applications grow, the network circuits can become overloaded. The fundamental problem in client-based networks is that all data on the server must travel to the client for processing. For example, suppose the user wishes to display a list of all employees with company life insurance. All the data in the database must travel from the server where the database is stored over the network to the client, which then examines each record to see whether it matches the data requested by the user. This can overload both the network and the power of the client computers.

Client–Server Architectures

Most organizations today use client–server architectures, which attempt to balance the processing between the client and the server by having both do some of the application functions. In these architectures, the client is responsible for the presentation logic, whereas the server is responsible for the data access logic and data storage. The application logic may reside on either the client or the server or be split between both (see Figure 11-3). The client shown in Figure 11-3 can be referred to as a *thick*, or *fat, client* if it contains the bulk of application logic. A current practice is to create client–server architectures using *thin clients* because there is less overhead and maintenance in supporting thin-client applications. For example, many Web-based systems are designed with the Web browser performing presentation, with only minimal application logic using programming languages like Java and the Web server having the application logic, data access logic, and data storage.

Client–server architectures have four important benefits. First, they are *scalable*. That means it is easy to increase or decrease the storage and processing capabilities of the servers. If one server becomes overloaded, you simply add another server so that many servers are used to perform the application logic, data access logic, or data storage. The cost to upgrade is much more gradual, and you can upgrade in smaller steps rather than spending hundreds of thousands to upgrade a mainframe server.

Client–server architectures can support many different types of clients and servers. It is possible to connect computers that use different operating systems so that users can choose which type of computer they prefer (e.g., combining both Windows computers and Apple Macintoshes on the same network). We are not locked into one vendor, as is often the case with server-based networks. *Middleware* is a type of system software designed to translate between different vendors' software. Middleware is installed on both the client computer and the server computer. The client software communicates with the middleware, which can reformat the message into a standard language that can be understood by the middleware assisting the server software.

For thin-client server architectures that use Internet standards, it is simple to clearly separate the presentation logic, the application logic, and the data access logic and design so

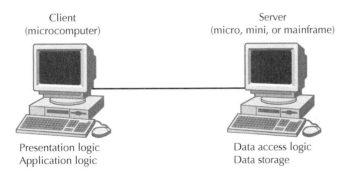

FIGURE 11-3
Client–Server
Architecture

that each is somewhat independent. For example, the presentation logic can be designed in HTML or XML to specify how the page will appear on the screen (see Chapter 10). Simple program statements are used to link parts of the interface to specific application logic modules that perform various functions. These HTML or XML files defining the interface can be changed without affecting the application logic. Likewise, it is possible to change the application logic without changing the presentation logic or the data, which are stored in databases and accessed using SQL commands.

Finally, because no single server computer supports all the applications, the network is generally more reliable. There is no central point of failure that will halt the entire network if it fails, as there is in server-based computing. If any one server fails in a client–server environment, the network can continue to function using all the other servers (but, of course, any applications that require the failed server will not work).

Client–server architectures also have some critical limitations, the most important of which is its complexity. All applications in client–server computing have two parts, the software on the client and the software on the server. Writing this software is more complicated than writing the traditional all-in-one software used in server-based architectures. Updating the network with a new version of the software is more complicated, too. In server-based architectures, there is one place where application software is stored; to update the software, we simply replace it there. With client–server architectures, we must update all clients and all servers.

Much of the debate about server-based versus client–server architectures has centered on cost. One of the great claims of server-based networks in the 1980s was that they provided economies of scale. Manufacturers of big mainframes claimed it was cheaper to provide computer services on one big mainframe than on a set of smaller computers. The personal computer revolution changed this. Since the 1980s, the cost of personal computers has continued to drop, whereas their performance has increased significantly. Today, personal computer hardware is more than 1,000 times cheaper than mainframe hardware for the same amount of computing power.

With cost differences like these, it is easy to see why client–server computing is so popular. The problem with these cost comparisons is that they ignore the *total cost of ownership*, which includes factors other than obvious hardware and software costs. For example, many cost comparisons overlook the increased complexity associated with developing application software for client–server networks. Most experts believe that it costs four to five times more to develop and maintain application software for client–server computing than it does for server-based computing.

Client–Server Tiers

There are many ways the application logic can be partitioned between the client and the server. The example in Figure 11-3 is one of the most common. In this case, the server is responsible for the data, and the client is responsible for the application and presentation. This is called a *two-tiered architecture* because it uses only two sets of computers, clients, and servers.

A *three-tiered architecture* uses three sets of computers (see Figure 11-4). In this case, the software on the client computer is responsible for presentation logic, an application server (or servers) is responsible for the application logic, and a separate database server (or servers) is responsible for the data access logic and data storage.

An *n-tiered architecture* uses more than three sets of computers. In this case, the client is responsible for presentation, database servers are responsible for the data access logic and data storage, and the application logic is spread across two or more different sets of servers.

FIGURE 11-4
Three-Tiered
Client–Server
Architecture

This type of architecture is common in today's e-commerce systems (see Figure 11-5). The first component is the Web browser on the client computer employed by a user to access the system and enter commands (presentation logic). The second is a Web server that responds to the user's requests, either by providing (HTML) pages and graphics (application logic) or by sending the request to the third component on another application server that performs various functions (application logic). The fourth component is a database server that stores all the data (data access logic and data storage). Each of these four components is separate, making it easy to spread the different components on different servers and to partition the application logic on two different servers.

The primary advantage of an *n*-tiered client–server architecture compared with a two-tiered architecture (or a three-tiered architecture with a two-tiered architecture) is that it separates the processing that occurs to better balance the load on the different servers; it is more scalable. In Figure 11-5, we have three separate servers, a configuration that provides more power than if we had used a two-tiered architecture with only one server. If we discover

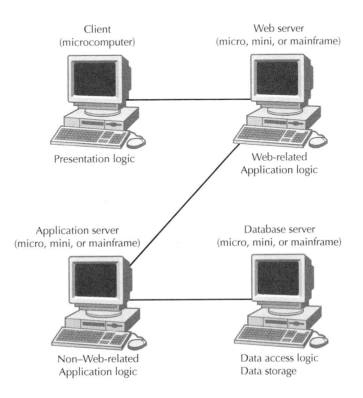

FIGURE 11-5
Four-Tiered
Client–Server
Architecture

that the application server is too heavily loaded, we can simply replace it with a more powerful server or just put in several more application servers. Conversely, if we discover the database server is underused, we could store data from another application on it.

There are two primary disadvantages to an *n*-tiered architecture compared with a two-tiered architecture (or a three-tiered architecture with a two-tiered architecture). First, the configuration puts a greater load on the network. If you compare Figures 11-3, 11-4, and 11-5, you will see that the *n*-tiered model requires more communication among the servers; it generates more network traffic, so you need a higher-capacity network. It is also much more difficult to program and test software in *n*-tiered architectures than in two-tiered architectures because more devices have to communicate to complete a user's transaction.

Selecting a Physical Architecture

Most systems are built to use the existing infrastructure in the organization, so often the current infrastructure restricts the choice of architecture. For example, if the new system will be built for a mainframe-centric organization, a server-based architecture may be the best option. Other factors such as corporate standards, existing licensing agreements, and product/vendor relationships can also mandate what architecture the project team needs to design. However, many organizations now have a variety of infrastructures available or are openly looking for pilot projects to test new architectures and infrastructures, enabling a project team to select an architecture based on other important factors.

Each of the computing architectures just discussed has its strengths and weaknesses, and no architecture is inherently better than the others. Thus, it is important to understand the strengths and weaknesses of each computing architecture and when to use each. Figure 11-6 presents a summary of the important characteristics of each.

Cost of Infrastructure One of the strongest driving forces to client–server architectures is cost of infrastructure (the hardware, software, and networks that will support the application system). Simply put, personal computers are more than 1,000 times cheaper than mainframes for the same amount of computing power. The personal computers on our desks today have more processing power, memory, and hard disk space than the typical mainframe of the past, and the cost of the personal computers is a fraction of the cost of the mainframe.

Therefore, the cost of client–server architectures is low compared to server-based architectures that rely on mainframes. Client–server architectures also tend to be cheaper than client-based architectures because they place less of a load on networks and thus require less network capacity.

Cost of Development The cost of developing systems is an important factor when considering the financial benefits of client–server architectures. Developing application software for client–server computing is extremely complex, and most experts believe that it costs four to

FIGURE 11-6
Characteristics
of Computing
Architectures

Characteristic	Server-based	Client-based	Client–Server
Cost of infrastructure	Very high	Medium	Low
Cost of development	Medium	Low	High
Ease of development	Low	High	Low to medium
Interface capabilities	Low	High	High
Control and security	High	Low	Medium
Scalability	Low	Medium	High

computers. The computers do not have to be of the same type. For example, they can be a mixture of Linux servers and mainframes. With grid computing, firms have the ability to add and remove computers to support a business process based on the current level of activity taking place in that particular business process. This provides an enormous amount of flexibility in configuring the underlying physical architecture that supports business processes.

Combining virtualization, service-oriented architectures, and grid computing is what all the hoopla is about with regard to cloud computing. Cloud computing is highly elastic and scalable, it supports a demand-driven approach to provisioning and deprovisioning of resources, and it supports a billing model that only charges for the resources being used. From a business perspective, cloud computing supports the idea of IT being a commodity.

The cloud can contain the firm's IT infrastructure, IT platform, and software. *Infrastructure as a Service (IaaS)* refers to the cloud providing the computing hardware to the firm as a remote service. The hardware typically includes the computing hardware that supports application servers, networking, and data storage. Amazon's EC2 (aws.amazon.com/ec2/) service is a good example of this. With *Platform as a Service (PaaS)*, the cloud vendor not only provides hardware support to a customer but also provides the customer with either package-based solutions, different services that can be combined to create a solution, or the development tools necessary to create custom solutions in the PaaS vendor's cloud. SalesForce.com is a good example of the vendor providing a package-based solution, Amazon's SimpleDB and Simple Query Service are examples of different services being supported, and Google's App Engine is an example of a cloud vendor providing good development tools. Like most things in IT, *Software as a Service (SaaS)* is not a new idea. SaaS has been around for more than 30 years. In the 1970s, there were many "service bureaus" that supported *timesharing* of hardware and software to many different customers; that is, they supported multitenancy. For example, ADP has supported payroll functions for many firms for a very long time. Today, SalesForce.com's CRM system is a good example of a SaaS cloud-based solution.

However, cloud computing must overcome certain obstacles before it becomes the primary approach to provision the physical architecture layer.[7] The first obstacle is the mixed level of cloud performance. One issue is whether the vendor has the resources to provide the firm with enough "power" during a peak load. The issue here is that a typical cloud vendor is supporting many different firms. If the vendor does not have enough computing resources to handle all of the firms' peak loads at the same time, then there will have to be some degradation of some or all of the firms' support. This is primarily a result of the unpredictability of the overall performance requirements with disk I/O and network traffic. Given the multitenancy typical of a cloud vendor's hardware, bottlenecks with disks will occur. However, given the dependency on networks, data transfer rates are critical. In an enlightening example, Armbrust and colleagues show that when dealing with large volumes of data, it is faster to transfer data using overnight shipping. In their example, they showed that if you were to transfer 10 terabytes of data with an average transfer rate of 20 Mbits/sec, then it would take more than 45 days to complete the transfer. If you shipped the data overnight instead, you would effectively be using a transfer rate of 1500 Mbits/sec.

The second obstacle deals with the level of dependency that a customer's firm has on a cloud vendor. Firms are dependent on cloud vendors based on the type of service that they are using (IaaS, PaaS, and SaaS), the actual level of service availability, and the potential of data lock-in. Currently, most cloud vendor's API to storage is proprietary. Consequently, the customer's data become "locked in" to the specific cloud vendors storage. This is also true for

[7] Michael Armbrust, Armando Fox, Rean Griffith, Anthony D. Joseph, Randy Katz, Andy Konwinski, Gunho Lee, David Patterson, Areil Rabkin, Ion Stoica, and Matei Zahara, "A View of Cloud Computing," *Communications of the ACM* 53, no. 4 (2010): 50–58.

much of the actual service APIs. Consequently, customers find themselves hoping that the cloud vendor will be the equivalent of a benevolent dictator that will act in the interest of the customer; otherwise, actual level of service being provided could suffer. Given the potential for data and/or service lock-in, a customer must pay close attention to the viability of the cloud vendor. If the vendor goes out of business, the customer could be following suit very quickly. If the cloud vendor also has outsourced to other cloud vendors, such as to a disk farm company, then they could find themselves in the same situation. This could lead to a cascading effect of business failures. Consequently, when a firm is considering outsourcing its IT area into the cloud, the firm had better understand the total risk involved.

The third major obstacle to cloud adoption is the perceived level of security available in the cloud. Not only does a firm have to worry about security from the outside, but due to multitenancy, the firm must seriously consider potential attacks from within its cloud from other cloud users. From a service availability perspective, a denial-of-service attack against another tenant within the cloud can cause performance degradation of the firm's systems. Finally, a firm must consider protecting itself from the cloud vendor. The cloud vendor is responsible only for physical security and firewalls. All application-level security tends to be the responsibility of the cloud customer. Obviously, security in the cloud is a very complex endeavor. Given the confidentiality and auditability requirements of Sarbanes–Oxley (SOX) and the Health and Human Services Health Insurance Portability and Accountability Act (HIPAA), security in the cloud becomes a major concern when a firm considers moving any of its confidential data, including e-mail, to the cloud. In many ways, when using a cloud a firm is simply taking a leap of faith that the cloud is secure.

UBIQUITOUS COMPUTING AND THE INTERNET OF THINGS[8]

Often, *ubiquitous computing* and the *Internet of Things (IoT)* are the beginning of the realization of all of the dreams (or nightmares) of science fiction writers. This ranges from the dystopian views portrayed in *Blade Runner* and the *Terminator* movies to the Precrime unit of *Minority Report* and finally to the extremely optimistic future portrayed in *The Jetsons* cartoon of the 1960s. Essentially, ubiquitous computing is the idea that computing takes place everywhere and in everything. With ubiquitous computing, computing becomes so engrained into everyday things that computing effectively disappears into the background. In other words, computing becomes so deeply rooted into everyday things that the things themselves seem to become magical. The IoT is the idea that, in addition to things having some form of computing capacity built into them, everyday things become connected via the Internet. So, in addition to having some form of computing capacity, everyday things can communicate with each other. This raises the importance of understanding mobile computing, social media, and cloud computing even further. Obviously, the opportunities (or pitfalls) that this provides may be endless.

Currently, there are two major approaches to support ubiquitous computing: general computing devices and specialized computing devices. General computing devices include devices such as smartphones and tablets. These devices can be loaded with many different apps that provide all types of computing and communication support. For example, your smartphone can be used as a GPS, an e-book reader, a music or video player, a game console,

[8] This section is based on material contained in Adam Greenfield, *Everywhere: The Dawning of the Age of Ubiquitous Computing* (Berkeley, CA: New Riders, 2006); Bo Begole, *Ubiquitous Computing for Business* (Upper Saddle River, NJ: FT Press, 2011); Adrian McEwen and Hakim Cassimally, *Designing the Internet of Things* (Chichester, West Sussex, UK: Wiley, 2014); David Rose, *Enchanted Objects: Design, Human Desire, and the Internet of Things* (New York, NY: Scribner, 2014); Gershon Dublon and Joseph A. Paradiso, "Extra Sensory Perception," *Scientific American* 311, no. 1 (July 2014): 36–41.

a WWW interface, a camera, a "tape" recorder, a restaurant advisor, etc. In other words, if there is an app for it, you can have it loaded on your smartphone to give you that capability. Today's smartphones are essentially general computers that happen to support voice communications, i.e., it also is a phone. And, like general-purpose computers, the smartphone typically requires you to activate the app before it can do anything for you. Even though it is very impressive to have that amount of computing capability at your fingertips, it only supports the dream of ubiquitous computing in a very limited manner. Essentially, from an information systems development perspective, this is not new; it is no different than having a computer connected to the Internet. Thus, developing apps for these devices should follow the same basic development approach used throughout this book.

The second approach, having specialized computing devices, goes a long way toward realizing the dream of ubiquitous computing. With this approach, we have so-called *enchanted objects* that can interact with each other. An enchanted object is an everyday object that has a very specialized processor embedded in it that augments the object such that the object seems to be magical. For example, an umbrella that, since there is a good chance of rain, lets you know that you should take it with you today, or a wallet that lets you know that you are reaching your monthly budget limits or that your account just received a deposit. In the case of the umbrella, the umbrella is connected to a weather app. If the forecast is for rain, the umbrella activates a set of LEDs in the handle that informs you that you should take it with you when you leave. In the case of the wallet, as you deplete your monthly budget, the wallet becomes more difficult to open, or if you receive a deposit to your account, the wallet "puffs" up to let you know that your wallet is fatter, i.e., you have more cash available.

The general information systems development approach used in this book is applicable to the development of enchanted objects. However, given that enchanted objects, by definition, are enhanced everyday things, additional issues must also be addressed. These issues include a set of unique design principles, a set of characteristics, and a set of levels of enchantment.

McEwen and Cassimally identify a set of unique design principles that need to be considered when developing enchanted objects.[9] First, enchanted objects should be in the background simply providing its message for you to receive at your leisure, not "in your face." This is in contrast with most apps today. Typically, apps will notify you about some topic at their leisure by interrupting you. Second, magic is a useful metaphor for people to adopt an enchanted object. The umbrella mentioned earlier is a good example of this principle. The umbrella simply sits by the door letting you know whether it wants to be taken with you or not. Third is the whole issue of privacy. With all of these enchanted objects "sharing" data about you, all of the issues related to Orwell's "Big Brother" creeps into focus. How will you keep anything secret and, possibly even more important, who actually owns the data being collected? However, this issue is not unique to enchanted objects. It is equally applicable to smartphones and their apps. Fourth, we need to consider how to "mash-up" a set of enchanted objects that are loosely connected to support a larger purpose. In fact, Brynjolfsson and McAfee suggest that this type of recombinant innovation may provide the basis for a new type of economy that will increase both progress and prosperity.[10] Fifth, the idea of affordances becomes increasingly important. For an enchanted object to be adopted, it must be very simple to use. The object itself must imply how to use it. The umbrella, for example, simply lets you know that you should take it with you by drawing your attention to it.

---

[9] Adrian McEwen and Hakim Cassimally, *Designing the Internet of Things* (Chichester, West Sussex, UK: Wiley, 2014)

[10] Erik Brynjolfsson and Andrew McAfee, *The Second Machine Age: Work, Progress, and Prosperity in a Time of Brilliant Technologies* (New York, NY: Norton, 2014).

Rose provides a set of characteristics that enchanted objects should possess if we are to adopt them.[11] First, they should be glanceable. The umbrella, again, is a great example. You don't have to do anything but glance at the umbrella to know whether you should take it with you or not. Second, enchanted objects should be gestureable. This is related to the idea of affordances. It must be intuitively obvious as to how to use an enchanted object. For example, years ago A.T. Cross Company sold a notebook and pen combination (CrossPad™) that you could use to take notes. The affordance of this product was the fact that you simply used a special pen to write your notes on the paper contained in the notebook. The enchanted part was the fact that the product also had a radio transmitter built into the pen that enabled it to store your notes in electronic form that could be uploaded to your computer later. Third, the enchanted object must be affordable. In this case, given the falling cost of computing hardware, if the object isn't that affordable at first, it should be fairly quickly. Fourth, the objects should be wearable. The Fitbit™ is a perfect example. You simply wear it like a watch. Fifth, an enchanted object should be indestructible. Obviously, this one would only be true as it is related to the underlying object. For example, the enchanted umbrella is as indestructible as any normal umbrella, but it is not as indestructible as other things in the real world. Sixth, an enchanted object must be capable of doing its thing with minimal interaction with the user. For example, you simply wear the Fitbit™ and plug it up at night to your computer, and it will update itself, recharge itself, update your profile, and be waiting for you to put it on in the morning. Seventh, an enchanted object should be loveable. By that we mean that they should be easy to anthropomorphize. We should enjoy using them, and we should miss them when we don't. Obviously, you should recognize that there are trade-offs among some of the characteristics and, as such, not all objects will possess all of them. However, as a designer, your enchanted objects should have as many as possible.

Rose also suggests a set of levels (or steps) of enchantment of which enchanted objects designers should be aware. For the first level, he suggests that enchanted objects should be augmented everyday objects that are connected to the network. This allows them to send and receive data that can be used by other enchanted objects or other systems. Given the amount of data to be collected about ourselves and everyone else for both current time and in the future, the second level for enchanted objects is to be able to be personalized such that they can interact with us in a customized manner. Currently, to a small degree Amazon and Netflix are already doing this, e.g., with their list of recommendations that they make to you. Their recommendations are based on your past interactions with them and matching those interactions to the interactions of others. The potential for this type of activity in health systems is enormous. The third level is where our enchanted objects interact with our social networks to automatically inform our colleagues, or a special subset of them, of our activities with the enchanted object. This again could be very useful in health systems where the object informs our physician's system or our health support group of certain types of positive (or negative) activities. The fourth level adapts gaming ideas to our enchanted objects, i.e., gamification. Fitbit™ is a perfect example of using gamification to keep a user intrinsically motivated to reach his or her individual goals. The last level is that designers of enchanted objects will improve their adoption if the objects can be part of a story; Rose refers to this as storyification. Through the use of stories, users can more easily understand the purpose of and the utility provided by the enchanted objects, thus increasing the likelihood of a user "bonding" with the enchanted object.

Given the potential of ubiquitous computing and the IoT, you should begin considering possible applications that may benefit from them. For example, today, through the use of RFID and GPS, it is possible to know the location of each and every one of a firm's inventory

---

[11] David Rose, *Enchanted Objects: Design, Human Desire, and the Internet of Things* (New York, NY: Scribner, 2014).

items. Even though it can be argued that an inventory item with an RFID tag that has GPS ability isn't an enchanted object, it is useful one. And, even though the cost of these types of augmentations is dropping, it can be further argued that you may not want to tag each and every item. However, before the enchanted object vision can become a reality, two possible technical problems will need to be addressed.[12] First, given the current set of communication networks, can the current networks handle the additional communication volume required? Do the Internet, cell phone, and WiFi networks have sufficient bandwidth to support all of these additional things? When you start to hook up everything to the Net, it is doubtful that the capacity is there. Second, is it reasonable to expect the simple special-purpose devices that are embedded in enchanted objects to handle the complexity of the required communication protocols of the existing networks? To address these problems could mean that a new physical architecture could be necessary.

GREEN IT[13]

Given all of the computing power being deployed to solve today's business problems, Green IT has become important. *Green IT* is a broad term that encompasses virtually anything that helps reduce the environmental impact of IT. Some of the topics included are e-waste, greening data centers, and the dream of the paperless office.

First, when it comes to disposing old electronic devices, care must be taken. Old computers contain very toxic material, including lead, PCBs, mercury, and cadmium. One of the major Green IT issues is how to dispose of this *e-waste*. One of the most disturbing trends in dealing with e-waste is the shipping of the e-waste from the developed world to the developing world where environmental standards are virtually nonexistent. Owing to "backyard recycling" techniques used in these locations, the toxic material contained in the e-waste shows up in the soil, water, and air. Alternatives to simply dumping old computers into the trash include extending the replacement cycles of the machines by converting the machines from Windows-based machines to Linux-based machines. Linux takes less "horsepower" to run than Windows. Therefore, for certain applications, a Linux-based desktop is more than sufficient to implement parts of the physical architecture layer.

Second, large data centers use as much electricity in a day as a small city. Consequently, given this level of power consumption, creating *green data centers* in the future will be crucial. There are a whole set of ways to create a green data center. One way is to pay very close attention to where the data center is to be located. Placing the data center in the shade of a mountain or tall building will reduce the cost of energy required. For example, HP placed one of its data centers in northeast England so that it could be cooled by the cold winds that blow onto shore from the North Sea.[14] Looking into alternative energy possibilities is another way to deal with energy consumption. For example, Google has been in the business of buying wind farms to generate the power for its data centers, and HP has shown how a cow manure-based methane power plant could be created to generate the power to run a data center in dairy country.[15]

[12] Francis da Costa, *Rethinking the Internet of Things: A Scalable Approach to Connecting Everything* (New York, NY: Apress Media, 2013).

[13] Caril Baroudi, Jeffrey Hill, Arnold Reinhold, and Jhana Senxian, *Green IT for Dummies*™ (Hoboken, NJ: Wiley, 2009).

[14] Andrew Nusca, "Smart Takes: HP Opens First Wind-Cooled Green Data Center; Most Efficient to Date," *SMART-PLANET* (February 11, 2010). Retrieved August 2014 from www.smartplanet.com/blog/smart-takes/hp-opens-first-wind-cooled-green-data-center-most-efficient-to-date.

[15] Google Data Centers, *Renewable Energy*. Retrieved August 2014 from www.google.com/about/datacenters/renewable.

The third way to consider making your IT infrastructure greener is to consider the cloud (see earlier section). With the cloud's virtualization capabilities, the number of high-powered servers and desktops can be reduced. However, you will need to perform some trade-offs between the obstacles of moving to the cloud and the move toward a greener IT. The fourth way to address the power demands for a modern IT infrastructure is by only purchasing Energy Star compliant electronics. The fifth way is to encourage employees to have their machines go to "sleep" to save energy when the machines have been idle for some period of time.

The *paperless office* idea has been around for a very long time. However, up until now, the idea has been more fantasy than reality. Today, with the advent of multiuse tablets, such as Apple's iPad™, the paperless office is becoming a reality. When considering the cloud and the apps available on the iPad™, it is possible not only to create a paperless office but also to have the paperless office effectively be a portable office.

INFRASTRUCTURE DESIGN

In most cases, a system is built for an organization that has a hardware, software, and communications infrastructure already in place. Thus, project teams are usually more concerned with how an existing infrastructure needs to be changed or improved to support the requirements that were identified during analysis, as opposed to how to design and build an infrastructure from scratch. Coordination of infrastructure components is very complex, and it requires highly skilled technical professionals. As a project team, it is best to allow the infrastructure analysts to make changes to the computing infrastructure.

Deployment Diagram

Deployment diagrams are used to represent the relationships between the hardware components used in the physical infrastructure of an information system. For example, when designing a distributed information system that will use a wide area network, a deployment diagram can be used to show the communication relationships among the different nodes in the network. They also can be used to represent the software components and how they are deployed over the physical architecture or infrastructure of an information system. In this case, a deployment diagram represents the environment for the execution of the software.

The elements of a deployment diagram include nodes, artifacts, and communication paths (see Figure 11-7). Other elements can also be included in this diagram. In our case, we include only the three primary elements and the element that portrays an artifact being deployed onto a node.

A *node* represents any piece of hardware that needs to be included in the model of the physical architecture layer design. For example, nodes typically include client computers, servers, separate networks, or individual network devices. Typically, a node is labeled with its name and, possibly, with a stereotype. The stereotype is modeled as a text item surrounded by "<< >>" symbols. The stereotype represents the type of node being represented on the diagram. For example, typical stereotypes include device, mobile device, database server, Web server, and application server. There are times that the notation of a node should be extended to better communicate the design of the physical architecture layer. Figure 11-8 includes a set of typical network node symbols that can be used instead of the standard notation.

An *artifact* represents a piece of the information system that is to be deployed onto the physical architecture (see Figure 11-7). Typically, an artifact represents a software component, a subsystem, a database table, an entire database, or a layer (data management, human–computer interaction, or problem domain). Artifacts, like nodes, can be labeled with both a

A node: ■ Is a computational resource, e.g., a client computer, server, separate network, or individual network device. ■ Is labeled by its name. ■ May contain a stereotype to specifically label the type of node being represented, e.g., device, client workstation, application server, mobile device, etc.	<<stereotype>> **Node Name**
An artifact: ■ Is a specification of a piece of software or database, e.g., a database or a table or view of a database, a software component or layer. ■ Is labeled by its name. ■ May contain a stereotype to specifically label the type of artifact, e.g., source file, database table, executable file, etc.	<<stereotype>> **Artifact Name**
A node with a deployed artifact: ■ Portrays an artifact being placed on a physical node.	<<stereotype>> **Node Name** <<stereotype>> **Artifact Name**
A communication path: ■ Represents an association between two nodes. ■ Allows nodes to exchange messages. ■ May contain a stereotype to specifically label the type of communication path being represented (e.g., LAN, Internet, serial, parallel).	<<stereotype>>

FIGURE 11-7 Development Diagram Syntax

FIGURE 11-8 Extended Node Syntax for Development Diagram

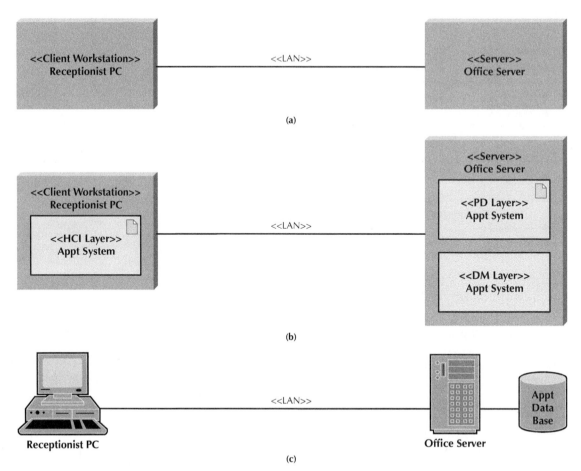

FIGURE 11-9 Three Versions of Appointment System Deployment Diagram

name and a stereotype. Stereotypes for artifacts include source file, database table, and executable file.

A *communication path* represents a communication link between the nodes of the physical architecture (see Figure 11-7). Communication paths are stereotyped based on the type of communication link they represent (e.g., LAN, Internet, serial, parallel, or USB) or the protocol that is being supported by the link (e.g., TCP/IP).

Figure 11-9 portrays three different versions of a deployment diagram. Figure 11-9a only uses the basic standard notation. Figure 11-9b introduces the idea of deploying an artifact onto a node (see Figure 11-7). In this case, the artifacts represent the different layers of the appointment system described in earlier chapters. Figure 11-9c uses the extended notation to represent the same architecture as portrayed in Figure 11-9b. As you can see, all three versions have their strengths and weaknesses. When comparing Figure 11-9a and Figure 11-9b, the user can glean more information from Figure 11-9b with little additional effort. However, when comparing Figure 11-9a to Figure 11-9c, the extended node notation enables the user to quickly understand the hardware requirements of the architecture. When comparing Figure 11-9b to Figure 11-9c, Figure 11-9b supports the software distribution explicitly but forces the user to rely on the stereotypes to understand the required hardware, whereas Figure 11-9c omits the software distribution information entirely. We recommend that you use the combination of symbols to best portray the physical architecture to the user community.

Network Model

The *network model* is a diagram that shows the major components of the information system (e.g., servers, communication lines, networks) and their geographic locations throughout the organization. There is no one way to depict a network model, and in our experience, analysts create their own standards and symbols, using presentation applications (e.g., PowerPoint) or diagramming tools (e.g., Visio). In this text, we use UML's deployment diagram.

The purpose of the network model is twofold: to convey the complexity of the system and to show how the system's software components will fit together. The diagram also helps the project team develop the hardware and software specification that is described later in this chapter.

The components of the network model are the various clients (e.g., personal computers, kiosks), servers (e.g., database, network, communications, printer), network equipment (e.g., WiFi connections, ethernet, cell phone network, satellite links), and external systems or networks (e.g., Internet service providers) that support the application. *Locations* are the geographic sites related to these components. For example, if a company created an application for users at four of its plants in Canada and eight plants in the United States and it used one external system to provide Internet service, the network model to depict this would contain twelve locations (4 + 8 = 12).

Creating the network model is a top-down exercise whereby we first graphically depict all the locations where the application will reside. Placing symbols that represent the locations for the components on a diagram and then connecting them with lines that are labeled with the approximate amount of data or types of network circuits between the separated components accomplish this.

Companies seldom build networks to connect distant locations by buying land and laying cable (or sending up their own satellites). Instead, they usually lease services provided by large telecommunications firms such as AT&T, Sprint, and Verizon. Figure 11-10 shows a typical network. The clouds in the diagram represent the networks at different locations (e.g., Toronto, Atlanta). The lines represent network connections between specific points (e.g., Toronto to Brampton). In other cases, a company might lease connections from many points to many others, and rather than trying to show all the connections, a separate cloud may be drawn to represent this many-to-many type of connection (e.g., the cloud in the center of Figure 11-10 represents a network of many-to-many connections provided by a telecom firm like Verizon).

This high-level diagram has several purposes. First, it shows the locations of the components needed to support the application; therefore, the project team can get a good understanding of the geographic scope of the new system and how complex and costly the communications infrastructure will be to support. (For example, an application that supports one site will probably have less communications costs as compared to a more-complex application that will be shared all over the world.) The diagram also indicates the external components of the system (e.g., customer systems, supplier systems), which may impact security or global needs (discussed later in this chapter).

The second step of the network model is to create low-level network diagrams for each of the locations shown on the top-level diagram. First, hardware is drawn on the model in a way that depicts how the hardware for the new system will be placed throughout the location. It usually helps to use symbols that resemble the hardware that will be used. The amount of detail to include on the network model depends on the needs of the project. Some low-level network models contain text descriptions below each of the hardware components that describe in detail the proposed hardware configurations and processing needs; others include only the number of users that are associated with the different parts of the diagram.

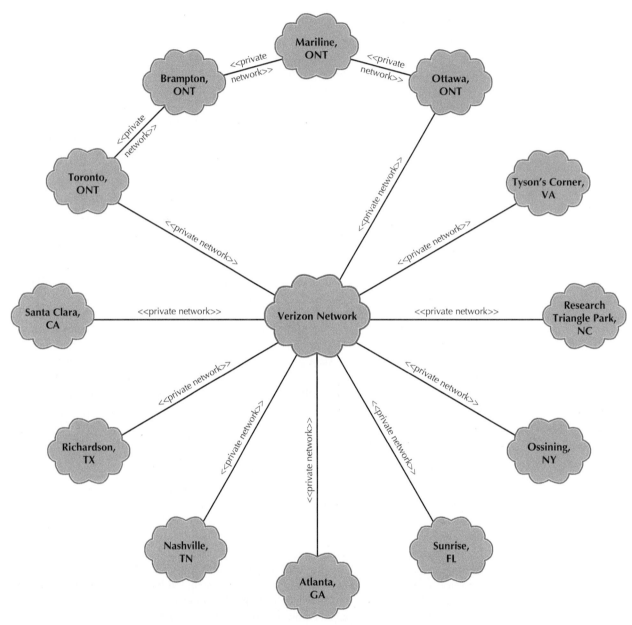

FIGURE 11-10 Deployment Diagram Representation of a Top-Level Network Model

Next, lines are drawn connecting the components that will be physically attached to each other. In terms of software, some network models list the required software for each network model component right on the diagram, whereas other times, the software is described in a memo attached to the network model. Figure 11-11 shows a deployment diagram that portrays two levels of detail of a low-level network model. Notice, we use both the standard and extended node notation in this figure. In this case, we have included a package (see Chapter 7) to represent a set of connections to the router in the MFA building. By including a package, we show only the detail necessary. The extended notation in many cases aids the user in understanding the topology of the physical architecture layer much better than the standard notation. We recommend using the symbols that get the message across best.

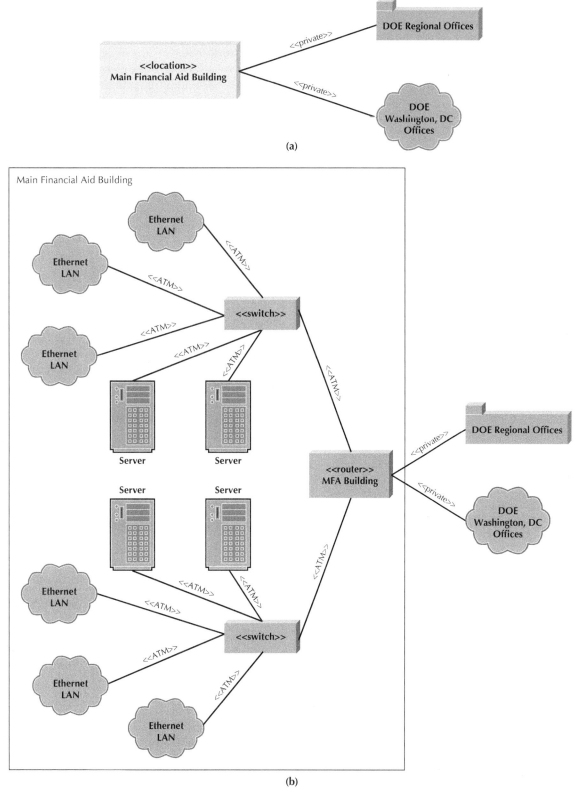

FIGURE 11-11 Deployment Diagram Representation of a Low-Level Network Model

Our experiences have shown that most project teams create a memo for the project files that provides additional detail about the network model. This information is helpful to the people who are responsible for creating the hardware and software specifications (described next in this chapter) and who will work more extensively with the infrastructure development. This memo can include special issues that affect communications, requirements for hardware and software that might not be obvious from the network model, or specific hardware or software vendors or products that should be acquired.

The primary purpose of the network model diagram is to present the proposed infrastructure for the new system. The project team can use the diagrams to understand the scope of the system, the complexity of its structure, any important communication issues that might affect development and implementation, and the actual components that need to be acquired or integrated into the environment.

HARDWARE AND SYSTEM SOFTWARE SPECIFICATIONS

The time to begin acquiring the hardware and software that will be needed for a future system is during the design of the system. In many cases, the new system will simply run on the existing equipment in the organization. Other times, however, new hardware and software must be purchased. The *hardware and software specification* is a document that describes what hardware and software are needed to support an application. The actual acquisition of hardware and software should be left to the purchasing department or the area in the organization that handles capital procurement. However, the project team writes the hardware and software specification to communicate the project needs to the appropriate people. There are several steps involved in creating the document. Figure 11-12 shows a sample hardware and software specification.

First, we need to define the software that will run on each component. This usually starts with the operating system (e.g., Windows, Linux) and includes any special-purpose software on the client and servers (e.g., Oracle database). This document should consider any additional costs, such as technical training, maintenance, extended warranties, and licensing agreements (e.g., a site license for a software package). The listed needs are influenced by decisions that are made in the other design activities.

Specification	Standard Client	Standard Web Server	Standard Application Server	Standard Database Server
Operating System	• Windows • Chrome	• Linux	• Linux	• Linux
Special Software	• Adobe Reader • VLC	• Apache	• Java	• Oracle
Hardware	• 816 GB Memory • 500 gig disk drive • Intel Core i6 • 2—22″ Monitors	• 32 GB Memory • 1 TB disk drive • Intel Core i7	• 32 GB Memory • 2–1 TB disk drives • Intel Core i7	• 64 GB Memory • 25 TB RAID • Intel Core i7
Network	• 100 Mbps Ethernet • WiFi	• 100 Mbps Ethernet	• 100 Mbps Ethernet	• 100 Mbps Ethernet

FIGURE 11-12 Sample Hardware and Software Specification

Second, we must create a list of the hardware that is needed to support the future system. With the advent of mobile computing (see Chapter 10), cloud computing (see earlier in this chapter), the IoT (see earlier in this chapter), and Green IT (see earlier in this chapter), this step is much more involved than it used to be. However, the low-level network model provides a good starting point for recording the project's hardware needs because each component on the diagram corresponds to an item on this list. In general, the list can include things like database servers, network servers, peripheral devices (e.g., printers, scanners), backup devices, storage components, and any other hardware component that is needed to support an application. At this time, you also should note the quantity of each item that will be needed.

Third, we must describe, in as much detail as possible, the minimum requirements for each piece of hardware. Typically, the project team must convey requirements like the amount of processing capacity, the amount of storage space, and any special features that should be included. Many organizations have standard lists of approved hardware and software that must be used; so in many cases, this step simply involves selecting items from the lists. Other times, however, the team is operating in new territory and is not constrained by the need to select from an approved list. This step becomes easier with experience; however, there are some hints that can help you describe hardware needs (see Figure 11-13). For example, consider the hardware standards within the organization or those recommended by vendors. Talk with experienced system developers or other companies with similar systems. Finally, think about the factors that affect hardware performance, such as the response-time expectations of the users, data volumes, software memory requirements, the number of users accessing the system, the number of external connections, and growth projections.

The last step to consider is to evaluate vendor proposals (see Chapter 7). The easiest way to do this is to create an *alternative matrix* (see Chapters 2 and 7). In this case, the evaluation criteria in the alternative matrix should include all architectural requirements, both optional and mandatory, and each criterion should be weighted. Some general criteria include CPU speed, bus speed, disk size, disk access time, cache size, cache speed, RAM size, RAM speed, data transfer rate, video RAM size and speed, monitor size, and printer resolution. Of course, in today's connected world, the networking hardware and software would also need to be specified, including routers, print servers, hubs, and switches. Mobile devices such as smartphones and tablets may be part of the physical architecture solution. Depending on the problem domain requirements, additional hardware and system software could be required, such as speech recognition and generation software and hardware, digitizing tablets, and possibly head-mounted displays, shutter glasses, force feedback pointing devices, and 3D printers.

Functions and Features   What specific functions and features are needed (e.g., size of monitor, software features)?

Performance   How fast does the hardware and software operate (e.g., processor, number of database writes per second)?

Legacy Databases and Systems   How well does the hardware and software interact with legacy systems (e.g., can it write to this database)?

Hardware and OS Strategy   What are the future migration plans (e.g., the goal is to have all of one vendor's equipment)?

Cost of Ownership   What are the costs beyond purchase (e.g., incremental license costs, annual maintenance, training costs, salary costs)?

Political Preferences   People are creatures of habit and are resistant to change, so changes should be minimized.

Vendor Performance   Some vendors have reputations or future prospects that are different from those of a specific hardware or software system they currently sell.

FIGURE 11-13
Factors in Hardware and Software Selection

Each of these types of specialized devices has its own specialized evaluation criteria. In a nutshell, when creating a hardware and system software specification, most systems analysts find that they need help from IT and CS personnel.

Depending on the overall cost and size of the project, one thing that should be seriously considered is the use of a benchmark. A *benchmark* is essentially a sample of programs that would be expected to run on the new physical architecture. Even though benchmarks can be expensive to create, they tend to provide a more realistic picture of how the proposed physical architecture layer will perform.

When evaluating hardware, there is a set of issues that you should recognize.[16]

- Not only should you provide sample programs for the benchmarks, but you also need to provide actual data. Otherwise, the benchmark results could be misleading.

- You need to carefully review the mix of system software and hardware. For example, in many cases, Linux performs better on the same hardware when compared against Windows, but some applications might not be available under Linux. Consequently, there may be some trade-offs that should be considered.

- When considering adding additional hardware, be sure to evaluate the additional hardware based on marginal utility, not actual utility.

- Do not specify the physical architecture before you understand the problem domain requirements. This might seem obvious, but when you consider the time it takes for a mainframe computer, a large number of servers, or a large number of client machines to be specified, ordered, and delivered, it can be tempting to specify the hardware and system software prematurely. This could lead to either under- or over-specification.

- Recognize the reality of *Parkinson's Law*. From an IT perspective, Parkinson's Law implies that regardless of the users' real needs, their imagined needs will always fill up whatever capacity the system has. Consequently, it is imperative that the physical architecture layer design be based on the current and expected future architecture of the problem domain layer.

- Do not limit choices to a single vendor. This is especially true when you consider commodity hardware, such as displays, desktops, and department-size servers.

- Given the rate of technological change that is taking place in IT, consider leading-edge ideas. For example, even though tablet computers have been around for a while, the iPad™ was not on most people's radar. Today, it is considered to be a game changer when considering client-based hardware. Consequently, you really must stay up to date when it comes to the design of the physical architecture layer.

NONFUNCTIONAL REQUIREMENTS AND PHYSICAL ARCHITECTURE LAYER DESIGN

The design of the physical architecture layer specifies the overall architecture and the placement of software and hardware that will be used. Each of the architectures discussed before has its strengths and weaknesses. Most organizations use client–server architectures for cost reasons, so in the event that there is no compelling reason to choose one architecture over another, cost usually suggests client–server.

Creating a physical architecture layer design begins with the nonfunctional requirements. The first step is to refine the nonfunctional requirements into more-detailed requirements that

---

[16] Alton R. Kindred, *Data Systems and Management: An Introduction to Systems Analysis and Design*, 2nd Ed. (Englewood Cliffs, NJ: Prentice-Hall, 1980).

are then used to help select the architecture to be used (server-based, client-based, or client–server) and what software components will be placed on each device. In a client–server architecture, one also has to decide whether to use a two-tier, three-tier, or *n*-tier architecture. Then the nonfunctional requirements and the architecture design are used to develop the hardware and software specification.

Four primary types of nonfunctional requirements can be important in designing the architecture: operational requirements, performance requirements, security requirements, and cultural/political requirements. Furthermore, each of these requirements must be fully verified and validated.

Operational Requirements

Operational requirements specify the operating environment(s) in which the system must perform and how those might change over time. This usually refers to operating systems, system software, and information systems with which the system must interact, but on occasion it also includes the physical environment if the environment is important to the application (e.g., it's located on a noisy factory floor, so no audible alerts can be heard). Figure 11-14 summarizes four key operational requirement areas and provides some examples of each.

Technical Environment Requirements *Technical environment requirements* specify the type of hardware and software system on which the system will work. These requirements usually focus on the operating system software (e.g., Windows, Linux, and Mac OS), database system software (e.g., Oracle), and other system software (e.g., Firefox). In today's distributed world, issues related to mobile computing (see Chapter 10), cloud computing (see the earlier section in this chapter), the IoT (see earlier section in this chapter), and Green IT (see the

Type of Requirement	Definition	Examples
Technical Environment Requirements	Special hardware, software, and network requirements imposed by business requirements	• The system will work over the Web environment with Internet Explorer. • All office locations will have an always-on network connection to enable real-time database updates. • A version of the system will be provided for customers connecting over the Internet via a tablet or smartphone.
System Integration Requirements	The extent to which the system will operate with other systems	• The system must be able to import and export Excel spreadsheets. • The system will read and write to the main inventory database in the inventory system.
Portability Requirements	The extent to which the system will need to operate in other environments	• The system must be able to work with different operating systems (e.g., Linux, Mac OS, and Windows). • The system might need to operate with handheld devices, such as Android and Apple iOS devices.
Maintainability Requirements	Expected business changes to which the system should be able to adapt	• The system will be able to support more than one manufacturing plant with six months' advance notice. • New versions of the system will be released every six months.

FIGURE 11-14 Operational Requirements

earlier section in this chapter) are very relevant. Consequently, it also includes all of the different types of hardware from mainframe computers to smartphones to IoT devices. Depending on the applications being deployed over the physical architecture, specialized hardware could be required, such as 3D displays, 3D printing, 3D sound systems, and tablets with accelerometers. With today's technology, the possible combinations of hardware that can be used to solve a problem are nearly endless. Consequently, this is one area where additional expertise might be required.

System Integration Requirements *System integration requirements* are those that require the system to operate with other information systems, either inside or outside the company. These typically specify interfaces through which data will be exchanged with other systems.

Portability Requirements Information systems never remain constant. Business needs change and operating technologies change, so the information systems that support them and run on them must change, too. *Portability requirements* define how the technical operating environments might change over time and how the system must respond (e.g., the system currently runs on Windows, whereas in the future the system might have to be deployed on Linux). Portability requirements also refer to potential changes in business requirements that drive technical environment changes. For example, in the future users might want to access a website from their cell phones.

Maintainability Requirements *Maintainability requirements* specify the business requirement changes that can be anticipated. Not all changes are predictable, but some are. For example, suppose a small company has only one manufacturing plant but is anticipating the construction of a second plant in the next five years. All information systems must be written to make it easy to track each plant separately, whether for personnel, budgeting, or inventory systems. The maintainability requirements attempt to anticipate future requirements so that the systems designed today will be easy to maintain if and when those future requirements appear. Maintainability requirements can also define the update cycle for the system, such as the frequency with which new versions will be released.

Performance Requirements

Performance requirements focus on performance issues, such as response time, capacity, and reliability. Figure 11-15 summarizes three key performance requirement areas and provides some examples.

Speed Requirements *Speed requirements* are exactly what they say: How fast should the system operate? First is the *response time* of the system: How long it takes the system to respond to a user request. Although everyone would prefer low response times, with the system responding immediately to each user request, this is not practical. We could design such a system, but it would be expensive. Most users understand that certain parts of a system will respond quickly, whereas others are slower. Actions that are performed locally on the user's computer must be almost immediate (e.g., typing, dragging, and dropping), whereas others that require communicating across a network can have longer response times (e.g., a Web request).

The second aspect of speed requirements is how long it takes transactions in one part of the system to be reflected in other parts. For example, how soon after an order is placed will the items it contained be shown as no longer available for sale to someone else? If the inventory is not updated immediately, then someone else could place an order for the same item, only to find out later it is out of stock. This is especially true when one considers NoSQL database that does not update all copies of the data immediately (see Chapter 9). Or how soon after an order is placed is it sent to the warehouse to be picked from inventory and shipped?

Type of Requirement	Definition	Examples
Speed Requirements	The time within which the system must perform its functions	• Response time must be less than 7 seconds for any transaction over the network. • The inventory database must be updated in real time. • Orders will be transmitted to the factory floor every 30 minutes.
Capacity Requirements	The total and peak number of users and the volume of data expected	• There will be a maximum of 100–200 simultaneous users at peak use times. • A typical transaction will require the transmission of 10K of data.
Availability and Reliability Requirements	The extent to which the system will be available to the users and the permissible failure rate due to errors	• The system will store data on approximately 5,000 customers for a total of about 2 MB of data. • Scheduled maintenance shall not exceed one 6-hour period each month. • The system shall have 99% uptime performance.

FIGURE 11-15 Performance Requirements

Capacity Requirements *Capacity requirements* attempt to predict how many users the system will have to support, both in total and simultaneously. Capacity requirements are important in understanding the size of the databases, the processing power needed, and so on. The most important requirement is usually the peak number of simultaneous users because this has a direct impact on the processing power of the computer(s) needed to support the system.

It is often easier to predict the number of users for internal systems designed to support an organization's own employees than it is to predict the number of users for customer-facing systems, especially those on the Web. How *does* Weather.com estimate the peak number of users who will simultaneously seek weather information? This is as much an art as a science, so often the team provides a range of estimates, with wider ranges used to signal a less-accurate estimate.

Availability and Reliability Requirements *Availability and reliability requirements* focus on the extent to which users can assume that the system will be available for them to use. Although some systems are intended to be used only during the forty-hour work week, some systems are designed to be used by people around the world. For such systems, project team members need to consider how the application can be operated, supported, and maintained *24/7*. This 24/7 requirement means that users might need help or have questions at any time, and a support desk that is available eight hours a day will not be sufficient support. It is also important to consider what reliability is needed in the system. A system that requires high reliability (e.g., a medical device or telephone switch) needs far greater planning and testing than one that does not have such high-reliability needs (e.g., personnel system, Web catalog).

It is more difficult to predict the peaks and valleys in use of the system when the system has a global audience. Typically, applications are backed up on weekends or late evenings when users are no longer accessing the system. Such maintenance activities need to be rethought with global initiatives. For example, what day(s) of the week is considered a "down" day. In different parts of the world, business does not take place every day. In some parts, Friday is sacred; in other parts, it's Saturday or Sunday. Consequently, political and cultural issues (described below and in Chapter 10) can impact the performance requirements. The development of Web interfaces, in particular, has escalated the need for 24/7 support; by default, the Web can be accessed by anyone at any time. For example, the developers of a Web application for U.S. outdoor gear and clothing retailer Orvis were surprised when the first order after going live came from Japan.

Security Requirements[17]

The primary purpose of the security requirements is actually to increase the trust that the users have with the system and its data. Good IT security protects the information system from disruption and data loss, whether caused by an intentional act (e.g., a hacker, a terrorist attack) or a random event (e.g., disk failure, tornado). In the past, security has been primarily the responsibility of the operations group—the staff responsible for installing and operating security controls, such as firewalls, intrusion-detection systems, and routine backup and recovery operations. However today, developers of new systems must ensure that the system's *security requirements* produce reasonable precautions to prevent problems; system developers are responsible for ensuring security within the information systems themselves. Furthermore, with the newer agile and DevOps approaches to developing systems, security must be at the forefront of any and all decisions. In fact, one of the major issues with the newer agile and DevOps approaches is the speed at which the software is deployed almost forces the developers to ignore security. Consequently, newer versions of DevOps now include security as a major aspect of the system that must be addressed.[18]

Security is an ever-increasing problem in today's Internet-enabled world. Historically, the greatest security threat has come from inside the organization itself. Ever since the early 1980s when the FBI first began keeping computer crime statistics and security firms began conducting surveys of computer crime, organizational employees have perpetrated the vast majority of computer crimes. For years, 80 percent of unauthorized break-ins, thefts, and sabotage have been committed by insiders, leaving only 20 percent to hackers external to the organizations.

In 2001, that changed. Depending on what survey you read, the percentage of incidents attributed to external hackers in 2001 increased to 50 to 70 percent of all incidents, meaning that the greatest risk facing organizations is now from the outside. Although some of this shift may be due to better internal security and better communications with employees to prevent security problems, much of it is simply due to an increase in differing threats, such as denial of service attacks, malware, phishing, ransomware, social engineering, spyware, trojan horses, and many others, by external hackers. Furthermore, given cloud computing and the IoT, security must be taken very seriously and be addressed as the system is being designed instead of simply an add-on that is considered after the system has been implemented.

Developing security requirements usually starts with some assessment of the value of the system and its data. This helps pinpoint extremely important systems so that the operations staff is aware of the risks. Security within systems usually focuses on specifying who can access what data, identifying the need for encryption and authentication, and ensuring the application prevents the spread of viruses (see Figure 11-16).

[17] For more information, see Brett C. Tjaden, *Fundamentals of Secure Computer Systems* (Wilsonville, OR: Franklin, Beedle, and Associates, 2004); for security controls associated with the Sarbanes–Oxley act, see Dennis C. Brewer, *Security Controls for Sarbanes–Oxley Section 404 IT Compliance: Authorization, Authentication, and Access* (Indianapolis: Wiley, 2006); William Stallings, *Effective Cybersecurity: A Guide to Using Best Practices and Standards* (Upper Saddle River, NJ: Pearson Education, 2019); and O. Sami Saydjari, *Engineering Trustworthy Systems: Get Cybersecurity Design Right the First Time* (New York, NY: McGraw-Hill, 2018).

[18] See, for example, Jim Bird, *DevOpsSec: Delivering Secure Software Through Continuous Delivery*, (Sebastopol, CA: O'Reilly Media, 2016); Len Bass, Ingo Weber, and Liming Zhu, *DevOps: A Software Architect's Perspective* (Upper Saddle River, NJ: Pearson Education, 2015); and Gene Kim, Jez Humble, Patrick Debois, and John Willis, *The DevOps Handbook: How to Create World-Class Agility, Reliability, & Security in Technology Organizations* (Portland, OR: IT Revolution Press, 2016).

Type of Requirement	Definition	Examples
System Value Estimates	Estimated business value of the system and its data	• The system is not mission critical, but a system outage is estimated to cost $50,000 per hour in lost revenue. • A complete loss of all system data is estimated to cost $20 million.
Access Control Requirements	Limitations on who can access what data	• Only department managers will be able to change inventory items within their own department. • Telephone operators will be able to read and create items in the customer file but cannot change or delete items.
Encryption and the Authentication Requirements	Defines what data will be encrypted where and whether authentication will be needed for user access	• Data will be encrypted from the user's computer to website to provide secure ordering. • Users logging in from outside the office will be required to authenticate.
Virus Control Requirements	Requirements to control the spread of viruses	• All uploaded files will be checked for viruses before being saved in the system.

FIGURE 11-16   Security Requirements

System Value The most important computer asset in any organization is not the equipment; it is the organization's data. For example, suppose someone destroyed a mainframe computer worth $10 million. The mainframe could be replaced, simply by buying a new one. It would be expensive, but the problem would be solved in a few weeks. Now suppose someone destroyed all the student records at your university so that no one knew what courses anyone had taken or their grades. The cost would far exceed the cost of replacing a $10 million computer. The lawsuits alone would easily exceed $10 million, and the cost of staff to find paper records and reenter the data from them would be enormous and certainly would take more than a few weeks.

In some cases, the information system itself has value that far exceeds the cost of the equipment as well. For example, for an Internet bank that has no brick and mortar branches, the website is a *mission-critical system*. If the website crashes, the bank cannot conduct business with its customers. A mission-critical application is an information system that is literally critical to the survival of the organization. It is an application that cannot be permitted to fail, and if it does fail, the network staff drops everything else to fix it. Mission-critical applications are usually clearly identified so that their importance is not overlooked.

Even temporary disruptions in service can have significant costs. The costs of disruptions to a company's primary website or the LANs and backbones that support telephone sales operations are often measured in the millions of dollars. Amazon.com, for example, has revenues of more than $10 million per hour, so if its website were unavailable for an hour or even part of an hour, it would lose millions of dollars in revenue. Companies that do less e-business or do telephone sales have lower costs, but recent surveys suggest losses of $100,000 to $200,000 per hour are not uncommon for major customer-facing information systems.

Access Control Requirements Some of the data stored in the system need to be kept confidential; some data need special controls on who is allowed to change or delete it. Personnel records, for example, should be able to be read only by the personnel department and the employee's supervisor; changes should be permitted to be made only by the personnel department. *Access control requirements* state who can access what data and what type of access is permitted: whether the individual can create, read, update and/or delete the data. The requirements reduce the chance that an authorized user of the system can perform unauthorized actions. The vast majority of these requirements have already been captured in the form of the actors and stakeholders with the real use case descriptions (Chapter 10), the associated classes with the CRC cards (Chapters 5 and 8), and the detailed version of the CRUDE matrix (Chapter 6).

There are several approaches to address access control. An *access control list* is associated with the asset for which you want to control access. For example, a file that you wanted to restrict access to a subset of users would have the users, along with the type of access being granted to them, listed in the access control list for the file. If a user was not in the list, the user would not be able to access the file. Furthermore, if a user was only granted read access, then the user could only read the file. We could actually implement this detailed level of control by capturing the access control lists in the pre-conditions of a method contract (see Chapter 8). Another approach would be to create a *capabilities list* with each user profile. In this case, the access controls would be associated with a specific user instead of a file. With the previous example, the capabilities list would show that the user had read access to the file. Finally, we could combine the access control and capabilities list approaches and require that access is only granted to an IT asset if both the access control list and the capabilities list match. This is the basis for the *access control matrix* approach. However, in terms of processing power requirements, the actual cost of these very low-level approaches may be prohibitive.

Role-based access control attempts to address some of the overhead associated with the access control list, the capability list, and the access control matrix approaches. With *role-based access controls*, access is limited by the role that the user is assigned. So instead of keeping track of the level of access being granted by the individual user, the controls are maintained at the role level. This could be captured with documentation associated with the actors that will be using the system. This is obviously a variation of the capabilities list approach. Furthermore, using operating system file level controls or using controls implemented through the DBMS would provide access controls at a less granular level. These approaches obviously require less processing power and less storage. As usual, it always comes back to cost–benefit analysis of the amount of risk a firm is willing to take on with regard to the cost of security.

Encryption and Authentication Requirements One of the best ways to prevent unauthorized access to data is *encryption*, which is a means of disguising information by the use of mathematical algorithms (or formulas). Encryption can be used to protect data stored in databases or data that are in transit over a network from a database to a computer. There are two fundamentally different types of encryption: symmetric and asymmetric. A *symmetric encryption algorithm* [such as Data Encryption Standard (DES) or Advanced Encryption Standard (AES)] is one in which the key used to encrypt a message is the *same* as the one used to decrypt it, which means that it is essential to protect the key and that a separate key must be used for each person or organization with whom the system shares information (or else everyone can read all the data).

An *asymmetric encryption algorithm* (such as *public key encryption*) is one in which the key used to encrypt data (called the *public key*) is different from the one used to decrypt it (called the *private key*). Even if everyone knows the public key, once the data are encrypted, they cannot be decrypted without the private key. Public key encryption greatly reduces the key-management problem. Each user has its public key that is used to encrypt messages sent to it. These public keys are widely publicized (e.g., listed in a telephone book style directory)—that's why they're called public keys. The private key, in contrast, is kept secret.

Public key encryption also permits *authentication* (or digital signatures). When one user sends a message to another, it is difficult to legally prove who actually sent the message. Legal proof is important in many communications, such as bank transfers and buy/sell orders in currency and stock trading, which normally require legal signatures. Public key encryption algorithms are *invertible*, meaning that text encrypted with either key can be decrypted by the other. Normally, we encrypt with the public key and decrypt with the private key. However, it is possible to do the reverse: encrypt with the private key and decrypt with the public key. Because the private key is secret, only the real user can use it to encrypt a message. Thus, a digital signature or authentication sequence is used as a legal signature on many financial transactions. This signature is usually the name of the signing party plus other unique information from the message (e.g., date, time, or dollar amount). This signature and the other information are encrypted by the sender using the private key. The receiver uses the sender's public key to decrypt the signature block and compares the result to the name and other key contents in the rest of the message to ensure a match.

The only problem with this approach lies in ensuring that the person or organization that sent the document with the correct private key is the actual person or organization. Anyone can post a public key on the Internet, so there is no way of knowing for sure who actually used it. For example, it would be possible for someone other than Organization A in this example to claim to be Organization A when, in fact, he or she is an imposter.

This is where the Internet's public key infrastructure (PKI) becomes important.[19] The PKI is a set of hardware, software, organizations, and polices designed to make public key encryption work on the Internet. PKI begins with a *certificate authority (CA)*, which is a trusted organization that can vouch for the authenticity of the person or organization using authentication (e.g., VeriSign). A person wanting to use a CA registers with the CA and must provide some proof of identify. There are several levels of certification, ranging from a simple confirmation from a valid e-mail address to a complete government-style background check with an in-person interview. The CA issues a digital certificate that is the requestor's public key, encrypted using the CA's private key as proof of identify. This certificate is then attached to the user's e-mail or Web transactions in addition to the authentication information. The receiver then verifies the certificate by decrypting it with the CA's public key and must also contact the CA to ensure that the user's certificate has not been revoked by the CA.

The encryption and authentication requirements state what encryption and authentication requirements are needed for what data. For example, will sensitive data such as customer credit-card numbers be stored in the database in encrypted form, or will encryption be used to take orders over the Internet from the company's website? Will users be required to use a digital certificate in addition to a standard password?

Virus Control Requirements *Virus control requirements* address the single most common security problem: *viruses*. Studies have shown that almost 90 percent of organizations suffer a virus infection each year. Viruses cause unwanted events—some harmless (such as nuisance messages), some serious (such as the destruction of data). Any time a system permits data to be imported or uploaded from a user's computer, there is the potential for a virus infection. Many systems require that all information systems that permit the import or upload of user files to check those files for viruses before they are stored in the system.

Cultural and Political Requirements

Cultural and political requirements are those specific to the countries in which the system will be used. In today's global business environment, organizations are expanding their systems to

---

[19] For more on the PKI, see http://datatracker.ietf.org/wg/pkix/charter/.

reach users around the world. Although this can make great business sense, its impact on application development should not be underestimated. Yet another important part of the design of the system's physical architecture is understanding the global cultural and political requirements for the system (see Chapter 10 and Figure 11-17).

Customization Requirements For global applications, the project team needs to give some thought to *customization requirements:* How much of the application will be controlled by a central group, and how much of the application will be managed locally? For example, some companies allow subsidiaries in some countries to customize the application by omitting or adding certain features. This decision has trade-offs between flexibility and control because customization often makes it more difficult for the project team to create and maintain the application. It also means that training can differ among different parts of the organization, and customization can create problems when staff moves from one location to another.

Owing to the use of different languages, in some cases, specialized hardware that has been customized to the local culture is required. For example, having specialized keyboards makes sense for any language that does not use the typical Roman alphabet, e.g., Arabic, Hebrew, Greek, Japanese, Korean, Mandarin, or Russian. There are also emulators available for many different languages. Depending on the users being served, assistive devices could be required, such as Braille devices, eye-tracking devices, head pointers, head/mouth stick keyboards, or adaptive ability switches. Depending on the cultural and political requirements, many different hardware platforms might need to be considered.

Legal Requirements *Legal requirements* are requirements imposed by laws and government regulations. System developers sometimes forget to think about legal regulations; unfortunately, forgetting comes at some risk because ignorance of the law is no defense. For example, in 1997 a French court convicted the Georgia Institute of Technology of violating French language law. Georgia Tech operated a small campus in France that offered summer programs for American students. The information on the campus Web server was primarily in English because classes are conducted in English, which violated the law requiring French to be the predominant language on all Internet servers in France. By formally considering legal regulations, you are less likely to overlook them. Another major example is the recent European court ruling regarding the user's right to be forgotten.

Type of Requirement	Definition	Examples
Customization Requirements	Specification of what aspects of the system can be changed by local users	• Country managers will be able to define new fields in the product database to capture country-specific information. • Country managers will be able to change the format of the telephone number field in the customer database.
Legal Requirements	The laws and regulations that impose requirements on the system	• Personal information about customers cannot be transferred out of European Union countries into the United States. • It is against U.S. federal law to divulge information on who rented what videotape, so access to a customer's rental history is permitted only to regional managers.

FIGURE 11-17 Cultural and Political Requirements

Another area that legal requirements can cause problems is with the *end-user license agreements*. When is the last time that you carefully have read the end user license agreement when you installed software on your machine? From an organizational perspective, this could cause problems. Some agreements commit the organization to allow access to the data that is processed by the software. Other agreements require that the organization be bound by the laws of a foreign country. Or, with a federal government system such as in the United States, the agreement could require that the organization to follow the laws of another state. So, from an organization perspective, the organization should restrict the installation of any software until the organization's lawyers clear it. Otherwise, a user could be granting access to an outside organization to organizational data and possibly to intellectual property. In other words, we need to have the "fine print" of the agreement read by an expert to prevent the accidental loss of organizational assets.

Synopsis

In many cases, the technical environment requirements as driven by the business requirements can simply define the physical architecture layer. In this case, the choice is simple: Business requirements dominate other considerations. For example, the business requirements might specify that the system needs to work over the Web using the customer's Web browser. In this case, the architecture probably should be a thin client–server. Such business requirements are most likely in systems designed to support external customers. Internal systems can also impose business requirements, but usually they are not as restrictive.

In the event that the technical environment requirements do not stipulate a specific architecture, then the other nonfunctional requirements become important. Even in cases when the business requirements drive the architecture, it is still important to work through and refine the remaining nonfunctional requirements because they are important in later stages of design and implementation.

VERIFYING AND VALIDATING THE PHYSICAL ARCHITECTURE LAYER

Like the models on the other layers, the infrastructure design and the hardware and software specifications of the physical architecture layer need to be verified and validated. Verifying and validating the design of the physical architecture layer fall into three basic groups.

First, we recommend verifying and validating deployment diagrams by ensuring that all of them are in fact consistent and balanced. For example, each of the nodes in a top-level network model deployment diagram should be associated with a separate deployment diagram that represents the low-level network model for the node.

Second, the hardware and software specifications should be consistent with the "lowest-level" network models. For example, if a low-level network model for an office describes a set of workstations, servers, printers, switches, routers, etc., then the hardware and software specification for that location should be the details for each of the IT artifacts for that location.

Third, once the system has been implemented, testing of the nonfunctional requirements becomes crucial. In this case, tests must be designed and performed for each of the nonfunctional requirements. For example, for the performance requirements, load testing must be performed to identify possible performance bottlenecks in the network. We will return to this topic in Chapter 12.

APPLYING THE CONCEPTS AT PATTERSON SUPERSTORE

Sam Wilson, the infrastructure analyst, took the lead in designing this layer. Sam was responsible for ensuring that the new system adheres to the infrastructure standards in place at Patterson while making sure that the infrastructure can support the new system. The team had to decide which architecture would best meet the needs of the Integrated Health Clinic Delivery system and to determine what software would be placed on which hardware. Next, the team had to map the network model on a deployment diagram. Accomplishing this task required close communication with the other layers, including the problem domain, data management, and human–computer interaction layers.

You can find the rest of the case at www.wiley.com/go/dennis/systemanalysis6e/casestudy.

CHAPTER REVIEW

After reading and studying this chapter, you should be able to:

- [ ] Describe the four major architectural components.
- [ ] Describe the three major physical architectures.
- [ ] Discuss the trade-offs in selecting a physical architecture.
- [ ] Discuss cloud computing.
- [ ] Describe Infrastructure as a Service, Platform as a Service, and Software as a Service.
- [ ] Describe the three primary obstacles to cloud computing.
- [ ] Discuss the potential impact of ubiquitous computing and the Internet of Things.
- [ ] Describe enchanted objects.
- [ ] Discuss the three general questions that Green IT tries to address.
- [ ] Create an infrastructure design using deployment diagrams.
- [ ] Create a high-level hardware and software specification.
- [ ] Describe how nonfunctional requirements may influence the actual design of the physical architecture layer.

KEY TERMS

24/7
Access control list
Access control matrix
Access control requirements
Alternative matrix
Application logic
Architectural component
Artifact
Asymmetric encryption algorithm
Authentication
Availability and reliability requirements

Benchmark
Business process
Capability list
Capacity requirements
Certificate authority (CA)
Client–based architecture
Client computer
Client–server architecture
Cloud computing
Communication path
Cultural and political requirements
Customization requirements
Data access logic

Data storage
Deployment diagrams
Enchanted objects
Encryption
End-user license agreement
E-waste
Fat client
Graphical user interface (GUI)
Green data centers
Green IT
Grid computing
Hardware and software specification
Hybrid cloud

Infrastructure as a service (IaaS)
Internet of Things (IoT)
Invertible
Legal requirements
Locations
Maintainability requirements
Middleware
Mission critical system
Multitenancy
Network
Network model
Node
N-tiered architecture

Operational requirements
Outsourcing
Paperless office
Parkinson's law
Performance requirements
Platform as a service (PaaS)
Portability requirements
Presentation logic
Private cloud
Private key
Public cloud

Public key
Public key encryption
Response time
Role-based access control
Scalable
Security requirements
Server
Server-based architecture
Service
Service-oriented architecture
Software as a service (SaaS)

Speed requirements
SQL (structured
query language)
Symmetric encryp-
tion algorithm
System integration
requirements
Technical environment
requirements
Thick client
Thin client

Three-tiered architecture
Timesharing
Total cost of ownership
Two-tiered architecture
Ubiquitous computing
Virtualization
Virtual memory
Virus
Virus control requirements
Web services

QUESTIONS

1. What are the four basic functions of any information system?
2. What are the three primary hardware components of any physical architecture?
3. Name two examples of a server.
4. Compare and contrast server-based architectures, client-based architectures, and client–server-based architectures.
5. What is the biggest problem with server-based computing?
6. What is the biggest problem with client-based computing?
7. Describe the major benefits and limitations of thin client–server architectures.
8. Describe the major benefits and limitations of thick client–server architectures.
9. Describe the differences among two-tiered, three-tiered, and *n*-tiered architectures.
10. Define *scalable*. Why is this term important to system developers?
11. What six criteria are helpful to use when comparing the appropriateness of computing alternatives?
12. Why should the project team consider the existing physical architecture in the organization when designing the physical architecture layer of the new system?
13. Name the three different types of clouds. How do they differ from one another?
14. What is meant by a service-oriented architecture?
15. Define virtualization. How does it relate to the cloud?
16. What are the differences among IaaS, PaaS, and SaaS?
17. What are the obstacles for provisioning the physical architecture layer with cloud technologies?
18. What, if any, are the issues related to security in the cloud?
19. What are SOX and HIPAA, and how could they affect a firm's decision to adopt cloud technology?
20. What is meant by ubiquitous computing? How about the Internet of Things?

21. What is an enchanted object? Give a set of examples of them.
22. What is e-waste?
23. What is the problem with backyard recycling of e-waste?
24. What is meant by a green data center?
25. How do tablets, such as the iPad™, enable the paperless office?
26. What additional hardware- and software-associated costs might need to be included on the hardware and software specification?
27. Who is ultimately in charge of acquiring hardware and software for a project?
28. What is a benchmark, and why is it important?
29. Why is Parkinson's Law relevant to the design of the physical architecture layer?
30. What do you think are three common mistakes that novice analysts make in architecture design and hardware and software specification?
31. Describe the major nonfunctional requirements and how they influence physical architecture layer design.
32. Why is it useful to define the nonfunctional requirements in more detail even if the technical environment requirements dictate a specific architecture?
33. What does the network model communicate to the project team?
34. What are the differences between the top-level network model and the low-level network model?
35. Are some nonfunctional requirements more important than others in influencing the architecture design and hardware and software specification?
36. What do you think are the most important security issues for a system?
37. Describe the different approaches to access control.
38. Why is it important to have end-user license agreements examined?

EXERCISES

A. Using the Web (or past issues of computer industry magazines such as *Computerworld*), locate a system that runs in a server-based environment. Based on your reading, why do you think the company chose that computing environment?

B. Using the Web (or past issues of computer industry magazines such as *Computerworld*), locate a system that runs in a client–server environment. Based on your reading, why do you think the company chose that computing environment?

C. Using the Web, locate examples of a mainframe component, a minicomputer component, and a microcomputer component. Compare the components in terms of price, speed, available memory, and disk storage. Did you find large differences in prices when the performances of the components are considered?

D. You have been selected to find the best client–server architecture for a Web-based order entry system that is being developed for L.L. Bean. Write a short memo that describes to the project manager your reason for selecting an *n*-tiered architecture over a two-tiered architecture. In the memo, give some idea as to what different components of the architecture you would include.

E. Think about the system that your university currently uses for career services, and suppose that you are in charge of replacing the system with a new one. Describe how you would decide on the computing architecture for the new system using the criteria presented in this chapter. What information will you need to find out before you can make an educated comparison of the alternatives?

F. Using the Web, find information on the effects that e-waste and backyard recycling has on developing countries. Based on you find, what Green IT policies would you suggest a firm put in place to minimize the negative effects of e-waste.

G. Using the Web, find examples of company's pursuing a Green IT strategy. Describe what they are doing.

H. Energy Star is a joint program between the US Department of Energy and the Environmental Protection Agency. What are the requirements for various IT devices to be certified as being Energy Star compliant?

I. Using the Web, find examples of firms using the cloud as a basis for the physical architecture layer. Describe exactly what they are doing.

J. Locate a consumer products company on the Web and read its company description (so that you get a good understanding of the geographic locations of the company). Pretend that the company is about to create a new application to support retail sales over the Web. Create a high-level network model that depicts the locations that would include components that support this application.

K. Create a low-level network diagram for the building that houses the computer labs at your university. Choose an application (e.g., course registration, student admissions) and include only the components that are relevant to that application.

L. An energy company with headquarters in Dallas, Texas, is thinking about developing a system to track the efficiency of its oil refineries in North America. Each week, the ten refineries—as far as Valdez, Alaska, and as close as San Antonio, Texas—will upload performance data via satellite to the corporate mainframe in Dallas. Production managers at each site will use a personal computer to connect to an Internet service provider and access reports via the Web. Create a high-level network model that depicts the locations that have components supporting this system.

M. Suppose that your mother is a real estate agent, and she has decided to automate her daily tasks using a laptop computer. Consider her potential hardware and software needs, and create a hardware and software specification that describes them. The specification should be developed to help your mother buy her hardware and software on her own.

N. Suppose that the admissions office in your university has a Web-based application so that students can apply for admission online. Recently, there has been a push to admit more international students into the university. What do you recommend that the application include to ensure that it supports this global requirement?

O. Based on the A Real Estate Inc. problems in Chapter 4 (exercises I, J, and K), Chapter 5 (exercises N and O), Chapter 6 (exercise D), Chapter 7 (exercise D), Chapter 8 (exercise A), Chapter 9 (exercise H), and Chapter 10 (exercises I and J), suggest a physical architecture design and portray it with a deployment diagram.

P. Based on the A Video Store problems in Chapter 4 (exercises L, M, and N), Chapter 5 (exercises P and Q), Chapter 6 (exercise E), Chapter 7 (exercise E), Chapter 8 (exercise B), Chapter 9 (exercise I), and Chapter 10 (exercises K and L), suggest a physical architecture design and portray it with a deployment diagram.

Q. Based on the gym membership problems in Chapter 4 (exercises O, P, and Q), Chapter 5 (exercises R and S), Chapter 6 (exercise F), Chapter 7 (exercise F), Chapter 8 (exercise C), Chapter 9 (exercise J), and Chapter 10 (exercises M and N), suggest a physical architecture design and portray it with a deployment diagram.

R. Based on the Picnics R Us exercises in Chapter 4 (exercises R, S, and T), Chapter 5 (exercises T and U), Chapter 6 (exercise G), Chapter 7 (exercise G), Chapter 8 (exercise D), Chapter 9 (exercise K), and Chapter 10 (exercises O and P), suggest a physical architecture design and portray it with a deployment diagram.

S. Based on the Of-the-Month-Club problems in Chapter 4 (exercises U, V, and W), Chapter 5 (exercises V and W), Chapter 6 (exercise H), Chapter 7 (exercise H), Chapter 8 (exercise E), Chapter 9 (exercise L), and Chapter 10 (exercises Q and R), suggest a physical architecture design and portray it with a deployment diagram.

MINICASES

1. The system development project team at Birdie Masters golf schools has been working on defining the physical architecture design for the system. The major focus of the project is a networked school location operations system, allowing each school location to easily record and retrieve all school location transaction data. Another system element is the use of the Internet to enable current and prospective students to view class offerings at any of the Birdie Masters' locations, schedule lessons and enroll in classes at any Birdie Masters location, and maintain a student progress profile—a confidential analysis of the student's golf skill development.

The project team has been considering the globalization issues that should be factored into the architecture design. The school's plan for expansion into the golf-crazed Japanese market is moving ahead. The first Japanese school location is tentatively planning to open about six months after the target completion data for the system project. Therefore, it is important that issues related to the international location be addressed now during design.

Assume that you have been given the responsibility of preparing a summary memo on the globalization issues that should be factored into the design. Prepare this memo discussing the globalization issues that are relevant to Birdie Masters' new system.

2. Jerry is a relatively new member of a project team that is developing a retail store management system for a chain of sporting goods stores. Company headquarters is in Las Vegas, and the chain has twenty-seven locations throughout Nevada, Utah, and Arizona. Several cities have multiple stores.

The new system will be a networked client–server architecture. Stores will be linked to one of three regional servers, and the regional servers will be linked to corporate headquarters in Las Vegas. The regional servers also link to one another. Each retail store will be outfitted with similar configurations of two PC-based point-of-sale terminals networked to a local file server. Jerry has been given the task of developing a network model that will document the geographic structure of this system. He has not faced a system of this scope before and is a little unsure how to begin.

a. Prepare a set of instructions for Jerry to follow in developing this network model.

b. Using a deployment diagram, draw a network model for this organization.

c. Prepare a set of instructions for Jerry to follow in developing a hardware and software specification.

3. Refer to the Professional and Scientific Staff Management (PSSM) minicase in Chapters 4, 6, 7, 8, 9, and 10. Based on the solutions developed for those problems, suggest a physical architecture design and portray it with a deployment diagram.

4. Refer to the Holiday Travel Vehicles minicase in Chapters 5, 6, 7, 8, 9, and 10. Based on the solutions developed for those problems, suggest a physical architecture design and portray it with a deployment diagram.

PART THREE
CONSTRUCTION, INSTALLATION, AND OPERATIONS

During construction, the actual system is built. Building a successful information system requires a set of activities: programming, testing, and documenting the system. In today's global economy, cultural issues also play an important role in managing these activities. Installing an information system requires switching from the current system to the new system. This conversion process can be quite involved; for example, cultural differences among the users, the development team, and the two groups can be quite challenging. Furthermore, not only does conversion involve shutting the old system down and turning the new one on, but it also can involve a significant training effort. Finally, operating the system may uncover additional requirements that may have to be addressed by the development team.

CHAPTER 12

CONSTRUCTION

$\mathbf{T}$his chapter discusses the activities needed to successfully build an information system: programming, testing, and documenting the system. Programming is time-consuming and costly, but except in unusual circumstances, it is the simplest for the systems analyst because it is well understood. For this reason, the systems analyst focuses on testing (proving that the system works as designed) and developing documentation.

OBJECTIVES

- Understand the basic issues related to managing programmers.
- Understand how cultural issues can impact the efficiency, effectiveness, and focus of software development teams.
- Be familiar with the different types of documentation.
- Understand how to develop documentation.
- Understand how object-orientation effects software testing.
- Understand the different types of and purpose of unit tests.
- Understand the different types of and purpose of integration tests.
- Understand the different types of and purpose of system tests.
- Understand the different types of and purpose of acceptance tests.

INTRODUCTION

When people first learn about developing information systems, they usually think immediately about writing programs. Programming can be the largest single component of any systems development project in terms of time and cost. However, it also can be the best understood component and therefore—except in rare circumstances—offers the fewest problems of all aspects of systems development. When projects fail, it is usually not because the programmers were unable to write the programs, but because the analysis, design, installation, and/or project management were done poorly.

Construction is the development of all parts of the system, including the software itself, documentation, and new operating procedures. Looking back at Figure 1-4, we see that the Construction phase of the Enhanced Unified Process deals predominantly with the Implementation, Testing, and Configuration and Change Management workflows. Implementation obviously deals with programming. Programming is often seen as the focal point of systems development. After all, systems development *is* writing programs. It is the reason we do all the analysis and design. And it's fun. Many beginning programmers see testing and documentation as bothersome afterthoughts. Testing and documentation aren't fun, so they often receive less attention than the creative activity of writing programs.

However, programming and testing are very similar to writing and editing. No professional writer (or good student writing an important term paper) would stop after writing the first draft. Rereading, editing, and revising the initial draft into a good paper are the hallmarks of good writing. Likewise, thorough testing is the hallmark of professional software developers. Most professional organizations devote more time and money to testing (and the subsequent revision and retesting) than to writing the programs in the first place.

The reasons are simple economics: Downtime and failures caused by software bugs[1] are extremely expensive. Many large organizations estimate the costs of downtime of critical applications at $50,000 to $200,000 *per hour*.[2] One serious bug that causes an hour of downtime can cost more than one year's salary of a programmer—and how often are bugs found and fixed in one hour? Testing is, therefore, a form of insurance. Organizations are willing to spend a lot of time and money to prevent the possibility of major failures after the system is installed.

Therefore, a program is usually not considered finished until the test for that program is passed. For this reason, programming and testing are tightly coupled, and because programming is the primary job of the programmer (not the analyst), testing (not programming) often becomes the focus of the construction stage for the systems analysis team.

The Configuration and Change Management workflow keeps track of the state of the evolving system. The evolving information system comprises a set of artifacts that include, for example, diagrams, source code, and executables. During the development process, these artifacts are modified. The amount of work, and hence dollars, that goes into the development of the artifacts is substantial. Therefore, the artifacts themselves should be handled as any expensive asset would be handled: Access controls must be put into place to safeguard the artifacts from being stolen or destroyed. Because the artifacts are modified on a regular, if not on a continuous basis, good version control mechanisms should be established. The *traceability* of the artifacts back through the various artifacts developed, such as data management layer designs, class diagrams, package diagrams, and use-case diagrams, to the specific requirements is also very important. Without this traceability, we will not know which aspects of a system to modify when—not if—the requirements change.

MANAGING PROGRAMMING

In general, systems analysts do not write programs; programmers write programs. Therefore, the primary task of the systems analysts during programming is . . . waiting. However, the project manager is usually very busy managing the programming effort by assigning the programmers, coordinating the activities, and managing the programming schedule.[3]

Assigning Programmers

The first step in programming is assigning modules to the programmers. As discussed in Chapter 8, each module (class, object, or method) should be as separate and distinct as possible from the other modules (i.e., cohesion should be maximized and coupling should be minimized). The project manager first groups together classes that are related so that each programmer is working on related classes. These groups of classes are then assigned to programmers. A good place to start is to look at the package diagrams.

---

[1] When I (Alan Dennis) was an undergraduate, I had the opportunity to hear Admiral Grace Hopper tell how the term *bug* was introduced. She was working on one of the early Navy computers when suddenly it failed. The computer would not restart properly, so she began to search for failed vacuum tubes. She found a moth inside one tube and recorded in the log book that a bug had caused the computer to crash. From then on, every computer crash was jokingly blamed on a bug (as opposed to programmer error), and eventually the term *bug* entered the general language of computing.

[2] See Billie Shea, "Quality Patrol: Eye on the Enterprise," *Application Development Trends* (November 5, 1998): 31–38.

[3] One of the best books on managing programming (even though it was first written more than 30 years ago) is that by Frederick P. Brooks, Jr. *The Mythical Man-Month*, 20th Anniversary Edition (Reading, MA: Addison-Wesley, 1995).

One of the rules of systems development is that the more programmers who are involved in a project, the longer the system will take to build. This is because as the size of the programming team increases, the need for coordination increases exponentially, and the more coordination required, the less time programmers can spend actually writing systems (see Chapter 2). The best size is the smallest possible programming team. When projects are so complex that they require a large team, the best strategy is to try to break the project into a series of smaller parts that can function as independently as possible.

Coordinating Activities

Coordination can be done through both high- and low-tech means. The simplest approach is to have a weekly project meeting to discuss any changes to the system that have arisen during the past week—or any issues that have come up. Remember, agile development approaches such as Scrum encourage daily meetings (see Chapter 2). Regular meetings, even if they are brief, encourage the widespread communication and discussion of issues before they become problems.

Another important way to improve coordination is to create and follow standards that can range from formal rules for naming files, to forms that must be completed when goals are reached, to programming guidelines (see Chapter 2). When a team forms standards and then follows them, the project can be completed faster because task coordination is less complex.

The analysts also must put mechanisms in place to keep the programming effort well organized. Many project teams set up three areas in which programmers can work: a development area, a testing area, and a production area. These areas can be different directories on a server hard disk, different servers, or different physical locations, but the point is that files, data, and programs are separated based on their status of completion. At first, programmers access and build files within the development area and then copy them to the testing area when the programmers are finished. If a program does not pass a test, it is sent back to development. Once all programs are tested and ready to support the new system, they are copied into the production area—the location where the final system will reside.

Keeping files and programs in different places based on completion status helps manage *change control*, the action of coordinating a system as it changes through construction. Another change control technique is keeping track of which programmer changes which classes and packages by using a *program log*. The log is merely a form on which programmers sign out classes and packages to write and sign in when they are completed. Both the programming areas and program log help the analysts understand exactly who has worked on what and the system's current status. Without these techniques, files can be put into production without the proper testing (e.g., two programmers can start working on the same class or package at the same time).

If a CASE tool is used during the construction step, it can be very helpful for change control because many CASE tools are set up to track the status of programs and help manage programmers as they work. In most cases, maintaining coordination is not conceptually complex. It just requires a lot of discipline and attention to tracking small details.

Managing the Schedule

The time estimates that were produced during project identification and refined during analysis and design almost always need to be refined as the project progresses during construction because it is virtually impossible to develop an exact assessment of the project's schedule. As we discussed in Chapter 2, a well-done set of time estimates usually has a 10 percent margin of error by the time we reach the construction step. It is critical that the time estimates be

PRACTICAL	12-1 Avoiding Classic Implementation Mistakes
TIP	

In previous chapters, we discussed classic mistakes and how to avoid them. Here, we summarize four classic mistakes in implementation[4]:

- *Research-oriented development:* Using state-of-the-art technology requires research-oriented development that explores the new technology because "bleeding edge" tools and techniques are not well understood, are not well documented, and do not function exactly as promised.

  Solution: If you use state-of-the-art technology, you need to significantly increase the project's time and cost estimates even if (some experts would say *especially if*) such technologies claim to reduce time and effort.

- *Using low-cost personnel:* You get what you pay for. The lowest-cost consultant or staff member is significantly less productive than the best staff. Several studies have shown that the best programmers produce software six to eight times faster than the least productive (yet cost only 50 to 100 percent more).

Solution: If cost is a critical issue, assign the best, most expensive personnel; never assign entry-level personnel in an attempt to save costs.

- *Lack of code control:* On large projects, programmers need to coordinate changes to the program source code (so that two programmers don't try to change the same program at the same time and overwrite each other's changes). Although manual procedures appear to work (e.g., sending e-mail notes to others when you work on a program to tell them not to), mistakes are inevitable.

Solution: Use a source code library that requires programmers to "check out" programs and prohibits others from working on them at the same time.

- *Inadequate testing:* The number one reason for project failure during implementation is ad hoc testing—where programmers and analysts test the system without formal test plans.

Solution: Always allocate sufficient time in the project plan for formal testing.

revised as construction proceeds. If a program module takes longer to develop than expected, then the prudent response is to move the expected completion date later by the same amount.

One of the most common causes for schedule problems is scope creep. Scope creep occurs when new requirements are added to the project after the system design was finalized (see Chapter 2). If you recall, Scrum encourages adding new requirements to the product backlog instead of letting the scope of the project change between sprints. Scope creep can be very expensive because changes made late in system development can require much of the completed system design (and even programs already written) to be redone. Any proposed change during construction must require the approval of the project manager and should only be done after a quick cost–benefit analysis has been done.

Another common cause is the unnoticed day-by-day slippages in the schedule. One package is a day late here; another one is a day late there. Pretty soon these minor delays add up and the project is noticeably behind schedule. Once again, the key to managing the programming effort is to watch these minor slippages carefully and update the schedule accordingly.

Typically, a project manager creates a risk assessment that tracks potential risks along with an evaluation of their likelihood and potential impact. As the construction step moves to a close, the list of risks changes as some items are removed and others surface. The best project managers, however, work hard to keep risks from having an impact on the schedule and costs associated with the project.

[4] Based upon material from Steve McConnell, *Rapid Development* (Redmond, WA: Microsoft Press, 1996).

Cultural Issues

One of the major issues facing information systems development organizations is the offshoring of the implementation aspects of information systems development. Conflicts caused by different national and organizational cultures are now becoming a real area of concern. With the potential of cloud computing (see Chapter 11) potentially enabling even more outsourcing, the potential of cultural conflict is even greater.

A simple example that can demonstrate cultural differences with regard to student learning is the idea of plagiarism. What exactly does plagiarism really imply? Different cultures have very different views. In some cultures, one of the highest forms of respect is simply to quote an expert. However, in these same cultures, there is no need to reference the expert. The act of quoting the expert itself is the act of respect. In some cases, actually referencing the expert through the use of quotation marks and a footnote may be viewed as an insult to the expert and the reader because it is obvious to the reader that the writer did not expect the reader to recognize the expert's quote. This expectation was caused by either the reader's own ignorance or the expert's lack of reputation. Either way, the writer would be insulting someone through the use of quotation marks and footnotes. These cultures tend to be collectivist in nature (see Chapters 10 and 13). Consequently, since the collective owns all ideas, there is no concept of theft of ideas. However, in the United States, the opposite is true. If a writer does not use quotation marks and footnotes to appropriately give credit to the source of the quote (or paraphrase), then the writer is guilty of theft.[5] Obviously, in today's global world, plagiarism is not a simple issue.

Another simple example of cultural differences, with regard to student learning, is the idea of students working together to complete homework assignments. Even though we all know that research has shown that students learn better in groups, in the United States, we view students who turn in the same assignment as cheaters.[6] In other cultures, individual performance is not as important as the performance of the group. Again, these cultures are collectivist in nature. Consequently, helping a fellow student to understand the assignment and to perform better in the class would be the expectation. Furthermore, this attitude extends to test taking. If a fellow student is struggling on a test and if you were from a collectivist culture, it would be your duty to allow your fellow student to copy your answer. Obviously, this is another example of a substantive cultural difference. From a business perspective, these different views of plagiarism and cheating could have serious implications for the protection of intellectual property.

As we stated previously, with offshore outsourcing, information systems development teams can be geographically dispersed and multicultural in their membership. Given the above issues and when we consider the cultural differences Hall and Hofstede identified (see Chapter 10), cultural issues add a new wrinkle in the management of developing a successful information system.[7] From an information systems development perspective, *context* could influence the ability of a team member to see (or not see) potential creative solutions that are out of the box or affect a team member's ability (or inability) to understand the entire problem under consideration. Furthermore, given this dimension, the level of detail in direction

---

[5] A wonderful little book on plagiarism is Richard A. Posner, *The Little Book of Plagiarism* (New York: Pantheon Books, 2007).

[6] In this case, the recent work of Roger Schank is very enlightening. For example, see Roger C. Schank, *Making Minds Less Well Educated than Our Own* (Mahwah, NJ: Lawrence Erlbaum Associates, 2004).

[7] See Geert Hofstede, *Culture's Consequences: Comparing Values, Behaviors, Institutions and Organizations across Nations*, 2nd Ed. (Thousand Oaks, CA: Sage, 2001); Geert Hofstede, Gert Jan Hofstede, and Michael Minkov, *Cultures and Organizations: Software of the Mind*, 3rd Ed. (New York, NY: McGraw-Hill, 2010); Edward T. Hall, *Beyond Culture* (New York: Anchor Books, 1981).

could be varied between cultures. Hofstede's *individualism* and *collectivism* dimension partially explains the results regarding plagiarism and cheating described above. Given the importance that intellectual property plays in IT, this potentially could be a real problem when offshoring development to a collectivist culture. Furthermore, Hall's *speed of messages* and context dimensions could also affect the way this could be addressed. Depending on the culture, too much detail could be insulting, but attempting to put this issue in to a contextual frame that is culturally sensitive is difficult.

When managing programmers in a multicultural setting, Hall's *time* dimension must also be considered. In *monochronic time* cultures, deadlines are critical. This is probably why *time-boxing* has been relatively successful as a method to control projects (see Chapter 2). However, in a *polychronic time* culture, a deadline is nothing more than a suggestion. Obviously, when managing programmers, understanding how the culture considers time is very important to have both a successful product delivery and a successful development process.

Hofstede's other previously mentioned dimensions are *power distance, uncertainty avoidance*, and *masculinity* versus *femininity*. Managing programmers in a culture with a high power distance value is different than with a culture with a low power distance. For example, in the United States, programmers see themselves as equals to their managers. In fact, in some firms, the president of the firm can be found "coding" solutions alongside of a brand new hire. This somewhat explains the growing popularity of agile methods (see Chapter 1). In comparison, in a high power distance culture, the president of the firm would never stoop to perform the same tasks as a new hire. It would be insulting to the president and embarrassing to the new hire.

With regard to uncertainty avoidance, the choice of systems development approach could be affected. In a culture that prefers everything to be neat and ordered, a systems development methodology that is very rule-driven would be beneficial. Also, development team member professional certification and team and firm ISO or CMMI certifications would lend credibility to the team, whereas in a culture that willingly takes on risk, certifications might not increase the perceived standing of the development team.

When managing programmers in a masculine culture, it is critical to provide recognition to the top-performing members of the development team and also to recognize the top-performing teams. On the other hand, when considering a feminine culture, it is more important to ensure that the workplace is a supportive, noncompetitive, and nurturing environment.

Hofstede has identified a fifth dimension, *long-* versus *short-term orientation*, which deals with how the culture views the past and the future. In a long-term focused culture, team development and a deep relationship with a client is very important, while in a culture that emphasizes the short term, delivering a high-quality product on time is all that really matters.

For years, project managers in the United States have had to bring together individuals from very different backgrounds. Moreover, there was always a common spoken and written language, English, and the melting pot idea that guaranteed some level of commonality among the team members.[8] However, in today's "flat world," there is no longer any common culture or common spoken and written language. From an information systems development perspective, the common languages tend to be UML, Java, SQL, C++, Objective-C, and Visual Basic, not English. However, at this time, there is no common culture. Consequently, understanding cultural issues will be extremely important for the near future to successfully manage international and multicultural development teams.

---

[8] People who grew up in different areas of the United States (e.g., New York City, Nashville, Minneapolis, Denver, and Los Angeles) are, in a very real sense, culturally different. For an interesting take on this, see Joel Garreau, *The Nine Nations of North America* (New York, NY: Avon Books, 1981). However, the prevalence of the Internet and cable TV has created much more of a shared culture in the United States than in many other parts of the world. Obviously, the Internet and cable TV also could affect the world in the long run.

DEVELOPING DOCUMENTATION

Developing documentation of the system must be done throughout system development. In many ways, the documentation of a system is a system. So, developing documentation can follow a similar, but simpler, approach as software development. In this case, creating use cases and developing the user interfaces to the documentation make sense. There are two fundamentally different types of documentation: system documentation and user documentation. *System documentation* is intended to help programmers and systems analysts understand the application software and enable them to build it or maintain it after the system is installed. System documentation is largely a by-product of the systems analysis and design process and is created as the project unfolds. Each step and phase produces documents that are essential in understanding how the system is or is to be built, and these documents are stored in the project binder(s). In many object-oriented development environments, it is possible to somewhat automate the creation of detailed documentation for classes and methods. For example, in Java, if the programmers use javadoc-style comments, it is possible to create HTML pages that document a class and its methods automatically by using the javadoc utility.[9] Because most programmers look on documentation with much distaste, anything that can make documentation easier to create is useful.

User documentation (such as user's manuals, training manuals, and online help systems) is designed to help the user operate the system. Although most project teams expect users to have received training and to have read the user's manuals before operating the system, unfortunately, this is not always the case. It is more common today—especially in the case of commercial software packages for microcomputers—for users to begin using the software without training or reading the user's manuals. In this section, we focus on user documentation.[10]

User documentation is often left until the end of the project, which is a dangerous strategy. Developing good documentation takes longer than many people expect because it requires much more than simply writing a few pages. Producing documentation requires designing the documents (whether on paper or online), writing the text, editing the documents, and testing them. For good-quality documentation, this process usually takes about three hours per page (single-spaced) for paper-based documentation or two hours per screen for online documentation. Thus "simple" documentation, such as a ten-page user's manual and a set of twenty help screens, takes seventy hours. Of course, lower-quality documentation can be produced faster.

The time required to develop and test user documentation should be built into the project plan. Most organizations plan for documentation development to start once the interface design and program specifications are complete. The initial draft of documentation is usually scheduled for completion immediately after the unit tests are complete. This reduces (but doesn't eliminate) the chance that the documentation will need to be changed due to software changes and still leaves enough time for the documentation to be tested and revised before the acceptance tests are started.

Although paper-based manuals are still important, online documentation is becoming more pervasive. Paper-based documentation is simpler to use because it is more familiar to users, especially novices who have less computer experience; online documentation requires the users to learn one more set of commands. Paper-based documentation is also easier to flip

---

[9] For those who have used Java, javadoc is how the JDK documentation from Sun is created.

[10] For more information on developing documentation, see Thomas T. Barker, *Writing Software Documentation* (Boston: Allyn & Bacon, 1998).

through and gain a general understanding of its organization and topics and can be used far away from the computer itself.

There are four key strengths of online documentation that all but guarantee it will become the dominant form for the 21st century. Searching for information is often simpler (provided the help search index is well designed) because the user can type in a variety of keywords to view information almost instantaneously, rather than having to search through the index or table of contents in a paper document. The same information can be presented several times in many different formats, so that the user can find and read the information in the most informative way (such redundancy is possible in paper documentation, but the cost and intimidating size of the resulting manual make it impractical). Online documentation provides many new ways for the user to interact with the documentation that is not possible in static paper documentation. For example, it is possible to use links or "tool tips" (i.e., pop-up messages; see Chapter 10) to explain unfamiliar terms, and one can write "show-me" routines that demonstrate on the screen exactly what buttons to click and text to type. Finally, online documentation is significantly less expensive to distribute than paper documentation.

Types of Documentation

There are three fundamentally different types of user documentation: reference documents, procedures manuals, and tutorials. *Reference documents* (also called the help system) are designed to be used when the user needs to learn how to perform a specific function (e.g., updating a field, adding a new record). Often people read reference information when they have tried and failed to perform the function; writing reference documents requires special care because the user is often impatient or frustrated when he or she begins to read them.

Procedures manuals describe how to perform business tasks (e.g., printing a monthly report, taking a customer order). Each item in the procedures manual typically guides the user through a task that requires several functions or steps in the system. Therefore, each entry is typically much longer than an entry in a reference document.

Tutorials—obviously—teach people how to use major components of a system (e.g., an introduction to the basic operations of the system). Each entry in the tutorial is typically longer still than the entries in procedures manuals, and the entries are usually designed to be read in sequence (whereas entries in reference documents and procedures manuals are designed to be read individually).

Regardless of the type of user documentation, the overall process for developing it is similar to the process of developing interfaces (see Chapter 10). The developer first designs the general structure for the documentation and then develops the individual components within it.

Designing Documentation Structure

The general structure used in most online documentation, whether reference documents, procedures manuals, or tutorials, is to develop a set of *documentation navigation controls* that lead the user to *documentation topics*. The documentation topics are the material that user wants to read, whereas the navigation controls are the way the user locates and accesses a specific topic. As such, using storyboards, windows navigation diagrams, and wireframe diagrams is useful (see Chapter 10).

Designing the structure of the documentation begins by identifying the different types of topics and navigation controls that need to be included. Figure 12-1 shows a commonly used structure for online reference documents (i.e., the help system). The documentation topics generally come from three sources. The first and most obvious source of topics is the set of

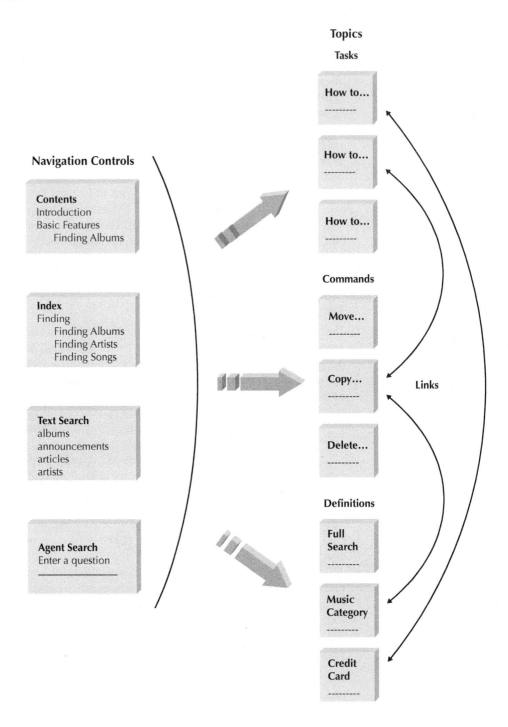

FIGURE 12-1
Organizing Online
Reference
Documents

commands and menus in the user interface. This set of topics is very useful if the user wants to understand how a particular command or menu is used.

However, the users often don't know what commands to look for or where they are in the system's menu structure. Instead, users have tasks they want to perform, and rather than thinking in terms of commands, they think in terms of their tasks. Therefore, the second and often more useful set of topics focuses on how to perform certain tasks, usually those in the use scenarios, WND, and the real use cases from the user interface design (see Chapter 10). These topics walk the user through the set of steps (often involving several keystrokes or mouse clicks) needed to perform some task.

The third topic is definitions of important terms. These terms are usually the use cases and classes in the system, but sometimes they also include commands.

There are five general types of navigation controls for topics, but not all systems use all five types (see Figure 12-1). The first is the table of contents that organizes the information in a logical form, as though the users were to read the reference documentation from start to finish. The index provides access into the topics based on important keywords, in the same way that the index at the back of a book helps us find topics. Text search provides the ability to search through the topics either for any text the user types or for words that match a developer-specified set of words that is much larger than the set of words in the index. Unlike the index, text search typically provides no organization to the words (other than alphabetical). Some systems provide the ability to use an intelligent agent to help in the search. The fifth and final navigation controls to topics are the hyperlinks between topics that enable the user to click and move among topics.

Procedures manuals and tutorials are similar but often simpler in structure. Topics for procedures manuals usually come from the use scenarios, WNDs, and the real use cases developed during interface design and from other basic tasks the users must perform. Topics for tutorials are usually organized around major sections of the system and the level of experience of the user. Most tutorials start with the basic, most commonly used commands and then move into more complex and less commonly used commands.

Writing Documentation Topics

The general format for topics is fairly similar across application systems and operating systems. Topics typically start with very clear titles, followed by some introductory text that defines the topic and then by detailed, step-by-step instructions on how to perform what is being described. Many topics include screen images to help the user find items on the screen; some also have tutorials and videos available online that demonstrate the functions of interest to the user. Most also include navigation controls to enable the movement among topics, usually at the top of the window, plus links to other topics. Some also include links to related topics that include options or other commands and tasks the user might want to perform in concert with the topic being read.

Writing the topic content can be challenging. It requires a good understanding of the user (or more accurately the range of users) and a knowledge of what skills the users currently have and can be expected to import from other systems and tools they are using or have used (including the system that the new system is replacing). Topics should always be written from the viewpoint of the user and describe what the user wants to accomplish, not what the system can do. Figure 12-2 provides some general guidelines to improve the quality of documentation text.[11]

Identifying Navigation Terms

As we write the documentation topics, we also begin to identify the terms that will be used to help users find topics. The table of contents is usually the most straightforward, because it is developed from the logical structure of the documentation topics, whether reference

---

[11] One of the best books to explain the art of writing is William Strunk and E. B. White, *Elements of Style*, 4th Ed. (Needham Heights, MA: Allyn & Bacon, 2000).

Guideline	Before the Guideline	After the Guideline
Use the active voice: The active voice creates more active and readable text by putting the subject at the start of the sentence, the verb in the middle, and the object at the end.	Finding albums is done using the album title, the artist's name, or a song title.	You can find an album by using the album title, the artist's name, or a song title.
Use e-prime style: E-prime style creates more active writing by omitting all forms of the verb to be.	The text you want to copy must be selected before you click on the copy button.	Select the text you want to copy before you click on the copy button.
Use consistent terms: Always use the same term to refer to the same items, rather than switching among synonyms (e.g., change, modify, update).	Select the text you want to copy. Pressing the copy button will copy the marked text to the new location.	Select the text you want to copy. Pressing the copy button will copy the selected text to the new location.
Use simple language: Always use the simplest language possible to accurately convey the meaning. This does not mean you should "dumb down" the text but that you should avoid artificially inflating its complexity. Avoid separating subjects and verbs and try to use the fewest words possible. (When you encounter a complex piece of text, try eliminating words; you may be surprised at how few words are really needed to convey meaning.)	The Georgia Statewide Academic and Medical System (GSAMS) is a cooperative and collaborative distance learning network in the state of Georgia. The organization in Atlanta that administers and manages the technical and overall operations of the currently more than 300 interactive audio and video teleconferencing classrooms throughout Georgia system is the Department of Administrative Service (DOAS). (56 words)	The Department of Administrative Service (DOAS) in Atlanta manages the Georgia Statewide Academic and Medical System (GSAMS), a distance learning network with more than 300 teleconferencing classrooms throughout Georgia. (29 words)
Use friendly language: Too often, documentation is cold and sterile because it is written in a very formal manner. Remember, you are writing for a person, not a computer.	Blank disks have been provided to you by Operations. It is suggested that you ensure your data are not lost by making backup copies of all essential data.	You should make a backup copy of all data that are important to you. If you need more diskettes, contact Operations.
Use parallel grammatical structures: Parallel grammatical structures indicate the similarity among items in list and help the reader understand content.	Opening files Saving a document How to delete files	Opening a file Saving a file Deleting a file
Use steps correctly: Novices often intersperse action and the results of action when describing a step-by-step process. Steps are always actions.	1. Press the customer button. 2. The customer dialogue box will appear. 3. Type the customer ID and press the submit button and the customer record will appear.	1. Press the customer button. 2. Type the customer ID in the customer dialogue box when it appears. 3. Press the submit button to view the customer record for this customer.
Use short paragraphs: Readers of documentation usually quickly scan text to find the information they need, so the text in the middle of long paragraphs is often overlooked. Use separate paragraphs to help readers find information more quickly.		

Source: Based upon material from T. T. Barker, *Writing Software Documentation* (Boston: Allyn & Bacon, 1998).

FIGURE 12-2 Guidelines for Crafting Documentation Topics

topics, procedure topics, or tutorial topics. The items for the index and search engine require more care because they are developed from the major parts of the system and the users' business functions. Every time we write a topic, we must also list the terms that will be used to find the topic. Terms for the index and search engine can come from four distinct sources.

The first source for index terms is the set of the commands in the user interface, such as open file, modify customer, and print open orders. All commands contain two parts (action and object). It is important to develop the index for both parts because users could search for information using either part. A user looking for more information about saving files, for example, might search by using the term *save* or the term *files.*

The second source is the set of major concepts in the system, which are often use cases and classes. In the case of the Appointment system, for example, this might include appointment, symptoms, or patient.

A third source is the set of business tasks the user performs, such as ordering replacement units or making an appointment. Often these are contained in the command set, but sometimes they require several commands and use terms that do not always appear in the system. Good sources for these terms are the use scenarios and real use cases developed during interface design (see Chapter 10).

A fourth, often controversial, source is the set of synonyms for the three sets of preceding items. Users sometimes don't think in terms of the nicely defined terms used by the system. They might try to find information on how to stop or quit rather than exit, or erase rather than delete. Including synonyms in the index increases the complexity and size of the documentation system but can greatly improve the usefulness of the system to the users.

DESIGNING TESTS

In object-oriented systems, the temptation is to minimize testing. After all, through the use of patterns, frameworks, class libraries, and components, much of the system has been tested previously. Therefore, we should not have to test as much. Right? Wrong! Testing is more critical to object-oriented systems than to systems developed in the past. Based on encapsulation (and information hiding), polymorphism (and dynamic binding), inheritance, reuse, and the actual object-oriented products, thorough testing is much more difficult and critical. Given the complexity of the development processes used and the global nature of information systems development, testing becomes even more crucial. Thus, object-oriented testing must be done systematically, and the results must be documented so that the project team knows what has and has not been tested. Testing object-oriented systems is therefore very complex. Consequently, a complete coverage of the topic is beyond the scope of this book.[12]

The purpose of testing is not to demonstrate that the system is free of errors. It is not possible to prove that a system is error free. The purpose of testing is to uncover differences between what the system actually does and what the system should do. In other words, the purpose of testing is to try and break the system. This is similar to theory testing. You cannot prove a theory. If a test fails to find problems with a theory, your confidence in the theory is increased. However, if a test succeeds in finding a problem, then the theory has been falsified. Software testing is similar in that it can only show the existence of errors. So, the point of testing is to uncover as many errors as feasible. It is simply not cost-effective to try to get every error out of the software. Except in simple examples, it is, in fact, impossible. There are simply too many combinations to check.

[12] For a good introduction to testing object-oriented software, see John D. McGregor and David A. Sykes, *A Practical Guide to Testing Object-Oriented Software* (Boston: Addison-Wesley, 2001). For a thorough coverage of testing object-oriented software, see Robert V. Binder, *Testing Object-Oriented Systems: Models, Patterns, and Tools* (Reading, MA: Addison-Wesley, 1999); this book provides more than 1,000 pages of information with regard to how to test the different artifacts and processes included in object-oriented systems development.

With our functional requirements, we focused our testing approach to ensure the fidelity of our problem domain representations through the use of role-playing and walkthroughs (see Chapters 4–8). These included the balancing of the analysis models and ensuring that all constraints (invariant, pre-conditions, and post-conditions) and method specifications were completed in such a way that they removed any ambiguity from the developer's intention of the detailed design of the classes that addressed the functional requirements.

With the design of the data management layer (Chapter 9), the focus of the verification and validation activities dealt with confirming that the problem domain classes were mapped properly to the type of object persistence chosen and that a set of data access and manipulation classes were designed. For example, when mapping the problem domain classes to a relational database format, a specific set of rules must be followed (see Figure 9-9). Testing the design of the human–computer interaction layer (Chapter 10) included the validation of all data input by using the constraints to guarantee that only valid data is allowed to enter the system. Furthermore, testing of the design of the user interface using heuristic evaluation, walkthrough evaluation, interactive evaluation, A/B testing, and formal usability testing was described. When considering testing the physical architecture layer (Chapter 11), the fidelity of the design of the network, hardware, and the deployment of the software must be guaranteed. As with the other layers, performing walkthroughs to balance the high- and low-level designs of the network and to confirm that the hardware specifications and the specifications of the software over the network and workstations were consistent was described.

In addition to testing the functional requirements across all layers, testing must also address all nonfunctional requirements: operational, performance, security, and cultural and political requirements. For example, performance testing of all interactions with the implementation of the system becomes important. For example, if queries run too slow, the optimization approaches described in Chapter 8 may be required on the problem domain, data management, human–computer interaction, and physical architecture layers. And, of course, once these optimizations have been designed and implemented, the optimizations will need to be further tested. As you can see, regardless of the systems development methodology used, testing is paramount to delivering successful information systems.

In general, there are four general types or levels of tests: unit tests, integration tests, system tests, and acceptance tests. Although each application system is different, most errors are found during integration and system testing. Before describing the specific types of tests, we describe the effect that the object-oriented characteristics have on testing and the necessary planning and management activities that must take place to have a successful testing program. Next we describe the four general types of tests. Finally, given the importance of the security nonfunctional requirements, we describe how security requirements affect testing.

Testing and Object Orientation

Most testing techniques have been developed to support non–object-oriented development. Therefore, most of the testing approaches have had to be adapted to object-oriented systems. The characteristics of object-oriented systems that affect testing the most are encapsulation (and information hiding); polymorphism (and dynamic binding); inheritance; and the use of patterns, class libraries, frameworks, and components. Also, the sheer volume of products that come out of a typical object-oriented development process has increased the importance of testing in object-oriented systems development.

Encapsulation and Information Hiding Encapsulation and information hiding allow processes and data to be combined to create holistic entities (i.e., objects). They support hiding everything behind a visible interface. Although this allows the system to be modified and maintained in an effective and efficient manner, it makes testing the system problematic. What do you need to test to build confidence in the system's ability to meet the user's need? You need to test the business process that is represented in the use cases. However, the business process is distributed over a set of collaborating classes and contained in the methods of those classes. The only way to know the effect that a business process has on a system is to look at the state changes that take place in the system. But in object-oriented systems, the instances of the classes hide the data behind a class boundary. How is it possible then to see the impact of a business process?

A second issue raised by encapsulation and information hiding is the definition of a "unit" for unit testing. What is the unit to be tested? Is it the package, class, or method? In traditional approaches, the answer would be the process that is contained in a function. However, the process in object-oriented systems is distributed over a set of classes. Therefore, testing individual methods makes no sense. The answer is the class. This dramatically changes the way unit testing is done.

A third issue raised is the impact on integration testing. In this case, objects can be aggregated to form aggregate objects; for instance, a car has many parts, or they can be grouped together to form collaborations. Furthermore, they can be used in class libraries, frameworks, and components. Based on all of these different ways classes can be grouped together, how does one effectively do integration testing?

Polymorphism and Dynamic Binding Polymorphism and dynamic binding dramatically affect both unit and integration testing. Because an individual business process is implemented through a set of methods distributed over a set of objects, as shown before, the unit test makes no sense at the method level. However, with polymorphism and dynamic binding, the same method (a small part of the overall business process) can be implemented in many different objects. Therefore, testing individual implementations of methods makes no sense. Again, the unit that makes sense to test is the class. Except for trivial cases, dynamic binding makes it impossible to know which implementation is going to be executed until the system does it. Therefore, integration testing becomes very challenging.

Inheritance When taking into consideration the issues raised about inheritance (see Chapter 8), it should not be a surprise that inheritance affects the testing of object-oriented systems. Through the use of inheritance, bugs can be propagated instantaneously from a superclass to all its direct and indirect subclasses. However, the tests that are applicable to a superclass are also applicable to all its subclasses. As usual, inheritance is a double-edged sword. Finally, even though we have stated this many times before, inheritance should support only a generalization and specialization type of semantics. Remember, when using inheritance, the principle of substitutability is critical (see Chapter 5). All these issues affect unit and integration testing.

Reuse On the surface, reuse should decrease the amount of testing required. However, each time a class is used in a different context, the class must be tested again. Therefore, any time a class library, framework, or component is used, unit testing and integration testing are important. In the case of a component, the unit to test is the component itself. Remember that a component has a well-defined API (application program interface) that hides the details of its implementation.

Object-Oriented Development Process and Products In virtually all textbooks, including this one, testing is covered near the end of system development. This seems to imply that testing is something that takes place only after the programming has ended. However, every product[13] that comes out of the object-oriented development process must be tested. For example, it is a lot easier to ensure that the requirements are captured and modeled correctly through testing the use cases, and it is a lot cheaper to catch this type of error back in analysis than it is in implementation. Obviously, this is also true for testing collaborations. By the time we have implemented a collaboration as a set of layers and partitions, we could have expended a great deal of time—and time is money—on implementing the wrong thing. So testing collaborations by role-playing the CRC cards in analysis actually saves the team lots of time and money.

Testing is something that must take place throughout system development, not simply at the end. However, the type of testing that can take place on nonexecutable representations, such as use cases and CRC cards, is different from those on code written in an object-oriented programming language. The primary approach to testing nonexecutable representations is some form of an inspection or walkthrough of the representation.[14] In the earlier chapters, we focused on verifying and validating the different analysis and design representations. We also made sure that the different representations were consistent and balanced. As such, we have dealt with testing the nonexecutable representations throughout the development process (see Chapters 4–11).

Test Planning

Testing starts with the development of a *test plan*, which defines a series of tests that will be conducted. One of the concerns that must be addressed through a comprehensive set of tests is to not limit the testing to the so-called *happy path* where testing only focusses on the *normal flow of events* of the use cases. Furthermore, the testing is limited to only ensuring that the code works when the tester provides the expected values. Not only should testing include the alternative paths through the use cases, but testing must also include all of the possible combinations of input data that could be in error. In other words, testing should include all of the *sad paths* through the use cases also. Because testing takes place throughout the development of an object-oriented system, a test plan should be developed at the very beginning of system development and continuously updated as the system evolves. For example, the representation of a class evolves from a simplistic CRC card to a set of classes that are implemented in a programming language. In Figure 12-3, we see a CRC card representation of an Order class that contains invariants. Each of these invariants must be tested and enforced for the Order class to be considered to be of sufficient quality. One simple invariant test would be to attempt to assign a value to the Cust ID attribute that was not associated with the Customer object that is contained in the Customer attribute. Another invariant test would be to try and assign more than one date to the Date attribute. Finally, a trickier invariant test would be to try to assign an integer value to the Shipping attribute. This one is more difficult because most programming languages allow an integer to be "cast" to a double. If the value contained in the Shipping attribute really is supposed to be a double, then casting the integer value to a double would be an error. These tests should be done using a walkthrough approach when the class is specified, as we did in Chapters 4–7. Furthermore, once the class has been fully

---

[13] For example, activity diagrams, use-case descriptions, use-case diagrams, CRC cards, class diagrams, object diagrams, sequence diagrams, behavioral state machines, package diagrams, contracts, method specifications, use scenarios, window navigation diagrams, storyboards, wireframe diagrams, real use cases, and source code.

[14] See Michael Fagan, "Design and Code Inspections to Reduce Errors in Program Development," *IBM Systems Journal* 15, no. 3 (1976); Daniel P. Freedman and Gerald M. Weinberg, *Handbook of Walkthrough, Inspections, and Technical Reviews: Evaluating Programs, Projects, and Products*, 3rd Ed. (New York: Dorset House Publishing, 1990). Also, Chapters 4–7 describe the walkthrough process in detail in relation to the verification and validation of the analysis models.

Front:

Class Name: Order	ID: 2	Type: Concrete, Domain
Description: An Individual who needs to receive or has received medical attention		**Associated Use Cases:** 3

Responsibilities	Collaborators
Calculate subtotal	
Calculate tax	
Calculate shipping	
Calculate total	

(a)

Back:

Attributes:

Order Number	(1..1)	(unsigned long)	
Date	(1..1)	(Date)	
Sub Total	(0..1)	(double)	{Sub Total = ProductOrder.sum(GetExtension())}
Tax	(0..1)	(double)	(Tax = State.GetTaxRate() * Sub Total)
Shipping	(0..1)	(double)	
Total	(0..1)	(double)	
Customer	(1..1)	(Customer)	
Cust ID	(1..1)	(unsigned long)	{Cust ID = Customer. GetCustID()}
State	(1..1)	(State)	
StateName	(1..1)	(String)	{State Name = State. GetState()}

Relationships:

Generalization (a-kind-of):

Aggregation (has-parts):

Other Associations: Customer {1..1} State {1..1} Product {1..*}

FIGURE 12-3
Order CRC Card (see
Figure 8-8)

(b)

implemented, a more rigorous approach is necessary. In fact, with agile and DevOps approaches, it is recommended that testing be fully automated.[15]

The test plan should address all products that are created during the development of the system. For example, tests should be created that can be used to test completeness of a CRC card. Each individual test has a specific objective and describes a set of very specific *test cases* to examine. In the case of invariant-based tests, a description of the invariant is given, and the original values of the attribute, the event that will cause the attribute value to change, the actual results observed, the expected results, and whether it passed or failed are shown. *Test specifications* are created for each type of constraint that must be met by the class.

Testing should not be limited to the functional requirements. Instead, testing must also consider all of the nonfunctional requirements. In this text, this includes operations testing, performance testing, security testing, and the testing of any and all cultural and political considerations. Given the incremental and iterative development nature of object-oriented systems development, the nonfunctional requirements should be verified and validated during the design and construction phases of the Unified Process. However, the nonfunctional requirements need to be thoroughly tested once they have been implemented during the construction and transition phases. Consequently, testing should be performed throughout the development process. Obviously, it is a lot easier to design tests when you are creating the different analysis and design representations than to wait and design them during the construction of the system. In fact, many of the agile approaches suggest creating the test either before or concurrently with the creation of the user stories that drive the creation of the system (see Chapter 3).

When testing an object-oriented system, given that the systems are built incrementally, being able to toggle on/off the different features that the system is supporting is useful. In this way, the testing can be somewhat localized and controlled. For example, for testing purposes, only certain user interface features could be toggled on. The other features could be toggled off by "graying" them out. Once the set of features have been tested, they can be toggled off and others toggled on. Obviously, this type of testing is not available until some code has been created. Also, in most cases, all classes that are supporting an application will not likely be finished at the same time. In those cases, depending on the language, toggles could be useful to test the parts of the system that has been implemented. With other languages, the programmer will have to write *stubs* for the unfinished classes to enable the completed classes around them to be tested. A stub is a placeholder for a class that usually displays a simple test message on the screen or returns some *hardcoded* value[16] when it is selected. For example, consider an application system that provides creating, changing, deleting, finding, and printing functions for some object such as CDs, patients, or employees. Depending on the final design, these different functions could end up in different objects on different layers. Therefore, to test the functionality associated with the classes on the problem-domain layer, a stub would be written for each of the classes on the other layers that interact with the problem-domain classes. These stubs would be the minimal interface necessary to be able to test the problem-domain classes. For example, they would have methods that could receive the messages being sent by the problem-domain layer objects and methods that could send messages to the problem-domain layer objects. Typically, the methods would display a message on the screen notifying

[15] Gene Kim, Jez Humble, Patrick Debois, and John Willis, *The DevOps Handbook: How to Create World-Class Agility, Reliability, & Security in Technology Organizations* (Portland, OR: IT Revolution Press, 2016); Steve Freeman and Nat Pryce, *Growing Object-Oriented Software, Guided By Tests* (Boston, MA: Pearson Education, 2010); Kent Beck, *Test-Driven Development by Example* (Boston, MA: Pearson Education, 2003).

[16] *Hardcoded* means written into the program. For example, suppose you were writing a unit to calculate the net present value of a loan. The stub might be written to always display (or return to the calling module) a value of 100 regardless of the input values.

the tester that the method was successfully reached (e.g., Delete item from Database method reached). In this way, the problem-domain classes could pass class testing before the classes on the other layers were completed.

In fact, testing could need to continue even after deployment. For example, Netflix uses a tool that they call *Chaos Monkey* that simulates major failures by constantly and randomly killing servers to ensure that their systems are fully recoverable.[17] Finally, realize that the results from testing could be the uncovering of additional functional and nonfunctional requirements. Again, given the nature of object-oriented systems development, this is somewhat expected.

Unit Tests

Unit tests focus on a single unit—the class. There are two approaches to unit testing: black-box testing and white-box testing (see Figure 12-4). *Black-box testing* is the most commonly used because each class represents an encapsulated object. Black-box testing is driven by the CRC cards, behavior state machines, and contracts associated with a class, not by the programmers' interpretation. In this case, the test plan is developed directly from the specification of the class: each item in the specification becomes a test, and several test cases are developed for it. *White-box testing* is based on the method specifications associated with each class. However, white-box testing has had limited impact in object-oriented development. This is due to the rather small size of the individual methods in a class. Most approaches to testing classes use black-box testing to ensure their correctness.

Class tests should be based on the invariants on the CRC cards, the behavioral state machines associated with each class, and the pre- and post-conditions contained on each method's contract. Assuming all the constraints have been captured on the CRC cards and contracts, individual test cases can be developed fairly easily. For example, suppose the CRC card for an order class gave an invariant that the order quantity must be between 10 and 100 cases. The tester would develop a series of test cases to ensure that the quantity is validated before the system accepts it. It is impossible to test every possible combination of input and situation; there are simply too many possible combinations. In this example, the test requires a minimum of three test cases: one with a valid value (e.g., 15), one with a low invalid value (e.g., 7), and one with a high invalid value (e.g., 110). Most tests would also include a test case with a nonnumeric value to ensure the data types were checked (e.g., ABCD). A really good test would include a test case with nonsensical but potentially valid data (e.g., 21.4).

Using a behavioral state machine is a useful way to identify tests for a class. Any class that has a behavioral state machine associated with it has a potentially complex life cycle. It is possible to create a series of tests to guarantee that each state can be reached. For example, Figure 12-5 portrays the behavioral state machine for the Order class just discussed. In this case, there are many transitions between the different states of an instance of the Order class. Tests should be created to guarantee that the only transitions allowed from an instance of the Order class are the ones specifically defined. In this case, it should be impossible for an Order object to go from the In process state to the Placed state without traversing the Ordered and Processing states via the Customer submits order, Order sent for credit authorization, and Authorization = Approved transitions. This state-based testing can be done throughout the development of the class via walkthroughs and role-playing early in the evolution of the class and more rigorous testing once it has been implemented in a programming language.

Tests also can be developed for each contract associated with the class. In the case of a contract, a set of tests for each pre- and post-condition is required. For example, the contract

[17] Gene Kim, Jez Humble, Patrick Debois, and John Willis, *The DevOps Handbook: How to Create World-Class Agility, Reliability, & Security in Technology Organizations* (Portland, OR: IT Revolution Press, 2016).

Stage	Type of Tests	Test Plan Source	When to Use	Notes
Unit Testing	**Black-Box Testing** Treats program as "black-box"	CRC Cards Class Diagrams Contracts	For normal unit testing	• Tester focuses on whether the class meets the requirements stated in the specifications.
	White-Box Testing Looks inside the program to test its major elements.	Method Specifications	When complexity is high	• By looking inside the unit to review the code itself the tester may discover errors or assumptions not immediately obvious to someone treating the class as a black box.
Integration Testing	**User Interface Testing** The tester tests each interface function.	Interface Design	For normal integration testing	• Testing is done by moving through each and every menu item in the interface either in a top-down or bottom-up manner.
	Use Case Testing The tester tests each use case.	Use Cases	When the user interface is important	• Testing is done by moving through each use case to ensure they work correctly • Usually combined with user interface testing because it does not test all interfaces.
	Interaction Testing Tests each process in a step-by-step fashion.	Class Diagrams Sequence Diagrams	When the system performs data processing	• The entire system begins as a set of stubs. Each class is added in turn and the results of the class compared to the correct result from the test data; when a class passes, the next class is added and the test re-run. This is done for each package. Once each package has passed all tests, then the process repeats integrating the packages.
	System Interface Testing Tests the exchange of with other systems	Use Case Diagram	When the system exchanges data	• Because data transfers between systems are often automated and not monitored directly by the users it is critical to design tests to ensure they are being done correctly.
System Testing	**Requirements Testing** Tests to whether original business requirements are met.	System Design, Unit Tests, and Integration Tests	For normal system testing	• Ensures that changes made as a result of integration testing did not create new errors. • Testers often pretend to be uninformed users and perform improper actions to ensure the system is immune to invalid actions (e.g., adding blank records).
	Usability Testing Tests how convenient the system is to use	Interface Design and Use Cases	When user interface is important	• Often done by analyst with experience in how users think and in good interface design. • Sometimes uses formal usability testing procedures discussed in Chapter 10.
	Security Testing Tests disaster recovery & unauthorized access	Infrastructure Design	When the system is important	• Security testing is a complex task, usually done by an infrastructure analyst assigned to the project. • In extreme cases, a professional firm may be hired
	Performance Testing Examines the ability to perform under high loads	System Proposal	When the system is important	• High volumes of transactions are generated and given to the system • Often done by using special purpose testing software
	Documentation Testing Tests the accuracy of the documentation	Help System, Procedures, Tutorials	For normal system testing	• Analysts spot check or check every item on every page in all documentation to ensure the documentation items and examples work properly.
Acceptance Testing	**Alpha Testing** Conducted by users to ensure they accept the system.	System Tests	For normal acceptance testing	• Often repeats previous tests but are conducted by users themselves to ensure they accept the system
	Beta Testing Uses real data, not test data	No plan	When the system is important	• Users closely monitor system for errors or useful improvements

FIGURE 12-4 Types of Tests

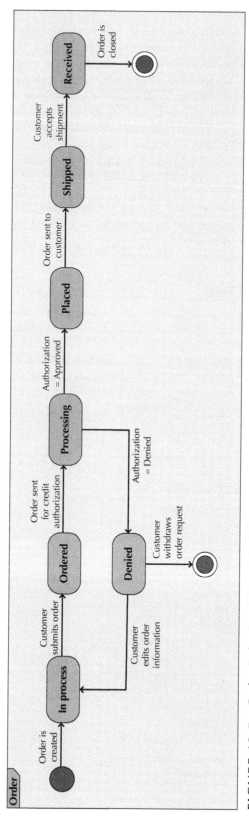

FIGURE 12-5 Order Behavioral State Machine (see Figure 6-22)

of the addOrder method of the Customer class shown in Figure 12-6 has both a pre- and post-condition that essentially requires the new order to have not existed with the instance of the Customer class before the method executes, and that the new order is associated with the Customer object after the method executes. Tests must be created to enforce these constraints. If the class is a subclass of another class, then all the tests associated with the superclass must be executed again. The interactions among the constraints, invariants, and the pre- and post-conditions in the subclass and the superclass(es) must be also addressed.

Finally, owing to good object-oriented design, to fully test a class, special testing methods might have to be added to the class being tested. For example, how can invariants be tested? The only way to really test them is to have methods that are visible to the outside of the class that can be used to manipulate the values of the class's attributes. However, adding these types of methods to a class does two things. First, they add to the testing requirements because they themselves have to be tested. Second, if they are not removed from the deployed version of the system, the system will be less efficient, and the advantage of information hiding effectively is lost. As is readily apparent, testing classes is complex. Therefore, great care must be taken when designing tests for classes.

Integration Tests

Integration tests assess whether a set of classes that must work together do so without error. They ensure that the interfaces and linkages between different parts of the system work properly. At this point, the classes have passed their individual unit tests, so the focus now is on the flow of control among the classes and on the data exchanged among them. Integration testing follows the same general procedures as unit testing: The tester develops a test plan that has a series of tests, which, in turn, have a test. Integration testing is often done by a set of programmers and/or systems analysts.

Method Name: addOrder	**Class Name:** Customer	**ID:** 36
Clients (Consumers):		
Associated Use Cases: addCustomerOrder		

Description of Responsibilities:
  Implement the necessary behavior to add a new order to an existing customer keeping
  the orders in sorted order by the order's order number.		

Arguments Received: anOrder:Order		
Type of Value Returned: void		
Pre-Conditions: not Orders.includes(anOrder)		
Post-Conditions: Orders = Orders@pre.including(anOrder)		

FIGURE 12-6
addOrder Contract (see
Figure 8-14)

From an object-oriented systems perspective, integration testing can be difficult. A single class can be in many different aggregations, because of the way objects can be combined to form new objects, class libraries, frameworks, components, and packages. Where is the best place to start the integration? Typically, the answer is to begin with the set of classes, a collaboration, that are used to support the highest-priority use case (see Chapter 4). Also, dynamic binding makes it crucial to design the integration tests carefully to ensure that the combinations of methods are tested.

There are four approaches to integration testing: *user interface testing,*[18] *use-case testing, interaction testing,* and *system interface testing* (see Figure 12-4). Most projects use all four approaches. However, like unit testing, integration testing must be carefully planned. In the case of use-case testing, only the aspects of the class and class invariants related to the specific use case are included in these use-case context-dependent class tests. In fact, typically use-case testing is performed one scenario at a time. In many ways, use-case testing can be viewed as a more rigorous role-playing exercise (see Chapter 5). Like unit testing, integration testing should be performed throughout the evolution of the system. In the early stages of the system's development, you should be working with the CRC cards and role-playing them. Later on, you will have the contracts and method specifications completed. Gradually, you will have implemented the problem domain classes, the user interface classes, and the data management layer classes in a programming language. As in unit testing, each time a new representation (diagram, text, program) is created, a new integration test needs to be performed. Therefore, as the system evolves to more completely support the use case, we can more rigorously test whether the use case is fully supported or not.

One of the major problems with integration testing and object-oriented systems is the difficulty caused by the interaction of inheritance and dynamic binding. This specific problem has become known as the *yo-yo problem*. The yo-yo problem occurs when the analyst or designer must bounce up and down through the inheritance graph to understand the control flow through the methods being executed. In most cases, this is caused by a rather deep inheritance graph; that is, the subclass has many superclasses above it in the inheritance graph. The yo-yo problem becomes even more of a nightmare in testing object-oriented systems when inheritance conflicts exist and when multiple inheritance is used (see Chapter 8). About the only realistic approach to testing through the yo-yo problem is through an interactive debugger that is typically part of a systems development environment, such as Eclipse, Netbeans, or Visual Studio.

System Tests

To ensure that all classes work together without error, systems analysts usually conduct the system tests. System testing is similar to integration testing but is much broader in scope. Whereas integration testing focuses on whether the classes work together without error, *system tests* examine how well the system meets both the functional and nonfunctional requirements, e.g., usability, documentation, performance, and security (see Figure 12-4).

The purpose of functional *requirements testing* is to ensure that the functional requirements uncovered are indeed met. Like integration testing, this is primarily driven by the system's use cases and their scenarios. However, in many cases, integration testing requires modifications to the system. So, the focus of requirements testing is to ensure that the modifications made did not cause additional errors.

Usability testing is essentially a combination of the user interface and use-case testing that takes place during integration testing. Where user interface and use-case testing focused on

---

[18] We describe some of the different types of user interface testing in Chapter 10.

whether the user interface works and whether the use case was supported, respectively, usability testing focuses on how *well* the user interface supports the use cases. That is, how efficient and effective the user interface is. In many cases, this could include formal usability testing (see Chapter 10).

Given that documentation is basically a system in itself, documentation testing should involve both unit and integration testing. In this case, the unit is a documentation entry, and the user interface is either the paper or help screen. From an integration testing perspective, the focus is on whether the documentation works or not. And, like system testing of the software, the focus of system testing of the documentation is how *well* the documentation works. The reason that documentation is not typically tested in parallel with the system, i.e., when the classes, use cases, and user interface are tested, is to minimize the amount of documentation testing required. Even though the documentation should be developed in parallel with the software, until the software is tested, it is unclear exactly what to test in the documentation. As the software "passes" its tests, the documentation that goes along with the software can then be finalized and tested.

Performance testing focuses on trying to break the system with regard to the amount of work the system can handle. These types of tests typically fall into two categories: stress tests and volume tests. The purpose of *stress tests*, also known as *load tests*, is to ensure that the system can handle a certain number of simultaneous requests. For example, if the system is supposed to be able to handle 10,000 simultaneous requests, a stress test would attempt to push the system into handling more than that. If the performance of the test is insufficient, various software and database optimizations (see Chapters 8 and 9) can be investigated. In other cases, additional hardware could be required. The purpose of *volume tests* is to push the implementation so that it may break when there is a large amount of data required to answer a user request. Again, if it is discovered that the system fails this type of test, then database and software optimizations and additional hardware could be required. For example, sometimes it is more efficient to create a set of temporary tables by "selecting" the data from the actual tables before "joining" the tables together. By performing the "selects" first, the "join" works on less data. In this case, it could both speed up and lessen the amount of temporary storage required to handle the request. In other cases, denormalization of the data and storing the data at multiple locations could be called for. You typically do not want the user to make a request for a report and have to wait "too long" for the report to be processed. In some cases, giving up some functionality to improve performance can be crucial to the success of the system. So, the results of performance testing can make or break a system.

Obviously, in today's networked world, security testing is crucial. *Security testing* involves three primary areas: authentication, authorization, and virus control. *Authentication testing* deals with ensuring that the logged in user is who he or she claims to be. Typically, this has been addressed with user IDs and passwords and through the use of encryption techniques (see Chapter 11). Today, in addition to these approaches, various biometric identifiers have been used, e.g., retinal scans and fingerprints. *Authorization testing* deals with ensuring that the logged in user actually has the authority to use the system(s) being accessed. Authorization has been controlled through the use of roles, access control lists, and capability lists. Security *roles* are the same as actor roles in a use-case model. Depending on the role being played by a user, different capabilities are made available to the user in the form of a *capability list*. However, in this case, a role can be specified down to the individual user level and not be limited to a group of users. Also, an *access control list* can be associated with each use case and with each class. In this case, an access control list specifies which roles have access to the resource (use case or class). Given that many system break-ins are a function of viruses, *virus controls* also need to be enforced. Anytime a file is received or sent by a user, the files should be scanned for potential viruses. This includes e-mail attachments, Web downloads, and the insertion of flash drives on desktop computers as well on all forms of "client" machines that can be attached to the system. Obviously, security requirements will impact the performance of the system. Therefore, trade-offs between these two sets of requirements may be necessary.

Acceptance Tests

Acceptance testing is done primarily by the users with support from the project team. The goal is to confirm that the system is complete, meets the business needs that prompted the system to be developed, and is acceptable to the users. Acceptance testing is done in two stages: *alpha testing*, in which users test the system using made-up data, and *beta testing*, in which users begin to use the system with real data but are carefully monitored for errors (see Figure 12-4).

Testing and Security Considerations[19]

There are many different types of security threats with which testing can help address. The first way to address security threats is to incorporate security concerns throughout the development process. This begins with identifying the different types of threats that could occur as early as possible with the development of the system. Once the different types of potential threats have been identified, then the appropriate approaches to security can be designed for both the IT artifacts created during the development process, e.g., CRC cards, and the most effective way to incorporate the security requirements into the actual system can be developed. As described in Chapter 11, there are different ways in which to address the security requirements. For example, there are different approaches to implement access controls. Depending on the approach chosen, different types of testing is appropriate. Next, we extend our coverage of security testing to include the unit and integration levels.

Typical unit testing attempts to uncover missing requirements. However, when unit testing the security requirements, we want to ensure that only authorized users will be able to execute the different methods of each class. As described in Chapter 11, this could be implemented as a set of pre-conditions that would be part of the method specification and implementation. Moreover, when considering the data management layer, we could implement access controls directly in the DBMS. We also could decide to encrypt all data stored in the DBMS. However, depending on the volume of data and the different types of access to the data that needed to be supported, this level of detailed security requirements implementation could be prohibitive in terms of the processing power required.

With integration testing, testers should be sure to incorporate both authorization and access control types of tests when testing the user interface and use cases. The basis of these tests should come from the use case descriptions, contracts, and method specifications. In addition to the typical input validations that must be performed, tests that can detect code insertions should also be performed. This simply implies that a more detailed set of user interface tests that guarantees that only valid data be allowed to pass from the user interface to the system. Furthermore, if encryption is to be used on the data captured by the user interface, appropriate tests must be performed to make sure that it works as expected. In many ways, this takes us back to the unit testing level. However, instead of testing classes, the unit is the individual field.

---

[19] For more information, see William Stallings, *Effective Cybersecurity: A Guide to Using Best Practices and Standards* (Upper Saddle River, NJ: Pearson Education, 2019); O. Sami Saydjari, *Engineering Trustworthy Systems: Get Cybersecurity Design Right the First Time* (New York, NY: McGraw-Hill, 2018); Len Bass, Ingo Weber, and Liming Zhu, *DevOps: A Software Architect's Perspective* (Upper Saddle River, NJ: Pearson Education, 2015); Gene Kim, Jez Humble, Patrick Debois, and John Willis, *The DevOps Handbook: How to Create World-Class Agility, Reliability, & Security in Technology Organizations* (Portland, OR: IT Revolution Press, 2016).

> ## APPLYING THE CONCEPTS AT PATTERSON SUPERSTORE
>
> While many of the activities, including testing and documentation, were done throughout the development process, the construction phase for phase one of the Integrated Health Clinic Delivery System was a busy time for the team who conducted integration, system, and acceptance testing for the system. In addition, they finalized user and system documentation of the system.
>
> You can find the rest of the case at www.wiley.com/go/dennis/systemanalysis6e/casestudy.

CHAPTER REVIEW

After reading and studying this chapter, you should be able to:

- ☐ Describe the basic issues related to managing programmers.
- ☐ Describe cultural issues as they are related to intellectual property.
- ☐ Describe how Hall's and Hofstede's cultural dimensions can affect systems development.
- ☐ Describe the different types of documentation associated with an information system.
- ☐ Describe how to develop the documentation of an information system.
- ☐ Describe how object-orientation effects software testing.
- ☐ Describe and discuss unit testing.
- ☐ Describe and discuss integration testing.
- ☐ Describe and discuss system testing.
- ☐ Describe and discuss acceptance testing.

KEY TERMS

Acceptance test
Access control list
Alpha test
Authentication testing
Authorization testing
Beta test
Black-box testing
Capability list
Change control
Chaos Monkey
Collectivism
Construction
Context
Documentation navigation control

Documentation topic
Femininity
Happy path
Hardcoded
Individualism
Integration test
Interaction testing
Load test
Long-term orientation
Masculinity
Monochronic time
Normal flow of events
Polychronic time
Power distance
Procedures manual

Program log
Reference document
Requirements testing
Role
Sad path
Security testing
Short-term orientation
Speed of messages
Stress test
Stub
System documentation
System interface testing
System test
Test case
Test plan

Test specification
Time
Time-boxing
Traceability
Tutorial
Uncertainty avoidance
Unit test
Usability testing
Use-case testing
User documentation
User interface testing
virus controls
Volume test
White-box testing
Yo-yo problem

QUESTIONS

1. Why is testing important?
2. How can different national or organizational cultures affect the management of an information systems development project?
3. What is the primary role of systems analysts during the programming stage?
4. In *The Mythical Man-Month*, Frederick Brooks argues that adding more programmers to a late project makes it later. Why?
5. When offshoring development, how could differences in Hall's context dimension of culture affect the contribution of a team member to the successful development of an information system? What about Hall's time or speed of messages dimensions?
6. What are Hofstede's five dimensions of cultural differences? How could differences in them influence the effectiveness of an information systems development team?
7. What are the common language or languages used today in information systems development?
8. Compare and contrast user documentation and system documentation.
9. Why is online documentation becoming more important?
10. What are the primary disadvantages of online documentation?
11. Compare and contrast reference documents, procedures manuals, and tutorials.
12. What are five types of documentation navigation controls?
13. What are the commonly used sources of documentation topics? Which is the most important? Why?
14. What are the commonly used sources of documentation navigation controls? Which is the most important? Why?
15. What is the purpose of testing?
16. Describe how object orientation affects testing.
17. Compare and contrast the terms test, test plan, and test case.
18. What is a stub and why is it used in testing?
19. What is the primary goal of unit testing?
20. How are the test cases developed for unit tests?
21. Compare and contrast black-box testing and white-box testing.
22. What are the different types of class tests?
23. What is the primary goal of integration testing?
24. How are the test cases developed for integration tests?
25. Describe the yo-yo problem. Why does it make integration testing difficult?
26. What is the primary goal of system testing?
27. How are the test cases developed for system tests?
28. What is the primary goal of acceptance testing?
29. How are the test cases developed for acceptance tests?
30. Compare and contrast alpha testing and beta testing.

EXERCISES

A. Different views of plagiarism and collaborative learning were described as examples of differences among different cultures today. Using the Web, identify other differences that could affect the success of an information systems development team.

B. Besides Hall and Hofstede, both David Victor and Fons Trompenaars have identified a set of cultural dimensions that could be useful in information systems development. Using the Web, identify their dimensions.

C. If the registration system at your university does not have a good online help system, develop one for one screen of the user interface.

D. Examine and prepare a report on the online help system for the calculator program in Windows (or a similar one on the Mac or Unix). (You will probably be surprised at the amount of help for such a simple program.)

E. Compare and contrast the online help at two different websites that enable you to perform some function (e.g., make travel reservations, order books).

F. Create an invariant test specification for the class you chose for the A Real Estate Inc. problem in exercise A in Chapter 8.

G. Create a use-case test plan, including the specific class plans and invariant tests, for a use case from the A Real Estate Inc. exercises in the previous chapters.

H. Create an invariant test specification for the class you chose for the A Video Store problem in exercise B in Chapter 8.

I. Create a use-case test plan, including the specific class plans and invariant tests, for a use case from the A Video Store exercises in the previous chapters.

J. Create an invariant test specification for the class you chose for the gym problem in exercise C in Chapter 8.

K. Create a use-case test plan, including the specific class plans and invariant tests for a use case from the gym membership exercises in previous chapters.

L. Create an invariant test specification for the class you chose for Picnics R Us in exercise D in Chapter 8.

M. Create a use-case test plan, including the specific class plans and invariant tests, for a use case from the Picnics R Us exercises in the previous chapters.

N. Create an invariant test specification for the class you chose for the Of-the-Month Club (OTMC) in exercise E in Chapter 8.

O. Create a use-case test plan, including the specific class plans and invariant tests, for a use case from the Of-the-Month Club (OTMC) exercises in the previous chapters.

MINICASES

1. Pete is a project manager on a new systems development project. This project is Pete's first experience as a project manager, and he has led his team successfully to the programming phase of the project. The project has not always gone smoothly, and Pete has made a few mistakes, but he is generally pleased with the progress of his team and the quality of the system being developed. Now that programming has begun, Pete has been hoping for a little break in the hectic pace of his workday.

Prior to beginning programming, Pete recognized that the time estimates made earlier in the project were too optimistic. However, he was firmly committed to meeting the project deadline because of his desire for his first project as project manager to be a success. In anticipation of this time pressure problem, Pete arranged with the Human Resources department to bring in two new college graduates and two college interns to beef up the programming staff. Pete would have liked to find some staff with more experience, but the budget was too tight, and he was committed to keeping the project budget under control.

Pete made his programming assignments, and work on the programs began about two weeks ago. Now, Pete has started to hear some rumbles from the programming team leaders that might signal trouble. It seems that the programmers have reported several instances where they wrote programs, only to be unable to find them when they went to test them. Also,

several programmers have opened programs that they had written, only to find that someone had changed portions of their programs without their knowledge.

a. Is the programming phase of a project a time for the project manager to relax? Why or why not?

b. What problems can you identify in this situation?

c. What advice do you have for the project manager? How likely does it seem that Pete will achieve his desired goals of being on time and within budget if nothing is done?

2. The systems analysts are developing the test plan for the user interface for the Holiday Travel Vehicles system. As the salespeople are entering a sales invoice into the system, they will be able to enter an option code into a text box or to select an option code from a drop-down list. A combo box was used to implement this, because it was felt that the salespeople would quickly become familiar with the most common option codes and would prefer entering them directly to speed up the entry process.

It is now time to develop the test for validating the option code field during data entry. If the customer did not request any dealer-installed options for the vehicle, the salesperson should enter "none"; the field should not be blank. The valid option codes are four-character alphabetic codes and should be matched against a list of valid codes.

Prepare a test plan for the test of the option code field during data entry.

CHAPTER 13

INSTALLATION AND OPERATIONS

This chapter examines the activities needed to install an information system and successfully convert an organization to using it. It also discusses post-implementation activities, such as system support, system maintenance, and project assessment. Installing the system and making it available for use from a technical perspective are relatively straightforward. However, the training and organizational issues surrounding the installation are more complex and challenging because they focus on people, not on computers.

OBJECTIVES

- Be familiar with the system installation process.
- Understand different types of conversion strategies and when to use them.
- Understand several techniques for managing change.
- Be familiar with post-installation processes.

INTRODUCTION

"It must be remembered that there is nothing more difficult to plan, more doubtful of success, nor more dangerous to manage than the creation of a new system. For the initiator has the animosity of all who would profit by the preservation of the old institution and merely lukewarm defenders in those who would gain by the new."

—Niccolò Machiavelli, *The Prince*, 1513

Although written almost 500 years ago, Machiavelli's comments are still true today. Managing the change to a new system—whether it is computerized or not—is one of the most difficult tasks in any organization. Because of the challenges involved, most organizations begin developing their conversion and change management plans while the programmers are still developing the software. Leaving conversion and change management planning to the last minute is a recipe for failure.

In many ways, using a computer system or set of work processes is much like driving on a dirt road. Over time, with repeated use, the road begins to develop ruts in the most commonly used parts of the road. Although these ruts show where to drive, they make change difficult. As people use a computer system or set of work processes, those systems or work processes begin to become habits or norms; people learn them and become comfortable with them. These systems or work processes then begin to limit people's activities and make it difficult for them to change because they begin to see their jobs in terms of these processes rather than of the final business goal of serving customers.

One of the earliest models for managing organizational change was developed by Kurt Lewin.[1] Lewin argued that change is a three-step process: unfreeze, move, and refreeze (Figure 13-1). First, the project team must *unfreeze* the existing habits and norms (the as-is system) so that change is possible. Most of system development to this point has laid the groundwork for unfreezing. Users are aware of the new system being developed, some have participated in an analysis of the current system (and so are aware of its problems), and some have helped design the new system (and so have some sense of the potential benefits of the new system). These activities have helped to unfreeze the current habits and norms.

The second step is to help the organization move to the new system via a *migration plan*. The migration plan has two major elements. One is technical, which includes how the new system will be installed and how data in the as-is system will be moved into the to-be system; this is discussed in the conversion section of this chapter. The second component is organizational, which includes helping users understand the change and motivating them to adopt it; this is discussed in the change management section of this chapter.

The third step is to *refreeze* the new system as the habitual way of performing the work processes—ensuring that the new system successfully becomes the standard way of performing the business function it supports. This refreezing process is a key goal of the *post-implementation* activities discussed in the final section of this chapter. By providing ongoing support for the new system and immediately beginning to identify improvements for the next version of the system, the organization helps solidify the new system as the new habitual way of doing business. Post-implementation activities include system support, which means providing help desk and telephone support for users with problems; system maintenance, which means fixing bugs and improving the system after it has been installed; and project assessment, evaluating the project to identify what went well and what could be improved for the next system development project.

Change management is the most challenging of the three components because it focuses on people, not technology, and because it is the one aspect of the project that is the least controllable by the project team. Change management means winning the hearts and minds of potential users and convincing them that the new system actually provides value.

Maintenance is the most costly aspect of the installation process, because the cost of maintaining systems usually greatly exceeds the initial development costs. It is not unusual for organizations to spend 60 to 80 percent of their total IS development budget on

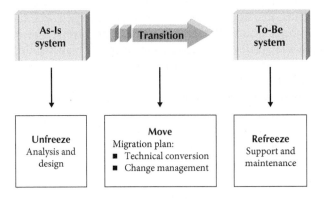

FIGURE 13-1
Implementing
Change

[1] Kurt Lewin, "Frontiers in Group Dynamics," *Human Relations* 1, no. 5 (1947): 5–41; Kurt Lewin, "Group Decision and Social Change," in E. E. Maccoby, T. M. Newcomb, and E. L. Hartley (Eds), *Readings in Social Psychology* (New York: Holt, Rinehart, and Winston, 1958), pp. 197–211.

maintenance. Although this might sound surprising initially, think about the software you use. How many software packages do you use that are the very first version? Most commercial software packages become truly useful and enter widespread use only in their second or third version. Maintenance and continual improvement of software is ongoing, whether it is a commercially available package or software developed in-house. Would you buy software if you knew that no new versions were going to be produced? Of course, commercial software is somewhat different from custom in-house software used by only one company, but the fundamental issues remain.

Project assessment is probably the least commonly performed part of system development but is perhaps the one that has the most long-term value to the IS department. Project assessment enables project team members to step back and consider what they did right and what they could have done better. It is an important component in the individual growth and development of each member of the team, because it encourages team members to learn from their successes and failures. It also enables new ideas or new approaches to system development to be recognized, examined, and shared with other project teams to improve their performance.

CULTURAL ISSUES AND INFORMATION TECHNOLOGY ADOPTION[2]

Cultural issues are one of the things that are typically identified as at least partially to blame when there is a failure in an organization. Cultural issues have been studied at both organizational and national levels. In previous chapters, we discussed the effect that cultural issues can have on designing the human–computer interaction and physical architecture layers (see Chapters 10 and 11) and the management of programmers (Chapter 12). The cultural dimensions identified by Hall and Hofstede included speed of messages, context, time, power distance, uncertainty avoidance, individualism versus collectivism, masculinity versus femininity, and long- versus short-term orientation.[3] In this chapter, we describe how these dimensions can affect the successful deployment of an information system that supports a global information supply chain.

Hall's first dimension, *speed of messages*, has implications for the development of documentation (see Chapter 12) and training approaches (see later in this chapter). In a culture that values "deep" content, so that members of the culture can take their time to thoroughly understand the new system, simply providing an online help system is not going to be sufficient to ensure the successful adoption of the new information system. However, in a culture that prefers "fast" messages, an online help system could be sufficient.

Hall's second dimension, *context*, also affects the adoption and deployment of a new system. In high-context cultures, it is expected that the new information system will be placed into the entire context of the enterprise-wide system. Members of this type of society expect to be able to understand exactly where the system fits into the firm's overall picture. Again, like the speed of messages dimension, this affects the training approach used and the documentation developed.

---

[2] A good summary of cultural issues and information systems is Dorothy E. Leidner and Timothy Kayworth, "A Review of Culture in Information Systems Research: Toward a Theory of Information Technology Culture Conflict," *MIS Quarterly* 30, no. 2 (2006): 357–399.

[3] See Geert Hofstede, *Culture's Consequences: Comparing Values, Behaviors, Institutions and Organizations across Nations*, 2nd Ed. (Thousand Oaks, CA: Sage, 2001); Geert Hofstede, Gert Jan Hofstede, and Michael Minkov, *Cultures and Organizations: Software of the Mind*, 3rd Ed. (New York: McGraw-Hill, 2010); and Edward T. Hall, *Beyond Culture* (New York: Anchor Books, 1981).

Hall's third dimension, *time*, can also effect the adoption and deployment of a new system. In a *polychronic time* culture, the training could need to be spread out over a longer period of time, when compared to a *monochronic* time culture. In a monochromic time culture, interruptions would be considered rude. Consequently, training could be accomplished in a small set of intense sessions. However, with a polychronic time culture, because interruptions may occur frequently, maximum flexibility in setting up the training sessions may be necessary.

Hofstede's first dimension, *power distance*, addresses how power issues are dealt with in the culture. For example, if a superior in an organization has an incorrect belief about an important issue, can a subordinate point out this error? In some cultures, the answer is a resounding no. Consequently, this dimension could have major ramifications for the successful deployment of an information system. For example, in a culture with a high power distance, the deployment of a new information system is dependent on the impression of the most important stakeholder (see Chapter 2). Therefore, much care must be taken to ensure that this stakeholder is pleased with the system. Otherwise, it might never be used.

Hofstede's second dimension, *uncertainty avoidance*, is based on the degree to which the culture depends on rules for direction, how well individuals in the culture handle stress, and the importance of employment stability. For example, in a high-uncertainty-avoidance culture, the use of detailed procedures manuals (see Chapter 12) and good training (see later in this chapter) can reduce the uncertainty in adopting the new system.

Hofstede's third dimension, *individualism* versus *collectivism*, is based on the level of emphasis the culture places on the individual or the collective. The relationship between the individual and the group is important for the success of an information system. Depending on the culture's orientation, the success of an information system being transitioned into production can depend on whether the focus of the information system will benefit the individual or the group.

Hofstede's fourth dimension, *masculinity* versus *femininity*, addresses how well masculine and feminine characteristics are valued by the culture. Some of the differences that could affect the adoption of an information system include employee motivational issues. In a masculine culture, motivation would be based on advancement, earnings, and training, whereas in a feminine culture, motivations would include friendly atmosphere, physical conditions, and cooperation. Depending on how the culture views this dimension, different motivations might need to be used to increase the likelihood of the information system being successfully deployed.

The fifth dimension, *long-* versus *short-term orientation*, deals with how the culture views the past and the future. In East Asia, long-term thinking is highly respected, whereas in North America and Europe, short-term profits and the current stock price seem to be the only things that matter. Based on this dimension, all the political concerns raised previously in this text become very important. For example, if the local culture views success only in a short-term manner, then any new information system that is deployed to support one department of an organization may give that department a competitive advantage over other departments in the short run. If only short-run measures are used to judge the success of a department, then it would be in the interest of the other departments to fight the successful deployment of the information system. However, if a longer-run perspective is the norm, then the other departments could be convinced to support the new information system because they could have new supportive information systems in the future.

Obviously, when reviewing these dimensions, we can see they interact with each other. The most important thing to remember from an IT perspective is that we must be careful not to view the local user community through our eyes; in a global economy, we must take into consideration the local cultural concerns for the information system to be deployed in a successful manner.

CONVERSION[4]

Conversion is the technical process by which a new system replaces an old system. The processes described here are related to the Deployment and Configuration and Change Management workflows of the Unified Process. Conversion moves the users from using the as-is business processes and computer programs to the to-be business processes and programs. The migration plan specifies what activities will be performed when and by whom and includes both technical aspects (such as installing hardware and software and converting data from the as-is system to the to-be system) and organizational aspects (such as training and motivating the users to embrace the new system). Conversion refers to the technical aspects of the migration plan.

There are three major steps to the conversion plan before commencement of operations: Install hardware, install software, and convert data (Figure 13-2). Although it may be possible to do some of these steps in parallel, usually they must be done sequentially at any one location.

The first step in the conversion plan is to buy and install any needed hardware. In many cases, no new hardware is needed, but sometimes the project requires new hardware such as servers, client computers, printers, and networking equipment. It is critical to work closely with vendors who are supplying needed hardware and software to ensure that the deliveries are coordinated with the conversion schedule so that the equipment is available when it is needed. Nothing can stop a conversion plan in its tracks as easily as the failure of a vendor to deliver needed equipment.

Once the hardware is installed, tested, and certified as being operational, the second step is to install the software. This includes the to-be system under development and, sometimes, additional software that must be installed to make the system operational. At this point, the system is usually tested again to ensure that it operates as planned.

The third step is to convert the data from the as-is system to the to-be system. Data conversion is usually the most technically complicated step in the migration plan. Often, separate programs must be written to convert the data from the as-is system to the new formats required in the to-be system and store it in the to-be system files and databases. This process is often complicated by the fact that the files and databases in the to-be system do not exactly match the files and databases in the as-is system (e.g., the to-be system may use several tables in a database to store customer data that were contained in one file in the as-is system). Formal test plans are always required for data conversion efforts (see Chapter 12).

FIGURE 13-2
Elements of a
Migration Plan

---

[4] The material in this section is related to the Enhanced Unified Process's Transition phase and the Deployment workflow (see Figure 1-18).

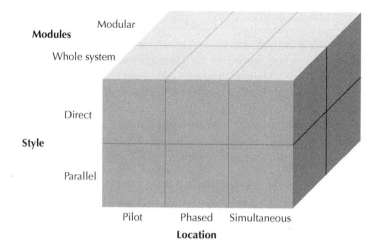

FIGURE 13-3
Conversion
Strategies

Conversion can be thought of along three dimensions: the style in which the conversion is done (*conversion style*), what location or work groups are converted at what time (*conversion location*), and what modules of the system are converted at what time (*conversion modules*). Figure 13-3 shows the potential relationships among these three dimensions.

Conversion Style

The conversion style is the way users are switched between the old and new systems. There are two fundamentally different approaches to the style of conversion: direct conversion and parallel conversion.

Direct Conversion With *direct conversion* (sometimes called cold turkey, big bang, or abrupt cutover), the new system instantly replaces the old system. The new system is turned on, and the old system is immediately turned off. This is the approach that we are likely to use when we upgrade commercial software (e.g., Microsoft Word) from one version to another; we simply begin using the new version and stop using the old version.

Direct conversion is the simplest and most straightforward. However, it is the most risky because any problems with the new system that have escaped detection during testing can seriously disrupt the organization.

Parallel Conversion With *parallel conversion*, the new system is operated side by side with the old system; both systems are used simultaneously. For example, if a new accounting system is installed, the organization enters data into both the old system and the new system and then carefully compares the output from both systems to ensure that the new system is performing correctly. After some time period (often one to two months) of parallel operation and intense comparison between the two systems, the old system is turned off and the organization continues using the new system.

This approach is more likely to catch any major bugs in the new system and prevent the organization from suffering major problems. If problems are discovered in the new system, the system is simply turned off and fixed and then the conversion process starts again. The problem with this approach is the added expense of operating two systems that perform the same function.

Conversion Location

Conversion location refers to the parts of the organization that are converted when the conversion occurs. Often, parts of the organization are physically located in different offices (e.g., Toronto, Atlanta, Los Angeles). In other cases, location refers to different organizational units located in different parts of the same office complex (e.g., order entry, shipping, purchasing). There are at least three fundamentally different approaches to selecting the way different organizational locations are converted: pilot conversion, phased conversion, and simultaneous conversion.

Pilot Conversion With a *pilot conversion*, one or more locations or units or work groups within a location are selected to be converted first as part of a pilot test. The locations participating in the pilot test are converted (using either direct or parallel conversion). If the system passes the pilot test, then the system is installed at the remaining locations (again using either direct or parallel conversion).

Pilot conversion has the advantage of providing an additional level of testing before the system is widely deployed throughout the organization, so that any problems with the system affect only the pilot locations. However, this type of conversion obviously requires more time before the system is installed at all organizational locations. Also, it means that different organizational units are using different versions of the system and business processes, which can make it difficult for them to exchange data.

Phased Conversion With *phased conversion*, the system is installed sequentially at different locations. A first set of locations is converted, then a second set, then a third set, and so on, until all locations are converted. Sometimes there is a deliberate delay between the different sets (at least between the first and the second), so that any problems with the system are detected before too much of the organization is affected. In other cases, the sets are converted back to back so that as soon as those converting one location have finished, the project team moves to the next and continues the conversion.

Phased conversion has the same advantages and disadvantages of pilot conversion. In addition, it means that fewer people are required to perform the actual conversion (and any associated user training) than if all locations were converted at once.

Simultaneous Conversion *Simultaneous conversion*, as the name suggests, means that all locations are converted at the same time. The new system is installed and made ready at all locations; at a preset time, all users begin using the new system. Simultaneous conversion is often used with direct conversion, but it can also be used with parallel conversion.

Simultaneous conversion eliminates problems with having different organizational units using different systems and processes. However, it also means that the organization must have sufficient staff to perform the conversion and train the users at all locations simultaneously.

Conversion Modules

Although it is natural to assume that systems are usually installed in their entirety, this is not always the case.

Whole-System Conversion A *whole-system conversion*, in which the entire system is installed at one time, is the most common. It is simple and the easiest to understand. However, if the system is large and/or extremely complex (e.g., an enterprise resource-planning system such as SAP or PeopleSoft), the whole system can prove too difficult for users to learn in one conversion step.

Modular Conversion When the *modules*[5] within a system are separate and distinct, organizations sometimes choose to convert to the new system one module at a time—i.e., using modular conversion. *Modular conversion* requires special care in developing the system (and usually adds extra cost). Each module either must be written to work with both the old and new systems or object wrappers (see Chapter 7) must be used to encapsulate the old system from the new. When modules are tightly integrated, this is very challenging and therefore is seldom done. However, when there is only a loose association between modules, module conversion is easier. For example, consider a conversion from an old version of Microsoft Office to a new version. It is relatively simple to convert from the old version of Word to the new version without simultaneously having to change from the old to the new version of Microsoft Excel.

Modular conversion reduces the amount of training required to begin using the new system. Users need training only in the new module being implemented. However, modular conversion does take longer and has more steps than does the whole-system process.

Selecting the Appropriate Conversion Strategy

Each of the three dimensions in Figure 13-3 is independent, so that a conversion strategy can be developed to fit in any one of the boxes in this figure. Different boxes can also be mixed and matched into one *conversion strategy*. For example, one commonly used approach is to begin with a pilot conversion of the whole system using parallel conversion in a handful of test locations. Once the system has passed the pilot test at these locations, it is then installed in the remaining locations using phased conversion with direct cutover. There are three important factors to consider in selecting a conversion strategy: *risk*, *cost*, and the *time required* (Figure 13-4).

Risk After the system has passed a rigorous battery of unit, system, integration, and acceptance testing, it should be bug free . . . maybe. Because humans make mistakes, nothing built by people is ever perfect. Even after all these tests, there might still be a few undiscovered bugs. The conversion process provides one last step in which to catch these bugs before the system goes live and the bugs have the chance to cause problems.

Parallel conversion is less risky than is direct conversion because it has a greater chance of detecting bugs that have gone undiscovered in testing. Likewise, pilot conversion is less risky than is phased conversion or simultaneous conversion because if bugs do occur, they occur in pilot test locations whose staff are aware that they might encounter bugs. Because potential bugs affect fewer users, there is less risk. Likewise, converting a few modules at a time lowers the probability of a bug because there is more likely to be a bug in the whole system than in any given module.

| Characteristic | Conversion Style | | Conversion Location | | | Conversion Modules | |
	Direct Conversion	Parallel Conversion	Pilot Conversion	Phased Conversion	Simultaneous Conversion	Whole-System Conversion	Modular Conversion
Risk	High	Low	Low	Medium	High	High	Medium
Cost	Low	High	Medium	Medium	High	Medium	High
Time	Short	Long	Medium	Long	Short	Short	Long

FIGURE 13-4 Characteristics of Conversion Strategies

---

[5] In this case, a module is typically a component or a package, i.e., a set of collaborating classes.

How important the risk is depends on the system being implemented—the combination of the probability that bugs remain undetected in the system and the potential cost of those undetected bugs. If the system has indeed been subjected to extensive methodical testing, including alpha and beta testing, then the probability of undetected bugs is lower than if the testing was less rigorous. However, there still might have been mistakes made in the analysis process, so that although there might be no software bugs, the software might fail to properly address the business needs.

Assessing the cost of a bug is challenging, but most analysts and senior managers can make a reasonable guess at the relative cost of a bug. For example, the cost of a bug in an automated stock market trading program or a heart–lung machine keeping someone alive is likely to be much greater than a bug in a computer game or word processing program. Therefore, risk is likely to be a very important factor in the conversion process if the system has not been as thoroughly tested as it might have been or if the cost of bugs is high. If the system has been thoroughly tested or the cost of bugs is not that high, then risk becomes less important to the conversion decision.

Cost As might be expected, different conversion strategies have different costs. These costs can include things such as salaries for people who work with the system (e.g., users, trainers, system administrators, external consultants), travel expenses, operation expenses, communication costs, and hardware leases. Parallel conversion is more expensive than direct cutover because it requires that two systems (the old and the new) be operated at the same time. Employees must then perform twice the usual work because they have to enter the same data into both the old and the new systems. Parallel conversion also requires the results of the two systems to be completely crosschecked to make sure there are no differences between the two, which entails additional time and cost.

Pilot and phased conversions have somewhat similar costs. Simultaneous conversion has higher costs because more staff are required to support all the locations as they simultaneously switch from the old to the new system. Modular conversion is more expensive than whole-system conversion because it requires more programming. The old system must be updated to work with selected modules in the new system, and modules in the new system must be programmed to work with selected modules in both the old and new systems.

Time The final factor is the amount of time required to convert between the old and the new system. Direct conversion is the fastest because it is immediate. Parallel conversion takes longer because the full advantages of the new system do not become available until the old system is turned off. Simultaneous conversion is fastest because all locations are converted at the same time. Phased conversion usually takes longer than pilot conversion because once the pilot test is complete all remaining locations are usually (but not always) converted simultaneously. Phased conversion proceeds in waves, often requiring several months before all locations are converted. Likewise, modular conversion takes longer than whole-system conversion because the models are introduced one after another.

DevOps and Continuous Delivery[6]

With the DevOps approaches to systems development, software updates are deployed in a continuous manner. For example, a software update is performed on AWS on the average

---

[6] Jez Humble and David Farley, *Continuous Delivery: Reliable Software Releases Through Build, Test, and Deployment Automation* (Boston, MA: Pearson Education, 2011); Gene Kim, Jez Humble, Patrick Debois, and John Willis, *The DevOps Handbook: How to Create World-Class Agility, Reliability, & Security in Technology Organizations* (Portland, OR: IT Revolution Press, 2016); and Sam Newman, *Building Microservices: Designing Fine-Grained Systems* (Sebastopol, CA: O'Reilly Media, 2015).

every 12 seconds, Google deploys software for its App Engine as often as once a day and updates to its search deploys multiple times a week. These levels of deployment give you the idea of how many and quickly software updates are being deployed today. This tends to work given that what is deployed is a microservice; not an entire system. A *microservice* is a single aspect of the overall system that is highly cohesive (see Chapter 7). In some cases, multiple versions of the same microservice will be deployed and tested using A/B testing (see Chapter 10).

The ability to deploy software in a continuous manner requires a deep level of problem domain understanding, a lot of infrastructure and automation. The creation of microservices requires a lot of factoring and decomposition for a microservice to be highly cohesive (see Chapter 7). The necessary infrastructure includes tools that support continuous integration, testing, monitoring, delivering, and deploying the software in real time. This infrastructure forms the deployment pipeline. This approach requires a lot of testing to be successful. Before the microservice is allowed to continue down the deployment pipeline, all tests relevant to that deployment stage must have been executed successfully. Otherwise, the deployment of the microservice is prevented and sent back to be reworked.

As with everything else regarding DevOps, the inspiration for this level of automation comes from lean manufacturing where the production line is halted until the problem is resolved. Consequently, the idea of a traditional conversion does not really apply. However, all of the issues described regarding risk, cost, and time are still relevant.

CHANGE MANAGEMENT[7]

In the context of a systems development project, change management is the process of helping people to adopt and adapt to the to-be system and its accompanying work processes without undue stress. There are three key roles in any major organizational change. The first is the *sponsor* of the change—the person who wants the change. This person is the business sponsor who first initiated the request for the new system (see Chapter 2). Usually, the sponsor is a senior manager of the part of the organization that must adopt and use the new system. It is critical that the sponsor be active in the change management process because a change that is clearly being driven by the sponsor, not by the project team or the IS organization, has greater legitimacy. The sponsor has direct management authority over those who adopt the system.

The second role is that of the *change agent*—the person(s) leading the change effort. The change agent, charged with actually planning and implementing the change, is usually someone outside of the business unit adopting the system and therefore has no direct management authority over the potential adopters. Because the change agent is an outsider, he or she has less credibility than do the sponsor and other members of the business unit. After all, once the system has been installed, the change agent usually leaves and thus has no ongoing impact.

The third role is that of *potential adopters,* or targets of the change—the people who actually must change. These are the people for whom the new system is designed and who will ultimately choose to use or not use the system.

In the early days of computing, many project teams simply assumed that their job ended when the old system was converted to the new system at a technical level. The philosophy was

---

[7] The material in this section is related to the Enhanced Unified Process's Transition and Production phases and the Configuration and Change Management workflow (see Figure 1-18). Many books have been written on change management. Some of our favorites are the following: Patrick Connor and Linda Lake, *Managing Organizational Change*, 2nd Ed. (Westport, CT: Praeger, 1994); Douglas Smith, *Taking Charge of Change* (Reading, MA: Addison-Wesley, 1996); Daryl Conner, *Managing at the Speed of Change* (New York: Villard Books, 1992); and Mary Lynn Manns and Linda Rising, *Fearless Change: Patterns for Introducing New Ideas* (Boston: Addison-Wesley, 2005).

"build it and they will come." Unfortunately, that happens only in the movies. Resistance to change is common in most organizations. Therefore, the change management plan is an important part of the overall installation plan that glues together the key steps in the change management process. Successful change requires that people want to adopt the change and are able to adopt the change. The change management plan has four basic steps: revising management policies, assessing the cost and benefit models of potential adopters, motivating adoption, and enabling people to adopt through training (see Figure 13-2). However, before we can discuss the change management plan, we must first understand why people resist change.

Understanding Resistance to Change[8]

People resist change—even change for the better—for very rational reasons. What is good for the organization is not necessarily good for the people who work there. For example, consider an order-processing clerk who used to receive orders to be shipped on paper shipping documents but now uses a computer to receive the same information. Rather than typing shipping labels with a typewriter, the clerk now clicks on the print button on the computer and the label is produced automatically. The clerk can now ship many more orders each day, which is a clear benefit to the organization. The clerk, however, probably doesn't really care how many packages are shipped. His or her pay doesn't change; it's just a question of which the clerk prefers to use, a computer or typewriter. Learning to use the new system and work processes—even if the change is minor—requires more effort than continuing to use the existing, well-understood system and work processes.

So why do people accept change? Simply put, every change has a set of costs and benefits associated with it. If the benefits of accepting the change outweigh the costs of the change, then people change. Sometimes the benefit of change is avoidance of the pain that might be experienced if the change were not adopted (e.g., if you don't change, you are fired, so one of the benefits of adopting the change is that you still have a job).

In general, when people are presented with an opportunity for change, they perform a cost–benefit analysis (sometime consciously, sometimes subconsciously) and decide the extent to which they will embrace and adopt the change. They identify the costs of and benefits from the system and decide whether the change is worthwhile. However, it is not that simple, because most costs and benefits are not certain. There is some uncertainty as to whether a certain benefit or cost will actually occur; so both the costs of and benefits from the new system need to be weighted by the degree of certainty associated with them (Figure 13-5).

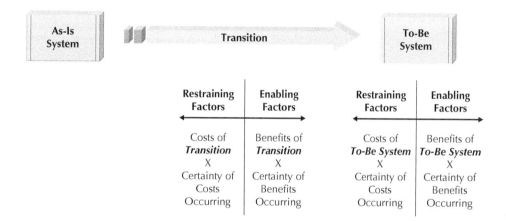

FIGURE 13-5
The Costs and
Benefits of Change

[8] This section benefited from conversations with Dr. Robert Briggs, research scientist at the Center for the Management of Information at the University of Arizona.

Unfortunately, most humans tend to overestimate the probability of costs and underestimate the probability of benefits.

There are also costs and, sometimes, benefits associated with the actual *transition process* itself. For example, suppose we found a nicer house or apartment than our current one. Even if we liked it better, we might decide not to move simply because the cost of moving outweighed the benefits from the new house or apartment itself. Likewise, adopting a new computer system might require us to learn new skills, which could be seen as a cost to some people or as a benefit to others, if they perceived that those skills would somehow provide other benefits beyond the use of the system itself. Once again, any costs and benefits from the transition process must be weighted by the certainty with which they will occur (see Figure 13-5).

Taken together, these two sets of costs and benefits (and their relative certainties) affect the acceptance of change or resistance to change that project teams encounter when installing new systems in organizations. The first step in change management is to understand the factors that inhibit change—the factors that affect the perception of costs and benefits and certainty that they will be generated by the new system. It is critical to understand that the *real costs* and *real benefits* are far less important than the *perceived costs* and *perceived benefits*. People act on what they believe to be true, not on what is true. Thus, any understanding of how to motivate change must be developed from the viewpoint of the people expected to change, not from the viewpoint of those leading the change.

Revising Management Policies

The first major step in the change management plan is to change the management policies that were designed for the as-is system to new management policies designed to support the to-be system. *Management policies* provide goals, define how work processes should be performed, and determine how organizational members are rewarded. No computer system will be successfully adopted unless management policies support its adoption. Many new computer systems bring changes to business processes; they enable new ways of working. Unless the policies that provide the rules and rewards for those processes are revised to reflect the new opportunities that the system permits, potential adopters cannot easily use it.

Management has three basic tools for structuring work processes in organizations.[9] The first are the *standard operating procedures (SOPs)* that become the habitual routines for how work is performed. The SOPs are both formal and informal. Formal SOPs define proper behavior. Informal SOPs are the norms that have developed over time for how processes are actually performed. Management must ensure that the formal SOPs are revised to match the to-be system. The informal SOPs will then evolve to refine and fill in details absent in the formal SOPs.

The second aspect of management policy is defining how people assign meaning to events. What does it mean to "be successful" or "do good work"? Policies help people understand meaning by defining *measurements* and *rewards*. Measurements explicitly define meaning because they provide clear and concrete evidence about what is important to the organization. Rewards reinforce measurements because "what gets measured gets done" (an overused but accurate saying). Measurements must be carefully designed to motivate desired behavior.

A third aspect of management policy is *resource allocation*. Managers can have clear and immediate impacts on behavior by allocating resources. They can redirect funds and staff

---

[9] This section builds on the work of Anthony Giddens, *The Constitution of Society: Outline of the Theory of Structure* (Berkeley: University of California Press, 1984). A good summary of Giddens's theory that has been revised and adapted for use in understanding information systems is an article by Wanda Orlikowski and Dan Robey, "Information Technology and the Structuring of Organizations," *Information Systems Research* 2, no. 2 (1991): 143–169.

from one project to another, create an infrastructure that supports the new system, and invest in training programs. Each of these activities has both a direct and symbolic effect. The direct effect comes from the actual reallocation of resources. The symbolic effect shows that management is serious about its intentions. There is less uncertainty about management's long-term commitment to a new system when potential adopters see resources being committed to support it.

Assessing Costs and Benefits

The next step in developing a change management plan is to develop two clear and concise lists of costs and benefits provided by the new system (and the transition to it) compared with the as-is system. The first list is developed from the perspective of the organization, which should flow easily from the business case developed during the feasibility study and refined over the life of the project (see Chapter 2). This set of organizational costs and benefits should be distributed widely so that everyone expected to adopt the new system should clearly understand why the new system is valuable to the organization.

The second list of costs and benefits is developed from the viewpoints of the different potential adopters expected to change, or stakeholders in the change. For example, one set of potential adopters may be the frontline employees, another may be the first-line supervisors, and yet another might be middle management. Each of these potential adopters, or stakeholders, may have a different set of costs and benefits associated with the change—costs and benefits that can differ widely from those of the organization. In some situations, unions may be key stakeholders that can make or break successful change.

Many systems analysts naturally assume that frontline employees are the ones whose set of costs and benefits are the most likely to diverge from those of the organization and thus are the ones who most resist change. However, they usually bear the brunt of problems with the current system. When problems occur, they often experience them firsthand. Middle managers and first-line supervisors are the most likely to have a divergent set of costs and benefits and, therefore, resist change because new computer systems often change how much power they have. For example, a new computer system may improve the organization's control over a work process (a benefit to the organization) but reduce the decision-making power of middle management (a clear cost to middle managers).

An analysis of the costs and benefits for each set of potential adopters, or stakeholders, will help pinpoint those who will likely support the change and those who might resist the change. The challenge at this point is to try to change the balance of the costs and benefits for those expected to resist the change so that they support it (or at least do not actively resist it). This analysis could uncover some serious problems that have the potential to block the successful adoption of the system. It may be necessary to reexamine the management policies and make significant changes to ensure that the balance of costs and benefits is such that important potential adopters are motivated to adopt the system.

Figure 13-6 summarizes some of the factors that are important to successful change. The first and most important reason is a compelling personal reason to change. All change is made by individuals, not organizations. If there are compelling reasons for the key groups of individual stakeholders to want the change, then the change is more likely to be successful. Factors such as increased salary, reduced unpleasantness, and—depending on the individuals— opportunities for promotion and personal development can be important motivators. However, if the change makes current skills less valuable, individuals might resist the change because they have invested a lot of time and energy in acquiring those skills, and anything that diminishes those skills may be perceived as diminishing the individual (because important skills bring respect and power).

	Factor	Examples	Effects	Actions to Take
Benefits of to-be system	Compelling personal reason(s) for change	Increased pay, fewer unpleasant aspects, opportunity for promotion, most existing skills remain valuable	If the new system provides clear personal benefits to those who must adopt it, they are more likely to embrace the change.	Perform a cost–benefit analysis from the viewpoint of the stakeholders, make changes where needed, and actively promote the benefits.
Certainty of benefits	Compelling organizational reason(s) for change	Risk of bankruptcy, acquisition, government regulation	If adopters do not understand why the organization is implementing the change, they are less certain that the change will occur.	Perform a cost–benefit analysis from the viewpoint of the organization and launch a vigorous information campaign to explain the results to everyone.
	Demonstrated top management support	Active involvement, frequent mentions in speeches	If top management is not seen to actively support the change, there is less certainty that the change will occur.	Encourage top management to participate in the information campaign.
	Committed and involved business sponsor	Active involvement, frequent visits to users and project team, championing	If the business sponsor (the functional manager who initiated the project) is not seen to actively support the change, there is less certainty that the change will occur.	Encourage the business sponsor to participate in the information campaign and play an active role in the change management plan.
	Credible top management and business sponsor	Management and sponsor who do what they say instead of being members of the "management fad of the month" club	If the business sponsor and top management have credibility in the eyes of the adopters, the certainty of the claimed benefits is higher.	Ensure that the business sponsor and/or top management has credibility so that such involvement will help; if there is no credibility, involvement will have little effect.
Costs of transition	Low personal costs of change	Few new skills needed	The cost of the change is not borne equally by all stakeholders; the costs are likely to be higher for some.	Perform a cost–benefit analysis from the viewpoint of the stakeholders, make changes where needed, and actively promote the low costs.
Certainty of costs	Clear plan for change	Clear dates and instructions for change, clear expectations	If there is a clear migration plan, it will likely lower the perceived costs of transition.	Publicize the migration plan.
	Credible change agent	Previous experience with change, does what he/she promises to do	If the change agent has credibility in the eyes of the adopters, the certainty of the claimed costs is higher.	If the change agent is not credible, then change will be difficult.
	Clear mandate for change agent from sponsor	Open support for change agent when disagreements occur	If the change agent has a clear mandate from the business sponsor, the certainty of the claimed costs is higher.	The business sponsor must actively demonstrate support for the change agent.

FIGURE 13-6 Major Factors in Successful Change

There must also be a compelling reason for the organization to need the change; otherwise, individuals become skeptical that the change is important and are less certain it will, in fact, occur. Probably the hardest organization to change is an organization that has been successful because individuals come to believe that what worked in the past will continue to work. By contrast, in an organization that is on the brink of bankruptcy, it is easier to convince individuals that change is needed. Commitment and support from credible business sponsors and top management are also important in increasing the certainty that the change will occur.

The likelihood of successful change is increased when the cost of the transition to individuals who must change is low. The need for significantly different new skills or disruptions in operations and work habits can create resistance. A clear migration plan developed by a credible change agent who has support from the business sponsor is an important factor in increasing the certainty about the costs of the transition process.

Motivating Adoption

The single most important factor in motivating a change is providing clear and convincing evidence of the need for change. Simply put, everyone who is expected to adopt the change must be convinced that the benefits from the to-be system outweigh the costs of changing.

There are two basic strategies to motivating adoption: informational and political. Both strategies are often used simultaneously. With an *informational strategy*, the goal is to convince potential adopters that the change is for the better. This strategy works when the cost–benefit set of the target adopters has more benefits than costs. In other words, there really are clear reasons for the potential adopters to welcome the change.

Using this approach, the project team provides clear and convincing evidence of the costs and benefits of moving to the to-be system. The project team writes memos and develops presentations that outline the costs and benefits of adopting the system from the perspective of the organization and from the perspective of the target group of potential adopters. This information is disseminated widely throughout the target group, much like an advertising or public relations campaign. It must emphasize the benefits and increase the certainty in the minds of potential adopters that these benefits will actually be achieved. In our experience, it is always easier to sell painkillers than vitamins; that is, it is easier to convince potential adopters that a new system will remove a major problem (or other source of pain) than that it will provide new benefits (e.g., increase sales). Therefore, informational campaigns are more likely to be successful if they stress reducing or eliminating problems rather than focusing on providing new opportunities.

The other strategy for motivating change is a *political strategy*. With a political strategy, organizational power, not information, is used to motivate change. This approach is often used when the cost–benefit set of the target adopters has more costs than benefits. In other words, although the change might benefit the organization, there are no reasons for the potential adopters to welcome the change.

The political strategy is usually beyond the control of the project team. It requires someone in the organization who holds legitimate power over the target group to influence the group to adopt the change. This may be done in a coercive manner (e.g., adopt the system or you're fired) or in a negotiated manner, in which the target group gains benefits in other ways that are linked to the adoption of the system (e.g., linking system adoption to increased training opportunities). Management policies can play a key role in a political strategy by linking salary to certain behaviors desired with the new system.

In general, for any change that has true organizational benefits, about 20 to 30 percent of potential adopters will be *ready adopters*. They recognize the benefits, quickly adopt the system, and become proponents of the system. Another 20 to 30 percent are *resistant adopters*. They simply refuse to accept the change and they fight it, either because the new system has more costs than benefits for them personally or because they place such a high cost on the transition process itself that no amount of benefits from the new system can outweigh the change costs. The remaining 40 to 60 percent are *reluctant adopters*. They tend to be apathetic and will go with the flow to either support or resist the system, depending on how the project evolves and how their coworkers react to the system. Figure 13-7 illustrates the actors who are involved in the change management process.

Sponsor	Change Agent	Potential Adopters
The sponsor wants the change to occur.	The change agent leads the change effort.	Potential adopters are the people who must change. 20–30 percent are ready adopters. 20–30 percent are resistant adopters. 40–60 percent are reluctant adopters.

FIGURE 13-7
Actors in the Change Management Process

The goal of change management is to actively support and encourage the ready adopters and help them win over the reluctant adopters. There is usually little that can be done about the resistant adopters because their set of costs and benefits may be divergent from those of the organization. Unless there are simple steps that can be taken to rebalance their costs and benefits or the organization chooses to adopt a strongly political strategy, it is often best to ignore this small minority of resistant adopters and focus on the larger majority of ready and reluctant adopters.

Enabling Adoption: Training

Potential adopters might want to adopt the change, but unless they are capable of adopting it, they won't. Careful *training* enables adoption by providing the skills needed to adopt the change. Training is probably the most self-evident part of any change management initiative. How can an organization expect its staff members to adopt a new system if they are not trained? However, we have found that training is one of the most commonly overlooked parts of the process. Many organizations and project managers simply expect potential adopters to find the system easy to learn. Because the system is presumed to be so simple, it is taken for granted that potential adopters should be able to learn with little effort. Unfortunately, this is usually an overly optimistic assumption.

Every new system requires new skills, either because the basic work processes have changed or because the computer system used to support the processes is different. The more radical the changes to the business processes, the more important it is to ensure the organization has the new skills required to operate the new business processes and supporting information systems. In general, there are three ways to get these new skills. One is to hire new employees who have the needed skills that the existing staff does not. Another is to outsource the processes to an organization that has the skills that the existing staff does not. Both these approaches are controversial and are usually considered only when the new skills needed are likely to be the most different from the set of skills of the current staff. In most cases, organizations choose the third alternative: training existing staff in the new business processes and the to-be system. Every training plan must consider what to train and how to deliver the training.

What to Train What training should you provide to the system users? It's obvious: how to use the system. The training should cover all the capabilities of the new system so that users understand what each module does, right? Wrong. Training for business systems should focus on helping the users to accomplish their jobs, not on how to use the system. The system is simply a means to an end, not the end in itself. This focus on performing the job (i.e., the business processes), not using the system, has two important implications. First, the training must focus on the activities around the system as well as on the system itself. The training must help the users understand how the computer fits into the bigger picture of their jobs. The use of the system must be put in context of the manual business processes as well as of those that are computerized, and it must also cover the new management policies that were implemented along with the new computer system.

Second, the training should focus on what the user needs to do, not what the system can do. This is a subtle—but very important—distinction. Most systems provide far more capabilities than the users will need to use (e.g., when was the last time you wrote a macro in Microsoft Word?). Rather than attempting to teach the users all the features of the system, training should instead focus on the much smaller set of activities that users perform on a regular basis and ensure that users are truly expert in those. When the focus is on the 20 percent of functions that the users will use 80 percent of the time (instead of attempting to cover all functions), users become confident about their ability to use the system. Training should mention the other little-used functions but only so that users are aware of their existence and know how to learn about them when their use becomes necessary.

One source of guidance for designing training materials is the use cases. The use cases outline the common activities that users perform and thus can be helpful in understanding the business processes and system functions that are likely to be most important to the users.

How to Train There are many ways to deliver training. The most commonly used approach is *classroom training,* in which many users are trained at the same time by the same instructor. This has the advantage of training many users at one time with only one instructor and creates a shared experience among the users.

It is also possible to provide *one-on-one training,* in which one trainer works closely with one user at a time. This is obviously more expensive, but the trainer can design the training program to meet the needs of individual users and can better ensure that the users really do understand the material. This approach is typically used only when the users are very important or when there are very few users.

Another approach that is becoming more common is to use some form of *computer-based training (CBT),* in which the training program is delivered via computer, either on CD or over the Web. CBT programs can include text slides, audio, and even video and animation. CBT is typically more costly to develop but is cheaper to deliver because no instructor is needed to actually provide the training.

Figure 13-8 summarizes four important factors to consider in selecting a training method: cost to develop, cost to deliver, impact, and reach. CBT is typically more expensive to develop than one-on-one or classroom training, but it is less expensive to deliver. One-on-one training has the most impact on the user because it can be customized to the user's precise needs, knowledge, and abilities, whereas CBT has the least impact. However, CBT has the greatest reach—the ability to train the most users over the widest distance in the shortest time—because it is much simpler to distribute than classroom and one-on-one training, simply because no instructors are needed.

Figure 13-8 suggests a clear pattern for most organizations. If there are only a few users to train, one-on-one training is the most effective. If there are many users to train, many organizations turn to CBT. We believe that the use of CBT will increase in the future. Quite often, large organizations use a combination of all three methods. Regardless of which

	One-on-One Training	Classroom Training	Computer-Based Training
Cost to develop	Low to Medium	Medium	High
Cost to deliver	High	Medium	Low
Impact	High	Medium to High	Low to Medium
Reach	Low	Medium	High

FIGURE 13-8
Selecting a
Training Method

approach is used, it is important to leave the users with a set of easily accessible materials that can be referred to long after the training has ended (usually a quick reference guide and a set of manuals, whether on paper or in electronic form).

POST-IMPLEMENTATION ACTIVITIES[10]

The goal of post-implementation activities is the *institutionalization* of the use of the new system—i.e., to make it the normal, accepted, routine way of performing the business processes. Post-implementation activities attempt to refreeze the organization after the successful transition to the new system. Although the work of the project team naturally winds down after implementation, the business sponsor and sometimes the project manager are actively involved in refreezing. These two—and, ideally, many other stakeholders—actively promote the new system and monitor its adoption and usage. They usually provide a steady flow of information about the system and encourage users to contact them to discuss issues.

In this section, we examine three key post-implementation activities: *system support* (providing assistance in the use of the system), *system maintenance* (continuing to refine and improve the system), and *project assessment* (analyzing the project to understand what activities were done well—and should be repeated—and what activities need improvement in future projects).

System Support

Once the project team has installed the system and performed the change management activities, the system is officially turned over to the *operations group*. This group is responsible for operating the system, whereas the project team was responsible for developing the system. Members of the operations group are usually closely involved in the installation activities because they are the ones who must ensure that the system actually works. After the system is installed, the project team leaves but the operations group remains.

Providing system support means helping the users to use the system. Usually, this means providing answers to questions and helping users understand how to perform a certain function; this type of support can be thought of as *on-demand training*.

Online support is the most common form of on-demand training. This includes the documentation and help screens built into the system, as well as separate websites that provide answers to *frequently asked questions (FAQs)*, which enable users to find answers without contacting a person. Obviously, the goal of most system support is to provide sufficiently good online support so that the user doesn't need to contact a person, because providing online support is much less expensive than is providing a person to answer questions.

Most organizations provide a *help desk* that provides a place for a user to talk with a person who can answer questions (usually over the phone but sometimes in person). The help desk supports all systems, not just one specific system, so it receives calls about a wide variety of software and hardware. The help desk is operated by *level-1 support* staff who have very broad computer skills and are able to respond to a wide range of requests, from network problems and hardware problems to problems with commercial software and problems with the business application software developed in-house.

The goal of most help desks is to have the level-1 support staff resolve 80 percent of the help requests they receive on the first call. If the issue cannot be resolved by level 1 support staff, a *problem report* (Figure 13-9) is completed (often using a special computer system designed to track problem reports) and passed to a *level-2 support* staff member.

---

[10] The material in this section is related to the Enhanced Unified Process's Production Phase and the Operations and Support workflow (see Figure 1-4).

- Time and date of the report
- Name, e-mail address, and telephone number of the support person taking the report
- Name, e-mail address, and telephone number of the person who reported the problem
- Software and/or hardware causing problem
- Location of the problem
- Description of the problem
- Action taken
- Disposition (problem fixed or forwarded to system maintenance)

FIGURE 13-9
Elements of a
Problem Report

The level-2 support staff members are people who know the application system well and can provide expert advice. For a new system, they are usually selected during the implementation phase and become familiar with the system as it is being tested. Sometimes the level-2 support staff members participate in training during the change management process to become more knowledgeable about the system, the new business processes, and the users themselves.

The level-2 support staff works with users to resolve problems. Most problems are successfully resolved by the level-2 staff. However, sometimes, particularly in the first few months after the system is installed, the problem turns out to be a bug in the software that must be fixed. In this case, the problem report becomes a *change request* that is passed to the system maintenance group (see the next section).

System Maintenance

System maintenance is the process of refining the system to make sure it continues to meet business needs. More money and effort are devoted to system maintenance than to the initial development of the system, simply because a system continues to change and evolve as it is used. Most beginning systems analysts and programmers work first on maintenance projects; usually only after they have gained some experience are they assigned to new development projects.

Every system is "owned" by a project manager in the IS group (Figure 13-10). This individual is responsible for coordinating the system's maintenance effort for that system. Whenever a potential change to the system is identified, a change request is prepared and forwarded to the project manager. The change request is a smaller version of the *system request* discussed in Chapter 2. It describes the change requested and explains why the change is important.

Changes can be small or large. Change requests that are likely to require a significant effort are typically handled in the same manner as system requests: They follow the same process as the project described in this book, starting with project identification in Chapter 2 and following through installation in this chapter. Minor changes typically follow a smaller version of this same process. There is an initial assessment of feasibility and of costs and benefits, and the change request is prioritized. Then a systems analyst (or a programmer/analyst) performs the analysis, which might include interviewing users, and prepares an initial design before programming begins. The new (or revised) program is then extensively tested before the system is converted from the old system to the revised one.

Change requests typically come from five sources. The most common source is problem reports from the operations group that identify bugs in the system that must be fixed. These are usually given immediate priority because a bug can cause significant problems. Even a minor bug can cause major problems by upsetting users and reducing their acceptance of and confidence in the system.

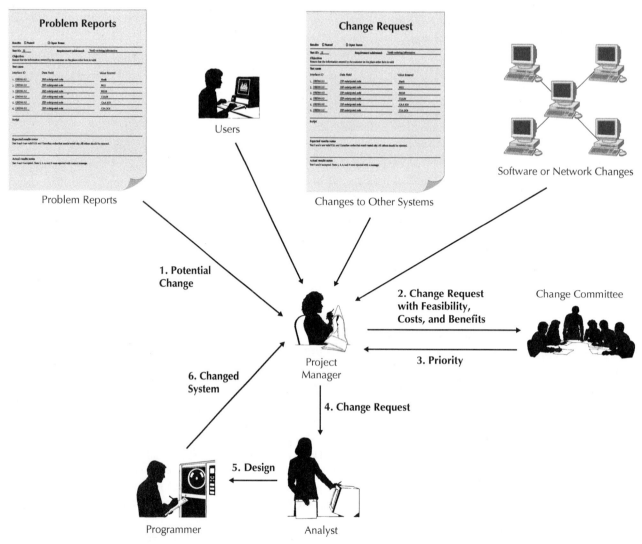

FIGURE 13-10 Processing a Change Request

The second most common source of change requests is enhancement to the system from users. As users work with the system, they often identify minor changes in the design that can make the system easier to use or identify additional functions that are needed. Such enhancements are important in satisfying the users and are often key in ensuring that the system changes as the business requirements change. Enhancements are often given second priority after bug fixes.

The third source of change requests is other system development projects. For example, if the doctor in the appointment problem decided that he or she would like to have a Web-based appointment system that would allow patients to directly interact with the current appointment system, it is likely that other systems, such as billing, would have to be modified to ensure that the two systems would work together. These changes required by the need to integrate two systems are generally rare but are becoming more common as system integration efforts become more common.

The fourth source of change requests is those that occur when underlying software or networks change. For example, new versions of Windows often require an application to change the way the system interacts with Windows or enables application systems to take advantage of new features that improve efficiency. Although users might never see these changes (because most changes are inside the system and do not affect its user interface or functionality), these changes can be among the most challenging to implement because analysts and programmers must learn about the new system characteristics, understand how application systems use (or can use) those characteristics, and then make the needed programming changes.

The fifth source of change requests is senior management. These change requests are often driven by major changes in the organization's strategy or operations. These significant change requests are typically treated as separate projects, but the project manager responsible for the initial system is often placed in charge of the new project.

Project Assessment

The goal of project assessment is to understand what was successful about the system and the project activities (and, therefore, should be continued in the next system or project) and what needs to be improved. Project assessment is not routine in most organizations, except for military organizations, which are accustomed to preparing *after-action reports*. The purpose of an after-action report is to simply provide an objective, rational description of everything that happened, good and bad, during an operation. Nonetheless, assessment can be an important component in organizational learning because it helps organizations and people understand how to improve their work. It is particularly important for junior staff members because it helps promote faster learning. There are two primary parts to project assessment—project team review and system review.

Project Team Review A *project team review* focuses on the way the project team carried out its activities. Each project member prepares a short two- to three-page document that reports and analyzes his or her performance. The focus is on performance improvement, not penalties for mistakes made. By explicitly identifying mistakes and understanding their causes, project team members will, it is hoped, be better prepared for the next time they encounter a similar situation—and less likely to repeat the same mistakes. This is especially true when something fails, e.g., the team misses a deadline, the system fails tests, or the system blows up while in production. This type of review has become known as *blameless post-mortems*. Likewise, by identifying excellent performance, team members will be able to understand why their actions worked well and how to repeat them in future projects. By supporting blameless post-mortems, the system development organization supports a *just culture*. A just culture, according to Dekker, is one that supports the idea of *psychological safety* where a team member knows that it is safe to admit to mistakes. In this way, the organization can learn about different mistakes and hopefully be able to avoid them in the future.[11] From a motivation perspective (see Chapter 2), supporting a just culture where the team members feel safe is critical to the development of "jelled" teams. And, having jelled teams is critical to the overall success of the systems development organization.

The project manager, who meets with the team members to help them understand how to improve their performance, assesses the documents prepared by each team member. The

---

[11] See Sidney Dekker, *Just Culture: Balancing Safety and Accountability,* 2nd Ed. (Surrey, UK: Ashgate Publishing, 2012); Sidney Dekker, *The Field Guide to Understanding "Human Error,* 3rd Ed. (Boca Raton, FL: CRC Press, 2014); and Gene Kim, Jez Humble, Patrick Debois, and John Willis, *The DevOps Handbook: How to Create World-Class Agility, Reliability, & Security in Technology Organizations* (Portland, OR: IT Revolution Press, 2016).

13-1 Beating Buggy Software

*H*ow do you avoid bugs in the commercial software you buy? Here are six tips:

1. *Know your software:* Find out if the few programs you use day in and day out have known bugs and patches, and track the websites that offer the latest information on them.

2. *Back up your data:* This dictum should be tattooed on every monitor. Stop reading right now and copy the data you can't afford to lose onto a second hard disk or Web server. We'll wait.

3. *Don't upgrade—yet:* It's tempting to upgrade to the latest and greatest version of your favorite software, but why chance it? Wait a few months, check out other users' experiences with the upgrade on Usenet newsgroups or the vendor's own discussion forum, and then go for it. But only if you must.

4. *Upgrade slowly:* If you decide to upgrade, allow yourself at least a month to test the upgrade on a separate system before you install it on all the computers in your home or office.

5. *Forget the betas:* Installing beta software on your primary computer is a game of Russian roulette. If you really have to play with beta software, get a second computer.

6. *Complain:* The more you complain about bugs and demand remedies, the more costly it is for vendors to ship buggy products. It's like voting—the more people participate, the better the results.

Based upon material from "Software Bugs Run Rampant," *PC World* 17, no. 1 (January 1999): 46.

project manager then prepares a summary document that outlines the lessons learned from the project. This summary identifies what actions should be taken in future projects to improve performance but is careful not to identify team members who made mistakes, i.e., a blameless post-mortem. The summary should be circulated as widely as possible to increase the potential for other members of the organization to learn from the team's experience. At the least, the summary should be circulated among all project managers to help them understand how to manage their projects better.

System Review The focus of the *system review* is to understand the extent to which the proposed costs and benefits from the new system identified during feasibility analysis were actually recognized from the implemented system. Project team review is usually conducted immediately after the system is installed while key events are still fresh in team members' minds, but system review is often undertaken several months after the system is installed because it often takes a while before the system can be properly assessed.

System review starts with the system request and feasibility analysis prepared at the start of the project. The detailed analyses prepared for the expected business value (both tangible and intangible) as well as the economic feasibility analysis are reexamined, and a new analysis is prepared after the system has been installed. The objective is to compare the anticipated business value against the actual realized business value from the system. This helps the organization assess whether the system actually provided the value it was planned to provide. Whether or not the system provides the expected value, future projects can benefit from an improved understanding of the true costs and benefits.

A formal system review also has important behavior implications for project initiation. Because everyone involved with the project knows that all statements about business value and the financial estimates prepared during project initiation will be evaluated at the end of the project, they have an incentive to be conservative in their assessments. No one wants to be the project sponsor or project manager for a project that goes radically over budget or fails to deliver promised benefits.

APPLYING THE CONCEPTS AT PATTERSON SUPERSTORE

In this chapter, we see how the first phase of the Integrated Health Clinic Delivery System transitions from development into production for use by the user community. Making this transition involved providing training to the users, including Clinic employees and clients. Ruby and the team conducted an assessment of the development process and each member's contribution. They also developed a plan for continued maintenance of the system.

You can find the rest of the case at www.wiley.com/go/dennis/systemanalysis6e/casestudy.

CHAPTER REVIEW

After reading and studying this chapter, you should be able to:

- [ ] Describe how Hall's and Hofstede's cultural dimensions can affect the adoption of an information system.
- [ ] Describe the technical and managerial issues related to system conversion.
- [ ] Discuss the three dimensions of system conversion.
- [ ] Discuss why people resist and accept change.
- [ ] Describe the major steps in a change management plan.
- [ ] Discuss the different strategies to motivate adoption of a new system.
- [ ] Discuss why training is crucial to the acceptance of a new system.
- [ ] Describe the different post-implementation activities that take place after the successful deployment of the information system.
- [ ] Describe the ideas of a just culture, blameless post-mortems, and psychological safety.

KEY TERMS

After-action reports
Blameless post-mortems
Change agent
Change management
Change request
Classroom training
Collectivism
Computer-based
    training (CBT)
Context
Conversion
Conversion location
Conversion modules
Conversion strategy
Conversion style
Cost
Direct conversion
Femininity
Frequently asked
    questions (FAQ)

Help desk
Individualism
Informational strategy
Institutionalization
Just culture
Level-1 support
Level-2 support
Long-term orientation
Management policies
Masculinity
Measurements
Microservice
Migration plan
Modular conversion
Modules
Monochronic time
On-demand training
One-on-one training
Online support
Operations group

Parallel conversion
Perceived benefits
Perceived costs
Phased conversion
Pilot conversion
Political strategy
Polychronic time
Post-implementation
Potential adopter
Power distance
Problem report
Project assessment
Project team review
Psychological safety
Ready adopters
Real benefits
Real costs
Refreeze
Reluctant adopters
Resistant adopters

Resource allocation
Rewards
Risk
Short-term orientation
Simultaneous conversion
Speed of messages
Sponsor
Standard operating
    procedure (SOP)
System maintenance
System request
System review
System support
Time
Training
Transition process
Uncertainty avoidance
Unfreeze
Whole-system conversion

QUESTIONS

1. What are the three basic steps in managing organizational change?
2. What are the cultural issues of which developers should be aware?
3. What are the major components of a migration plan?
4. Compare and contrast direct conversion and parallel conversion.
5. Compare and contrast pilot conversion, phased conversion, and simultaneous conversion.
6. Compare and contrast modular conversion and whole-system conversion.
7. Explain the trade-offs among selecting between the types of conversion in questions 4, 5, and 6.
8. What are the three key roles in any change management initiative?
9. Why do people resist change? Explain the basic model for understanding why people accept or resist change.
10. What are the three major elements of management policies that must be considered when implementing a new system?
11. Compare and contrast an information change management strategy with a political change management strategy. Is one better than the other?
12. Explain the three categories of adopters you are likely to encounter in any change management initiative.
13. How should you decide what items to include in your training plan?
14. Compare and contrast three basic approaches to training.
15. What is the role of the operations group in system development?
16. Compare and contrast two major ways of providing system support.
17. How is a problem report different from a change request?
18. What are the major sources of change requests?
19. Why is project assessment important?
20. How is project team review different from system review?
21. Why are the ideas of psychological safety, blameless post-mortems, and a just culture important when performing a project team review?
22. What do you think are three common mistakes that novice analysts make in migrating from the as-is to the to-be system?
23. Some experts argue that change management is more important than any other part of system development. Do you agree or not? Explain.
24. In our experience, change management planning often receives less attention than conversion planning. Why do you think this happens?

EXERCISES

A. Suppose you are installing a new accounting package in your small business. What conversion strategy would you use? Develop a conversion plan (i.e., technical aspects only).
B. Suppose you are installing a new room reservation system for your university that tracks which courses are assigned to which rooms. Assume that all the rooms in each building are "owned" by one college or department and only one person in that college or department has permission to assign them. What conversion strategy would you use? Develop a conversion plan (i.e., technical aspects only).
C. Suppose you are installing a new payroll system in a very large multinational corporation. What conversion strategy would you use? Develop a conversion plan (i.e., technical aspects only).
D. Consider a major change you have experienced in your life (e.g., taking a new job, starting a new school).

Prepare a cost–benefit analysis of the change in terms of both the change and the transition to the change.
E. Suppose you are the project manager for a new library system for your university. The system will improve the way students, faculty, and staff can search for books by enabling them to search over the Web, rather than using only the current text-based system available on the computer terminals in the library. Prepare a cost–benefit analysis of the change in terms of both the change and the transition to the change for the major stakeholders.
F. Prepare a plan to motivate the adoption of the system in exercise E.
G. Prepare a training plan that includes both what you would train and how the training would be delivered for the system in exercise E.
H. Suppose you are leading the installation of a new DSS to help admissions officers manage the admissions

process at your university. Develop a change management plan (i.e., organizational aspects only).

I. Suppose you are the project leader for the development of a new Web-based course registration system for your university that replaces an old system in which students had to go to the coliseum at certain times and stand in line to get permission slips for each course they wanted to take. Develop a migration plan (including both technical conversion and change management).

J. Suppose you are the project leader for the development of a new airline reservation system that will be used by the airline's in-house reservation agents. The system will replace the current command-driven system designed in the 1970s that uses terminals. The new system uses PCs with a Web-based interface. Develop a migration plan (including both conversion and change management) for your telephone operators.

K. Develop a migration plan (including both conversion and change management) for the independent travel agencies that use the airline reservation system described in exercise J.

L. For the A Real Estate Inc problem in Chapters 4 through 12:
   1. Prepare a plan to motivate adoption of the system.
   2. Prepare a training plan that includes both what you would train and how the training would be delivered.
   3. Prepare a change management plan.
   4. Develop a migration plan.

M. For the A Video Store problem in Chapters 4 through 12:
   1. Prepare a plan to motivate adoption of the system.
   2. Prepare a training plan that includes both what you would train and how the training would be delivered.
   3. Prepare a change management plan.
   4. Develop a migration plan.

N. For the gym problem in Chapters 4 through 12:
   1. Prepare a plan to motivate adoption of the system.
   2. Prepare a training plan that includes both what you would train and how the training would be delivered.
   3. Prepare a change management plan.
   4. Develop a migration plan.

O. For the Picnics R Us problem in Chapters 4 through 12:
   1. Prepare a plan to motivate adoption of the system.
   2. Prepare a training plan that includes both what you would train and how the training would be delivered.
   3. Prepare a change management plan.
   4. Develop a migration plan.

P. For Of-the-Month Club problem in Chapters 4 through 12:
   1. Prepare a plan to motivate adoption of the system.
   2. Prepare a training plan that includes both what you would train and how the training would be delivered.
   3. Prepare a change management plan.
   4. Develop a migration plan.

MINICASES

1. Nancy is the IS department head at MOTO Inc., a human resources management firm. The IS staff at MOTO Inc. completed work on a new client management software system about a month ago. Nancy was impressed with the performance of her staff on this project because the firm had not previously undertaken a project of this scale in-house. One of Nancy's weekly tasks is to evaluate and prioritize the change requests that have come in for the various applications used by the firm.

   Right now, Nancy has five change requests for the client system on her desk. One request is from a system user who would like some formatting changes made to a daily report produced by the system. Another request is from a user who would like the sequence of menu options changed on one of the system menus to more closely reflect the frequency of use for those options. A third request came in from the billing department.

   This department performs billing through a billing software package. A major upgrade of this software is being planned, and the interface between the client system and the bill system need to be changed to accommodate the new software's data structures. The fourth request seems to be a system bug that occurs whenever a client cancels a contract (a rare occurrence, fortunately). The last request came from Susan, the company president. This request confirms the rumor that MOTO Inc. is about to acquire another new business. The new business specializes in the temporary placement of skilled professional and scientific employees and represents a new business area for MOTO Inc. The client management software system will need to be modified to incorporate the special client arrangements that are associated with the acquired firm.

How do you recommend that Nancy prioritize these change requests for the client/management system?

2. Sky View Aerial Photography offers a wide range of aerial photographic, video, and infrared imaging services. The company has grown from its early days of snapping pictures of client houses to its current status as a full-service aerial image specialist. Sky View now maintains numerous contracts with various governmental agencies for aerial mapping and surveying work. Sky View has its offices at the airport, where it keeps its fleet of specially equipped aircraft. Sky View contracts with several freelance pilots and photographers for some of its aerial work and also employs several full-time pilots and photographers.

The owners of Sky View Aerial Photography recently contracted with a systems development consulting firm to develop a new information system for the business. As the number of contracts, aircraft, flights, pilots, and photographers increased, the company experienced difficulty keeping accurate records of its business activity and the utilization of its fleet of aircraft. The new system will require all pilots and photographers to swipe an ID badge through a reader at the beginning and conclusion of each photo flight, along with recording information about the aircraft

used and the client served on that flight. These records are to be reconciled against the actual aircraft utilization logs maintained and recorded by the hangar personnel.

The office staff was eagerly awaiting the installation of the new system. Their general attitude was that the system would reduce the number of problems and errors that they encountered and would make their work easier. The pilots, photographers, and hangar staff were less enthusiastic, being unaccustomed to having their activities monitored in this way.

a. Discuss the factors that might inhibit the acceptance of this new system by the pilots, photographers, and hangar staff.

b. Discuss how an informational strategy could be used to motivate adoption of the new system at Sky View Aerial Photography.

c. Discuss how a political strategy could be used to motivate adoption of the new system at Sky View Aerial Photography.

3. For the Holiday Travel Vehicles problem described in Chapters 5 through 12:
a. Prepare a plan to motivate adoption of the system.
b. Prepare a training plan that includes both what you would train and how the training would be delivered.
c. Prepare a change management plan.
d. Develop a migration plan.

4. For the Professional and Scientific Staff Management problem described in Chapters 4, and 6 through 11:
a. Prepare a plan to motivate adoption of the system.
b. Prepare a training plan that includes both what you would train and how the training would be delivered.
c. Prepare a change management plan.
d. Develop a migration plan.

INDEX